心同虛空超法界　量包宇宙入微光

His mind, identical with empty space, transcends the Dharma Realm.
His scope, enveloping the universe, enters ethereal light.

# 髙山仰止眾中尊
## Revered as a Lofty Mountain; venerated among the multitudes.

光明寶戒紹心印——1968年於美國三藩市佛教講堂「楞嚴暑期班」結束，傳授菩薩戒
Brilliant, precious precepts connect with the mind seal. — Transmission of the Bodhisattva Precepts at the culmination of the Shurangama Summer Session, 1968, at the Buddhist Lecture Hall, San Francisco

自利利他覺行圓——1978年於馬來西亞
Benefiting himself and benefiting others brings the perfection of enlightenment and practice!
— 1978, in Malaysia

正法久住願弘深——於馬來西亞
How vast and deep his vow that the Proper Dharma long abides! — In Malaysia

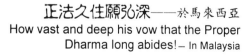

大慈大悲救群生
Great kindness and great compassion rescue the multitudes.

大喜大捨益含萌——於萬佛聖城總辦公室
Great joy and great giving benefit all creatures.
— Administration Office, the City of Ten Thousand Buddhas

任運來往剎那中——於美國萬佛聖城
How easily he comes and goes in the blink of an eye!
— At the City of Ten Thousand Buddhas, USA

# 實相無相離諸相

**The actual appearance, devoid of any appearance, is beyond all appearances.**

龍華會上慶歡欣
——1994年4月於美國洛杉磯長堤聖寺

Such a joyous celebration in the Dragon Flower Assembly! — April 1994, at Long Beach Sagely Monastery, Los Angeles, USA

萬行同入般若門
——1990年9月於臺灣五股寶纈禪寺

Each of the myriad practices enters the doors to prajna. — September 1990, at Baoxie Dhyana Monastery, Wugu, Taiwan

逍遙法界任優游
——1990年於加拿大溫哥華卑詩大學校園

Traversing the Dharma Realm in perpetual amusement.
— 1990, on the campus of the University of British Columbia, Vancouver

仁慈善濟化群萌——1990年9月於臺灣
Humane compassion and wholesome aid
transform teeming throngs. – September 1990,
in Taiwan

觀機逗教當如是
——1994年3月27日觀世音菩薩聖誕法會於萬佛
聖城五觀堂
Contemplating which teaching is timely – thus is
the Way! – Celebration of Guanshiyin Bodhisattva's
Birthday on March 27, 1994, in the Five Contemplations
Hall, City of Ten Thousand Buddhas

盛德遠播被海外——1988年於臺灣臺中
Bounteous virtue disseminated far across the seas.
— 1988, in Taichung, Taiwan

# 歸去來兮仰高風
## Returning--how revered and exalted!

大教普利化西東

——1993年1月於臺灣法界佛教印經會

Benefiting all with his extensive teaching, he transforms
West and East. — January, 1993, Dharma Realm Buddhist Books
Distribution Society, Taiwan

因人說法演實權——1993年4月7日於洛杉磯長堤聖寺花園上人壽宴

Speaking the Dharma in accord with people, he proclaims both actual and provisional.
— On the Master's birthday, April 7, 1993 at Long Beach Sagely Monastery, Los Angeles

拔苦與樂救倒懸——1993年1月於臺灣
He extricates those who are hanging upside-down from suffering and gives them happiness.
— January 1993, in Taiwan

# 法界悠哉共樂觀
## The Dharma Realm is yours!
## Enjoy it together!

萬方向化三寶興
——1994年5月29日於法界聖城開幕典禮

Those from myriad places are transformed and the Triple Jewel flourishes. — Ritual of Cutting the Cake, May 29, 1994, at the Sagely City of the Dharma Realm

弘揚正教度坤乾
——1994年4月於法界聖城

Propagating Proper Dharma to rescue women and men! — April 1994, at the Sagely City of the Dharma Realm

人天同慶佛開眼
——1994年4月24日
於法界聖城上人壽宴

People and gods rejoicing and the Buddhas watching!
— The Master's birthday celebration, April 24, 1994, at the Sagely City of the Dharma Realm, Sacramento

# 金山寺中般若堂
## In the Prajna Hall
## at Gold Mountain Monastery

誰能悟得娘生面
——1993年9月7日於金山聖寺剃度典禮

Who can recognize his own face when
he first entered the womb?
— Ceremony for Entry into Monastic Life,
September 7, 1993, at Gold Mountain Sagely Monastery

十方共聚選佛場
——1992年12月26日於三藩市金山聖寺上堂說法

Those of the ten directions gather at this Buddha-
selecting site. — Speaking Dharma from the High Seat,
December 26, 1992, at Gold Mountain Sagely Monastery in
San Francisco

許汝自在又清涼
——金聖寺講經法會

Promising you comfort,
ease and coolness!
— A Dharma lecture at
Gold Sage Monastery

# 大轉法輪一字多

## In the mightiest turning of the Dharma Wheel, even a single word is excessive!

### 講說放光天懸蓋
──1991年2月10日於國際譯經學院

The lecture itself sends forth a canopy of light that hovers in the sky.
— February 10, 1991, at the International Translation Institute

### 聖人演教接群品
──1993年10月23日於舊金山灣柏林根市國際譯經學院，布希總統競選記者招待會（右二：上人。右三：德文斯基部長）

The sages speak the teachings to draw in all.
— October 23, 1993, Press Conference for President Bush's Election Campaign, at the International Translation Institute in Burlingame, San Francisco Bay Area (Second right: Venerable Master, Third right:. Director of Veterans' Administration Derwinski)

### 光明永照未來際──1991年於國際譯經學院
The brilliance eternally illumines all future time.
— 1991 at the International Translation Institute

### 松柏耐寒人仰慕

——1993年4月30日於法界佛教總會總辦事處
會晤臺灣前行政院院長郝柏村先生

Pines and cedars that endure the cold win our
esteem!— April 30, 1993 at Dharma Realm Buddhist
Association Headquarters with Taiwan's
ex-Prime Minister Mr. Bo-cun Hao

### 常常接引願無窮

——1994年4月於柏克萊法界宗教研究院，會晤
柏克萊大學宗教聯合研究所院長格林·布克先生

Always and ever welcoming, his vows are
never-ending!— April 1994, at the Institute of World
Religions in Berkeley with the President of the Graduate
Theological Union, Dr. Glenn Bucher, and his wife

### 影響眾生化無緣

——1993年11月31日於舊金山柏林根法界佛教總
會總辦事處前，並柏林根市市長哈理遜先生（右
四）暨其夫人等合影

Influencing beings and transforming those with
whom they have yet to create affinities.
— November, 31, 1993, in front of the Dharma Realm
Buddhist Association Headquarters (Burlingame) with the
Mayor of Burlingame Mr. "Bud" Harrison and his wife and
others.

# 今輔譯場演摩訶
## Now, a place for translation--
## to help proclaim the Mahayana!

# 洛城龍宮甘露灑

**At the dragon palace in Los Angeles,
sweet dew is diffused.**

法雨遍灑潤群生——長堤市福祿壽聖寺
Sprinklings of Dharma rain abound, nurturing all living things.
— Blessings, Prosperity and Longevity Sagely Monastery at Long Beach

法雲普蔭利萬物
——1993年6月於洛杉磯長提市長堤聖寺佛殿
In the ample shade of the Dharma cloud, all beings
gain benefit. — June 1993, in the Buddha Hall at Long Beach
Sagely Monastery, Long Beach

# 華嚴大教遍三千

**The magnificent Flower Adornment Teaching fills the three-thousand world system.**

大匠無巧亦無拙——於華嚴聖寺題字

The greatest artisan is neither skilled nor clumsy
— Writing calligraphy at Avatamsaka Sagely Monastery

佛法妙理本無說
——1994年於金佛聖寺十週年紀念

Wondrous principles of Buddhism are basically ineffable.
— 1994, at the Tenth Anniversary of Gold Buddha Sagely Monastery

法尚應捨有無說
——1992年8月，歡迎上人到西雅圖

Since even the Dharma must be renounced, there is nothing to say.
— Welcoming the Master to Seattle, August 1992

有緣無緣咸攝化──於華盛頓華嚴精舍
Those with affinities and those without are all gathered in and taught. — Avatamsaka Hermitage on the East Coast

覺後一字更嫌多──1992年8月
於美國西雅圖金峰聖寺上堂說法
After awakening, a single word is excessive! — Speaking Dharma from the High Seat, August 1992, at Gold Summit Sagely Monastery, Seattle

可惜對面人不識──於1986年夏，華嚴聖寺佛像開光
What a shame there's no one who recognizes him!
— Opening the Light on the Buddha images, summer of 1986, Avatamsaka Sagely Monastery

山僧介紹結法緣──於加拿大華嚴聖寺
Introducing mountain Sanghans and tying up Dharma affinities.
— Avatamsaka Sagely Monastery, Canada

住持佛法功勳普
——1976年於洛杉磯市
舊金輪寺
How all-pervasive the merit in hosting and supporting the Dharma!— 1976, at the former Gold Wheel Monastery, Los Angeles

高山仰止慕前賢
——1994年3月20日於金輪聖寺
Behold the magnificent mountains; emulate worthy ones of old.
— March 20, 1994, at Gold Wheel Sagely Monastery

見賢思齊自承當
——1993年1月23日於洛杉磯市
皈依法會
Meeting worthy ones, we will naturally strive to emulate them. — Taking Refuge ceremony on January 23, 1993, Los Angeles

# 虛空包含萬有
## Empty space contains all that exists.

心燈永續古今傳——1995年檀香山虛雲寺眾弟子，舉行追悼宣公上人及誦《華嚴經》法會
Continue unceasingly the mind's lamp, transmitting it from past to present. — Disciples at Empty Cloud (Hsu Yun) Monastery holding Memorial Services for the Master and reciting the *Avatamsaka Sutra,* l995 in Hawaii

眾流奔海泯西東
——1995年馬來西亞芙蓉皈依弟子等，舉行追悼宣公上人法會
All waters rush to the sea, obviating West and East.
— Disciples and others join the Memorial for the Venerable Master, l995 in Furong, Malaysia

仰望慈恩再來臨
——1995年馬來西亞紫雲洞眾弟子舉行追悼宣公上人及誦《華嚴經》法會
Reverently hoping that he who was so compassionate and kind will come back to us soon. — Disciples at Ziyundong (Purple Cloud Grotto) Temple holding Memorial for the Master and reciting the *Avatamsaka Sutra,* 1995 in Malaysia

祖師傳心昭大道

**The Patriarch's Mind-transmission illumines the Great Way**

# 荷擔我佛大家業
## Carrying on the enormous task of our Buddhas!

✻ 於香港  In Hong Kong

✻ 於香港  In Hong Kong

✻ 於香港  In Hong Kong

思惟靜慮即禪那　摩訶般若菩提芽
栽培灌漑勤精進　悟無生忍赴龍華
—宣公上人作—

*Stilling thoughts is Chan.*
*Mahaprajna, a Bodhi sprout.*
*Nurture and water it with diligent effort*
*and, awakening to Patience with Non-arising,*
*join the Dragon Flower Assembly.*
— by Venerable Master Hua —

✻ 於香港  In Hong Kong

✻ 於香港觀音洞  At Guanyin Cave in Hong Kong

✹ 於美國 In America

✹ 於香港 In Hong Kong

✹ 於香港 In Hong Kong

✹ 於香港 In Hong Kong

✹ 於香港 In Hong Kong

✹ 於美國 In America

# 大教總持無人我

**The all-encompassing import of Great Teaching is devoid of self and others**

✳ 1954年冬　at the end of 1954

✳ 於香港慈興禪寺灑淨儀式
A Ceremony for Sprinkling the Boundaries at Cixing (Flourishing Compassion) Dhyana Monastery, Hong Kong

✳ 於美國　In America

✸ 於香港  In Hong Kong

✸ 於香港西樂園  Western Bliss Gardens, Hong Kong

✸ 於香港佛教講堂  Buddhist Lecture Hall, Hong Kong

慈觀悲觀喜捨觀　普度眾生化大千
有緣無緣同攝受　離苦得樂返本源
—宣公上人作—

*Contemplating with kindness, compassion, joy, and giving,*
*he rescues beings and transforms the triple-thousand worlds.*
*Those with and without affinities are together gathered in*
*so they leave suffering, attain bliss, and return to their origin.*

— by Venerable Master Hua —

# 虛空塵剎好優遊

**How skilled in roaming through space and traversing lands like dust-motes!**

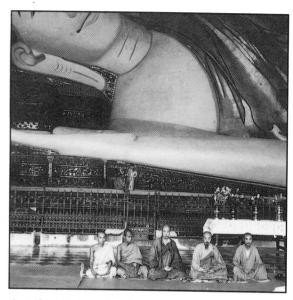

❋ 於泰國（中：上人） In Thailand (center: Master)

❋ 於緬甸（左：上人） In Burma (left: Master)

本於一僧紀攝情缽習眾學國苑律佛中
苑香二五念影形時托實僧留出學教國
島四三

❋ 於香港，中國佛教律學苑出國留學僧實習托缽時情形（右三：上人）
In Hong Kong. Photo commemorating the Chinese Buddhist Vinaya Academy's overseas program when the Sangha members were about to go on alms rounds (Third right: Master)

✳於緬甸（右一：上人）　In Burma (far right: Master)

✳1974年於錫蘭菩提樹　1974 at the Bodhi Tree in Ceylon

✳於緬甸　In Burma

虛空法界一口吞　自性寂然非內外
如是如是如是因　無始無終無古今
—宣公上人作—

*Swallow space and the Dharma Realm in a single gulp!*
*Your own tranquil nature is neither inside nor out.*
*So it is, so it is, the causes are just so*
*Without beginning, without end, and not in the past or present.*
*— by Venerable Master Hua —*

## 法海汪洋無不度　衆生與我離自他
—宣公上人作—

*The sea of Dharma is so immense that none cannot be saved.*
*Distinctions of self and others do not exist between living beings and me.*
— by Venerable Master Hua —

✳1962年於檀香山　I962, in Hawaii

✳1973年11月18日於美國三藩市金山禪寺　November 18, I973 Gold Mountain Dhyana Monastery, USA

宣化老和尚示寂週年
暨
萬佛聖城成立廿週年
紀念專集

# IN MEMORY OF THE
## FIRST ANNIVERSARY OF THE NIRVANA OF
# VENERABLE MASTER HSUAN HUA
### AND THE
## TWENTIETH ANNIVERSARY OF THE
# CITY OF TEN THOUSAND BUDDHAS

# 宣化老和尚示寂週年
## 暨
# 萬佛聖城成立廿週年
## 紀念專集

翻譯
佛經翻譯委員會
出版
法界佛教總會
佛經翻譯委員會
法界佛教大學

IN MEMORY OF THE
FIRST ANNIVERSARY OF THE NIRVANA OF
VENERABLE MASTER HSUAN HUA
AND THE
TWENTIETH ANNIVERSARY OF THE
CITY OF TEN THOUSAND BUDDHAS

Translation by the
Buddhist Text Translation Society

Buddhist Text Translation Society
Dharma Realm Buddhist University
Dharma Realm Buddhist Association
Burlingame, California U.S.A.

Published and translated by:

**Buddhist Text Translation Society**
Dharma Realm Buddhist University,
Dharma Realm Buddhist Association

**First edition 1996**

03 02 01 00 99 98 97 96          10 9 8 7 6 5 4 3 2 1

ISBN 0-88139-557-9

Notes:  Pinyin is used for the romanization of Chinese words, except for proper names which retain familiar romanizations.

*Addresses of the Dharma Realm Buddhist Association's branch offices are listed at the back of this book.*

# 編者的話

> 往復無際，
> 動靜一源，
> 含眾妙而有餘，
> 超言思而迥出者，
> 其為法界歟！

上人遺產，量周法界；上人囑命，心包法界。上人正法，普施法界眾生，值上人示寂週年，特出追思第三集，期略窺一二無盡寶藏。

上人教化，多軌重重，謹列禪七、念佛、觀音法門、上人自詮楞嚴咒，以為修行核心。開示摘要，短短數語，針對無盡話題，開示自在。上人泯門戶，大開方便門，過現未來眾生，入得門來，咸認門門互含圓融，一如上人所言。

> 炳然齊現，猶彼芥瓶；
> 具足同時，方之海滴；
> 一多無礙，等虛空之千燈；
> 隱顯俱成，似秋空之片月；
> 法門重疊，若雲起長空；
> 萬行芬披，比華開錦上。

獅子吼，大智大勇，正直不阿，對末法邪師邪眾，不愧當頭棒喝。當齊心，宣正法。

不辭勞，廣建道場，沿革歷史，略為陳示；並溯上人法脈，遠源六祖。照片選輯，略見世人殷殷向上人致意；不可見者，芸芸法界眾生，亦紛紛致敬。上人加持，無時不在，過去如是，未來亦復如是。

一九九六年五月二十日

# A Note from the Editor

*Going and returning with no border;*
*Movement and stillness have one source;*
*Embracing multitudes of wonders, more remains.*
*Overstepping words and thought by far:*
*This can only be the Dharma Realm!*

What a legacy the Master left for us: encompassing nothing less than the Dharma Realm itself! What a mandate he gave us: to make our scope equal to the Dharma Realm! This third memorial volume, published in observance of the first year, offers a glimpse of some minute portion of the priceless legacy of Proper Dharma that the Venerable Master so selflessly bestowed upon all beings of the Dharma Realm.

In this third memorial volume, Chan meditation, Amitabha Buddha's name, Guanyin Bodhisattva's Dharma doors, and the powerful Shurangama Mantra, described in the Master's own words, are featured as core practices from among the Master's multifaceted teachings. Further, short sayings selected from the Master's prolific body of instructions display the magnitude of topics he handled with ease. Ignoring sectarianism, the Master opened the doors of Buddhism's myriad expedients, and as multitudes of beings in the past, present, and future enter them, they find them to be mutually inclusive, just as the Master said they were.

*Clearly arrayed, they are like mustard seeds in a jar;*
*Completely simultaneous, they are like drops of water in the sea.*
*One and many are unobstructed, like a thousand lamps in space;*
*Hidden and revealed are realized together, like a crescent moon in the sky.*
*Dharma doors pile up in layers, like clouds billowing in space;*
*Myriad practices unfurl profusely, like flowers blooming on brocade.*

The Lion's Roar also issues forth from these pages to expose with astute wisdom and uncompromising candor those who are contributing to the Dharma's demise. Surely we must stand united in perpetuating the Proper Dharma.

The beginnings of many of the Way-places the Master founded with ceaseless toil are described herein. And the Master's own roots, stemming from the first Six Patriarchs in China, are traced. Photos show people throughout the world paying tribute to the Master; unseen, are the multitudes of beings throughout the Dharma Realm also making obeisance. This volume attempts to tell some of how the Master aided and continues to aid us all.

May 20, 1996

# 目 錄

# CONTENTS

不立文字傳衣缽　　本來無物泯言說
悟澈心源破迷倒　　了達性海遊太虛
一華五葉續慧命　　萬古千秋度世佛
曹溪法水流沙界　　洗滌眾生垢沉痾

*Without relying on language, the robe and bowl are transmitted.*
*Originally there's not a single thing, so words are done away with.*
*Awakening to the mind's origin, one smashes through delusion.*
*Understanding the nature's sea, one roams through space.*
*With a five-petalled flower, the wisdom life continues.*
*For tens of thousands of years, the Buddhas have been saving the world.*
*Caoxi's Dharma water flows to worlds as many as grains of sand,*
*Washing away living beings' severe illnesses of defilements.*

宣化老和尚追思紀念專集

# 佛爲什麼入涅槃？
## WHY DID THE BUDDHA ENTER NIRVANA?

宣公上人講述
Lectures by the Venerable Master Hua

【編按】：很多人對上人的圓寂覺得很突然，也覺得來得太快；但是大善知識及祖師們的出世與入滅都有其必定的因緣。《法華經》〈如來壽量品〉中解釋了佛爲什麼入涅槃。上人在一九七〇年講解這一品時，曾作了類似之譬喻，這個譬喻對目前的情形也是很恰當的寫照。故謹節錄上人對這一品之講解如下：

釋迦牟尼佛對所有菩薩摩訶薩說：

一切世間天人及阿修羅都說，釋迦牟尼佛在淨飯王那個宮殿出來，到山裏邊去，離伽耶城大約有五里路，在那兒坐菩提樹下修行，坐在那兒四十九天，就成佛了。

各位善男子，要是講到我實實在在成佛到現在，那個時間可沒有法子能算得過來，有無量無邊百千萬億那由他劫。只可以用一個譬喻來告訴你們。譬喻什麼呢？譬如百千萬億那由他阿僧祇那麼多的世界，假使有一個人，把這麼多的三千大千世界像磨墨似的，把它抹成微塵了。然後向東方走，走過五百千萬億那由他阿僧祇國，就放下一粒微塵，像這樣子把這一些微塵都放沒有了。你說這一切世界的數目多不多啊？你們用你們的心思來思想，用你們最巧的算數師來計算，知道它數目有多少嗎？

我很清楚地告訴你們，沒有數量這麼多的世界，或者下一粒微塵的世界，或者過五百千萬億那由他阿僧祇國都沒有下微塵的。現在無論下一粒微塵和沒有放下一粒微塵這麼多的世界，都把它們磨成微塵，這一粒微塵就算它一個大劫，我成就佛道以來到現在，那個數目比這個數目加倍都不止，比這個又多了百千萬億那由他阿僧祇劫這麼長的時間。

*Editor's Note:* For many people, the Venerable Master's passing into stillness seemed too sudden and too soon. However, Great Good Knowing Advisors and Patriarchs appear in the world and leave the world for good reason. The *Dharma Flower Sutra* in particular, in Chapter Sixteen, "The Thus Come One's Life Span," discusses why the Buddha manifests entering Nirvana. In explaining that chapter in 1970, the Venerable Master drew parallels which are applicable to the present situation. Excerpts from that commentary appear below.

Shakyamuni Buddha said to all the Bodhisattvas Mahasattvas:

All gods, humans, and *asuras* in the world say that Shakyamuni Buddha now, having left the palace of the Pure Rice King and gone to a place about five miles from the city of Gaya to sit beneath the Bodhi tree to cultivate, became a Buddha after sitting there for forty-nine days.

Good men, I actually realized Buddhahood a long time ago. If you want to talk about how long it's been since I became a Buddha, there's no way to calculate the time. It was limitless, boundless hundreds of thousands of myriads of *kotis* of *nayutas* of eons ago. All I can do is try to draw an analogy to give you some idea. What is it analogous to? Suppose a person were to grind into fine motes of dust five hundred thousand myriads of *kotis* of *nayutas* of *asamkhyeyas* of three thousand great thousand world systems. Then, suppose he traveled to the east across five hundred thousand myriads of *kotis* of *nayutas* of *asamkhyeyas* of lands, and there he deposited one mote of dust. Suppose he continued in this way, traveling to the east, dropping one mote of dust every time he passed through that many lands, until all the motes of dust were gone. Would you say that was a great number of worlds? If you had the best mathematician and the most advanced technology, could you find the total?

I shall now explain this clearly for you. If all these numberless world systems, whether a dust mote were deposited in them or not--this includes all the worlds in which a dust particle was dropped, as well as the five hundred thousand myriads of *nayutas* of *asamkhyeyas* of lands where a mote of dust was not dropped--now, if all those many worlds were ground together and reduced to fine dust motes, and if each dust mote were counted as a great *kalpa*, the time that has

我自從那個時候開始到現在，常常就在這個婆婆世界，給眾生說法，教化一切眾生。不單在這個婆婆世界，我來說法教化眾生；在其他的世界，我也給一般的眾生來說法，百千萬億那由他阿僧祇國，我都用種種的方法，也不怕苦，也不怕難，來教化眾生。遇著種種根性的眾生，我就給他說種種法。

釋迦牟尼佛在數不盡這麼多大劫以前，已經就成佛了，所以他所度的這些菩薩弟子，充滿三千大千世界的虛空，都是他的弟子。

我在這麼長的時間，我說在然燈佛的時候，我的名字叫善慧，遇見然燈佛給我授記，說：「汝於來世，當得作佛，號釋迦牟尼。」我又說然燈佛在什麼時候、怎麼樣入涅槃。我所說的這一些個法，現在實實在在地告訴你，我這些說法是方便法門，是對眾生的根性，而說這種過去因地的事情，你們不要拿它當實在的。

假設這個世界上的眾生，他到我這個地方來，我就要先觀察觀察他的根性因緣。我所應該度的，無論哪個地方我都自己說這個佛法，並且說這個名字，可是在美國就叫一個名字，在中國又叫一個名字，在日本又叫一個名字，在德國、在法國，各處這個名字不同，但是都是這個人。年紀或者大一點、老一點，或者小一點，也就現身說法，對這個徒弟就說了，說：「我現在要入涅槃了。」其實佛也沒有生、也沒有滅，在常寂光中常常說法，又用種種的方便，說微妙不可思議這種法，令眾生發歡喜心。

釋迦牟尼佛說如來觀眾生的根機，來給眾生說法，他看見眾生歡喜小乘法的，就說小乘法；歡喜大乘法，就說大乘法。這個德行薄的人，你對他說佛法，他不會相信的；業障重的人，你給他講佛法，他也不會相信的。那麼必須要善根深厚，你給他講佛法，他才能相信。給這一般根基淺、善根也薄的人，就說這種方便法門，說：

我在少年的時候，十九歲就出家了，出家之後，我就得到無上正等正覺了。可是要是問我真正成佛到現在，這個時間遠得就像前邊所說的，有這麼長遠的時間，我用方便的法門來教化

passed since I became a Buddha would exceed even that by hundreds of thousands of myriads of *kotis* of *nayutas* of *asamkhyeyas* of eons. From that time on, I have always remained in the Saha world speaking the Dharma to teach and transform beings. I have been speaking Dharma to teach beings not only in this Saha world, but also in other worlds. In hundreds of thousands of myriads of *kotis* of *asamkhyeyas* of lands, I use all kinds of methods, not fearing suffering, not fearing difficulty, to teach and transform living beings. Meeting with living beings with all different kinds of faculties, I speak all different kinds of Dharmas for them.

Shakyamuni Buddha, uncountable great kalpas ago, had already become a Buddha. Therefore, the Bodhisattva disciples he has taken across are so many. They fill up empty space throughout the three thousand great thousand world systems. The Buddha continued:

In the midst of that long period of time, I said, "At the time of Dipankara Buddha, my name was Good Wisdom. When I met Dipankara Buddha, he bestowed a prediction upon me. He said, 'In the future, you will become a Buddha called Shakyamuni.'" I also said that at such-and-such a time, Dipankara Buddha would enter Nirvana. But to tell you the truth, I was just speaking expediently. I spoke of such events to accord with living beings' faculties. You shouldn't think it was actually the case.

Good men, if a living being comes to where I am, I contemplate his faculties and his causes and conditions. For the sake of those I should take across, no matter where they are, I will personally speak the Buddhadharma. What's more, I will say my name, although the names by which I refer to myself are different. In America I'm called by one name. In China I'm called by another. In Japan I have another name. In Germany, France, in all the places I appear, I go by different names, but the person is the same in all cases. And my age may be older or younger. I appear in a body and speak the Dharma. I tell my disciples, "I am about to enter Nirvana."

Actually the Buddha has no birth or demise. Within Eternal Stillness and Light, he is always speaking the Dharma. He employs various expedient devices, speaking the wonderful, inconceivable Dharma to make living beings happy. The Buddha observes the dispositions of living beings. Then he speaks the Dharma for them. When he sees living beings who like the Small Vehicle Dharmas, he teaches them the Small Vehicle Dharmas. If they like the Great Vehicle Dharmas, he teaches them the Great Vehicle Dharmas. People of scanty virtue will not be able to believe the Buddhadharma if you speak it for them. Those with heavy karmic obstacles won't believe it either. One must have deep and thick good roots to believe the Buddhadharma. Shakyamuni Buddha continues:

To people whose foundations are shallow and whose good roots are scant, I speak expediently, saying, "I left home when I was nineteen. After I left home, I gained the Unsurpassed,

一切眾生，令一切眾生都改邪歸正，改惡向善，迴小向大，來發菩提心。所以我才說我年少出家，然後成道，說法教化眾生。

如來所說這一切的經典、這種法門，都是預備來度脫眾生，因為眾生有八萬四千種的塵勞，所以佛就說出八萬四千個法門，每一種法門是對治眾生的塵勞。就好像醫生治病一樣，要是頭痛的人，醫生就給治頭痛的藥；腳痛的人就要治腳痛；全身痛就要用治全身的這種藥來治這種病，這叫對症下藥。佛說法也是這樣子，眾生貪心重的，就給他說不淨觀，說：「你不要貪，貪是最不清淨的。」多瞋眾生就慈悲觀；愚癡眾生就因緣觀，用種種的方法來對治眾生種種的毛病。或者說其他佛的事；或以自己的身來以身作則，給眾生做個榜樣，做個模範，對眾生來說法；或者說他身給人做榜樣、做模範；或者講一講自己本生、本事這種因緣；或者講一講其他的佛、菩薩、聲聞、羅漢的因，來給眾生做一個模範。所有我所說的，都是實實在在的，沒有一點虛假的。

如來的這種知見是如實的知見，真實的知見。在佛的本身來講，沒有生，也沒有死；也沒有退，也沒有出。退就是退到三界裏邊來，出就是超出三界。在佛的本體上來講，沒有生死，也沒有出入，也沒有退，也沒有出，沒有一個住世，也沒有一個滅度。不是像一般凡夫，見這個三界是實有的，凡夫見到什麼都是真的，見到假的他認為是真的。那麼二乘他觀一切諸法空相，他見三界如空花，都是空的，這是二乘的見解。所以二乘就入虛，凡夫就入實，那麼在佛的份上，也沒有實也沒有虛，就好像在這個太虛空裏頭，包羅萬有而不礙虛空，虛空也不礙萬有，萬有也不礙虛空，也就是真空不礙妙有，妙有不礙真空，互不相礙的。不像一般三界的眾生，見有三界可出，不是這樣子，他是與虛空為一體了，沒有一、也沒有異。不像三界所有的眾生，見到三界，有一個三界；在佛的份上來講，沒有生死，也沒有三界。如來才是真正的一個覺悟者，知道這一切的法，如來所見的，不會錯的。

因為所有一切眾生各有各性，我們人就有人性，不單有人性，又有佛性，也有菩薩性，也有聲聞性，也有緣覺性。這個人裏邊分出有聖人的性，

Proper and Equal Enlightenment." In truth, however, I became a Buddha a long time before that. The length of that time is as in the analogy I explained before. I'm using expedient methods to teach living beings, enabling all living beings to change from the deviant and return to the proper, to change evil into good, to turn from the small and go toward the great, bringing forth the Bodhi mind. It's for this reason that I speak of having left home when young, having realized the Way, having spoken the Dharma, and having taught and transformed living beings.

The Buddha spoke the Sutras, setting forth the Dharma-doors, in order to save living beings. Living beings have 84,000 varieties of afflictions. The Buddha taught 84,000 Dharma-doors to counteract those afflictions. The Buddha works like a physician curing illnesses. If someone has a headache, the doctor prescribes a certain kind of medicine. If someone has a sore leg, he prescribes another kind of medicine, and someone with the flu gets yet another prescription. In the same way, the Buddha "prescribes" Dharmas. To living beings plagued with much greed, he prescribes the contemplation of impurity. He encourages them not to be greedy, and he points out the impurity of desire. To living beings with big tempers, he recommends the contemplation of compassion. To stupid living beings, he prescribes the contemplation of causes and conditions. He uses these various methods to cure the illnesses of living beings. He may speak of his own deeds or of the deeds of another Buddha. He may manifest his own body, to personally guide living beings, or he may manifest a body of someone else as a guide. He may talk about his own deeds from this and former lives, or he may relate the causes and conditions of other Buddhas, Bodhisattvas, Hearers, or Arhats, as an inspiration to living beings. But all that he says is true. There is nothing false in it whatsoever.

The Buddha's knowledge and views accord with truth and principle. On the Buddha's part, there is no birth or death, no retreating or advancing. There is no retreating into the triple realm and no transcending of the triple realm. On the part of the Buddha, there is no existence in the world or passage into extinction; there is no birth or death. Common people see the three realms as real. Whatever common people see, they take it as true. Even the false they consider to be true. Those of the Two Vehicles contemplate all dharmas as empty marks. They see the three realms as flowers in space, that is, as unreal, nonexistent, and empty. Common people take the three realms as real; those of the Two Vehicles take the three realms as unreal. To the Buddha there is nothing real or unreal, just as all things are contained within empty space but do not obstruct empty space. Empty space does not obstruct the myriad forms of existence, and the myriad forms of existence do not obstruct empty space. This is the same principle as True Emptiness not obstructing Wonderful Existence, and Wonderful Existence not obstructing True Emptiness. The Buddha is not like ordinary living beings who view the triple realm as something they must transcend. Having become one with empty space, there is neither oneness nor difference for the Buddha. The Buddha, unlike living beings, does not see the triple realm as the triple realm. To the Buddha, there is no birth, no death, and no triple

有凡夫的性，又有智慧的性，有愚癡的性。又有種種的憶想，又分別一切的事情。因爲這種緣故，佛想令這一切種種欲、種種性、種種行、種種憶想分別的種種眾生，令他們生出善根，以種種的因緣、譬喻、言辭、種種說法，從這麼遠以來到現在，每一天、每一個月、每一年，都是作佛事，暫時間也沒有停過。

佛的壽命是不生不滅的，沒有生滅的，所以到現在有無量無邊這麼多的那由他阿僧祇劫了，他是常住在常寂光淨土裏邊，也不生也不滅的。

> 我成佛這個時間就這樣長遠，要是說起來我在以前行菩薩道那時候的壽命，比我前邊說那個數目更長，那個時間更久，所以說比我成佛以來這個數目還多。可是我現在說要滅度了，實實在在地告訴你，不是滅度，這是方便說法，說我要滅度了。我就是示現滅度，也是用這種方便的法門，來教化一切的眾生。

怎麼佛滅度又說沒有滅度，沒有滅度又說滅度了；由示生滅而說沒有生滅，沒有生滅又現出來這麼一個生滅，這是什麼道理呢？佛本來不生不滅的，假設他久住在這個世界上，不入涅槃的話，沒有德行的人，就是沒有善根的人、業障重的人，就不想種善根了。爲什麼呢？他生出一種依賴性，他以爲：「佛在這兒，我這個善根暫時先不種了，等慢慢地我再種這個善根！」他要等一等，不想即刻就種善根。所以佛若示現滅度，人一看沒有所依靠了，就要種善根了。這是很淺顯的一個道理。

記得我在東北的時候，我有很多很多皈依弟子，我教他們修行，他們也不修行。有的說：「我們要慢慢來修行。」有的說：「我現在沒有時間。」等我從東北走了之後，有人給我來信說：「某某人以前不修行，現在修行了。」因爲師父不在這兒了；師父在這兒，他還不會修行，那麼現在是很用功修行了。這是在東北，那麼在香港的時候，我也有一些皈依弟子，他們也是馬馬虎虎的，我走了之後，他們知道沒有師父是很困難的問題了，所以也寫信希望我回去，那麼我誰也不理他。人就是這麼樣子，天天若見著，他就不覺得是重要的；你若見不著，他沒有法子了，就覺得重要了。所以佛不久住於世，就是因爲德薄之人，他不種善根，佛在世長了，

realm. The Thus Come One is one who is truly awakened to all dharmas and who makes no mistake in what he sees.

Each living creature has its own nature. Each person has a human nature. Each person also has a Buddha nature, a Bodhisattva nature, a Hearer nature, and a Pratyekabuddha nature. And so a human being has the nature of a sage and a common nature--a wisdom nature and a stupid nature. Living beings also have various ideas, thoughts, and discriminations. Wishing to lead living beings to produce the roots of goodness, the Buddha employs diverse causes and conditions, analogies, and expressions to explain the various dharmas, carrying out the Buddha work without respite, day after day, month after month, year after year.

The Buddha's life span knows no birth or death. For limitless and boundless *nayutas* of *asamkhyeyas* of eons, he has been dwelling constantly in the Pure Land of Eternal Stillness and Light, neither produced nor extinguished. The Buddha says:

> It has been such a very long time since I became a Buddha, yet the life span I realized when formerly practicing the Bodhisattva path is even longer than that. As I now proclaim that I am about to enter the stillness, I am not really passing into the stillness. I manifest entering the stillness only as an expedient to teach and transform living beings.

Why does the Buddha, although he does not become extinct, still announce his extinction? Why does he manifest production and extinction when for him there is actually no production or extinction?

If the Buddha were to stay in the world a long time, remaining long in the world and not entering Nirvana, those of scanty virtue who do not plant good roots would become even more lazy. Those with heavy karmic obstacles would not plant good roots. They would grow dependent on the Buddha, thinking, "The Buddha's here. I don't need to plant good roots right now. I'll get to it later." They would wait around. That is why the Buddha manifests as entering the stillness. Once he has entered Nirvana and people see that they have nothing to rely on, they will get busy and plant some good roots. This is a very obvious principle.

When I was in Manchuria, I had a lot of disciples. I taught them how to cultivate, yet they didn't cultivate. Some said they wanted to take their time. Others said, "I don't have time right now." After I left Manchuria, I started to get letters that said, "So-and-so, your disciple in Manchuria, didn't cultivate before, but now he is cultivating because his teacher isn't here. He's working very hard now."

When I was in Hong Kong, my disciples were pretty relaxed about their cultivation. After I left, they realized how hard it is without a teacher, and they all wrote letters to me asking me to come back. I didn't pay any attention to them, however. People are like that. If you see something every day, you don't think it's important. When it's taken away from you, you realize how important it is. So the Buddha doesn't remain in the world for a long, long time, because if he did, people of scanty virtue would fail to plant good roots. They

他善根慢慢地再種也不晚。因為人不種善根，不供養三寶，所以他就會貧窮，會下賤，就貪著財、色、名、食、睡這五欲。

世間的事情就這麼奇怪，越沒有他越貪，越有他越放下了。你看釋迦牟尼佛，這個財、色、名、食、睡，他都具足，然後他都放下了。那些個窮人，財、色、名、食、睡，他都不具足，不具足他就要貪。具足和不具足、他有沒有，這種的境界都是有一種業報的因緣。你若沒有善根，不做善事，你就不會得到好的這種果報。那麼要怎麼樣才能得到好的果報呢？你就要種善根、做善事，才能結善果，有好的果報。好像那些個窮困的人，越窮他就越貪；那些有錢的人，他就沒有那麼大的貪心，因為他有，所以他就不貪。若是有錢的，他還貪，那就是等於窮人一樣，所以才說：「善人就不怨人」，他不怨恨人。「怨人是惡人」，他若怨恨人，這就是惡人。「賢人就不生氣」，那個聖賢的人，就很少生氣的。就有的時候生氣也不是真生氣，是隨這個境界現出這種的樣子。生氣的人是什麼呢？「生氣的人就是愚人」。「富人他就不佔便宜」，若真正富貴的人，他不歡喜佔便宜的，歡喜佔便宜的人都是窮人。窮人他才想佔人家的便宜，他是利益自己。

沒有善根，所以他就貧窮下賤，就貪財、貪色、貪名、貪食、貪睡，貪這個色、聲、香、味、觸，這五欲的境界。他因為貪著五欲，所以就總有一些個憶想，好像無論什麼事情，或者什麼貴重的東西，他沒有得到的時候，他就想要得到。已經得到了，他又怕丟了，又怕把它失去了。這都是憶想妄見。這種妄知妄見，這種憶想，也就好像網羅那麼樣子，把你真正智慧就都給遮蓋住了。這一切眾生善根也沒有，也貧窮下賤了。貪著五欲這種的眾生，如果佛常在這個世界上不入涅槃，他們就生出一種驕慢，就很放肆、很不守規矩了。他們因為天天能看見佛，時時能看見佛，佛也不入滅，他常見佛，就會生出一種厭怠心來了。就好像你沒有到佛教講堂的時候，希望趕快去、趕快去，到佛教講堂去學佛法去。到這兒學了幾個月，或者學一年、半年，就跑了：「啊！學佛法也是這樣子，沒有什麼意思啊！到外邊去總自由，到這地方天天又要來聽經，起早貪黑的，太辛苦了！」沒來的時候就歡喜來，來到這兒學的時間久，就生出一種厭怠，就不願意過

would just choose to wait instead. But those who do not plant good roots or make offerings to the Triple Jewel remain poor and lowly, and they covet the five desires--wealth, form, fame, food and sleep.

The affairs of the world are just that strange. The "have-nots" are greedy, and those who have everything can't put it down. Shakyamuni Buddha, as a crown prince, had a surfeit of all the five desires, but he put them all down. People who haven't had their fill of the five desires are greedy for them. Whether a person "has" or "has not" is a matter of karmic retribution. If you don't have good roots and do no good deeds, you won't have a good reward. How can you get a good reward? Plant good roots and do good deeds, then you will reap a good fruit and gain a good reward. The poorer people are, the greedier they are. People who have a little money aren't as greedy.

People who are wealthy and are still greedy might as well be poor. It's said, "Good people don't hate others; hateful people are not good. Noble people don't get angry; those who get angry are not noble." Sometimes sages get angry, but not really. It's just something they manifest according to certain circumstances. People who get angry are stupid. Rich people don't grab for bargains. People who like bargains are poor people. Poor people are always looking for a deal, hoping to benefit themselves.

Because they don't plant good roots, they are poor, lowly, and greedy for the five desires: wealth, form, fame, food, and sleep or forms, sounds, smells, tastes, and tangible objects. Being greedy for the five desires, they are always plotting about how they can appropriate something they want or how they can hold on to something they have. They are opportunistic and take advantage of situations, using wrong knowledge and views. These schemes and false views are like a net that covers up one's genuine wisdom.

Seeing the Thus Come One constantly present and not entering the stillness, they would become arrogant and lax. They would not follow the rules, and they would act indifferent. If they see the Buddha every day, all the time, and the Buddha does not enter Nirvana, they get tired of him.

This is similar to how, before you came to the Buddhist Lecture Hall, you thought, "I must quickly go and study the Buddhadharma." But once you've been here for a few months or a year, you run away. "Studying the Buddhadharma isn't that great," you decide. "It's kind of boring. I'd rather go where I can be free and not have to listen to lectures every day. It's too hard getting up so early and not resting until late." Before you came here, you were really looking forward to it. Once you have been here studying for a while, you become dissatisfied with the lifestyle, and you get lazy. Perhaps when you first arrived here, you were more vigorous than anyone. You got up earlier and went to bed later than anyone else. You listened to the Sutras regardless of what else was going on. In all respects you were vigorous.

這種生活了，就懶惰了。或者初初到這兒，很勤力的，很精進的，睡也比別人睡得晚，起也比別人起得早，聽經一定來聽，無論哪一個課程都是很精進的，不願意懈怠。時間一久了，就生出一種懈怠了。因為常常在這兒學，就不能想：「我是不容易遇著這個佛法，你看現在在西方來講，從來就沒有研究佛法的，我怎麼這麼幸運呢！我這麼年輕就遇著真正的佛法到西方國家來了，這真是太難得了。」所以就甚至於，也不吃飯，也不睡覺，一定要來學佛法，不單一天、兩天，一個月、二個月這樣子，時時刻刻、年年月月都是這樣子，都是精進，生難遭想：「你說我要是死了，我怎麼會學佛法？我現在沒有死，我就有這一個生命，我一定要學佛法。」要生這種不容易遭遇的想。

你看！你的父親、你的祖父、你的老祖父，往上數七代、八代以上去，恐怕也都沒有學過佛法。你們現在居然就學佛法，這就叫超祖拔宗了。你祖宗都不懂佛法，你們現在懂了，現在學佛法了。不要學了佛法，又當耳邊風，聽過去就沒有事了，好像：

聰明乃是陰騭助，陰騭引入聰明路，
不行陰騭使聰明，聰明反被聰明誤。

我在講《楞嚴經》的時候，已經就講過，居然你們大家誰也不要了，又送回來，這樣子未免把光陰都空過了。所學的佛法必須要每一天溫習它一遍，我以前學的什麼佛法啊？我睡不著覺，我想一想：「《楞嚴經》上都講的誰？講的有個月光童子，他修什麼三摩地來的？喔！修這個水觀定，啊！他怎麼樣子啊？」就想一想。這過去學的想一想，那麼今天新學的又想一想，這種雖然也是妄想，但是這種妄想是幫助你法身慧命的，是往上走的，是君子上達的。你若想一想：「哦！我以前吸marijuana，這個東西不錯，我現在再把它拿起來再吸一吸。」這就又入了魔的境界了，又退回去了。所以你不要有這種的妄想，以前做過的事情不對的，現在一定要把它改了；改了之後，再就不要做了，這才對呢！

你要對這個佛法生難遭難遇的想，尤其有的青年人遇著一些災難，更應該發出來一種懇切至誠的心，生一種難遭難遇的想。這個不單你超祖拔先，比你祖父都有善根，這個佛法恐怕一百個大劫、一千個大劫、一萬個大劫也不容易遇到這個佛法的。

釋迦牟尼佛成佛以來，這個數目算不過來了，你要知

But after a while, because you are constantly surrounded by it and are always studying here, you are unable to think, "It's really difficult to encounter the Buddhadharma, especially now in the West. No one here in the West has ever really had a chance to study the Buddhadharma. How could I be so fortunate? Here I am so young, and I have met the real, true Buddhadharma. It has come here to the West! This is incredibly rare. I don't care if I eat or sleep, but I am certainly going to study the Buddhadharma-- not for just a day or a week or a month or two, but always, year after year, remembering always how rare it is. If I were dead I couldn't study the Buddhadharma. Now, while I am still alive I am certainly going to study it." Keep in mind how rare it is to meet with the Buddhadharma.

Think of your grandparents and great-grandparents and ancestors for generations back who never had a chance to study the Buddhadharma. Now, all of a sudden, you have the chance! This is called "transcending your ancestors." Your ancestors never understood the Buddhadharma, but you are now studying the Buddhadharma.

You shouldn't let the Buddhadharma that you are studying pass by like wind blowing in one ear and out the other. You should make an effort to remember it, not like the verse I taught you during the *Shurangama Sutra* session that none of you remembered:

*Intelligence is aided by hidden virtue.*
*Hidden virtue leads one along the path of intelligence.*
*Failing to do good deeds in secret, thinking yourself smart,*
*You end up outsmarting yourself.*

If you cannot remember it, you are wasting your time. You should review it every day. Go over your lessons each day. For example, before you go to sleep you can reflect, "The *Shurangama Sutra* lessons--The Youth Moonlight, what *samadhi* did he study? Was it the water-contemplation *samadhi*?" And also review your new lessons. Granted all this is false thinking, but this kind of false thinking is helpful in the elevation of your Dharma body and wisdom life. The superior person takes the high road.

Don't review your bad habits, thinking, "I used to smoke marijuana. Should I try it again?" If you do, you have entered a demonic state; you have retreated. Don't have false thoughts like that. The things that you did wrong before, you should change. Once you have changed, don't slip back and do them again.

Consider how difficult it is to meet the Buddhadharma. Young people who have been through traumatic experiences should especially bring forth real sincerity and consider how hard it is to encounter the Buddhadharma. Not only have you transcended your ancestors with your good roots, but in hundreds of thousands of ten thousands of great eons, it's not easy to meet the Buddhadharma.

Shakyamuni Buddha's realization of Buddhahood actually took

道，我們做人以來，這個數目也是算不過來的。我們做人，今生做人，來生做人，這個和佛的作佛這種情形雖然不同，但是都大同小異的。

雖然這麼長的時間，你沒遇到佛法，你們現在想一想，這個世界上，你說遇到佛法的人多呀？是遇不著佛法的人多？你們算一算。就算佛教的國家，也有信天主教的，也有信耶穌教的，是不是啊？就是在佛教的國家，也不一定完全都懂得佛法的，你們想一想有多少人不懂佛法？在表面上好像是懂了，實際上佛法的內容、道理，一點都不通，所以這個佛法不容易遭遇的，要生出一種難遭難遇這種想。又要恭敬三寶，因為佛若久住於世，眾生就沒有這種難遭難遇的想了，也沒有恭敬心了。佛看見這些個眾生現在都不恭敬了，就說：「我入涅槃了。」

有的人聽見說是做人和作佛一樣這麼長的時間，他就生出一種歡喜心，說是：「這也不錯，我雖然沒有作佛，我做人也可以做這麼長的人，生生世世都做人，啊！那我就不要成佛了，我就做人好了。做人，吃一點好東西，穿一點好衣服，住個好房子，買一個好的車，再買一個好的飛機，哦！或者再有錢多，將來這個火箭發明到月宮去，我可以到那地方去旅行一下，這也都是不錯的。」啊！你這個主意雖然很聰明，但是可沒有把握，你沒有一定可以靠得住這個把握。

我雖然說你做了這麼長時間的人，這是大約說的。其實這麼長的時間，你不單做人，什麼都做過，你又到過天上去，見過那個天主；你又到過地下、地府裏去，見過那個地主；你又到過人間，又見過這個人主。各處你都去過，甚至於月宮，你早就去過了，不過你去完了，你忘了，去回來，你又忘了。就好像你小時做的什麼事情，長大的時候，有很多就忘了；你昨天做的事情，今天也就忘了，是不是有這個感覺？甚至於就十二點鐘你所做的事情，到一點鐘的時候就忘了。說：「誰給你多少錢。」「啊！沒有呀！」就忘了。你看這是不是？今生的事情，你都忘了，何況前生再來生的事情，你怎麼會不忘呢？

佛成佛是不變隨緣，隨緣不變，他永遠都是不變更的。做人，隨時都會變的，變貓、變狗、變那個小蟲子各處去爬，變那個鴿子各處去飛，什麼都會變

place uncountable eons ago. And you should know that we have been ordinary beings for an equally unreckonable period of time. Think about how long you have wandered in a human body.

Although the situation in becoming a Buddha is, of course, not the same as continuing an ordinary existence, the time factor is similar. Although it has been such a long time since you met the Buddhadharma, consider this: In this world would you say that there are more people who encounter the Buddhadharma or more who do not? Figure it out for yourself. Even in Buddhist countries, many believe in Christianity, right? Even in Buddhist countries not everyone understands the Buddhadharma. Think about how many people don't understand it. They may appear to understand it, but they haven't penetrated the doctrines at all. It's not easy to meet the Buddhadharma. You should consider how rare it is to encounter. You should pay reverence to the Triple Jewel.

If the Buddha remained long in the world, people wouldn't think of the Buddhadharma as rare, and they wouldn't be reverent. Seeing that living beings weren't being reverent toward him, the Buddha said, "It's time to go. I'm entering Nirvana!"

Hearing that, someone is thinking, "Being a person and becoming a Buddha take the same length of time." They are happy and say, "That's not bad. I may not get to be a Buddha, but if I can be a person for such a long time, life after life, then I don't need to become a Buddha. I'll just be a person, eat some good food, wear some nice clothes, live in a fine house, buy a good car, a plane--or if I'm really rich and rocket technology develops to that point, I'll go for a vacation on the moon! That won't be bad at all."

That is a fairly intelligent plan, but you cannot guarantee that it will happen; there is no way to know with certainty if you can do it. I said that we have been people for a long time, but that was just an estimate. Actually, during all this time, not only have you been a person, but you've been everything else as well. You've been up to heaven and met God, and entered the earth to see one in charge of the earth. You've also roamed among human beings, meeting the leaders. You've been all around. In fact, you went to the moon a long time ago, too. But you forgot, just as you have forgotten a lot of things you did as a child. There are even times when you forget the things you do from one day to the next. In fact, sometimes by one o'clock in the afternoon you can't remember what you did at noon. If you forget the things you do in this life, how much more likely are you to forget the things you did in your previous lives.

We say that the Buddha does not change but accords with conditions, and accords with conditions but does not change. He is forever unchanging. But as a person, you can turn into something else anytime. You can turn into a cat, a dog, a little bug crawling around, or a pigeon flying through the air. Take, for example, the article in yesterday's paper in which people wanted to become animals--cats, dogs, tigers, lions, eagles, frogs, mice, and so forth. Everything is made from the mind alone; you become what you want to be.

的。所以你若不相信，在前幾天那個報紙上都登過了，居然就有那麼多人願意做貓的，願意做狗的，願意做老虎的，願意做獅子的，願意做鷹的，願意做蛤蟆、老鼠，什麼都有願意做的。你看！他願意做他就去做。這一些個畜生，很多種類的眾生，都是一切唯心造，你心裏願意做什麼就做什麼了。說：「那我心裏願意成神，會不會成？」也會的。你願意做什麼都可以，因為你所願意就會達到你的目的。因為有這種道理，所以我們願意成佛就會成佛的，若不願意成佛就不成佛。我們做人是很危險的，作佛是很平安的。你願意危險，你就做危險的事情；你願意快樂平安，你就去做快樂平安的事情。

因為前邊所說這個道理，所以如來用這個方便法門為眾生說法。你們應該知道，諸佛出世是不容易遇見，百千萬億劫都不一定遇見佛出世，非常難遭難遇的。是什麼道理呢？這一些沒有善根、德行薄的人，要經過很長很長的時間，無量百千萬億那麼多個大劫，或者有善根的就會見到佛；或者沒有善根，就是在無量百千萬億劫這麼長的時間，也見不著佛。你看多困難！因為這種的緣故，我才作這種的說話。你們要知道，如來是不容易得見的，不是小善根、薄德行的人所能見到的。

所有這一切的眾生，聞佛說這個佛不容易遇著，他們就會生難遭難遇的這種想，心裏就戀慕於佛，戀慕於法，戀慕於僧，所以見到佛也非常歡喜，見到佛法也非常歡喜，見到僧人更歡喜，就好像人渴了喝水似的，渴仰於佛。他生出一種戀慕，生出一種渴仰的思想，這無形中，就會種善根了。因為這樣子，所以如來雖然不真實的滅度，而說自己滅度了；其實佛現在還是在靈山來說法呢！不單我釋迦牟尼佛這樣說法，就過去一切諸佛也都是這樣說法。他們為的教化眾生，所說的法都是真實不虛的法。

現在舉出一個譬喻，譬喻有這麼一個最好的醫生，能善治諸病。這個醫生聰明有智慧，他明白怎樣處理藥方，用什麼藥可以治什麼病，一切的病，他都可以治。這個醫生有很多小孩子。這小孩子有多少呢？有十、二十，乃至一百。這十就是十地菩薩；二十就是聲聞、緣覺這二乘；一百也就是十法界變成百數了。

這個最好的醫生因為有特別的緣故，有特別的事，

"Well, I want to become a god. Can I do that?" you ask.

Yes, you can. You can be whatever you want. Because you have a wish and an intention, you can arrive at your aim. Based on this principle, if we want to become Buddhas, we can do so. If you don't want to become a Buddha, you won't. Being a person is very dangerous. Being a Buddha is very peaceful. If you like danger, then do dangerous things. If you prefer peace and quiet and happiness, then do peaceful and happy things.

For that reason, because of the doctrines just discussed, the Thus Come One uses skill-in-means in speaking the Dharma for living beings. You should know that it is difficult to encounter a Buddha appearing in the world. In a hundred million eons, a Buddha may not appear in the world even once. What is the reason? Those of scant virtue, who do not have good roots, may pass through limitless hundreds of thousands of myriads of *kotis* of eons--such a long time, so many great kalpas--during which time they may see a Buddha or they may not. If they have good roots, they may see a Buddha. If they don't, then throughout all that time they will not encounter a Buddha. Consider how difficult it is! Because of that, I tell them that the Thus Come One is difficult to get to see. Those of few good roots and little virtue cannot see the Buddha.

All these living beings, listening to the Buddha's words, will realize how difficult it is to get to encounter the Buddha. They will long to meet a Buddha, the Dharma, and the Sangha. And so when they encounter the Buddha, they are extremely happy. When they meet the Dharma and the Sangha, they are also exceptionally happy. They were as if thirsty, and upon gazing at the Buddha, had their thirst quenched.

They will then, simply by virtue of cherishing that thought of longing and thirst, plant good roots. That is why the Thus Come One, although he does not really become extinct, still speaks of passing into extinction. In reality, the Buddha is presently on Vulture Peak speaking the Dharma. Not only does Shakyamuni Buddha speak Dharma in this way, all the Buddhas speak in this way. For the sake of teaching and transforming living beings, they speak such Dharma, which is entirely true and not false.

The Buddha then brings up an analogy: It is as if there were a good physician, wise and intelligent, who can cure all illnesses. He is well-versed in the medical arts and skillful at healing the multitude of sicknesses. The man also has many sons--ten, twenty or even a hundred. "Ten" represents the Bodhisattvas of the Ten Grounds. "Twenty" represents those of the Two Vehicles--the Hearers and the Pratyekabuddhas. "A hundred" represents the Ten Dharma Realms times the Ten Suchnesses.

The excellent physician is called away on business, and he travels to a far-off country to heal someone, or on tour. Meanwhile, the children are not yet grown. It's a physician's home, and there are many medicines in it. The children get hold of

到其他的國家去，或者給人治病，或者去旅行，所以遠至餘國。這一些個小孩子因爲都沒有長大，這個醫生家裏有很多的藥品，小孩子就把這個毒藥給吃了。他以爲：啊！這毒藥是糖水呢！因爲年紀小，他又不知道什麼叫毒，什麼叫糖，看見這兒有一瓶東西，本來是毒藥的，他以爲是什麼juice，他就拿著喝了，喝了就中毒了。這個毒藥一發作了，就不舒服，不好受了，不好受就悶亂了，心裏發狂了，發顛了，就在地下打滾。這時候，這個好的醫生在其他國辦事辦完了，就回來了。回到家裏，所有的小孩子都飲了毒了，或者毒得糊塗了，毒得什麼也不知道了，或者還有多少明白，很遠就看見父親回來了。這小孩子就都很歡喜，就歡迎父親回來，又有的給父親叩頭，有的就給打個問訊，說：「唉！這回父親可回來了，我們都很幸運還能看見父親。」這一些個沒有失心的小孩子就說：我們太愚癡了，也不知道這個毒藥這麼厲害，我們以爲是糖水，或者是什麼蘋果水、橘子水，或者可口可樂之類的；歡喜喝酒的，就以爲這是酒，於是乎拿過就都喝，誰不知道是毒藥。願請父親您給我們救療，給治一治這個病，你教我們多活一個時期，把壽命再延長一點。

這良醫是誰呢？方才不是説比喻嗎？良醫就是佛，佛就譬如良醫。這些小孩子是誰呢？就是一切眾生。因爲在佛沒有到我們這兒來，或者已經到這個世界來，又入涅槃到其他的世界去，這時候因爲我們沒有眞正智慧，所以就亂吃東西。眾生就是以食爲天，食色性也，小孩子一生出就會吃奶，什麼也不懂呢，你給他東西，他就會吃，又吃拳頭，又吃手指頭，總而言之，有什麼東西他就要吃，這是他本性。所以我們眾生也都像那個小孩子歡喜吃，這一吃，就吃了毒藥了。

什麼叫毒藥呢？這個旁門外道，那個邪道，這都叫毒藥。旁門左道，他講的道理不徹底、不究竟，這都等於毒藥一樣。這個毒藥，他吃了若知道是毒藥，還有一點辦法可以救的，就怕他吃得太多了，根本就不知道是毒藥了。他以爲這回他可得到長生不老丹了，吃了這個東西，現在什麼也不知道了，這大約永遠都不會死了，可生天堂了，到天國樂園了。因爲什麼他吃毒都不知道呢？就因爲他迷得太深了，毒得太深了，這種毒入到骨髓裏頭去了，所以就失心，就不明白眞理了。不失心的有人給他一講，他還可以懂了，還可以明白眞理。

some poisonous concoction and drink it, thinking that it is a sweet-tasting drink. Children don't know any better. They can't tell the difference between poison and something good to drink. They think it's a bottle of some kind of juice, and they drink it up. When it takes effect, the pain, which is unbearable, causes them to roll on the ground in delirium.

Just then their father, the good doctor, finishes his business and returns home. Because they drank the poison, some have lost their senses and are totally oblivious. Some of them still have some sense and recognition left. Seeing their father at a distance, they are all delighted. They bow to him, kneel, and inquire after him. "Welcome back in peace and safety. We are really fortunate to be able to see our father again." Those who have not completely lost their senses speak up and say, "In our foolishness, we took some poison by mistake. We thought it was syrup or apple juice or cola or something, and we swallowed it." Those who like to drink alcohol see the poison as alcohol. Who would have known it was poison? "We pray that you will rescue and heal us, and will restore our lives to us. Father, will you save us, so we can live for a while longer?"

Above we said this was an analogy. Who is the good doctor? The Buddha, of course. The children are all living beings. Maybe these living beings live at a time when the Buddha is not in the world, or maybe the Buddha was in the world but has already entered Nirvana and gone to some other world. The father's leaving refers to the Buddha's entering Nirvana, so beings have no chance to meet him. When the Buddha goes away, living beings are not careful about "what they eat." It is said, "Living beings take food as heaven." It's also said, "Food and sex come naturally." Children start drinking milk from the moment they are born. They don't know very much, but they know how to eat. They suck their thumbs or suck their fingers; whatever you give them they put in their mouths. And so, acting on this instinct, the children here managed to poison themselves.

What is the poison? The poisons are the deviant sects and cults and externalist ways, the teachings of nonultimate religions. If after the children have taken the poison, they know it is poison, then there is a chance they can still be saved. But if they've taken a lot of it and don't even realize that it's poison, thinking they have taken the nectar of immortality or something, they are hard to save. Having taken it, they are senseless, but they think they will never die. They think they have been born into some heavenly paradise. They are so deeply immersed in their confusion that they don't even know they have been poisoned. The poison has penetrated all the way to their bones and marrow. So some have lost their senses, that is, they don't recognize true principle. Others have not lost their senses, and they are still receptive to understanding the truth.

The doctor's returning is an analogy for the Buddha's appearing in the world. The Buddha, having finished his work of

等佛回来，這是佛出世了，這個醫生從他國回來了，就譬如佛在其他的世界教化眾生完了之後，又到這個世界來教化眾生。教化眾生一看，這一些個眾生都喝旁門外道這個毒，毒得太深了，不容易救治了，但是這一些個眾生有的還有聰明的，所以見著佛就很歡喜，向佛叩頭，頂禮問訊，就說：「我們這一些個眾生太愚癡了，請佛慈悲，給我們一點藥，救療我們，把我們這個毒給解除去，令我們壽命再增長，再延長，不會毒死我們。」所以佛看眾生這麼樣可憐，就用種種的藥，來解除眾生這個毒。但是有的就歡喜服，病就好了，這邪知邪見也就沒有了；有的不歡喜服，不歡喜吃這個藥，他這個毒就不能解。不相信佛法的人，就等於不服，不吃這個最好的醫生給的藥一樣。

現在講的是這個良醫，良醫就是譬如佛。我們再講庸醫，庸醫就是殺人的，良醫是救人的。什麼是庸醫呢？就是這一些個旁門外道，佛教不是佛教，道教不是道教，儒教不是儒教，婆羅門不是婆羅門，這一些九十六種旁門外道，這都叫庸醫。

這個良醫見著自己這一班小孩子都中毒了，非常地苦惱，發狂了這個樣子，於是乎就依照藥書上藥性這種經的方法，就找一點最好的、可以解毒的這種藥和這種草。這個藥草的顏色也非常好，味也不苦，也很美味的，很甜的，看得也很好看，滋味又甜。然後把它搗碎了，又用篩子篩一篩。這就是用種種的法來教化這二乘的人，令他們都由阿含經過方等般若，在般若的時候，這就等於搗篩和合。這個良醫給這一班小孩子，令他們吃這種的藥，就說：「這個藥是最好的一種藥，看著也好看，這個味道又非常香，也非常地甜，非常好，你們這一班小孩子，快一點把這個藥吃下去。吃下藥，你們病就好了，你這一切的痛苦就都解除了，沒有了。」

這一班小孩子裏邊，那個還沒有發狂、沒有發神經、還清醒的這種人，見著這個良藥，色也好，味道也好，就把這個藥吃了。在般若之後，就到了法華的時候，就是這個法華的妙法，這叫良藥。把這個良藥吃了之後，這個病統統都好了，完全都好了，什麼病也沒有了。什麼病也沒有，就是把這個見惑、思惑、無明惑都破了，破了之後，就開悟了，這就什麼病都好了。還有其他中毒中得深的，已經發了神經這一類的小孩子，見到他父親來了，雖然也

teaching and transforming living beings in other worlds, comes again to this world to teach and transform living beings. He sees that these living beings have been poisoned by adherents of deviant cults and outside ways, and are almost beyond help. Some of them, however, are fairly intelligent. When they see the Buddha, they are very happy. They bow respectfully to the Buddha and say, "We living beings are too stupid. Please be compassionate, Buddha, and give us some medicine to counteract this poison. We want to live a bit longer and don't want to die."

Seeing how pitiful living beings are, the Buddha uses various kinds of "medicines" to counteract their respective poisons. Some of them are happy to take the medicine, and they get well; they get rid of their deviant knowledge and deviant views. Others, however, do not wish to take the medicine. They do not expel the poison, which causes them not to believe in the Buddhadharma.

The Buddha is likened to a good doctor. But there are inept doctors who kill people. Good doctors save people. The quacks represent the leaders of deviant cults and sects and externalist ways. They may say they are Buddhists, but they don't act like Buddhists. Or they may say they are Taoists, but they don't act like Taoists. They may claim to be Confucianists or Brahmans or any one of the ninety-six externalist sects.

The good doctor sees that his children have taken poison. Seeing his children delirious and in such agony, the father consults his medical texts, which describe the properties of different medicines, and then searches for wholesome herbs possessed of good color, aroma, and flavor--not bitter, but actually very sweet--perfect in all respects. He then pounds, sifts, and mixes them together. This represents the Buddha using various Dharmas to teach and transform those of the Two Vehicles. Having passed through the Agamas and Vaipulya periods, arriving at the Prajna period is likened to "pounding, sifting, and mixing."

The good doctor says to his children, "This is an excellent medicine. It looks good, smells good, and is very sweet to the taste. It is exceptionally fine medicine. Quickly take it, children, and you will get better and all your pain and suffering will be relieved."

Among the children are those who have not lost their senses, but are relatively alert. Seeing the wholesome and aromatic medicine, they immediately take it and their sickness is completely cured. After the Prajna period comes the Dharma Flower/Nirvana period. The Wonderful Dharma of the *Dharma Flower Sutra* is called "excellent medicine." The children's sickness being "completely cured" means they have broken through the delusions of views, the delusions of thought, and the delusions of ignorance. Having done that, they gain enlightenment and have no more illnesses.

Although the others who were badly poisoned and who have

很歡喜地問訊他的父親，也想要叫他父親給他治病；可是他父親這個良醫給他的藥，他不肯吃。就是給他說法華經，他不相信，不肯信受奉行。這是什麼道理？因為他這個毒氣入得太深，把他本來那清醒的心都失去，都糊塗了。對於這種顏色又好，滋味又香的藥，他說這個不是好藥，這個藥吃了他更糊塗。所以他就不相信這個妙法。佛也就像這個良醫似的，給眾生說法，用這最妙的法來教化眾生，眾生他若不相信，佛也沒有辦法一定叫他相信的。

這個父親看見這一些個中毒的小孩子太可憐了，他們都是因為中毒中得太深了，所以心裏就有一種顛倒，心裏都不清楚了。雖然他們看見我很歡喜的，他們求我，叫我給他們治這個病，我給他們選擇這麼好的藥品，他們也不願意吃這種藥。我現在應該想一個方便法門，設出來一個方便法門，使令這一班中毒的小孩子，能吃我所給他們預備的這種藥。

所以他就這樣講了，說：「你們各位小孩子應該知道，我現在年紀已經衰老了，我死的時候，很快就到了，我給你們預備這種好的良藥，最好的藥品，我現在給你們留在這個地方，你們這一班中毒的小孩子可以拿來吃，吃了它，你不要憂愁你這個病不會完全好，你服下我這個藥，你的病就會好的。」這麼教誨這些小孩子之後，又到其他的國家去了，然後派一個人回來告訴這一些小孩子，說：「你的父親現在已經死囉！」

所以佛示現入涅槃也就是這樣子，佛預備一切的法，這都是良藥。因為看眾生中的毒太深，不肯相信佛法，所以就設方便法門，說是佛入涅槃了；實際上，佛也沒有生，也沒有滅，在佛的境界上是不生不滅，不垢不淨，不增不減的。那麼因為眾生，所以就設出這麼一個方法來，說是入涅槃。

這一班中毒的小孩子，聽見他父親在其他的國家喪亡了，雖然他們把本心已經失去了，但是還懂得他父親已經死了，所以就心裏非常地憂惱，就作出這麼一種的想念，說：「我父親在的時候，他慈悲愍念我們，他很疼愛我們的，對我們非常好，他能以救護我們，令我們沒有病。現在父親捨棄我們了，在很遠的地方，在其他的國家死亡了，現在我們又孤獨又沒有依靠了，沒有人來救護我們了，沒有人來做我們的恃怙了。」心裏就很悲傷，很感嘆的。

already gone crazy rejoice in their father's arrival, inquire after his well-being, and seek to be cured of their illnesses, they refuse to take the medicine. The Buddha speaks the *Dharma Flower Sutra*, but they do not believe it. They are unable to believe, accept, and practice it.

What is the reason? The poisonous vapors have entered them so deeply that they have lost their senses. They are muddled and confused, and so they say that the medicine with good color and aroma is not good. They profess that if they take the medicine, they will not gain any advantage. They don't believe the Wonderful Dharma.

The Buddha, like the good doctor, speaks the Wonderful Dharma for living beings. He uses the most magnificent Dharma to try to teach and transform living beings. But if living beings do not believe him, the Buddha has no way to force them to believe.

The father then thinks, "How pitiful are these children. The poison has entered too deeply and has confused their minds, and they are unclear. Although they rejoice to see me and ask me to rescue and cure them, still, once I give them this excellent medicine, they refuse to take such good medicine as this. I should now set up an expedient device to induce them to take this medicine."

Immediately he says, "You should know that I am now old and weak, worn out, and my time of death has arrived. I will now leave this good medicine right here for you to take. You children who have ingested poison can use it. Don't worry about not getting well. Just take the medicine, and you shall certainly recover." Having instructed them in this way, he then goes away to another country and sends a messenger back to announce to the children, "Your father is dead."

The Buddha's manifesting entry into Nirvana is also like this. The Buddha prepared all these Dharmas to be good medicines because he sees that living beings are so severely poisoned that they are unable to believe in the Buddhadharma. For that reason he sets up the expedient Dharma-door of entering Nirvana. In reality, the Buddha does not undergo production and extinction. The Buddha's state is one of no production and no extinction, no defilement and no purity, no increasing and no decreasing. His entering Nirvana is an expedient device for the sake of saving living beings.

When the children who have been poisoned hear that their father, off in some other country, is dead, their hearts are struck with grief. Although they have lost their senses, they understand that their father has died, and they are extremely distraught. And they think, "If our father were here, he would be compassionate and pity us, and we would have a savior and protector. He really cherished us. He was so good to us. He would have saved us from our sickness. Now, he has forsaken us to die in another country. He left us and went somewhere far, far away. Now he is

因為心裏有這種悲傷，有這種感嘆，心就醒悟了。醒悟什麼呢？說：「哦！這個藥是我父親在生的時候留下的，說是可以治病。這個顏色也非常地好，這個味也非常香，非常美好。」於是乎就把這個藥拿來吃了，所中這種毒、這個病就都癒了，都好了。就是不信這個外道法，而信佛法了；一信佛法，這邪知邪見就沒有了，這叫病癒了。這個父親本來是沒死，聽見他兒子這個病統統都好了，完全都好了，於是乎沒有好久，他父親就回來了，令所有這一班中毒的小孩子，又都看見他的父親了。

或者會有人這樣說：「這個良醫盡打妄語，他盡說假話，他有打妄語的罪。」會不會有人這麼樣講呢？那麼請問佛的這位菩薩就答覆佛說：「不會的，世尊。」釋迦牟尼佛也說了：

> 我所說的法也就是這個樣子，我說阿含、方等、般若，然後說法華涅槃，也就是像這個良醫是一樣的。我已經成佛沒有數量沒有邊際，有百千萬億這麼多那由他阿僧祇劫了。因為想要教化眾生的緣故，用這個方便說法，為實施權這個道理，所以才對眾生說：「哦！我要滅度了。」就好像那個醫生到其他的國家，說他已經死了，是一樣的道理。這個也沒有人可以說：「哦！佛是打妄語，佛也盡說虛假的話。」

自從我得佛果以來，很長很長的時間，所經過這一切的劫數已經有無量百千萬這麼多的大劫，這個阿僧祇劫也不知道有多少了。經過多少個阿僧祇，我常常是在這個世界各國來說法教化眾生，所有無數億這麼多的眾生，我教化令他們成就佛道。

從我最初成佛到現在，有無量無邊這麼多的那由他阿僧祇劫，我都是因為想要教化眾生的緣故，方便現涅槃。也就好像這個醫生走到其他的國家，叫一個人回來告訴他這些個小孩子說，他已經死了。為什麼呢？就叫這一些個小孩子自己沒有一種依賴心了，就要吃他所預備這個良藥。用個方便法門，說：「佛要入涅槃了，你們大家有什麼問題趕快問了，有什麼不明白的趕快說了。」實實在在的，佛沒有滅度，沒有入涅槃，常常在這個地方來說法教化眾生，我常常都住到這個娑婆世界，這靈鷲山上，

dead, leaving us orphaned with no one to rely upon. No one will save us now. No one will offer us support and protection." Constantly grieving, their minds then become awakened. They understand that the medicine their father offered them when he was alive has good color, aroma, and flavor. They take it immediately, and their poisonous sickness is completely cured. They believe in the Buddhadharma and no longer believe in the dharmas of externalist ways. As soon as they came to believe in the Buddhadharma, they got rid of all their deviant knowledge and deviant views.

The father, who really hasn't died, hearing that his children have been completely cured, then comes back. All the children who had previously been poisoned see their father.

Perhaps someone will say, "This good physician has committed the offense of false speech. He didn't tell the truth." Now, could anyone rightly say the good doctor has lied? The Bodhisattva who had been questioning the Buddha replied, "No, World Honored One." Shakyamuni Buddha said:

> I, too, am like that. The Dharma I have spoken is that way as well. I spoke the Agamas, the Vaipulya teachings, the Prajna teachings, and then the Dharma Flower/Nirvana teachings in the same way, just like the good doctor. I realized Buddhahood limitless, boundless, hundreds of thousands of myriads of *kotis* of *nayutas* of *asamkhyeyas* of eons ago. For the sake of living beings, in order to teach and transform them, I speak expediently, bestowing the provisional for the sake of the real, and say that I am about to enter Nirvana. This is like the doctor going to another country and then sending back the message that he has died. And no one can say, "Oh, the Buddha was lying."

I attained Buddhahood limitless hundreds of thousands of myriads of *kotis* of *asamkhyeyas* of eons ago. During all those uncountable eons, I always speak the Dharma in different lands and countries, to teach and transform countless millions of living beings, so they enter the Buddha-Way.

And from the time I attained Buddhahood until now, throughout these limitless *asamkhyeyas* of eons, in order to teach and transform living beings, I expediently manifest Nirvana. This is like the doctor who went to another country and sent back a messenger to tell his children he was dead. When his children heard that, they no longer relied upon their father, but took the medicine instead. Thus I expediently said, "The Buddha is going to enter Nirvana. All of you should ask whatever questions you have. Hurry up! If there is something you don't understand, get it cleared up right away." But in truth I do not really enter Nirvana.

I remain here always speaking the Dharma, teaching and transforming living beings. I always stay right here on

以種種的神通這種力量，使令一切的顛倒眾生，就是我沒有滅度，他們也看不見了。雖然我就在他旁邊，因為這個眾生顛倒，他也看不見我。因為這個些個顛倒眾生，他被無明來迷住了，雖然近我，他也看不見。

大家看見我入滅了，要供養我的舍利，這時候他們就統統都生出來一種懷念，愛戀而仰慕的心，生出一種渴仰，想要見佛。眾生既然生出一種信服的心來了，他們這個心也直了，意念也都柔軟了，也不那麼剛強了，現在他們也都想要見佛了：「現在佛入涅槃了，我們現在若再見著佛可好了。」就生一種稀有的心，難遭難遇的心。甚至於把自己的生命做布施，他們都不可惜了，他們都不吝惜他們的生命了，就是為求佛法布施他們的生命，他也都願意了。

所以在求佛道受戒的時候，都在頭上燃香疤，這都是不惜身命的一種表現；你若惜命：「我這很痛的！」就捨不得不惜生命這樣子來燒身供佛。

佛為什麼要滅度而說沒有滅度呢？在這一種的道理上，是為開悟的人，就沒有滅度；沒有開悟的人，就以為佛滅度了。你要是開悟，得三身四智五眼六通，就和佛常常在一起，你都在佛的身邊，所以這叫常見於佛。你若沒有得到這種的境界，就佛雖然在你的身邊，你也看不見佛。所以為什麼說佛沒有滅度？就是他能和證得五眼的人常常相見的，所以佛沒有滅度；要是一般沒有五眼的人，就是不能相見，所以以為佛是滅度，實際佛也沒有滅度。

這一切眾生，不惜生命來求佛法，這時候就有一種感應道交，因為眾生的心真誠了，所以在這個時候，我釋迦牟尼佛和一切的大比丘僧、比丘尼等等，一同出現於靈鷲山這個靈山法會。所以在天臺智者大師，念誦《法華經》，入到法華三昧，親見靈山一會，儼然未散，所以他就得到一旋陀羅尼。由這一點證明，就是現在釋迦牟尼佛還仍然在靈鷲山那兒說法教化眾生呢！

佛常常在靈鷲山來為眾生說法，並沒有入滅，因為以方便權巧這種方法的緣故，所以才現出來有滅和不滅，這非滅是滅，所以就滅而不滅，生而未生。那麼在其他的國家裏頭，有這一切的眾生，他們若

Vulture Peak in the Saha World and, using the power of spiritual penetrations, I cause inverted living beings, although near me, not to see me. That means that even though I do not really enter Nirvana, I make it so they don't have an opportunity to see me. Although they are right beside me, because they are upside down, they do not see me.

The multitudes see me as passing into extinction, and they extensively make offerings to my sharira. At this time, they all start thinking about how much they long for and admire me, and their hearts look up to me in thirst. They long to see the Buddha.

Living beings are then faithful and subdued, straightforward, with compliant minds. They are not stubborn any longer. They just single-mindedly wish to see the Buddha. "Now the Buddha has gone to Nirvana! Oh, if we could only see the Buddha once again!" They realize how rare the Buddha is and how difficult it is to encounter him. If they had to give up their very lives, they would do so without regrets.

When you seek the Buddha-Way and take the precepts, you burn some incense scars on your head. This represents that you are willing to give up your life for the sake of the Buddhadharma. If you still care for your own life, that burning will cause unbearable pain, and you won't be able to go through with it. To burn the body as an offering to the Buddha represents that you are willing to give up your life for the sake of the Dharma.

Why does the Buddha say that he doesn't actually pass into extinction? The principle works like this: For those who are enlightened, there is no extinction. Those who are unenlightened think that the Buddha enters extinction. If one is enlightened and has the Three Bodies, the Four Wisdoms, the Five Eyes, and the Six Spiritual Penetrations, then one is with the Buddha at all times; one is always right next to the Buddha. That is called "always seeing the Buddha." If you have not attained that state, then although the Buddha is actually right beside you, you cannot see him. The Buddha says he does not pass into extinction because he is always present for those who have been certified to the attainment of the Five Eyes. Those without the Five Eyes cannot see the Buddha, and they conclude that he has become extinct. Actually, the Buddha does not become extinct.

When people get to the point that they do not even care about their own lives as they seek the Buddhadharma, there is a response of the Way because of their extreme earnestness. At that time, Shakyamuni Buddha and the Sangha assembly of Bhikshus and Bhikshunis all appear together on Spiritual Vulture Mountain. Thus Great Master Zhi Zhe of the Tiantai School entered the Dharma Flower *samadhi* when reciting the *Dharma Flower Sutra*, and he personally saw the Dharma assembly on Spiritual Vulture Mountain still taking place--it had not dispersed. He obtained the "Dharani of a Single Revolution." That

生一種恭敬心，而歡喜見佛，我在其他的國家給他說無上法。

你們各位沒有聽說過這種的道理，所以你們就說：「佛滅度了。」其實我沒有一個滅度，也沒有一個不滅度，這個不生不滅，又也有生，又也有滅。我看見所有諸眾生都埋沒在五欲裏邊，埋沒在這個財、色、名、食、睡裏邊，苦惱就是在這個財色名食睡裏邊貪戀。因爲他們都貪著到五欲上了，所以我也就不現身爲他們說法，令這一切的眾生，生出一種好像好飢渴似的，好仰慕這種心。因爲他們心裏生出一種戀慕的心，所以就出現爲這眾生來講說佛法。

爲什麼眾生就有見佛的？有不見佛的？爲什麼佛滅度了，又說沒有滅度？沒有滅度，又說滅度了？什麼原因呢？這都是佛的神通力所變現的。所以才說，生而未生，滅而未滅，這都是佛的神通力的緣故，所以眾生就有見，有不見。與佛有緣的，就隨時都可以見佛；與佛沒有緣的，隨時都見不著佛。那麼說：「我若與佛沒有緣，我見不著佛，那怎麼辦呢？」你就要種善根、結佛緣，供養三寶——供養佛、供養法、供養僧。你在三寶面前修供養，修的時間久了，你自然就有佛緣了嘛！你如果不種善根，始終都不會有佛緣的，所以就要種善根。

你們來皈依三寶的人，以後或者到其他的道場裏邊，或者到其他的廟上去住的時候，不要以爲不給錢是一種好處，因爲你是在家人，到這個道場，無論哪一個道場，屬於佛教的。不屬於佛教呢，那是不管。若屬於佛教的，到無論哪一個道場都應該發一種供養心，要供養三寶，不要叫三寶來供養你。因爲你要是叫三寶來供養你，那你就一生不如一生了。你看那一些個人，爲什麼他就富貴？就因爲他供養三寶，才能有福。爲什麼那些個人窮，就因爲他不供養三寶，所以他就一生比一生窮。那麼你們是凡皈依我的弟子，無論以後到任何的道場去，都應該生一種供養心。

釋迦牟尼佛於阿僧祇劫，就是無量無數無邊那麼多的時間，他常常住在靈鷲山上而爲眾生說法，或者到其他的世界，或者到其他的國土裏邊去。眾生看見有一切水、火、風三災、八難這種劫，可是這靈鷲山和其他我所住的地方都安隱，不會被這三災所害。我所住的地方，有很好的花園子，很好的樹林子，一切的堂

proves that even now the Buddha is still present on Spiritual Vulture Mountain, speaking the Dharma, teaching and transforming living beings. He has not passed into extinction. But using clever expedient devices, he manifests "extinction" and "nonextinction." He speaks of and manifests birth and passing into extinction, but they are not real. For living beings in other lands, those who are reverent, faithful, and longing to see the Buddha, he speaks the supreme Dharma. The Buddha says:

> All of you have not heard this doctrine, and you think I entered extinction. For me there is no production or extinction, although I speak of it. I see living beings in misery, drowning in the five desires: wealth, sex, fame, food, and sleep. Since they are greedy for the five desires, I refrain from manifesting for them. I do not manifest and speak the Dharma for them, because I want to cause them to look up in thirst. Then, when living beings are filled with longing, I emerge and speak the Buddhadharma for them.

Why is it that some living beings see the Buddha and others do not? Why is it that the Buddha says he is entering extinction and then does not? These are all transformations worked by the power of the Buddha's spiritual penetrations. So we say, "There is production and yet no production. There is extinction and yet no extinction. Those who have affinities with the Buddha can see him any time; those lacking affinities never get to see him." You say, "If I have no affinities with the Buddha and cannot see him, then what should I do?" Plant good roots, create affinities with the Buddha by making offerings to the Triple Jewel--the Buddha, Dharma, and Sangha. If you cultivate merit and virtue before the Triple Jewel, after a while you will naturally have affinities with the Buddha. If you do not plant good roots, you will never have affinities with the Buddha. So you ought to plant good roots.

When people who have taken refuge with the Triple Jewel visit other temples or monasteries, they should not think they can get a good deal by staying there without paying. As laypeople, whenever you go to a Buddhist temple, you should wish to make offerings to the Triple Jewel, not ask that the Triple Jewel make offerings to you. If you ask the Triple Jewel to support you, you will be bound to fall lower in each successive life. Why are some people so wealthy? They made offerings to the Triple Jewel. People who do not make offerings to the Triple Jewel become poorer and poorer in each successive life. Those of you who have taken refuge with me should always bring forth the initiative to make offerings at any temple you visit in the future.

For countless *asamkhyeyas* of eons, Shakyamuni Buddha constantly speaks Dharma for living beings at Spiritual Vulture Mountain, as well as in other lands. Living beings may see the calamities of wind, water, and fire, or the eight difficulties, but

閣，用種種七寶來莊嚴這個寶妙樓閣。眾生在這一個莊嚴的道場裏邊遊樂，一切的三界諸天，來擊這個天鼓，天鼓鳴空，常常在給佛作伎樂。常常在天上雨最適意、最歡悦的這種華，你一看這種華，心裏就歡喜得不得了。這華散在佛上，和供養大眾。

我這個常寂光淨土永遠都不會毀壞的，可是眾生自己有這種煩惱的見給燒盡了，所以又憂愁又恐怖，有種種的苦惱。爲什麼呢？就因爲有這個惡見，有這個眾生的見。這一切有罪的眾生，以他這種惡業的因緣，他們要超過無量無數無邊這麼多的阿僧祇劫，聽不見佛的名字，聽不見法的名字，也聽不見僧的名字。

你説這個世界上，佛沒有出世以前，沒有人知道佛法，所以也就沒有人見著佛，也沒有人聽見佛這個名字。所以須達多長者一聽見佛的名字，就毛孔悚然，也不知道是怎麼回事，他毛孔就都豎起來了，因爲從來就沒有聞見這三寶的名字。

所有修功德、種善根的人，他又柔和，心又直，沒有委曲心，他們就都能見著我；那一些個有罪的眾生，他就見不著我。所以有罪的人，就連一個佛像都看不見，你能看見佛像，這是你的罪業減輕了。你若有功德，才能見著佛，才能見著法，才能見著僧。有善根的人，常常見佛的人，我就説佛的壽命長，因爲若不壽命長，他怎麼可以常常見呢？常常見佛，就因爲佛的壽命長。那麼常常不見佛的人，我就給他説佛不容易遇著，最難遭難遇。我的智慧力量是這樣子，這個智慧的光明照到無量的世界，無量的眾生發無量的菩提心。

這個壽命沒有數量那麼多的大劫，怎麼樣得來的呢？就因爲久修放生的善業所得來的，所以才能壽命長。你若想你的壽命長，你就要放生，能多放生你壽命就長了。

你們這一般有智慧的人，你不要對我所説的話生出一種疑惑心來。你把你這種懷疑的心斷了它，令它永遠永遠都沒有了，對佛法不要生疑心，佛所説的話是實實在在的，沒有虛假的。就好像那個良醫，對於藥書、藥性，他都非常地熟悉，他知道這寒的藥治什麼病，熱的藥治什麼病，溫的藥治什麼病

Vulture Peak and all the other places where the Buddha is present are peaceful. They cannot be harmed by the three calamities but are always filled with fine gardens and groves, and halls and pavilions adorned with the seven treasures. In the adorned Bodhimanda of the Buddha, the beings wander happily.

The heavenly beings throughout the Three Realms make the heavenly drum resound throughout space, making music for the Buddha. And *mandarava* flowers, flowers which "accord with one's intent" and make people extremely happy as soon as they see them drift down, are scattered on the Buddha and the great assembly.

The Buddha's Pure Land of Eternal Stillness and Light will never be destroyed. But living beings with their afflictions see it being burned entirely, and they become worried, terrified, and miserable. They are miserable because of all their evil views. All these beings with offenses, because of their evil karma, pass through boundless, uncountable eons without hearing the name of the Buddha, the Dharma, or the Sangha.

Before the Buddha appeared in the world, no one knew about the Buddhadharma; no one had ever seen the Buddha or heard the Buddha's name before. When the Elder Sudatta heard the word "Buddha" all the hairs on his body stood straight up on end, although he did not know why. That was because he had never heard the names of the Triple Jewel before.

People who have practiced merit and virtue and planted good roots, who are compliant, agreeable, and honest--not crooked--will all see the Buddha. People with offenses cannot see him; they cannot even see a Buddha image. If you can see a Buddha image, it will lessen your offense-karma. In order to see the Buddha, the Dharma, or the Sangha, you must have merit and virtue. To those with good roots who always see him, the Buddha speaks of the length of the his life span. If it were not this way, how could they see him? For those who pass through long, long periods of time before they get to see the Buddha, he speaks about how the Buddha is difficult to encounter. Such is the power of his wisdom. The Buddha's wisdom light shines throughout limitless worlds, and limitless living beings bring forth the Bodhi mind.

The Buddha's life span of limitless eons was attained through long cultivation and work. The Buddha did the good work of liberating life. If you want to have a long life, you should liberate life. The more life you liberate, the longer your own life will be.

Those of you with wisdom should not have doubts about what the Buddha has said. Cut them off entirely and forever. Do not have doubts about the Buddhadharma. Get rid of them, for the Buddha's words are real, not false.

平常的藥治什麼病，他知道寒熱溫平，這一切的藥性，他都明白，所以你不要生懷疑，他因為想要治發狂、中了毒這一些個小孩子病的緣故，他本來沒有死，他說他死了。所以這些小孩子一看爸爸已經死了，於是乎就要吃這個藥了。

好像佛所說的佛法，留下這種種的藥方。要是佛在世，你就：「不要緊，等一等慢慢再學佛法，反正佛現在也在這兒。」那麼就不著急學佛法。現在佛入涅槃了，你見佛也見不著了，所以要研究佛法了，要來講經說法了，聽經了。要是佛在世，佛會說法嘛！還要聽什麼經呢？就沒有人聽經了。沒有人可以說這個醫生用這種方便法門來給他兒子治病，這是虛妄的，這是有罪了。

我告訴你，我是世間之父，所以救度這個世界上一切苦患的眾生，也就好像這一些個眾生都中了毒似的。本來我實實在在的也沒有入涅槃，但是因為眾生顛倒，我就說入涅槃了。我為什麼說入涅槃呢？因為眾生若天天見著我，就生出一種驕傲縱恣的心，就不守規矩了，不依照佛法來修行了。很放逸，很不守規矩的，著到這個五欲，財色名食睡上，或者著到這個色聲香味觸上，墮落到地獄、餓鬼、畜生這三惡道裏邊去。

我常常知道眾生的這種思想，他想什麼，他或者修行和不修行，我都知道。

我告訴你們，你們現在我這些皈依弟子，你們誰修行、不修行，我也知道，你們誰守規矩、不守規矩，我都知道。那守規矩的人，就天天來聽經；不守規矩的人，就天天要往外跑。這暑假班也是這樣子，你守規矩的，無論哪一個課程，都來守規矩；不守規矩的人上這課，他做那個事。你們必須要認真去學習佛法，不要馬馬虎虎。我講經費這麼多的氣力，你不要以為很容易的，講經也是很費氣力的。

那麼眾生有修行和不修行的，這個眾生應以佛身得度者，佛就現佛身而為說法；應以眾生身得度者，佛就隨類應現，變種種的眾生，去度種種的眾生，為眾生說種種的法。所以佛常常都這樣想，想用什麼方法能使令眾生，得到無上的道法，很快很快就成就佛的這種法身。

They are like the clever expedients of the physician who is knowledgeable about the different kinds of medicines--cool, hot, warm, and neutral--and who, to cure his insane children who had been poisoned, says he is dead, although he is actually alive. When the children think their father is dead, they finally take the medicine.

The Dharma spoken by the Buddha is like good medicine. As long as the Buddha remained in the world, living beings thought they would take their time about studying the Dharma; they were not eager to study it. When the Buddha entered Nirvana and they no longer had access to him, they decided to study the Buddhadharma and lecture the Sutras. As long as the Buddha was in the world, they could just listen to the Buddha, but they did not care to have Sutra lectures. So no one can accuse the doctor, who expediently tries to save the lives of his children by saying that he is dead, and say that he has committed an offense of false speech. The Buddha says:

> I, too, am a father to the world, saving all living beings from suffering and woe. Basically, I do not enter Nirvana, but because living beings are confused, I say I am entering Nirvana. I say this because if living beings saw me every day they would grow arrogant and sloppy. They wouldn't follow the rules and cultivate according to the Dharma. They would be attached to the five desires of wealth, sex, fame, food, and sleep, or else to forms, sounds, smells, tastes, and tangible objects, and then they would tumble into the three evil paths of the animals, ghosts, and hell beings.

> I keep track of all the thoughts in the minds of living beings. I know what they are thinking, and whether or not they are practicing the Way.

As for those of you who have taken refuge with me, I also know whether you are practicing the Way or not. I know very well whether or not you follow the rules. Those who follow the rules come to the Sutra lecture every day, while those who don't go out every day. It's also this way in the Summer Session. Good students obediently attend every class, while unruly ones find other things to do during classtime. You should seriously apply yourselves to studying the Buddhadharma. Don't be casual about it. You shouldn't think it's such a simple matter for me to lecture on the Sutras. It takes a lot of energy.

If a person can be saved by means of a Buddha body, the Buddha appears as a Buddha and speaks Dharma for that person. If a person can be saved by means of another kind of being, the Buddha will take the appropriate form and save that person. The Buddha is always thinking, "How can I cause living beings to realize the supreme Way and to quickly attain the Dharma body of a Buddha?"

# 中國六代祖師血脈傳承
## A BRIEF HISTORY OF THE
## FIRST SIX BUDDHIST PATRIARCHS IN CHINA

## 第一代祖師──達摩大師

菩提達摩，菩提是個覺，達摩是個法，從覺法大師這地方來論，菩提達摩在印度是第二十八代祖師。菩提達摩為什麼不在那兒做祖師，跑到中國來呢？因為在以前授佛記，佛曾經預先說過，到第二十八代的時候，這個大乘佛法應該傳到震旦，震旦就是中國。

所以菩提達摩由印度坐船到中國的時候，當時中國的佛法似有似無，好像有佛法，又好像沒有佛法。為什麼這樣講呢？因為當時有佛法只是在那兒做表面上的工作，誦經呀、研究經典呀、講經呀，甚至於連拜懺都沒有，這是當時一般的學者就拿著佛法當學問來研究，就是互相討論研究。

所以神光法師──二祖慧可，當時就講經說法，講經講得很有感應，講得天花亂墜。天花亂墜並不是人人都看得見的，當時因為也有有善根的人，他就得到天眼。五眼六通，五眼是得到了，六通還談不到，就看見慧可大師一講經，天上就有天女散花，地湧金蓮，從地裏頭湧出金蓮了，神光法師就坐在金蓮花上來講經。你看真是很神氣，這就是研究經典。

但是經典所說的道路是應該修行，可是沒有什麼人修行。為什麼沒有人修行？就因為都怕苦，沒有什麼人真正打坐。當時有一個誌公祖師，他是參禪打坐的，他也是得五眼的。那麼一般人都怕苦，不修行，沒有認真去參禪打坐的。也就好像現在你們一樣，坐在那兒，等一等這個腿痛了，就想把腿伸開這麼搖搖晃晃地把它摩擦一下。因為人都是人嘛！都怕吃苦頭，當時就有這個情形，和現在差不多。這叫似有佛法而沒有佛法，似有似無。

所以達摩祖師一看中國的大乘根性成熟了，應該把這個大乘的佛教帶到中國，於是乎也不怕路程遙

## The First Patriarch
## Great Master Bodhidharma

In the name Bodhidharma, "Bodhi" means enlightened and "Dharma" means the teachings . In the sequence of great masters who enlightened to the Dharma, Patriarch Bodhidharma was the twenty-eighth Patriarch in India. And so why didn't he stay in India and be a Patriarch? Why did he go to China? Well, previously Shakyamuni Buddha made a prediction that from the Twenty-eighth Patriarch on, the Mahayana ("Great Vehicle") teaching would be transmitted to China.

And so when Bodhidharma sail from India to China, the Buddhadharma already existed in China, yet it was as if it were not there at all. Although there were people who studied, there were few who lectured or recited the Sutras and repentance ceremonies were seldom practiced. Cultivation was superficial. Scholars engaged in debates and discussions, but none of them truly understood.

When Dharma Master Shenguang (the Second Patriarch Huike) explained the Sutras, the responses were tremendous! The heavens rained fragrant blossoms and a golden-petaled lotus rose from the earth for him to sit upon. However, only those with good roots, who had opened the heavenly eye, were able to see that. There are five eyes and six spiritual penetrations. Some had attained the five eyes, but there wasn't anyone with the six spiritual penetrations. When Great Master Huike began explaining the Sutra, heavenly maidens would scatter flowers and a golden lotus would well up from the earth. Master Shenguang would sit upon that golden lotus to explain the Sutra. Wasn't that a fine spiritual atmosphere in which to investigate the Sutra?

But, the principles in the Sutras must be cultivated, and yet at that time in China nobody really cultivated. Why not? It was because they were afraid of suffering. No one truly meditated. Well, there was Venerable Patriarch Zhi, who practiced meditation and attained the five eyes. But most people didn't seriously practice meditation because they feared suffering. Now, in America, it is just the same. People sit in meditation. However, as soon as their legs begin to ache, they wince and fidget and then gently unbend and rub them. People are just people and everyone avoids suffering as much as possible. That's the way it was then; that's the way it is now. That's what I meant when I said, although there was Buddhadharma, it was as if there wasn't.

遠、旅行辛苦，來到了中國。你說到了中國怎麼樣呢？中國當時的人看不起外國人，說這是摩羅剎來了，摩羅剎和尚，講話也不懂，語言也不通，所以小孩子一看見達摩祖師就跑了。為什麼呢？看他那麼長的鬍子，就很害怕；大人一看小孩子跑了，就以為這個印度人是不是來抓小孩子來的？所以就叫小孩子更不要接近他。你看不要說是度大人，他連小孩子都度不到，都沒有人敢接近他。

於是他就到廣州，再從廣州到南京，去聽神光法師在那兒講經。達摩祖師一看，法師在這兒講經，他就聽經。聽完了經，他就請法，說：

「法師，你在這兒做什麼呢？」

神光法師說：「我講經呀！」

達摩祖師說：「你講經做什麼？」

神光法師說：「我講經教人了生死呀！」

達摩祖師說：「噢！你教人了生死，生死怎麼樣了法呢？你所講的經，黑的是字，白的是紙，你用什麼教人來了生死？」

神光法師一聽，問得他也沒話講了，心想：「自己用什麼教人了生死呢？」就惱羞成怒，發了脾氣了。

哦！你看他講得天花亂墜，地湧金蓮，也一樣發脾氣，所以我就說似有似無。發了脾氣怎麼樣呀？他就拿起他這個武器，他的武器是什麼？就是一串念珠。他這個念珠，不是我這個星月菩提，我這個不太重，很輕。他那個念珠是用鋼鐵造的，用鋼鐵造的這個念珠做什麼呢？就是預備同人打的時候，就用這個念珠來做兵器、做武器。他這時候一發脾氣，這法師若發了脾氣，那不得了！那簡直像洪水，山崩地裂似的，他說：「你現在來謗法！」拿起念珠照著達摩面上就打了一念珠。

雖然達摩祖師大約會武術，因為他未加防避，想不到他這麼樣子厲害，說不過就要動粗，所以就把達摩祖師的牙給打掉兩顆。

因為他是聖人，據說祖師、聖人的牙被人打掉了，他若是吐在地上，據一般的傳說——是這樣子不是這樣子，你不要問我，我是這麼樣講，我們先講明白了，不要說為什麼？什麼理由？沒有理由，講就是講，沒有理由的，你不要問——吐到地下，就要三年不下雨。

達摩祖師一想：「噢！這若三年不下雨，你說要餓死多少人！我來度眾生、救眾生，這不是殺眾生了？」於是乎把這兩顆牙像吃油餅似的，把它吃到肚裏頭去；油餅沒有那麼硬，他就像吃骨頭似的，吃到肚裏

Patriarch Bodhidharma saw that the roots of Mahayana, the Great Vehicle Buddhadharma, were ripe in China. Fearing neither the distance nor the hardship of travel, he took the Dharma there. The Chinese, who looked down on foreigners at the time, called him a "barbarian monk" because he talked in a way no one understood. When the children looked up at the bearded Bodhidharma, they ran away in terror. Adults feared that he was a kidnapper and so told their children to stay away from him. So you see, he didn't even get to teach children, much less the adults, because nobody dared to approach him.

Patriarch Bodhidharma went to Guangzhou, and then to Nanjing, where he listened to Dharma Master Shenguang explain the Sutras. After listening to the Sutra, Patriarch Bodhidharma asked, "Dharma Master, what are you doing?"

"I am explaining Sutras," Shenguang replied.

"Why are you explaining Sutras?"

"I am teaching people to end birth and death."

"Oh?" said Bodhidharma, "Exactly how do you do that? In this Sutra which you explain, the words are black and the paper is white. How does this teach people to end birth and death?"

Dharma Master Shenguang had nothing to say. How did he teach people to end birth and death? He fumed in silence. Then, even though heavenly maidens rained down flowers and the earth gave forth golden lotuses, Dharma Master Shenguang got angry. That is what I mean when I say that the Buddhadharma existed in China but it was if it were not there at all!

What happened when he got angry? He grabbed his weapon. What was it? His recitation beads. His beads weren't lightweight like these "stars and moon Bodhi" beads of mine. His recitation beads were made of iron. He had them made that way intentionally so he could use them as a weapon when the need arose. This time his wrath was extreme. He reddened with anger and raged like a tidal wave smashing a mountain. As he whipped out his beads, he snapped, "You are slandering the Dharma!" and cracked Patriarch Bodhidharma across the mouth.

Although Patriarch Bodhidharma had some skill in the martial arts, he was caught unprepared. He hadn't expected such a vicious attack— that being unable to reply, the Dharma Master would resort to brute force. As a result, the blow knocked two of Patriarch Bodhidharma's teeth loose.

Now he was a sage, and there is a legend about the teeth of sages. Don't ask me whether or not it's true. I'm just relating the legend. Let's just get it clear first and not ask why it's so. If you ask the reason--there's no reason. It's just what they say--don't ask me why! Anyway, it's said that if a sage gets his teeth knocked loose and he spits them out on the ground, it won't rain for three years.

Patriarch Bodhidharma thought, "If it doesn't rain for three years, just image how many people will starve! I have come to China to save living beings, not to kill them!" And so Patriarch Bodhidharma did not let his teeth fall to the ground. Instead, he swallowed them, just like he was eating a pancake; well, pancakes aren't that hard--it was more like eating a bone! He

頭去了，吃到肚裏頭於是乎就走了。外來的人被人欺負也就算了，打掉牙也不能到政府那兒去告這個神光，出家人要忍辱嘛！況且他是個祖師，更應該忍辱，於是乎就走了。

走到半路上，遇到一隻鸚鵡；這隻鸚鵡在籠子裏邊圍著，可是這隻鳥比神光法師就聰明得多，牠認識菩提達摩是一位祖師，牠就說了：

> 西來意，西來意，
> 請你教我出籠計。

你看達摩祖師對人沒有知音，對於這個小鳥，遇到一個知音。什麼叫知音呢？就是認識他。

達摩祖師一聽，這個小鳥這樣請教他，他也就很高興，就教牠一個方便法，這不是實法，這是權法。他說：

> 出籠計，出籠計，
> 兩腿伸直，兩眼閉，
> 這便是你出籠計。

這好像秘密的妙訣，這是秘密法，所以他說話沒有那麼大聲，我現在講的恐怕比達摩祖師說的聲音要大，他一定告訴那個小鳥說：「出籠計，這便是你出籠計。」他一定是這樣講的，為什麼呢？他若講得聲音大了，被旁人聽見，這個方法也行不通了。所以你看這個地方，這位祖師用心良苦呀！

方法教會了，這小鳥說：「好了，這可以，我現在明白怎麼樣是出籠計了！」於是乎，小鳥看見牠的主人遠遠地來了，這時候牠就把這個方便法用出來，腿也伸直，眼睛也閉上了，就等著主人來親近牠。

這主人天天回來都要看一看、玩一玩牠，這是他最心愛的一隻小鳥，可以和他談話，又可以給他消愁、解悶，所以回來先要看看這隻鳥。這主人回來一看，哇！甚至於就要哭起來了！怎麼呢？這小鳥在籠子裏頭，躺在那地方不動彈了。他比兒子死了都焦急，他兒子若死了，他恐怕都沒有看得那麼重要。於是乎他把這籠子門打開，把小鳥拿出來放到手上，這還是熱的，熱呼呼的沒有涼，因為牠是假裝死，所以牠身上的暖氣不會沒有的。這主人把小鳥放在手裏轉著看，嗯！不動了，翻過來看，掉過來看，看來看去，把手打開看看？噢！把這個手一打開，你說這個小鳥怎麼樣？呼！飛了！飛了，這隻小鳥的出籠計靈了。

swallowed them and made his exit. Foreigners are bound to be bullied and after all, he couldn't go to the government and file suit against Dharma Master Shenguang for knocking his teeth out. Those who have left home have to be patient! How much more must a Patriarch forbear! And so he just left.

On the road, he met a parrot imprisoned in a wicker cage. However, this bird was much more intelligent than the Dharma Master Shenguang. Recognizing that Bodhidharma was a Patriarch, the bird said.

> *Mind from the West.*
> *Mind from the West.*
> *Teach me a way*
> *To escape from this cage.*

Although Patriarch Bodhidharma hadn't been able to find any people who really understood who he was, this parrot recognized him. Hearing the bird's plea for help, Bodhidharma was pleased and taught the bird an expedient method-- a provisional, not a real, Dharma. He said,

> *To escape the cage,*
> *To escape the cage,*
> *Put out both legs,*
> *Close both eyes.*
> *This is the way*
> *To escape from the cage!*

It was a secret Dharma--sort of like a secret password, and so it's for sure the Patriarch whispered it. He didn't say it so loudly as I am speaking now! He certainly must have used a very small voice: "To get out of the cage--this is what you must do to escape!" He spoke softly like that. Why? If he said it out loud so that others heard him, then the method would not work. From this we can see how much trouble the Patriarch took to be kind.

The parrot listened attentively and said, "All right! Now I understand how to get out of the cage!" When the bird saw his owner approaching in the distance, he applied the method--sticking his legs out straight and closing his eyes, he waited for his owner to come close.

Every day when the owner came home, he always played with this bird that he was so fond of. Talking to it would cheer him up. And so, as usual, upon his return, he first went to check on his bird. But this time when he looked in the cage he was shocked. He practically burst into tears. How come? His little bird lay on the floor of the cage unmoving. He couldn't have been more upset if his son had died. In fact, it's likely that this bird meant even more to him than his own son! He pulled opened the cage door and gently placed the little bird in his hand. It was still warm. It must have just died, he assumed, that's why the heat hadn't yet left its body. The owner peeked at the little thing, turning his hand this way and that. It didn't even quiver. Slowly he open his

可是我們現在都在籠子裏，我們這個出籠計怎麼辦呢？我們人哪，你不要以為自己是自由的，不要誤解自由，說是我願意吃就吃，我願意喝酒就喝酒，願意做什麼就做什麼，我不守規矩也可以，這就是自由！那簡直太混帳了，那叫誤解自由。你真正自由，要能生死自由，我願意飛到天空就飛到天空，我願意鑽到地裏頭就鑽到地裏頭去，你要有這個本事，才是自由，好像那隻小鳥似的。

現在講這個《六祖壇經》，本來我講得不好，不是客氣，是真的。但是雖然我講得不好，可是敢講；那麼也有的講得好的，可是他不敢講。等我這個講得不好的人先講一次，以後講得好的就可以跟著來講。那麼將來你們有很多時間、很多機會可以聽《六祖壇經》，可是那個講得好的，是從講不好的這兒生出來的，要明白這一點。我現在講得雖然不好，將來你們開智慧了，比我講得就更好，因為我現在沒有開智慧，和你們是一樣的。但是你們可都要把它用筆記一記，等你們開了智慧，就知道我講得是對不對。現在我相信還不能知道我講得是好？是不好？等你們開智慧了，噢！原來他這地方講錯了，是不是呀？那時候就明白了，可是那要等二十年之後。

神光法師把印度來的和尚打掉了兩顆牙，和尚也沒有來反攻他，以為這回是得到好處了，勝利了，把外國和尚都給打了。可是把外國和尚給打了，無常鬼卻來了，這無常鬼戴著一頂高帽子，到這裏來說：「法師，你今天壽命應該盡了，閻羅王派我來請你去，你今天就應該死了。」

神光法師一聽，「噢！怎麼我還要死嗎？我也要死嗎？我講經講得天花亂墜，地湧金蓮，講得這樣好，還不能了生死嗎？這個世界上到底有沒有人了生死呢？」就問無常鬼。

無常鬼說：「有。世界上有了生死的。」

神光法師說：「是哪一個？你可以告訴我，我跟他學一學這個了生死的法。」

無常鬼說：「哪一個呀？就是你剛才打掉兩顆牙的那個黑臉和尚。他呀！閻羅王就管不了他了，不單管不了他，閻羅王天天都要拜他，都要向他叩頭頂禮，來恭敬他。」

神光法師說：「噢！他就是了生死的和尚呀！那麼好了，我要跟他去學這個了生死的法門，你這無常鬼，你這個鬼大哥，等一等再叫我去，可以不可以呀？我現在真是想要了生死的，所以你同閻羅王講一講，給我一點時間，讓我去學這個法門。」

hand... PHLLRTTPHLRTTPHLRTT! The bird broke loose from his hand and flew away! It had escaped from the cage!

But we are still in a cage right now! How do we escape? As to human beings--you shouldn't think you are free. Don't misinterpret freedom saying, "I am really free. If I want to eat, I eat; if I want to drink, I drink. I can do anything I please. I can ignore the rules if I want to! That's what I call freedom!" Don't think you are quite so clever. That's a misinterpretation of freedom. To be truly free, you must be free of birth and death, and then, if you wish to fly into space you can fly into space, and if you wish to burrow into the earth, you can burrow into the earth. If you can do that, you will gain the kind of freedom that the little bird gained.

As I explain the *Sixth Patriarch's Dharma Jewel Platform Sutra*, I do not lecture well. This is not polite talk; it's true. Even though I do not speak well, at least I dare to lecture. There are many who could lecture well, but who do not dare to speak. After I, who don't speak well, have finished lecturing, those who are eloquent can give their explanations. Then, in the future you will have many opportunities to hear the *Sixth Patriarch Sutra*. However, let's be clear about one thing: the source of those eloquent explanations will be this simple explanation. I don't explain well, because I'm just like you in that I haven't opened my wisdom. And so, in the future when you people open your wisdom, you will be able to speak better than I. But for right now, you can take notes and then when you open your wisdom you will be able to tell if what I am saying now is right or not! I believe that at present you have no way to judge if I am explaining well or not. But once your wisdom opens, then, "Aha! Basically he explained that passage wrong!" Right? You'll understand then, but that might be twenty years from now!

Dharma Master Shenguang knocked out two of that Indian monk's teeth, and since the monk didn't retaliate, the Dharma Master figured he had the advantage— that he'd won the victory. He'd put a barbarian monk in his place. But not long after he struck the barbarian, the Ghost of Impermanence, wearing a high hat, paid a call: "Dharma Master, your life ends today," said the ghost. "King Yama has sent me to escort you. Today you are supposed to die."

Master Shenguang was astounded. "What? I still have to die? Why must I die? I speak Sutras so well that flowers rain down from the heavens and golden lotuses well up out of the earth, yet I still have not ended birth and death? Tell me," he said to the Ghost of Impermanence, "is there a person in this world who has ended birth and death?"

"There is," came the reply. "There's someone in this world who has ended birth and death."

"Who?" asked Dharma Master Shenguang. "Tell me, and I'll follow him to learn the way to end birth and death."

"He is the black-faced Bhikshu whose teeth you knocked out. King Yama has no control over him. Not only that, King Yama bows in respect to him everyday!"

"Oh! That monk has ended birth and death! Fine, then I

無常鬼說：「你真有誠意，這也未嘗不可，也都可以通融通融。」

神光法師一聽，無常鬼答應他了，高興得不得了，連鞋也忘了穿，打了赤足就後面追達摩去。

追達摩，達摩在前面走，他就在後面追，一追，追到這兒，看見這隻小鳥，達摩祖師幫助牠得到自由了。他就想：噢！原來就是這麼回事，要裝死，要裝一個活死人。那麼達摩也不理他，就前頭走，他就後頭跟著，一跟就跟到洛陽的熊耳山。達摩祖師就在那兒打坐、面壁。達摩在那兒坐禪，神光就在那兒跪著；達摩祖師在那兒坐了九年、面壁九年，神光法師就在那兒跪了九年。

以前我講這個公案的時候，有一個小孩子，他聽我講，聽得很高興，就問我說：「那麼他跪了九年，有沒有吃飯呢？」這小孩子他就想起問有沒有吃飯，當時我答他，在這九年如果不吃飯，怎麼可以活著呢？就是達摩祖師吃飯的時候，他也吃飯；達摩祖師打坐的時候，那麼他也打坐，可是在書上沒有記載這個事情，我也沒有講明這問題。這小孩子來問這個問題，可見他一天到晚就是想著吃飯，所以他怕神光法師在那兒跪著沒有飯吃。其實這小孩子並不是掛著吃飯，講起來他是非常有善根的，他由五歲就開始給父親、母親天天叩頭，等到十一歲的時候遇著我。他問我那時候是十一歲，並不是五歲，我要說的是他五歲的時候就能孝順父母。

神光法師在那兒跪了九年，有一天下大雪，達摩祖師在那兒打坐，神光法師就在那兒跪著，雪下得沒到腰了，把神光法師的腰都給埋上了，他還是在那兒跪著求法。達摩祖師回頭看，說：「你幹什麼在這兒這麼樣子，下這麼大雪，你還在這兒跪著幹什麼呀？」

神光法師說：「我要了生死！以前我講經不能了生死，現在我要了生死了，請祖師傳給我這個了生死的法門！」

達摩祖師說：「你看這個天，下的是什麼呀？」

神光法師說：「噢！這下的是雪。」

「這個雪是什麼色的啊？」

神光法師說：「雪當然是白色的囉！」

達摩祖師就給他出一個題目，來考他一下，說：「你等著天什麼時候下紅雪，那個時候我就傳法給你；如果不下紅雪的話，你就不要希望了。你這麼惡的一個和尚，一念珠就把我牙打掉了兩顆，我不向你報仇已經就是最慈悲了，怎麼又會傳給你法呢！」就出了這麼一個題目，來考神光法師一下。

這個題目出來了，可是神光法師就把這個文章給作成了！這個文章怎麼樣作的呢？他一看，牆上有一把刀，

want to follow him to learn the Dharma-door of ending birth and death. Please, Old Brother Ghost, could you wait a bit to take me away? I am determined to end birth and death! Could you speak to King Yama on my behalf to see if he can't give me a little more time so I can go learn this Dharma-door?"

"All right," said the ghost. "Since you are sincere, King Yama will wait."

Dharma Master Shenguang was delighted. He was so quick to rush after Patriarch Bodhidharma that he forgot to put on his shoes. On he ran, barefoot, until he met the parrot whom Bodhidharma had freed, and suddenly he understood, "Oh! That's what it's all about! I have to play dead. I have to be a living dead person!"

Bodhidharma walked on, ignoring the barefoot Dharma Master following behind. Arriving at Bear's Ear Mountain in Loyang, the Patriarch sat down to meditate facing a wall. Patriarch Bodhidharma sat meditating there for nine years, and for nine years Dharma Master Shenguang knelt beside him.

Earlier, when I spoke this public record, an eleven year old child asked me, "During the nine years he knelt, did he eat or not?" I replied, "How could anyone kneel for nine years without eating and still live? When the Patriarch meditated, Shenguang knelt, and when the Patriarch ate, Shenguang ate." But this is not recorded in the books. One might think that the child was always thinking about eating and so he worried about Dharma Master Shenguang not getting anything to eat. Actually, the child who asked the question was not really attached to eating. He had very good roots, and he began bowing to his parents every day when he was only five. He was eleven when he met me and asked me this question.

One day a great snow fell, and it rose in drifts as high as Dharma Master Shenguang's waist. Yet he continued to kneel, seeking the Dharma. Finally Patriarch Bodhidharma asked him, "Why are you kneeling here in such deep snow?"

"I want to end birth and death," replied Shenguang. "When I was lecturing Sutras, I was unable to end birth and death. Please, Patriarch, transmit the Dharma of ending birth and death to me."

"What do you see falling from the sky?" asked Bodhidharma.

"Snow," said Shenguang.

"What color is it?" asked Bodhidharma.

"It's white of course."

Then Patriarch Bodhidharma gave him his test topic: "When red snow falls from the sky," he said, "I will transmit the Dharma to you. If there's no red snow, then you've no hope of receiving the Dharma. You're such a wicked monk! You knocked out two of my teeth with one swipe of your recitation beads. The fact that I haven't taken revenge already counts as being too compassionate! Do you really expect me to give you the Dharma?" That was the test that the Patriarch

這把刀是修道人的戒刀。這個戒刀就是預備有要犯戒的時候，逼不得已，一定要犯這個戒了，寧可自己把自己的頭割下來也不犯戒，保持這個戒體，預備這樣用的。那麼神光法師把這個刀拿下來，一刀就把這個臂斬斷了，斬斷了一條臂，這是作文章了，這是考試的題目，他作這個文章。

斬斷了，就有血流了，他把血和到雪裏面，雪雖然是白色的，經過血一染，它就變成紅色的。於是乎神光法師或者拿一個東西，中國人有畚箕，掃地裝塵土的那種東西。就把這個雪撮了一畚箕，紅雪、白雪這麼一攪和都變成紅雪，就說：「祖師你看，現在是紅雪了！」

達摩祖師一看，「真的嗎？啊！這真是紅雪了！」這本來早就在意料之中，就是要考驗他這個真心。那麼一看見這個，達摩祖師就很高興了：「噢！我到中國還真是沒有白來這一次，還遇著你這麼一個真心求法修道的人，把自己的臂膀都不要了，這是真有一點誠心。」於是乎就給他說這個以心印心的法門，教他直指人心、見性成佛這種的法門。

那麼神光法師聽了說法之後，這時候臂痛了，以前他沒有想到這個臂，就只是想方法教這個雪變成紅色，把臂痛也忘了。達摩祖師把這個法給他講完了之後，他這時候生了分別心了：「啊，我剁下來這個胳臂好痛！」他就對達摩祖師說：「啊！我現在心很痛，請祖師替我安心。」

達摩祖師就說：「你把你的心拿來給我，我才可以幫助你。把你這個心安好了，才不會痛。」

神光法師自己就找自己的心，心在什麼地方？東西南北四維上下，所有的地方都找遍了，覓心了不可得！對達摩祖師說：「我找不著心，沒有。」

達摩祖師說：「我與汝安心竟！」我給你已經安好了，安完了你這個心。

在這個地方，要講起來這個法是無量無邊的，達摩祖師對神光法師所說的法，也是妙不可言的，所以才說「萬法歸一一歸合」。萬法就是歸於一，一又歸到什麼地方呢？合就是人一口，這念一個「合」字。「神光不明趕達摩」，神光不懂這個「合」字的意思，所以就去追趕達摩祖師。「熊耳山前跪九載」，在熊耳山這個地方跪了九年。「只求一點躲閻羅」，只求達摩祖師指點他這一點點，來了生脫死，躲過閻羅王。這是神光法師遇到達摩祖師的一段經過。

達摩祖師到中國，曾經被人用毒藥下了六次，誰來毒他呢？當時北魏有一個法師叫菩提流支，又叫光統

Bodhidharma gave to Master Shenguang.

How did Dharma Master Shenguang complete this test? Cultivators of the Way carry a knife to protect the substance of their precepts. A true cultivator would rather cut off his head than break a precept.

In reply to the test topic, Dharma Master Shenguang drew his precept knife, and with one slice, cut off his arm. His blood flowed on the new fallen snow. He scooped up a bucket full of crimson snow, set it before Patriarch Bodhidharma, and said, "Patriarch, do you see? The snow is red!"

Patriarch Bodhidharma said, "So it is, so it is." He had tested Shenguang's sincerity, and now the Patriarch was extremely happy. "My coming to China has not been in vain. I have met a person who dares to use a true mind to cultivate the Way, even forsaking his arm in search of the Dharma." The Patriarch then spoke the Dharma door of "Using the mind to seal the mind." It is the Dharma door that points straight to the mind to see the nature and realize Buddhahood.

While hearing this Dharma, Dharma Master Shenguang didn't think about the pain in his arm, and before that he had thought only of making the snow turn red. But once Patriarch Bodhidharma finished speaking the Dharma for him, his discursive thought arose: "My arm really hurts!" he said. "My mind is in pain. Please, Patriarch, quiet my mind."

"Find your mind," said Patriarch Bodhidharma. "Show it to me and I will quiet it for you. Then you won't feel any more pain."

Dharma Master Shenguang searched for his mind. Where was his mind? He looked in the north, east, south, west, in the intermediate points, and up and down. It was simply not to be found anywhere! At last he said to Patriarch Bodhidharma, "I can't find my mind! It is nowhere to be found."

"I have already finished quieting your mind!" said the Patriarch. At this place, if I wanted to discuss this Dharma, the meanings would be infinite and boundless. Those few words of Dharma spoken between Patriarch Bodhidharma and Dharma Master Shenguang are ineffably wonderful. And so it's said, "The myriad dharmas return to the one; the one returns to unity." *Ten thousand dharmas return to one. Where does the one return?* The character for "unity" (合) is composed of "person", "one" and a "mouth." *Shenguang did not understand, and ran after Bodhidharma.* He did not understand the meaning of "unity" and so he pursued Patriarch Bodhidharma. *Before him at Bear's Ear Mountain he knelt nine years, seeking a little something to escape King Yama.* He didn't ask for much from Patriarch Bodhidharma; he just wanted to end birth and death so he could avoid Yama, King of the Dead. This is some of what transpired when Patriarch Bodhidharma and Dharma Master Shenguang encountered each other.

While Patriarch Bodhidharma was in China, he was poisoned six times. Dharma Master Bodhiruchi of Northern Wei who was also called Vinaya Master Guangtong was extremely jealous of him. He prepared a vegetarian meal which contained

律師，他最妒忌達摩祖師，所以就做一些齋菜來供養達摩祖師；但是這菜飯裏邊下了最毒的這種毒藥，無論任何人吃了都會死的，就這麼來供養達摩祖師。達摩祖師知道不知道這個飯裏有毒呢？知道！知道可是他還是照吃可也，就把這個毒飯給吃了。吃了之後，就叫人給他拿來一個盤子，他就吐了，吐出來變成什麼呢？這個毒藥完全都變成蛇了，這是一次。

那麼以後，菩提流支看毒不死達摩，也不知道是怎麼回事，第二次又來下毒藥，加倍下毒，以前沒有毒死你，這回下多一點毒藥。就用另一種更毒的這種毒藥來毒達摩，達摩也是又把它吃了，吃了之後，怎麼樣呢？坐到一塊大石頭上，把這個毒藥屙出去，屙出毒藥的這個力量把這石頭都給毒爆了，毒破壞了，一塊大磐石也破壞了，那麼這是第二次。

以後又有三次、四次、五次、六次，吃了六次毒藥。達摩祖師就對神光說：「我到中國來，是因為中國有大乘根性的人，大乘根性的眾生，所以我把大乘的佛教帶到中國來。現在已經傳法有人了，接續我這個法有人了，那麼我就不留在這兒了，我現在就要死了。」

這個神光法師由達摩祖師傳給他法之後，就給他改名字叫慧可，說他的智慧真可以了，夠了。那麼這慧可大師就問達摩祖師，說：「你在印度有沒有傳法的徒弟呢？是不是也要給這個袈裟，用這個衣缽袈裟來做憑據呢？」

達摩祖師說：「沒有。在印度，我傳法是傳法，但是不用這個衣缽袈裟來表信。因為印度的人心都很直率的，他修道，得道就說得道。有人證明他是開悟得道，這就是得道了；如果沒有人來給證明，他自己不會說我得了道，我證了果，我又是阿羅漢了，我又是菩薩。沒有，不會這麼講的，所以那裏的人都很正直。中國的人不同，中國大乘根性的眾生是多，可是打妄語的人也多。修道沒有成道業，他說他成道了；沒有證果，他說他證果了。所以要用衣缽袈裟來表明這種證據。所以現在傳給你這個衣缽袈裟，你好好保持著。」

神光法師，就是這慧可大師聽達摩祖師這樣地囑咐他，也就明白傳法的這種意義了。

達摩祖師於是乎就死了，人就把他用棺材裝起來埋到墳裏，沒有事了。可是就在這同時，魏朝有一個使臣叫宋雲，在葱嶺附近，就是中國終南山那一帶——在路上碰見達摩祖師，達摩祖師拿著一隻鞋，對宋雲講：「你的國王今天死了，你趕快回去呀，你的國家有事。」

宋雲就問說：「那麼大師您到什麼地方去？」

他說：「我回印度去。」

a lethal drug, and offered it to the Patriarch. Well, did the Patriarch Bodhidharma know that it was poisoned? He knew! Although he knew it was poisoned, he ate it anyway. Then he vomited the food on to a tray, and it was transformed into a pile of writhing snakes. That was the first time.

After that unsuccessful attempt, Bodhiruchi tried again, using an even more potent poison. Again, Patriarch Bodhidharma ate the food. Then he sat atop a huge boulder and relieved nature. The boulder crumbled into a heap of dust. That was the second time.

After that there were the third, fourth, fifth and sixth times he was poisoned. One day, Patriarch Bodhidharma said to Dharma Master Shenguang, "I came to China because I saw people with the Great Vehicle disposition. Now I have transmitted the Dharma and I am not going to stay here any longer. I am ready to complete the stillness."

With the transmission of the Dharma, Dharma Master Shenguang received the name "Huike" which means "Able Wisdom," evidence that his wisdom was truly up to the task; it was sufficient. Great Master Huike asked Patriarch Bodhidharma, "In India, did you transmit the Dharma to your disciples? Did you also give the robe and the bowl as certification?"

"I transmitted the Dharma in India," replied Bodhidharma, "but I did not use the robe and the bowl as a token of faith. Indian people are straightforward. When they attain the fruition, they know they must be certified. If no one certifies them, they do not say, 'I have attained the Way! I have certified to the fruition! I have given proof to Arhatship! I am a Bodhisattva!' They do not speak like that. People there are upright and straight."

"Chinese people, however, are different. Many Chinese have the Great Vehicle disposition, but there are also many people who lie. Having cultivated without success, such people claim to have the Way. Though they have not certified to the fruition, they claim to be certified sages. Therefore I will transmit the robe and bowl to prove that you have received the transmission. Guard them well and take care." Great Master Huike listened to Patriarch Bodhidharma's instructions and thereupon understood the Dharma transmission he had received.

After his death the Patriarch's body was placed in a coffin and buried. There was nothing unusual about his funeral. However, right at that time, an official from Northern Wei called Song Yun met Patriarch Bodhidharma on the road to Zhongnan Mountain in the Congling Range. When they met, Patriarch Bodhidharma was carrying one shoe in his hand. He said to Song Yun, "The king of your country died today. Return quickly! There is work to be done."

The official asked, "Great Master, where are you going?"

"Back to India," he replied.

"Great Master, to whom did you transmit your Dharma?"

"In China after forty years, there will be someone able ('Ke')." "Able" was a reference to Great Master Huike.

「大師，您這個法傳給誰了？」

達摩祖師說：「在中國四十年以後，可是也。」我的法在中國四十年以後，可是也，可就是說的慧可。

宋雲回到他自己的國家北魏，就說這件事：「我那天走到蔥嶺，就是終南山那一帶，遇見菩提達摩了。他說他回印度，他告訴我，就是我遇到他那一天，是我們的國王死了。我現在回來，果然正是那一天，他怎麼會知道呢？」

這些人說：「達摩已經早就死了，你怎麼會碰見他呢？」於是乎大家都不相信這個宋雲講的話。「他已經死了，你怎麼會遇著他，我們大家把他的墳打開看看。」於是乎把達摩祖師的墳墓就給打開了，打開一看，這棺材裏什麼也沒有，就剩一隻鞋。

那麼究竟達摩祖師到什麼地方去了呢？以後就沒有人知道，恐怕現在來到美國了也不一定。不過沒有人認識他，他可以改頭換面，隨便千變萬化的。他到中國，就說他一百五十歲，走了還是一百五十歲，到什麼地方去？也沒有人知道。說是去考查歷史，歷史上也沒有這些個問題，沒有地方考據去，這是達摩祖師一生到中國大概的意思。

這二祖神光爲求佛法，把臂斷去一條，我們爲求佛法，這個腿痛一點，可千萬不要斷去它，因爲斷去就不會走路了。這個腿痛一點，就忍著一點，應該想一想，二祖慧可大師把臂都斷了，我們現在還不需要斷臂啊，所以打坐的時候，不要怕痛。

在達摩祖師沒有來之前，他派過兩個徒弟到中國，孰不知到中國受了很大的氣，被人欺負。他這兩個徒弟的名字叫什麼呢？一個叫佛馱，一個叫耶舍。兩個徒弟到中國就傳這個頓教法門，就是禪宗這個道理。那麼到什麼地方講，人家都不睬他，沒有人和他講話的，所有的和尚都默擯他。默擯就是不和他講話，你自己講什麼也沒有人聽，所以自己也沒有意思，就要走了。

一走就走到盧山，盧山那時候有個志遠法師，他是專門講念佛的。那麼去見這個遠公大師。志遠大師就說：「你們兩位是印度的和尚，你們傳的是什麼法啊？怎麼這些個人就不理你們呢？」

佛馱、耶舍就把手伸出來，因爲大約講話也講不太通，只會很少的中國話，所以就這麼把手伸出來，說：「這個手做拳，拳做手，這個快不快？手做拳，拳做手，這快不快？」遠公大師說：「很快的！」他說：「菩提、煩惱也就是這麼快！」遠公大師當時也就開悟了：「哦！菩提、煩惱原來沒有分別啊！沒有什麼兩樣！菩提就是煩惱，煩惱即菩提，煩惱即菩提！」遠公大師這樣

Song Yun returned to his country of Northern Wei and reported the incident. "Recently, in Congling, I met the Patriarch Bodhidharma who told me that the king of our country had died and instructed me to return to the capital. When I arrived I found it exactly as he had said. How did he know?"

His countrymen scoffed, "Bodhidharma is already dead. How could you have met him on the road?" People didn't believe Song Yun. "He's already dead, how could Song Yun have met him? Let's open his coffin and take a look!" But when they dug up the grave, they found that the coffin was empty. There was nothing inside but one shoe.

Well, where did Patriarch Bodhidharma go? No one knows. Perhaps he came to America. But no one can recognize him, because he can change and transform according to his convenience. When he came to China he said he was one hundred and fifty years old, and when he left he was still one hundred and fifty years old. No one knows where he went after that. No historical references can be found. This has been a general discussion of Patriarch Bodhidharma's life in China.

The Second Patriarch Shenguang (Huike) cut off his arm for the sake of the Dharma. We ought to remember this when our legs ache in meditation. We don't need to cut off our arms now, but at the very least, we should be patient with the pain. We should think, "The Second Patriarch Great Master Huike cut off his arm and we don't have to do that, so the least we can do is not fear the pain when we are meditating!"

While still in India, Patriarch Bodhidharma sent two of his disciples, Fotuo and Yeshe, to China to transmit the sudden enlightenment Dharma-door--the principles of the Chan School of meditation. Who would have thought that when they got to China they would be totally ostracized and bullied. No matter where they went to speak, everyone snubbed them. No one would talk to them; all the monks kept silent and ignored them. Since no one would listen to them, it was meaningless to remain, so they decided to leave.

On their way out they passed through Lu Mountain where they met the Great Master Zhiyuan (Huiyuan), who promoted the practice of reciting the Buddha's name. Master Yuan asked, "What Dharma do you two monks from India transmit that causes people to pay you so little respect?"

Fotuo and Yeshe used sign language because they probably knew very little Chinese. Raising their arms in the air, they said, "Watch! The hand makes a fist and the fist makes a hand. Is this not quick?"

Master Yuan replied, "Quick indeed."

"Bodhi (enlightenment) and affliction," they said, "are just that quick."

At that moment, Great Master Yuan became enlightened and said, "Aha! Bodhi and afflictions basically are not different! They are non-dual. Bodhi is affliction and affliction is Bodhi." Having gained such an understanding, Great Master Yuan made abundant offerings to Fotuo and Yeshe.

子明白了，就供養他們兩位。沒有好久，他們兩個人在同一天就都死了，他們兩個的墳現在還在廬山那兒。

達摩祖師在印度，一聽說兩個徒弟被人欺負得這麼樣子，以後兩個徒弟也都死了。自己就想：「我去給看一看。」於是乎就到中國來。那麼到中國來，收了很多中國徒弟。當時他在熊耳山那兒面壁九年，不知多少人去皈依、禮拜，拜他做師父。其中有三個人，達摩祖師臨圓寂的時候說：「我到中國來，我這個法傳了三個人。一個得到我的髓，一個得到我的骨頭，一個得到我的肉。」所以他自己也沒有身體了，自己把身體都分給人了。那麼誰得到他的髓呢？就是慧可得到達摩祖師的髓；道育禪師，得到達摩祖師的骨，就這骨頭；這道濟比丘尼，就是那個總持比丘尼——我講《法華經》的時候，不是說有一個比丘尼死了之後，在她口裏生出一朵青蓮花來？就是這個比丘尼——她得到達摩祖師的肉，她把達摩祖師的肉都給吃了；道育禪師把達摩祖師的骨頭都給啃了；慧可祖師把達摩祖師的髓都給喝了，所以達摩祖師這連身體都沒有了。所以各位不要在美國找，找不著了。

# 第二代祖師——慧可大師

接下來我們講二祖。神光——慧可法師被人把頭給割去了。慧可法師死的時候，是被政府把他殺了。殺了可殺了，但是他不流血，流的是像牛奶似的，他的血都變白色的。因為他這樣子，所以就很多人又信佛了，當時皇帝也改過了，知道是錯了，知道他是真菩薩。

慧可大師他在家姓姬，是出生在北齊的時候。達摩祖師是在梁武帝的時候，到第二祖已經換了北齊的時代。慧可大師以前的名字叫神光，為什麼叫神光呢？因為他降生的時候，他的父母看見有一個金甲的神人，放大光明。這個金甲的神人，大概就是護法韋陀菩薩，來保護著這一位祖師出世。

這一位祖師生來非常地聰明，記憶力非常之強，所謂「目下十行字，耳聽百人音。」怎麼叫目下十行字？並不是說他這一看，就看十行，而是你普通的人看這一行，看這一趟字的時間，他可以看十趟，就這麼快，非常迅速；耳聽百人音，你一百個人同時講話，他都可以聽得清楚，他的分別力就這麼樣。因為有金甲的神人放光，所以名字就叫神光。

可是這一位祖師脾氣最大，講話不投機就想打。在四十歲以前，連講經說法都帶著一個鐵念珠來行俠仗義，

Shortly thereafter, the two died on the same day, in the same place. Their graves may still be seen at Lu Mountain.

Patriarch Bodhidharma, hearing that his two disciples had been scorned by the Chinese and had both died, decided to go to China take a look himself. While the Patriarch was sitting at Bear's Ear Mountain, many people came to bow to him and were received as his disciples. Among them were three individuals whom Patriarch Bodhidharma mentioned when he was about to enter Nirvana. He said, "I came to China and transmitted my Dharma to three people. One received my marrow, one received my bones, and one received my flesh." After the transmission, the Patriarch himself no longer had a body. Great Master Huike received the marrow and Chan Master Daoyu received the bones. And then there was Bhikshuni Zongchi. When I lectured on the *Dharma Flower Sutra* didn't I tell you about how a blue lotus flower grew from her mouth after she died? That Bhikshuni received Patriarch Bodhidharma's flesh. She consumed the Patriarch's flesh; Dhyana Master Daoyu consumed the Patriarch's bones, and Patriarch Huike consumed Patriarch Bodhidharma's marrow. In the end, Patriarch Bodhidharma had no body at all. And so don't look for him in America; you won't find him.

## The Second Patriarch
## Great Master Huike "Able Wisdom"

Now we will discuss the Second Patriarch. Shenguang--Great Master Huike. He was executed by the government, but after his head was chopped off, what flowed from his neck was not blood, but a white milky substance; his blood had turned white. Because of that, many people came to believe in Buddhism, and the emperor also repented, admitting he was wrong, for he realized that the Patriarch was a real Bodhisattva.

Great Master Huike, whose family name was Ji, was born during the Northern Qi dynasty (550-577 A.D.). Patriarch Bodhidharma was in China during the reign of Emperor Wu of the Liang dynasty. By the time of the Second Patriarch, the government had already changed to the Northern Qi. Great Master Huike's given name was Shenguang "Spiritual Light" because when he was born, his parents saw a golden-armored spiritual being emitting light. This spiritual being was most likely Weituo Bodhisattva, coming to offer protection to this Patriarch at his birth.

Not only was the Patriarch exceptionally intelligent, but he had an excellent memory as well. He was one who "could read ten lines to others' one and distinguish a hundred people's conversations." To "read ten lines to others' one" means he was fast--a speed reader! In a gathering of one hundred people, all talking at once, he could be clear about each conversation.

有不平的事情，他就要給平一平。因為這個，所以見到達摩祖師，他就用念珠打菩提達摩，結果跪了九年，自己又把臂斬斷了一隻。你想想，要是沒有脾氣，怎麼能捨得把自己這個臂一刀就斬斷了。這就是有一股脾氣，有火氣，所以把自己的臂斬斷了。斬斷了也不覺得痛，得法之後才覺得痛，為什麼他覺得痛了？因為他有脾氣，如果沒有脾氣的話，就算斬掉了也不會痛的。痛就是有煩惱，所以會痛。

這一位祖師在四十歲遇到菩提達摩祖師，得法之後，又隱遁了四十年。為什麼要隱遁？就因為當時有一位菩提流支——光統律師他們這一黨，專門和達摩祖師的弟子作對，甚至於見到就想要殺。你看！連菩提達摩祖師都是被他們用毒藥來毒，所以何況他的徒弟呢！慧可大師雖然是很大的脾氣，但因為聽他師父菩提達摩的指教：「你應該隱遁，躲避這些人來和你作難。」所以他就隱遁了四十年。

前面不是講，宋雲問達摩祖師，他傳法給誰？他說：「四十年後，可是也。」四十年後有位慧可大師，就是我的傳法人。那麼等到四十年之後，慧可大師弘揚佛法，教化眾生，就遇到三祖僧璨大師，把這個法就傳給僧璨大師，他吩咐僧璨大師說：「你好好保護著這衣缽，這是作證據的。你也應該隱遁，不然的話，也會對你不利。」說這話之後，菩提流支——這光統律師的徒黨，他的徒弟和他這一黨又來尋仇，又來想要殺慧可大師。

那麼慧可大師在這時候就假裝瘋狂了，就是crazy，發顛、發神經病。在發神經病的期間，有這些有緣的人，他就度。他雖然是有神經病，但是和眾生有緣，所以很多人就相信這個慧可大師。可是菩提流支的徒弟，這一班黨徒，還是放不下，還是妒忌障礙，於是就到政府那裏把他告了，告這個慧可大師。拿什麼理由告呢？說：「這個不是個人哪，他是個妖怪啊！所以迷得這麼多人來崇拜他，根本他就不是個人。」就這樣到政府裏去告，政府就把這種的情形奏給皇帝。

當時皇帝就下了一道聖旨，就是詔書，命令當地的有司、當地的官，去把慧可大師給捉起來，就審問他，說：「你到底是人？是妖怪？」你猜這慧可大師怎麼說？他說：「我是妖怪。」

可是這大地方官一聽到他這樣講，知道他是冤枉，是受人妒忌，就叫他自己想清楚，說：「你想清楚了！你到底是個什麼？」

慧可大師說：「我實實在在是妖怪，我真正地是個妖怪。」

那麼既然這樣，真是一個妖怪，這國法不能允許妖怪

The Great Master, however, had great anger; whenever he disagreed with someone, he was ready to fight. Forty years earlier he even wore iron recitation beads when he lectured Sutras to level the opposition and dispense justice. Remember? He used his iron beads to strike the Patriarch. But later, he knelt for nine years in quest of the Dharma, and it was his great anger which enabled him to cut off his arm and feel no pain. It was also because of this anger that he later felt pain. Unafflicted by anger, he would have felt no pain. Pain is just an affliction and affliction is the cause of pain.

The Second Patriarch was forty years old when he met Bodhidharma. Having obtained the Dharma, he went into hiding for forty years. That was because Bodhiruchi--Vinaya Master Guangtong--and his gang, who had made six attempts on the life of Patriarch Bodhidharma, also wished to kill his disciples. So although Great Master Huike had great anger, he nevertheless obeyed his teacher, Patriarch Bodhidharma, who told him, "You should hide away to avoid these people who want to make things difficult for you." That's why he went into hiding for forty years.

I mentioned earlier that when asked to whom he transmitted the Dharma, Patriarch Bodhidharma told Song Yun: "After forty years, there will be someone able ('Ke')." When Great Master Huike was eighty, he began to propagate the Buddhadharma, teaching and transforming living beings. He met and transmitted the Dharma to the Third Patriarch Sengcan, saying, "Protect this robe and bowl well, for they certify that you have received the Dharma Seal. You too should go into hiding to avoid danger." Later, the disciples of Bodhiruchi (Vinaya Master Guangtong) tried to kill Master Huike, who feigned insanity to lessen the jealousy of his rivals. Although he pretended to be insane, he still had tremendous affinities with living beings and so a great many people still believed in and were taken across by him. But Bodhiruchi's disciples, still jealous and obstructive, wouldn't leave him alone. They reported Great Master Huike to the government, accusing him of being a weird inhuman creature. "He confuses the people who follow him," they charged; "He is not even human." The situation was reported to the emperor, who ordered the district magistrate to arrest him, and Great Master Huike was locked up and questioned:

"Are you human or are you a freak?" asked the Magistrate.

"I'm a freak," replied Great Master Huike.

The magistrate knew that the Patriarch was saying this to avoid jealousy, so he ordered him to tell the truth. "Speak clearly," he demanded, "what are you?"

The Great Master replied, "I'm really, truly a freak; absolutely for sure!"

Governments can't allow strange freaks to roam the earth, and so Great Master Huike was sentenced to a public beheading. Aii ya! This world is totally unreasonable. The Second Buddhist Patriarch gets mistaken for weird creature!

The Patriarch told his disciples, "I must undergo this

在世界上，於是乎奏明皇帝，就要把他問斬了，就要斬首示眾，要把這個妖怪給殺了。唉！你說世界有沒有真理！一個第二代祖師，這個政府就說他是妖怪，是個妖精。

在這個時候，二祖慧可大師就對著他這一班徒眾說：「我是應該受這個果報的。我傳的這個佛法，到第四代的時候，只落到名相上，就是有名有相，著到相上。」說完這話，二祖慧可大師就落淚了。落淚並不是怕死，並不是說政府要殺他，他怕死，哭起來了。因為二祖這個脾氣最大，就是死，或什麼的他也不怕；他若怕死，他也不會承認他是妖怪。二祖最神氣，你看死就死了嘛！怕什麼！你說我是妖怪，我就是妖怪！你看這個脾氣。若不是有脾氣，怎麼會這樣子，這就是一股勁兒，你說是妖怪就妖怪了，沒關係。

那麼哭了之後，就叫劊子手，說：「你來殺吧！」劊子手拿著刀照他頭上就砍了一刀。你猜怎麼樣？你猜不著呢！你一定想：「這一定像砍到鐵上、石頭上，這個頭砍不掉的，因為他是祖師，有神通嘛！」你會這樣想。不是的。這一刀就把頭給砍掉了，再也不會長出來了。那麼砍掉頭怎麼樣呢？沒有血出，所出的是什麼呢？就像牛奶似的白漿。

說：「這個未免太神化了！」就是這麼神化。你信就信，你不信就算了，這沒有什麼理由可講的。那麼你信，我可以給你用一個簡單的道理講一講，為什麼他冒白漿，不流血呢？這是人到一種純陽體了，他所有的血都變成白色。你說我不信，當然你不信啦！你若信，你也成了第二代祖師了嘛！

這個有司一看這種情形——這個妖怪不流血，這真是妖怪了！於是乎就具實以奏，說：「這個真是妖怪。我把他殺了，他頭掉了，沒有血流出來，只流出好像牛奶那種白色的漿，並且他這個面目，死了還和活著一樣。這證明這真是妖怪了。」

但是到皇帝那兒，皇帝知道。皇帝那兒怎麼知道呢？因為在印度第二十四祖——師子比丘，也是被人殺了，砍掉了頭，不流血，冒白漿。這印度第二十四代祖師師子比丘也是這樣的，這是證明這個人的體純陽無陰了，陰都變成陽了，這叫白陽世界。

這個白陽世界是為什麼呢？就因為他無漏了。什麼無漏了？就因為他自己沒有無明了。那麼說：「你方才講這個慧可大師脾氣很大的，那麼有脾氣，怎麼會沒有無明呢？」你比我聰明，我還沒想到這個問題，你想到這個問題令我也多了一點知識。你要明白，慧可大師我說他這個脾氣，這是大仁、大勇、大智、大慧的脾氣，並

retribution. "I have transmitted the Buddhadharma. But by the time of the Fourth Patriarch, the Dharma will only be a name and an appearance." When he finished speaking, he wept. He wasn't crying because he was afraid of dying. It's not that, having been sentenced to death, he was scared and cried. The Second Patriarch had a big temper; he feared nothing— even death. If he had been afraid to die, he would not have claimed he was a weird creature. The Second Patriarch was a courageous man, and so he looked death square in the eye. When he finished crying he faced the executioner and said: "Come and kill me!"

The executioner raised his ax and swung it towards the master's neck. What do you suppose happened? You are probably thinking, "He was a Patriarch with great spiritual power. Certainly the blade shattered and his neck was not even scratched." No. The axe cut off his head, and his head didn't grow back. However, instead of blood, a milky white fluid flowed onto the chopping block.

Someone says, "Now really, that's going too far." Well, if you believe it, that is fine. If you don't believe it, then just pass it off it as being too unreasonable. However, for those of you who do believe, I can give you a simple explanation of why blood did not flow from the Patriarch's neck: when a sage enters the white yang realm his blood becomes white because his body has completely transformed into yang, leaving no trace of yin. You say you can't believe it? Of course you can't. If you could, you could become a Second Patriarch!

When the executioner saw that the Master did not bleed, he exclaimed, "Hey! He really is a freak! I chopped off his head, but what came out was not blood, it was this milky white fluid. And his face looks exactly as it did when he was alive! That proves he was strange." But when the emperor was informed, the emperor knew. How did he know? He remembered that the Twenty-fourth Indian Patriarch, Aryasimha, had also been beheaded and had not bled, but a white milky fluid had poured forth. Since the Twenty-fourth Indian Patriarch had been like that, it proved that this person's body was also entirely yang without any yin. When the yin turns to yang, that's called the white yang realm.

How does one attain the white yang realm? It's the result of no outflows. What doesn't flow out? Well, it means he didn't have any ignorance. You may object, "But you just said that Great Master Huike had great anger. Since he had a temper, how could he have been devoid of ignorance?" You are certainly more clever than I, for I did not think of this question. But now that you have brought it up, I've increased my awareness a bit. You should understand that when I said Great Master Huike had a temper, I meant the temperament that stems from great humaneness, great courage, great knowledge, and great wisdom. I wasn't talking about petty anger like yours and mine which explodes like firecrackers, "Pop! Pop! Pop." His anger was wisdom that enabled him to recognize the workings of cause and effect so that he never

不是像你我好像炮仗似的那個脾氣，啪似地響了！你要聽明白，他這個脾氣和一般脾氣不同。他這個脾氣就是智慧，有智慧他就能認出因果循環，一切的道理都不違背了。所以你這一問，我又要多說這麼多話。大仁、大智、大勇、大慧，這是他的脾氣。

那麼這樣子，皇帝知道這是真正的肉身菩薩，所以就生大懺悔，說：「這真菩薩在我們國家裏，我們都不能保護，現在居然把他殺了。」於是乎，他大生慚愧，令這些文武大臣全都皈依這位妖怪。所以他雖然死了，又收了這麼一些個徒弟。二祖神光的大略事蹟是這樣。

# 第三代祖師 ——僧璨大師

在隋朝的時候，這是僧璨法師弘法，他是第三位祖師。這一位祖師，誰也不知道他是從什麼地方來的？姓什麼？叫什麼？沒有人知道。他來見二祖的時候，是一個什麼樣子呢？是一個身上生了很多的瘡，很多的癩疱。這個癩疱在身上，這兒也長一個，那兒也長一個，很多很多的，通身都是，就像那個大痲瘋一樣。人長那種病，要和一般的人都隔離，因為恐怕會傳染，就是這種病。他就這樣來見二祖，二祖問他說：「你從什麼地方來啊？你來到這個地方幹什麼啊？」這個大痲瘋的人說什麼呢？他說：「我來皈依和尚，學習佛法。」二祖說：「你病得這個樣子，污濁邋遢，你身上這麼樣不乾淨，你怎麼可以學佛法呢？」

這個病人，你猜他說什麼？二祖本來很聰明，他比二祖更聰明。他說：「我這個有病的人和你這個和尚，這個心有什麼分別，心有什麼不同？」

二祖一聽，咦！這個人有點來歷，就說：「你不要講，不要講，我知道了。」於是乎把法就傳給他，就這麼樣傳的。傳了之後，說：「你好好保護著、愛護這個法，你也要避一避，因為菩提流支這個印度和尚，他自己是印度人，但是他專門妒忌印度和尚。我現在接的是菩提達摩的法，他的徒弟就想把菩提達摩的徒弟都給殺完了。所以現在我傳法給你，你切記不要出鋒頭，不要教人知道，你要藏起來。」於是乎，這個三祖僧璨法師也就學他師父的樣子，假裝發瘋癲這種病，到各處去默默中來教化眾生。

他正趕上後周武帝滅佛法，於是也就跑到山裏面住了十多年。他住的這個山有很多狼熊虎豹；等他到這兒住的時候，這些狼熊虎豹都不知道搬家搬到什麼地方去了，都沒有了。

did anything against principle. Since you asked, I must explain: Great humaneness, great knowledge, great courage, and great wisdom--that's what his temper was made of!

Realizing that the man he had executed was a Bodhisattva in the flesh, the emperor felt deeply repentant. "A true Bodhisattva came to our country," he said, "and instead of offering him protection, we kill him." Then, with utmost shame and remorse, the emperor had all the officials take refuge with this weird creature. Thus, even though the Second Patriarch was already dead, he still accepted this group of disciples. The general biography of the Second Patriarch Shenguang ends here.

# The Third Patriarch
# Great Master Sengcan "Brilliant Sanghan"

The Third Patriarch, Sengcan of the Sui Dynasty, was of unknown family and origin. When he first came to visit the Second Patriarch, his body was covered with repulsive sores like those of a leper. As a rule, lepers were isolated in those days, for fear of contagion.

But he came in that condition to see the Second Patriarch. "Where are you from?" asked the Second Patriarch. "What are you doing here?"

The leper answered, "I have come here to take refuge with the High Master and to study and cultivate the Buddhadharma."

"You have a loathsome disease and your body is filthy. How can you study the Buddhadharma?"

The Second Patriarch was clever, but Dhyana Master Sengcan was even more clever. "I am a sick man and you are a high master," he said, "but in our true minds where is the difference?"

Hearing his reply, the Second Patriarch knew that he was no ordinary person. He quickly answered, "Don't say any more! Don't talk! I know!" and immediately transmitted the Dharma to him. After the transmission he said, "You should protect this Dharma well. You also must go into hiding, because Bodhiruchi, who is an Indian monk, is very jealous of Indian monks, and the Dharma that I have received is from Patriarch Bodhidharma. Bodhiruchi's disciples want to kill Bodhidharma's disciples. Be very careful and let no one know that you have received this transmission from me. Hide away!" After that, the Third Patriarch used the same technique as his teacher. He feigned insanity and went about quietly teaching and transforming beings.

During the persecution of Buddhism by the Emperor Wu of the Northern Zhou dynasty (reigned from 561-577 A.D.), the Third Patriarch fled into the mountains for more than a decade. While he hid there, the tigers, wolves, leopards, and other fierce animals all left the area.

When he encountered Dharma Master Daoxin, he transmitted the Dharma to him, making him the Fourth Patriarch. After

直到有一次，他見到道信祖師，就把這個法傳給道信，道信祖師這是第四祖。

那麼傳了之後，他就設了一個千僧齋。千僧齋就是請一千個和尚來吃齋，他的徒弟有不知多少都到這兒來吃齋。吃完齋的時候，你説他怎麼樣啊？他説：「你們大家都認爲坐著死，這是最好了，你們現在看看我，我給你們來一個特別的樣子，我這個生死自由。」

怎麼樣子呢？説完這話，一隻手攀著一個樹枝子——就在當時千僧齋那個地方，前面有一棵大樹，他手扳著樹枝子——腳翹起來了，並不是上吊，但是可就死了，奮然而化。就這麼手扳著樹枝子，就圓寂了。究竟他多大歲數？是什麼地方人？姓什麼？叫什麼？也沒有人知道。這是三祖大略的事蹟。

有一個人在這兒聽經，這會兒就害怕了，害什麼怕？説：「第一個祖師菩提達摩，被人用毒藥毒死了，第二個祖師被人殺了，第三個祖師抓著樹枝也就這麼死了。這做祖師太沒有意思了！太危險囉！我無論如何不願意做這個祖師。」你就想做也不可能做，因爲你怕死。做祖師的就要不怕死，拿著死和生沒有分別。所謂前面講這個「煩惱即菩提，生死即涅槃；遊戲人間，教化眾生。」這才能做祖師。你這麼膽小，連死你都怕，那怎麼可以做得祖師，你連祖師的徒弟都做不成呀！因爲什麼呢？你有所恐懼，有所怕。

祖師都是不怕苦，不怕難，也不怕死，也不怕生。前面講那個佛馱、耶舍——達摩祖師那兩個徒弟，不是説嗎？「你手做拳，拳做手，你看快不快？」遠公大師説：「快！」他説：「煩惱即菩提，生死即涅槃，也是這麼快。」所以你不要怕死就可以做祖師。現在誰可以不怕死，我都封他做祖師。那麼上面説的這是第三祖。

# 第四代祖師——道信大師

第四祖又是一個特別樣兒，怎麼特別樣呢？他很小就出家，跟著僧璨祖師來學習佛法。他六十年長坐不臥，總是這麼坐著不臥，他眼睛也常常閉著不睜開，但可不是睡覺，你不要誤會了，他閉著眼睛來用功。可是眼睛一睜開，怎麼樣啊？哦，一般人一看見他這個眼睛，就都打戰顫，嚇得——哦！就都好像地震了似的，嚇得那個樣子，常常是這樣。爲什麼呢？誰也不知道，他就有這種威德。

他是什麼時候的人？唐朝的時候。在唐朝貞觀十七年的時候，皇帝聽説這個第四代祖師在這兒，就派一個使

the transmission, Master Sengcan invited a thousand Bhikshus to a great vegetarian feast and a vast number of his disciples also attended the banquet. After they had eaten, what do you suppose he did? He said, "You think that to sit in a full lotus is the best way to die. Watch! I'll show you something different to demonstrate my independence over birth and death!"

The Master walked to the base of a large tree, leaped up, grabbed a strong branch, and right then and there, in front of the thousand Bhikshus, he entered Nirvana. It's not that he was hanged, mind you. He passed away peacefully swinging from the tree by one hand! No one knew how old he was. No one knew where he came from. No one knew his name. That's a general description of the Third Patriarch.

Someone is afraid and thinks, "The First Patriarch was poisoned, the Second Patriarch was beheaded, the Third Patriarch died hanging from a tree. It's totally meaningless to be a Patriarch. It's much too dangerous. No matter what, I don't want to be a Patriarch." With this attitude, even if you wanted to be a Patriarch you could not. Patriarchs do not fear death. For them, there is no distinction between life and death. "Afflictions are Bodhi; birth and death are Nirvana. They roam in the human realm teaching and transforming living beings." Someone like that can be a Patriarch. As long as you are a coward, as long as you fear anything, not to mention being a Patriarch, you cannot even be a Patriarch's disciple.

Patriarchs are not afraid of suffering, not afraid of difficulty, not afraid of death, and not afraid of life. Like Fotuo and Yeshe, those two disciples of Patriarch Bodhidharma, said, "The hand makes a fist; the fist makes a hand. Is that fast or not?" The Venerable Yuan said "Fast!" They said, "Afflictions and Bodhi, birth and death and Nirvana, are just that fast!" And so don't fear death and then you can be a Patriarch. Right now, if there is anyone who doesn't fear death, I will make him a Patriarch. Above has been a discussion of the Third Patriarch.

# The Fourth Patriarch
# Great Master Daoxin "Faith in the Way"

The Fourth Patriarch was also a strange character. While very young, he left home under Master Sengcan and for sixty years he sat in Dhyana concentration, without lying down to rest. Although he seldom opened his eyes, he wasn't asleep. He was working at cultivation. When he did open his eyes, everyone shook with terror. People would shudder and tremble as if enduring an earthquake when they saw his eyes. Why? No one knew. Such was the magnitude of his awesome virtue.

Hearing of the Master's great virtue, in the seventeenth year of the Zhenguan Reign of the Tang dynasty (643 A.D.), the emperor sent a messenger to invite him to the palace to

臣，去請他到皇帝那兒，皇帝要供養他，要拜他做師父。你看，要是到現在，不要說皇帝請我去，就不請，我都要去見皇帝，來攀緣一下，何況他來請我呢，怎麼可以不去？可是你說他怎樣啊？他不去！他説：「我年紀太老了，走路也走不動囉！吃飯也不香囉！我老得多病，不能到京裏去了。」

這個使臣就回去對皇帝一説，皇帝説：「你再去，一定要把他請來！你就説皇帝説的，無論如何你要去，你就老了，怎麼樣老，也都要去的。請你，你就要去的。」所以這使臣又來了，就對他講：「皇帝説無論如何，你就老，就怎麼樣子，現在我們用人把你抬著也要抬去的。我們給你預備個轎子，把你抬到京裏去。」那時候因為沒有飛機，不是交通這麼方便。

四祖説：「哦！不行的，我不去，我太老了，不可能去了。如果你一定要我去，你把我這個腦袋斬下來拿去，但是我心始終不去的。」

使臣一聽，他這麼樣講，沒有辦法，怎麼可以把他腦袋斬去拿給皇帝呢？就回去對皇帝説：「這個和尚真是特別古怪，性情真是太不近人情了。皇帝您請他來，他説就是把他頭斬了拿來，他心也不來，也不來見皇帝。」

皇帝説：「好！你就去把他的頭給我拿來。」於是乎就用這個盒子裝上一把刀，説：「你到那兒，就拿這把刀把他頭給斬了。」這使臣説：「好！」等臨走的時候，皇帝對他又説：「無論如何，你不能傷這和尚，你不能殺這個和尚。」

啊！這個使臣現在明白了，於是乎到那兒就説：「老和尚啊！你現在倒是去不去？皇帝叫我拿這把刀來就是斬你頭的，這把刀是皇帝賜給我的。你若不去，他就叫我拿這把刀，把你頭給割下來，拿著你的頭去見皇帝。」

這個道信祖師説：「好啊！那是最好了，我這個頭能見到皇帝，這一生真是特別地光榮。好啦！你現在就來斬我的頭啦！」於是把頭就伸出來。這個使臣拿著刀正比量著他的頭，一看見他把頭伸過來了，趕快把這把刀又放到盒子裏了。

道信祖師這麼閉著眼睛等他斬頭，等了大約十分鐘，恐怕有的。這是大約的，也不一定，你不要執著，説一定十分鐘。或者十一分鐘，或者九分鐘，都不一定的。那麼看他沒有斬，道信禪師就説了：「喂！你怎麼不斬哪？」他發了脾氣了，好像二祖似的。

這使臣就説：「皇上叫我，只是這麼講一講，不能傷和尚。」

receive the offerings of the emperor, who wanted to bow to the Patriarch as his teacher. Think about it, the way things are now, not to speak of being invited by the emperor, people would attempt to wedge themselves into the court unasked! How much the more would they go if invited! But the Great Master, the Fourth Patriarch, refused the invitation saying, "My age is advanced. I don't walk well, and I have no appetite. I'm old and sick. I cannot travel to the capitol."

When the messenger delivered the Patriarch's reply, the emperor said, "Go back and tell him that the emperor says that no matter how old he is or how difficult the journey, I have ordered him to come to the palace."

The messenger returned to the Patriarch and said, "Master, regardless of your health, you must come to the emperor's court. We will carry you back in a sedan chair if necessary!" At that time, since there were no airplanes, travel was difficult.

"No, I cannot go," replied the Patriarch. "I am too old and ill. Take my head if you must, but my heart will not go."

The messenger thought, "There is nothing to do but to go back without him. I cannot take his head to the emperor." The messenger then hurried back to the emperor. "Your Excellency, this Bhikshu is very strange; he is hardly human. He said you may have his head, but his heart will not move! He has no intention of coming to see the emperor."

"Very well, go get his head," replied the emperor. He put a knife in a box and gave it to the messenger saying, "Slice off his head."

"Fine." the messenger replied. Then, when the messenger was about to set out, the emperor told him, "Under no circumstances should you harm this Bhikshu. You must not kill this monk." Ah, with that, the messenger understood.

He returned to the Fourth Patriarch and said, "Venerable Master, ultimately are you going or not? The emperor has given me this knife with the orders that if you refuse to come, I am to cut off your head and take it back to the emperor."

Patriarch Daoxin said, "Fine! If my head gets to see the Emperor, then that will be great glory. Good! You may remove my head now." And he stuck out his head. The messenger had taken out the knife and been sizing up his head. But when he saw the Great Master stick out his head, the messenger quickly put the knife away.

Meanwhile, Patriarch Daoxin closed his eyes and waited calmly for his head to be cut off. He waited for about ten minutes. Maybe it was ten minutes, maybe it was nine or eleven. Don't become attached. It's not for sure precisely how long he waited. But nothing happened. Finally Master Daoxin got angry, just like the Second Patriarch, and shouted, "Hey! Why don't you slice off my head!"

"The emperor had no intention of harming you," the messenger quickly replied. "He was just bluffing."

The Patriarch heard this and laughed aloud. Then he said, "Now you know there is still such a person in the world!" meaning, a person who does not fear death.

The family name of the Fourth Patriarch Daoxin was Si-Ma.

四祖道信大師哈哈一笑說：「啊！你現在知道這個世界還有人吧！」就是還有不怕死的人。

四祖道信禪師，俗家姓司馬，名字叫信，所以出家的名字就叫道信。司馬這個姓這在漢朝和晉朝可以說是貴族的人，因為晉朝皇帝就姓司馬，漢朝有一個司馬遷和司馬相如，作文章都作得非常好。這第四祖他是很有名望的家族，從小就出家修道，他活了七十二歲，但是六十年都是脅不著席，就是不躺著睡覺，他的成就是有一種不可思議的境界。

有一次他在山上修道，湖北這個城就被土匪給圍困住了。城被圍困了一百多天，道信禪師看見城裏邊，水都沒有了，井也乾了，水的來源也沒有了。水、火和飲食有重要的關係，沒有水，人就不能有生命。於是乎，信禪師就到城裏邊來，教化所有的城民，教這個官和民都念「摩訶般若波羅蜜多」。一念「摩訶般若波羅蜜多」，沒有好久，賊、土匪就都散去了、退了，井裏這水又都有了，這是一種感應道交的情形。

在這個時候，他用佛眼觀察，自己應該到什麼地方去住去？他一看，湖北那兒有一個山，這個山叫破頭山，這名字很不好的，那個地方有一股紫氣圍繞，紫雲在那地方籠罩著。這紫雲就是一種祥瑞的表現、吉祥的意思，於是乎他就到這個山上去住，那麼給這個山改了一個名字，叫什麼名字呢？叫「雙峰山」，因為它有兩個山峰。

有一次他教化眾生，遇到很剛強難化的眾生，他教他改惡向善，他就改善向惡，不聽教化。以後他就用種種的權巧方便法門，結果把這剛強眾生也教化得改惡向善了，知道自己是錯誤的。他弘揚佛法，有四十多年，所教化的眾生如稻麻竹葦那麼多，「稻麻竹葦」就是表示太多了，那數量不知有多少。

有一次他告訴他的徒弟圓一法師，說：「你要給我造一個塔，我要走了。」這圓一法師就給他造塔。有一次他就問：「這個塔造好了沒有呀？」圓一法師說：「已經造好了。」造好了，怎麼樣呢？在永徽二年，永徽是唐朝一個皇帝的年號。二年這時候，閏九月二十四日，道信祖師從來也沒有生過病，可是在這一天，他就坐在那兒奄然而化，就圓寂了。沒有什麼人知道他圓寂，他也沒有告訴大家說我要走了，沒有告假。

圓寂之後，就把他裝到這個塔裏邊，封上了。這是用石頭造的塔，本來用鐵都鎖著的。過了一年，這個塔自己就開了，鎖也都開了，大家就看見這第四祖在裏邊，還是在那兒端然正坐，和活著的時候一樣，一點都沒有變。

His personal name was Xin "Faith," and when he left-home, that name became part of his ordained name "Faith in the Way." Si-Ma was an honorable ancestral name. Both Emperor Si-Ma of the Jin dynasty and the historian and skilled writer Si-Ma Qian of the Han dynasty had this name. The Fourth Patriarch, who had such famous ancestors, left the home-life to cultivate when he was very young. He lived seventy-two years, sixty of which were spent without lying down even once to sleep. The Fourth Patriarch's realm of accomplishment was inconceivable.

While Master Daoxin was cultivating in the mountains in Hubei, a nearby city was besieged by bandits for more than a hundred days. Master Daoxin saw that there was no water in the city--the wells were dry and there was no more flow from the source. Water, fire and food and drink are vital to life. Deprived of water, the inhabitants of that city would not be able to go on living. And so, Master Daoxin left his mountain retreat to teach and transform the people. He taught the officials and populace all to recite "Mahaprajna-paramita." After they recited for a time, the bandits scattered and fled and water reappeared in the wells. That was a response based on the Way which Master Daoxin had.

When the Fourth Patriarch decided to build a temple, he looked with his Buddha eye and saw Broken Head Mountain in Hubei. The name is not a good one, but the area itself was surrounded by a purple cloud of energy. Observing this auspicious sign, the Master went there to dwell, changing its inauspicious name to "Double Peak" Mountain, after its shape.

The Master used expedient dharmas to teach living beings how to discard their bad habits. These stubborn living beings, however, often discarded what was good and continued doing evil, refusing to listen to instructions. But the Master persisted and by using all kinds of skill-in-means caused these stubborn living beings to realize their mistakes and change. He propagated the Dharma for more than forty years, transforming living beings greater in number than seedlings of rice, stalks of hemp, shoots of bamboo, or blades of grass.

One day the Fourth Patriarch said to his disciple, Dharma Master Yuanyi, "You should build me a stupa. I am going to leave." Later he asked, "Is the stupa ready?" to which Master Yuanyi replied "yes." In the second year of Yonghui, of the Tang dynasty (651 A.D.), on the twenty-fourth day of the ninth lunar month, Patriarch Daoxin, who had never been ill, sat down and peacefully entered Nirvana. Very few people knew of his passing, since he had not announced it to the assembly. He didn't say good-bye.

His disciples locked his flesh body securely in the stone stupa. A year later the iron locks fell away and the stupa opened by itself. Looking in, everyone saw the Fourth Patriarch still sitting in full lotus, appearing the same as he had when alive. At that time the Fifth Patriarch Hongren was delighted when he saw his teacher's appearance. The Master's

在這個時候，第五代祖師弘忍，又看見師父的相好，就非常高興。雖然像活著的時候一樣，但是這個肉都乾了，一定都沒有什麼肉了。於是乎用漆布把這個身體貼上金，保護這個真身，直到現在還有，這是第四祖。他教化的眾生非常之多，那麼他的入室弟子、傳法弟子，就是第五祖弘忍大師。

## 第五代祖師 ──弘忍大師

從西天到東土，歷代祖師各有各的特長，各有各的密行，各有各的來歷不同，現在略略說一說五祖大師的經歷。五祖大師生在湖北雙峰山黃梅縣這個地方，俗家姓周，七歲就被送到廟上修行。大約是他父親、母親都是篤信佛教，覺得世俗這種生活煩煩惱惱，爭爭吵吵，貪而無厭，從生至死，沒有什麼真正的價值。所以有小孩子，在七歲的時候就把他送到廟上，跟著四祖道信禪師出家。

道信禪師一見這個小孩子，就知道他是法門的龍象，就儘量栽培他。栽培他，並不是說天天給他吃點好的，穿點好的，住一點好的，這麼樣栽培他。他是天天叫他勤勞工苦作──清潔的工作呀、煮飯、燒水、煲茶呀這一類的，總而言之，什麼工作都叫他做，叫他沒做過的要做一做，試一試這種工作的味道。

白天他是勤勞工苦作，任勞任怨，不和同等的沙彌打架，也不拌嘴，就是那麼認真腳踏實地地用功修行。誰說他不對，他就很歡喜地接受，很歡喜地改過自新。七歲的時候，就是這樣一天一天修行，白天做一切的事，工作護持道場，晚間就參禪打坐，認真用功。不是到晚間就趕快睡覺了，一早起也睜不開眼睛，爬不起來，不是這樣的。晚間練習坐單，坐那兒用功，修這一切的行門。一切的行門是什麼呢？就是自己誦經、持咒、拜佛、禮懺、研究學問，在這忙裏偷閒來用功修行，時間一分一毫也不叫它空過去；白天做一切的工作，也正是用功修行，晚間還是參禪打坐，也是認真修行，所謂時時刻刻都痛念生死。不多說一句話，不少做一份活，做一切的工作也儘量把它做好了，話不說那麼多，不和任何人爭，不和任何人去吵，這是五祖弘忍大師。什麼叫弘忍？就是什麼他都忍，忍不了的，他也要忍；讓不了的，他也要讓。

經過這麼樣，到十三歲的時候，四祖大師觀察他可以受具足戒了，所以給他授具足戒。受戒之後，十三歲就做比丘了，他身量也長得高高大大的，身高八尺

body had not decayed, but the flesh had dried out. The Fifth Patriarch wrapped the body with lacquered cloth and gilded it to protect this "true body." To this day the Fourth Patriarch's body still exists. He taught and transformed a vast number of disciples; his "room-entering" disciple, that is, the disciple who received the Dharma transmission, was the Fifth Patriarch, Great Master Hongren.

## The Fifth Patriarch
## Great Master Hongren "Vast Patience"

From West to East, each of the Patriarchs had his own special points, his own secret practices, and his own background. Now, we'll discuss in general the experiences of the Great Master, the Fifth Patriarch. The Fifth Patriarch lived on Double Peak Mountain in Huangmei County, Hubei Province. His family name was Zhou. His parents, devoted Buddhists who felt that worldly life with its afflictions, fighting, and avarice was meaningless, sent their son to the monastery at the age of seven to leave home with the Fourth Patriarch, Great Master Daoxin.

Dhyana Master Daoxin knew at once that the boy had great potential, so he undertook to train him seriously. Instead of spoiling him with good food, nice clothing, and a fine place to live, he made the boy do chores every day. As a child, Great Master Hongren cleaned the monastery, cooked, heated the water, steeped the tea, and so forth. He did every kind of work there was to do, so he got a taste of each and every task.

During the day he diligently did manual labor, bearing the weariness, bearing grievances. When the other Shramaneras (novices) wanted to fight with him, he would not retaliate. He remained intensely involved in applying real effort to his cultivation. When people criticized him, he accepted it gladly, eagerly changing his faults and renewing himself. Starting from age seven, he cultivated like this day in and day out. During the day he did all kinds of chores to protect the Way-place, and then at night he sat in meditation, investigating Chan. During the night the Master sat there working hard at developing his skill in meditation. It's not that as soon as evening came he rushed off to rest, and then in the morning couldn't crawl out of the sack. He wasn't like that! He practiced at night. He cultivated every kind of practice: reciting Sutras and mantras, bowing to the Buddhas, bowing in repentance, and studying the teachings, never letting a moment go by in vain. He sustained the thought of birth and death as a painful reminder. Although he spoke very little, he worked very diligently and never fought or argued with people. His name, Hongren, means "Vast Patience," because he was always patient and able to yield.

When he was thirteen, the Fourth Patriarch observed that he was mature enough and allowed him to receive the complete precepts and become a Bhikshu. The Fifth Patriarch was eight feet tall and had an extraordinary appearance. His eyes were full of spirit, and he was extremely circumspect in his speech

，相貌奇特。什麼相貌奇特呢？他這個眼睛有神，口不隨便講話，天天都是謹言慎行的。一看他就看得出，他是時時刻刻行住坐臥都在用功，不把光陰空過。四祖一看，觀察他是載道之器，可以弘化一方，所以就把衣缽傳給這弘忍大師，他做這個五祖，是在中國第五代的祖師。從釋迦牟尼佛一代一代傳下來，傳到中國的五祖，這叫傳授心法，以心印心，直指人心，見性成佛的法門。

五祖大師的戒行精嚴，修行是特別認真的。在當時也有一些土匪常常到城裏頭去打家劫舍，搶金銀財寶。有一次土匪就把湖北這個城給圍上，弘忍大師忍不住了，就想要救這城裏頭的老百姓，於是乎他就下山了，從東山那地方到湖北城裏去。這些土匪一見著弘忍大師來了，就嚇得丟盔卸甲望影而逃。為什麼這樣子？因為弘忍大師雖然是一個人下山來的，就是有隨從，大約也不過三三兩兩這樣子；可是這些土匪就看到完全都是穿金盔金甲的天兵、天將，好像從天上下來的天神一樣，身穿著金盔金甲，手拿著寶劍，這麼威武奇揚的。土匪一見到這樣的情形，就嚇得望影而逃，就跑了；也不用一刀、一鎗、一箭，他們就嚇得撤退了。那麼這是什麼原因呢？很簡單，我告訴你們各位，就因為弘忍大師他誦持〈楞嚴咒〉。在《楞嚴經》上說過：誦持〈楞嚴咒〉的人，常常有八萬四千金剛藏菩薩隨從他、保護他，到必要的時候就救他、擁護他，所以土匪一見著弘忍大師就嚇跑了。這可以說是金剛藏菩薩顯聖，也可以說是弘忍大師修行的功德、威德，把他們都懾伏了。

那麼以一個修道的人，能不用一兵一卒，把土匪給嚇跑了，這就是有真正的功夫才能這樣子；若沒有真正的功夫，怎麼會有這樣的感應道交？因為這種種的靈異，所以四方的比丘都望風而歸，聽到五祖這個道風，就都去到他那兒學習佛法。所以當時在五祖的座下，常常有千餘人在那兒來求法。

這個四祖大師，唐太宗召請他到宮裏頭去，想要供養他。那麼有其師必有其徒，五祖弘忍大師也是在唐高宗的時候，很多次皇帝請他到宮廷裏邊來，要供養他；他每一次都婉拒了，也不到宮廷裏頭去受皇帝的供養。這種高風亮節不是一般人所能明白的，可以說是他本著

富貴不能淫，貧賤不能移，威武不能屈。

這是一種頂天立地的大丈夫的行為，不是一般求名求

and manner. It was obvious that he was mindful of his practice in every moment. Seeing that he would become a worthy teacher of people, the Fourth Patriarch transmitted the robe and bowl to Great Master Hongren, making him the Fifth Patriarch in China. That transmission, which came down from Shakyamuni Buddha, generation by generation, is a mind-to-mind transmission of the mind seal passed straight to a person's mind. It is the Dharma-door of seeing the nature and realizing Buddhahood.

The Fifth Patriarch held the precepts very purely and cultivated with great diligence on East Mountain in Hubei Province. During that time thieves often entered a nearby city to steal gold, silver, and valuables. Once, when he saw a horde of bandits besieging that city in Hubei, he was unable to be patient any longer. And so the Great Master "Vast Patience" went down the mountain toward the city, intending to rescue its inhabitants. When the bandits saw him, they were terrified, dropped their weapons and armor and retreated as fast as they could. Why? It was because although Great Master Hongren had actually come alone down the mountain, or perhaps with just a few others, what the thieves saw accompanying the Patriarch was a retinue of golden-armored heavenly soldiers and generals armed with jeweled weapons, manifesting awesome virtue and brightness. The alarmed thieves ran away and the siege was broken without the use of a single sword, gun, or arrow.

How was the Great Master able to accomplish that? It was very simple! I'll tell you how. The Fifth Patriarch cultivated and recited the Shurangama Mantra. The *Shurangama Sutra* says that if you constantly recite the Shurangama Mantra, eighty-four thousand Vajra Store Bodhisattvas will protect you from all danger. On the one hand, the thieves were frightened off by the Vajra Store Bodhisattvas, and on the other, they were subdued by awesome virtue of the Great Master himself.

To be able to intimidate a horde of bandits without using a single weapon, one must have genuine skill in cultivation. Based on many responses of this sort, Bhikshus from all quarters were drawn to the Fifth Patriarch's place to study the Dharma. Often there were more than a thousand people studying under him.

The Emperor Taizong of the Tang dynasty had tried without success to invite the Fourth Patriarch to the palace to accept offerings. As it was with the teacher, so it was with the disciple, and so Great Master Hongren also received many invitations from Emperor Taizong. But, like his teacher, he refused them all and did not go to the palace to receive the emperor's offerings.

Not tempted by wealth and honor,
Unchanging in poor and lowly circumstances,
Not submissive to power and coercion.

That kind of resolute, heroic spirit is beyond the understanding of ordinary people who covet fame and riches and who im-

利、迷戀財、色、名、食、睡這一類的人所能了解的。由他這一點看來，這是佛教和其他任何宗教不同的地方。

在唐朝咸亨的時候，他就對門人說：「我要走了。」叫門人給他造一個塔，用石頭造的。他又問：「這個塔造好了沒有？」門人告訴他：「造好了。」於是乎他就端然正坐，無疾而終。

可是在他入滅以前，他告訴人，說我傳法的人有十個。這十個人每一個都可以教化一方，都可以做一方的法主。

這十個人是他教化眾生以來，所挑選的十個嗣法的人。因為他告訴六祖大師說：「衣為爭端，止汝勿傳。」說從你這兒就不傳這個衣了，有這個衣，大家就爭這個衣，這是一個亂的開始。

他嗣法的人有十位，這十位就是神秀、智詵、慧藏、玄約、老安、法如、智德、義方，又有惠能大師，又有一個叫劉主簿。那麼這十個人都是接五祖法脈的嗣法門人，都可以做一方的教化主。那麼說完這話，他就入滅了。以上，這是五祖大師簡略的行狀是這樣子。

這十位五祖大師的嗣法門人，每一位都有他的特長，或者是智慧第一的，或者是品行第一的，或者有道德第一的，或者有容忍第一的，或者有喜捨第一的，或者有慈悲第一的，或者有教化第一的，或者有修行第一的。總而言之，是各有所長，所以他們都值得做一般人的師表，做人天師，做眾生的依止師，做眾生的善知識。

總括起來說，他們這十位沒有自伐的。什麼叫自伐呢？就是自己讚歎自己，自誇其德，表露自己與人不同，就是顏淵說的：「願無伐善」那個「伐」。願無伐善，就是不說自己的特點，不說自己的長處，也沒有自誇的。不會自己誇讚自己，說我小的時候如何如何；中年的時候、讀書的時候如何如何，都是出乎其類，拔乎其萃，與人不同；也不會說我老年的時候，如何如何；也不會到處誇耀自己有多少皈依弟子，多少人相信自己。總而言之，不會像毛澤東似的，神化自己，自吹自擂，自命不凡。凡是聖賢的人，都不會有這個毛病，也不會自大、驕傲，也不會自滿。

總而言之，他們都有優秀的這種德行，注重德行，不會圖虛名、好假好，在表面上用功夫，自欺欺人。這十位不驕傲、不爭、不貪、不求、不自私、不自利、不打妄語，這是這十位教化主的行狀，那麼要一一詳細說，要很多時間，這簡略的，大約就是這樣子。

merse themselves in wealth, sex, fame, food, and sleep, and yet it is just that which makes Buddhism outstanding.

In the fifth year of the Xianxiang reign of the Tang dynasty (674 A.D.), the Fifth Patriarch said to his disciples, "Build me a stupa. I am going to leave." Later he asked, "Is the stupa ready?" His disciples replied that it was. He then sat upright and passed away without sickness.

But before the Fifth Patriarch entered Nirvana, he made a public announcement: "Ten people have received my Dharma transmission. These ten will become Dharma Hosts in ten different areas where they will establish Bodhimandas to preserve and spread the teaching among living beings." The Fifth Patriarch had already advised the Sixth Patriarch, Great Master Huineng, "Since the robe is a source of contention, it should stop with you. Do not transmit it." He said, "Everyone will want to fight over the robe, since it is the token of transmission. And so you should not pass it on. Turmoil and tumultuous times are at hand."

His ten Dharma heirs were: Dharma Masters Shenxiu, Zhixian, Huizang, Xuanyao, Laoan, Faru, Zhide, Yifang , as well as Great Master Huineng and also Recordkeeper Liu. These ten people who received the Fifth Patriarch's Dharma-pulse were advised to go each to a different place to teach and transform living beings. Shortly after announcing this, the Master entered Nirvana. Above has been a general description of events surrounding the Fifth Patriarch.

Each of the ten who received the Fifth Patriarch's Dharma-transmission had his own strong points. Some were foremost in wisdom, some foremost in good character, foremost in virtue in the Way, foremost in patience, foremost in joyful giving, or foremost in compassion. Or perhaps they excelled in teaching others or in their cultivation. They were qualified to be good models for people, to be teachers of gods and humans, to be places of reliance for the multitudes, and to be Good and Wise Advisors for living beings.

None of them boasted of his own merit or tried to put on a special style. As Yenyuan said, "I would hope not to boast of my own goodness." None of them discussed his own special points; no one talked about his qualifications. They never praised themselves saying things like, "When I was young, I was like this and like that; in my prime, my level of scholarship was such-and-such. In my old age, I could do this and do that." Nor would they brag about how many disciples they had or how many people believed in them. In general, they weren't like Mao Zedong, turning themselves into legends, claiming extraordinary destiny. True sages and virtuous ones are not arrogant like that.

They were men of outstanding virtue, who emphasized virtuous conduct and did not desire fame or expend their energy in superficial ways that were only cheating themselves and cheating others. These ten individuals were not arrogant, did not contend, were not greedy, did not seek, did not pursue self-benefit and did not lie. To attempt to describe the behavior

現在在這兒研究歷代祖師，我們每一個人要迴光返照，自己選擇一個，我要學哪一位祖師，哪一位祖師是我的一個榜樣，我願意照著他這樣去修行。我們要這樣想，聽經才有用，對我們自己的身心、生死上才有幫助。我們如果聽經是經，我是我，我和這個經分開了，和這個祖師也分開了，那始終我們不能得到利益。我們要：

見賢思齊焉，
見不賢而內自省也。

哪一位祖師我們最佩服，我們就要向他看齊，向他學習，這才不把這個時間浪費了。

好像方才聽說這個五祖大師七歲就出家，他就不和他的同類沙彌打架，也不爭、也不拌嘴，就是天天好好地工作，好好地任勞任怨，這才真正懂得怎麼叫出家了，懂得要怎麼了生死。如果你出家了，還天天吵架，天天打架，天天罵架，這個和沒有出家是一樣的，我們人人都要猛省這一點。

萬佛城叫「法界佛教總會」，所謂

無不從此法界流
無不還歸此法界

在萬佛城的人，都是凡夫，也都是一般的人，到這萬佛城。萬佛城這個地，雖然說是個聖地，雖然說是造就佛、造就菩薩、造就祖師的地方；可是我們剛一來到這地方，誰也不是佛，誰也不是菩薩，誰也不是祖師，未免就掛一漏萬，有很多的事情都是美中不足、不能盡善盡美、不能圓滿的。要是都圓滿了，我們就成佛、成菩薩、做祖師了，不做凡夫了。

我們在這兒都是凡夫俗子，都一點一點去自己的習氣毛病，所以無論哪一位做事，都有一些個出入，有一些個不圓滿的地方。不過我們到這兒來，都是想要圓滿，都是想要往好的學，我們這一個想要圓滿、想要好好修行、想要見賢思齊，這一個心，這是最寶貴的。就怕我們有過不能改，知善不能行，就只是自私自利，那就完了。

我們每一個人能有這一念要成佛的心，要行菩薩道的心，要本照普賢菩薩那十大願王，去發這十大願，這就一定會達到你所希望的目的。我們現在不圓滿的地方，大家都互相包涵一點，互相諒解一點，所謂

and style of each of these ten teaching hosts would take a long time; this has just been a summary.

Now as we study the Patriarchs of the past, we ought to reflect upon ourselves. We should each choose a Patriarch to learn from and to serve as our model in cultivation. If we reflect in this way when we listen to the Sutra lectures, then the lectures will help us to cultivate our bodies and minds and to end birth and death. If we listen to the Sutras, but the Sutras remain Sutras and we remain ourselves, separating ourselves from the Sutras, separating ourselves from the Patriarchs, then we won't gain any benefit at all.

When we see worthy ones,
    we should strive to be like them.
When we see unworthy ones,
    we should reflect upon ourselves.

We should strive to be like the Patriarch we most admire. Then we won't have wasted our time.

For example, we heard earlier that after the Fifth Patriarch left home at age seven, he never argued or fought with the other novice monks. He worked hard every day, putting up with the fatigue and blame. He really understood what leaving home was all about. He knew the way to end birth and death. If you fight, argue, and scold people all day long after you leave home, then basically you're the same as before you left home. We should all take note of this.

The City of Ten Thousand Buddhas is under the auspices of the Dharma Realm Buddhist Association.

*There is nothing which does not flow forth from*
    *the Dharma Realm,*
*And nothing which does not return to the Dharma Realm.*

The people at the City of Ten Thousand Buddhas are all ordinary, common people. Although the City is a sages' ground, a place where Buddhas, Bodhisattvas, and Patriarchs are created, no one is a Buddha, a Bodhisattva, or a Patriarch when he or she first comes here. Nothing is perfect right now. If everything were perfect, then we would have already become Buddhas, Bodhisattvas, and Patriarchs, and would not be ordinary people.

We are ordinary people who are trying to change our bad habits little by little. Therefore, we will inevitably make mistakes in our work and not do a perfect job. However, we have come here in the hope of improving ourselves through cultivation. This resolve to perfect ourselves and emulate the sages is extremely precious. It's only to be feared that we have faults but refuse to change them , or that we know what is good but refuse to do it. If we are selfish and only seek to benefit ourselves, then we are finished. If each of us makes the resolve to become a Buddha, to practice the Bodhisattva Path, and to follow Universal Worthy Bodhisattva in making his Ten Great Kings of Vows, then we will certainly reach our goal. Meanwhile, we should be tolerant of each other's shortcomings. As it's said,

忍是無價寶，
人人使不好，
若能會用它，
事事都能好。

我常對各位講「一切是考驗」，我們在多生多劫，不知道造了什麼罪業，不知道和哪一位有什麼因果，有什麼不圓滿的地方，所以就會有很多的問題發生，很多不如意的問題發生。那麼在這個時候，就是「一切是考驗，看我怎麼辦」，看看我自己怎麼辦？不是看爾怎麼辦？看爾是往外看了。

一切是考驗，
看爾怎麼辦？
對境若不識，
須再從頭煉。

這是

一切是考驗，
看**你**怎麼辦，看你自己怎麼辦？
對境若不識，
須再從頭煉。

一切是考驗，
看**他**怎麼辦？
你若明白他了，也就不會埋怨他了，
對境若不識，
須再從頭煉。

這幾句話都是反求諸己的話，你不要看你、我、他，你要學那個菩薩。菩薩的行狀是

真認自己錯，
莫論他人非，
他非即我非，
同體名大悲。

你常常有個大悲心，憐憫一切眾生：我要教化眾生，感化不動眾生，是我的德行不夠；我的德行若圓滿了，能萬德莊嚴，沒有不被我所化的。我化不了，就是德行還沒有萬德莊嚴。這樣一想，就不會向外馳求了

*Patience is a priceless jewel*
*Which no one knows how to use.*
*If you could make use of it,*
*Everything would turn out fine.*

As I often say to you, "Everything is a test." We don't know what offenses, what causes and effects, what bad things we may have done to others throughout many lives and many eons in the past, which causes us to now encounter a lot of trouble and impediments. So now, when we face these troubles, we must remember: "Everything is a test, to see what I will do." We should look at ourselves, not look outside to see what someone else will do.

*Everything is a test*
*To see what you will do.*
*If you don't recognize what's before you,*
*You'll have to start anew.*

Everything is a test
To see what **you** will do.
If you don't recognize what's before you,
You'll have to start anew.

What will you yourself do in this situation?

Everything is a test
To see what **he** will do.
If you understand others, then you won't blame them anymore.
If you don't recognize what's before you,
You'll have to start anew.

These verses tell us to seek within ourselves. Don't look at you, me, or him. Be like the Bodhisattvas. A Bodhisattva says:

Truly recognize your own faults.
Don't discuss the faults of others.
Others' faults are just my own.
To be of the same substance is called great compassion.

Always bring forth great compassion and pity for all living beings. If living beings don't listen to you when you try to teach them, think: "I must not have enough virtue. If I were adorned with the ten thousand virtues, no one would fail to listen to me." Contemplating in this way, you won't seek outside. You will truly reflect upon yourself, seek within yourself when things don't go your way.

If you care for others,
But they don't respond to your kindness,
Reflect on your own humaneness.

If you try to correct people,
But they don't listen,
Reflect on your own wisdom.

If you greet people,
But they ignore you,

，不會到外邊去找，這叫真正地迴光返照，反求諸己，行有不得，皆反求諸己。

愛人不親反其仁，
治人不治反其智，
禮人不答反其敬，
行有不得，皆反求諸己。

我們若能這樣子，不要說聖賢，就是佛菩薩，我們都可以很快地就達到他們的果位了。

「愛人不親反其仁」，你愛護一個人，人家和你遠遠的，很疏遠的，不敢接近你。反其仁，你要迴光返照，看看我這個仁愛人的心，夠不夠？這是愛人不親反其仁。「治人不治反其智」，好像我做師父的，教化徒弟，徒弟不聽。我要迴光返照，我這個做師父的，是不夠德行吧？所以這個徒弟才出叛徒，才不聽話，這是反其治。

「禮人不答反其敬」，你對人行個禮，人家不睬你，望都不望你，你要反求諸己，看看我是不是很恭敬地向人行禮？這是禮人不答反其敬。

「行有不得」，不得，就是不怎麼好，不圓滿。你所行所作，覺得不對的地方，「皆反求諸己」，都要自己反回來看看自己對不對。

五祖大師把這個衣缽傳給六祖。五祖繼承四祖的道統，所以當唐高宗以皇帝的尊嚴，要請他到宮廷去供養，很多次他也不接受。因為他這樣自尊，不隨隨便便受國王的邀請，國王更加對他崇敬；於是乎就把宮廷裏頭最珍貴的藥品，和最尊貴的寶貝，叫使臣送去給他，去供養他。可是五祖大師也不因為拿這些珍貴的藥品和寶貴的東西，就生大我慢，生大執著，他心裏沒有這些個東西。所以他就把所有的珠寶、藥材又散給大家，於是乎他就入滅了。

由摩訶迦葉到菩提達摩這二十八代祖師，傳到中國後，這第五代祖師大概的行狀是像以上所說的。

## 第六代祖師——惠能大師

惠能大師，在中國又叫六祖，是廣東新州那兒的人，他以前是北方人，以後因為他祖先搬到廣東，在新州那個地方落戶了。父親姓盧，三歲父親就死了。母親寡居，沒有嫁人，守她這個兒子。他打柴來維持生活。

有一天，他賣柴到一個店裡去，裡邊一個客人在那

Reflect on whether your respect is true.

Whenever you fail in your endeavors,
Seek the cause within yourself.

If we can be like that, then we will soon attain to the position of Buddhas and Bodhisattvas, how much the more that of sages and worthies.

*If you care for others, but they don't respond to your kindness, reflect on your own humaneness.* If you care for others, but they keep their distance and are afraid to approach you, contemplate to see if you are deficient in kindness.

*If you try to correct people, but they don't listen, reflect on your own wisdom.* For example, if my disciples don't listen to me, I have to reflect on whether I have sufficient virtue to be their teacher. It must be due to my lack of virtue that my disciples are rebellious and disobedient.

*If you greet people, but they ignore you, reflect on whether your respect is true.* If you greet someone, but he doesn't even look at you, ask yourself: Did I greet him with genuine respect?

*Whenever you fail in your endeavors, seek the cause within yourself.* If you do not obtain the result you expect, always seek the reason in yourself. Reflect to see if you did something wrong.

The Fifth Patriarch transmitted the robe and bowl to the Sixth Patriarch in order to perpetuate the Dharma transmitted to him by the Fourth Patriarch. And so, when the Emperor Gaozong of the Tang dynasty invited the Fifth Patriarch to the palace to receive offerings, the Fifth Patriarch, just like his teacher the Fourth Patriarch, declined his invitations many times. As a result of this, the emperor became even more respectful and sent a variety of precious gifts, including rare medicinal herbs, as an offering to the Great Master. These expensive gifts from the emperor did not make the Fifth Patriarch arrogant or attached to his own importance. The Great Master simply distributed them among the assembly and entered Nirvana shortly thereafter.

Starting from Patriarch Mahakashyapa, there were twenty-eight generations of Patriarchs in India, culminating with Bodhidharma, who became the First Patriarch in China. Great Master Hongren was the Fifth Patriarch in China.

## The Sixth Patriarch
## Great Master Huineng

Great Master Huineng, who was the Sixth Patriarch in China, was from Xinzhou in Canton. His ancestors were originally from northern China, but later moved south and settled in Canton. His father, of the Lu family, died when the Master was only three years old. His mother remained a widow and took care of her son. The Master chopped and sold firewood to support them.

誦《金剛經》，他聽見「應無所住而生其心」就開悟了。他以居士身，就到嵩山五祖弘忍大師那兒去。在那兒就做苦工，在黃梅道場，他舂米舂了八個月。

五祖知道這時候應該傳法給他了，因為他在那兒服勞幾個月，也不打妄想，只是用功，所以知道這個時間對了，就叫大家都寫一首偈頌來。

那個神秀就偷著寫了一首偈頌，說是：

身是菩提樹　心如明鏡臺
時時勤拂拭　勿使惹塵埃

六祖到那兒一看，也作了一首，說：

菩提本無樹　明鏡亦非台
本來無一物　何處惹塵埃

其實這就是批評神秀的偈頌。因為神秀那個偈頌是在修道的時候，所以他要時時勤拂拭。六祖大師是已經過來人，他是過河不需舟了。所以他說「菩提本無樹，明鏡亦非臺，本來無一物」，本來什麼也沒有。「何處惹塵埃」在什麼地方有這個塵埃可惹呢？這是這麼說的。

黃梅就也沒有說什麼，就記得這個人。因為當時那學佛法的人，也都是互相妒忌障礙的，你怕我得到這個祖師位，我怕你得到這個祖師位，所以都在那守候著，想接這個衣鉢。就好像現在這個修行，你也想要開悟，他就想要成佛，他也想要什麼，總是有一個東西在那兒障著，總是功夫不相應的。

那麼五祖在晚間就把衣鉢傳給六祖大師，也把修行的這種道傳給他了，叫他晚間就連夜跑。你看那時候都這樣的，現在更不如那個時候囉！

五祖對他說：

有情來下種　因地果還生
無情亦無種　無性亦無生

「有情來下種」，要有情，有這個生機，要有這種生生化化的這種的功能，才能下種。「因地果還生」，也就是因為有這個地，種了花才生。這

Once when he was selling firewood to a shop, he noticed a customer reciting the *Vajra (Diamond) Sutra*. Upon hearing the words of this Sutra: "One should produce that thought which is nowhere supported," he became enlightened. As a layperson, he went to the monastery of the Fifth Patriarch Hongren in the Sung Mountain Range. There in the Huang Mei Way-place, he did manual labor, threshing rice for eight months. The Fifth Patriarch, knew that the time had come to transmit the Dharma to him, because the Patriarch was aware that, during those months of bitter toil, the newcomer had not had any false thinking, but had single-mindedly worked at developing his skill. That's how the Patriarch knew that the time was right, and so he asked those in the Great Assembly to write verses and submit them.

Master Shenxiu [the Fifth Patriarch's senior disciple] secretly wrote this verse:

*The body is a Bodhi tree,*
*The mind like a mirror stand.*
*Time and again brush it clean,*
*And let no dust alight.*

When the Sixth Patriarch saw it, he wrote another verse:

*Originally Bodhi has no tree,*
*The bright mirror has no stand.*
*Originally there is not a single thing:*
*Where can dust alight?*

This verse is a criticism of Shenxiu's verse. The line "Time and again brush it clean" describes the process of cultivation. The Sixth Patriarch, being one who was already beyond that stage, was someone who has "crossed the river" and no longer "needed the raft." And so he said, "Bodhi has no tree; the bright mirror has no stand. Originally there is not a single thing." To begin with, there is nothing at all, "Where can dust alight?" Where could there be any place for the dust? That's what he meant.

The Fifth Patriarch, Great Master Huangmei, said nothing when he saw the second verse, but he remembered the person who wrote it. At that time people who studied the Buddhadharma were mutually jealous and obstructive. You were afraid I might get the Patriarchate and I was afraid you would get it. So everyone was biding his time, hoping to receive the robe and bowl. And so they were competing with each other, just like the way people cultivate now: you want to get enlightened; he wants to become a Buddha; and she, what does she want? There's always something obstructing them so their efforts bring no response. Well, the Fifth Patriarch transmitted the robe and bowl to the Sixth Patriarch in the middle of the night. After imparted the essentials of cultivation to him, he told the Great Master to flee in the night. It was that dangerous back then; now it is even worse.

The Fifth Patriarch spoke this verse to Great Master Huineng:

*With feeling comes the planting of the seed.*
*Because of the ground, the fruit is born again.*
*Without feeling there is no seed at all.*
*Without that nature there is no birth either.*

個「無情亦無種」，若沒有這個生機了，也沒有種子了，就有地也沒有用。「無性亦無生」，也沒有什麼性命，也沒有什麼生生的這個能力。

這就是説，修道用功，你不要怕有妄想，你就有妄想，你能引開，不給妄想轉，還繼續修行；你也不怕有意念；有意念，你能以不跟著這個意念跑，那也都沒有關係的。所以你要能收攝身心，不跟著那妄想跑。所以無性亦無生，你若沒有這個生——生性，他也沒有這生機了，沒有生機也就沒有生性。

六祖大師得到這個衣缽，得到正法眼藏了，之後就和打獵的人在一起住。以後他看時機成熟了，就到廣州聽印宗法師講《涅槃經》，那時就有兩個僧人，這個就説風在那兒動，那個僧人就説幡在那兒動，那個風你看不見的，那個幡是有形的，他就説他那個理，他就講他的理。六祖大師就説了，不是風動，不是幡動，是仁者心動；你心裡動了，你心裡若不動，什麼都沒有了嘛！

所以在這個時候，他就把衣缽拿出給人看，也出家了。大家就請他到曹溪那個地方去建立道場，因為以前那兒有個智藥尊者，説是一百七十年以後有肉身菩薩，在這兒弘揚佛法。那時候，正是一百七十年以後，所以他到那兒去修南華寺——曹溪道場。以後接他的法就有三十多個人，南嶽和青原這二位是其中的上首。

在唐朝先天二年他就圓寂了，年紀是七十六歲。唐憲宗就封他一個諡號，叫大鑑禪師。塔叫靈照之塔。後人作贊曰：

應無所住　　碓柴生花
本來無物　　總欠作家
黃梅夜半　　誤賺袈裟
流傳天下　　五葉一花

説那《金剛經》上説無所執著。舂米和斬柴，在這裡邊好像開花了似的，就言其他在那兒修行。本來什麼也沒有的。他還差一點，就是猶欠篩在的意思。黃梅禪師在夜半傳給他法，這個袈裟被六祖大師給得去了，這衣缽就流傳到世界。這一花開五葉，這五葉就是雲門、法眼、臨濟、曹洞、溈仰。這一花五葉流傳到現在。

所以我説：

*With feeling comes the planting of the seed.* There must be a life force, the ability to generate and transform, before the seed can be planted.

*Because of the ground, the fruit is born again.* The seed planted into the ground can grow and bear fruit.

*Without feeling there is no seed at all.* If there is no life force, there is no seed and the ground will be useless.

*Without that nature there is no birth either.* If there is no nature and life, there is no productive force. In cultivating the Way, don't be afraid of idle thoughts. If idle thoughts come, simply set them aside, avoid being turned by them, and continue cultivating. Don't be afraid of thoughts. As long as you don't let your mind wander off and follow those thoughts, they are not a problem. Gather in your body and mind; don't pursue your false thoughts. If there is no birth, no productive nature, there is also no life force.

After the Sixth Patriarch received the robe and bowl and the Proper Dharma Eye Treasury, he went to live among hunters. Many years later, seeing that the conditions were ripe, he went to Guangzhou where Dharma Master Yinzong was giving lectures on the *Nirvana Sutra*. There he met two monks arguing over the topic of a flag in the wind. One said the wind moved; the other said the flag moved. The first one said that the wind is invisibly moving the visible flag. Each expressed his own principle. The Sixth Patriarch told them, "The wind is not moving, nor is the flag. Your minds, Kind Sirs, are moving. If you minds were not moving, then there would be nothing at all."

Then he showed everyone the robe and bowl, and he left the home-life. Afterwards people invited him to establish a monastery in Caoxi, where in the past (502 A.D.) the Venerable Wisdom Medicine (Jnanabhaishajya) had made a prophecy, saying that after one hundred and seventy years, a Bodhisattva in the flesh would proclaim the Buddhadharma there. It was then exactly one hundred and seventy years after the prophecy, and so the Great Master went to Caoxi and constructed Nanhua Monastery--The Caoxi Way-place. Later on he transmitted the Dharma to over thirty people, of whom Masters Nanyue and Qingyuan were the leaders.

The Great Master completed the stillness in the second year of the Xiantian reign of the Tang dynasty, at the age of seventy-six. Emperor Xianzong conferred upon him the posthumous title of Dhyana Master Dajian ("Great Example"). A stupa was built called the Lingzhao ("Spiritual Illumination") Stupa. A praise says:

*One should be nowhere supported;*
*Splitting wood, opening like a flower;*
*Originally, there is nothing at all;*
*He was like rice waiting for the sieve.*
*From Huangmei, in the middle of the night,*
*He unexpectedly obtained the robe.*
*Circulating the teaching to all under heaven,*
*One flower blooms with five petals.*

The first line refers to the principle of non-attachment spoken of in the *Vajra Sutra*. Threshing rice and chopping wood, the Sixth Patriarch progressed in his cultivation, like a flower opening up. Originally, there is not a single thing. But he was still not quite ready, just

不立文字傳衣缽
本來無物泯言説
悟澈心源破迷倒
了達性海遊太虛
一華五葉續慧命
萬古千秋度世佛
曹溪法水流沙界
洗滌眾生垢沉痾

沒有一個什麼證書，也沒有一個什麼文字的證明，就傳這衣缽給六祖。不像現在有個畢業證書啊，他那什麼也沒有，所以説本來無一物，什麼都沒有的，所以也沒有什麼可説的，泯言説。什麼叫破迷倒？把這個心——真心的那個源頭——明白了，所以也不迷了，也不顛倒了。好像我們人，這有一種情情愛愛，這都是迷倒，把它迷著。若明白了，這些個本來都沒有的，爲什麼要被這一些個東西來支配？你要明白這個性海是大而無外，小而無內。

法界爲體有何外
虛空是用無不容
萬物平等離分別
一念不生絕言宗

你若能這個樣子啊，就了達性海全是空洞的。遊太虛，遊到那沒有一點點無明在裡頭的大海。

從六祖大師以後傳來——有雲門，有法眼，有曹洞，有臨濟，有潙仰，這是叫一花開五葉，續佛的慧命。萬古千秋這個佛都在這兒教化世人。曹溪的水流到盡虛空遍法界去，恆沙世界去。把眾生這個無明煩惱，這些大病，都給洗乾淨了。

like threshed rice waiting for the sieve. Dhyana Master Huangmei transmitted the Dharma to him in the middle of the night, covering the Sixth Patriarch with his *kashaya* sash. His teaching, signified by the robe and bowl, circulated throughout the world. The five petals of the flower represent the Yunmen, the Fayan (Dharma Eye), the Linzi, the Caodong, and the Weiyang sects. These five sects have been transmitted down to the present time. And so I said,

*Without relying on language, the robe and bowl are transmitted.*
*Originally there's not a single thing, so words are done away with.*
*Awakening to the mind's origin, one smashes through delusion.*
*Understanding the nature's sea, one roams through space.*
*With a five-petalled flower, the wisdom life continues.*
*For tens of thousands of years, the Buddhas have been saving*
*the world.*
*Caoxi's Dharma water flows to worlds as many as grains of sand,*
*Washing away living beings' severe illnesses of defilements.*

There was no written document certifying the transmission of robe and bowl from the Fifth Patriarch to the Sixth Patriarch. Not like now when you can get a certificate of graduation. He had nothing at all in the way of proof. And so it's said that originally, there was nothing at all. Since there isn't anything, then there is nothing to be said. Smashing through delusion means understanding the source of the true mind. And so he was not confused and not upside-down. People who still have emotion and love are confused and upside-down. They get confused by those things. We need to understand that originally those things do not exist, and so why should we be controlled by them? You should realize that the "sea" of the nature is so great there is nothing outside of it, and yet so small there is nothing within it.

*With the Dharma Realm as substance, what could be outside?*
*With empty space as function, what is not included?*
*The myriad things are level and equal, apart from discrimination.*
*With not a single thought arising, words and speech are ended.*

If you can be like this, you will understand that the sea of the nature is completely empty. You will roam in the great void, roaming until there isn't a trace of ignorance to be found in the great sea.

Starting with the Sixth Patriarch, the Yunmen, Fayan, Caodong, Linzi, and Weiyang sects have been passed down to the present--they are five petals of a single blossom, perpetuating the Buddha's wisdom. For tens of thousands of ages, the Buddhas have been teaching the people of the world. The waters of Cao Creek have circulated throughout space and the Dharma Realm, flowing to worlds in number like the sands of the Ganges, washing away living beings' severe illnesses of ignorance and affliction.

# 白山黑水育奇英
## ——上人事蹟
# White Mountains and Black Waters
# Nurture Rare Talent
## Events in the Life of the Venerable Master

佛經翻譯委員會提供
Compiled from the Venerable Master's lectures by the editorial staff

在中國東北有一個山，叫長白山，爲什麼叫長白山呢？因爲它終年積雪，一年到頭都有雪。那個山底下有一個縣，東邊有一個城，西邊有一個城，所以叫雙城縣。我家在東北的山裏，剛進山的地方，是很有名的山，叫韶達子戶，那就是長白山最後的地方。長白山那個脈最後就落到雙城縣那兒，所以雙城縣的文化很高，出了很多偉大的人物，這近百年來，盡大臣、將軍，出了有二、三十個，于斌也是雙城縣的人。

當我記得事情的時候，就聽我母親告訴我，以前怎麼樣怎麼樣，不過那些事情都是一種虛妄的，我也不願意再提它了。

我生來有一些壞習氣，就是好哭。由出生就哭，哭了好幾天，哭得人晚上都不能睡覺，白天又要去做工，所以就很疲倦。但是最後那天不哭了，因爲大約這幾天哭得也累了，人也疲倦，也都睡著了；睡著了，就有人到家裏來偷東西，本來是一個窮苦家庭，有一點什麼比較值錢的東西，都被賊給偷去。由這個之後，就不哭了。哭的時候，就好像有什麼自己很不願意的事情，這小孩子就哭了，大約是有這麼樣情形。

我父親弟兄五個，父親那一輩，有幾個女的我不知道。我這一輩，有五個男的，三個女的，我是最小的。所以父母最寵愛，把我慣得很古怪的，一天到晚我一個人就這麼坐著，坐在那兒一天不講話也可以；就不願意講話，所謂沉默寡言。我生來和人不同的地方，我不隨便談論人家的是非，我不隨便說一句話；從小就是這樣子，不隨便講話。我講出話來，如果不真的，我不講，打妄語是不行的。

我生來性情與一般的小孩子好像合不來，生來就很孤獨的，也不願意去和任何人玩耍。那時候也沒有其他什麼本事，只會哭，一哭就哭一天一夜、兩天兩夜、三天三夜，這麼哭。誰惹到我，我就專門哭，一哭就哭得要往死了哭，也不吃東西，心裡有個什麼想法呢？心裡知道我父親、母親都捨不得我，我一不吃東西，豁出來不要命了哭，這樣子父親、母親一定心裡就軟了，就要向我投降。就這麼樣子壞，旁的什麼也不懂，不願意講話，也不願意玩，就是這麼楞頭楞腦的一個孩子。人家說什麼也不懂，人家幹什麼，自己也不知道，什麼也不懂，就是很傻的。傻得什麼樣子呢？我記得在還不會走的時候，就會爬，那時候剛在懂不懂事之間，和其他的小孩子在一起就好像在比賽爬著跑似的。那個小孩子跟不上了，他就在後邊咬我的腳後跟子，我也不知道，咬痛了就哭。本來那小孩子要咬腳，應該就懂得打，懂得和他打架啊！可是我

In Manchuria (northeastern China), there is a range of mountains called the Changbai (Eternally White) Mountains. They are so named that because they are covered with snow all year around. At the foot of these mountains is a county named Shuangcheng (Twin Cities), because there is one city in the eastern part of the county and one in the western part. My home was in these mountains in Manchuria. When you first enter the mountains, there is a famous mountain called Shaodazihu, which is the end of the Changbai Mountains. The end of the Changbai range falls into Shuangcheng County. That's why the county is so culturally advanced and has produced many great people. In the last hundred years, twenty or thirty great ministers and generals have come from Shuangcheng County. Cardinal Yubin was also from Shuangcheng County.

The earliest memory I have is of my mother telling me about various things that happened in the past. However, those things are all unreal, and I don't want to bring them up again.

Ever since birth, I had some bad habits, such as liking to cry. When I was born, I cried for several days straight. Since people worked all day and were kept awake by my crying at night, they ended up very tired. Finally I stopped crying, probably because I was worn out after crying for so many days. Everyone else was tired too, so we all went to sleep. While we were fast asleep, a thief came and plundered our house. Basically we were a very poor family, but he stole whatever was worth any money. After that, I didn't cry anymore. Probably the reason I cried was that I was unhappy about something--that's why most children cry.

In my father's family, there were five boys and I am not sure how many girls. In my family, there were five boys and three girls. Since I was the youngest child, my parents loved me most and spoiled me until I became a very strange child. All day long I would just sit there. I could sit for a whole day without talking. I didn't like to talk. I preferred silence. One thing that's different about me is that I have never liked to gossip about other people. In fact, I never say anything casually. I've been that way ever since I was little. If something is not true, I will not say it. I simply cannot tell a lie.

When I was little I didn't like to be with other kids. I was a loner. I didn't like to play with the others. The only thing I knew how to do then was cry. I could cry continuously for one, two, or three days and nights. If anyone made me upset, I would cry. And when I cried, I cried as if I were ready to die. I refused to eat. I knew that if I refused to eat and cried as if I didn't want to live, my parents' hearts would soften and they would give in to me. That's how bad I was. All I knew is that I didn't want to talk, and I didn't want to play. I was a really dull kid. I didn't understand anything people said, and I never paid attention to what they did. I was totally out of it, like an idiot. How stupid was I? I remember once, before I learned to walk, I was having a crawling race with another kid. When the other kid couldn't keep up with me, he bit down on my heel. It hurt,

不懂，就會哭，也不知道怎麼樣來打對方。現在想起來，這都是一種很愚癡的地方。

在我有生以來，脾氣很倔強，性情特別剛強，剛強到什麼樣呢？無論什麼事情，寧可折而不彎的，就是斷了可以，你叫我彎彎一點，是不可以的。性情既然剛強，當然在小的時候就很霸王的，霸王霸到什麼程度呢？在七、八歲的時候，就願意當孩子王。和小孩子在一起玩的時候，我願意管著其他的小孩子，他們都要聽我招呼，誰若不聽我招呼嘛？我就打他，就要叫他向我投降。不單這樣子，而且還最歡喜打抱不平，無論前後村的玩童、小孩子，我看見哪一個如果做什麼事不公道，我就是不要命，也要幫助這個人主持公道，為朋友犧牲，我覺得這是最光榮的，所以常常「路見不平，拔刀相助」。可是講公道話，有的人不佩服你，就要打。我和人打架，那時候雖然小，可是很勇敢的，在十歲時，敢和二十歲的，比我大那麼多的人打架。那時候也不怕死，打得頭破血流，遍體鱗傷，也不在乎，一定要把對方打服了，那才算。就這樣剛強的一個人，對我父母非常忤逆，不聽話，常常惹禍，叫人找到家裏來，給我父母很多的麻煩。但是和一般同等的小朋友在一起，自己願意怎麼樣呢？就願意做皇帝。你看小的時候，就願意做皇帝，小孩子怎麼做皇帝？就把土培得高高的，自己坐到上邊，這就是登基坐殿，就叫一般的小孩子在那兒叩頭，要三呼萬歲。這樣一個人，怎麼樣也想不到會信佛的。

我家那兒是窮鄉僻壤的地方，雖然東北文化最高就是哈爾濱，哈爾濱文化最高就是雙城縣，雙城縣文化最高就是拉林鎮，可是還那麼孤陋寡聞。我住的家庭和一般人的家庭，距離大約有一百步，所以孤伶伶的一個農人住的宅子。這宅子是用泥造的，一個泥屋，草山的房，所以很破舊的。在這個環境裏頭，從來就沒有看見過，也沒有聽說過小孩子死的、活的，因為看見那時候年紀也小。

有一次，記得好像十一、二歲的時候，到郊區和一般的小孩子玩耍，在那荒地上就遇到一捆草，這捆草裏邊就捆著一個小孩子，這小孩眼睛閉著，又不喘氣。我從來也沒有看過這種事情，以為他在睡覺，我就去叫這小孩子也起來一起玩。其他小孩子說：「他已經死了，你叫他幹什麼？」這時候自己也不懂得什麼叫死，也不能問他們怎麼叫死了？問他們好像自己不好意思似的。於是乎，回到家就問我母親：「今天我遇到一個小孩子用草捆著，在荒地上睡著了，我問他們這是怎麼回事？旁的小孩子都說是死了，什麼叫死

and I cried. I should have known to retaliate, but I didn't even know enough to do that. All I could was cry. Now that I think of it, I was really stupid.

Ever since I was born, I have had a tough temper and a stubborn streak. No matter what it was, I would rather break than bend and yield a little. Being so obstinate, of course I was a real tyrant when I was little. How tyrannical was I? When I was seven or eight years old, I wanted to be the king. When all the neighborhood kids were playing together, I wanted to boss them around. They all had to take orders from me. If they didn't, I would beat them up until they gave in.

I also liked to play Robin Hood. Whenever I saw any of the kids being bullied or treated unfairly, whether it was in the front village or the back village, I would fight for justice on his behalf, not caring if I died. I considered it a great glory to give up my life for a friend. And so whenever I saw unjustice, I would go to the rescue. Even though I was on the side of justice, sometimes the kids wouldn't respect me and would fight back. Even though I was young, I was a brave fighter. At the age of ten, I would tackle twenty-year-olds, even though they were much bigger than me. Since I wasn't afraid of death, I would fight until I was bruised and bleeding and covered with wounds. I didn't care--I was simply determined to defeat my opponent. That's how stubborn I was. I was terribly rebellious and disobedient to my parents. I caused so much mischief outside that people would come to my home to complain. I gave my parents a lot of trouble.

When I was with kids of the same age as me, what did I do? I set myself up as the king. Take a look: even as a child, I had the ambition of being the king! I piled up a dirt mound and then sat on top of it--it was my throne--and told the other kids to bow to me and say "Long live your Majesty!" No one ever expected such a person as me to end up believing in the Buddha.

My home was in a poor rural village. Even though Harbin was the most culturally developed part of Manchuria, Shuangcheng County was the most developed part of Harbin, and my native town of Lalin was the most developed part of Shuangcheng County, I was still very ignorant and unlearned. My house was about a hundred paces from the nearest neighbor. It was an isolated farmer's thatched mud cottage, rather old and rundown. Growing up in this environment, I had never seen or even heard of children dying. I may have seen a child being born, but I was too young to remember. But I had never seen a dead child.

One time when I was around eleven or twelve, I was playing in a field with some other kids. We came across a child wrapped inside a straw bundle. Its eyes were closed and it wasn't breathing. This was something new to me. Thinking the child was asleep, I called to him to come play with us. The other children said, "He's dead. What are you calling him for?" Even though I was already eleven or twelve at the time, I didn't understand the meaning of death. I was too embarrassed to ask

？爲什麼這個小孩子會死呢？」我不懂得這個死。你看就這麼孤陋寡聞，十幾歲還不懂得什麼叫死，足見這個人是很少和一般人接觸來往。

我母親説：「死啊，人人都會死，不過有早死、晚死，有老死、少死。有的時候小孩子死了，就用草把他捆上，丟到荒街上；年老了也會死，病了也會死，種種的死法不一樣。」我覺得人生既然要死，活著幹什麼？沒有意思啊！「人是不是能不死呢？怎麼樣才能不死？」我覺得死很沒有意思。我母親也沒有話講，也不會答。當時有個親戚，姓李，叫李林，他説：「你想不死嘛！那容易。」我説：「怎樣容易呢？」他説：「你除非出家修道，做和尚，或者做老道，修道去，做和尚就修行成佛，做老道就修行成仙，就會不死了。」我記住這個修道能不死，這是有出路了。這時候我就不願意死，覺得死沒有什麼大意思，生了又死，死了又生，這又有什麼好玩的？沒有什麼意思，所以從那時候發心要出家，於是乎就和母親商量，要求出家、修道。母親説：「你出家是好事，我不能阻攔你。但是現在你不能出家，等到我死了之後，你願意幹什麼就幹什麼。我活著，你應該一起住在家裏，你不能出家。」那麼許可我出家，但是不許可即刻出家，於是我説那好啦！所以我就這麼等著。

我小時候，是一個不孝順的孩子、很不守規矩的。怎麼樣不守規矩呢？脾氣特別大，特別歡喜和人打架，打架的對象都是比我大的孩子。在十二歲以前，是以打架爲我的本行，一天要是不打架，一天就不吃飯。最歡喜什麼呢？最歡喜吃好東西。誰若有什麼東西吃，你無論在家裏、外邊，若不給我吃，怎麼樣也不行，一定要爭，也要貪，也要求，也要自私，也要自利，甚至於變個方法也要打妄語。我又歡喜騎馬，就在馬身上站著跑，也願意拿刀弄槍的，來學武術。

等到十二歲的時候，有一天，自己忽然覺得我這個人怎麼這麼頑皮？這麼樣不守規矩？覺得自己做人沒有多大意思，這樣地野蠻，這樣不守法紀；我對父母也不孝順，令父母費了很多精神，覺得很對不起自己的父母，也對不起一些小朋友，也對不起所有的親戚。這樣一想，就生大慚愧，於是乎從十二歲那一年，知道以前所行所作都不對了，將來還可以有自新的機會。我要改過自新，改惡向善，諸惡不作，眾善奉行。這時候也不知道什麼叫佛的戒律，止惡防非完全不懂。雖然不懂，可是我所行所作，和佛的戒律默默中相符合。在這個時候，我覺得修行要做種種的功德，要培福培德，才能修行，不然會著魔的。我想我在家裡不孝順父母，那麼我要學

the other kids, so when I returned home I asked my mother. I told her, "Today I saw a child wrapped in straw, sleeping in the field. When I asked the other kids what was wrong with him, they said he was dead. What does that mean? Why did he have to die?" That's how ignorant I was--at eleven or twelve I didn't understand the meaning of death. From this you can see that I had very little contact with people.

My mother replied, "Everyone must die. Some die sooner than others. Some die old, others die young. When children die, people may bundle them up in straw and leave them in the fields. Some die of old age, some of disease. People die in many different ways." I thought, "If we all have to die, then what's the point of living? It's meaningless!" "Isn't there a way to escape death? What can I do to avoid dying?" I asked. I felt that dying was really pointless. My mother didn't know how to answer me.

There was a relative at our home named Lin Li, who said, "You don't want to die? That's easy enough." "How is it easy?" I asked. He said, "You have to leave home and cultivate the Way; that is the only method. Either become a Buddhist monk and practice to achieve Buddhahood, or become a Taoist and practice to achieve immortality. Then you won't die." Learning that the only way to escape death is to cultivate the Way, I asked my mother for permission to leave the home-life. She said, "Your wish to leave the home-life is a good one, and I cannot stop you. However, you should not leave home right away. When I die, you may do whatever you wish. But while I am alive, you should stay at home with me." I agreed to wait.

When I was little, I was a very unfilial child. I didn't follow the rules. I had a big temper and loved to get into fights. I always fought with children who were older than me. Before I turned twelve, I lived on fighting. If I didn't fight for day, I would go without food that day. And I loved to eat good food. If someone had something good to eat but didn't share it with me--it didn't matter whether it was at home or outside--I would fight for my share. I was greedy; I sought for things; I selfishly thought only of benefiting myself; and I even found ways to lie.

This continued until I turned twelve. One day, I suddenly realized how incredibly naughty and unruly I was. It seemed pointless to be like that--so wild and rebellious. I felt sorry for being so unfilial to my parents. I also felt sorry for behaving so badly towards my friends and relatives. I felt great shame and remorse. At the age of twelve, I knew that everything I had done in the past was wrong, but that I could make a fresh start. And so I turned over a new leaf. I changed my faults and turned towards goodness, and resolved to refrain from all evil and practice all good deeds. I did not know anything about the Buddhist precepts, which "stop evil and prevent mistakes." Nevertheless, what I was doing was in accord with the precepts.

46

好，先得從父母開始。於是乎，沒人教我，我就決定先要報答父母恩，我下決心對父母悔過、認錯，然後就向父母叩頭求懺悔。

最初給我父親、母親叩頭的時候，把父親、母親都嚇了一跳，他們說：「做什麼？這不是過年，也不是過節，你叩什麼頭？」我當時就說：「父親、母親，您們生我已經十二歲了，我從來就是一個最不孝順的人，給您們惹了很多的麻煩、很多的禍患，令你們憂心。這十多年也沒有聽過您們一句話，只是我行我素，一意孤行，我實在對不起您們。我以前給您們做兒子做錯了，從今天開始我要改過自新，我不要像以前的性情那麼剛強。以前惡劣的習慣，我都要改了它，我以後要好好孝順您們二位。」父母聽我這麼樣一說，就流淚了，我就說：「您們不要哭，以後我天天給您們二位老人家叩頭、悔過，以後再也不會對你們忤逆不孝了。」我父親就說：「你既然知道錯了，那沒有關係，你不要叩頭了。以後只要你聽話一點，不那麼頑皮，我們就覺得很好了，叩不叩頭沒有關係的，你總給我們叩頭，我們也不好意思。」雖然他們這樣說，不要我叩，但是我有一個強脾氣，我要做的事情，誰也擋不住，誰不許可也不行，就照常叩頭。從這個以後，我就天天給父親、母親叩頭。

叩了一個時期，就覺得這個世界上，不是單單我父母親對我好，這個世界上有五大恩。這五大恩是什麼呢？就是天地君親師，這些都應該報恩的。我居住在這天地之間，天能覆我，地能載我，這都是有恩的，所以給天叩三個頭，又給地叩三個頭，報天地負載我的恩。君是國家的元首，我也應該報恩；當時雖然是民主時代，不是君主時代，但是那個舊思想還有，所以就向國家元首叩三個頭。親就是父母。師，當時也沒有讀書，也沒有修道，所以還沒有師父。但是我就想到我要出家修行，將來一定會有師父；我如果讀書也要有師父，我現在雖然沒有遇到我師父，但是我預先就要拿出我至誠懇切的恭敬心，先給我師父來叩頭，不要對師父不孝順。那時候也不知有個天主，也不知有個地主，也不知有個人主

I intuitively knew that if I wanted to cultivate, I had to do many meritorious deeds to foster blessings and virtue. Otherwise, it would be easy to become possessed by a demon. If I wanted to become a better person, I had to start by being filial to my parents. Without anyone telling me to do this, I wanted to repay my parents' kindness. I made up my mind to confess my faults in front of my parents. I decided to bow to them to seek their forgiveness.

The first time I bowed to my parents, they were shocked. "What are you doing?" they demanded. "It isn't New Year's or some special holiday. Why are you bowing to us?"

"Father and Mother," I said, "you have raised me for twelve years. I have been most unfilial and I have given you much trouble and worry. In all these years, I have never listened to you, but have stubbornly followed my own will. I have not been a good son. From today onwards I will change my stubbornness and my bad habits. I will be filial to you from now on." My parents wept as they listened. "Please don't cry. I will bow to you in repentance every day, and I will not be so rebellious."

"You don't have to bow," said my father. "It will be enough just to listen to us and do what you are told. If you keep bowing to us, we will feel embarrassed." Even though they asked me not to bow, I was still so obstinate that no one could stop me from doing what I wanted to do. And so from that time on I bowed to my father and mother every day.

After bowing to my parents for a while, it occurred to me that besides my parents, there were others in the world who were good to me. There are five main sources of kindness we should repay, namely: heaven, earth, the national leader, our parents, and our teachers. Living in this world, I am sheltered by the heavens and supported by the earth. To repay their kindness, I made three bows to heaven and three to earth. I also made three bows to the national leader to repay his kindness. In monarchic times the Chinese people considered themselves indebted to the emperor, and this idea carried into the era of the Republic. Since I was neither attending school nor cultivating the Way, I had no teacher. Yet I knew that if I wanted to leave home, I would need a teacher. If I went to school, I would also need a teacher. Therefore, with the utmost sincerity and respect, I bowed to my teacher in

，不過聽人說有天地君親師，所以就給天叩三個頭，地叩三個頭，國家元首叩三個頭，又給父親叩三個頭，母親叩三個頭，又給我老師也叩三個頭。

你們各位想一想，這個人沒有見到師父之前，預先就給師父叩頭。所以我出家之後，我對長一輩的人，從來就沒有發過任何的脾氣，就是他們對不對，對我好不好，我都沒有發過脾氣。可是，現在居然要受這個果報，一天到晚我的徒弟都對我發脾氣，甚至於我要給徒弟叩頭。這個門已經開了，我想將來哪一個徒弟再對我發脾氣，我就給他叩頭，沒有旁的辦法，我也不用任何的勢力來壓迫人，我只可以用這個方法。因為我沒有道德嘛！只可以學這個沒有能力的人。

以後叩了一個時期，覺得還不夠，於是乎又給世界上古今的聖人叩頭。我聽人說聖人是生而知之的，這個世界大聖人是對人有好處的，我應該來感謝他們，就給大聖人叩頭。又給大賢人叩頭。以後又想，這個世界有一些大善人，他們幫助人做善，救濟人，我應該感謝他們，所以也向大善人叩頭。以後加上天下大忠臣、大孝子、大偉人、大哲士、大英雄、大豪傑、節夫、義婦，關帝公，岳武穆，所有古今的名人差不離地我都叩遍了；總而言之，世界好的這一類人，我都要給他們叩頭。因為他們能影響我，諸惡不作，眾善奉行；他們能影響我怎麼樣做一個無愧於天地的正人君子，所以我要感謝他們，向他們叩頭頂禮。

這樣每一天就增加叩頭的數量，最後大惡人我也給他們叩頭，我做什麼事情都好大喜功，願意找那個大的。給大惡人叩頭，希望他改惡向善，發菩提心，皆共成佛道。因為大聖人、大賢人、大善人、大孝子、大英雄、大豪傑，我都給他們叩頭。然後又打了妄想，我說大聖人、大賢人、大善人，我都給他們叩頭，感謝他們；這些不善的人、大惡人、大壞人、大無賴、大流氓，他們怎麼辦呢？於是乎我又向他們叩頭。人家是給佛叩頭，給菩薩叩頭，給大菩薩、大佛來叩頭。我那時候就很愚笨的，就想起大惡人、大壞人，在世界上，這些人很可憐的，他們在六道輪迴裏，愈輪愈轉，離佛道愈遠，所以我希望給他們迴向，令他們都改過自新，改惡向善。

以後我又想，這一般普通的人，各國的民族，各國的人士，我對他們也應該要恭敬，我想以前我可能有對不起世界各國民族的地方，於是我向天下所有眾生來叩頭頂禮，乃至最後連螞蟻，我也給牠叩頭，蚊蟲我也給牠叩頭。為什麼要給牠們叩頭呢？我想我以前也做過螞蟻，也做過蚊蟲，種種的眾生我都做過。現

advance. I certainly didn't want to be unfilial to my teacher. At that time I didn't really know about heavenly lords, earthly rulers, or human leaders. But I had heard people talk about heaven, earth, the national leader, parents, and teachers being the five sources of kindness, so I bowed three times to heaven, three times to earth, three times to the national leader, three times to my father, three times to my mother, and three times to my teacher.

Can you imagine a person bowing to his teacher even before he has met him? And so after I left the home-life, I never lost my temper at those who were elder to me. Whether they were right or not, whether they were good to me or not, I never got mad at them. Yet now I must undergo this retribution: my disciples get mad at me all day long. It's gotten to the point that I have to bow to my disciples. Since I've already opened the door, in the future I will bow to any disciple who gets angry at me. There's no other way. I can't use force to oppress people. Since I lack virtue, I can only use this method of someone who has no abilities.

After an interval, I still felt I wasn't doing enough, so I started bowing to the sages of the past and present. Having heard that sages are wise from birth and that they benefit people, I thought I should thank them. And so I bowed to the great sages and worthies. Then I reflected that I should also bow to virtuous people, in order to thank them for doing good deeds and rescuing people. Later I also added to my list loyal ministers, filial children, great people, wise scholars, brave heroes, and faithful husbands and wives. I bowed to Lord Guan Yu, to General Yue Fei, and to just about every renowned figure in history. In general, I bowed to all the good people in the world. They could influence me to avoid doing any evil and to practice all good deeds, and to be an upright and good person with a clear conscience. That's why I wanted to bow to them in gratitude.

In this way, I increased the number of bows. Later on, I also bowed to the most evil people as well. Whatever I do, I like to do it on a grand scale. I bowed to bad people, hoping they would mend their ways and become good, bring forth the resolve for Bodhi, and attain the Buddha Way.

I had been bowing to the great sages and worthies, great virtuous ones, great filial sons and daughters, and great heroes, but then I thought, "What about the big evil-doers, the big bad guys, and the big outcasts? What about them?" And so I began bowing to them as well. Other people bow to the great Buddhas and great Bodhisattvas, but I very foolishly thought of the big evil-doers and the bad guys. These people are very pitiful, because the longer they turn in the six paths of rebirth, the farther they get from the Buddha Way. So I wished to transfer merit to them, hoping they would reform and renew themselves and become good.

Later, I thought I should also show respect to ordinary people of all nationalities, because in the past I might have mistreated them in some way. As a result I began bowing to all

在我雖然做人了，這些老朋友我還不能把他們忘了，所以我要給他們也叩頭。我給他們叩頭的時候，我就想我以前也是個小螞蟻，向牠們來恭敬；也是一個小蚊蟲，向牠們來恭敬。我覺得我和這些最微細的眾生都是一樣的，所以我應該來引導度脫牠們，早成佛道。這是我叩頭的原因。

我這樣叩頭，一路一路增加，增加到最多的時候，我記得增加到每一次叩頭要兩個半鐘頭，增加到八百三十三個頭的樣子，增加這麼多。那麼我叩頭，不是在房裏叩頭，是到外邊就這麼望空來遙拜。在什麼時候叩呢？一早起，人都沒起身時，我到外邊去叩我這個迷信的頭；晚間在人都要睡了之後，我又到外邊去叩我這個沒有什麼理由的頭，就這樣不叫人知道。

你們各位想一想，這要不是愚癡，怎麼會也沒有人教，我就會叩這個迷信的頭、沒有什麼理由的頭呢？那麼自己一路一路就增加到這麼多，而且每一天是風雨不誤的。我在外邊，下雨也叩頭，颱風也叩頭，下雪也叩頭。打雷、下雨、颱風，是風雨無阻的都到外邊去叩頭。下雨時，雨水把我身上都淋濕了，我也不管；下雪時，我的雙手就放在雪地上叩頭。為什麼要這樣呢？這就表示自己那時候是以一種真誠的心，實際就是愚誠。

這樣叩了十多年個頭，以後我想每天早晨叩頭要兩個多鐘頭，叩八百三十幾個頭；晚間又要兩個鐘頭，叩八百三十幾個頭，一天兩次。這樣一想，叩頭要四個鐘頭，應該把它減少一點，做一些旁的事情。那麼八百三十幾個頭，我就縮成五個頭，把它濃縮起來。

第一個是頂禮盡虛空、遍法界十方三世一切佛法僧三寶；第二個頭也是給佛法僧三寶來頂禮；第三個頭還是給佛法僧三寶頂禮。第四個頭是給誰頂禮呢？就是給大聖人、大賢人、大孝子、大善人、大英雄、大豪傑、大偉人、大哲士，甚至這些大惡人、大壞人，統統的，盡虛空、遍法界十方三世一切眾生，都包括在內。蚊蟲是我的好朋友，我也給牠們頂禮；螞蟻也是我的好朋友，我也給牠們頂禮。因為我過去生中，不知殺了多少蚊蟲、螞蟻，我實在對不起牠們；包括一切其他的眾生在內，無量劫以前，我不知道傷害過多少眾生的生命，所以現在都要向牠們來叩頭贖罪，希望牠們不怪我。我常對人講笑話，我說你們現在雖然給我叩頭，實際上，我在有生以來已經給你們各位叩頭了，不過你們不知道，但是你們心裏知道。所以誰向我叩頭，現在都是還我的頭呢！所以我也不能受，也不能拒，這是第四。

of the living beings in the world, including ants and mosquitoes. Why did I bow to them? I figured that I have also been an ant, a mosquito, and other kinds of creatures in the past. Now that I am a human being, I can't forget about my old friends. When I bowed to them, I thought: "I am paying respect to you, because I used to be an ant and a mosquito myself." I identified with the smallest beings and felt that I ought to guide them to quickly accomplish Buddhahood. Those were the reasons I bowed.

I kept increasing my bows until I was making 833 bows each time, which took me two and a half hours. I bowed outside the house in the open air. Every morning before the others got up, I would go outside and bow my "superstitious" bows. At night after everyone had gone to sleep, I again went outside to bow. I had no real reason for bowing like this; I simply didn't want people to know.

Think it over: if I wasn't foolish, why would I bow so many bows every day, rain or shine? No one had told me to bow these superstitious, senseless bows. Wind, rain, thunder, and snow couldn't stop me. I bowed regardless of the weather. I didn't care if the rain drenched me. When it snowed, I continued bowing, putting my bare hands on the snow-covered ground. Why did I do this? It was to show my sincerity. I was sincere to the point of foolishness.

For more than ten years, I bowed two hours in the morning and two hours in the evening, making eight hundred and thirty-some bows twice a day. I was bowing four hours a day. I wanted to decrease the bowing time and do some other things, so I condensed the eight hundred thirty-some bows to five bows.

The first bow is to the eternally dwelling Buddhas, Dharma, and Sangha pervading empty space and the Dharma Realm in the ten directions and the three periods of time. The second and third bows are also to the Triple Jewel of the Buddhas, the Dharma and the Sangha. Whom do I bow to on the fourth bow? I bow to the great sages, great worthies, great filial sons and daughters, great virtuous ones, great heroes, and great scholars, and all other beings in the past, present, and future throughout empty space and the Dharma Realm, including great evil-doers and great bad guys. This includes my good friends the mosquitoes and my good friends the ants. I also bow to them. Who knows how many mosquitoes and ants I killed throughout countless eons in the past? Now I feel truly sorry toward them and toward all living beings, for I do not know how many of them I have killed in past lives. Now I feel I should bow to them to compensate for my offenses. I hope they will not bear a grudge against me.

I often joke with people and say, "You are bowing to me now, but actually I've bowed to each of you in the past. You may not know it consciously, but perhaps in your heart you know. Therefore, you are simply returning my bows! That's why I can neither accept nor refuse your bows." That's the fourth bow.

第五個頭呢，我是頂禮盡虛空、遍法界十方三世一切諸佛所說的波羅提木叉、所說的戒律。因為有佛的戒律，我才能依照這個道路，往佛道上走。這個戒律對我的恩德是無量無邊的。

所以我每逢叩頭的時候，都是這樣子做。我相信世界上沒有一個愚癡的人，像我這麼愚癡。人人都比我有智慧，他們都不屑於像我這種的思想、行為和作法，都覺得我太可憐了。因為這樣的行為，所以不要說在家人，就連出家人都是看不起我的，都是抵制我的。你們誰若信我，你們要深深地了解，可能是上了一個大當，可能不是大當，因為你慈心下氣，能對一切眾生都來結緣，這是好的。

我在很小的時候，有一次作夢，夢見自己走在路上，那路就像那個篩子的窟窿那樣，底下就不知多深。那個路就像羅網似的，在上面可以走，但是一不小心一定就掉下去了，就在這麼一個路上走。等我走到沒有窟窿的地方，沒有網羅的地方，到那個平安的康莊大道了。再往後邊看，那個路上不知多少人跟著我來，老的、年輕的，什麼樣都有，哪個國家也都有。不知道是不是現在走的路？

我生在一個貧苦的家庭，家裡很窮的，要去做工才有飯吃，這就等於要飯一樣的，所以我稱自己叫乞士，你看這麼小的時候就叫乞士。那時家裏自己有一點地，只夠維持一年的生活，所以也沒有那麼早讀書。

我小的時候割地，那時候我十四歲吧？是十三歲？我有哥哥，譬如割高粱，他割半喇子，半喇子就是割三條壟，割六條壟是整的。我比他小五歲，他割半喇子，我割整的。高粱不容易割，我那個子小，不容易，雖然我年紀輕，還小；可是我有方法，我會用力，就割這個地，根本我就不用多大力量。我拿鐮刀割，可是我這麼抱著，這一抱，一下子就可以割十幾根。那個高粱也高，我把它都抱到一起，我胳臂一伸，伸到最後那地方，往那麼一割，這麼一條子都割下來，他們大人都沒有像我那麼多的。我也沒人教我怎麼做，我就看著，我也不一定照著他們那個，我有我的方法；總而言之，都能勝過他們。

那時候，我也做過生意，和人家合股來做生意，譬如一個人拿出五千塊錢來，三個人應該拿出一萬五；一個人五千，三個人就一萬五。我們做生意怎麼樣呢？這三個人最後就我一個人拿錢，那兩個人都不拿錢，就是單單等著賺錢，把我拿這五千塊錢都給吃去了，他們不拿錢，完了，把我的錢也都給弄沒有了，然後就算了。這樣差不離的一般人一定要打官司啊，又

On the fifth bow, I bow to the Pratimoksha, the precepts, spoken by the Buddhas of the past, present, and future throughout the ten directions of the Dharma Realm. The Buddha's precepts guide me on the path to Buddhahood. The kindness and benefit of the precepts is infinite and boundless.

This is how I always bow. I don't think there is anyone in the world as stupid as I am. Everyone is smarter than I am, and they don't think much of my way of thinking and acting. They think I am very pitiful. Not only laypeople, but even left-home people look down on me and boycott me. If you have faith in me, you should realize that you are taking a big loss. On the other hand, it might not be a loss, because by learning to be kind and humble, you can create affinities with everyone, and that's a positive thing.

When I was little, I dreamed I was walking on a road which was gutted with holes like those of a sieve. They were very deep holes, and if I wasn't careful I could slip and fall into one of them. When I walked past the holes onto a safe, smooth highway, I glanced back and saw a great many people following me--old and young, people of all ages and nationalities. I wonder if that's the road I'm walking on now.

I was born in a destitute family, and we had to work to get our daily meals. It was a beggar's life. That's why I nicknamed myself "Mendicant." You see, at such a young age I was already calling myself a mendicant. We owned a little plot of land that was just big enough to support us through the year. That's why I didn't go to school when I was young.

When I was thirteen or fourteen, I could cut double the amount of grain that my brother, who was five years older than me, could cut. For example, if he could cut three rows of sorghum, I could cut six. Sorghum is pretty tough to cut, especially for someone as young and small as I was. But I had my method, and I knew how to use my strength. Actually, I didn't use much strength. Sorghum grows very tall, but I would grab a big bunch of stalks and then stretch my arm as far as I could reach and cut through the whole bunch in one cut. None of the adults could cut as much as I could. No one taught me this method. I watched the way they did it, but I didn't follow their way. I had my own way, and I could cut more than they could.

I also did business then. For example, if each person invests five thousand dollars, then three people should invest fifteen thousand. But when I invested my share, the other two didn't. They just wanted to make money, so they used up the five thousand that I invested without putting in any money of their own. Most people would sue their partners if this happened to them, but I didn't want to fight with them. I was always willing to suffer a loss. I didn't care about getting advantages. I'm still that way now. I think taking a loss in order to benefit others is the very best thing. That's why I often refer to myself as a stupid person. I'm willing to do the things that others wouldn't do. I'm really very stupid!

I didn't have a chance to go to school when I was young.

50

争啊！可是我不和人争。我什麼事情都吃虧的，不注重佔便宜，到現在還是這個樣子，我覺得吃虧利人，這是一個最好的事情。所以我常常説我是一個很愚癡的人，也就這樣子，人家不願意的事情，我就要做，這真是very stupid！

我在幼童的時候失學，沒有受教育，在我沒有出家以前，我就到處去尋找了生脱死的方法。北方有很多旁門外道，我都參加過，所以一些外道的法，我都知道。好像在北方有一種外道叫理門，他這個理門不念旁的，就是念一句。那最高的領袖坐到那地方，受人的禮拜，人人都向他叩頭頂禮，他的心裏就專念什麼呢？他就念「南無喝囉怛那哆囉夜耶」，就念這一句，這就是那個理門的法。他在那個地方也裝模作樣，坐到那個法座上，正中間坐的這個叫「領正」，旁邊這個叫「幫正」，有三個人坐到這個地方，就像放燄口似的。人去代理，代理他傳什麼呢？就傳一個密法。他這個密法，叫你伸出手來，就這麼樣寫「觀世音菩薩」五個字。寫完了，就這麼篆上了；篆上了以後，就不要出口念，要念就在心裏念，念「觀世音菩薩、觀世音菩薩」，在心裏念，不出口。這個法呢，父子不過，妻子不傳，父親對兒子也不能説的，就夫婦也不能講的。得到這五個字，這叫「五字真言」，然後就再告訴你：「閉口藏舌，舌尖頂上顎，繫託心念，意根法現。」這講得好妙、好神秘的。在北方有這麼一個外道，它就是怎麼樣呢？主要就是不喝酒、不抽菸，這叫「戒菸酒會」，又叫「代理公所」。這種道在中國近一百年以來，很盛行的。它所仗著什麼呢？就是這一句。那個做法師的，在正座上坐著，就念這個「南無喝囉怛那哆囉夜耶」，就這麼一句。因為以前這些個門徑我都走過，所以我都知道。我也參加過天主教的彌撒，耶穌教的這種安息會，我也都參加過，到處我都來研究他們這個教義；孔教、老子的道教、佛教、回教，我也都研究過。

以後到了十五歲，才開始在私塾裏讀書，讀了半年，我記得十五歲那一年，三月初十上學，舊曆八月十三放假。冬天日本人來，就沒有讀了。十六歲又讀一年書，十七歲讀了一年書，前前後後合起來是兩年半。我記得在讀書的時候，一開始讀得很慢，笨得不得了，笨得怎麼樣呢？讀一遍也記不住，讀兩遍也記不住，不知道怎麼樣背書，不知道怎麼樣子remember？譬如我讀《百家姓》的時候，因為在家裏聽我母親念過，所以那時候聽一遍，我就會了，就能背，也不用怎麼念。一旦念《三字經》的時候，這《三字經》沒

Prior to leaving the home-life, I went in search of someone who could teach me the way to end birth and death. There were many cults and non-Buddhist religions in northern China, and I visited them all. I'm familiar with all their doctrines. For example, there was a sect called the Door of Principles (Limen) that exclusively recites one line of mantra. When their High Master sits there receiving bows from people, he recites in his mind the single phrase, "Na mo he la dan nuo duo la ye ye." That's the teaching of Limen. They put on airs, sitting up there on their Dharma seats. The one in the middle is called the "leader" and those on either side are called "helpers." The three of them sit there, just like in the ceremony for feeding ghosts with flaming mouths. Their representatives transmit a secret Dharma. They tell people to hold their hand out and then they write the words "Guan shi yin pu sa" (Guanshiyin Bodhisattva) on it. Then they "seal" it and tell the people to recite "Guan shi yin pu sa" in their minds, but not out loud. And the people are forbidden to transmit the Dharma to anyone, even to their own parents, spouse, or children. They call it the "Five Character True Words" and instruct people:

*Close your mouth, hide the tongue.*
*Let the tip of the tongue touch the roof of the mouth.*
*Keep reciting with the mind,*
*And the Dharma will manifest.*

It sounds very mysterious. Mainly this sect advocates abstaining from alcohol and smoking, so it's known as the "Society for Prohibiting Smoking and Alcohol" and also the "Representative Association." It's been flourishing in China for the last hundred years. The whole "religion" is based on the one phrase, "Na mo he la dan nuo duo la ye ye," that the "Dharma Masters" recite. I've been to all these cults and know what they're about. I also attended Catholic Mass and Christian Sabbath. I wanted to study the teachings of every religion-- Confucianism, the Taoism of Lao Zi, Buddhism, Islam--I investigated them all.

At the age of fifteen, I studied for half a year at the village school. I remember school started on the tenth of the third lunar month and ended on the thirteenth of the eight month. In winter the Japanese came and there was no school. I studied for two full years when I was sixteen and seventeen, and so altogether I received two and a half years of schooling.

At first I was slow to learn--incredibly dull. I couldn't remember my lessons no matter how many times I read them. Since I had heard my mother recite *The Hundred Surnames* at home, I could memorize it right away. But I had never read or heard *The Three Character Classic* before. I would study the first few lines:

*People at their birth are by nature good.*
*Their natures are close to the Way,*
*But their habits take them away from it.*
*If there is laxness in teaching them,*

有念過，也沒有聽過，就六句書：

人之初，性本善， 性相近，習相遠，
苟不教，性乃遷， 教之道，貴以專。

這麼樣子讀，左讀也不會，右讀也不會，讀來讀去也不會；那麼讀會了，在炕上背得滾瓜爛熟的，記得很清楚。那時候讀書要背書，拿了這個書本到先生那兒去，要把書交給先生，然後掉過背向著先生，眼睛不看這書本子，再把它念出來。我本來都記得清清楚楚，念得很熟很熟的，一到地下，到先生那兒，把面一背，怎麼樣呢？一個字也想不起來了，連個「人」字也想不起來了，就這麼奇怪！

所以小孩子你叫他好好讀書，他很困難；學一些下流的動作，他非常熟行，非常地聰明，不學自通。好像小時候我看人家賭牌九，又叫天九牌，有三十二張天九牌，四個人來賭，有一對天、一對地、一對人，這是最大的；又有皇上，有這三隻六套。這三十二張天九牌，我到那兒一看，沒有五分鐘，我都記得了，把這三十二張天九牌，哪裏什麼樣的，我回去自己就做一副，做得很漂亮的。你看！讀書讀得沒有法子記得住，記這個東西，也不需要師父教，也不需要老師來怎麼樣教你一遍，就看他們那麼玩，不超過五分鐘就統統都記得了。你看！學賭錢的東西，沒有人教就會了；學讀書，有人教也讀不出，讀不好，都忘了。

為什麼忘了？自己也莫名其妙！而且很多天都是這樣子。我就想：這是什麼道理呢？怎麼在炕上念得那麼熟，一下地就都忘了？奇怪！是不是沒給聖人叩頭呢？我細研究，原來什麼都不是，我已經給聖人叩很多頭了；我入學也叩頭，沒入學以前我就給聖人叩頭，這個理由不存在的。不存在，我就來研究，一研究這個讀書，喔！我知道是為什麼了。因為害怕，怕先生那個大菸帶鍋子，一背錯，就爆頭。所以在炕上專心讀書，下地到先生那兒，就好像見了閻羅王似的，一害怕，這心就散了；心一散，把所有讀的書都忘了，不能背了，就想著這個菸帶鍋子會不會來？明白這個，以後就不怕了，挨打就打嘛！怕什麼？之後我在炕上專心讀書，在下地的時候還是專心讀書，再念多少，就背多少，一字不差的。

我讀一個月書之後，研究出什麼問題呢？就找著讀書的門徑。一入門，就好辦了，讀書不單記得快，而且還永遠也不忘。等讀《大學》的時候，讀得就很快。最初是很慢的，以後讀得就很快，讀得怎樣？那時

*Their natures will change.*
*The way to teach them is to be single-minded.*

But no matter how I tried, I couldn't memorize them. In those days, studying consisted mainly of memorizing lessons. Whenever you memorized a passage to the point that you could rattle it off easily without thinking, you would go to the teacher, give him your book, and then turn around with your back to him and recite from memory. Well, I had finally memorized the lines very clearly, but as soon as I turned my back to the teacher, my mind blanked out and I couldn't even think of the first word. It was just that strange!

So you see? If you try to teach children to study well, it's very difficult for them. But when it comes to less noble things, they are really smart. No one needs to teach them. I remember watching people gamble when I was little. There's a cardgame called Heavenly Nine, which uses thirty-two cards and has four players. The biggest combination was a pair of "heaven," a pair of "earth," and a pair of "people." There's also an "emperor" and "three singles and six sets." It took me only five minutes to remember what the thirty-two cards looked like, and when I returned home I made a very pretty set of my own. Take a look! When it came to studying, I was a hopeless case. People tried to teach me to study, but I always failed and forgot my lessons. Yet when I saw these cards, no teacher had to explain them to me, but I committed them to memory in five minutes!

Why did I forget my lessons? I was really puzzled. This had gone on for many days. I wondered, "What's going on? How come I remember it so well when I'm on the *kang* (brickbed), but forget everything as soon as I get down from it? Is it that I haven't bowed to the sages?" No, I had already made many bows to the sages, even before I entered school. So that wasn't a valid reason. I looked into it some more and finally discovered that it was because of fear. I was afraid that if I made a mistake in reciting, the teacher would bop me over the head with his big pipe. And so, as soon as I went to the teacher, it was like seeing King Yama. All my concentration fled, and I forgot everything I'd memorized. All I could think was: "Is the pipe going to come down on my head?" Once I understood, I was no longer afraid. If I was in for a beating, so be it! What was there to fear? From then on, I maintained my concentration both on the brickbed and on the floor. I could remember everything I read without forgetting a single word.

After being in school and looking into this problem for a month, I found the path to studying. Once I entered the door, so to speak, everything became easier. Not only could I memorize things quickly, but I never forget them afterwards. When I began *The Great Learning*, at first I was very slow, but after a while my study progressed rapidly. What I covered in one day, others could not cover in twenty days. How could I do this? It was because I had discovered the secret to studying. I simply used single-minded concentration--I have no other method but this. When I studied, I didn't think about other things--such as

我讀一天的書，旁人二十天也讀不了，相差這樣子。爲什麼這樣呢？因爲得到讀書的門徑了，我念書也沒有旁的絕妙方法，就是一心不亂，在那兒專心讀書，旁的什麼也不想。不想吃，也不想喝，也不想怎麼穿好衣服，住好地方，什麼妄想也不想，就專一。專一，專到怎樣呢？我告訴你們，這是一個最妙的法門，怎樣妙法？我在這兒讀書，你旁邊作戲、打鼓，或者吹喇叭、吹簫、吹笛子，或者打鐘，我可以聽不見。本來可以聽見的，但是我可以叫這個心不跟著你的音樂去跑，就能把這個心管住。心不外緣，心不旁驚，不到旁的地方去，讀書就是讀書，把心放到讀書上，不打妄想。這樣所讀的書，一讀就會，很快就會了。

在我最初讀書，讀三十遍恐怕也不會，等得到這個法門，你一專一，能管得住這個心的時候，就很巧妙的，讀頭一遍就能記得大半，讀第二遍就完全都記得了；若讀第三遍之後，就永遠不忘了，是這樣子的。那麼讀兩遍就可以背得出來了，當時教我那個老師，他就這樣讚歎過我，他說：「啊！看你這個樣子，一點都不聰明，你眞是和顏回差不多了。啊！看你樣子不聰明，但是你記憶力這麼好。」我一聽他這麼樣讚歎，就生了一種貢高心，我說：「我怎麼可以比得了顏回呢？並且我也不願意比顏回，爲什麼呢？顏回他聰明太過了，變成一個短命鬼，我如果和顏回一樣，會不會和顏回一樣的年紀就死了？」然後我就給自己起一個別名，叫什麼名字呢？叫如愚子，這就是一個貢高的名字。本來壽命長和短沒有什麼分別，你要是怕短命，這就是著住到壽者相；你若歡喜長命，這更是著住到壽者相，所以我不願意學顏回的短命，也不願意學彭祖的長命。

我在讀書的時候，也很頑皮的，在學校裏頭對對聯，我讀書時有三十多個學生，差不多有二十五個都找我去當槍手，你說這怎麼辦？我就模仿他們寫的字，給他們對。有一次我記得，老師出的：「鴻雁空中過」，我給同學當槍手對了一個：「麋鹿山內遊」。完了，先生就看這個人說：「這是你對的嗎？」他說：「是。」先生說：「你能想出這樣的好句子來？」哈！回憶起來，小孩子這些經過，也很好笑的。我知道這個讀書的竅門了，我一讀《弟子規》：

弟子規，聖人訓，
首孝弟，次謹信。
汎愛眾，而親仁，
有餘力，則學文。

eating, drinking, wearing nice clothes, or living in a nice place. I had no random thoughts at all. What was the extent of my concentration? I'll tell you, this is a most wonderful method. When I studied, people could be putting on a play, beating drums, blowing trumpets, playing flutes, or ringing bells beside me, but I wouldn't hear them. Actually I could hear them if I wanted to, but I could also tell my mind not to pursue those sounds. I could control my mind and keep it from running after external states. Once I set my mind to studying, I didn't think of anything else. In that way, I mastered what I studied very quickly.

In the beginning, I might read a lesson thirty times without understanding it. But once I discovered the method, once I could concentrate my mind, it was really wonderful. After reading it once, I would remember most of it. After the second time, I remembered the whole thing. By the third time through, I would never forget it. Seeing that I could memorize anything after reading it twice, my teacher praised me, saying, "From the looks of you, I would never have thought you were so intelligent. You really are a lot like Yan Hui. Even though you don't look smart, you have a marvelous memory." I became proud, thinking, "How could I compare to Yan Hui? Anyways, I don't want to be like Yan Hui. He was so intelligent that he ended up dying young. If I'm like him, won't I die young too?" I gave myself an arrogant nickname: "Like-a-Fool." Basically, there's no difference between a long life and a short life. If you're afraid your life will be short, then you are attached to the mark of a life span. If you would like to have a long life, you're even more attached to the mark of a life span. That's why I don't want to be short-lived like Yan Hui, and I don't want to be long-lived like Peng Zu [the Methusaleh of China].

I was quite mischievous in school. When we had to match couplets, probably twenty-five of the thirty-some students in our class asked me to write matches for them. I imitated their handwriting and helped them write couplets. I remember once the teacher gave the first line: "The goose flies through the air." I wrote a match for my classmate: "The deer roams in the hills." When the teacher saw it, he looked at my classmate and asked, "Did you write this?" "Yes," said my classmate. The teacher said, "I never would have thought you could come up with such a good match." It was pretty funny.

Once I knew the secret to studying, I read the Standards for Students. The first few lines give the major themes:

*These standards for students are guidelines*
*Handed down to us by the sages.*
*First be filial and fraternal,*
*Next be careful and honest.*
*Cherish all living beings,*
*And draw near to good-hearted people.*
*Whatever energy you have left*
*Should be devoted to study.*

這是前面幾個大題目。「弟子規」，這是做弟子的規矩，弟子規也包括做子女的規矩。所謂弟子，弟就是人家的徒弟，或者兄弟，這也包括做兒子的。

「聖人訓」，這聖人留下的教訓。聖人這個教訓說什麼呢？「首孝悌」，首先要盡孝盡悌，孝是孝順父母，悌是悌於兄長。「次謹信」，這是應付一切世間的世法，我要謹言慎行，謹謹慎慎的，又鄭重其事地來說話。「汎愛眾」，廣泛地博愛地來對大眾。「有餘力，則學文」，再有空閒的時候，還學更多的文字般若。下面說得更明顯了，

父母呼，應勿緩；
父母命，行勿懶。

父母教，須敬聽；
父母責，須我承。

冬則溫，夏則清；
晨則省，昏則定。

出必告，返必面，
居有常，業無變。

一讀這個書，我就想，這書這麼好，教人做人的道理，說得清清楚楚的。由這個，我就得到了讀書的方法，當我走路眼睛看著路，心裏背書、口裏背書。我就背一遍又一遍，來回來回背；要是熟了，每一天都要溫習一、兩遍，就這樣讀完一本書，永遠都不忘了。這叫路上。

還有枕上：這個枕上，就是枕頭上，睡覺的時候，不想旁的，就想書。書上怎麼說的，然後自己想：「古人著書立說，就是給後人留下一個法則，我能不能照這個法則去做呢？我能不能效法呢？」就這樣地揣摩，我說：「好！這一句話我將來一定要躬行實踐的，我要這樣做。」我讀什麼書，我就想我會不會這樣子？我會不會說這話？我把它就當自己，想這話和我說得差不多，那就記住了。無論讀哪一段書，都是往自己的身心性命上來回叩，來把它算一算。

就這樣子，這三上，枕上、路上，還有什麼呢？廁所上。在廁所，你讀書是最快的地方。你看那個時候，雖然是短短的一個時間，可是你那時候讀書，很好讀的，想不起來的也想起來了，為什麼呢？

These are rules for students and disciples, as well as for sons, daughters, and brothers and sisters. These rules are teachings left by sages. The sages teach us first of all to be filial to our parents and respectful to our brothers and elders. Secondly, we should accord with worldly conventions and be cautious in our speech and behavior. We should speak seriously and in earnest. We should regard all beings with universal kindness. Then, if we have any spare time, we should learn more literary Prajna. The next lines are even more clear:

*When father and mother are calling,*
*Answer them right away.*
*When they give you instructions,*
*Obey without hesitation.*

*When your parents instruct you,*
*Respectfully do as you're told.*
*When your parents scold you,*
*You should compliantly accept it.*

*In the winter make sure they are warm.*
*In the summer make sure they are cool.*
*Each morning cheerfully greet them.*
*At night wish your parents a pleasant rest.*

*Before going out, tell your parents.*
*Let them know when you return.*
*Dwell in a fixed place*
*And finish what you begin.*

When I read this book, I thought it was wonderful, for it sets forth clearly the principles of how to be a good person. I would memorize my lessons as I walked. Keeping my eyes on the road, I recited the text from memory both with my mouth and in my mind. If it was a new lesson, I would recite it over and over. If it was an old lesson, I would review it once or twice every day. That way, once I finished a lesson, I would never forget it. That's on the road.

I also memorized on the pillow. When I went to bed, I reviewed my lessons. After reviewing them, I would ask myself: "The sages handed down these teachings as standards for those of later generations to follow. Can I follow these standards? Can I emulate the sages?" That's how I grasped the intent of the teachings. I would say: "Okay, I'm going to apply this sentence in my life. I'm really going to do it." No matter what I studied, I would ask myself if I would act or speak that way. I would treat the text as if I were speaking it myself, and then I'd be able to remember it. I would take every passage and use it as a standard to measure my own life and behavior.

I had three places for studying: on the pillow, on the road, and on the toilet. I studied the fastest in the toilet. Even though you're only in the toilet for a short time, it's a great place to study. You can remember what you couldn't remember before. Why? You have samadhi. If you single-mindedly concentrate on your studies

這是一種三昧，你在那個時候，什麼妄想也沒有，你專心一讀書，都想起來了，所以那個時候不能空過。你三上，這一懂了，

　　讀書法，有三到，
　　心眼口，信解要。

這眼睛看著書，心裏就想著書，口裏就念這個書，這是三而一、一而三了，這心眼口都合作了，這叫三到。這個方法我得到了，以後念什麼書也不困難。可是一般聰明的小孩子，他一離開課本，就和書分家。我不是，我是和這個書本合而爲一，所以讀得也快，記得也快，我的讀書經過就是這樣子。那時候讀四書五經都不困難，念一遍就記得了。

　　我最得力的地方，就是我最後那個老師，是個秀才，山東人，叫郭錦堂，字叫如汾。他大約就是要仿照唐朝郭子儀那個行爲，郭子儀叫汾陽王，所以他說自己叫如汾。那麼這個老師學問很好，寫的字不太好，可是學問好。我讀什麼書，他看我讀得快，就給我講什麼書，讀什麼書講什麼書。他隨講，我懂了，一讀更容易了。好像報任少卿書，那是古文最長的一篇，大約有二千三百多字。那篇文章，我的老師讀了一宿讀會了，能背得出，他就和我說，他怎麼讀那篇文章，讀得怎麼樣快，然後就說看你的了！這時是吃完午飯，睡一個鐘頭午覺，在這一個鐘頭，我就看這個書，也沒睡覺，看了兩遍，能背得出了。第二天我給他一背，把他嚇壞了：「這個你……，哦！我都要讀一宿，你讀一個多鐘頭就會了！」這篇文章難是難，但是我很專一的，你看看我不睡覺，在那兒看這個書，這很專心的。

　　因爲這個，所以說起來人都不相信的，我有一位同學，他讀了十五年書，我讀兩年半，還把他超過去兩部書。我把五經四書都讀了，古文八本，我讀有七本，醫書讀了十五、六本。十八歲的時候就沒有書讀了，也很少世俗的醫生讀那麼多書的。那時候，醫學、易卜、星象我都涉獵過，可是我都不做，都不精；會批八字，但是我不批，因爲這個不究竟，雖然它也是真的，但是那都是在路上走呢！在那兒繞彎子。

　　我讀藥書，讀了十五、六本，因爲我父親想叫我行醫，說是可以賺錢。等我讀完了書，那時候可以給人看病了，什麼病我都懂，因爲我那個老師也是醫生，他給人看病，也叫我幫著看脈。讀完書，我

and have no other thoughts, you'll be able to remember everything. That way the time you spend there won't go by in vain.

Once you understand the three "on's," you should also know:

*When you're pursuing your studies,*
*On three places focus attention:*
*Your mind, your eyes, and your mouth.*
*It's essential to have faith and understanding.*

You look at the book with your eyes, think about it with your mind, and read it with your mouth. They are three, yet one; one, and yet three. The mind, eyes, and mouth work together.

Once I discovered this method, studying no longer presented any difficulty. Many children are very smart, but once they leave their books, they forget their studies. I, however, became one with my books, so I studied and memorized them very quickly. Those were my experiences with studying. I did not find the *Four Books* and *Five Classics* difficult to study either. After reading through them once, I was able to remember them.

The person who benefitted me the most was my last teacher, Jintang Guo, also known as Ru Fen ("Like Fen"). He was a *xiu cai* (a graduate of the first degree) from Shandong province. He probably wanted to model himself after Ziyi Guo of the Tang dynasty, who was also known as Yangwang Fen. That's why he called himself "Like Fen." This teacher was very learned, although his calligraphy was not that good. Seeing that I was a fast learner, he would explain for me whatever text I happened to be studying. Once I understood his explanation, the text was even easier to study. For example, there's the "Report on the Letter to Ren Shaoqing," which has about 2,300 characters and is one of the longest classical texts. My teacher had memorized it in one night. He told me how quickly he had mastered this text, as if challenging me to see how fast I could learn it. That was after lunch, when we had a one hour nap period. During that hour, I read the essay twice and memorized it. When I recited it to my teacher the next day, he was shocked, "You... I studied it for one night, but you mastered it in an hour!" Although the essay was difficult, I was very concentrated. You see? Instead of taking a nap, I studied the essay.

You won't believe this, but I had a classmate who had studied for fifteen years. I only studied for two and a half years, but I was ahead of him by two books. I studied the *Four Books* and *Five Classics*, seven of the eight volumes of ancient literature, and fifteen or sixteen medical texts. By the time I was eighteen there was nothing left for me to study. Few ordinary doctors had studied as many books as I had. I had studied medicine, divination with the *Book of Changes*, and physiognomy, but I didn't practice any of these; I wasn't an expert at them. I knew how to tell fortunes based on people's date and time of birth, but I didn't do it, because it isn't ultimate. Even though the results are true enough, they are only a detour on the path.

I had studied so many medical texts because my father had wanted me to practice medicine, knowing that doctors made a good living. By the time I finished my studies, I knew how to treat

也不敢做醫生，為什麼呢？因為我雖然很窮，沒有錢，可是我不願意賺錢，我討厭這個錢。我說這個東西，是一個很邋遢的東西，很不乾淨；來路不明，更不乾淨。我說假如一百個人，我給人治好了九十九個半，剩半個我把人家生命給耽誤了，這怎麼能對得起這個人呢？因為這個，所以我也沒有做醫生。這是我讀書的經過。

為什麼要說這個？就是我們人無論做什麼要專心，不打妄想。你若專一其心，才能有成就；你若不專一其心，你就是天資怎麼樣聰明，也是不行的。

古人說齊國裏有一個善於下棋的人，叫弈秋。這個弈秋教兩個徒弟下棋，一個徒弟，弈秋叫他怎麼樣走那個棋，他就怎麼走，所以就把棋招精通了，一下棋的時候就勝利。那麼另外一個人呢，他也是學著下棋，可是他在那兒一邊學嘛，一邊就打妄想。想什麼呢？他說空中來這一幫雁，這幫雁有大雁在頭裏領著，我這一箭就先把那個大雁射下來，我這個箭這麼準。就想這個，結果他學這個下棋的棋招，一天不如一天——只因一招錯，輸了滿盤棋。我們學佛法也要專一其心，不要像那個學下棋似的。我們在這兒拜佛，說老佛爺啊！你保佑著我啊！快點生意做好了、發財了，我好報答你啊！這樣子，我相信佛他不管這個事的。為什麼呢？你在那兒不是拜佛，是在拜自私呢！在那兒一邊拜佛，一邊要發財。這個拜佛不是賭錢，也不是下棋。所以這一點雖然是很粗淺的道理，我們各位細戳其味，學佛法也要拿出至誠懇切的真心來。

我記得我一開始修行的時候，就念《地藏經》和《法華經》。大約十五歲那年，冬天的時候，我最初第一次遇著《地藏經》，有三卷，上卷、中卷、下卷。以前根本就沒有看過佛經，頭一次看佛經，好像是在妙蓮長老那兒得到《地藏經》，是他用筆寫，然後再印的。他是前清一個翰林，做過道台。這個人說起來善根也不錯，大約是個秀才，以後就做道台，道台就轉任到杭州那地方。到那兒，他就穿著便衣去看扶鸞，也沒有人認識他，不知道他是當地的地方官，那時他還沒有真正地上任，就是早幾天去等著接任，還沒有接呢！這時候他沒有事情，就跑去那兒。聽說有地方扶鸞，他就去參加。扶鸞，這也不是道家的，也不是佛家的，它就是一種旁門左道的事情，也有真的、也有假的。那麼到那地方參觀，他一進門口，這鸞壇就叫了，說這個人來了，叫他聽命。他就很奇怪，也沒有人知道他，

sick people. I had an understanding of all the various diseases, because my teacher was also a doctor, and he asked me to help him take the pulse of his patients. However, I didn't dare to be a doctor. Even though I was very poor, I didn't wish to make money. I detested money. I thought it was filthy and unclean, especially if it was obtained in an improper manner. I thought, if I cure ninety-nine and a half out of one hundred patients, but harm half a life, how could I ever face that person? That's why I didn't become a doctor. These were my experiences in studying.

I relate these experiences to illustrate that no matter what we do, we should concentrate on it and not have idle thoughts. You have to concentrate in order to accomplish something. If you don't concentrate, then no matter how intelligent you are, you won't succeed.

In the ancient state of Qi, there was a master chess player named Yi Qiu who had two disciples. One disciple made moves exactly the way his teacher instructed him to, and he also became a master chess player who won every game. The other disciple learned to play chess on the one hand, but indulged in idle thoughts on the other. For example, he thought: "Look! There's a flock of geese flying overhead. With a single arrow, I could shoot down that big goose in the lead." Because he was distracted by such thoughts, his skill in chess deteriorated with each passing day. "With one wrong move, you lose the whole chess game." Studying Buddhism also takes concentration. We shouldn't be like the second disciple of the chess master. When some people bow to the Buddha, they pray, "Buddha, protect me. Let my business prosper so I can get rich quick! Then I'll be able to repay you!" If you pray like that, the Buddha won't pay any attention. Why? You're not bowing to the Buddha, you're bowing to your own selfishness! You bow to the Buddha, hoping to get rich. Bowing to the Buddha isn't gambling, nor is it a chess game. This is a shallow principle, but we can ponder it well. In studying the Buddhadharma, we have to be totally sincere.

When I first began to cultivate, I read the *Earth Store Sutra* and the *Lotus Sutra*. In the winter of my fifteenth year, I saw the three rolls of the *Earth Store Sutra* for the first time. It was in three volumes, I believe. I had never read a Sutra before. I think it was at the Elder Miaolian's place that I first saw the Sutra. He had written it by hand and then printed it. He had been a *hanlin* scholar and an official in the former Qing dynasty. He had quite a few good roots. He was probably a *xiucai* and then an official in Hangzhou. When he went to Hangzhou, he wore civilian clothes and went to visit a medium. No one recognized him or knew that he was a local official. He hadn't officially assumed his post yet, because he had come several days early. Since he had nothing better to do, he went to attend this session with the medium. These mediums are part of a cult that is neither Taoist nor Buddhist. Some are real, others are not. As soon as he walked in, the medium announced his arrival and told him to follow orders. He was astonished because the medium called his name--Zhang Hancheng--even though no one knew him there. He knelt there to accept instructions. The instructions were: "You were very filial in

怎麼把他名字叫出來了──張翰承，他就跪在那兒聽訓。聽訓，就說他：「你前生很孝順，是某某人，所以今生才作官，你要做一個清官，不要做一個貪官污吏，你要好好幹。」就這麼地把他嚇出一身汗：「奇怪！他怎麼說出我的來歷。」

回去，躺著睡覺。他本來想抽大菸，也不想抽了；睡幾天，起來了，說要去遊西湖。遊西湖，把菸具都帶著，大菸也都帶著，旁人以為他要到西湖拼命地抽，他說不是，到了西湖，當船走到西湖中間，他就把這個菸和菸槍都丟到湖裏，以後就把大菸戒了。之後，他開始一路一路學佛法，最後就出家。他因為這個儒教的底子不錯，寫字也寫得很好。

我得到他寫的經，回去就念。《地藏經》念全部要用這麼高的精進香，北方那種精進香要兩個鐘頭，我點一支精進香跪那兒慢慢念這部經，正念一部，這香也完了。一天就念一部，在中午的時候念。念了一個時期，把腿都跪破了，因為是在磚地上跪著的，什麼也不墊，就那麼硬挺。本來也有墊子，但是我不用，就是愚癡到那個程度上，把膝蓋都跪破，還是不用墊子，反正你破就由著你破，我不管你，我還是那麼念。所以這是我念《地藏經》頭一次的經驗，那時的體會是一言難盡的，總覺得身心都清淨、舒暢。我看你們現在坐那兒的時候，那個禪凳子已經有膠墊子，還要墊多一個；跪到地下，一定要有個墊子來墊著，一點苦也吃不了，這情形都比你們的師父聰明得多。我那時候蠢得那個樣子，就不願意墊墊子，就願意叫這個膝蓋破了、流血，覺得這是應該的。你們現在不單沒有破，沒有流血，就是痛一點點，也覺得這是對不起自己這個膝蓋了。由這個證明，你比師父是聰明得太多了。

我記得我過去看《法華經》，看得眼睛流血。為什麼流血呢？因為很多天也沒有睡覺，跪在那個地方看《法華經》，愈看愈願意看，愈念愈願意念，念得把吃飯也忘了，睡覺也忘了，所以自己眼睛流出血來都不知道。等這血淌到這個經上，把經也給染紅了，這才知道，哦！從眼裏不是流眼淚，是流紅血了。知道眼睛它不幫忙了，所以也就不得不休息，這是我記得我看《法華經》看得這個樣子。說：「唉！那法師你這太愚癡了！」不錯！我若不愚癡，眼睛就不會流血，像你那麼聰明，眼睛絕對不會流血，對不對呀？你在心裏都笑起來了，說：「是這樣子。」不好笑出來，心裏頭笑起來，在心裏頭說：「我當然是比你聰明。」但是你比我聰明，

your previous life; that's why you have become an official in this life. You should be an honest official. Don't be corrupted by bribes. Do a good job." He broke into a sweat and thought, "This is really strange! The medium has just told me my past."

He went back and went to sleep. He had been an opium smoker, but now he didn't want to smoke anymore. After resting for several days, he got up, collected his pipes and opium, and went to West Lake. Everyone thought he was going to have a smoking spree on West Lake. When he got to the middle of the lake, he threw his pipes and opium into the lake. After he quit smoking opium, he learned Buddhism and eventually left the home-life. He had a pretty good foundation in Confucianism and his calligraphy was also good. As I said before, he was a *xiucai* and a *hanlin* scholar.

I obtained a copy of the Sutra he had written, and I took it back to recite. When I recited the Sutra all the way through, I would light a long stick of incense known as "vigorous incense" in northern China. It burned for exactly two hours. I would kneel there and recite the Sutra slowly, and when I finished, the incense would also finish burning. I would recite the entire Sutra once every day at noon. After a while, my knees broke open and bled because I knelt on the brick floor without any cushions. There were cushions, but I didn't use them even when my knees broke open. That's how foolishly stubborn I was. I continued reciting and paid no attention to my knees. "Break open if you want, I don't care" was my attitude. It's hard to describe that first experience reciting the *Earth Store Sutra*. There was a sense of purity and refreshing comfort in body and mind.

Now I take a look at all of you sitting there. The bench is already padded, yet you insist on adding another cushion. When you kneel on the ground, you have to have a cushion for your knees. You can't endure even a little hardship. You are all much more intelligent than your teacher. I was so foolish then that I didn't want a cushion. I wanted my knees to break open and bleed. I felt it was right. Not to mention letting them break open and bleed, you can't even bear to let your pampered knees take a little pain. This just shows that you are much smarter than your teacher.

I remember long ago, I would read the *Dharma Flower Sutra* until my eyes bled. Why did they bleed? Because I didn't sleep for many days. I just knelt and read the Sutra. The more I read it the more I wanted to read it and recite it. I forgot about eating and sleeping. When my eyes started to bleed, I didin't notice, until the blood fell on the text. Then I knew, "Oh, those aren't tears, that's blood!" Since my eyes were acting up like that, I had to rest. That's how I read the *Dharma Flower Sutra*.

You say, "Dharma Master, you are really too stupid."

Right. If I was as intelligent as you, my eyes wouldn't have bled.

Perhaps you are laughing to yourself, "That's right. That's the way it is."

You may be more intelligent than me, but you are still my disciples. No matter how smart you are, you are still studying

你現在可是做我的徒弟，你再聰明也要跟我學。

不單念《法華經》念得這個樣子。我還記得過去……。你不要以為你師父現在是個法師，我過去什麼都做過，做過皇帝，也做過宰相；總而言之，什麼都做過，這是我記得的，雖然不太清楚，馬馬虎虎有這麼回事。所以現在不願意做皇帝，也不願意做轉輪聖王，太麻煩了。做什麼就有什麼麻煩，讀書有讀書的麻煩，做工有做工的麻煩，做生意有做生意的麻煩，作官有作官的麻煩，當和尚有和尚的麻煩。麻煩雖然是有，可是你若會做，麻煩都不足為麻煩，你能把這個境界轉過來，就是不麻煩，逆來順受，

> 反者道之動，
> 弱者道之用。

無論做什麼事情，你若放不下，都是麻煩；你若放得下，就不麻煩了。什麼叫放得下呢？就是我常常對你們講的，Everything's okay! No problem. 就是這個。你若能這麼樣，你也變成妙人了。

在我讀書的時候，也有麻煩，開始讀書很笨，誰也看不起我，說：「從來也就沒有遇著這麼笨的一個人，讀了八句《三字經》都背不出來。」等我一入門了，讀得很快的。讀得很快是好嘛，可是讀得快又有麻煩。讀得慢，人看不起；讀得快了，有的人就妒忌，有的人就羨慕。老師嘛，也不會做老師，就讚歎我，對我同學說：「我教了五、六十年學，沒遇著這麼能讀書的學生，這個人將來一定會做大事。」你們各位要注意，這樣一讚歎我，怎麼樣啊？這個麻煩就來了。什麼麻煩呢？女同學的麻煩來了。這我不解釋，你們大家都明白，都懂這個，這個是人人都很熟行的，也都很內行的，所以我講了這麼久也沒人笑，現在這麼多人笑起來。這個女同學的麻煩來了，她打什麼主意，你們大家也會明白。就因為老師讚歎我，說將來能做大事，她要看一看是怎麼樣一個大事法？

等我下地背書的時候，這個女同學就用腳踢我。用這個腳踢，我也不懂這個，雖然那個時候十六歲了，可是說一句不好的話，就是不解風情，不懂溫柔，也不知道女孩子這心理是幹什麼？當時我把眼睛一瞪，就又發起脾氣了，我說：「我要打死你啊！你想幹什麼？」把這個女同學嚇得一縮脖子、一伸舌頭，就跑了。這個麻煩算退去了；退去了，你猜怎麼樣啊？她就託媒人到我家裏和我母親講，說什麼也不要，只要答應就可以了，也不要錢，也不要什麼禮物。就因為

with me.

I remember in the past, I read a lot of Sutras like that until my eyes bled. But you shouldn't think that I was always a Dharma Master. I have done everything. I was an emperor, and a minister, all kinds of things. I remember it, more or less. That's why I'm not interested in being an emperor or a politician, or even a wheel-turning sage king. It's too much trouble. Everything is a lot of trouble. Students have the troubles of students, workers have the troubles of workers, business people have business troubles, officials have official troubles, and monks have monks' troubles. However, if you know how to do what you're doing, the troubles don't present any problem. If you can turn the state around, it's not troublesome. Take things in stride.

*Adversity moves the Way.*
*Yielding carries the function of the Way.*

Anything you cannot let go of becomes a trouble. Once you let go of it, it's no longer troublesome. Being able to put it down means saying, "Everything's okay, no problem." If you can do that, you'll be a wonderful person.

When I was studying, I also had my share of trouble. At first when I learned very slowly, everyone looked down on me, saying, "We've never seen such a dullard. He can't even memorize eight lines from the *Three Character Classic*." Once I got the hang of it, I learned very fast. Learning fast is a good thing, but it also has its troubles. No one thought much of me when I was a slow learner, but when I became a quick learner, some people were jealous or envious. My teacher, who didn't know how to be a teacher, praised me in front of my classmates, saying, "In my fifty or sixty years of teaching, I've never had such a capable student as this. He will certainly do great things in the future." As soon as he praised me like that, the trouble came. What trouble? Girls. I think everyone understands what I mean. I don't have to explain, because everyone is an expert in this area. You didn't laugh at all while I talked for so long, but now everyone is laughing. I'm sure you all know what my girl classmate had in mind. My teacher had said I would do great things, and she wanted to see what kind of great things I could do.

When I got down from the brickbed to recite my lesson, the girl gave me a kick. I didn't know what she was up to. Even though I was sixteen, I knew nothing about romance. I didn't understand the mentality of girls. I glared at her and furiously said, "You want me to beat you up?" The girl ran away in fright, and I thought I'd gotten rid of that trouble. Guess what? She sent a matchmaker to my house to speak with my mother. The matchmaker said they didn't want anything--no money or gifts--simply my mother's agreement. My mother was overjoyed. When I returned home, she told me, "Your classmate sent a matchmaker over saying her family didn't want anything

58

這個學生讀書讀得好，她這個女孩子就迷上了。這麼和我母親一說，我母親高興得不得了，我回家，就對我講，說：「某某你同學的家裏請媒人來說親，說只要我們答應，她什麼條件也沒有，什麼都不要，就白把一個女孩子送過來。」我說：「那您怎麼樣啊？您有沒有答應她啊？」我母親說：「我要等你回來問問你。」我說：「您說問問我，這還算您聰明。您沒有作主意，如果您答應的話，您今天答應，我明天就去出家去。」我母親說：「你不能出家。」我說：「您不叫我出家，您就不要答應這個女孩子。」我母親說：「那好。」就這樣子，把這個麻煩又退了。這是在十六歲遇到這樣的麻煩。

九一八事變那時候，我年紀小，不太懂事情，也不知道什麼叫國？什麼叫家？以後日本打到中國，我就覺得日本來了，這麼殺人放火，到處摧殘中國的老百姓，這是沒有天理的，它憑什麼把中國這樣來蹂躪、糟蹋，就想要去參加革命來打日本，把它消滅了，把他們驅逐出去，令中國的人民安居樂業；可是怎樣也沒成功，沒有能遂我的志願，所以沒能挽回天意。當時我不恨，我覺得我恨他們，這沒有用的，我要想法子來對付他們。我那時候對付日本的方法，就是用一個「火」字，我就預備到什麼地方都用火攻他。我想它那時候以火攻火，它也屬於火，所以以毒來攻毒，我就用種種的方法，主要的宗旨就是用火攻它。譬如把他住的地方都給燒了，叫他無家可歸。我本來想要投筆從戎去創革命，可是沒有成功，以後就走到出家這個途徑上。我出家以後，一生的遺憾就是沒有報國。因為既然不能為國流血流汗，我願意做一個出世的、弘揚佛法的一份子。

在日本投降的前五年，我早就說過，日本一定完了。我那時候也就是按著五行來推測，到那時候它就衰了，沒有了。等日本投降之後，中央政府也沒有接收廣島，共產黨也沒有佔領，中國那時候到處是妖魔鬼怪，大街上走的，不是完全人啊！妖魔鬼怪都有，不過人不認識，多得很。那時候無政府了嘛！無拘無束，沒有人管，你看那時候跳神的也多，扶鸞的也多，出會的也多了。這些東西出來，都是群魔在那個地方亂舞。可是幸虧有人會誦〈楞嚴咒〉，他們雖然出來晃一晃，也沒有做什麼大怪。但是在沒有政府的時候，也是一個不好的時候，那些妖魔鬼怪、牛鬼蛇神，什麼都出世了。因為沒人管他們，一般人是不知道這個事情，我是深深地有經驗，對於這些問題，我是很清楚的，所以說沒有政府的味道，我經驗過。

except our permission. They were willing to send their daughter over with no conditions."

"Did you agree?" I asked.

"I waited for you to come home so I could ask you," my mother replied.

"At least you had enough sense not to make the decision on your own. If you had given your agreement today, I would be leaving home tomorrow."

My mother said, "You must not leave home."

I said, "If you don't want me to leave home, then don't promise this girl anything."

"Fine," said my mother.

That's how I got rid of the trouble I encountered when I was sixteen.

When the Mukden Incident of September 18, 1931, occurred, I was still young and didn't understand very much. I didn't have any sense of what "country" and "family" were. Later when the Japanese attacked China and went about murdering and setting fires, destroying the Chinese people, I felt it was totally unjust. What right did they have to lay waste to China? I wanted to join the revolution to drive the Japanese out so that the Chinese people could once again live in peace and safety. However, in the end I failed to carry out my resolve. I wasn't able to reverse the tides of destiny. I didn't hate the Japanese, because I knew hatred was useless. I only tried to think of ways to counteract them. My idea was to attack them with fire. Since they belonged to the element fire, I would fight fire with fire, for example, setting fire to their dwellings. I wanted to write articles to stir up a revolution, but I didn't succeed. Later I chose to walk the path of monkhood. My lifelong regret after I became a monk was that I wasn't able to fulfill my patriotic duty. Since I wasn't able to sweat and toil for the sake of my country, I decided to rise above worldly affairs and propagate the Buddha's teachings.

I had predicted the surrender of the Japanese five years before it happened. Based on the theory of the five elements, I predicted that their presence in China would weaken and then disappear by that time. After the Japanese surrendered, when the central government had not accepted the island of Guang and the Communists had not yet taken control, there were many, many ghosts, demons, and weird beings on the streets of China. Some of the "people" walking on the streets were actually ghosts and freaks, but no one recognized them. There was no government and there were no laws at that time, so it was total anarchy. Witch doctors and spirit mediums were widespread. They were basically demons wreaking havoc. Luckily there were still people who recited the Shurangama Mantra, so even though the demons made an appearance, they didn't do any great mischief. Anarchic times are not pleasant at all. At that time all the ghosts, demons, and weird beings came out, because there was no one to watch over them. Most people weren't aware of these things, but I saw very clearly what was going on. I have tasted the flavor of anarchy.

我當初做小孩子的時候，本來是一個不會說話的人，連慢講話都不會，很遲鈍，什麼話都不會說，等於啞吧差不多，天天坐在家裡，也不願意去和人玩耍。可是從十六歲我參加道德會，就學講演，天天練習說話，也就會講演了。會講演呢，以後研究佛法了，我就練習說法給大家聽，我知道多少就給大家講多少，不知道的當然就不能講了。我也參加佛教會很多事情，雖然年紀輕，但是我願意為佛教來服務。所以我十六歲的時候，就跑到廟上給人講《六祖壇經》，看了《六祖壇經》，我就寫了一副對聯，我說：

頓漸雖殊，成功則一，何分南北；
聖凡暫異，根性卻同，莫論東西。

當時我也講《金剛經》、《彌陀經》，這些小部經典，我都給大家講，又講其他種種的佛法。那時候，我有的字還不認識呢！可是我就給大家講，因為中國的文盲很多，我認幾個字如果不給大家講一講，大家永遠也不知道佛法是做什麼？佛教是做什麼？所以我十六歲就以弘揚佛法為己任，到今天練習得不會講也會講幾句，不會說也會說幾句。那時候我就學會讀〈大悲咒〉，我一看到〈大悲咒〉的時候，覺得非常歡喜，坐到火車上就開始讀，讀了有三十分鐘，下火車後，居然就能把〈大悲咒〉給背誦出來了。以後，就得到四十二手眼，修習四十二手眼幾年，以後也因為種種的因緣，遇到有病的人也不怕，就給人治病。治病用〈大悲咒〉和四十二手眼，一治就把病給治好了。

我這個人生來，什麼狼蟲虎豹也不怕。天魔、地魔、神魔、鬼魔、人魔，都不怕，沒有我恐懼的東西。為什麼我不怕呢？因為我不怕死，從小生來就不怕死，什麼也不怕。我記得在很年輕的時候，學習佛法，以為我定力夠了，自己以為自己不得了了，很自滿的，就說起狂話來了。說什麼狂話呢？我說一般人都是怕魔，我就是魔怕，魔他怕我，不是我怕魔。你說這話說得狂不狂？說魔他怕我，我說天魔、地魔、神魔、鬼魔、人魔，無論什麼魔，我也不怕的。說完這話之後，你說怎麼樣啊？這魔就來了，你猜什麼魔來？病魔來了。這病魔一來，你說怎麼樣呀？這回我也怕魔了，不是魔怕我，而是我怕這個魔，怕這個病魔。因為這個病一來，行動也不自由了，好像披枷戴鎖似的，這個身體也不聽話了。你教它走，它就走不動；你教它坐著，也坐不起來，一天到晚就躺到炕上，也不能飲水，也不能吃飯，讓這病魔纏住了。這時候我一想，我是說錯話了，我說：「人家

As a young child, I didn't even know how to speak slowly--that's how dull I was. I was no better than a mute. I sat at home every day, not wanting to play with other kids. When I joined the Virtue Society at sixteen, I practiced speaking every day and gradually learned to lecture in public. Then I studied Buddhism and taught the Dharma to others, explaining as much as I understood. I participated in many activities in the Buddhist society as well. Despite my youth, I was eager to serve Buddhism. And so at the age of sixteen I went to a temple to lecture on the *Sixth Patriarch Sutra*. After reading this Sutra, I wrote a couplet which says:

*Although sudden and gradual are not the same,*
*When the work is complete, they are one: why divide*
*    north and south?*
*Holy and common differ temporarily, but*
*Their basic nature is the same. Don't argue about*
*    east and west.*

I also lectured on other short Sutras such as the *Vajra Sutra* and the *Amitabha Sutra*, and taught people the Buddhadharma. Even though I was not fully literate myself, I was willing to lecture. There were so many illiterate people in China, and if I didn't teach them as much as I knew, they would never understand what Buddhism was about. At sixteen, I took it upon myself to propagate Buddhism. And so, after so many years of practice, I can now speak and lecture a little bit.

I also knew how to recite the Great Compassion Mantra in those days. The first time I saw the Great Compassion Mantra, I was extremely delighted. I started reading it when I boarded the train. When I got off the train half an hour later, I could recite it from memory. Then I learned the Forty-two Hands and Eyes. After cultivating them for several years, I began curing people's illnesses. Using the Great Compassion Mantra and the Forty-two Hands and Eyes, I was able to cure any illness.

In my life I have never been afraid of anything. I don't fear wild beasts, heavenly or earthly demons, spirit or ghost demons, or even human demons. Why not? It's because I am not afraid of death. I remember that as a young student of Buddhism, thinking that I had enough samadhi, I became arrogant and made a wild statement. I said, "Everyone is afraid of demons, but I'm not. Demons are afraid of me! Heaven demons, earth demons, spirit, ghost, and human demons--I'm not afraid of any demons at all." Guess what happened after I said that? A demon of sickness came.

And when it came, it was I who feared the demon, not the other way around. When the sickness came, my body wouldn't listen to orders--I couldn't even walk around or sit up. I was so sick that I lay on the bed from morning to night, unable to eat or drink. I thought, "I spoke foolishly, and now

都怕魔，我是魔怕我。」現在這個病魔來找我了，我還是抵抗不住這個病魔，那時候大約十七、八歲的時候。

這一病，你說病得怎麼樣？病得什麼也不知道，就是奄奄一息，要死了。可是在將要死而沒死這個時候，又生出一種境界來。什麼境界呢？就見著東北的三個王孝子。這三個王孝子，是兩個出家人，一個在家人，出家這兩個王孝子，有一個是老道，一個是和尚；在家這個王孝子，是一個老年人。他們三個人來，就把我帶走了，教我出去和他們玩一玩，我隨著就跟他們出去了。很奇怪的，一出門口，走路這個腳就不沾地了。雖然不是坐飛機，可是也到虛空裏頭，又不是騰雲駕霧，就在虛空裏頭行，就從這個房子頂上走，往下邊一看，那個房子都很小的，也看到很多人。

這麼樣走，走到什麼地方去呢？走到所有的廟裏，名山大川，中國的五臺山、峨嵋山、九華山和普陀山，四大名山都去遍了。到什麼地方，都見到很多人，也見到很多的廟宇，各處去參觀。那時候不但中國的地方，外國的地方也到了很多，有一些是白頭髮、白眉毛、綠眼睛的外國人。到那個地方，很快就走了，那麼就好像什麼呢？我告訴你，就好像看電影似的，看完了這一幕，那一幕又來了；看完這一幕，那一幕又來了。電影那個銀幕是一幕一幕地轉變，不是你看電影的人到銀幕那個地方去；我看電影是我到銀幕那個地方去。不是那個銀幕動，而是自己覺得同這三個人，連我四個人，各處去看這些電影。那時候，看見很多很多東西，也聽見很多很多的事情。以後呢？就回來了。回到自己的門前，把自己的門開開，向房裏一看，怎麼床上還有一個我，在那個地方呢？當覺得還有一個我的時候，本來是兩個我，現在又變成一個了。就這麼一覺得的時候，就變成一個了，這時候就有呼吸，也有動轉了。當時我父親在我身邊，我母親也在我身邊看著我，就說：「他沒有死，又活了！」這樣子，我覺得什麼叫沒有死，又活了？自己一看自己：啊！躺到床上，不會動彈了。自己一想起來：啊！我是有病了。一問我父親、母親，說我已經七、八天的時間，和我講話也不知道，一切一切都人事不省了，現在又有知覺了，知道我還沒有死。

由這一趟之後，就變成一個「活死人」，我自己想我已經死了，我這是又生出來一個人。由此之後，也不那麼狂了，不說：「我不怕魔，是魔怕我。」我知道病魔我是怕的，這東西做不得主，這個魔是厲害的。現在我告訴你們每一個人，千萬不要說這種的話，不要說：「我什麼也不怕！」你什麼也不怕，那將來就有所怕了。那麼說：「我什麼都怕。」你什麼都怕，那也不對的。

a demon of sickness has found me and there is nothing I can do." I was seventeen or eighteen at the time.

I was so sick I went into a coma and was on the verge of death. Suddenly I saw the three Filial Sons of the Wang Family of Manchuria. Two of them, a Buddhist Bhikshu and a Taoist Master, had left the home-life, and the third was an elderly layman. They came and took me out to play. As soon as we went out the door, our feet left the ground and we rode the clouds and drove the wind. We took off from the roof of the house and when I looked down, the house was already very small and I could see a lot of people.

We met a lot of people and traveled everywhere, to all the scenic spots in China and all the temples, on Mount Wutai, Mount Emei, Mount Jiuhua, Mount Putuo, and others. We also visited foreign lands and saw people who had blond hair and blue eyes. It was like a movie, scene after scene quickly passed. Frame after frame, we actually went to those places. We saw many sights and heard many things.

When we returned, I opened the front door and saw myself lying on the bed inside the house. "How can this be?" I thought, and as soon as I was aware that there were two of me, the two changed into one. My mother and father were at my bedside watching me. When they saw me begin to breathe again, they cried, "He's alive! He hasn't died!" "What are they talking about?" I wondered. Then I discovered I was lying on the bed unable to move, and remembered I was sick. My parents told me I had been unconscious for seven or eight days. They had thought I was dead.

After this experience, I considered myself a "living dead person," one who had been born again. After that, I never spoke recklessly. I did not claim to fear no demons, because I knew the demon of sickness was too powerful for me to overcome. Now, I also advise all of you never to brag that you don't fear anything, because if you do, something will happen to make you afraid. Nor should you say that you fear everything. In general don't make such claims. Talking in that way is useless.

Another strange thing happened to me at that time. I began to feel that I had some real skill in cultivation. When I was in Manchuria, before I became sick, I was active in the Virtue Society. What did I do there? I was one of the leaders. We would lecture on morality, humaneness, and righteousness, and exhort people to do good deeds. When I exhorted others to do good, did I do good deeds myself? Yes, I did even more good deeds myself. I didn't preach without practicing. One day I read an article about the virtuous behavior of a man named Zhang Yaxuan. The article said that a woman named Yu (the niece of Zhang Xueliang's wife) had become infatuated with Zhang Yaxuan and knelt in front of him hysterically demanding that he marry her. Zhang Yaxuan, seeing that it was not a good situation, gently persuaded her to give up her wish.

When I read this article while sitting beneath a tree, I

總而言之，不要講這些沒有用的話。

當時，我還有一件事情，講起來真奇怪。什麼事情呢？我那時候修行，覺得自己有點功夫了。因為在東北，在我沒病以前，我就參加道德會。在道德會上幹什麼的？在道德會做總科長，就講道德、說仁義的，專門勸人家做好事。那麼勸人家做好事，我自己做不做好事呢？我自己更做好事，不是說單勸人家做好事，自己不做好事。這個時候，有一天我拿著一本書，看書看到有一篇講張雅軒這種很好的行為。書上講有一個女人叫余淑嫻，就是余鳳至（張學良的太太）的姪女。余淑嫻喜歡張雅軒，就佯狂跪倒，像發狂似的跪到他面前，就要求他，說她一定要嫁給他。張雅軒一看，這是不對的，這是不好的兆頭，就委曲婉轉把她勸退了。我看見他的行為這樣好，於是乎我在樹底下就發願。發什麼願？我就對著天好像講鬼話似的這麼講，我說：「天哪，天哪！張雅軒這種行為，我一定要效法他。」說完之後，自己就覺得後悔了：「唉！我要遇著這個事情幹什麼呢？這有什麼意思呀！我為什麼要遇到這個事呢？這簡直不是自己太愚癡了。」說完之後，覺得生這個念頭是不對的。你說怎麼樣呀？很奇怪地，隨著這一天晚間，女魔就來了。本來白天那是道德會的辦公室，晚間因為那是單一個房間，女人的宿舍和男人的宿舍就連著的，北方都是炕，這中間有一道牆，牆就用木板子夾的，底下還有道縫。她隔著這個牆從這道縫就把手伸過來，就不老實了。我當時就知道：「哦！白天發那個願，晚上就遇到這種魔考，來試驗我，看我究竟能不能效法張雅軒？這真是不可思議的。」那怎麼辦呢？我就不理她，她就退了。是有這麼一次，從這個我知道，你如果有什麼願力，默默中菩薩或者就來試驗你，所以不要說自滿的話。

還有一次，我晚上那是作夢的樣子，就夢見我到一個家庭去住了，這家庭有二個女人，老的大約五、六十歲，年輕的有二十多歲，就這麼二個人。我在北炕上，她們就在南炕上住，晚上睡覺，又像睡著、又像沒睡著，這個年輕的女人，就到北炕上，把我抱起來了，就往南炕她躺的那地方拖。一拖，我心裏想：「這是幹什麼？一定不懷好意。」我問她：「妳幹什麼？妳幹什麼？」她也不講話。然後我知道大約這不是人吧！就想起念觀音菩薩來了，我說：「南無大悲觀音菩薩……」，這一念觀音菩薩，什麼也沒有了，可是這兩邊肋被她夾得痛了有一個禮拜。你說是真的，它不應該什麼也沒有了；你若說是假的，它又是痛。就遇到這麼一個事情。

我十五歲開始才讀書，因為我覺得我小的時候失學，沒有受過很良好的教育，這是我一生很大的一個遺憾。

admired his conduct and immediately made a vow: "Heaven, I will definitely emulate the conduct of Zhang Yaxuan." I regretted the statement as soon as I said it. I thought, "Why would I want something like that to happen to me? It was stupid of me to say that." I felt that my vow was wrong. What happened then? It's very strange, but that very evening, a woman demon came. The room that served as the office of the Virtue Society was used as a women's dormitory at night. The brick beds (which we use in northern China) in the women's dorm were separated from those in the adjacent men's dorm by a wooden wall with a gap at the bottom. She reached her hand through the gap and tried some hanky-panky. I thought, "This is inconceivable. I made a vow to imitate Zhang Yaxuan today, and now a demon has come to test me to see if I can really do it." What did I do? I ignored her, and then she stopped making advances. From this, I know that if we make vows, the Bodhisattvas will come to test us. We should never make arrogant statements.

Another time, I had a dream in which I was staying in a house with two women, one in her fifties or sixties, the other in her twenties. I was sleeping on a brickbed on the north side of the house, and they were on one at the south side. At night, when I was neither asleep nor fully awake, the young woman came to the north side, embraced me, and started dragging me towards her brickbed. I knew she was up to no good. "What are you doing? What are you doing?" I shouted. There was no answer and I thought, "She's probably not a human!" Then I recited, "Homage to the Greatly Compassionate Bodhisattva Guanyin." As soon as I recited, everything disappeared and I woke up. But the portion of my body that she embraced ached for a week. You may say it was real, but then everything disappeared; say it's unreal, but the aching was there. That was another experience I had.

I didn't attend school until I was fifteen. It is one of my greatest regrets that I was not able to receive a proper education. Thus I was very eager to promote education. After attending school for two and a half years, at the age of eighteen I began a free school in my own home. I didn't collect tuition, but taught the students for free, teaching them what I myself had learned and studied in school.

I was teaching in a culturally undeveloped area in the mountains, and I called the school "Toad Hall." In the autumn, the toads would crawl under the rocks. If you turned up a rock, you would see lots of little toads. It is said that these toads were used for imperial tributes. I taught over thirty students, spending day after day with them. Why did I volunteer to teach them? Was it a honorable position being the leader of the kids? No. Since it had been difficult for me to study, I sympathized with other children who didn't have the opportunity to go to school. I knew that poor families couldn't afford to send their children to school. At that time in China, education was not widespread and the literacy rate was extremely low. I hoped all the young people could have

雖然沒有讀好書，但是我很熱心教育，自己認識幾個字不多，書也懂的還不少，所以我就願意在我讀二年半書之後，我十八歲那年就在自己的家裏成立義務學校，不收錢，就這麼盡義務教人讀書，我把我所學的、所讀的書，就盡我一番的能力來教導一些學生。

那是在山裏邊沒有文化的地方，我在那裏教義學，那兒叫蛤蟆堂，什麼叫蛤蟆堂？就是一到秋天，那蛤蟆都鑽到石頭底下去了，你把這石頭一揭開，都是小蛤蟆，很多，據一般人說那種蛤蟆是進貢的。那時小孩子有三十多個，我一個人教，就一天一天陪著學生，在一起做孩子王。為什麼我要做孩子王，還不收錢呢？是不是這孩子王很光榮的？也不是。因為我讀書很困難的，我就很同情其他的學生沒有機會讀書。我想沒有錢讀書的人，都是家裏很困苦艱難的。當時中國教育不普及，文盲也太多，我很希望所有中國的青年學子，都在很小的時候能有機會讀書，令他們有相當的學識，所以我也不求代價，不求取任何的學費，每天義務來教，我稱自己做老師，成立一個學校、私塾，教這些青年的文盲。

我又想，這世界為什麼壞的呢？世界壞的原因，就因為這一個「錢」字，錢把各行各業都支配得顛顛倒倒。那時候，我就教義務學，不要錢。我想做老師是為教育而教育，不是為的錢，不是為的名，也不是為的利來教書，所以我就願意提倡這個義務學校。「學生不需要收學費，老師也不要錢」，這樣子才真見得出老師是為教育而教育，不是為錢而教育。因為我知道我沒有錢，不能讀書，我就想到其他的貧苦兒童想要讀書也沒有錢，所以義務學校不收學費，也不收紙、筆、墨的雜費，什麼費都不收，我還給預備書本，預備紙筆墨，免得學生應該讀書的時候，因為沒有錢，就不能到學校去讀書。所以就這樣我教這些小孩子，陪著他們來讀書。

這樣教了一個時期，因為那時候，不知是氣候，還是什麼關係，在山裏頭就有這一種病流行，這種病叫什麼呢？叫羊毛疔。大人很多人都生這個羊毛疔，這羊毛疔是在身上它凸出一個小包包，前七後八，前邊有七個，後邊有八個。那個小包包不太高，小小的，就像火柴頭那麼大，可是它鼓起來，你用火材頭一扎它，它這個包塌下去就不起來了，這是羊毛疔的一種症狀。鼓起來這個包，你用針一挑，那裏頭，咦！是真有羊疔。你若認識，挑破了它，出一點血，就好了，沒事了；不挑破呢？一定死的，所以這種病如果不治，死不用多少天，三天就死了；但是若有人懂得怎樣治，它很快也就好了。這種病就是來得這麼厲害。

我在那兒教義學，我教的學生，同在一天就有十幾個

the opportunity to go to school and receive an adequate education. That's why I started a tuition-free private school and worked without pay teaching those illiterate children.

I also thought to myself, "Why is the world going bad? It's because of money. Money has deluded the members of every profession and every line of work." That's why I taught without asking for pay. I thought a teacher should teach for the sake of educating students, not for the sake of money, fame, or benefit. I wanted to promote the idea of free education--students don't pay tuition, and teachers don't ask for a salary. Only then can teachers show that they are devoted to teaching rather than to making money. Since my family hadn't been able to pay for my schooling, I knew that the children of other poor families had no money either. That's why I didn't collect any tuition or material fees. I supplied the books, brushes, and ink. I didn't want children to be unable to study because of lack of money.

During that period, there was an epidemic going around called "Sheep's Hair Lumps." The disease may have been due in part to the climate. Many adults came down with it and grew blisters on their body--seven in the front and eight in the back. The blisters were about the size of matchstick heads, and would collapse if you poked them with a match-stick. If you pricked them with a needle, there was really sheep's hair inside. If the sick person's blisters were pricked and bloodletting was done, the person would get well. Recovery was very rapid if the sick person received the proper treatment. However, if no one treated the disease by pricking the blisters, the person would die in three days. That's how lethal a disease it was.

When I was teaching, in a single day over ten of my students came down with the "sheep's hair lumps." I had learned to treat the disease after watching others do it, and so I was able to cure my students very quickly. But when one of my favorite students, named Li Youyi, who was intelligent, well-behaved, and a good student in every respect, came down with the disease, I was a little worried and the fire rose in me. When fire rises, it's easy to catch the disease. After I finished pricking this student's blisters, he went home and recovered. But then I fell sick and was in terrible pain. Seeing the little blisters on my chest, I knew I had "sheep's hair lumps."

I couldn't prick my own blisters and cure myself, and no one else knew how to treat the disease. Then I lost my temper and declared, "Guanshiyin Bodhisattva, I want to help the people of the world. You shouldn't let me get sick like this! If I really cannot contribute anything to Buddhism, I might as well die right now. I won't treat myself or find anyone to treat me; I'll just wait for death." I could have taught the others how to prick the blisters, but I was sick and in no condition to go and call someone else. I thought, "I have offered my life to Buddhism. If Buddhism has no use for me, I might as well die! If Buddhism still needs me, then

都生了羊毛疔。這羊毛疔我看人家挑這個羊毛疔，我也去學會了，也就會治這個病。這十幾個學生都生羊毛疔，我就都給他們治好了，即刻治就都給治好了。最後我很喜歡的一個學生，他姓李，好像叫李有益，這個學生很聰明，讀書也好，也守規矩，每一樣都是優等的，我對這個學生也很愛惜的。這個學生也生羊毛疔了，當時我心裡有一點著急，上點火。可是誰一著急上火，就容易生這個病。我一給他挑，挑完了，這個學生就回家去。沒有事，我這個病就來了，頭痛得不得了，我一看，也是前後心上都有小疙搭，我知道我也生羊毛疔。

自己生了羊毛疔，自己刀不能解自己的把，自己不能給自己治，旁人也沒有人會治，於是乎，我那時候又發了脾氣了。發什麼脾氣啊？我說：「觀世音菩薩，我是幫助世界人的，你不應該叫我也生這種病啊！好啦！我真要是一個對佛教沒有貢獻的人，我現在就願意生羊毛疔死了算了，我也不治了，我就等著死，我不找人來給我挑。」我會挑，但是旁人沒有人會的，要我教，我自己生病，我不便叫旁人。我說：「我是獻身佛教的，如果佛教不用我，我就生羊毛疔死了算了；如果佛教裡還需要我的話，我就不治也會好的。」這時候頭痛得好像就要兩半那樣，我也不管，就忍著、忍著，眯了一陣子，就睡著了。睡著睡睡，怎麼樣呢？就不能呼吸了，氣喘不出來了，就彎得醒了，醒了就覺得好像有什麼東西在喉嚨這兒堵著似的，呼吸氣也沒有了。沒有，自己心裡頭明白不能喘氣了，就用力往前一咳，咳嗽出來有十多團這個羊毛，哦！這個每一團都像羊毛似的。這麼吐出之後，我這個羊毛疔也沒有治，它就好了。由這個我知道我是對佛教，還可以做一點事情，那時候我知道我自己是屬於佛教的。

之後，我母親有了病，癱瘓了。我一邊教書，一邊就服侍我母親的病。什麼病呢？也不知道是什麼病，也不能走路，也不能翻身，大約半年多，那時候大小便都要我來幫助她，做這一切的飲食，什麼都我給她。老年人病了，身上有一股臭味，但是我也不厭煩，毫不勉強地盡心竭力來服侍母親。我雖然是個男人，但是也沒有其他人來照顧我母親。那時候我就各處找好醫生來治我母親，也治不好。這麼樣在十八歲那一年，我也常常打餓七；這打餓七，有時候是七天，有的時候是十八天，有的時候是三十六天，這麼一邊教學，還一邊打餓七。為什麼打餓七呢？因為希望用至誠懇切的心，感應道交，令我母親的病早一點痊癒。

那時候，白雲河有個狐仙，在那兒顯靈，贈醫施藥，一千里地以外的人，都來求藥。這個狐仙是怎麼個來歷

I will get well without treatment."

My head hurt so badly it felt like it would split into two, but I paid no attention. I patiently bore the pain and fell asleep. As I slept, I stopped breathing and woke up gasping for air. Something was stuck in my throat and I couldn't breathe. I coughed forcefully, and up came a dozen or so lumps of sheep's hair--it really looked like sheep's hair! As soon as I spit them out, I recovered--without treatment. From this, I knew that I could still do a little work for Buddhism. I knew then my life truly belonged to Buddhism.

Afterwards, my mother became sick and was confined to bed. I continued teaching on the one hand, and tended to my mother's sickness on the other. I don't know what her sickness was, but for over half a year she could neither walk nor turn over in bed. I helped her go to the bathroom, prepared her food, and did everything for her. My mother's body had a foul·odor because she was old and sick, but I didn't mind the smell at all. I exhausted my strength and did my very best to take care of her. Although I was a young man, there was no one else who could take care of her. I searched everywhere and found a lot of good doctors to treat my mother, but none of them could cure her. During this period (my eighteenth year) I often fasted--sometimes for seven days, or for eighteen or thirty-six days. While fasting, I continued to teach in school. Why did I fast? It was to show my extreme sincerity in praying for my mother's recovery.

At that time there was a spirit called the Fox Immortal at White Cloud River (Baiyunhe) who bestowed medicine upon those who prayed to him. People came from over a thousand miles away to seek medicine from the spirit. When the Japanese had their base there, the Fox Immortal also dwelt in the barracks, but later it chased the troops away. The Japanese army had secretly built an electrically run oil cauldron near their base, and they shipped Chinese prisoners in by the trainload to be boiled in it. It's not known how many people they boiled to death.

Probably the Fox Immortal was upset by what was happening. He transformed himself into a white-haired old man and walked into the area. The Japanese chased after him carrying their guns, but he ran into their armory and blew it up. After two such explosions, the Japanese knew they couldn't stay there any longer and so they moved out. That's how powerful the Fox Immortal was.

After the Japanese left, the Fox Immortal began giving medicine to those who sought it. All one had to do was go to his place, set out a bowl with a red cloth over it, and make a request. Whatever medicine one prayed for would appear in the bowl. I went to the Fox Immortal seeking medicine for my mother. I set out the bowl, knelt down, asked for help, and waited. I knelt for three days and three nights, but no medicine appeared in the bowl. Later, after I left the home-life, the Fox Immortal possessed one of my

呢？日本軍隊到那兒駐防的時候，那個狐仙原來也在那個軍營裡住著，後來他就把日本軍隊給攆跑了。怎麼攆跑的呢？這日本軍隊不知從什麼地方抓來很多中國人，用火車載到白雲河那個地方，火車門一打開，人一走出來，就走到熱油鍋裡頭去，被活活炸死，有很多人在那兒炸死都不知道。這個時候大概狐仙也看得不高興了，所以就變成一個有白鬍子的老人，到那個地方去和日本人鬥。日本人看見這個老人，就拿槍追他，一追，這老人就跑到軍藥庫裡頭去，軍藥庫就自己爆炸了。這樣爆炸了兩次，日本人知道沒有辦法在那兒住，所以都搬離那個地方，這隻狐仙就有那麼大的本領。

日本人走了之後，他就贈醫施藥顯靈，無論多遠去的人求藥，只要用紅布包著一個碗，到那兒跪著一禱告，這碗裡就會有藥，或者藥丸，要什麼藥就有什麼藥，這麼樣靈驗。我因為母親有病，也到那個地方去求藥。可是我在那兒跪了三天三宿，打開紅布看看，還沒有藥；再打開看看，還是沒有藥，所以求不到，以後也就不求了。等到我出家以後，這隻狐仙就附在我親戚身上，也要皈依我，我就問牠是誰？牠說牠就是白雲河贈醫施藥的狐仙。我就和他算賬，我說：「當初你贈醫施藥，我去求藥，你怎麼不給我藥？你現在還想來皈依我！」這狐仙就說：「那時候你跪在那兒，我只看到一片金光，什麼也看不見，所以我沒有辦法給你藥。」求不到藥，我自己也懂中藥，就到藥材店給我母親買了一點藥，回去熱煎，可是吃了也不好。那麼不好，果然沒有多久我母親就死了，當時是在三月十九那天。我母親死了，我手裏頭連一個penny也沒有，窮得不得了，家裏也很窮的。雖然那麼窮，但是我教學也不收錢，還是做義務的事情，所以我這人生來是很笨的，就不知道怎樣去利益自己，只知道利益旁人，這不是我自誇其德來講的，這是個人的個性，生來是這樣子，就願意捨己為人。

等我母親死了，我把我幾個哥哥都叫去，他們都沒去，就這個三哥那時候去。去了，我問他：「母親故去了，我們要買一個什麼樣的棺材？」他說：「哎！我們這個環境還買什麼棺材，我們現在吃飯都沒有錢，哪有錢給買棺材？」我說：「那怎麼辦呢？」他說：「用幾塊木板釘一個火匣子，埋葬起來就算了嘛！」我說：「這個好像對不起母親似的，生我們這麼多個子女，死了連個棺材都沒有。」我對他說這樣是不好的，我到街上去賒一賒看看。

我就到拉林鎮去賒棺材。因為我參加道德會，在家的時候就在道德會做總科長，我在街上認識一些人，我就到棺材鋪姓田那兒，這人叫田老埠。怎麼叫老埠呢？他

relatives and sought to take refuge with me. When he identified himself as the Fox Immortal of White Cloud River, I said, "When I went to seek your help, you didn't give me any medicine. How can you have the gall to ask to take refuge with me?" The Fox Immortal said, "When you were kneeling there, I couldn't give the medicine to you because I was blinded by a golden light."

Having failed to obtain medicine from the Fox Immortal, I went to the herbal shop myself and bought some medicinal herbs and decocted them for my mother. But she still didn't get well. Not long after that, on the ninth day of the third lunar month, my mother died.

I didn't have a single penny on the day she died. My whole family was destitute. Despite our poverty, I taught school for free. That's the kind of stupid person I was. I didn't know how to benefit myself, but only wanted to help others. I'm not boasting about my virtue--my temperament really is that way--I only wish to renounce myself to help others.

When my mother died, I summoned my brothers, but only my third elder brother came. I said to him, "What kind of coffin should we buy for our mother?"

"How can we buy a coffin when we're so poor?" he asked. "We can't even afford our meals, much less a coffin."

"Then what should we do?" I asked.

"Just nail a few boards together and make a box to bury her in!" said my brother.

"It doesn't seem right," I said. "She raised so many sons and daughters, and yet she doesn't even have a coffin for her burial." I said I would go take a look on the streets.

I went into the town of Lalin to buy a coffin. Since I had been a supervisor at the Virtue Society before I left home, I knew some people in town. I went to see Mr. Tian, who sold coffins. He was known for being a sharp dealer. As soon as he saw me, he said, "Have you come to buy a coffin?"

"I don't have any money right now. Will you let me buy one on credit?"

"Fine," he said. "Pay me back whenever you have money." So the coffin was taken care of, and I made arrangements to ship it home. As I was about to leave, Mr. Tian handed me three hundred dollars, saying, "If you don't have money to buy a coffin, then for sure you won't have the money to hold a funeral. Take this money and pay me back when you can." I knew he had faith in me, and so I accepted the money. Three hundred dollars was quite a sum in those days. It would be equivalent to 30,000 Hong Kong dollars nowadays. Everything was very cheap in those days (forty or fifty years ago), and there was no inflation.

I returned home on the nineteenth of the third lunar month. I placed my mother's body in the coffin, hired some musicians, ordered some food, and arranged for people to carry the coffin. The funeral was set for the next day. However, the warm spring winds had melted the winter snow

的嘴很黑，好罵人，是個跑江湖的，水陸兩碼都通，他開棺材鋪。我到那兒，這賣棺材的老板認識我，說：「喔！你來買棺材。」我說：「我沒有錢，你賒給我可不可以？」他說：「好！我賒給你。你賒到什麼時候有，什麼時候給。」這棺材沒有問題了，就想法子往回運棺材。臨走的時候，田老埠又借給我三百塊錢，他說：「你既然買棺材都沒有錢，一定沒有錢辦喪事，我借給你三百塊錢，你拿去用，什麼時候有，什麼時候給我。」因爲他對我很有感情，很有信心的。我說好啊！那時候三百塊錢是很好用的，拿港幣來講，差不離可以頂現在三萬塊錢來用，因爲那時候什麼東西都很便宜的，這是四、五十年以前的事情，那時候錢沒有卯呢！

我回來正是春天三月十九那一天，我買了一個棺材，又有三百塊錢，所以就把母親的屍首盛殮起來，雇吹鼓手，買了飯菜，請一些人抬這個棺材，準備第二天往墳上送，發殯出去。可是春天三月十九，正是解凍的時候，東北跑洮兒河水，路上又有水又有泥，那個土水和泥，非常泥濘，很不容易走的。我住的地方距離墳塋地大約還有七、八里路吧！這七、八里路，人若抬重，那路我覺得不能走，這樣泥濘，又水里嘎嘰的不容易走。這樣我心裏就打妄想，在晚上大約二點鐘的時候，我就想人抬著這一個棺材，走路是不方便，我怎麼能對得住人呢？這時候我就有所求了，求什麼呢？就求佛菩薩來幫助我，幫助我什麼呢？我說：「我沒有什麼人緣，也沒有天緣，如果諸佛菩薩和上帝能今天晚間，在沒天光以前，或者下雪，或者上凍，這個路就好走了。」下雪，若下一寸的雪墊到這泥濘上邊，也差不多結凍的樣子，就會容易走路了；如果上凍呢，也會好走一點。我晚上這樣一祈禱，啊！很奇怪的，等到雞叫的時候，果然下雪了，也上凍了，這個水就結成冰，冰上面又有雪，這雪下有一寸這麼厚，所以幾十個人抬著棺材走到墳上去，也沒有什麼困難。我想這是佛菩薩特別的感應。

我離墳塋地有七、八里路，二十多個人抬著棺材往墳上送，一早起，天還剛要一亮，就抬著棺材往墳上送，恰好也有點陰天，太陽就不出來，人抬著棺材也不太累。送到墳上，這墳地也刨一個坑，把棺材埋到土裏，做一個墳的樣子，埋好了，哦！太陽出來了，這雪也開始化了，幫忙的人也都回自己家去，我就坐到墳上那兒不走，他們有人問我，爲什麼還不走？我說我要在這兒陪陪我母親，那時候就準備在那兒守孝；可是在我母親墳沒有埋好之前，我從來沒有告訴任何人說我想要守孝。所以這一些人都很驚奇，就勸我回去；無論誰說什麼，我也不聽，我就像聽不見似的，就坐那個地方。那時候

and the roads were muddy and hard to travel. The family burial ground was two or three miles away, and I was worried that it would be very difficult for the pall bearers to transport the coffin on the muddy, slippery roads. That night, I prayed to the Buddhas and Bodhisattvas and to the Heavenly Lord, saying, "I don't have many affinities with people or with heaven, but it would be best if either snow fell or the ground froze before dawn." If an inch of snow covered the ground, or the ground became frozen solid, it would provide traction for easy walking. Strangely enough, the temperature dropped and an inch of snow fell on the frozen ground right before dawn. I knew this was a special response from the Buddhas and Bodhisattvas.

Over twenty people began sending the coffin to the burial ground as soon as it was light. The cloudy weather made it less tiring to carry to coffin. After the service, the sky cleared and the snow began to melt. As people started to leave, I sat down beside the grave. When people asked why I didn't leave, I told them I wanted to keep my mother company. I had not told anyone before my mother's burial of my intention to stay by the grave to observe filial piety. They tried to persuade me to go home, but I was deaf to their pleas. I didn't feel sad. I just thought, "Mother, even though you've passed away, I will keep you company so you won't be lonely." I was nineteen then.

A lot of people are curious about what it was like sitting by the grave, so I'll tell you some more. The first day I sat by the grave, a big test came. The daytime was uneventful, but that evening, a large pack of wolf dogs closed in. These dogs had been trained by the Japanese. They were extremely fierce and were known to eat people. Rich people used them as watch dogs to guard their homes and set them loose at night. These wolf dogs would gather in a pack at night and go on raids, sort of like a guerrilla unit. They moved with military precision. Seeing me sitting there all alone beside the grave, the dogs anticipated making a good meal out of me. There were several dozens of them. They formed a circle around me and started closing in. At first they were fifty or sixty paces away, and they came closer and closer, looking very menacing. The bolder ones led the attack, and the more timid ones brought up the rear. How could I defend myself against a whole pack of wolf dogs? Even fending off one wolf dog would not be easy.

I figured I had only two choices: I could surrender, or I could fight. As for fighting, I was weaponless: I didn't have a gun, or a hand grenade, or a knife, or even a wooden stick or a bamboo rod. How could I resist the attacking dogs? Then I thought to myself: "I'll just sit here and pay no attention to the dogs. They can bite me, tear at my flesh, drink my blood. I'm mourning for my mother, and if I die, then so be it." Under the circumstances, I resigned myself to die. What else could I do? I shut my eyes and waited.

The dogs advanced until they were only thirty paces away.

心裏也不是難過，只是想：「母親，您死了，我願意在這兒陪著您，您就死了，也不會覺得寂寞。」就這樣在墳上守孝，這大約是十九歲的時候。

有些人希望聽聽在墳上守孝又是什麼滋味，所以今天簡單地再說一說。在守孝的第一天，就遇到大考驗，什麼考驗呢？白天沒有什麼事情發生，等到晚間天一黑，附近的狼狗都出來了，就來麻煩我。這些都是日本時代的一些狼狗，都會吃人的，有錢人把牠養在家裏守護門口，到晚間把牠放到門外邊，這些狼狗就想出來，到各處去打游擊，做狼狗的游擊隊。牠們這個游擊隊是有相當的訓練，隊伍非常整齊，有條不紊的。牠們看見在墳的旁邊有一個人在那兒坐著，這是牠們的目地物，是牠們可以裹腹的一種好食糧，於是就有幾十條狼狗，做一個圓形的包抄，四面八方向前進攻。首先是離得五、六十步遠，牠們一邊示威，一邊往前闖，膽大的就往前走得快一點，膽小的就在後邊那麼來跟著。四面八方來的狼狗有幾十條，你說怎麼辦？一個人要打這麼多的狼狗，不要說打這麼多，就打一條狼狗，也不容易的。

這時候遇到這種的情形，要當機立斷，或者投降，或者是和牠們來對敵。對敵呢，什麼武器也沒有，手槍啊、手榴彈哪，刀槍劍戟，十八般兵刃也沒有，連一個木頭棍子，連一個竹枝子也沒有，你說怎麼樣作戰？怎麼樣對抗這一群狼狗？這時候自己想一想：「好了！我坐

Seeing me sitting there motionless, they dared not advance further. What did they do then? From all sides, the several dozen wolf dogs slunk low to the ground and inched their way in--like a carpet being rolled up. They crept forward cautiously, snarling and growling, getting closer and closer, until they were only ten feet away from me. Then, for no apparent reason, they all started yelping and snapping at each other--this dog bit that one, and that one bit the other one. It was as if someone were beating them. Suddenly the whole pack turned and ran. That was the first day. I passed the test of the dogs and escaped being eaten.

When people try to do good things, their offenses will seek them out. If people want to become Buddhas, they will be tested by demons. Since I was doing a good deed by staying beside my mother's grave, my karmic creditors were bound to find me. Probably the dogs were my enemies from lives past, and so they came to attack me when I was totally defenseless. I did not resist them (although I didn't surrender either), and in the end they ran off in defeat. (You could say Manchuria had also put up no resistance to the Japanese army, but it ended up being occupied by the Japanese, so the comparison is not very apt.) Actually, it wasn't I who caused them to retreat, for I hadn't made a single move, said a single word, or even so much as breathed on them. They simply started fighting among themselves and then left and never came back.

After the dogs left, mosquitoes came. There shouldn't have been any mosquitoes in March, but a huge swarm of mosquitoes appeared the second evening. They were big

在這個地方，不管牠，牠願意咬就隨牠咬，願意吃我的肉就給牠吃肉，願意喝血就給牠喝血，反正我是為我母親守孝，我就死了，也死得其所。」那時候，真是逼著你視死如歸，你不如歸也不行了。所以把眼睛一閉，似睜不睜的，看看牠們的行動怎麼樣？

這時候，牠們由五、六十步進攻到三十幾步遠，牠們看我在那兒也不動，有點不敢往前攻了。這時候怎麼樣呢？牠們就趴到地下，來做一個地甑式的進攻，四邊幾十條狼狗趴那兒往前捲地甑這麼走，慢慢爬，試探著，一步一步地這麼往前爬著來，一邊爬，一邊叫，一邊咬，來示威。這樣子，由三十多步遠，牠們就趴在那地方往前進攻，我還是不動彈。那麼越走越近，越走越近，進攻到十幾尺遠這個時候，也不知道是為什麼？啊！牠們都互相叫起來，自己就打起來了，這個狗咬那個狗一口，那個狗就咬那個狗一口，互相這麼一咬，喔！就好像被人打了似的，回頭就都跑了。那麼這樣子，這是第一天第一關——狗關——過了，闖過這個狗腹之難。

這個人想要好，就冤孽來找；想要成佛，就先要著魔。在這兒守孝，也可以說是一件善事；可是你要做善事，這個冤孽債都要來找。好像這個狗的難關，這可能是我過去生中，和這一些狗有這些冤冤相報的這種因果，所以牠們在我什麼防備也沒有的時候，就出其不意，攻其無備，來進攻我。可是我不來和牠們敵對，也不投降，但是就是不抵抗，好像東北被日本佔領了一樣，東北這個不抵抗，結果被日本真地給佔領了；我這個不抵抗呢，就把牠們打敗了，所以這有點不同。那麼我把牠們打敗，我想並不是我，我根本也沒有動手，連話也沒有說一句，連一口氣也沒有向牠們吹過，這樣子，牠們自己就互相打起來，然後都垂翅敗歸，就跑了，以後再也不來了。

本來三月間在我東北沒有蚊子，可是也不知為什麼第二天晚間蚊子來了。這個蚊子啊，喔！都是很大的蚊子，叫得也很響，白天沒有，晚間就出來了，就要來喝血，不是一隻、兩隻蚊子，不知多少，這蚊子也是無數那麼多。當時我就想：「咦！這三月間不應該有蚊子，這些蚊子從什麼地方來的？天氣還很冷呢！牠們怎麼會來？」自己一想：「喔！這也是一個難關，昨天是狗的難關，今天是蚊子的難關來了。」這蚊子我可以把牠們都打死，但是我若打死牠們，我怎麼能對得起我母親，好了！我發一個布施心，我說：「請你們儘量來喝血，當飲茶這麼飲，我請客。」我就把上身的衣服都脫下來，那麼這衣服一脫下來，就都來啦！牠們一落到身上；可是落到身上，然後不咬，在身上各處爬一爬，又都飛了

mosquitoes, buzzing noisily and hungry for blood. I thought: "It's only March, and the weather is still very cold. Where did all these mosquitoes come from? This must be another test--yesterday it was dogs, today it's mosquitoes." I could have slapped the mosquitoes, but if I killed them, how could I face up to my mother? And so I said, "You're all welcome to drink my blood. Please be my guests." I took off my shirt and bared my upper body. They landed on my body and crawled around, but then flew away without biting. After that, no mosquitoes ever bothered me again. There were many mosquitoes in the wilderness, but I never got bitten even once. Yet the people who came to visit me were bitten so much that they joked, "Ah! So many doctors giving us shots!" That's how I passed the mosquito test on the second day.

You all think it's very funny and sounds like a fairytale, but I assure you it wasn't fun at all. If I hadn't taken off my shirt and been willing to let them drink their fill, they might not have left me in peace. My thoughts at the time were: "You may drink my blood dry and let me die here, but I won't seek revenge. And when I become a Buddha, you mosquitoes will be the first ones I take across. I want to be your friends." And so when the mosquitoes landed on me, they wanted to be my friends, too. They couldn't bear to drink my blood. I don't know if this was a response. All I know is that when I offered my blood to them, they didn't want it anymore. That's why, after leaving home, I called myself the Mosquito Bhikshu. I often used this penname because my names To Lun and Hsuan Hua gave people a headache. Later I also used the name "Mosquito." Today I have told you the story behind these nicknames.

Some people think I'm just telling stories. You can think of them as tall tales if you like. I'll tell you another story. What test was in store for me on the third night? You'll never guess. It was ants--thousands of them. As I sat there, they crawled on my body and bit me all over. I knew they were either trying to drive me away or testing my sincerity. Again, I showed no resistance. I thought, "You may want to drive me away, but I won't drive you away." I relaxed my body and thought, "If you want to crawl onto my head, go ahead. Crawl on my face if you like. You can crawl into my ears, up my nose, into my mouth--wherever you want. I can bear it." After about half an hour, the ants left. Strange! After that, not a single ant ever came to disturb me. The ants probably saw that they couldn't take over the territory so they went somewhere else.

From these three incidents, I realized that if we don't put up any resistance to our enemies--if we can regard our enemies as friends--then they will eventually come to see us as friends too. That's how I gave myself the penname "Little Ant." Now you have a little ant and a little mosquito lecturing the Sutra for you. That's why very few people come to listen; everyone is afraid of being bitten by the mosquito and

宣化老和尚追思紀念專集

，你說奇怪不奇怪？從此以後，不但沒有蚊子，而且無論什麼時候，我在墳上守孝的時候，蚊子不來咬我了。那蠻荒野地很多蚊子，可是冬天、夏天也沒有蚊子來咬了。我那兒來的客人，他們都被蚊子給叮了，他們說：「哦！這麼多打針的，這麼多的醫生。」蚊子咬，他們說是打針的。可是我在那兒坐，牠們不咬。這是第二天晚間這個蚊子關也打破了。

你看！講起來是不是像神話似的，你們各位聽得是很好笑的吧！這個真不是很好玩的，當時若沒有一個布施心，若不把衣服脫了，飽牠們的腹，牠們也不一定就善罷干休的。當時我就想怎麼樣呢？我自己想：「好！我布施給你們這個血，你們就是把我血都給榨乾了，我就是死在這兒，也不會來報復你們。我不但不報復你們，我若成佛的時候，我要度這一些蚊蟲，我現在開始就要做蚊蟲的朋友，我要和你們做朋友。」這樣一想，所以蚊子落到身上，牠也就要和我做朋友，牠們也就捨不得喝我的血了。你看這個不知道是不是感應力，總而言之，我一真發出這個布施心，牠們又不要了，這是第二天這個蚊子關。由這個之後，我出家，就叫蚊子比丘。我有個筆名，有的時候寫字，因為我這個度輪和宣化，人看見都很頭痛的，我就寫蚊子比丘。那麼現在聽經的，有人會見到我寫字署名是「小蚊子」，就是從這兒來的，我今天告訴你們清楚一點。

有人心裏想：「啊！這是講故事。」不錯！講故事，你就當故事聽好了。我再給你講個故事，那麼第三天晚間是什麼關呢？你們誰也想不到，誰猜也猜不著，就是什麼呢？螞蟻關。這個螞蟻也是無千無萬的，晚間哪，喔！我坐到這個地方，牠往身上都跑遍了，各處這麼跑到身上也咬。這時候，我想這個螞蟻來撐我，不叫我在這兒守孝，或者也是試驗我，看看我心真不真吧！既然是你來想要撐我，可是我不撐你，我就把手腳都鬆弛開，隨便你願意怎麼爬，我也不驅除你。你就是願意往我頭上爬就頭上爬，願意臉上爬就臉上爬；願意往耳朵裏爬嘛，我也是忍受著；往鼻子裏爬、口裏爬，隨便你怎麼爬。這樣一想，過了有半點多鐘的時間，咦！這些螞蟻也都撤退了。這又過一個螞蟻關，你們說這個奇怪不奇怪？由這個之後，我那兒連一隻螞蟻也不來了。螞蟻到這兒大約也是看看這個地盤，可是怎麼樣子想做霸王也霸不了，所以也就都跑了，一起到旁的地方去。

由這三種情形之後，我知道我們人，只要我們存著一個沒有敵人的心，不和任何人敵對，他就對我敵對，我還是拿他做朋友。這樣子，始終會感化到他，也會把你當成朋友。所以，我以後也有一個筆名叫「小螞蟻」，

having the ant mess up their clothes. Those of you who dare to come are willing to be friends with the ants and mosquitoes. I won't say anymore today, or I might scare you all away!

On the fourth day, the mosquitoes, ants, and dogs were gone, and the rats came. The big ones were as large as cats. I don't know if they were like the huge rat that fell from the roof in Taiwan, but they were pretty big. At first I thought they were cats, but upon taking a closer look I saw that there were white rats and grayish ones, and rats with poor eyesight that burrowed in the ground in the beanfields. There were also rats called "big-eyed thieves," because they have large eyes. These rats could jump three feet high in the air. As I sat there, all the rats--too many to count--swarmed over me and tried to jump on my head. Now, I had been powerless to defend myself against the wolf dogs, and I could have killed the ants and mosquitoes but I didn't. It would have been difficult to fight against the rats because there were so many of them. However, when they tried to jump on my head, I put up my hand to block them. They immediately bit my hand until it bled. Then I thought, "Fine, I won't resist. Go ahead and bite me." I left them alone, and about twenty minutes later, they all ran off. That was the test of rats on the fourth day.

On the fifth day, I was surrounded by all kinds of poisonous snakes--big, small, long, and short. Usually snakes were not seen in that area, but that day they all came preparing to bite me. Again I thought, "Go ahead and bite me. If I die, so be it!" But none of them bit me. On the sixth day came a swarm of centipedes out of nowhere. They were three or four inches long. I've seen similar ones at Flourishing Compassion Monastery on Lanto Island and Western Bliss Gardens in Hong Kong, but I'd never seen such large centipedes in that part of Manchuria. The grass rustled as they came crawling closer on all sides, menacing me. I thought to myself, "What's going on here? I've been attacked by dogs, mosquitoes, ants, rats, snakes, and now centipedes. Well, no matter what comes, I'll just let them bite me." Since there was no fear or hatred in my heart, they dispersed and vanished on their own.

There was something different on the seventh day: a rare fragrance filled the air--a fragrance that was not of this world. After the tumultous first seven days, everything settled down. While I was sitting by the grave, no one had brought me any food and I resigned myself to starving. But after the seventh day, my father came bringing me food. He was in his seventies, and he urged me to go home, crying as he talked. Although I wasn't really hungry after seven days of not eating, I forced myself to eat. Then I asked my father not to bring me any more food. I said I wouldn't accept food or other things from my own family. All these things happened to me as I sat beside the grave, but I never encountered any ghosts. Sometimes I ate grass roots and

這個筆名也是這麼來的。我現在和大家講經，就是一隻小螞蟻和一隻小蚊蟲子在這裡講經，所以沒有人來聽，因為每個人都怕蚊子咬，怕一些螞蟻爬上你們的衣服，把這弄得很骯髒。現在來聽法的，大家都是願意和蚊子、螞蟻做朋友，所以你們就敢來聽。今天就講這麼多，再講多一點呢，恐怕就會嚇走你們了。

在昨天講到有這個狗的難，又有蚊子的難，又有螞蟻的難，今天我講一個老鼠的難。第四天老鼠來了，蚊子不來了，螞蟻也不來了，狗也不來了，那麼老鼠跑來了。大的老鼠像貓似的，那是不是和臺灣從那個房上掉下來十四斤那麼大的老鼠一樣，我是不知道，總而言之，很大。我當初以為牠們是貓，仔細一看，有的是白的老鼠，有的是灰灰的老鼠；有的是在這豆地裏頭，叫豆豕子這種老鼠，這種老鼠眼睛不太好，但是牠是在地下各處鑽的；還有一種老鼠叫大眼賊，這種老鼠很大的眼睛，會跳，一跳能跳起三尺多高。所以我在那兒坐著，牠們就也不知有多少，總而言之，沒有數量，就往我身上爬，又往我身上跳，想往頭上跳。這樣子，狗我打是打不過的；那蚊子是能打得過，可是我也沒有打牠；螞蟻也可以把牠們打死，我也沒有打，因為犯殺戒，所以可以把牠們都殺了，但是沒有殺牠們。這個老鼠來了，本來太多了，也不容易打的，但是牠往頭上跳，我就用手搪牠，一搪，哦！牠就把我這個手抓住就咬，把我手都咬得流血了。這樣子，然後我自己又想：「哎呀！不抓牠了，由牠咬去了！」一不理牠呢，也沒有好久，大約有二十多分鐘吧！牠們也自己都跑了。所以這第四天是這個老鼠難來了。

第五天呢，也不知道什麼地方來一班毒蛇，很多，大的、小的、長的、短的這個蛇就來了。本來我那個地方，蛇是平時看不見的，可是那天晚間牠們都來了，來了也要咬我。我也是：「哎呀！就給牠咬了，咬死算了！」結果也都不咬。第六天來的是什麼呢？是百足。這個百足也不知有多少，也不知從什麼地方來的？這個百足大的有三、四寸那麼長，我在大嶼山的慈興寺見過這麼大的百足，在西樂園也見過，可是在那以前我沒有見過百足那麼大條的。這一次這個百足來了，也是四面來包圍往上爬，把那個草都爬得唰唰響，很有威風的樣子。在這個時候，我想：「這又是狗，又是蚊子，又是螞蟻，又是老鼠，又是蛇，又是百足，這簡直地，這是怎麼回事呢？啊！不管牠了，不論你什麼來，給你咬算了。」這個心一對牠們不生恐懼心，也不生慎恨心，結果嘛，牠們也都自動地撤退了。

第七天呢，來的這個不同了，什麼呢？有一股香味。

leaves when I felt hungry. Once I found a mushroom and ate it, and for the whole day I wanted to laugh; thus I knew there was a laughter-inducing chemical in the mushroom. That period of living by the grave was one of great hardships.

I built an A-shaped hut out of some branches tied in bundles. When it snowed outside, the inside of the hut would also turn white; when it rained, it was also wet inside. The hut didn't keep out the wind, snow, or rain. Spending my days reciting Sutras, reciting the Buddha's name, and sitting in meditation, I developed a great sense of mental peace.

When I read *The Romance of the Three Kingdoms* in my youth, I cried for three days when I reached the part about Lord Guan being killed. I was sorely grieved that such a loyal and righteous man had to be so brutally murdered. Yet when my own mother died, I didn't shed tears. I think I probably was too sad to even cry.

While living beside my mother's grave, I continued to bow. During that time I also left the home-life. My goal in leaving home was to end birth and death, to cut off the endless rounds of birth and death. I had nicknamed myself "Mendicant" as a young child, and now I really was one who lived on alms--a monk. My father did not know of my wish to leave home until I was living beside the grave. My father was an alcoholic who spent all his money on liquor. He would walk nearly two miles to and from town to buy eight ounces of liquor, and he would drink four ounces at a time. After drinking his fill, he would sleep. After I left Manchuria, my father was sick for three days, stopped eating, and then sat up and entered the stillness. I have invited my third eldest brother to America and I'm supporting him now, because I want to repay him for supporting my father. Everything I do is motivated by the wish to be filial. Some people speak about practicing filial piety for a certain number of years, but my filial obligations have no time limit.

In remembrance of my father and mother, I dare not commit any mistakes. If I were to do something wrong, I would be an unfilial son. If you ask me how many years I practiced filial piety, I would answer that I'm still practicing now--I don't know how many years it has been, but my filial piety has no limit. I wish to be kind to all elderly people. I want to support everyone's parents, in order to repay everyone's kindness. People have praised me for my filiality to my parents, but I feel my practice is very imperfect. Therefore, I wish to treat all old folks as my own parents. I contemplate all men as my fathers and all women as my mothers. I truly see all people as my parents in past lives and as future Buddhas. I remember how filial and loyal Yue Wumu (General Yue Fei) was. Before every meal, he would remember the two Song dynasty emperors, and then he would take his meal while shedding tears of gratitude. I especially admire heroes like him; they are the most excellent people in the world. As for me, I am not worthy to be people's teacher.

這股香味啊，簡直人間沒有這股香味，覺得異香滿鼻。等過了這七天以後，就比較平靜下來了，所以這七日的難關都打破了。那時候，我坐在墳上那兒，也沒有人送飯，我也打算餓死在墳那個地方，打算也不吃東西，自己也就不吃飯，什麼時候餓死算了。那麼餓餓，到第七天以後，就有人送飯來。誰給我送飯呢？是我父親，我父親那時候已經七十多歲了，拿飯給我。他叫我回去，不要再守孝了，也就一邊講話一邊落淚。本來七天沒有吃飯也不覺得餓，我勉強把這飯吃了。之後，我就告訴我父親，我說：「以後不要給我送飯了，我家裏人送來的飯、東西，我不吃的。」這是一開始在墳上有這樣的情形。是不是也見到鬼呢？沒有見著鬼。可是在守孝的時候，有的時候餓了，草根、樹葉也都吃過。還有一次餓，沒有東西吃，我到那個草地裏去找出一個蘑菇，這個蘑菇吃了怎麼樣？整天也要笑，以後知道這蘑菇裏頭有笑菌，吃了就會笑。說起來，這個也是很苦的。

那時我用十幾捆樹楷搭一個A字形的茅篷，這個茅篷外邊下雪，裏邊也是白的，因為那個茅篷有透風的地方，漏雪；外邊下雨呢，裏邊也是濕的，就這麼一個地方。我住在那兒是坐著，天天也就是念經、念佛、坐禪，心裏覺得很平安。我年輕的時候，讀《三國演義》，看到關公被殺的那一段，我哭了三天。因為我覺得關公這樣忠義的人，還慘遭殺身之禍，心裏實在太悲痛了，所以很感慨就落淚了。可是我母親死那麼大一件事，我沒有掉過淚。為什麼？因為那時候可能也哭不出來。

母親死了之後，我在墳上守孝，還繼續叩頭，那時候已經出家。出家就為了想不死，想截斷這生死的長流，不再生了又死，死了又生，在生死的長流裡流轉。小的時候我就叫自己是乞士，這時候果然就做一個要飯的。我父親不知道我想出家，等我守孝的時候，他才知道。父親是一個好喝酒的人，有錢一定去買酒，到街上來回五里路，買半斤酒，半斤酒喝兩次，一次喝四兩，兩次喝半斤。自己一個人跑到街上買，自己拿回來自己喝。喝完了酒嘛！就睡覺。我出來之後，父親圓寂了，他是坐著圓寂的，病了三天，也不吃東西，然後坐起來就圓寂了，那時我已經離開東北。我把三哥接來，養一養他，也報答他那時候養我父親，有這種關係，所以我不能不理他。我一舉一動都是本照孝念來做的，不是說像某一個人守孝有多少年，我這是無限期的。

我不敢做錯事，也就因為我父親、母親；我若做錯事，這就是個不孝的子弟，因為我時時刻刻都追念我父母，所以什麼錯事我都不敢做的。你問我守孝幾年，我到現在還是一樣在守孝，這是沒有限期的，我也不知道是

When I was practicing filial piety beside my mother's grave, several times the villagers thought my hut had caught on fire, but when they came, there was no fire. There was also an earthquake one night. I was sitting in dhyana, and everything was empty--there was no self and no others--when suddenly I felt a movement, an agitation. I thought to myself, "Ah, what is this demon that can shake my body this way? Its strength is certainly formidable." I didn't realize it was an earthquake. The next day someone came to tell me there had been an earthquake--a very strange earthquake. During it, the well where I sat had spouted fire. This was a water-well, not a volcano, and yet fire had come forth from it. There are many strange things in the world.

I believe someone is thinking, "I'm sure that beneath the well there was a vein of sulphur which fed a volcano, and that is why the well spouted fire." Maybe that's the way it was.

One day at dusk, the Sixth Patriarch came. I saw a monk wearing a gray robe, in his fifties or sixties. He explained some principles to me, telling me how to cultivate, and said that in the future I might come to America. He also told me what kind of people I would meet. After saying that, he disappeared. I wasn't asleep when I saw him, and I found it very strange.

When Japan invaded Manchuria, I was mourning beside my mother's grave. Meanwhile, somebody told me that the Japanese had seized a lot of Chinese people and put them into labor camps. They didn't have enough food to eat or clothes to wear and so a lot of people starved to death and froze to death. It was extremely bitter. I pondered this situation and the severity of their plight, and then I made a vow to eat one meal a day. I wished to save my breakfast and dinner for those who didn't have food to eat. Somebody might say this kind of attitude is very stupid. Well, you can say it's very stupid because those hungry people might not directly receive the food which I saved. But all of you should know it's the law of the conservation of matter. The food I didn't eat will remain in the world. Since it remains in the world, somebody will get to eat it. So I made this vow to eat one meal a day. The *Sutra in Forty-two Sections* says, "Bhikshus take only one meal a day at noon, pass the night beneath trees, and are careful not to acquire worldly things." That's why I vowed to take one meal a day.

I also vowed not to wear padded cotton clothing. During the winters in Manchuria, the temperature often dropped to 33 or 34 degrees below zero. When the temperature dropped to 38 degrees below zero, people would freeze to death. But even in such cold weather, I wore only three layers of clothing. Whether in winter or summer it was always the same, I did not even put on an extra sweater. By my vow I saved the cotton for those who didn't have clothes to wear. I transferred it to them. Did they obtain benefit from it? This again is a case of the law of conservation of matter. Some-

幾年了。因爲這個，我對老人都特別好，也就是這個原因，我就是要養大家的老。爲什麼我要養大家的老？我是還報大家，因爲人人稱讚我怎麼樣盡孝，我實在是抱歉得很，沒有圓滿。所以，我要以所有的老年人做我的父母，是男子皆是我父，是女子皆是我母，我心裡頭真是作這樣的觀想，都是過去的父母，未來的諸佛。我因爲看著岳武穆那麼孝、那麼忠，精忠報國，每逢吃東西，都要紀念徽欽二帝，吃東西，都是感激地痛哭流涕那個樣子。對這一類的人，我都是特別佩服的，這真是天地的精華。我這個呢，還不足爲人師。

在守孝的時候，我那兒本來沒有著火，有幾次，鄉下人就看著火了，去一看，啊！沒有什麼。那時候也經過一次地震。有一天晚間我正在那兒坐禪呢！正在無人無我，什麼都空了，忽然間就覺得動了，這樣晃晃悠悠地晃起來。我自己就想：「哦！這是什麼魔，他可以把我這個身體都搖動起來，這個魔的力量是不小。」就這樣子，也不知道是地震。等第二天有人來告訴我說：「喔！這是地震。」我才知道是地震。那個地震很奇怪的，這井裡本來應該是往上有水的，那次地震，我那地方有一個井，就往上出火，井裡會冒火。火山會冒火，這個井也不是火山，它也冒火，所以這世界奇奇怪怪的事情很多。我相信有人想：「喔！那一定是那個井底下有琉璃，也是火山的脈，所以往外冒火。」也許是這樣。

有一天，也不是白天，也不是晚間，就是天將要黑的時候，六祖大師到我這兒，我看見一個和尚來，穿著灰袍子，五、六十歲的樣子。和我講一些道理，告訴我怎麼樣修行，說你將來，或者會到西方美國去，會遇到一些什麼樣的人。就這樣，說完了，忽然間就沒有了。這時候也不是在睡覺，看到這個，就覺得很奇怪的。

正在日本侵略中國東北的時候，那時我在母親墳上守孝，就有人告訴我，說：「日本人把中國人抓去做勞工，到那地方一天也吃不飽，餓死很多人；也不給衣服穿，唉！太苦了！」我想起這麼多沒有衣服穿、沒有飯吃的人，餓死很多人，凍死很多人，所以我就發願，我願意一天吃一餐，把我早晨這一餐和晚間這一餐，都留給沒有飯吃的人吃。有的人就說：「這種行爲太愚癡了。」可以這麼說，是很愚癡，因爲沒有飯吃的人或者他不能直接得到我所剩下的飲食。但是各位要知道，物質不滅，我不吃的東西，這飲食始終會在世界存在的。它在世間存在，始終是有人會來吃的。所以我發這個願一天吃一餐。我看《四十二章經》，那上面說：比丘，日中一食，樹下一宿，慎勿再矣。因爲這樣我發願吃一餐。

由此之後，我又發願不穿棉衣服。我在東北天氣冷的

body would use it for sure. From the time I made that vow not to wear padded clothes, I didn't feel cold even in very chilly weather. Later on, I even went without socks and shoes, and I could walk with bare feet on icy ground at any time. My feet didn't get frozen.

That reminds me of a funny thing that happened. I had an eighteen-year old fellow student who was a very energetic young man. He saw me walking on the icy ground without wearing socks and shoes, and he wanted to try it out. But he hadn't taken more than 100 steps when his feet completely froze and then swelled up. He couldn't endure it any more and hurriedly ran into the temple. It took six months before he was able to walk again. At that time, I was twenty years old, and I could bear the cold, but even though he was younger, he couldn't. How could I bear it? It had to do with my vow not to wear padded clothes. Since I didn't wear padded clothes, I didn't feel cold at all. Since I didn't eat so much food, I didn't feel hungry.

Before when I wasn't eating one meal a day, I had to eat five small bowls of food at each meal, which means a total of fifteen bowls a day. But after I vowed to eat one meal a

時候，零下三十三度，三十四度是常常有的；如果零下三十八度的時候，一定會凍死人。我冬天、夏天就穿三層布，也不穿毛線衣服。我把棉花省下來，給沒有衣服的人穿，迴向給他們。他們能不能得到呢？這也是一種物質不滅的方法，這物質存在著，一定會有人用的。在那麼冷的天氣，我也不怕凍，甚至以後我鞋也不穿，襪子也不穿，在那個雪地上可以隨便走，腳凍不壞的。

講起這個，有一個很可笑的故事，我有一個徒姪，他十八歲，很年輕，朝氣很大的。他看我不穿鞋、不穿襪子，他也試試看。在那個雪地上走了一百多步遠，他凍得那個腳胖得很厲害，受不了，他趕快跑到廟上去，結果在廟上半年不能走路。你看看，我那時二十多歲，他十八歲比我還年輕，我受得了，他卻受不了。不單他受不了，和我差不多年齡的，他們都受不了，我可以受得了。怎麼這樣呢？就因為我發願不穿棉衣服，以後不穿棉衣服也不凍，不吃那麼多飯也不餓。

在以前不是吃一餐的時候，我每一餐要吃五碗飯。這五碗，三五一十五碗，雖然不是很大的碗，是普通吃飯的碗，年紀輕的人差不多都可以吃五碗飯，我因為身體也不小呀！所以吃五碗飯。但是發願吃一餐以後，最多只吃三碗飯，不論大小碗；大碗吃兩碗，小碗吃三碗，並不是自己節量食，是吃多了就覺得不舒服，所以不吃也不餓了。人就是要有願力，你有願就會滿你的願，我吃一餐就是這個原因。

我的弟子多數都是吃一餐的，不單出家人吃一餐，在家人很多都吃一餐，他們也都願意學我這個笨法子，在科學時代用這個笨法子來修行。真是啊！可以說是不會算賬，不會算數。又可以說算得很清楚，我們不吃的東西，給其他人吃，和其他人結這飲食緣，相信盡未來際都不會餓死，因為我們怕餓死，所以把應該吃的東西，留它一些慢慢吃。古人又有這麼兩句話：

減衣增福，減食增壽。

我想自己不會活得很長命，所以少吃一點，這個壽命或者會長一點。這不一定是這樣，不過我和你們各位講一講這個笑話。

我們吃一餐就是要依照佛制來修行，佛是主張比丘日中一食，樹下一宿，在什麼地方住，最多不超過三天，因為超過三天，或者就有人來供養。那麼說不受人供養嗎？受是受，但是不應該存一個貪供養的心。你若是在什麼地方一住，時間久了，一定就有緣法了。所謂「久坐有禪」，就會有禪定的功夫，「久住就有緣」。比丘

day, I could manage with three bowls of rice at most. If the bow was a big one, I ate two bowlfuls. If the bowl was a small one, I ate three bowlfuls.

It is not that I put myself on a diet. Actually I feel uncomfortable when I eat too much. And so even though I was eating less, I didn't feel hungry at all. From this, people should recognize the power of vows. If you make vows, you will be able to fulfill them. This is the story behind why I eat one meal a day.

Most of my disciples also eat one meal a day. Not only do the left-home people eat one meal a day, but a lot of the laypeople also eat one meal a day. They like to learn my stupid method. In this scientific age, they want to use this stupid method to cultivate. You can say that they don't know how to calculate. But from another viewpoint, they can be said to be calculating very clearly. They give away the food which they don't eat and save it for other people. This is creating food-affinities with other people. So, I believe they will never starve to death to the ends of time. It is because we're afraid that we'll starve that we save some food for future use. The ancients had a saying,

*If one decreases the clothes one wears,*
*One's blessings will grow.*
*If one decreases the food one eats,*
*One's lifespan will increase.*

Because I think that my lifespan will probably not be too long, I want to decrease my intake of food in order to increase my lifespan. Actually this is not true. I'm just joking with you!

We have to follow the Buddha's instructions to cultivate. The Buddha said, "Bhikshus should eat one meal a day, and sleep each night under a different tree." They should not dwell for more than three days in the same place, because if they do, people may come to make offerings. But shouldn't they receive any offerings? They are allowed to accept offerings, but they should not accept the offerings out of greed. Once you live in a place for a long period, Dharma conditions will arise. It is said,

*Sitting for a long time, one attains samadhi.*
*Dwelling for a long time, one develops affinities.*

Therefore, unless a Bhikshu has some important matter to attend to, it is better that he travel around. So in China left-home people travelled around everywhere and paid respects at every famous temple. This is called "hiding one's light." Not wanting to show off or sell their cultivation, wherever Bhikshus dwelled, they would not stay for over three nights.

When I was practicing filial piety beside my mother's grave, there was a controversial issue. Some people thought it was right and good, while others thought it was wrong and

若是沒有什麼重要關係的時候，各處雲遊是最好的。所以中國的出家人要到各處去參方，到各大叢林去參方，這就叫韜光晦跡，不願意顯修行叫人知道，不願意一天到晚到各處賣修行。

我在守孝的時候，還有一件事情不知道對不對？有人說是對，有人說不對。對的人他就說好，不對的人他就說是壞。什麼事情呢？那時候村子很多人供養我，有的買一點這個東西，有的就送一點那個東西；總而言之，都是可以吃的，可以穿的，這些東西。當時就有一個比丘，這個比丘他的神通大得很，什麼神通呢？專門能吃，他也是一天吃一餐，他這一餐吃多少東西呢？這麼大的碗，大約裏邊最低限度可以裝十磅，ten pounds，他可以吃這麼三大碗，他吃得快得很，很快很快的，哦！和那餓鬼吃東西是一樣的。這個比丘這麼大的神通，他想我在那兒守孝，一定也是沒有東西吃，於是乎他就送了一筐裏二外八，用竹子織的筐，這麼一筐裏二外八。

什麼叫裏二外八呢？趙州和尚不懂得這是什麼。趙州和尚已經八十多歲了，有一天人家問他說：「老和尚，你什麼都知道，你知道裏二外八是什麼？」這一問，把老和尚給問住了。趙州和尚知道這東西是吃的東西，但是不知道叫什麼名字，就說：「拿來給老僧吃了它。」那麼這個人以為他懂。叫什麼名字，他沒有說出來，但是他說拿來給老僧吃了它，這個人就以為他認識這個裏二外八了。實際上呢！這個趙和尚他不知道這個叫什麼名字。那麼回去，就生大慚愧心：「這個東西叫什麼名字，我都不認識，你說這修道修得連吃東西的名字都不知道，這真是修的糊塗道，唉！還要出去當參學去。」

但是當參學，自己的眼睛也不幫忙了，這個牙也掉了很多，腿也罷工了，就是腿也不幫忙，走路很困難，這個腿總想罷工，那怎麼辦呢？和這個侍者商量商量看。這侍者就是天天來幫他展具啊！提香爐啊！總來侍候他的一個出家人。他就把侍者找來，和這個侍者開了一個小小的會議，就說：「喂！我和你借一點東西，你可不可以借給我啊！」侍者一聽，和尚要借東西，這怎麼可以不借呢！就說：「你借什麼？只要我有的東西，你借什麼，我都可以借給你。」趙州說：「你說可以就可以啦！不要問我借什麼，你回去睡覺去，睡完了覺，我再告訴你。」這個侍者也莫名奇妙了，那麼和尚叫他回去睡覺，就去睡囉！

這侍者回去一睡覺，這一覺醒了，自己照鏡子一看，自己那個年輕的身體，不是自己了，自己變成和尚了，有八十多歲，哦！很長的鬍子也白了，牙也掉了，啊！變一個老翁，就是趙州這個樣子，啊！變成趙州和尚了

bad. It was the matter of many villagers making offerings to me of all kinds of food, clothing, and things. There was another Bhikshu who had great spiritual powers. What kind of spiritual powers? The ability to eat. He took only one meal a day, but he had a huge bowl that could hold ten pounds of food, and he could eat three bowlfuls a day. He ate really fast, too, like a hungry ghost! He thought that I probably didn't have any food to eat living beside the grave, and so one day he sent me a big basket of steamed dumplings. Those dumplings have a colloquial name, which is "inside two and outside eight."

Dhyana Master Chao Zhou didn't know what "inside two and outside eight" referred to. At that time he was over eighty years old. One day someone asked him "Do you know what an inside two and outside eight is?" The old monk was unable to answer the question. He knew it was food, but didn't know the reason behind that name. So he said, "Bring them to me, and I will eat them." The person had assumed that Master Chao Zhou knew he was talking about steamed dumplings, but actually the monk didn't know. As a result Master Chao Zhou remorsefully thought, "Here I have been cultivating for such a long time, and I don't even know the meaning behind the name of this kind of food. What have I been cultivating? A muddled path? I should go out and investigate."

Although he wanted to go out and study, his eyes were failing, his teeth had fallen out, and his legs had gone into retirement. What could he do? He decided to have a chat with his attendant. He called him in and asked him, "May I borrow something from you?" The attendant thought, "If my master wants something, how can I not lend it to him?" Therefore he said, "Anything that the Venerable Master would like, I am willing to lend him." Master Chao Zhou said, "As long as you agree to it, that's fine. You don't have to ask me what thing I want to borrow. Now run along and go back to sleep."

The attendant felt this was a rather strange request, but he went back to sleep. The next morning on waking up he took a look in the mirror and just about had a fit! He saw that he now had a long beard and teeth that were falling out; in fact, he looked exactly like the old monk Chao Zhou. He was panic-stricken, "Oh no, this is terrible! How did I come into this body of the old master?" He ran off to find Master Chao Zhou. When he entered the master's room, he found himself standing there. This terrified him even more, so that he was screaming and yelling, "What's happening?"

Master Chao Zhou comforted him in a gentle voice, "Don't stir up a scene. I will return your body to you eventually. You needn't be afraid. Now you'd better stand in for me as the Abbot, while I go out to investigate a little."

So Master Chao Zhou went from the south to the north in his investigation. In the northern region, he saw people making steamed dumplings. As they kneaded the dough,

。這個侍者嚇壞了，啊！這一回可糟了，真糟糕了。我怎麼跑到和尚這個身上來了？就去找和尚算賬，到那兒看看自己去。走到自己住的房裡一看，自己也睡醒了在那地方，他說這是怎麼一回事？

趙州就說：「不要吵，不要吵，慢慢地我還給你，你不要怕。但是你現在替我做和尚，我出去參方。」這年輕的「侍者」就走了，年輕的就是這趙州和尚，本來他八十多歲，他把這個侍者二十多歲的身體給換去了，換去就走，從南方就到北方，到了北方一看，人家做那個裏二外八，裏邊用二個手指頭，外邊用八個手指頭，原來是什麼呢？北方那兒叫窩窩頭。窩窩頭有些人恐怕還不知道，這個裏邊是空的，做的時候，這兩個大拇手指頭放在裡邊，四個手指頭放到外邊這麼做，做完了，蒸熟了可以吃。趙州就問：「這個叫什麼？」那個人就告訴他：「哦！你連這個都不知道，這個叫窩窩頭。」趙州：「喔！原來這個東西叫窩窩頭。」那好了！知道這個名字就回來了，回來把侍者這個年輕的身體就還給侍者，自己又回到自己那個老態龍鍾的身上去。為什麼呢？他因為老的身體走路是很不方便的，太不聽招呼了，所以他換一個年輕的。所以說：「趙州八十還行腳」，他八十歲了還去行腳，不過他行腳不是他自己，是他換了這個身體去，所以這叫「裡二外八」。

當時這個比丘給我送來一筐這個東西，一筐有五、六十個。這比丘叫什麼名字？叫止一，意思大約也是一天只吃一餐；但是吃得很多。那麼他看我在那兒守孝，怕我餓壞了，就送了一筐這個東西給我。這個東西一天吃不了，他以為他大約一、兩天就可以吃完這些東西；但是給我，我吃了有半個多月，也沒有吃完這個東西，沒有吃完，我就慢慢吃這個東西，吃到最後，大約有三個禮拜吧，才吃完。天天吃這個，那沒有問題；可是當時天氣也熱，熱得不得了，最後這個窩窩頭裏邊、外邊都長了這麼長的毛，差不多有一寸半那麼長。我也沒有管它，沒有把它拿到外邊去吹吹風，或者曬一曬，它就不會長毛了。我那時候也很懶的，一天吃飽了就坐著，什麼也不管，結果最後天氣熱的時候，就長那麼長的毛。

這時候，我把這個毛拿走了，把這個窩窩頭也都吃了。但是這個東西真難吃，和那個糞的味道是一點也沒有分別；甚至於比那個糞還臭，還難吃啊！現在要是一想起來這個味道，甚至於要作嘔。當時你說這壞得這個樣子，如果丟了它嘛！人家來供養，尤其是一個出家人來供養，那時候我僅僅是一個沙彌；若不丟它，這東西真難吃，吃得又辣又臭，從來都沒有吃過那麼難吃的東西。有的人到那兒去，看我吃這個東西，就不叫我吃，說

they used two fingers to knead the inside of the dumpling, while eight fingers remained outside to shape the exterior of the dumpling. He asked the people, "What is the name of this food?" They answered, "You don't know what this is called?! This is 'inside two and outside eight'--steamed dumplings!"

Suddenly Master Chao Zhou understood. There was nothing else to do, so he came home and returned the young body to his attendant, and crept back into his old, weak, and worn body. So it's said, "Chao Zhou went out to travel at the age of eighty." However, he didn't do it in his own body. He traded bodies with his young attendant, because his own body was falling apart and not fit for travel. That's the story of 'inside two and outside eight.'

At that time, a Bhikshu sent me a basket of those dumplings, also called "*wowotou*," about fifty or sixty of them. This was a Bhikshu who ate one meal a day. He was afraid I would starve to death, so he offered me these dumplings. He probably could have finished them in a day or two, but I ate them slowly and took three weeks to finish them. On the last day, the steamed dumplings had developed long mold, about one and a half inches thick. I didn't expose them under the sun or let the wind dry them. I was very lazy at that time. After eating, I usually sat there and didn't pay attention to anything. As a result, the food developed long mold when the weather got hot. At that time I wiped away the mold and ate all the *wowotou*'s. This kind of food was really hard to eat--it stank even worse than excrement. Even now, thinking of them makes me want to vomit. However, I couldn't throw them away, because they were offerings made by a left-home person, and I was only a novice. On the other hand, they really tasted terrible. Other people who saw me eating them told me not to eat them, saying I would get sick. "And what if I get sick?" I asked. "Then you won't be able to cultivate," they said. "I'm perfectly willing to die, how much the more get sick!" I replied. I had put mind and body down, so I could eat anything, no matter how bad it tasted. I ate them, but nothing happened to me and I didn't get sick.

While I was practicing filial piety beside the grave, I went to leave the home-life. Before leaving home, I had taken refuge with Great Master Chang Ren, who, despite being illiterate, spoke very elegantly. Great Master Chang Ren was the Abbot of the temple. He had practiced filial piety beside his parents' graves for six years, during the second three years of which he didn't eat cooked food and didn't speak to people. Living at the temple where I left home were forty or fifty Bhikshus, but sometimes as few as a dozen. When I first arrived at the temple, the Abbot was out begging and none of the Bhikshus knew me. "I know the Abbot, and I want to leave the home-life," I said, and they welcomed me.

After leaving home, I practiced austerities, but not the

這個吃了會生病的。我説：「生病！什麼叫病啊？」「生病就是你在這兒就不能修行了。」我説：「那死了更好，何況病呢！」當時真是把身心都放下了，所以吃這種東西也可以吃，我相信當時怎麼難吃的東西，我都可以吃的。吃完了也沒有病，什麼事情也沒有。

守孝之後，然後就出家。我沒出家以前就皈依常智大師，他是一個不認字的人；雖然不認字，可是他所説的話，都是文縐縐，一套一套的。廟上的方丈和尚是常仁大師，他守孝守六年，後三年不吃熟的東西，也不講話。在冰天雪地的地方，三年沒講話，也不吃熟的東西。廟上有四、五十個和尚，有的時候二、三十，有的時候十幾個，有的時候三、四十，也不一定。我到廟上出家，那時方丈和尚沒有在廟上，其他人也沒有人認識我。方丈可能到外面化緣去了，廟上那些和尚，就把我留在廟上出家。我説：「我認識方丈和尚。」大家都很高興的，很歡迎。出家以後，就要做什麼呢？要做苦行。我做的苦行和你們的不同，你們只是打打字、念念經啦，或者是其他的工作。那廟是很大一個鄉下的廟，有很多工作；掃廟的院子，也要掃一個鐘頭才能掃完。我在廟上收拾廁所、洗廁所，這是我第一個工作。但是那廁所不是現在這種的廁所，那種是在地下挖個坑，然後把它拿出來放到一邊去，那種味道很「香」的，因為修道人不願意聞香味，所以把這個糞搬到另外一個地方去。這個工作是由我來做，因為我是初發心，對於這個香塵還沒有斷，所以天天收拾這個工作，也都不太討厭。

在廟上我要做種種的工作，譬如燒飯、掃地，煲茶水、作菜，收拾廁所、倒痰罐；沒有人做的事情，都由我來做。下雪的時候，我就會早一點把路都打掃乾淨，方便大家上殿。平時人家沒起身，我就先起身；好像人四點鐘起身，我在兩點鐘就起來，把有雪的地方都收拾乾淨；等其他人起身做早課時，就沒有雪了，這是我的工作，可是做了很久，也沒有人知道。

雖然小的時候我是尚武善鬥，歡喜和人打架，但是當我出家之後，盡被人家打啊、罵啊，常常是受氣的。到什麼地方，誰也看不起我，就一點什麼能力也沒有，就這麼樣一個人。我在廟上，師兄弟都欺負我，罵我，有的時候還打我。等到方丈和尚過了一個時期回來，回來一見到我，他説：「啊！你來了。」我説：「我來了。」出家以後，他就和大家開會，要在廟上選首座和尚。首座和尚就是除了方丈和尚，就是首座，等方丈退位了，就首座做和尚、做方丈。那麼有幾十個和尚，方丈和尚誰他也不選，他要選我來做首座和尚。問大家，大家都反對，説：「他一個剛出家的，怎麼可以做首座和尚呢？」方丈和尚説：「那

ones you practice. You type, recite Sutras, and so forth, but in the big rural temple where I lived, there was a lot of outside work to be done. Sweeping the courtyard alone took an hour. My first job was to clean the toilets, which weren't flush toilets, but pit toilets, and every day the waste had to be removed because the cultivators did not want to smell the odor. They gave this work to me because I had just left home and had not yet cut off my attachment to smells. I did it every day and didn't mind it too much.

I did various chores at the temple, such as sweeping. When it snowed I got up before everyone else at two o'clock and swept the walkways so that they were clear at four when everyone else got up to go to the Buddha hall and recite Sutras. I did this work for a long time without anyone else knowing.

Although I had loved to fight with people as a child, after leaving home I was often beaten, scolded, and bullied by others. Everyone looked down on me, thinking I was totally incapable. The other monks at the temple took advantage of me, scolded me, and even struck me at times.

When the Abbot returned and saw me he said, "So you have come!"

Yes," I said, "I have."

After I had formally left home, he called a meeting, wishing to elect a head monk, a position second only to the Abbot. When the Abbot retires, the head monk becomes the new Abbot. Among the several dozen monks, the Abbot wanted to choose me. Everyone objected, "He has just left home. How can he be the head monk?"

"Very well," said the Abbot. "Let's go before the image of Weitou Bodhisattva and draw names." Oddly enough (Weitou Bodhisattva must have wanted to give me some work to do), they drew three times and my name came up each time. No one said a word because I had been elected by Weitou Bodhisattva himself. At that time I was still a novice monk.

Later, when the Abbot wanted to make me a manager, I thought, "It's too much trouble. If he tells me to do it, I won't touch money. How will he expect me to be the manager then?" So I said, "All right, but I will not touch money. Other people must handle and count it. That is my condition." That's how I started holding the precept of not touching money.

Unusual things happened when I held this precept. Whenever I went to the train station near the temple, I didn't bring money to buy a ticket, because I couldn't hold money. I would sit and wait for someone who knew me to come and offer to buy me a ticket. If no one came I just waited, but strangely enough, whenever I went to the station, someone would come and ask me where I wanted to go and then buy me a ticket. And so in Manchuria there

我們在韋陀菩薩前，大家來抽籤。」就求籤，寫上幾個人的名字，誰有資格做首座就寫上，到那個籤筒裏搖，搖出來看是誰的名字，就是誰。搖了幾次，哎呀！很奇怪！這大約是韋陀菩薩他要給我找一點工作，搖了三次，都是我的名字跳出來。大家也不敢反對了，這韋陀菩薩安排的；所以我在廟上就做首座，那時我還是沙彌。做首座以後呢，方丈和尚又想教我當家，當家就是做boss（老闆）之類的。我一想：「這個太麻煩了，好了！你教我當家，我不拿錢，你看這個家怎麼當法？」所以他教我當家，我說：「可以的。但是我不拿錢，旁人拿錢旁人數，我無論到什麼地方，我都不拿錢的，我當這麼個家就可以。」這樣子呢，就持銀錢戒囉！

持銀錢戒，很奇怪的，我出門多數是自己出去，去搭火車。廟上離火車站很近的，沒有巴士，有火車站。搭火車要買票的；你要拿錢買票，這也是拿錢了。我就到那兒等著，我到什麼地方去，我在火車站那兒等著，看有熟人來，他就給我買票，我就去；沒有熟人來，我就在那兒等。但是很奇怪的，每逢我到什麼地方去，在火車站等火車，一定有人來給我買票的，問我到什麼地方去，然後就給我買票。所以我在東北，有一段的時期和錢分開家，我手裏不摸這個錢。

我在十九歲時，那時候我還是做沙彌呢！就有很多人要皈依我。為什麼要皈依我呢？他們看我好像和一般人不一樣似的。在冬天的時候，我也不穿鞋，也不穿襪子，在那雪地上走，不管它凍不凍。冬天、夏天都穿著三層布，不穿棉衣服。一般人看見天氣零下三十四、五度，也凍不死這個人，認為這是很特別了，於是乎就很多人都皈依我。我本來不願意收，但是他們又很誠懇的，跪在我面前，幾個鐘頭那麼跪著。我記得在東北有一個關忠喜，他住在貝因河旁邊，這地方接近山，所以他生來這個膝蓋就很大的。他是一個外道的老師，什麼外道呢？就是一個收元道的老師，他的徒弟有三千多。那麼入他這個道呢，要花很多錢，為什麼要花錢呢？他有很多寶貝，每一個寶貝賣一千塊錢；他有幾百個寶貝，就賣幾萬塊錢。什麼寶貝呢？他這個寶貝只有個名字，但是你看不見這個寶貝，怎麼說呢？他說：「這沒有到時候，這寶貝也不能交給你；等到時候，這個世界變了，那個寶貝就給你了，給你，你就可以用了。」他三、四千個徒弟都很相信他，他這時大約有五十多歲了。

有一天，他知道這騙人的事情靠不住，連他也沒有寶貝來保護自己的生命，他知道自己離死這條路很近了，很接近死的時候。他怕臨死的時候不懂修道，就會手忙腳亂，於是乎就發心各處去求道。在東北那個地方旁門外道很多

was a short period during which money and I parted company. I didn't touch money.

When I was nineteen and still a novice, many people in Manchuria wanted to take refuge with me. Why? They saw that I was different from ordinary people. I walked barefoot in the snow in wintertime, and I wore only three layers of cloth all year round and never wore padded clothing. People saw that I could do this without freezing even when the temperature dropped to 34 or 35 degrees below zero, and so they wanted to take refuge with me.

I didn't want to accept them as disciples, but they were extremely sincere and knelt in front of me for several hours without getting up. I remember a non-Buddhist teacher named Guan Zhongxi who lived by Beiyin River in Manchuria. He had large knees characteristic of people living near the mountains. His religion was called the Shouyuan Sect, and he had over three thousand disciples. One had to pay a considerable sum to join his religion. Why was that? He had hundreds of treasures for sale at a thousand dollars each. What kind of treasures were they? The treasures existed in name only, and he would explain, "The time is not right and so I can't give them to you now. When the time comes, the world will change and you will have your treasures." His three or four thousand disciples all had great faith in him. He was over fifty years old then.

Later, he knew that he could not rely on his business of cheating people. He didn't have any treasures to protect his own life. Knowing that the time of his own death was approaching, he was afraid that without understanding how to cultivate the Way, he would die in panic and confusion. Therefore, he went to pay visits all around. Whenever he heard that a person had attained the Way, he would call on that person no matter how far away he was, and request instruction on cultivating the Way. Taking his nephew Guan Zhanhai with him, he went around visiting for three years. His surname Guan is the same as that of the warrior Lord Guan, so he is probably Lord Guan's descendant. After three years, he still had not discovered the Way, and was very anxious. Every day he thought, "Alas, death is upon me, and I still don't understand how to cultivate. This is terrible!" His nephew planned to remain single and follow him to cultivate. So the two of them became fanatics of the Way.

One day, I went to his home. Strange to say, before I went there, Guan Zhanhai had a dream. In his dream, I had already come to his home and was sitting on his brick bed. He knelt in front of me and begged me to teach him to cultivate the Way. In the dream, he saw me peel a layer of skin from his body, tearing it off with both hands and throwing it on the ground. It was the skin of a pig. He thought, "How could I have a layer of pig skin on my body?" In the dream, he heard me say, "You aren't

，又是收元道、又是玉盧門、又是如意門，多得很，講不出來那麼多。我告訴你，所有的外道我都參加過。這個人呢，他也各處去訪道，參訪善知識。他聽某一個人有道，就算離得很遠他也會去拜訪這個人，向他求道。他很誠心的，一訪訪了三年，身邊帶著一個姪子，叫關占海，訪了三年呢，也沒有訪到道，就很憂愁，天天都在那兒想：「啊！就快死了，還不懂得修行，這是最壞的一件事。」他的姪子也不預備結婚，就預備和他一起修道，就跟著他，兩個人都變成「道迷子」，被這個道迷住了。

有一天，我到他家裏去，很奇怪的，關占海那時候大約是二十一、二歲的樣子，在我沒去之前，他就做了一個夢。做什麼夢呢？他夢到我去他家，坐在炕上，他和叔叔就跪到我面前，請我教他們怎麼樣修道。在這個夢中他就覺得，我在他身上，從頭頂這麼一剝，就剝下一張皮來。這張皮剝下來之後，用兩手這麼一扯，扯下來就放在地上。他一看，這張皮是什麼皮呢？原來是豬皮！他就說：「我身上怎麼有一張豬皮呢？」在夢中他就聽我說：「你不吃齋，你盡吃豬肉，將來就會有個豬皮披到身上了。」這麼樣子，他就很害怕的，「噢！做豬又骯髒，又……，有什麼用呢？」於是乎就醒了。第二天，很奇怪的，我就到他家裡了，他不認識我，但是在夢中他見著了，他就問他叔叔，說：「你認識這個人嗎？」他叔叔說：「我認識，他沒有守孝以前我就認識。他守孝之後，我沒有見過，但是我可認識他。」他就對他叔叔講了，說：「昨天晚間我做惡夢，夢見這個人到我們家裡來了，今天他真來了！」他叔叔說：「真的嗎？你做什麼夢？」他就對他叔叔一講，說怎麼樣子夢到我給他剝下一張豬皮來，他跪到我面前來求道。他叔叔說：「噢！他是個有道的人哪，把道送到我們家裡來了！我們兩個人一定要向他求道。」兩個人這麼互相你對我講一講，我對你講講，講完了，兩個人就到我坐的那房裡，把門關上，不叫他家裡人進來，兩個人到我面前就跪下了，跪下就向我求道。我說：「你不要發神經病了，你向我求什麼道？我有什麼道？我的道就是吃飯、睡覺，沒有旁的。我和你是一樣的，我不懂道。」他說：「噢！我知道你守孝。」因為他叔叔知道我守孝，在我母親墓上修道，他想去見我，總也沒有時間見，但是他認識我，知道是我。說：「這一回你到我們家裡來，給送道來了，我的姪子昨天晚間就做夢，夢見你給他剝下一張豬皮。」我說：「你盡胡說八道，我怎麼會給他剝下一張豬皮，他也不是個豬！」他說：「真的！無論如何你要教我們修行了。」我說：「我不會教你們修行

vegetarian, and you eat pork. In the future you will have a pig skin on your back." He was scared stiff and said to me, "Oh no! Pigs are filthy and useless!" Then he woke up.

When I showed up at his house the next day, the nephew asked his uncle, "Do you recognize that monk?" His uncle said, "Yes, I knew him before he practiced filial piety beside the grave." Then the nephew said, "Last night I dreamed that this person came to our house, and now he is actually here."

His uncle was excited. "Really?" he said. "What did you dream?" After he related the dream, his uncle said, "This person has the Way and he has brought it to our house. The two of us must certainly seek the Way from him." After talking, they went into the room where I was sitting, closed the door, and knelt before me to request the Way.

"Have you both gone insane? I said. "What do you want from me? I'm just the same as you. I don't understand the Way."

"We know you cultivate filial piety," they said. The uncle, who knew that I had cultivated filial piety beside my mother's grave, had wanted to meet me, but had never found the time. He said, "We know you have brought the Way to our home, for my nephew had a dream last night. In the dream, you peeled a pig skin off his body."

"You're confused," I said. "He's not a pig. How could I peel a pig skin off him?"

"But it's true," he said, "and no matter what, you have to teach us how to cultivate!"

"I can't teach you to cultivate, but if you want to find a teacher, I can help you look."

"We've looked everywhere, but we haven't found one. Wherever we go it's always the same. They all have a big reputation, but no genuine skill."

"I can take you around," I said. They had wanted to bow to me as their teacher, but I didn't know if they really had faith in me. I never did anything casually.

I took them to meet Great Master Chang Ren and many other great cultivators. But after meeting with them, they were always dissatisfied. After sending them everywhere for two years, they still insisted on taking me as their teacher. But I was still a novice monk and did not want to take disciples. Finally, they knelt before me and refused to get up. "It's useless to talk about whether or not I have the Way," I said. "First learn to sit in full lotus and then I will teach you."

Then I taught them to sit in lotus posture. I instructed them to sit with their backs erect, not leaning to the front or back, or letting the head droop, but sitting with determination and resolve. They practiced sitting every day.

The nephew had no trouble, but the uncle's bones were old and he had big kneecaps, which stuck up about fifteen inches in the air when he tried to sit cross-legged. But the uncle kept trying. He pushed his knees down over and over.

，你若想找師父呢，我可以幫忙介紹你認識多一點善知識，你看哪一個善知識有道呢，你就向他求道好了。」他說：「我們各處找，找了三年，也沒有找著，到哪個地方，都是光有個名，真功夫沒有。」我說：「我可以帶你們去。」他本來想拜我做師父，我也不知道他們是真的、是假的；是真相信我，是假相信我，是試驗我？我做事情也不是隨隨便便做的。

我就帶他們去見常仁大師，見很多這些修行的高人，見著，一談話，他就覺得不滿意。我又帶他各處訪道，訪了有兩年，他也不滿意，到什麼地方他也不皈依，也不拜師父，然後叔姪兩個一定要拜我做師父。我那時候，我還是沙彌呢！我不想收徒弟，兩個人就跪到我面前不起來。以後我就教關忠喜結雙跏趺坐，我說：「你不用講我有道沒有道，在沒有見到善知識以前，我先教你一個用功的方法。什麼呢？你就先練習雙跏趺坐，你把這個坐修好了，練得不痛了，我再來教你。」

這個時候，我就教他怎麼樣結上雙跏趺坐，在坐的時候怎麼樣一個姿勢，要端然正坐，也不前仰，也不後仰，也不低著頭，要把頭直起來，不要像沒有骨頭的樣子，這個腰骨要挺起來，這個表示自己有一種志氣。教他之後，他果然依照這個法來修行，天天就練雙跏趺坐。

他的姪子可以坐，但是他因為骨頭老了，膝蓋上這地方有一個大骨頭節，他坐著，這腿就不能貼床上，這樣支起了一尺多高。他天天就這麼揉，用手這麼揉來揉去，揉、揉……，等到七十多天吧，我又到他家裡去了。去一看他，怎麼樣啊？他本來是膝蓋大的，現在這膝蓋腫得有兩、三個膝蓋那麼大，腫得很大，也不能走路了。我說：「你怎麼搞的？你現在還有沒有坐啊？」他說：「我有坐啊，我就練習這個雙跏趺坐，把腿練得胖得這麼大，現在也不能走路了，連這個車轍都不能邁過去，連這個門檻子也不能邁了！」我說：「哦！你這樣子，那不要練習這個坐囉！你這麼樣子太痛苦囉！」你猜他說什麼？「不要練？我就快死了，我若不練，我死的時候怎麼辦哪？我現在就寧可我這個腿腫了，它怎麼樣子我都要練，除非死，那我就不管了，不然我就一定要練這個坐。我現在發願，一定要把這個雙跏趺坐練好它！」我說：「你這個腿這樣子，你是受不了的。」「受不了？受不了，才要受呢！」我聽他說這話，啊！有點門路了。我就說：「那好囉，你不怕死，你就練習囉！」然後我就走了。

走了，到一百天的時候，我又到他家裡去了，一看他，這回走路，腿也消了，也不腫了。我就問他，我說：「怎麼樣？你現在是不是不練習這個坐啦？」他說：「

When I returned after seventy days, I noticed that his knees were swollen. They were so sore, in fact, that he couldn't even step over a cart rut.

"You shouldn't sit in full lotus," I told him. "Are you still practicing?"

"I am," said the uncle. "My knees are swollen, but I can sit in full lotus."

"You shouldn't continue," I told him. "You won't be able to bear it."

"What do you mean?" said the uncle. "I'm about to die and if I don't practice now, what will I do then? No matter what, I'm going to practice meditation. If I die, that's another matter, but as long as I'm still alive, I'm going to practice."

"Do what you like," I said, and left. When I returned a hundred days later, I noticed that the uncle's legs were no longer swollen. "You're not still sitting, are you?" I asked.

Guan Zhongxi smiled. "I can sit in full lotus," he said, "and no matter how long I sit, it doesn't hurt and my legs don't swell." Then I taught him how to apply effort in meditation. The uncle was incredibly happy and sat in meditation every day. After cultivating for three years, about three months before his death, he gathered his family together and said, "On such and such a day, at such and such a time, I'm going to leave; I'm going to die. The only wish I have is to see my teacher once again. But I don't know where he is now, and so I cannot see him." Then on the appointed day, he sat upright in full lotus, and without any illness, he died. That evening, many of the villagers had the same dream; they dreamed that they saw the uncle accompanied by two youths in dark robes, being taken to the West.

The uncle, originally a non-Buddhist, later studied the Proper Dharma and cultivated without fear of pain or suffering. Even if he died, he wanted to practice meditation, and so eventually he had some accomplishment. If he had stopped practicing when his legs swelled up, I don't think he would have accomplished what he did. Cultivators have to suffer for a time before they can realize infinite happiness. If you can't bear suffering temporarily, you can't attain eternal bliss. Guan Zhongxi is a good model for all of us. If we wish to obtain true samadhi and wisdom, to obtain eternal bliss, we must first undergo a period of suffering.

Well, the nephew didn't die, and one day as we were walking down the road, he suddenly knelt, clutched my sleeve, and begged to become a disciple. I said, "I have no cultivation. What's the point of taking refuge with me?" He said, "I'm determined to take refuge with you, no matter what." I brushed him off and left. After walking about a mile, I turned around and saw the boy still kneeling. I returned and saw that he was crying, and so I felt compelled to accept him as a disciple. He was my first disciple. He was truly filial and always thinking of his teacher.

我現在這個坐可成功了！坐多久也不痛了，這個腿也不腫了。你來過之後，以後我再結雙跏趺坐，一點一點這腫就消了，也不痛了，所以現在坐得很好。」我說那這回好了，我就教他一個修行的方法，就是參禪怎麼樣用功，怎麼樣打坐，教他這種的功夫。噢！他高興得不得了，以後在家裡天天都修行打坐。修了大約有三年吧，等他臨終的時候，他預先在三個多月以前就知道了，就告訴他家人說：「某月某日某時我要走了，現在我唯一心裡覺得放不下的，就是沒有見到師父，我若能見一見師父，那是最好，我最高興了。可惜他現在不知在什麼地方？我也見不著他，在什麼時候我就要走了。」那麼到時候他就結上雙跏趺坐，也沒什麼病痛就走了。在他走的這天晚間呢，村裡頭很多人都做夢，夢見有兩個穿青衣服的童子，帶著他往西方去了。

這一個人呢，他本來是個外道，他知道要求正法，以後能不怕苦，不怕痛，腿腫了，他寧可死，他也要修行，要練習打坐，結果他有所成就。假如那時候，他腿腫，就不去練習，相信他就不會有所成就。所以我們修道的人要忍一時的痛苦，才能成就無窮的快樂。你若是不忍暫時的痛苦，那永久的快樂，你也得不到。關忠喜他這種行為可以做我們一個榜樣，我們若想真正得到定，得到智慧，一定要犧牲一時的痛苦，成就永遠的快樂。

以後他姪子沒有死，有一天我們走到路上，他就把我這個袖子給抓住了，抓住就跪在我面前，要求要皈依我。我說：「我也沒有什麼修行，你皈依我，這算是怎麼一回事？」他說：「無論怎麼樣，我就要皈依。」我把袖子一甩，就走了，也不看他，也不睬他。我走了之後，那麼走大約有一個mile這麼遠，回頭看看，他還在那兒跪著。這時候我心裏頭覺得：「嗯！回去看看他，他究竟在那兒幹什麼？」回去一看，他跪在那兒哭，我就勉強收他做我的皈依弟子，這是我第一個徒弟。這個徒弟對我最孝順不過，他常常無論什麼事情都很掛著師父

所以以後我就發願，我說我因為沒有什麼道德，不配做人的師表，可是竟有這樣誠心的人，來要皈依我。我就發了一個可以說是不大不小的願。這個願就是說凡是皈依我的人，他若不成佛嘛，我自己也不成佛，我要等著他。這是我一念的真心，對我的皈依弟子，是這樣子，究竟你們皈依我之後，你們對師父怎麼樣，那我不計較。總而言之，你們要是能依教奉行，你們將來一定有成佛的機會。今天我把我發這個願的緣起，對你們各位說一說。所以你們各位皈依我之後，一定要修行，努力向前，勇猛精進，不要躲懶偷安，好逸惡勞，要改惡向善，改過自新，向這個菩提路上勇猛精進；你們若不修

Later I made a vow, because while I had no virtue and was not worthy of being a teacher of others, there were people who sincerely requested to take refuge with me. My vow was neither great nor small. I vowed that if any being who has taken refuge with me--whether human or nonhuman, or a god, dragon, or member of the eightfold division--has not become a Buddha, I will not become a Buddha. I will wait for him or her. This shows my sincerity towards my disciples. How they treat me after taking refuge is of no concern to me. In general, if you practice in accord with the teachings, you will definitely have the chance to become a Buddha. Why did I make such a vow? I feel that if someone takes refuge with me and I fail to help him realize Buddhahood, I have not done my job and am not worthy to be his teacher; I am not even fit to be his disciple. Today I have told you the reasons I made this vow. After you take refuge with me, you must certainly advance vigorously in your practice. Don't be lax and lazy. Change your faults, reform yourselves, and proceed forward on the Bodhi path. If you fail to cultivate, you will delay your teacher from attaining Buddhahood.

After I failed to start a revolution in my youth, I left the home-life and later went around curing people's illnesses. Although I had studied the texts on Chinese medicine, I didn't use my medical knowledge to cure disease. I relied instead on the Shurangama Mantra and the Great Compassion Mantra. I used the Forty-two Hands and Eyes in the Great Compassion Mantra and the thirty-two dharmas in the Shurangama Mantra to subdue the heavenly demons and those of outside ways. I used the power of samadhi to capture and overcome those demonic and weird creatures. In this life alone, I have encountered countless demonic beings who transformationally appear in human form. When most people hear this, they don't believe it because they aren't aware of these strange and mysterious phenomena.

I remember there was a time in Manchuria when the Japanese had surrendered, but the Nationalist government had not officially taken power in Harbin, nor had the Communist party completely occupied Manchuria. Many demons, ghosts, and weird creatures appeared in the world at that time. These demonic beings had remained in hiding and had not dared to be so wild when we had a government. But during the period when we had no government, these demonic beings all came out of hiding. I remember one of the most important demons I met at that time was a several thousand year old demon. I will tell you her story now, but don't be afraid. She doesn't harm people anymore.

It is said that this big demon leader was a ghost in the Zhou dynasty, which was several thousand years ago. Since I haven't studied history very thoroughly, I'm not sure if it was three or four thousand years ago. This "As-you-will Demon Woman" did nothing but harm people back in the Zhou dynasty. She did things that transgressed the laws of heaven. Later a person who had spiritual powers shattered

行，那把師父都給耽誤得不成佛了。

　　我年輕的時候，因爲創革命創不成，就出家了，以後就各處給人治病。我雖然念過醫書，可是我給人治病，我不用醫書，那時就憑〈楞嚴咒〉、〈大悲咒〉。〈大悲咒〉上有四十二手，〈楞嚴咒〉有三十二套法，我用這個法來降伏天魔、制諸外道，這是一種三昧的功夫、定力，專門降妖捉怪的。我這一生，變化人形的妖怪，我遇到不知多少，你一般人聽起來，都不會相信的，不知道這個東西這麼奇怪，這樣微妙。我記得在東北的時候，那時候正是日本人投降了，國民政府也沒有正式接收哈爾濱，那麼共產黨也沒有完全接收，有的地方接收了，有的地方沒有接收，就在這個時候，妖魔鬼怪都出世了。我們有政府的時候，妖魔鬼怪他都遁形了，沒有那麼瘋狂；沒有政府的時代，妖魔鬼怪都出世了。我記得當時最要緊的，我遇到一個幾千年的魔，我對你們各位講講，你們各位不要害怕，我先說清楚，這個大魔她現在不會害人了。

　　這大魔頭據說是周朝時代的一個鬼，周朝到現在已經幾千年了，我因爲對歷史沒有什麼研究，所以不知道是三千年？是四千年？不知道。這個如意魔女，她在周朝的時候，就專門害人，做一些犯天條的事情，以後就被有神通的人，用雷把她劈碎了。那麼雷劈了她，但是沒有完全把她消滅了，這個魔本來是個鬼怪，以後她自己又修煉，就聚精會神把所散的這種靈氣又聚集到一起，修成一種魔術，就變成一個魔，雷也沒有法子打她了。當時因爲沒有政府，她就出來各處去作怪，各處去要人的命。爲什麼魔要人的命呢？就是因爲要增加自己的勢力和眷屬的勢力。每逢這個魔魔死一個人，其餘的魔就來恭賀他說：「你眞有本事！」就像我們作官的，陞官似的，就那樣子。因爲魔多殺一個人，就增加一種勢力，這個鬼的勢力也聽魔招呼的。這個如意魔女她已經害過九十九個人，她如果能抓到一百個人的靈魂，就是害死一百個人，她在魔王裏頭呢，就是勢力最大的，一切的魔民、魔子、魔孫都要聽她的號令了，她做魔王的首領，被她捉去那些靈魂都做她的眷屬，都聽她的招呼。現在九十九個，就差一個，因爲這樣子，所以她各處去找人，就想要害人。等以後遇到我，她也皈依三寶，改邪歸正了，這也是魔皈依佛的一個例證。這個要是說起來啊，可以寫一本書的。

　　在二十七年以前，大約是在中華民國三十四年（西元一九四五年）二月十二這一天，我在東北周家棧這個地方，有一個「道德會」。道德會，就是講道德的地方，天天都講演。這個會上有我幾個皈依弟子，所以每逢從

her with thunder, but didn't completely destroy her. She had been a ghost before, but then she cultivated and gathered her scattered energy and spirit back together, perfected her demonic skills, and turned into a demon that was invulnerable to thunder. In the interval when there was no government, she went around causing trouble and taking people's lives, because she wanted to increase her power and the power of her retinue. Each time she caused a person's death, the other demons would congratulate her: "You're really powerful!" It's similar to how other officials act toward an official who has just been promoted. A demon's power increases with the number of people it kills, until even ghosts have to follow its orders.

The "As-you-will Demon Woman" had killed ninety-nine people by then, and if she could capture the soul of one more person--killing a hundred people in all--she would become the most powerful demon king, and all the common demons would have to listen to her orders. She would be the leading demon, and all the souls she had captured would become her retinue and would have to obey her. She lacked only one more soul, so she went around looking for a victim. Later when she met me, she took refuge with the Triple Jewel and reformed herself. Thus she's an example of a demon who took refuge with the Buddha. I could write an entire book on this.

Twenty-seven years ago [1945], on the twelfth day of the second month, I passed through the Zhou family station in Manchuria. In the town there was a Virtue Society whose members met daily for lectures on morality. Since some of the members were my disciples, I would usually stay in the town for a few days when I passed through.

This time I met a Chinese astrologer who cast people's horoscopes by looking at the eight characters (two for the year, two for the month, two for the day, and two for the hour) of their birth. His horoscopes were very efficacious. He cast my horoscope and said, "You should be an official. Why have you left home? Had you wanted to, you could have been a great official."

"I haven't any idea how to be an official," I said. "But I do know how to be a Buddhist monk, and so I have left home."

"What a pity," said the astrologer, and he looked at my hands. "At the very least," he said, "you could have been a top-ranking imperial scholar."

"No," I said. "I couldn't even have come in last."

He looked my hands again and said, "Oh, this year something very lucky will happen to change your life!"

"What could that be?" I asked.

"After the tenth of the next month you will be different from now," he replied.

"Different in what way?"

"Right now, all the people within 1000 *li* [350 miles] believe in you, but after the tenth of next month, everyone

那兒經過的時候，我就到那地方住幾天。

住幾天就遇到一個不知姓什麼的批八字的先生。怎麼叫批八字呢？就是你年上兩個字，月上有兩個字，日上有兩個字，時上又有兩個字。他給人批八字批得很靈的，我就請他給我批一批囉！我把我的八字告訴他了，他就給我批，他說：「喔！你啊！應該去作官去，怎麼來出家了呢？你若作官，會做很大的官。」我說：「官怎麼樣做呢？我都不會，也不知道怎麼樣作官，怎麼可以做呢？我會做和尚，所以我現在出家。」他說這個太可惜了。這是在周家棧，這個批命的他這麼給我批。

然後又看我的手，他說：「噢！你這個手，最低限度，你可以中一個頭名狀元。」我說：「現在我連最後那一名都中不了了，還中頭名？」然後他又細看說：「哦，你啊！今年是走運了！今年你有吉祥的事情。」我說：「有什麼吉祥的事情呢？」他說：「你過下個月初十，你就和現在不同了。」我說：「怎麼樣不同法呢？」

他說：「以前一千里地以內的人相信你，過了初十之後，一萬里地以內的人就都相信你了。」我說：「這個怎麼會這樣子呢？」他說：「到時候你就知道了！」說完了這話，我又住了兩天。

大約是二月十四、十五的樣子，我就到那個鑲白旗四屯。鑲白旗四屯有我的皈依弟子，他叫夏遵祥，他那年已經六十多歲了。他家裏有三十多口人，種了很多地，可以說是個財主。在那一個鄉下，他是最有錢的。這個老人從來也不相信佛，什麼都不相信，等見著我來了，他就相信，要皈依。不單他一個人要皈依，全家都要皈依，所以他全家就都皈依我。以後我每逢到那個地方，就到他家裏去住。他家裏三十多口人，我一去，都高興得不得了。在那兒住了大約有十天的樣子，就又有七、八十人都皈依，大約是七十二個人也都來皈依。

皈依之後，等到二十五這天，我就坐著夏遵祥他家裏的車到雙城縣去，他家裏離雙城縣有七十多里路。這車要一早起三點多鐘就開始走。這時候雖然說三月間，正是冷的時候，冷得不得了。這個趕車的人和跟車的人都要穿著皮衣、皮襖、皮褲，戴著皮帽子。我呢，那時候是很窮的，穿的衣服就三層布，這一個衲袍是三層布，穿的褲子也是兩層布的褲子——夾褲；穿鞋是穿鞋，沒有穿襪子，就穿羅漢鞋，有窟窿的那種鞋。一早這車就走了，我坐在車上邊，戴著個帽子，也遮不住耳朵。那是一個合掌巾，那種帽子就好像人合著掌那個樣子的，你們看見濟公戴的那個帽子，就那個樣子的。

坐在車上，七十里路，從三點鐘大約坐到一早七點鐘吧！到了城裏了，天也光了。這趕車的老闆和跟著車的

within 10,000 *li* [3500 miles] will believe in you."

"How can that be?" I asked.

"When the time comes, you will know," he said.

Two days later, on the fourteenth or fifteenth of the second month, I went to the village of Xiangbaichi, fourth district, and stayed with my disciple Xia Zunxiang, who was over sixty years old and had a family of over thirty people. He was one of the richest landowners in the area and had never believed in Buddhism or anything else. But when he saw me, he believed in me and wanted to take refuge with me. He and his whole family took refuge, and every time I went to the village I'd stay at his house. His family of over thirty was extremely happy to see me this time. I stayed with them for ten days, and about seventy-two people came to take refuge.

On the twenty-fifth, I set out in Mr. Xia's cart for Shuangcheng County. Since it was over seventy *li* [25 miles] away, we left at three o'clock in the morning.

Although it was early spring, the weather was bitter cold. The driver and the attendant were dressed in fur coats, trousers, and hats. Being very poor, I wore only my usual rag robe made of three layers of thin cotton cloth, trousers made of two layers of cloth, open Arhat sandals with no socks, and a hat shaped like folded palms that didn't cover my ears. That was the kind of hat that Master Ji Gong wore.

We rode from three in the morning until dawn, reaching the city at seven in the morning. The driver and the attendant thought I would freeze to death, since I was so insufficiently dressed. They had stopped repeatedly to exercise and keep warm, but I had remained in the cart from the beginning of the trip. When we arrived at the eastern gate of Shuangcheng County and I got out of the cart, the driver exclaimed, "Oh, we thought surely you had frozen to death!"

I stayed with friends, Dharma protecting laymen, for more than ten days, and on the ninth of the third month, I returned to Xia Zunxiang's home in Xiangbaichi. When I arrived, he told me that one of my recent disciples, the daughter of Xia Wenshan, had fallen dangerously ill. She hadn't eaten or drunk water for six or seven days. She did not speak, and she looked fiercely angry, as if she wanted to beat people.

Then her mother came. "Master," she said, "my daughter became very ill a few days after taking refuge. She won't talk, eat, or drink, but just glares and sticks her head on the bed. She doesn't sleep either. I don't know what illness she has."

At that time I was with Han Gangji, who was able to look into people's past lives and could know their causes and effects. I said to the mother, "I can't cure her, so it's useless to ask me. However, my disciple Han Gangji has opened his five eyes and knows people's past, present, and future affairs. You should ask him."

Han Gangji had also taken refuge on the twenty-fifth of

人心裏想，一定會把我凍死在車上，因為穿的衣服也少，又在這車上。他們都坐坐車，下來跑一跑，因為不跑就凍得不得了，一定要下來活動活動。我在車上，由一出門口，就坐在車上，沒有下來。到雙城縣的東門外，把車停住了，我從車上下來。這個趕車的一看：「哦！還沒有凍死他！」他以為我一定會凍死。

二十五這天我到雙城縣，那裏有一些個善友，有一些個護法居士，我到他們家裏去，也住了十多天。等三月初八又回到鑲白旗四屯，到夏遵祥的家裏。他就告訴我了，他說有一個夏文山，他有一個女兒，就是在我打皈依的時候一起皈依的，她最近有病了，病得很厲害，六、七天不吃東西、不喝水，也不講話，就很大的脾氣，發脾氣要打人的樣子。他沒說有個老太太來過。等到初九這一天，她的母親聽說我回來了，就來找我，對我講，說：「師父啊！我這個女兒皈依之後沒過幾天，就病了。病得很厲害，她也不講話，也不吃東西，也不喝水，天天都瞪著眼睛，把頭紮到炕上，屁股撅起來，也不睡覺，不知道她這是個什麼病？」

當時就有一位叫韓崗吉，這韓崗吉他有宿命通，能看前因後果，人一切的因果循環報應，他都知道，他也在旁邊。我就對她講，我說：「我也不會給人治病，她什麼病，你問我是不行的。現在我有皈依弟子叫韓崗吉，他是開五眼的，能知道人的過去未來，前生是怎麼回事，他也知道；你今生什麼事情，他也知道，你問他去。」她就問這個韓崗吉。

這韓崗吉也是在我到雙城縣，二十五號以前的時候皈依的。他皈依的時候，本來我不收他，為什麼不收他呢？因為在我沒出家以前，他和我是很好的朋友，在道德會上是同事。因為他開眼了，我出家之後，他見到我，他開眼一看，他說：「原來你生生世世都是我的師父來著！」所以就要皈依我。我說：「我不能收你做徒弟，我們本來都是老朋友來著，我怎麼可以收你做徒弟呢？」他說：「不是，我自己現在知道我自己……。」他說如果我不收他皈依，這一生他就要墮落了。說這話之後，他就跪在地上不起來，一定要皈依。我就一定不收他。經過大約有半點多鐘，時間不太長。我就問他，我說：「皈依我的人，都要依教奉行，你現在這麼大的本事，又知道過去，又知道未來，又知道現在，你知道是知道，你會不會有一種貢高的心，不聽師父的教訓？」他說他一定會聽的：「師父！你教我赴湯我就赴湯，教我蹈火就蹈火。赴湯蹈火，在所不辭！」就是到了滾水裏頭去，那有一鍋滾水，師父你教我去，我就跳到那滾水裏去，煮熟了也不要緊，這叫赴湯。蹈火，那有一堆火

the second month. At first I had refused to take him as a disciple, because before I had left home, the two of us had been good friends and had worked together in the Virtue Society. After I left home and Han Gangji opened his five eyes, he saw that, life after life, I had always been his teacher. And so he wanted to take refuge with me.

I said, "We're good friends; how could I take you as a disciple?"

"But if I don't take refuge with you, I shall certainly fall in this life," Han Gangji said, and he knelt on the ground and refused to get up.

I was just as determined not to accept him, but after perhaps half an hour, I finally said, "Those who take refuge with me must follow instructions. You have talent; you know the past, present, and future. Is it possible that it has caused you to become arrogant? Will your pride prevent you from obeying my instructions?"

"Master," he said, "I'll certainly obey. If you tell me to throw myself into a cauldron of boiling water, I'll do it. If you tell me to walk on fire, I'll walk. If I get boiled or burned to death, that's all right."

"You'd better be telling the truth," I said. "If I give you instructions, you can't ignore them."

"No matter what it is," he said, "if you tell me to do it, I will do it, and fear no danger whatsoever."

And so Han Gangji was one of the seventy-two people who took refuge on the twenty-fifth.

Hearing that one of my disciples was sick, I told Han Gangji, "You can see people's causes and effects, and you know how to diagnose illnesses. Now my disciple is sick. Take a look at her."

Han Gangji sat in meditation and made a contemplative examination of the illness. Suddenly his face blanched with terror. "Master," he said, "we can't handle this one. It's beyond our control."

"What do you mean?" I asked.

"There's no way we can subdue this demon," he said.

"What kind of demon is it?" I asked.

"The demon who is causing the illness is extremely violent and can assume human form to bring chaos into the world and injury to humankind."

"What makes the demon so fierce?" I asked.

"The demon was a ghost long ago in the Zhou Dynasty," he said. "Because it didn't behave properly, a virtuous man with spiritual powers shattered it with thunder. But the ghost's spirit did not completely disperse, and through gradual cultivation it later fused into a powerful demon that could fly and vanish and appear again, at will. Now it has taken the form of an old woman and it goes around capturing people for its retinue. I don't think we're any match for her. We can't deal with this one."

，你教我到那火上走，我也要去的。我說：「真的？可是你不能將來我有事情教你做的時候，你不幹啊！」他說：「無論什麼事情，師父您教我做，我一定做的，就算有什麼危險我也不怕的。」那好啦！於是乎在這七十二個人裏頭，他也就皈依了。

這一次我就叫他，我說：「你會看因果，能給人家看病，現在我這皈依弟子有病了，你給看一看啦！看這病是怎麼樣來的？」他就坐那兒一打坐，這麼一觀想，這要作觀想的。這一觀想，哦！他面色即刻就變了，看他面都嚇白了，嚇得那個樣子，不得了了，就害怕了，告訴我：「師父！這個事情不能管的！這個事情啊，我無論如何管不了的！」我說：「怎麼樣不要管呢？」他說：「管啊，我們也沒有法子降伏這個魔。」我說：「怎麼樣一個魔呢？」他說：「這個魔啊，可太厲害了，她能變化人形，在這個世界搗亂害人，這個魔才厲害！」我說：「怎麼那麼厲害？你說一說看。」他說：「這個魔，周朝那時候是一個鬼，因為她不守規矩，做了違背天意的事情，受果報了，就被一個有道行、有神通的人，用雷把她劈碎了。但是她這個靈性還沒有完全散，所以以後她慢慢地煉，又聚回到一起了，現在她就煉成一個魔。這回煉成了，她也不怕雷，她的神通特別大，她能飛行變化，忽然就沒有了，忽然又有了。現在這個魔變一個老太婆的樣子，到處抓人，想要把人弄死，就做她的眷屬。我想我們也沒有她道行那麼深，不管這個閒事好。」我說：「我們若管怎麼樣呢？」他說：「如果我們管這閒事，連我們的生命都要賠上，這是惹不得。」他就嚇得這個樣子。

他說她因為被雷劈過，以後她又修成了，她煉一種法寶，這種法寶是專門避雷的。這法寶是什麼煉的呢？就是那個女人生小孩子，小孩子初初生出來外邊的那層皮，那層包小孩子的皮。她用那層皮修煉，煉成一個黑帽子，她把這個帽子戴到頭上，什麼雷也打不了她了，雷因為怕污穢的東西。西方人認為雷是沒有人來支配的。普通的雷可能是沒有人支配，但是有一種特別的雷，就是有一種神，用雷來懲罰世間的妖魔鬼怪的。她煉成這個帽子，這個雷就劈不了她了。她又煉成兩個法寶，是兩個圓圓的球，這就是上吊死的人那個眼珠子，她煉成了。她若給人戴上她這帽子，這個人靈魂就會被她捉去，就變成她的眷屬了。那麼她這個球，如果打在人身上，人就會死了。就這麼厲害，所以什麼她也不怕的。

所以韓崗吉看出來，她是這麼厲害的一個魔鬼，就告訴我，說：「師父啊！這事情不能管的！」我說：「那不能管，這有病的怎麼辦呢？」他說：「這個有病的，

"What would happen if we tried?" I asked.

"We might lose our lives as well," said Han Gangji. He was really scared.

"The demon has refined a magic weapon," he continued. "It's an exclusive anti-thunder device: a black hat made out of the thin membranes that cover the bodies of newborn children. When she wears the hat, the thunder cannot hurt her, because thunder has a great aversion to filth."

Westerners think that thunder has no one controlling it, and while that may be the case for ordinary thunder, there is a special kind of thunder that is used by gods to punish the goblins, demons, and ghosts who wander throughout the world.

In addition to the black hat, which protected her from thunder, she had refined two other magic weapons: two round balls, which were originally the eyeballs from a human corpse. If she put her hat on someone, his soul would fall under her control, and he would become one of her followers. If she hit someone with one of the two round balls, he would immediately die.

Han Gangji saw that she was such a fierce demon and said, "Master, we can't handle this one."

"Then what will become of the sick girl?" I asked.

"She will certainly die; there's no way to help her," he said.

"I can't allow her to die. If she weren't my disciple I'd pay no attention, but she took refuge with me on the twenty-fifth of last month.. If she hadn't taken refuge with me, I wouldn't care whether the demon took her life or not. But she took refuge with me, so I can't allow the demon to take her life. I've got to do something."

"You take care of it, then," said Han Gangji, "but I'm not going."

"What?" I said, "When you took refuge, you promised me that you would jump into boiling water or walk on fire if I asked you to. Now it's not even boiling water or fire; why have you decided to back out? If you're afraid to go, then you don't have to be my disciple anymore."

Han Gangji had nothing to say. He thought it over. "If you appoint some Dharma-protecting gods to take care of me..."

"Don't shilly-shally!" I said. "If you're going to go, go. But don't vacillate!"

He said no more and followed me. When we arrived, the girl was lying on the bed with her head on the pillow and her bottom sticking up in the air; it was an embarrassing sight. Her eyes were as wide as those of a cow, and she glared with rage at me.

I asked the girl's family, "What is the cause of the illness?"

They told me that seven or eight days earlier, an old

那一定死的！沒有辦法的！」我說：「死？怎麼可以的！她若是沒有皈依我，當然我不管。那麼她上個月二十四號皈依我的，還沒有多久呢！」我說：「她若不皈依我，這個魔鬼抓她去、不抓她去，我不管。現在已經皈依我了，我就不許可這魔鬼抓她去，叫她死。我一定要去管這個事。」他說：「師父啊！那您要去管，我不能跟您去的！」我說：「什麼？你當初皈依的時候，你說『赴湯蹈火，在所不辭』，現在還不一定是湯，不一定是火呢！你怎麼就辭了呢？你若不敢去，我就不要你做我的皈依弟子。」我這一說，他也沒有話講了。沒有話講，想一想就說：「師父！那你把你的護法派給我幾個，我才敢管這個事。」我說：「你不要囉嗦了！跟著走就是了，囉嗦什麼？」他聽我這樣講，也不敢囉嗦了，就跟著我去了。去到那地方，這個有病的人，頭衝著床下，紮到這枕頭上，屁股就撅起來這麼樣子，很難看的。但是很大脾氣，眼睛瞪著有牛眼睛那麼大；啊！尤其看見我，更不高興，眼睛瞪得更厲害。我就問他們家裏，有病的原因。他說，前七、八天，在他們這條屯外邊有個孤墳，就有一個老太婆，三尺多高，大約有五十多歲，穿著雨藍色的布衫，頭上梳兩個小辮辮。這個辮子不是向後邊梳的，她的辮是向前邊這麼樣梳的。那麼穿著黃褲子、黃鞋，手裏拿著黑帽子，這麼怪里怪氣的樣子，就在這孤墳哭。

當時我有一個皈依弟子姓夏，也是一個老太婆，在路上走路，見著這個魔女在一個孤墳那地方哭，就去勸她說：「妳為什麼哭得這麼悲哀呀？不要哭啦！」她哭什麼呢？這姓夏的老太婆就聽她的聲音在那兒哭：「我那個人哪！我那個人哪！」像蚊蟲那麼叫，聽得有聲無形的這麼哭，一邊哭一邊要找她那個人。那麼姓夏這個女居士，就問她說：「你從什麼地方來啊？」她說：「你不要和我講話，我是個鬼！」這樣把我這皈依弟子給嚇得就走了。走了，可是她也跟著這個人就來了，跟著她後邊走，一走走到鑲白旗四屯。那條屯有圍牆，四邊都有

fence（圍牆），有四個門，到門外邊她就不敢進來。我那個皈依弟子進這個屯裏來了，她就在門外邊停止了，還是照常哭說，她那個人哪！她那個人哪！這麼不進去。她為什麼停止呢？我相信那門口是有門神，就擋著不准她進去，所以她也不敢進去。

這時候，夏遵祥他家裏那個大轂轆車從外邊回來了，

有一個老太婆，三尺多高，大約五十多歲，穿著雨藍色的布衫，頭上梳兩個小辮辮。辮子不是向後邊梳的，是向前邊這麼樣梳的。穿著黃褲子、黃鞋，手裏拿著黑帽子，這麼怪里怪氣的樣子，就在這孤墳哭。

An old woman, about three feet tall and in her fifties, had been sitting beside an isolated grave outside the village. She was wearing a dark blue gown and had braided her hair backwards in two plaits that went up her head in back and hung down across her temples. She was wearing yellow trousers and shoes and holding a black hat, looking quite strange, and she was crying mournfully beside the grave.

---

woman, about three feet tall and in her fifties, had been sitting beside an isolated grave outside the village. She was wearing a dark blue gown and had braided her hair backwards in two plaits that went up her head in back and hung down across her temples. She was wearing yellow trousers and shoes and holding a black hat, looking quite strange, and she was crying mournfully beside the grave.

Hearing her cries from the road, the elderly Mrs. Xia (who was also my disciple) went to comfort her, saying, "Why are you so sad? Please don't cry." What was she crying about? Mrs. Xia heard her crying in a barely audible voice, "Oh my person, oh my person..." She kept looking for her "person." Mrs. Xia asked her, "Where are you from?"

She said, "Don't talk to me, I'm a ghost!" Mrs. Xia was so frightened that she left. But the old woman walked behind Mrs. Xia and followed her all the way to the village gate.

這個車套著馬，這馬一看見這個東西就認識！人不認識這個東西，馬認識。馬一見到這個東西，就毛起來了，就驚了。這一驚，這車跑到城裏去了，她就藉著這個車往門裏頭跑的時候，跟著就進來了。大約那守門的神在那兒也慌上來了，一看這馬驚了，這門神也一楞，她趁著這一楞的期間，就混進這個村裏頭來了，這叫趁虛而入。混進村裏頭，就到一個姓尤的家裏，這姓尤的叫尤忠實。到他家裏，她就一邊進他門口，一邊也是找她那個人。尤忠實就問：「妳幹什麼啊？」她說：「我找我那個人。」這樣子，以後她望望這個姓尤的，她說不是你們的家，然後從他家裏就出來了。出來，就在這一條村這個馬路上，這時候，就有三、四十人圍著這老太婆，就問她：「姓什麼？」她說：「我也沒有姓」。問她：「叫什麼名字？」她也沒有名。再問她：「妳是什麼地方人啊？妳到這兒來幹什麼？」她說：「我是個死人，我是鬼啊！我就找我那個人哪！找我所要的那個人哪！」這大夥因為人多，聽她說是鬼，也都不怕她，於是乎就叫她老傻太太。因為她講話瘋瘋癲癲的，又說她是鬼呀，又說她是魔呀！這麼樣胡說亂講的，大家以為她講瘋話，就叫她老傻太太，傻不拉嘰的這麼樣子。這麼樣子，就有三、四十人圍著她看，看她很特別的樣子，就覺得她奇奇怪怪的，就好像一個怪物這麼看她。她手裏拎著這個黑帽子這麼走，一邊走，好像一個什麼也不懂的人，大家就跟著圍著她，這些人也不知道她從什麼地方來的，這樣就走到夏文山家後邊的牆。那牆是用土木造的土牆，大約有八尺多高，北方那土牆，上邊還有那個roof。她到牆後邊，把她這個黑帽子往前一撕，就撕到院牆裏邊去了，她隨著往前一蹦，就一跳也跳到院子裏頭去了。啊！八尺多高的牆，任何人都跳不進去的牆，她跳進去了。

當時圍著她的這三、四十人，就說：「喔！這老傻太太原來會武術，會功夫！她武術這麼好，八尺多高一跳就跳進去。」於是乎，這一班人就跑到前面門裏邊去看。然後夏文山的兒子叫夏遵全——那時候他是個學生，也皈依我，他也是皈依沒有兩個禮拜，是二十四日皈依這一班人——就趕快跑，從前面大門跑進來，在院子裏就叫，說：「媽媽、媽媽！老傻太太到我們家裏來了，您不要害怕！」他媽媽巴著脖子從玻璃鏡向外一看，也沒有什麼；一回頭呢，哦！看見一個很奇怪的老太婆已經到炕邊上了，要上炕，身體爬到炕上一半，在下邊還有一半，一邊爬，一邊就找「我那個人」，就這麼樣子。這時候她就問：「妳找誰啊？妳找誰啊？我們也不認識你，來幹什麼？」她也不講話。不講，夏遵全的母親

There must have been a spirit guarding the gate, because the old woman wouldn't go in. The village was surrounded by a wall and had a gate on each of the four sides. Mrs. Xia went in, but the old woman stayed outside the gate, crying. I think the spirit guarding the gate must have kept her from going in.

At that moment Xia Zunxiang's horse cart returned to the village. When it reached the gate the horse saw the woman and shied in fright, for horses can recognize things that people cannot see. As the horse cart went careening through the gate, the old woman followed it in. Probably the spirit who guarded the gate had his back turned, and in the confusion, she went sneaking through.

The old woman ran to the house of Mr. Yu Zhongbao and continued to look for her "person." She looked at Mr. Yu and then ran out of the house onto the street, where she was surrounded by thirty or forty curious onlookers who asked her, "What's your last name?"

"I don't have a last name."

"What's your first name?" She didn't have a first name, either. "Where are you from? What are you doing here?" they asked.

"I'm a corpse--a ghost. I'm looking for my 'person.'" she said. Because there was such a crowd, they were not afraid when they heard her say she was a ghost. They called her "stupid old woman" because of her crazy talk. They looked at her as if she were a freak. She continued to walk as if in a stupor until she reached the back wall of Xia Wenshan's estate. She then threw her black hat over the eight-foot dirt wall, and in one jump, leapt right over after it. No one else could have jumped over the wall, but she made it.

"The stupid old woman knows kung fu!" the crowd screeched, and they ran around and went in through the front gate to watch her.

Xia Wenshan's son Xia Zunquan, who had also taken refuge on the twenty-fourth, ran in the door. "Mama! Mama! The stupid old woman is in our house, but don't be afraid."

His mother looked out the window, but saw nothing strange. When she turned around, there was the old woman crawling up on the brick bed. She was halfway on the bed and halfway on the floor, looking for her "person."

"Whom are you looking for? What do you want?" shouted the mother, but the old woman made no reply.

Seeing the old woman's strange behavior, the mother said to her daughter, "This woman is really weird. We'd better recite the Great Compassion Mantra."

When those people had taken refuge, I had taught them to recite the Great Compassion Mantra. I had said to them, "Each of you should learn to recite the Great Compassion Mantra. It will be of great help to you. If you are in danger and distress and you recite it, Guanyin Bodhisattva will

看見她很奇怪的樣子，就覺得不是路了，於是乎就對她女兒說：「哎呀！這麼怪的一個人，也不出聲，我們要念〈大悲咒〉。」之前她們皈依我的時候，我就教那一班人念〈大悲咒〉。我說：「你們每一個人都應該學〈大悲咒〉，將來會有用的。你們這屯子將來有什麼問題，遇到什麼危急的時候，你念〈大悲咒〉，觀音菩薩就會保護著你，就能消災免難。」於是乎，他們就有很多人學習〈大悲咒〉。這有病的女孩和她媽媽兩個人就念上〈大悲咒〉了，就念「南無喝囉怛那哆囉夜耶……」。這麼一念，這個老傻太太就從炕上，順著炕沿慢慢、慢慢就躺到炕沿底下，像死人一樣，就不動彈了。她們一看，這不得了，這若死在家裏，出人命啦！於是乎，她也不敢動這個老女人，就去報告農公會了。那時候已經是共產黨，在鄉下有農公會，這農公會的會長就拿著槍來了。到這兒，看見有這麼一個老年的女人躺在地下，好像要死的樣子，於是乎，這農公會的會長就伸手一提，用一隻手就把這個老女人拿起來了，拿到外面去，放在地下，就教她這麼走。等她走到農公會裏邊，就問她：「妳是哪裏人呀？妳幹什麼來的？」她就對著這些個人說她是死人，說：「你不要問我，我就是死人，我也沒有姓，也沒有名，也沒有住的地方；我到什麼地方，就住在什麼地方。」這個農公會的會長聽她這麼講，看她這個樣子，也都很驚恐了，於是乎帶著槍就把她向屯外邊送，向西邊送。頭一次，送了五十幾步遠，這個人回來了，等到屯的門口回頭一望，這老女人還跟在後邊。於是乎就又向遠處送她，這一回就送出七十幾步遠，這個人又回來了，走到半路上，這個老女人又跟著回來。最後這一次，就有三、四個鄉屯裏頭的人一同又往遠處送她。這回送出一百五十多步遠，就叫她趕快走，不走就用槍打她。農公會的會長，就在那兒往空中放了兩槍，這個老女人隨這槍聲就趴在地下。本來不是打她，但是她嚇得就趴在地上，大約她以為又是打雷了。這回大家回來一看，她沒有跟著回來，於是這會長和農公會裏幾個辦事的人員，就回到屯裏頭去了。

這個老的女人雖然走了，可是夏文山家裏，他的女兒，大約十七、八歲吧！由這個老太婆到家裏，然後又走了之後，這個女孩就跪到炕上，頭往炕上一趴，屁股撅起來，眼睛睜得圓圓的，也不說話，也不吃東西，晚間也不睡覺，頭就好像在床上叩頭那麼樣子。就是我前邊

protect you." Since then, many of them had been reciting the Great Compassion Mantra.

The mother and her daughter began immediately to recite the mantra. Just as they recited the first line of the mantra, *Na mo he la da nuo duo la ye ye*, the old woman slipped to the ground and lay inert, exactly like a corpse.

Seeing that, the family was greatly upset. If somebody were to die in their home, it would not be good.

They went for the sheriff. When the sheriff saw the old woman lying on the floor as if she were dying, he picked her up with one hand and set her outside. Then he took her to the village courthouse for questioning. "Where are you from?" he asked, "and why have you come here?"

"Don't ask me," she said. "I'm a corpse. I have no name and no home. I just live wherever I am."

Frightened by her strange talk and behavior, the sheriff escorted her at pistol point some fifty paces outside the village. But when he returned to the village gate, she was right behind him. The second time he took her seventy paces from the village, but on the way back he discovered that she was following him again. Finally, he and three or

---

這個女孩就跪到炕上，頭往炕上一趴，屁股撅起來，眼睛睜得圓圓的，也不說話，也不吃東西，晚間也不睡覺，頭就好像在床上叩頭那麼樣子。後邊這個身就高起來，七、八天也不吃東西，就中魔了，也治不好。

The daughter lay on the bed with her head buried in the pillow and and her bottom sticking up in the air. She glared in rage and didn't speak, nor did she sleep at night. She looked as if she were making bows on the bed. She didn't eat for seven or eight days. She had been possessed by a demon.

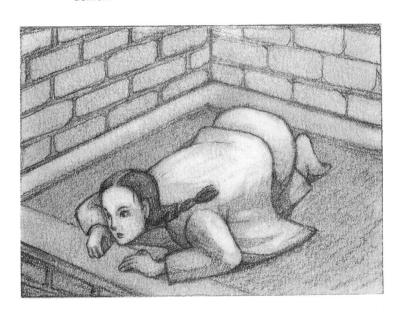

說的她這個頭紮在枕頭上，後邊這個身就高起來這麼樣子，七、八天也不吃東西，就中魔了，也治不好。

我沒有到她家裏以前，我和韓崗吉說：「你說一管這閒事，就會死的，我現在就寧可我自己死，我也要管的。我告訴你，現在因為這個有病的人是我的皈依弟子，我不知道我就不管了，我現在知道我這皈依弟子要被魔抓去，因為她皈依我，她有問題了，我應該來幫助她解決她這個問題，這我才能對得起這皈依弟子。那麼現在有病這個人一定死，這我不允許的，我不能看著她死了不管，我要救我這個徒弟，我不能見死不救的，這是一個理由。再者，我要救這個魔。你說這個魔，誰也管不了她，但是她盡傷天害理，造罪多端來害人，她造罪造得多了，一定還是會有人管得了她，將來她一定受果報，終究是會遭天譴的。她修煉了這麼多年，如果有人來把她消滅了，這也是很可惜的。所以現在我要救這個魔，叫她改邪歸正，不要再做惡事，她就是有本領令我死了，我都要去救她去，這是第二個理由。第三個理由，我要救全世界所有的一切眾生，如果我現在不把她收伏了，將來世界上受害的人一定是很多，我現在要救所有會被她害的人，不再被這個魔來傷害。因為有這三個理由，所以無論如何我要管這個閒事，我一定要去的。」所以就到這有病的人家裏了。

當時這個農公會會長也來了，聽我們一談論起來，一個禮拜以前來的這個老傻太太就是個魔鬼，他也就想起來了，他說：「哦！難怪那天，她在地上躺著，我用一隻手把她拿起來，一點都不費力，輕輕的，就像拿一張紙那麼輕，好像沒有東西似的。當時我也不覺悟，也不覺得怎麼這麼輕的一個人，若不說我也想不起來，現在一講起來，知道這的確是個魔鬼了，難怪我一提她，像一張紙那麼輕。」

這樣子呢，我們就要把這個魔鬼又找來。怎麼樣找呢？在〈楞嚴咒〉有五種法。五種法裏有「息災法」——息災法，就是人有什麼災難，可以把它息了。有「吉祥法」——有不吉祥的事情，可以變成吉祥。有「勾召法」——勾召法，就是妖魔鬼怪無論他離多遠，隨時可以把他捉來。又有「降伏法」——降伏法，就是魔鬼他來了，你能降伏他。有這種的法，所以當時我用那個〈楞嚴咒〉，把這個如意魔女給硬捉來了。她到這兒，一進門口的時候，她帶著一股臭氣。這股臭氣腥臭得不得了，人一聞到那腥臭的氣就作嘔，就要嘔吐的那個樣子。

她進來了，就用她所煉的那個帽子，想用她這法寶往我頭上來撒；一撒，這個帽子也撒不到我的頭上。那麼她這個帽子沒有用了，又拿出她這個圓圓的球想來打，

four other deputies took her 150 paces outside the village and said, "Get out or get shot!" and they fired two shots in the air.

The old woman fell to the ground in terror, thinking the shots were thunder, which had destroyed her before. This time she didn't follow them back to the village.

Although the old woman was gone, Xia Wenshan's daughter, who was seventeen or eighteen at the time, fell sick. After the old woman left their house, the daughter lay on the bed with her head buried in the pillow and and her bottom sticking up in the air. She glared in rage and didn't speak, nor did she sleep at night. She looked as if she were making bows on the bed. She didn't eat for seven or eight days. She had been possessed by a demon.

Before we went to Xia Wenshan's home, I said to Han Gangji, "You said that if we tried to handle the matter we would die. Well, I would rather die than not save one of my disciples. First of all, this sick girl has taken refuge with me. She has been possessed by a demon, and I have to help her out of this trouble. I can't just stand by and let her die. Secondly, I must save the demon. You say no one can control her, but she has committed so many offenses and harmed so many people that there's bound to be someone who can subdue her. She's bound to be punished. If she were to be destroyed, it would be a great pity, for she has cultivated diligently for many years. Even if she has enough power to kill me, I'll still save her and teach her to be good. Finally, I must save all living beings in the world, and if I don't subdue her now, in the future many people will be harmed by her. For these three reasons, then, I'm going to work."

Just then the sheriff happened by and overheard us saying that the old woman was a demon. "No wonder!" he exclaimed. "That's why I was able to pick her up with one hand, just as if there were nothing there at all. It didn't occur to me at the time, but now I realize she's a demon. She was as light as a sheet of paper."

We then had to find the demon. How did we do that? There are five kinds of dharmas in the Shurangama Mantra. One is the *dharma for extinguishing calamities*. If you are due to suffer a calamity, you can use this dharma to avert it. There is also the *dharma for creating auspiciousness*, which turns inauspicious events into auspicious ones. With the *dharma of summoning and hooking*, you can catch goblins, demons, and ghosts no matter how far away they are. There is also the *dharma of subduing and conquering*, which allows you to subdue any demon that comes. I employed these dharmas from the Shurangama Mantra to capture the As-You-Will demon woman.

When she entered the room, she had about her an intense and nauseating stench. She came in and tried to put her magic weapon--the black hat--on my head, but couldn't get it on me. Then she took out her round balls and tried to hit

也打不到我身上，那麼她帶了很多寶貝都用出來了，都沒有功效，沒有用了。她在這個時候才知道是不行了，就想要跑。要跑！回頭一看，東西南北，四維上下都擋著，什麼地方也跑不了。因為她一來的時候，我已經就結界，就好像擺上一個陣似的。那麼她沒有地方跑了，上邊也有人看著她，下邊也有人看著她，左右前後都有護法天龍八部在這裏堵著，她跑不了，沒有法子，就跪下來。跪下，就哭起來了，對我說：「我真想不到今天遇到我的剋星了，請你原諒我，把我放了。」我說：「放你是不能不放你，除非你改邪歸正，皈依三寶，我可以原諒你；你如果不改邪歸正，我是不能原諒你的。」她點頭說可以，那麼當時我就給她說法，說這個「四諦法」，說「十二因緣法」，又說這「六度法」，她即刻就明白了。明白了，她就要皈依三寶，發菩提心了。那麼這樣子，我就給她說了皈依，另給她起個名字，叫「金剛如意女」。

皈依之後，我當時有一個小葫蘆，那小葫蘆很小的一個，我就把她放到那葫蘆裏。以後她就常常跟著我到各處去度人。可是跟著我到各處走，想不到她還是不老實，她的本性是一種魔性，我們每逢到什麼地方，她就放出一股又腥又臭的那麼一股毒氣；跟著我到什麼地方，都有這股的味道。這股毒氣比什麼都腥，我聞到也沒有什麼問題，可是一般的人一聞到這種毒氣，就都頭暈眼花的受不了，就都作嘔。以後我一看，她跟著我不行了，我就派她回東北喇拔喇子，到吉林省蛟河縣磊法山「萬聖玲瓏洞」那地方去修行，現在她還在那兒修行。這是我個人在東北沒有政府狀態的情形之下，遇到這麼樣一個大魔頭，這是一件大事。

我有很多這個奇奇怪怪的皈依弟子都派到那兒，都叫他們在那地方修行。這個地方，我自己也到過這個山上。以後她修行很快就有了一點神通，常常到各處去救人去。不過她救人呢，也都不教人知道說是她怎麼樣救人。因為你教人知道這事情，所謂「善欲人見，不是真善；惡恐人知，便是大惡。」你做的好事，願意教人知道，那不是真的好事；你做的壞事，怕人知道，那才是壞事。所以這個如意魔女，結果也變成一個佛的眷屬了。

那個地方，怎麼叫「萬聖玲瓏洞」呢？因為一個洞有三個洞門，在這邊可以看到那邊，那邊又可以看到這邊，玲瓏透體的那個樣子。好像這個玻璃杯裏面裝著什麼，一看就知道了，這叫玲瓏，不是一定說是glass（玻璃），就是裏邊可以看到外邊，外邊又可以看到裏邊。這一個洞，有三個洞門，這三個洞門都互相通的。在那裏邊，有一個廟，造這個廟的材料，都是用羊馱上去的。

me, but they missed my body.

Both of her magic weapons had failed. Knowing she was finished, she turned to run, but when she first arrived, I had set up an invisible boundary that would trap her no matter where she tried to go. The gods, dragons, and others of the eightfold division of Dharma-protectors watched her from the left, right, front, rear, above, and below. Seeing that she couldn't get away, she knelt and wept. She said, "I never thought I would meet my subduer today. Please forgive me and let me go."

"I will certainly let you go, but I can only forgive you if you reform and take refuge with the Triple Jewel," I said.

She nodded in acquiescence. I then spoke the Dharma for her. I explained the Four Noble Truths, the Twelve Causes and Conditions, and the Six Perfections. She immediately understood, resolved to realize Bodhi, and asked to take refuge with the Triple Jewel. I accepted her and gave her the name "Vajra As-You-Will Maiden."

I had a small hut then, and I let her stay in there after she took refuge. Later she often followed me around to save people, but her basic make-up was that of a demon, and no matter where she went she emitted an overwhelming stench. The putrid odor didn't bother me, but it made most people so nauseated that they wanted to vomit. Seeing that it wouldn't do for her to follow me, I sent her to Leifa Mountain in Jiaohe County, Jilin Province, to cultivate in the Exquisite Cave of the Ten Thousand Saints. She is still there now. She was a great demon leader that I encountered in Manchuria when there was no government in force there.

I have sent many of my strange and unusual disciples there to cultivate, and I have also been there myself. She cultivated vigorously and soon attained spiritual powers and could rescue people. When she rescued them, she didn't like it to be known, since good done hoping others will know is not true good, and evil done in secret for fear that others will know is truly great evil. Thus, the former demon woman became one of the Buddha's followers.

Why is the cave called the "Exquisite Cave of the Ten Thousand Saints"? It's said to be exquisite because it has three entrances, which are mutually visible to each other. It's like a glass cup, in that one can see in from the outside and out from the inside. The three entrances to the cave are mutually connected. Inside the cave there is a temple made of bricks and lumber that were carried up the steep mountain crags on the backs of goats. One goat could carry two bricks or a piece of lumber at a time. Off the western entrance of the cave, there is another cave called the Cave of Lao Zi. Off the eastern entrance is the Dripping Water Cave, which drips enough water to satisfy a troop of ten thousand men and horses. The cave in the back is called the Cave of Patriarch Ji, named after Ji Xiaotang, a native of Manchuria who, in the Ming Dynasty, subdued five ghosts, one of whom was the Black Fish Spirit. The Black Fish Spirit was a Ming

這一隻羊或者馱兩塊磚，或者一塊木頭，這麼用羊運上去的，因為那個山很高。在那個洞裏邊，西邊這個洞門口，外邊又有一個「老君洞」——老子的洞。東邊這個洞門口，就有一個「滴水洞」。滴水洞那個洞裏，有這個水往下滴答、滴答這麼滴水。這個水啊，在那兒千人萬馬都夠吃的。後邊那個洞出去，就是「紀祖洞」；紀祖洞，就是紀曉堂。紀曉堂是我東北的人，他收過五個鬼，他又在磊法山這兒，捉過這個黑魚精。這黑魚精是在明朝那時候，在北京作官的，叫黑大人。他姓黑，但是他不是個人，他是魚。紀曉堂知道了，就要收拾他，知道他有一天會在這個山這兒過，紀曉堂就在那兒等著他。等他從那兒過，紀曉堂會「掌手雷」，用掌手雷就把黑大人給打死在那個地方。

那山上的洞，誰也不知道有多少？你今天查有七十二個，明天就有七十三個，後天你再數，或者就有七十個。總而言之，它沒有一定的數目。曾經有一個人到那個山上去，看見兩個老年人在那兒下棋，他在那兒看看，就咳嗽了一聲。咳嗽一聲，這兩個有很長鬍子的老人一看，嘿！他怎麼來了？這個石頭自己有個門就關上了！他就在那兒跪著，一跪就跪死在那個地方。現在他的墳，還在那個石頭洞的門外邊。你看！人家求道、求法，跪死在那地方都不起來了。所以那個山有很多神仙。

我遇到一個李明福，他會武術，跑得才快呢！跑得像猴子那麼快。我到那個地方的時候，我也是一早起到山上去，一早大約四點多鐘到山上，就看到他在那兒拜佛。他後邊這個頭髮，束得有七、八斤重，頭上桿著一個簪，從來也不洗。他的面目很小的，小眼睛、小鼻子、小嘴巴、小臉，這麼很小的。但是他力量很大的，他以前給人家做鐵道，那個鐵道軌，八個人抬一條，他一個人可以拿兩條。一個人拿兩條，這麼一個胳臂夾一個，就這麼有力量。他叫李明福，究竟他多大年紀？什麼時候的人？沒有什麼人知道他。我到那兒遇到過這麼一個奇怪的人。

今天我大約也是心血來潮了，把我這個事實講給你們大家聽聽，我對你們所講的，這不是講故事、不是自造的，這是實實在在，一個真實的事情！你們大家一定很多人都不相信的，但是這是事實。我說過之後，你們各位信，也可以；不信，也可以，信不信由你！不過我說的是真話。

Dynasty official in Beijing called Blackie the Great. His last name was Black, but he wasn't a human; he was a fish. Ji Xiaotang knew this and was determined to capture him. He knew that "Blackie" would pass by the mountain one day, and so he waited for him. When he passed by, Ji Xiaotang released thunder from the palm of his hand and killed him.

No one actually knows how many caves there are in Leifa Mountain. Each time you count them, the number is different--seventy-two today, seventy-three tomorrow, and maybe seventy the day after that.

A man once went there and saw two old men playing chess in a cave. When he coughed, the two long-bearded men said to themselves, "How did he get here?" and then the stone gate of the entrance closed by itself. The man knelt there seeking the truth from them until he finally died. His grave may still be seen outside the Stone Door Cave. How sincerely he sought for the truth!

There are many spirits and immortals up in the mountain. One was a man named Lee Mingfu, who had mastered kung fu and could run as fast as a monkey. Once I visited the cave at four in the morning and saw him bowing to the Buddha. His hair, which he never washed, was held by a hairpin and matted in a lump that weighed five or six pounds. His facial features--eyes, nose, and mouth--and his body, were very small, but his body was strong. He alone could carry two railroad tracks so heavy that eight ordinary men would be needed to carry one; he would tuck one track under each arm. No one knew how old he was or where he was from. He was one of the strange men I met there.

I was very inspired today, and that's why I told you these things. These are true stories; I didn't make them up. Most of you probably don't believe them. Whether you believe or not is up to you. But I have told you the truth.

# A FEW SCENES OF
# THE MASTER TEACHING IN THE WEST
# 上人弘化西方掠影

Oldy But Goody
好古

The
Venerable
Master
at the
Buddhist
Lecture Hall.

宣化上人
於佛教講堂

When the Master set out for America, he had a 10-day stop-over in Japan. He visited a temple where Chinese Dharma Masters were staying and upon entry detected their acute jealousy. Although it was his practice to take one meal a day at noon, when tea and refreshments were served, the Master decided to take a bite of food so as not to appear to be too different from the others and risk arousing their jealousy even more. He accepted six or seven fried soy beans and ate them.

Immediately he knew that the beans were loaded with deadly poison. Although he knew, he chose not to give any indication at the time, and did not dispel the poison from his body at once as the First Patriarch of China, Bodhidharma, had done when he spit it out on a tray one time, and on a rock another time, when he was poisoned by jealous people. Although the poison did not kill the Master, it lodged in a single place in his body and a painful sore formed on his lower leg.

Having been unsuccessful in poisoning the Master to death, one of the jealous monks went on ahead to San Francisco, the Master's destination, to campaign against him. After the founding of the Buddhist Lecture Hall in San Francisco in 1958, word of the Master's virtue, compassion, and cultivation had spread and many people sought to take refuge with him, sight unseen.

The jealous monk did his best to dissuade people: "He claims he never eats after noon, but I watched him with my own eyes while he ate one afternoon in Japan," he reported, failing to mention that he and the other monks had put poison in the food. But his skilled persuasion caused many who had planned to welcome the Master at the airport upon his arrival to change their minds and decide not to go.

Jealousy comes in many forms. One kind was this intense jealousy his contemporaries felt toward the Master--they wanted the rewards that came to the Master. Another kind of jealousy was harbored by some of his disciples--they didn't want to share the Master with anyone. One such disciple was a young, unmarried man in his early thirties who came to the Master because he wanted to learn *gung fu,* for he could see at a glance that the Master possessed skill. The Master always tried to save whoever drew near and so he used expedients to try to help this disciple, allowing him to accompany him and attend to some of the matters involved in doing the Buddha's work.

That's how it happened that this disciple accompanied the Master when he took a trip to the Southwestern States and visited the Hopi Indians. The Master felt deep concern about the pitiful conditions under which the Hopis were forced to live--their dwellings being no better than crude sheds fit for animals. It appeared that in the Hopi religious tradition was something about a prediction that eventually a savior would come to help their tribe--one who could be recognized by his red robe, black hat, and a symbol resembling a swastika on his chest. Needless to say,

上人前往美國途中，在日本停留了十天。有一天下午，拜訪了一間有中國法師的寺廟。上人一進去，就發覺這些法師懷著強烈的嫉妒心。雖然上人日中一食，但他們拿出茶點招待時，為免顯得與他們不一樣，更增加他們的嫉妒心，上人就吃了六、七粒炸黃豆。

一吃下去，上人就知道豆裡有毒，能毒死人。但是，當時上人不動聲色，也沒有馬上將毒排出體外；就像中國佛教禪宗第一代祖師——達摩大師，當他被嫉妒的人兩度下毒時，一次將毒吐到盤中，一次吐到石頭上。這毒沒能毒死上人，上人將毒擠到小腿下面，以後這一點就成為經常疼痛的毒傷。

這次毒殺上人計劃沒成功，其中一位和尚就先到上人的目的地——舊金山，去散佈謠言，來攻擊上人。一九五八年舊金山的佛教講堂成立以後，上人的德行、慈悲以及修行，弘揚開來。那時有很多人，雖然尚未見過上人，但都想皈依上人。

這個嫉妒的和尚盡情地煽動，說：「他說他下午從不吃東西，但我在日本時，有一天下午親眼看到他吃東西。」但他卻不說他和其他幾個和尚下毒的事。他能言善道，讓很多人改變心意，取消了原訂到機場歡迎上人的計劃。

嫉妒來自好幾個方向。一個是上人同期的同參，嫉妒心很強，想要得到上人所有的好處。另一個是上人的弟子們，心胸狹窄的嫉妒，想獨自擁有上人。其中的一位是一位年輕、單身、約三十歲的男眾，他接近上人的目的是為了想學功夫，因為他一眼就看出上人有一身特殊功夫。上人總是想要去度化接近他的人，他用了很多方便法去度他，讓他陪著參與一些有關佛教的工作。

一次這位弟子陪同上人到美國西南部的一個州，他們去拜訪荷比印第安人。上人看到他們擠在一個像給畜生住的簡陋的寮棚內，他很同情他們這種可憐的處境。在荷比人的宗教裡，一直流傳著一個預言：「會有一個救世主出現來幫助他們，他的特徵是穿著紅袍、戴頂黑帽、在胸前有一個卍字。」

上人受邀去為他們演講時，不用說，這荷比人一看到上人穿著紅迦裟，戴著黑帽，因沙漠的炎熱而赤

宣化老和尚追思紀念專集

when the Master, who had been invited to speak to them, appeared before them in his red precept sash and black cap, bare skinned to the waist, due to the desert heat, so that the *wan* character burned on his chest was clearly visible--the Hopis were filled with a mixture of awe, joy, and hope. Transcending language barriers, the Master recited the Shurangama Mantra for them. The whole tribe was deeply moved. Wishing to draw nearer, they approached the disciple who was accompanying the Master, leaving their names and addresses and asking if there were any chance to see the Master again.

But that disciple's jealousy obstructed the situation and he not only failed to give them the opportunity to take refuge with the Master, he also did not keep their names and addresses and refused to arrange interviews for them. [Note: That disciple died within few years after that incident, without ever being able to open his heart and do the good deeds that might have saved him from his untimely death.]

That was also the year of the Cuban Missile Crisis--a tense moment in history when the Soviet Union began a missile base installation on Cuba. President Kennedy gave Russia and Cuba an ultimatum: The US was prepared to go to war if the installation preparation continued.

裸右肩，露出胸前的卍字，他們的內心夾雜著敬畏、喜悅及希望。上人突破語言的障礙，爲他們念〈楞嚴咒〉。整個荷比族的人都被感動了。他們希望能更接近上人，就去找上人的隨從——這位弟子，留下他們的名字及地址，而且請問是否能再有機會見上人。

但是因爲這位弟子的嫉妒心阻礙了這件事情，他不僅沒有給他們皈依上人的機會，也沒有留下這些人的名字及地址，沒有幫他們安排見上人。〔註：這位弟子在這事情幾年後就過世了。在他死前，他都一直沒有打開心胸做一些善事，如果他放開心胸或許可以讓他免於早死。〕

在那一年也發生了古巴飛彈危機事件，當蘇聯在古巴開始建立飛彈基地時，是歷史上緊張的一刻。甘迺迪總統給蘇俄及古巴一個最後通牒：如果這基地還繼續建造，美國將準備發動戰爭。這情況在當時是非常緊張的。

**The Master during his early 35-day fast for world peace.**
**爲了世界和平，上人絕食三十五天。**

For those three reasons--the Cuban Crisis, the Hopi plight, and the poison in his system--the Master began a fast dedicated to world peace. The method of fasting, one of Guanyin Bodhisattva's Greatly Compassionate Dharmas, normally stipulates no food or water whatsoever for the first few days of fasting, and then only one-half cup of water per day for the duration of the fast.

Near the end of the 35-day fast, to the surprise and relief of everyone, the Soviet Union unexpectedly, voluntarily withdrew the missiles and the Crisis abated. During that time, civil rights movements began bringing the nation's attention to the plight of the Native Americans. And by the end of the fast, the poison had been dispelled, leaving just a permanent scar on the Master's leg.

爲了三樁事－古巴飛彈事件、可憐的荷比族，以及他自己的毒傷，上人開始絕食，並把功德迴向世界和平。「絕食」是觀音菩薩大慈悲法之一，方法是開始的前幾天不吃任何食物，也不喝水，然後每天喝半杯水。

在三十五天快結束時，大家都很驚訝，同時也放下心來，因爲蘇聯出乎意料之外，自動撤回飛彈，也停止建造基地。同時，民權運動也將美國人的注意力集中到美國土著的身上。餓七結束，上人的毒傷也消失了，僅在小腿上留下一個疤。

## The Master with young disciples in San Francisco.

Jimmy Wong discovered the Buddhist Lecture Hall in San Francisco's Chinatown even before the Master came to America. While studying Taijiiquan there, he heard about the Master's virtue and decided to write the Master. "I wrote him a letter to say hello and asked him when he was going to come to America," says Jimmy. "I was about thirteen at the time." Kim Lee, who was fourteen at the time, had been a Buddhist all his life and as soon as he saw the Master, he begged to be allowed to become a disciple. He and Jimmy were among those who received the first transmission of the Three Refuges given by the Master in America. Kim's Dharma name became Guo Qian "Fruit of the Yang Energy" and Jimmy's name became Guo Ren "Fruit of Humaneness."

The two boys devoted much of their time and energy to helping the Master and the Buddhist Lecture Hall. Kim learned printing and Jimmy joined him in helping print many materials for the Buddhist Lecture Hall in those early days. Kim made a vow to help print Buddhist texts and even now, in 1996, Kim is still the Association's printer.

Among all the experiences he gained in drawing near to the Master during those early years, Jimmy vividly remembers one event which made a deep impression on him. It was the Master's 35-day fast. During that time, the Buddhist Lecture Hall was virtually Jimmy's "second home." And so during that fast, Jimmy stayed close to the Master and was filled with wonder at the Master's incredible skill. Jimmy personally witnessed that during the entire thirty-five day fast, the Master took no more than one cup of water each day, and during the last two weeks, he did not even take the water. Nothing at all passed through his lips. Yet, Jimmy noted, whereas most people would have been debilitated after the first week or so, the Master continued his regular full day of monastic duties throughout the entire time.

傑米黃（照片右下角）在上人到美國前，就已經在舊金山的中國城發現了佛教講堂。當時他在那裡學太極拳，他聽到有關上人的德行後，就決定寫信給上人。傑米説：「在信上我只是問候上人，以及詢問上人何時會到美國？」李錦山（照片左下邊）那時候十四歲，一直是佛教徒，當他看到上人時，他立刻要求做上人的弟子。他和傑米黃是上人在美國第一批皈依的弟子之一。李錦山的法名是果乾，而傑米黃的法名是果仁。

這兩個男孩子為了幫助上人及佛教講堂，投入大量的時間與精力。一開始，因為李錦山學過印刷，黃果仁協助他一起幫忙佛教講堂印刷各種資料。李錦山發願幫忙印刷佛教書籍，一直到現在，李錦山還是我們的印刷者。

在早期那幾年，黃果仁都一直在上人身邊，在他所有的經歷中，他清清楚楚地記得一件令他印象深刻的事情，那就是上人絕食三十五天。在那段期間，佛教講堂實際上可以説是黃果仁的第二個家。而且在上人絕食的期間，黃果仁離上人很近，他對上人不可思議的奇蹟很佩服。黃果仁本人可以證明，上人在整個絕食期間，每天喝水不超過一杯，甚至在最後的兩個星期，上人連水也不喝。沒有任何東西經過他的嘴唇。黃果仁也注意到，一般人在第一週左右就會軟弱無力了，但在整個三十五天，上人還是繼續照常在寺廟全天地工作。

**Dr. Ron Epstein, who introduced many, many Americans to the Master (the majority of those in that early group of left-home and lay disciples).**

易象乾博士介紹了許多許多的美國人到上人處
（他們大部份是上人早期的出家及在家弟子）

Dr. Ron Epstein, who is now a Professor in the College of Humanities at San Francisco State University, comments:

During the Cuban missile crisis, the Master fasted for 35 days. There are newspaper articles in the archives about the Master fasting to help to resolve the Cuban missile crisis. I think Shr Fu was in a couple of locations in Chinatown, starting out in a basement location.

———————————————————

This is a translation of the caption at right of photo.

Dharma Master To Lun, who recently arrived from Hong Kong and is lecturing Sutras at the Buddhist Lecture Hall here in San Francisco, is now in the twelfth day of a total fast for the sake of world peace and harmony among humankind. This is the fifth fast the monk, who is in his fifties, has undertaken.

舊金山州立大學哲學教授—易博士說：

在古巴危機時，上人絕食三十五天。在我們檔案室收集的報紙中，也有報導上人打餓七幫助化解古巴飛彈基地危機。……我想師父曾在中國城兩個地方待過，第一次是在地下室那個地方。

法師絕食　期求世界和平

廿七日三藩市訊。度輪法師。昨在華埠沙加免度街七三一號佛教講堂。絕食已至第十二日。期求世界和平。人類免除殘暴及增進健康。據謂此爲其五十餘年來第五次絕食。彼于六月前由香港抵達三藩市。最近每日上午四時起床。穿起法袍。端坐絕食。尚無計劃何時停止。

The *Chinese Times* article titled "Seeking World Peace," dated September 27, 1962 read:

Dharma Master To Lun has been fasting for twelve days at the Buddhist Lecture Hall, 731 Sacramento Street, in order to seek for world peace, for the abolishment of cruelty, and for good health for all humankind. It's said that this is the fifth fast the monk, now in his fifties, has conducted. He arrived in San Francisco from Hong Kong six months ago. During this fast, he rises at 4 am, dons his precept sash, sits upright in meditation, and fasts. When his fast will terminate is not known.

# The Monk in the Grave

*Each of you now meets a monk in the grave.*
*Above, no sun and moon; below, no lamp.*
*Affliction and Enlightenment--ice is water.*
*Birth, death, and Nirvana; form is just emptiness.*
*Let go of self-seeking, be apart from the false.*
*When the mad mind ceases, enlightenment interpenetrates.*
*Awakened, attain to the bright store of your own nature.*
*Basically the retribution body is the Dharma body.*

# 墓中僧

各位今遇墓中僧　上無日月下無燈
煩惱菩提冰是水　生死涅槃色即空
放下攀緣離諸妄　歇止狂心覺圓融
悟得自性光明藏　原來報身即法身

In the summer of 1969, at a guest lecture given at the University of California at Berkeley in an "Introduction to Buddhism" class, the Master explained this verse he composed during his years of semi-seclusion in the early sixties.

*Each of you now meets a monk in the grave.* You young capable people who are endowed with wisdom will no doubt ask this monk in the grave, "How did you get there?" I don't know either. You should not ask me that question. It is not important. How this monk in the grave got in there and how he got out does not pose a problem. However, I will tell you what the grave is like.

*Above, no sun and moon; below, no lamp.* What does this describe? Ignorance. It is ignorance that has no name. Although it has no name, it is still necessary to destroy it. Not only do I have to destroy ignorance, you also have to destroy ignorance. You say, "I haven't entered the grave, how can you call me ignorant?" Well, you haven't entered the grave yet, but in the future you certainly will. You can't avoid it. You definitely have to go in the future, because of the ignorance you have now. Having ignorance means not having any brightness. Even the highest Bodhisattvas still have a bit of "ignorance that creates appearances" which has not yet been destroyed. Therefore, all the way from Bodhisattvas down through the Nine Dharma Realms--including us ordinary people--all beings have ignorance. That's why the Buddha said that ignorance is afflictions; afflictions are Bodhi. But in order to turn afflictions into Bodhi we have to have some *gung fu*--spiritual skill. And so the third line of the verse says:

一九六九年夏天，上人應柏克萊加州大學「基本佛教」課程邀請爲客座演講，在演講中，上人解釋這首他在一九六○年早期隱居時期所作的偈頌。

**各位今遇墓中僧。**你們這些稟賦聰明又有能力的年輕人，毫無疑問的會問這個墓中僧，「你是怎麼進去的？」我也不知道，你們不用問此問題，這個問題也不關緊要。這個墓中僧又怎麼進出墓中呢？這也不成問題，我會告訴你們，這墓是什麼樣子的。

**上無日月下無燈。**這像是什麼呢？無明。無名的「無明」，就是沒有名字的「無明」。雖然沒有一個名字，我們必須要破無明。不但是我要破無明，你們也要破無明。你們會說：「我又沒有跑到墳墓去，怎麼也要破無明呢？」現在是沒有去，可是將來一定要走上這條路，免不了的。既然將來一定要去，所以現在也是有無明。有無明，就沒有光明。在等覺菩薩的地位上，還有一分的生相無明未破。所以由菩薩算起的九法界的眾生，包括我們凡夫，都有無明。因此佛說無明即煩惱，煩惱即菩提。可是我們得有功夫，才能將煩惱轉變成菩提。所以第三句偈頌是：

**煩惱菩提冰是水。**因爲人人有煩惱，所以人人才

*Affliction and Bodhi--ice is water.* Because everyone has afflictions, everyone also has Bodhi. Everyone knows how to get afflicted; but we've all forgotten about Bodhi! If we forget about Bodhi then we cannot make use of it. It's like ice which originally was water but, because of a cold atmosphere, turned to ice. If there's a warm spell, it can melt the ice back into water. This is an analogy for afflictions and Bodhi. The cold atmosphere is afflictions; and the opposite, the warm sunshine, is Bodhi. What creates the cold atmosphere? Greed, hatred, and stupidity do it. What is the warm sunshine? Precepts, samadhi, and wisdom. We should diligently cultivate precepts, samadhi, and wisdom and put to rest greed, hatred, and stupidity. That is turning afflictions into Bodhi. It's also melting the ice into water. But this is only an analogy. Don't get attached and say, "Ice is water; afflictions are Bodhi," for fear you might then go on to say, "Well, I'll just hang onto my afflictions. After all, they're Bodhi! And since ice itself is water, I'll just keep the piece of ice and see if it turns into water." That's not the right attitude. Although everyone can become a Buddha, we have to cultivate before that can happen. How do we cultivate? We must rely in the Buddhadharma to cultivate and find a Bright-eyed Good and Wise Advisor who will teach us the methods of cultivation.

*Birth, death, and Nirvana; form is just emptiness.* Everyone is afraid of birth and death. However, if there weren't any birth and death, there wouldn't be any Nirvana. Nirvana must be found within birth and death. Once you find Nirvana it is not necessary to seek any more. Don't "ride a donkey trying to find a donkey." We don't have Nirvana at present because we are still caught up in birth and death. If you end birth and death, then Nirvana is yours--there will be no need to search for it. And so it's said that form is just emptiness. Nirvana, too, is just emptiness.

*Let go of self-seeking, be apart from the false.* If you want to certify to the emptiness of people, the emptiness of dharmas--the emptiness of birth, death, and Nirvana--you must let go and see through it all. Don't keep holding on, unable to let go. If you can let go, then that's called being apart from the false. If you cannot leave the false, you are involved in climbing on conditions and you cannot get rid of your obstructions. If you are able not to know either birth or death, then you won't have any attachments at all.

*When the mad mind ceases, enlightenment interpenetrates.* You must stop your mad mind and your ambitious tendencies. "How do I stop?" you ask. Just stop! Is there still a "how"? Just stop! When the mad mind ceases, then you enlighten to the perfect unobstructed interpenetration of the Buddhadharma. The Buddha said, "All living beings have the wisdom and virtuous characteristics of the Buddhas. It is only because of false thinking and attachments that they are unable to certify to the attainment." He also said, "When the mad mind ceases, that ceasing is Bodhi."

有菩提。人人都會起煩惱，可是卻把菩提忘了。要是忘了它，就不用它。就像冰，本來是水，因冷而結冰；如有一股暖氣，就可把冰變成水。這就是煩惱和菩提的譬喻。這一股冷氣，就是煩惱；相反的，要是有陽光，就變成菩提。什麼是冷氣？貪瞋癡是也。什麼是陽光？就是戒定慧。要是「勤修戒定慧，息滅貪瞋癡」，就是轉煩惱為菩提，也就是冰變水了。這只是個譬喻，不可又執著「冰即水」、「煩惱即菩提」。否則，你又會說：「那我就留著煩惱好，因為煩惱就是菩提；即然冰就是水，我就留著這塊冰，把它當水看。」不可如此。雖然人人可成佛，可是要修行。如何修行呢？須依佛法去修，或參訪明眼善知識，教我們方法去修行。

**生死涅槃色即空。**人人怕死，可是要是沒有生死，亦無涅槃。涅槃需要在生死中去找。找到涅槃後，就不必再繼續找了，不要「騎驢覓驢」。現在我們還沒有得到涅槃，因為我們還有生死；要是生死已了，涅槃就是你自己的，不必再找了。所以說色即是空，涅槃也是空。

**放下攀緣離諸妄。**想要證得人空、法空，生死涅槃皆空的境界，就要放下看破，不要執著不放。這就叫做離諸妄。不離諸妄，就是攀緣，就是不能除一切罣礙。你要不知生，不知死，就沒有任何執著。

**歇止狂心覺圓融。**把狂心野性停止。怎麼停止？停止就是停止，還有個什麼「怎麼」停止呢？狂心一停，就覺悟一切佛法圓融無礙。就是佛所說的：「一切眾生皆有如來智慧德相，但以妄想執著不能證得。」又說：「狂心若歇，歇即菩提。」

**悟得自性光明藏。**自性就是光明藏，要是能悟得自性本來就是光明藏，則證「**原來報身即法身。**」自性的大光明藏，就是如來藏性。原來未受業報的報身就是法身。所以我們現在正在受善報或惡報，這都是我們在過去生中所做的善業或惡業。如果我們做善業，我們就受善報；如果我們做惡業，我們就受惡報。悟得本來面目，悟得自性光明藏。

那像是什麼呢？學生就是教授，教授就是學生，沒有分別。佛即眾生，眾生即佛。明白這個道理，就是真正光明，否則就是無明。

*Awakened, attain to the bright store of your own nature.* Your own nature is a bright storehouse of light. If you can awaken to that bright treasury of light inherent in your own nature, then you can certify to the fact that *basically the reward body is the Dharma body.* The bright light treasury of your own nature is the Treasury of the Thus Come One. The reward body, prior to undergoing karmic retribution, is the Dharma body. And so we are now undergoing the rewards or retributions for whatever karma we created in the past. If we created good, then we receive a good reward. If we created evil, then we receive an evil retribution. But you must actually become enlightened--see your original face--before you can be certified as having perceived the light of your own nature.

What's it like when that happens? Students become professors and professors become students. Everyone is the same. Buddhas are living beings; living beings are Buddhas. If you understand this principle, you have genuine understanding. If you have not yet understood, then you still have ignorance.

Dr. Epstein comments:

What I remember, which may not be clear, about why the Master moved out of Chinatown was that, when he lectured on the Dharma, many of those in the assembly would not pay attention. They would talk and gossip, and even though he told them that their behavior was not proper, they continued not to take the Dharma seriously. And so he decided to move out of Chinatown. He found a flat at the corner of Sutter Street and Webster Street, near the present-day Japantown (which had not yet been built) and on the edge of the Fillmore District. A lot of the Buddhists in Chinatown were very unhappy with him for moving out of Chinatown; very few people came to see him.

...As I had the opportunity to be around the Master more, I became more and more interested in meditation. Slowly, through sitting with the Master and meditating, I began to get more of an idea who he was, and because of some special experiences I had with him when I was meditating, I came to see him not merely as a very kind, older Chinese monk, but as a truly extraordinary person; somebody, who, as far as I could see, had no self and was both very powerful and very compassionate. That realization radically trans-

易博士説：

有關上人為什麼搬出中國城一事，我記得的可能不是很清楚，大約是因為當他在講經時，很多人並不專心聽，他們在下面講話、聊天，甚至在上人告訴他們這態度不正確後，他們仍舊我行我素，不把佛法當一回事。所以上人決定搬出中國城。他在沙特街及維柏士街交叉處找到一棟樓房，很靠近現在的日本城（當時還沒有日本城）。這地方是在費摩區邊，中國城的一些佛教徒對師父搬出中國城一事很不諒解，也就沒幾個人去看上人。

……當我接近師父一段時間，我對打坐愈來愈有興趣。慢慢的因為與師父一起打坐，我開始有一些感覺，上人是誰？因為當我打坐時，我有一些特殊的境界，對我而言，上人不只是原來那位慈祥的中國老和尚，而變成了一位很特別的人，這個人就我所看的，是沒有我相，是非常的有力量又非常的慈悲。當我更進一步認識上人以後，我對上人及佛教的態度完全改觀了，我變得對佛法更有興趣，我用嚴肅的態度去研究，雖然當時我對佛教或皈依還不甚瞭解。

formed my whole attitude towards him and Buddhism, and I became more seriously interested in studying Buddhadharma, although I still didn't understand very much about it or know anything about taking refuge.

In July of 1967 the Master moved back to Chinatown and opened the Buddhist Lecture Hall, which occupied the oldest Chinese temple in America. The Master himself made a several-foot high white plaster Buddha image, which he placed in front of the old Taoist altar. Later, the images of Shakyamuni Buddha, Medicine Master Buddha, and Amitabha Buddha arrived from Hong Kong.

Dr. Epstein comments:

At the end of that summer, which was the summer of 1967, the Master had decided to move back to Chinatown. Just before I left to go to graduate school at the University of Washington in Seattle, I remember helping to move to the Tien Hou Temple on the fourth floor of a building on Waverly Place in Chinatown. Later that fall I wrote to the Master and asked him whether I could come and meditate over the Christmas break at the temple. He wrote me back a letter saying, "You are welcome to my place. There is no heat and cold. Hope will see you soon." At that time I had met a number of people in Seattle who were interested in Buddhism. They had heard about the Master from me, and so out of curiosity some of them dropped in for brief periods during the two weeks I was meditating at the temple. While I was there, I decided to take refuge, and Jon Babcock, who later was one of the translators during the Shurangama Sutra Session, took refuge as well.

We went back to Seattle and set up some places where people could get together and meditate. Then we got together the people who were interested in Buddhism and we wrote a letter to the Master to invite him to come to Seattle to have a meditation session over our Spring Break.

When the Master received our letter inviting him to go to Seattle to conduct a meditation session, he dictated a letter saying that he could not come to Seattle to hold the meditation session there, because if he did, there would be an earthquake in San Francisco. And as long as he stayed in San Francisco, there would not be an earthquake. And so he suggested that we come to San Francisco instead and have the meditation session there.

A number of people who were interested in Buddhism went to San Francisco to participate in the meditation session, along with some people living in San Francisco. At the end of that session, a summer study and meditation session was planned during which the Master would lecture on the *Shurangama Sutra*. That 1968 summer session was 96 days long.

一九六七年七月，上人搬回中國城，開放了佛教講堂，當時這地方是全美國最古老的中國廟。上人親自做了一尊數呎高的白石膏佛像，放在道教的神座上。後來，釋迦牟尼佛、藥師佛及阿彌陀佛的佛像都從香港運來了。

易博士又說：

在一九六七年夏天快結束的時候，師父決定搬回中國城。那時正是我要回西雅圖華盛頓州立大學念研究所，我記得我幫忙搬回位在中國城天后廟街一棟房子四樓的天后廟。稍後在秋天的時候，我寫了一封信給上人，問他我是否可以在聖誕節期間回去廟裡打坐。他回信說：「歡迎你來，這裡不冷不熱，希望很快的能見到你。」在那個時候，我在西雅圖遇到了一些對佛教很有興趣的人。他們聽我講過上人事蹟，由於好奇心，在我到廟裡打坐的兩個星期，一些人就順道來看一看。當我在那裡的時候，我決定皈依上人，還有一位白先生也同時皈依上人，他後來也是暑假楞嚴講修班的的口譯者之一。

我們回到西雅圖以後，找了大家可以打坐的地方。後來我們對佛法有興趣的人，共同寫了一封信給上人，邀請他在我們的春假期間到西雅圖主持一個禪七。

當上人收到我們邀請他到西雅圖舉行禪七的信時，他口述請人代筆說，他不能到西雅圖辦禪七，因為如果他離開舊金山，那舊金山就會發生地震。只要他待在舊金山一天，舊金山就不會有地震。所以他建議我們到舊金山，他會在舊金山舉辦一個禪七。

一些對佛教有興趣的人就到舊金山參加禪七，當時上人身旁已經有一些舊金山的美國人跟著他。當禪七結束時，我們就計劃在暑假期間，請上人舉辦一個楞嚴經講修班。這就是一九六八年暑期，有九十六天那麼長。

**The Master at Buddhist Lecture Hall requesting
the Buddhas of the ten directions.**

上人在佛教講堂恭請十方諸佛

The Master's deep affinities with young Americans coupled with his lofty virtue and astute wisdom were obvious during that first summer.

Dr. Epstein comments:

All through this time the Master was very, very patient. I think that's important to stress. Even though at that time Americans didn't know anything about Buddhism, and didn't know the proper etiquette, the Master was very, very patient in trying to teach people. He never got upset with anyone and did what amounted to a lot of baby-sitting and entertaining. He taught us how to cook. He sat with us during almost all the meditation sits. He told Buddhist stories to entertain everyone, and tried to help people sort out their personal problems. It was truly miraculous that he was able to bring this first summer session to a successful completion.

上人與這些年輕美國人深厚的緣份、他高尚的德行及智慧教化，在這第一期的暑假班流露無遺。

易博士說：

在這段期間，上人是非常非常地有耐心。有一點非常重要需要提出的，縱使在那段期間，這些美國人對佛教一點也不瞭解，也不知道應有的禮儀，師父一直非常非常耐心地教導這些人。上人從來沒有對任何一個人表示不愉悅，而且都是做一些哄小孩、逗小孩的工作。他教我們煮飯；幾乎每支香都陪我們一起打坐；說佛教故事娛樂我們；也試著幫助我們解決個人問題。他能把這第一個暑假班圓滿結束，真地是一件奇蹟的事情。

**The Master, kind and approachable,
used many expedients in teaching young Westerners.**

**慈祥、平易近人的上人，用各種方便法門度化西方的青年人。**

Terri Nicholson, Dr. Epstein's sister, comments:

Actually the first time I visited the Buddhist Lecture Hall was only briefly in January of 1969. I was fifteen at the time. I remember the Master saying, "Oh, so *you're* here."

My lasting impression of that first meeting with the Master is how surprised I was that he was so humble. I'd heard about the Master from my brother, and my impression was that he would be awesome and perhaps unapproachable. And yet when I arrived, the Master was dressed in a white T-shirt and gray pants; he was helping to move furniture. He was totally unaffected. I think that was my strongest impression--his total lack of any airs of being a great master or of having disciples. He just worked right along with everyone else and didn't at all put himself up as being special. I didn't come back again until January 1973.

[Note: Mrs. Nicholson later resided at the International Institute for the Translation of Buddhist Texts and became the Principal of Instilling Goodness School when it was founded there in 1973. When the school moved to the City of Ten Thousand Buddhas, she also moved with the school and continues to guide its development.]

易博士的妹妹易果參居士補充：

事實上一九六九年一月我第一次去佛教講堂時，停留時間很短。當時我才十五歲，我記得師父對我說：「喔，妳也來了！」

我永遠都記得第一次見到上人時的印象，當時我是多麼地驚訝，上人是如此平易近人。我從我哥哥那裡聽到上人的事蹟，我總認為他應該是一位令人敬畏或者是不可親近的人。但當我到了佛教講堂時，上人穿著一件白色汗衫，一條灰褲子，正在幫忙搬家具，一點不做作。我想我對上人最深的印象是：他完全沒有擺出一個大法師的架子或有很多弟子的樣子。他與每個人一樣地做工，沒有把自己擺得高高的，一副特殊的模樣。一直到一九七三年的一月，我都沒有再回去過。

（註：果參居士回來後就住在國際譯經學院，同時也是一九七三年成立育良小學時的校長。當學校遷移到萬佛城後，她也隨著搬到萬佛聖城，繼續指導學校發展。）

## Shurangama Sutra Session Graduation Ceremony: Alan Nicholson receives his award.

Alan, who dedicated his mastery of carpentry talents to the renovation of Gold Mountain Dhyana Monastery and later the City of Ten Thousand Buddhas, still resides at the City with his wife Terri and their family.

At the end of that summer session, the Master conducted a precept ceremony in which almost all the disciples took the Five Precepts and the Ten Major and Forty-eight Minor Bodhisattva precepts. One of the disciples who had participated in the entire session left the home-life and received the Shramanera (Novice) Precepts. Subsequently in 1969 he and four other Americans, three of whom were also full participants in the session, received full ordination at Haihui Monastery near Keelung, Taiwan. The five were the first Americans to become fully ordained members of the Buddhist Sangha.

倪果歸居士把他對木工的才能奉獻
出來，起先幫忙裝修金山禪寺，後
來又在萬佛聖城服務，目前他與他
的太太果參及家人居住在聖城。

在暑假講修班結束時，上人舉辦了
一次傳戒典禮，幾乎所有的弟子都
受了五戒及十重四十八輕菩薩戒。
暑假班的一位弟子在當時出家受沙
彌戒。接著在一九六九年，他和其
他四位美國人（其中三位曾是暑假
班的學生）到臺灣基隆的海會寺受具足戒。這
五位成為美國第一批受具足戒的佛教僧人。

## Notes taken by disciple Guo Yi prior to departure to Haihui Monastery in Keelung, Taiwan.

### October 27, 1969

The Master said:

往臺灣基隆海會寺受戒，
臨行前師父開示，果逸筆記。

一九六九年十月二十七日記錄

上人說：

I eat only once a day because I know that many of the world's people are hungry and I wish to offer my food to them. Eating only once a day at noon is in accord with Shakyamuni Buddha's rules.

In cultivating the Way, do not look at the faults of others. Speak of their good points instead. This is to have "virtue with respect to the mouth." If you don't have that kind of virtue, then no matter what you say, no one will believe you. With virtue in the three karmas of body, mouth, and mind, you will be respected on first sight. People will know by your bearing that you have virtue.

In the future I will transmit the Dharma to ten people: five left-home and five lay disciples. When you understand and can teach the *Shurangama Sutra*, the *Dharma Flower Sutra,* and when you have studied the *Avatamsaka Sutra,* you will separate and travel in the ten directions to be Dharma hosts and teach those with whom you have conditions.

In Buddhism you stand on your own two feet! Don't worry! Everything will be very easy.

我每天只吃一餐，是因為我知道在這個世界
上仍有很多人在饑餓中，而我希望將我的糧
食布施給他們。日中一食是佛制。

在修行的路上，不要看別人的過錯，相反的
要稱讚別人，我們要修「口德」。如果你沒
有口德，無論你說什麼，別人都不會相信你
。如果你身、口、意三業都具足德行，別人
第一眼看到你，就會尊敬你。他們從你的言
行舉止，就可以看出你的德行。

以後我會傳法給十個人：五個出家人、五個
在家人。當你們領悟了《楞嚴經》、《法華
經》，又可以講這二部經時，而且你們也研
究過《華嚴經》，你們要當個法主，分別遍
遊十方去教化與你們有緣的眾生。

在佛教中，你們要自己站起來！不要擔心！
每件事都會很簡單的。

## October 28, 1969

No one is to have a special style. We are a corporation and no one is first or last. Don't praise or slight others, and don't listen to them when they praise or slight you. You must do everything correctly and show them that Americans can cultivate the Way. Don't listen to praise and don't praise yourselves. Maintain "virtue with respect to the mouth" at all times and never speak of the faults of anyone. If people start talking falsely, just go away. Don't dirty your ears. These small points are the easiest to violate and are therefore the most important. Don't even think of the bad points of other people.

## October 29, 1969

Let me tell you what my work is: it is coarse work, like that of a brick maker. Bricks are made from mud and are used to make buildings, but if you let the mud dry by itself, it will crumble. You must fire it first, and then it won't fall apart. For a year the five of you have been fired and fired and now the time is ripe. You are bricks that won't fall apart and turn into mud. The bricks are fired, and later they will be used to build a house, a Dharma house, and they will be a firm and solid foundation.

Long ago a Bodhi seed was planted and now it bears fruit and you are going to receive the precepts. But you must tend the tree and nourish this fruit so that all who see it will want to eat it. Don't be the kind of fruit that has to be eaten in order to find out if it's sweet. People should know at a glance.

But don't let yourselves be eaten, either. Then, like the bricks, you won't fall apart. These words are difficult to put into practice.

Protect one another; protect one another's vows.

The most important thing in cultivation is samadhi. Recognize your own original nature. What is it? How do you recognize it? It is clear, pure, and unstained. Faced with worldly situations, do not react. Whether you meet with good conditions or with demons, do not let your heart be moved.

If they say you are good, if they say you are bad, whatever they say, pay no attention. You have followed me long enough to know better than to let your mind be moved by joy or sorrow.

And as to good and evil: there is no way you can say that someone is entirely good or entirely evil. Shakyamuni

一九六九年十月二十八日記錄

自己不要有一個特別的樣子。我們是一個團體，沒有一個人是第一或最後。不要讚嘆或輕視別人，你們也不要去聽別人對你的讚嘆或輕視。你們要很正確的做每一件事，讓他們看看美國人也是可以修行。不要聽別人的讚嘆，也不要自己讚嘆自己。隨時注意「口德」，不要講別人的過錯。如果別人在講是非時，你就走開，不要髒了你的耳朵。人很容易在這些小地方犯錯，所以這點特別重要，你們甚至連想也不要去想別人的過錯。

一九六九年十月二十九記錄

讓我告訴你們我的工作是什麼？那是很粗重的工作，就像一個磚瓦匠。磚是由濕泥所做成的，用來蓋房子。如果你把濕泥放著讓它乾了，那水泥就會碎掉。濕泥首先必須要用火來烤，才不會散開。一年來你們五個人一直被烤了又烤，現在是時候了。你們就像是磚一樣，不會再分散成為濕泥了。這些磚經過火烤後，就可以用來蓋房子，一個法房子，而且他們都是很穩定及堅固的基礎。

很久以前，佛的種子已經種下了，現在是結果的時候，你們就要去受戒了。你們必須要好好照顧這棵樹，孕育出好的果來，讓所有人看到這個「果」時就想要吃。不要變成一種讓人先要嚐甜不甜，才吃的「果」。你要讓每個人在一看到這「果」時，就知道是甜的。

但是你們也不要讓自己被吃掉了。你們要像磚一樣，不要碎掉了。這些話做起來是很困難的。

你們要彼此保護；要保護彼此的誓願。

在修行上最重要的是三昧。要認識自己原有的自性，那是什麼？要怎樣才能認識？自性是很清淨、純潔、無污染的。面對世間一切的境界，不要被轉動。無論你遇到善緣或魔，都不要讓你的心搖動。

如果人家說你好，如果人家說你壞，無論他們說什麼，都不要在乎。你們跟著我的時間已經夠長了，都會知道不要被高興或悲哀，轉動你的心。

說到善與惡：你不能說一個人完全好或完全壞。例如，釋迦牟尼佛有很多人讚嘆，同時也有很多人想要破壞僧團。提婆達多是最壞的一個，但他也有很

Buddha, for example, was praised by many people, and yet there were also many who tried to destroy the Sangha. Devadatta was the worst of men, but many disciples studied his practices. Some people even call the Buddha's disciples pigs and dogs. Don't let your heart move. Turn the situation, don't let it turn you. If you can know things without knowing them, then that's truly wonderful.

Good and evil come not from others, but from yourself. If you are good and others say that you are evil, you yourself know that you are right. But if you do evil and others say you are good, you are still a fraud. Turn the state. If you are right, it doesn't matter what people say.

I am happy that you want to leave the home-life, and in the future you must spread the Buddhadharma and make it great and vast. But you must not beg or take advantage of situations. Haven't I told you that those who leave the home-life under me must follow my Three Conditions? These Three Conditions are very important. As one who has left the home-life,

> Freezing, I do not scheme,
> Starving, I do not beg, and
> Dying of poverty, I ask for nothing.

Unless you meet these Three Conditions, you cannot leave home under me.

Spread the Buddhadharma, but have no mark of "self." Just that is the Proper Dharma. In Buddhism there is no such thing as suffering or difficulty. You must help others and not be selfish. Greed, hatred, and stupidity-- turn them, just like you turn over your hand. Before I was greedy, now I am not. Before I was hateful, now I am not. Before, I was stupid, now I am not. Turn it around, turn it over. This is the Mind Seal of all Buddhas which is being transmitted to you. Do you understand?

Don't have a 'self.' Put your 'self' to one side and help others. But do not think, "I am helping others. I am a Bodhisattva." What is done is done; put it aside. This is "letting all the appearances of dharmas be empty" and there is nothing higher. Sutras are explained just to tell you this. And so don't look elsewhere; you won't find it.

The Old Man of Mount Wei (the First Patriarch of the Wei Yang lineage) was given a sack of silver, but he didn't touch it. Three years later, the donor returned and it was still there, right where he left it. With that kind of samadhi power, you will surely succeed!

Are you enlightened? This is the last speaking of the Wonderful Dharma. Any questions?

While the five were in Taiwan, the Master paused in his lecturing of the *Dharma Flower Sutra* and spoke the *Amitabha*

多的弟子跟隨他學法。有些人甚至叫佛的弟子是豬，或狗。不要讓你的心被轉動了。要心能轉境，而不被境所轉。如果你可以知道而當做不知道，那就是最妙的了。

善與惡不是來自別人，而是來自你自己。如果你是好的，而別人說你壞，你自己知道你是對就好了。但如果你做壞事而別人說你好，那你還是一個愚癡的人，要轉這個境界。如果你是對的，就不要在乎別人說什麼。

我很高興你們願意出家，將來你們必須弘揚佛法，讓佛法遍佈更遠、更廣。但是你們不可以去化緣或攀緣。我不是曾經告訴你們，想要跟著我出家的人必須遵守三大宗旨？這三大宗旨是非常重要的。做一個出家人，必須

> 凍死不攀緣
> 餓死不化緣
> 窮死不求緣

除非你能夠遵守這三大宗旨，否則你不能跟著我出家。

弘揚佛法不可以有我相，那才是正法。在佛教中，沒有痛苦或困難的事情。你們必須幫助別人，不可以自私。轉貪、瞋、癡，就像翻手掌一樣。以前我貪心，現在我不貪心；以前我憎惡，現在我不憎惡；以前我愚癡，現在我不愚癡。轉過來，把它翻過來，這是所有佛祖的心印，現在傳給你們，你們都瞭解嗎？

不要有個「我」，把「我」放到一邊，去幫助別人。但也不要想，我正在幫助別人，我是一個菩薩。無論你做了什麼，把它忘了，這是「諸法空相」，沒有比這境界更高了。佛經就是告訴你這些，不要到其他地方去找，你找不著的。

曾經有人供養溈山老人（溈仰宗第一代祖師）一袋銀子，但他碰都不碰它。三年以後，這布施者回來，這黃金還在原地。有這樣的三昧定力，你就成功了。

你開悟了嗎？這就是妙法的最後一句了。有什麼問題嗎？

當五位弟子到臺灣受戒時，上人暫停講《法華經》，

*Sutra* during their absence. Once the five returned, the Buddhist Lecture Hall became busier and busier and the number of disciples kept increasing.

The *Seattle Times* published a large, front-page article and photo of the Master's five left-home disciples on Monday, November 10, 1969. The following is an excerpt from the article:

(Taipei, Formosa AP) Five young Americans, including four University of Washington students, hoping to become Buddhist monks and nuns began studying today at the Haihui Buddhist Temple in the Northern Formosan city of Keelung. The five arrived in Formosa Oct. 31. (...) If they stick to their schedule, they will be ordained into the priesthood December 1. All have studied Buddhism in the United States and will return there in December to take up duties in San Francisco's Buddhist Lecture Hall.

改講《阿彌陀經》。當他們五人回來後,佛教講堂變得比以前更忙碌,上人的弟子不斷的增加。

西雅圖時代報在一九六九年十一月十日星期一,以一大篇幅的首頁報導上人的五位出家弟子,並刊登了他們的照片。以下面節錄其中一段報導如後:

【臺灣臺北訊】五位年輕美國人,其中四位是華盛頓州立大學學生,今天於臺灣北部基隆的海會寺開始學習,希望成為佛教的比丘及比丘尼。他們在十月三十一日抵達……。如果他們能完成所有課程,到十二月一日他們就正式成為僧人。他們都是在美國學習佛法,十二月受完戒將返回美國佛教講堂,繼續他們的職責。

**The Master with his left-home and lay disciples on roof of Buddhist Lecture Hall in 1970.**

**一九七〇上人與出家及在家弟子於佛教講堂屋頂**

This roof became a much-used natural extension of the Buddhist Lecture Hall--an open-air classroom where we translated, memorized, did taiji, and worked on our own self-study and practice when time permitted. Translation and language study were the major emphases in the daily schedule of the five newly left-home disciples. The schedule was like this:

我們經常利用佛教講堂的屋頂做些事情,很自然地這屋頂就成為講堂的一部份。那是一間露天的房間,我們在那裡翻譯、背經、打太極拳;如果我們有時間的話,也是在那裡自修做功課。翻譯及學習語言,是這五位新出家弟子每天功課中最主要的一部份。他們的課程如下:

| morning recitation | 4:30 to 5:25 am |
| meditation | 5:30 to 8:30 am |
| Sutra translation | 8:30 to 10:30 am |
| Sutra translation | 2:00 to 4:00 pm |
| Chinese lessons | 5:00 to 6:45 pm |
| Sutra lectures | 7:00 to 9:00 pm |

| 早　課 | 早上4:30 ～ 5:25 |
| 打　坐 | 早上5:30 ～ 8:30 |
| 譯　經 | 早上8:30 ～10:30 |
| 譯　經 | 下午2:00 ～ 4:00 |
| 中文課 | 下午5:00 ～ 6:45 |
| 聽　經 | 晚上7:00 ～ 9:00 |

宣化老和尚追思紀念專集

# Taking Refuge

Among those who became disciples are Bob and Fran Laughton (not yet married then) and Barbara Waugh (who later had the rare good fortune of having the Master preside at her marriage to Ernie at the Buddhist Lecture Hall). Barbara and Fran both became nurses who now practice in the Ukiah Valley and regularly worship with their families at the City of Ten Thousand Buddhas.

Bob and Fran were over ten years without children and after multiple tests had been told it would be impossible to have any. They prayed sincerely to Guanyin Bodhisattva, and eventually Fran bore two strong and healthy sons--a feat that the doctors found incredible.

皈依的弟子中有果同及果通夫婦（當時他們尚未結婚），以及果須（後來她有一個罕有的好運，就是在佛教講堂上人主持她與 Ernie 的婚禮）。果須及果通兩位後來都是護士，她們現在在瑜伽鎮當護士，她們兩人定期與家人到萬佛聖城參加法會。

果同及果通結婚十年都未有小孩，在經過多次的檢驗後，醫生告知他們不可能有小孩。他們就很虔誠地向觀世音菩薩祈求，後來果通生了兩個強壯健康的兒子，讓醫生視爲不可思議的事情。

## More Take Refuge　更多的皈依弟子

The number of disciples kept growing and the Buddhist Lecture Hall somehow accommodated the expanding assembly. In this group of disciples taking refuge is one who would leave home, earn a Ph.D., publish monthly Sanskrit lessons in the Buddhist journal *Vajra Bodhi Sea*, and translate for the Venerable Master.

上人的皈依弟子愈來愈多，但佛教講堂怎麼樣也還是包容得下。相片中這一群皈依的弟子，有一位後來出家，也拿到博士學位。她以後也在每個月的《金剛菩提海》寫〈梵文專題〉，同時也爲上人翻譯。

# The Master's Chinese Lessons
## 上人的中文課

The lesson reads: "A worthy one of old said, 'If anyone is killed, it is as if I killed him myself. If anyone has been cheated, it is as if I cheated him myself.' At all times, look within. 'If you offend before heaven, you have no place to pray.'"

課文是「古人名言：『倘有一人被殺，如吾殺之。一人被欺，如吾欺之。時刻反省，庶不致獲罪於天無所禱也。』」

Daily Chinese lessons began as soon as the Shurangama Sutra Session ended. Through those precious lessons, which the Master faithfully taught, regardless of how busy, how weary, how pressured, or how sick he might be, we learned everything from the criteria for being good people all the way to the method for becoming Buddhas. Words cannot express how much of the Master's life-blood, how much of his soul and spirit went into educating his disciples!

「楞嚴經講修班」結束之後，接著立刻每天上中文課。上人不管多忙、多累、有多少壓力、或身體多不舒服，他都盡心盡力地親自教我們。經由這些寶貴的中文課，我們學會了，從如何做一個好人到如何成佛。上人爲教育弟子所付出的心血及精神，不是言語可以表達的。

## Dharma Instruments class led by Guoshi Tan.
## 譚果式的法器課程

Using the classical method, everyone tapped the table with his/her right and left hands in time to the beats of the drum and bell.

她使用傳統方法教每個人用左右手配合鐘鼓的節拍，在桌上練習拍打著。

宣化老和尚追思紀念專集

## Guoshi Tan acting as cantor during a ceremony.
## 譚果式在法會中當維那

In those early days, Madalena Liu, Guo-shi Tan, would come regularly to the Buddhist Lecture Hall to teach the monks, nuns, and laity how to play the traditional Dharma instruments. It was Guo-shi and her sister Guo-zheng who helped register the Sino-American Buddhist Association [later renamed the Dharma Realm Buddhist Association] in the State of California in 1958. They have followed the Master since his days in Hong Kong, when they took refuge while in their teens.

早期，譚果式經常來佛教講堂教比丘、比丘尼及在家居士傳統的法器。在一九五八年譚果式及她的姐姐譚果正，幫忙在加州註冊成立了中美佛教總會（法界佛教總會前身）。她們是從上人到香港時，就一直跟隨著上人，皈依上人時她們才十幾歲。

## The Master pleased and at ease amidst the bustle of the Lecture Hall.
## 上人和悅的、從容的穿梭在佛教講堂緊張又喧鬧的活動中

You know, in those early days, the Master would, on rare occasions, take us disciples on outings. Sometimes we would go to the "one-man temples" of Chinese monks who came to settle in the Bay Area. In the car on the way to such places that had expensive interior decoration--fine furnishings and thick carpets--the Master would quietly teach and re-teach us the rules of etiquette:

你知道嗎？在早期，上人偶爾會帶著我們去參訪。有時候我們去拜訪幾家「精舍」，那是一些中國和尚來到灣區後，就自己花錢買房子，建立自己的小廟。當我們開車到這些屋裡有昂貴裝潢、上等家具及厚地毯的精舍時，在車上上人反覆地叮嚀我們一些規矩：

Take off your shoes at the door. Don't look around as if you were thinking to steal something. Don't spill your tea. Don't ever go off alone in a room or place where you can't be seen; otherwise the host will worry about what you are up to or what you are going to take or break. Don't pick up anything! Don't take books off the shelves. Don't say things to challenge or embarrass the Dharma Master.

It was very obvious that our visits upset those Dharma Masters. As we trekked up to their doors, they would look at us aghast, for we didn't "fit" their environment at all!

How different their attitude was from the Master's kind and open acceptance of us! His patience and expedients drew us like magnets! He not only "put up" with our messes and mistakes, he slowly taught us how to clean up our messes and mend our mistakes. And how different those Dharma Master's "temples" were from the plain, often old, but always roomy and functional Way-places that the Master established for the Sangha and laity to reside in! The question is often asked why so many young people gravitated to the Master and wished to become part of his Sangha and cultivate. These are two big reasons!

**Excerpt from the article "Demon-cutting Sword" that appeared in the first issue of *Vajra Bodhi Sea*:**

Readers, beware! There are also among you false teachers: "Zen-masters," "Lamas," "Yogins," and "gurus"-- smooth swindlers seeking only profit and fame. In every bookstore, on every campus, among the young and the old, resorting to flattery, koans, and intellectual Zen, false patriarchs peddle their wares, saying, "You are a Buddha. I am a Buddha. We are all enlightened! Listen to me. Just BE! Be free!"...They gather naive and deluded "disciples" who are unable to distinguish the real from the false.

The Master also sent us out among the local American Buddhist "Patriarchs" occasionally and they didn't like us much either. Here is a quote from the speech Sam Lewis ("Sufi Sam") gave at the Wesak celebration conducted by the Master's left-home disciples, which some San Francisco officials called, "...the first organized attempt to celebrate this...birthday." Sam's disgruntled comments are:

I regret that I have to correct certain political men...The Dharma was introduced into this city in the last century...I remember especially the celebration fifty years ago which was the first time I went in any official capacity...Recently I have been on tour and when I returned I found the young people of this country...no, it is many years since we who are outcasts said, "The time will come when the Dharma will be established in

在門口脫掉鞋子。不要東張西望地好像想偷東西。喝茶時不要灑出來。不要單獨到沒人看到你的房間或地方，否則這主人會一直擔心你會做什麼，或者你會拿什麼或者你會打破什麼東西。不可以拿任何東西！不要在書架上拿書出來。不要對法師說些令人難堪的話。

很明顯地，那些法師對我們的拜訪都很不高興。當我們漫不經心大步地走到門口時，他們很不歡迎地看著我們，因為我們跟他們的格調實在格格不入！

和上人的慈悲及接受我們的態度比較起來，他們是多麼地不一樣！師父的耐心、權巧方便就像吸鐵石一樣吸住我們。上人不僅忍耐我們的邋遢及所做的錯誤，他還慢慢地教我們如何收拾乾淨及改正錯誤。那些法師的「精舍」與上人的道場又是多麼地不一樣！上人為僧團及在家人所建立的是一個雖樸素、老舊，但卻寬敞、又符合我們需要的道場。有人常問：「為什麼上人能吸引這麼多的年輕人，願意跟他出家及修行？」上面所說的兩點是最主要的因素。

**節錄自第一期金剛菩提海之「斬魔劍」一文：**

讀者們小心！你們之中也有偽裝的善知識─譬如「禪師」、「喇嘛」、「瑜伽師」、「上師」，都是一些求名求利的滑頭騙子。在每一個書店、校園裡，他們不論老少都使出諂媚法，講公案，或者講口頭禪說「你是佛，我是佛，我們全都開悟了！你聽我的，這是這樣，放任自由吧！」……他們聚集了一些天真無知、分不出真假的「弟子」們。

上人偶爾也會派我們到當地的美國佛教「祖師」那兒，他們也不喜歡我們。這裡我引用一段山姆‧路易士在上人的出家弟子所舉辦的釋迦牟尼佛聖誕慶祝法會中之演講詞。當時因為一些舊金山政府人員曾宣稱：「……這是第一次有組織公開地來慶祝釋迦牟尼佛聖誕。」山姆就很不高興地批評說：

我很遺憾我必須糾正這些政府人員……，佛法已經引進到這個城市一百年了……。我特別記得在五十年前，我第一次舉辦了這種慶祝典禮……。最近我出了一趟遠門，當我回來時，發現這國家的年輕人……不是，在很多年前，我們這些被擯除在佛教外的人，就曾經說過：「總有一天，年輕人會把佛

America, and established by the young." This prediction of us outcasts is fulfilled tonight in these young beautiful souls who have taken over and given us this holy celebration.

It was only after Sam's untimely death that he admitted that the Master was transmitting the Proper Dharma. He came back in dreams to his disciples, urged them to take refuge with the Master, and told them he regretted not having gone to study with the Master while he was alive.

And there was another "American Patriarch" who proclaimed that "Everybody is Buddha," meaning that since everybody was, he was too. Dr. Epstein comments:

At that time in San Francisco there were all kinds of strange Buddhist groups which claimed to be Buddhist but were not. And there were a number of Americans who had aspirations to be Patriarchs. They wanted recognition from the Master, because they recognized the Master in some way or another and felt that the Master could give them some kind of certification or verification of being the First American Patriarch. Of all those strange people, Joe Miller was probably the most intelligent and astute. Joe was the President of the San Francisco Theosophical Society and had his own disciples. Probably I first met Joe Miller and his wife in the winter of 1967-68, when I went to the Buddhist Lecture Hall to meditate. The Master then had public meditation from 7-8 in the evening. Joe Miller had very complicated conditions with the Master for many past lives, and the Master indicated that he had tried to teach Joe Miller for a long time. He was one who drew near to the Master and whom the Master was unable to teach successfully. I remember the Master saying that Joe Miller was already causing him trouble back in the Tang dynasty or the Song dynasty. He and his wife also attended parts of the Shurangama Summer Session until he was publicly scolded for his improper behavior. He left and after that only had infrequent contact with the Master.

But there were also others, including Sam Lewis, or Sufi Sam, who started the American Sufi Order, and who used to come around with his disciples. There was another fellow, whose name I can't recall, who had a group of Zen mountain climbers and fire walkers. The first issues of *Vajra Bodhi Sea* have some oblique references to these people in sections about the demon-cutting sword and the demon-pounding pestle. When those issues of *Vajra Bodhi Sea* came out, some of the people got very upset, because they recognized that the articles were directed at them, even though their names were not mentioned.

法在美國建立起來的。」這些取代我們原有地位的完美青年人做到，他們舉辦了這麼一個神聖的慶祝法會。

就在山姆不幸過世後，他承認了上人是把正法傳到了美國。他託夢給他的弟子，積極地要他們皈依上人，並且告訴他們說他很遺憾，當他活著的時候，沒有跟上人學佛法。

也有另一位自稱是「美國祖師」的人，他曾經宣說：「每一個人都是佛」，意思是說因為每一個人都是，所以他也是佛。易博士說：

當時在舊金山有一些奇怪的佛教團體，他們說自己是佛教徒，但卻似是而非。另外有一些個美國人渴望著當祖師。他們想要得到上人的印證，因為他們有一種感覺，認為上人可以證明他們是美國第一代祖師。在這些奇怪的人中，周米勒可能是最聰明、最能幹的一位。他是舊金山通神協會會長，也有自己的弟子。一九六七年底、六八年初的冬天，當時我在佛教講堂打坐，那是我第一次遇到周米勒夫婦。那時上人每晚上七點到八點對外開放禪坐班。周米勒在過去的幾世中與上人有很複雜的因緣，而且上人曾表示他想要教化周米勒已經好長一段時間了。周米勒接近上人，但上人卻未能將他度化成功。我記得上人說過，回溯到唐朝或宋朝時代，周米勒就已經開始給上人惹了一些麻煩。他和他的太太也參加部份暑假楞嚴經講修班，直到被上人公開譴責他的行為不端後就離開。從那次走後，他就很少再與上人接觸。

但是還有一些其他的人。包括山姆，他開始創立了美國回教的密宗派，他和他的弟子也一起到佛教講堂。另外還有一個人，我不記得他的名字，他有一群爬山禪人及一些會走火的人。早幾期《金剛菩提海》裡面，在講到斬魔劍及降魔杵的篇幅中，曾經隱約地提到這些人。當這些《金剛菩提海》出版時，其中一些人非常不痛快，雖然在文中沒有提他們的名字，但他們認為這些文章講的是他們。

## Chinese Lessons: Water and Mirrors

## 中文課：水鏡回天錄

淨其意志，回心向善，發精進勇猛心，立志修成道果。廣度同倫，共登彼岸，與諸上善人，歡聚一處，不退菩薩，永作伴侶。

予之水鏡回天錄所以作也，亦即為此。然此事說來容易，行之甚難。何以故？眾生行善，耳提面命，三誨五教，猶不奉行。若遇惡緣，念念增長，無教自通。迷途知返者鮮矣。

故譬如水中之月，鏡裡之花，有影而無形，此正所謂不可希望之希望，不可成就之成就。故名之曰「水鏡回天」云爾。

"With great heroism let us direct our thoughts toward the good; resolve to cultivate and realize the results of the Way; take other across and reach the other shore together; join the assembly of a superior and good people in one place; and forever be companion of irreversible Bodhisattvas.

"This is the very purpose for which this book *Reflections in Wate and Mirrors Turning Back the Tide of Destiny* was written. Th purpose is easy to discuss but very difficult to achieve. Why? I trying to get living beings to do good, you may grab them by th ear, admonish them three times and teach them five times, and sti they do not alter their conduct. Yet if they encounter bad ways the advance without faltering and learn without any need for instruc tion. Those who understand that they should turn away from th path of confusion are few indeed!

"Like the moon reflected in water, like flowers in a mirror--a these things are merely images without any substance. It may b said to be hoping for that which is without hope, trying to accom plish what cannot be accomplished. It is for this reason that thi book is called *Reflections in Water and Mirrors Turning Back th Tide of Destiny*."

**The Assembly at the Buddhist
Lecture Hall, San Francisco**

舊金山佛教講堂法會一幕

# 金輪聖寺
# 成立的經過及其沿革
## HISTORY OF GOLD WHEEL SAGELY MONASTERY

宣公上人一九九三年三月三十一日開示於長堤聖寺
A talk by the Venerable Master Hua on March 31, 1993, at Long Beach Sagely Monastery

**上人：**洛杉磯這道場成立多少年了？

**胡果相：**一九七六年開始。

**上人：**啊！一九七六年開始，就從他們三步一拜的時候，對不對？

**胡果相：**對！

**上人：**三步一拜以前就開始！

**胡果相：**對，先開始的，然後三步一拜。

**上人：**妳把這個前面的經過，給大家講一講，我們搬了多少次家。

**Venerable Master:** When was our first monastery in Lo Angeles established?

**Helen Woo:** In the beginning of 1976.

**Venerable Master:** Ah, that was when those two monks bega their "Three Steps One Bow" pilgrimage, right?

**Helen Woo:** Yes.

**Venerable Master:** The monastery was founded before th pilgrimage started!

**Helen Woo:** Yes.

**Venerable Master:** Why don't you tell everyone about th history of our temples here, how many times we moved, and s forth?

胡果相：在一九七六年的時候，因為我剛信佛，想找一位好的師父，但不知道在三藩市就有那麼好的師父，還特地到臺灣去尋師。等回來時，才發現好師父就在美國，所以很興奮，就想到舊金山去皈依上人。那時講好大家一起去，結果人越來越多，本來可擠一輛轎車，結果租一輛巴士都不行了。我們又不認識師父，也不好意思說請師父過來，後來倪偉然給師父打電話，師父很慈悲答應了我們，從三藩市來洛杉磯給我們一起皈依。

皈依那天差不多有二百多人，臨時租了個俱樂部的大廳。那天很熱，小孩子有幾個月大的，老人有八十多歲的，一起皈依，師父很慈悲，帶了很多出家人來。後來師父和一些法師，每個月都來洛杉磯，給我們講開示。我就開始想：我們應該有個道場了。開始時是在一九七六年，找了個小房子，本來是個托兒所，那就是我們金輪寺的開始。有了金輪寺後，恆實法師和恆朝法師就開始三步一拜了。

上人：那時候有一些個居士發菩提心。現在的成就，都是那時候紮下的根。現在的地方也比那時候的大，又有兩個地方了。

胡果相：大概過了兩三年，在漢廷頓道，就是在南巴沙地那市跟阿罕布拉市中間交接的地方，我們找到一個稍微大點的地方，可以坐一百五十人左右，但是很舊，也不太合用，就一邊修，一邊補，又加廁所，就這麼用了一陣子。大概待了兩年後，那時師父就找到個大的道場，在六街。因為那是個舊教堂，很舊很破爛了，那時萬佛城有幾位男居士來發心要修，花了一年多才修好。就在六街待了好幾年，後來碰到一個好機會，找到五十八街現在的金輪寺。

我們找到金輪寺現在的地方，那時師父正在臺灣弘法，很忙。因為洛杉磯大地震剛過，我看這地方建築表面好像不行了，要塌了似的，房子都是大裂紋，尤其底下。這棟房子本來是值一百多萬，但是他們賣的人看房子都是大裂紋，不能蓋公寓，所以要價特別低。我想也許當初建得很堅固，所以帶了一位結構工程師去看。一看之下，知道那些裂紋都是表面的，房子地基特別堅厚，非常好，是現在的建築物所不能比的。師父就買下來，後來有一些居士發心裝修，這就是現在的金輪寺。

上人：這是金輪寺成立和沿革的經過。

Helen Woo: In 1976, when I first believed in Buddhism, I was trying to find a good teacher. I went especially to Taiwan to look for one and didn't realize that there was such a wonderful teacher in San Francisco until I was back. I was so excited that I wished to go there to take refuge. At that time, some of us decided to go together. More and more people joined us, until there were so many of us that we could not fit in one car, and even a bus was too small. However, since we had not met the Venerable Master, it didn't seem right to ask him to come to Los Angeles.

Finally Weiren Ni called the Master, who kindly consented to come to L.A. to hold the Refuge-taking ceremony. On that day, more than two hundred people, ranging from several months to over eighty in age, took refuge with the Master in the very hot hall of a club that we had rented. The Master was very kind, and he had brought several left-home disciples along. When the Master and his disciples began coming to L.A. to give lectures on a monthly basis, I thought we should have a temple here, and so I found a small house that was formerly a nursery school. That was the beginning of Gold Wheel Monastery in 1976 [editor's note: Helen later remembered this was in 1977], and soon afterwards Dharma Masters Heng Sure and Heng Chau began their pilgrimage of bowing once every three steps.

Venerable Master: At that time some laypeople made the Bodhi resolve. They planted the roots for the accomplishments of today. Now we have a bigger place; in fact, we have two temples now.

Helen: Two or three years later, on Huntington Drive where South Pasadena and Alhambra meet, we found a larger place that could accommodate 150 people. It was a very old building and not suitable for our needs. We had to repair it and add a restroom. Two years later, the Master found a large, old church building on Sixth Street. Because it was quite rundown, several laymen from the Sagely City of Ten Thousand Buddhas came down and spent more than a year renovating it. Many years passed before we had the good fortune of finding the present site of Gold Wheel Monastery, on Avenue 58.

When we found the present site of Gold Wheel Monastery, the Venerable Master was away on tour in Taiwan. The big earthquake had just hit L.A., and the building looked like it was going to fall apart. There were many huge cracks in it, so the price was exceptionally low. Thinking that it still might be a very sturdy building, I took a structural engineer to inspect it. He found that the cracks were superficial and the foundation was very solid, much more so than in modern buildings. The Venerable Master bought it and some lay people renovated it, and thus we have the present Gold Wheel Sagely Monastery.

Venerable Master: That's the history and background of Gold Wheel Monastery.

# KINDNESS, COMPASSION, JOY, AND GIVING
# ENSURE AN ENDURING PEACE
# 慈悲喜捨永保和平

In l962, when the Venerable Master entered the United States for the first time,
Buddhism's monastic tradition was virtually unknown to Americans.

一九六二年，上人第一次來美國時，美國人對傳統的佛教寺廟不甚了解。

Oldy But Goody　好古

In the Golden Age of Buddhism in China, there was a network of Buddhist monasteries through that vast land. Shakyamuni Buddha's teachings flourished and the Patriarchs of China systematized them into schools of practice. During that long span of Buddhism's rise and flourishing, China was rich in the Dharma and the entire country benefited from the presence of the large community of Buddhists who, by actively applying the principles of Buddhism to their lives, served as a protection and support for their nation and the entire world.

In l962, when the Venerable Master entered the United States for the first time, Buddhism's monastic tradition was virtually unknown to Americans and there were no Buddhist facilities appropriate for housing the Buddhist Sangha and pure laity in the West at that time.

Today, in l996, thirty-four years later, there exists a network of Buddhist monasteries throughout the United States and Canada that links with monasteries in Southeast Asia to form a vast monastic complex spanning East and West. The Venerable Master is the single, vital, moving force that brought this monastic structure into being and nurtured it so that it could stand strong without reliance when the time came for him to loose his supportive hold.

Last year, the Master let go, and all over the world, beings mourn. The grief, held deep inside and carried quietly, is a common bond shared by all who knew him. And all of us who knew him intend to spread his teachings and carry on his work—filling those pure monastic facilities with ceaseless sounds of Dharma; with training centers for those just beginning to study; with pure Sanghans and laity who are dedicated to maintaining the daily schedule of study and practice so carefully given us by the Master; with communities of Buddhists who understand how to make offerings in a way that simultaneously supports and protects the purity of the Sangha community; with homes for the aged where their years are venerated and the fruits of their experiences valued and respected; and with schools to educate the young and give them a foundation in morality and humaneness so they can become beneficent leaders of the future.

Twenty years ago, a group of Buddhists in Los Angeles was inspired to look for a facility that could serve as a Way-place, so that they could invite the Master and his Sangha to Southern

佛教在中國最鼎盛時期，寺廟如網一般地佈滿在整個遼闊的土地上。佛教盛行，中國的祖師們也各自依其修行法門而形成宗派。在這一段全盛時期，中國佛法興盛，因爲有這麼多的僧團及佛教徒，在日常生活中修行，不僅護持了中國，甚至於整個世界都護持了。

一九六二年上人來美國時，那時美國人對傳統的佛教寺廟不甚瞭解，而且當時在西方也沒有一處大叢林，可供佛教僧團及眞正發心修行的在家居士們居住。

在三十四年後的今天，一九九六年，佛教寺廟如網般地遍佈在美國及加拿大地區，聯結了東南亞的佛寺。師父憑著他一個人的力量帶動建立了這麼多的寺廟，同時他一直培育到他們可以獨立了，他就放手。

去年上人「放手」了，舉世同悲。凡是認識上人的人，都有這份深蘊內心無言的悲哀。但是我們知道師父的人，要堅強起來繼續弘揚他的教法，肩負起他的佛事：在他所建立的清淨道場，要繼續法音不斷；要成爲初學佛法者的訓練中心；道場內的僧團及在家居士是清淨的，且願意維持師父所交待每天應作的功課及修行；並且也是一處給懂得依法供養的人去護持三寶的清淨；設安老院，讓年老的人有所安置，並善用其人生經驗；成立學校，教育年輕人，奠定其仁義道德的基礎，使其成爲未來能利益人的主人翁。

二十多年前，洛杉磯一群佛教徒受感召去尋找一個處所，做爲佛教道場，以便邀請上人及其僧團到南加州來弘揚佛法、修行。他們最後終於找到了地方，上人命名爲「金輪寺」。從此上人定期

California to propagate the Dharma and cultivate the Way there. They found a place and the Master gave it the name Gold Wheel. The Master began to travel to Gold Wheel Monastery regularly. His tasks there were many. First, he continued his fundamental universal teaching of getting people to recognize and confront their faults and afflictions and then getting them to accept and use methods for changing those faults and renouncing those afflictions. After stopping evil, he taught them to do good. The Master tirelessly trained this growing group of laity in the behavior appropriate for protectors of the Proper Dharma, while at the same time ever-reminding his left-home disciples of their behavior as members of the Orthodox Sangha. Also, he secured the boundaries and protected the earth, for the Los Angeles area—the entire West Coast in fact—was constantly receiving predictions of earthquakes, not to mention all the other natural disasters and man-made calamities that occurred nonstop. How skillful and all-encompassing the Master's expedients were in seeing to the success of all these things!

For instance, on May 7, 1977, the second Three Steps One Bow pilgrimage was launched from that first Gold Wheel. In the great scheme of things, it was undoubtedly no accident that the Master's Bhikshu disciples bowed once every three steps up the West Coast—spanning the distance from Los Angeles near the Mexican border to Mount Baker near the Canadian border. It was also surely no coincidence that the time frame of the first bowing pilgrimage included that gripping moment when a stray comet was discovered to be hurtling straight for our earth, followed by the sweet relief when it missed up by cosmic inches. When it was all over and nothing had happened, the Master led us in Praying for Peace in Seattle.

Nor could it have been chance that the second pilgrimage began shortly after we prayed for rain in Golden Gate Park. Those bowing monks, who headed north from Gold Wheel's Bodhimanda, venerating the *Avatamsaka Sutra* with every step, passed through drought-stricken Southern California where the earth was so barren and brittle that the top crust would crumble underfoot to send one plunging into empty pockets of illusory dust. As the monks repeatedly chanted "Homage to the *Great Flower Adornment Sutra*," the sweet dew of Dharma, welling forth from the Perfect Teaching, moistened the sterile valleys and brought relief to the starving and thirsty.

And every step of the way, the laity of Los Angeles protected and supported. How many times did they drive long, hot hours to bring offerings to the monks and to join them in bowing? The Master guided both the monks and the protectors, teaching them each their proper roles. The lay community grew and the second Gold Wheel was bigger. The Master continued his work of securing the boundaries and protecting the earth by lecturing the entire *Earth Store Sutra* during his monthly visits to Los Angeles.

Always careful to conserve, the Master often chose to be driven to Los Angeles rather than to fly there. Whoever accompanied the Master in the car had to be prepared to 1) give impromptu lectures

赴金輪寺。上人在金輪寺有多重的使命。首先，上人用他一貫基本的教化，先讓人瞭解並且看清楚自己的過錯、煩惱，然後再設法讓其改過遷善，斷除煩惱。在他們停止做惡事後，上人就教他們做善事。上人不厭倦地教導日益增多的居士們，如何正確地做一個護持正法的護法者，在這同時也不斷地提醒他的出家弟子，如何做好一個正法僧團的僧人。另外他為保護這片土地，為此地結界，因為洛杉磯地區，甚至整個美國西海岸，常受地震之威脅，又有其他種種天災人禍，層出不窮。從上人同時成功地兼顧這麼多的使命，我們就可以看出上人的方法是如何地善巧及周全。

舉例來說一九七七年五月七日第二次三步一拜行腳就是由金輪寺出發。從這麼一件大事中，我們可以瞭解，上人的比丘弟子分別從鄰近墨西哥邊界的洛杉磯沿著西海岸，三步一拜到接近加拿大邊界的貝克山，毫無疑問地這是非比尋常的。在第一次舉行三步一拜時，發生了一件絕非偶然的事情——當時彗星直衝地球而來，最後卻以毫釐之差閃過了地球。事過境遷，大家鬆了一口氣，什麼事也沒發生，然後上人帶領著我們在西雅圖祈禱世界和平。

就在我們去金門公園祈雨後不久，絕非偶然地，第二次三步一拜行腳就開始了。這兩位三步一拜的行者，從金輪寺向北方開始朝拜，每一步都是禮敬《華嚴經》，當他們經過鬧旱災的南加州時，土地十分貧瘠、乾裂，每踏前一步，就從龜裂的地面陷入中空的地內，揚起很大的灰塵。而兩位行者不斷地誦念「南無大方廣佛華嚴經」，於是從圓教中就生出法的甘露，潤澤了這不毛之地的盆地，解除了其乾渴飢饉。

行者每一步都受到洛杉磯地區信眾們的鼓勵和支持。不知有多少次，信眾們在大熱天下開車開了很長一段路程，為他們送來食物並陪著他們拜一段路。上人教導了行者和信眾們各人所應盡的職責。在家信眾們越來越多，第二個金輪寺比較大一點。上人繼續每個月來洛杉磯結界安定大地，並且講解全本《地藏經》。

上人一向節儉，多次南下洛杉磯，都是坐車而不搭飛機。凡與上人同車的人都準備接受考驗：（一）就上人即興出的題目說法，（二）背誦並解

on any topic the Master might introduce; 2) recite from memory and explain any one or several of the infinite Buddhist lists chosen at random by the Master; 3) recite passages of the *Shurangama Sutra* or the entire Shurangama Mantra from memory; and 4) never, ever fall asleep from the moment the car started until the moment it arrived. After several hours of riding in the car, the Master would usually arrive at Gold Wheel in the late evening. Clusters of disciples would be there to greet him, no matter how late it was. Surrounded by the Los Angeles gathering of disciples, who, so delighted to see him after a month's interval, couldn't resist asking their questions and telling their troubles to him right then and there, the Master would patiently listen, thoughtfully answer, and entertain them until they were filled with the joy of Dharma—far into the wee hours of the night.

The community of lay disciples in L.A. kept growing and the third Gold Wheel was even bigger. While it was under renovation, Guanyin Bodhisattva appeared in the sky one afternoon, astride that watery, fish-dragon creature of hers. The skeptical may demand: "Who said it was Guanyin?" Well, some of the toughest, most hard-to-fool guys in the world said so. Guo Rui and his men—the ones who were part of the gang that shot up San Francisco Chinatown's Golden Dragon Restaurant—said so. They were renovating Gold Wheel on that day and when she appeared, they stood outside the monastery staring up at her there in the clouds, with their mouths open in awe. They saw her with their own eyes. Even Dr. Woo, driving home from a long day of treating the sick saw "something strange" in the sky that evening—right at the spot where she appeared. And I, who was at the second Gold Wheel at the time, heard their eye-witness accounts moments after she finally withdrew.

When the Master sent a huge white jade Shakyamuni Buddha to preside as host at the third Gold Wheel, the group of male disciples who volunteered to transport the several-ton image found their task nearly impossible. The graceful image was so heavy they could hardly budge it. As they heaved and hoed the last few feet and then, with a valiant final effort, set the image on its altar—at that very instant, the heavenly dragons let loose an earth-shaking thunderclap that shook the entire Monastery. I was there and witnessed that spectacular certification. What a grand finale!

Always, the Master worked on to insure that peace prevailed in the South. In April of 1978 the Master hosted a three-day Medicine Master Repentance Dharma Assembly—a first in the U.S. His verse manages to capture in a few words all I have struggled to describe above and breathes whispers of things that hadn't even happened yet.

> *Medicine Master's Dharma meeting ushers in good luck.*
> *The City of Los Angeles avoids calamities.*
> *Good and faithful donors alike are vigorous.*
> *Human and divine protectors are busy, busy all.*
> *Sincerity brings responses of more blessings and long life.*
> *Joy and giving, kindness, compassion insure a peace to come.*
> *Shocking heaven and shaking earth like springtime thunderclaps,*
> *The resounding drums and ringing bells alter the ten directions.*

釋上人由無數佛學名相中抽出的名相，（三）背誦部份《楞嚴經》或全部〈楞嚴咒〉，（四）從車子起動到抵達終點，全程都不能打瞌睡。經過數小時車程，通常抵達洛杉磯時都已經晚上很晚了。可是一群弟子不管多晚，都會在那裡等候歡迎師父來臨。這些洛杉磯的信眾，在看到一個月未見的上人時，都圍繞在師父的身邊，忍不住當場就向師父請示或述說他們的問題；然而師父總是耐心地傾聽，並且一一解答他們的問題、哄他們，直到他們法喜充滿，而那時已經是深夜了。

洛杉磯地區的信眾日增，第三個金輪寺也更大了。在裝修這個新的金輪寺時，有一天下午，天空出現了觀音菩薩相，騎在她那條魚龍身上。有人懷疑說：「是誰說那是觀音？」就是最頑固、不容易信服別人的人說的；就是果銳居士和他那一幫人——以前舊金山金龍飯店血案那幫人說的。那天，當觀音菩薩現相時，他們正在裝修金輪寺，他們站在寺外凝神注視著雲中的觀音菩薩，驚訝得嘴都張開了，他們都親眼看見了。就連胡醫生在看了一整天病人之後，當他晚上開車回家的路上，就在觀音出現那個方向的空中也看到了「奇怪的景像」。而我本人當時正在第二個金輪寺，當觀音菩薩隱沒之後，我親耳聽到那些人細述他們所看到的景像。當上人送來一座巨大、白玉雕的釋迦牟尼佛像到金輪寺做為主尊時，一群自願幫忙搬佛像的男居士，幾乎搬不動那尊幾噸重而精緻的玉佛像。就在他們使出渾身解數的力量，搬動最後那幾呎，將佛像安放在佛座上的那一剎那，天龍忽然轟然一聲放出雷響，震動了整個金輪寺，這個殊勝的場面是我本人親身經歷的。這個圓滿的安座是多麼雄偉壯觀！

為了安定南加州，上人的工作總是沒有休息的一刻。一九七八年四月師父在金輪寺主持了一場三天的藥師懺法會，在美國這還是第一次。當時上人並作了一首偈頌，他只用了少少的字就將我上列吃力描述的事情表達出來了，並且對當時尚未發生的事情，透露了些許的訊息。

藥師法會降吉祥，洛杉磯市免災殃
善信檀越同精進，人天護法各奔忙
至誠感應增福壽，喜捨慈悲保安康
驚天動地春雷震，暮鼓晨鐘化十方

# 長堤聖寺
# 成立的經過及其沿革
## HISTORY OF LONG BEACH SAGELY MONASTERY

宣公上人一九九三年三月三十一日開示於長堤聖寺
A talk by the Venerable Master Hua on March 31, 1993, at Long Beach Sagely Monastery

**上人：**長堤聖寺成立前後及經過，你們都應該知道。

**胡果相：**我們非常幸運有這麼好的一個地方。這本來是個天主教修女靜修的地方，她們在這裡住了四十年，完全閉關不出去；所以裡面還有醫院，又可以自己做麵包、小餅的。有的人也供養她們，但是她們不對外開放。只有前面小小那地方，是教堂，是她們唯一開放的一點點地方，後面都有鐵柵攔住的。她們住了四十年，後來管理的人覺得這地方不適合了，就搬到聖塔巴巴拉去蓋新的地方。那時機緣到了，師父來看，也覺得很好。

**Venerable Master:** You should all know how Long Beach Sagely Monastery was established.

**Helen:** We are very lucky to have such a fine place. It used to be a Catholic convent. The nuns lived a cloistered life here for forty years. Since they never went out, they had their own clinic and their own bakery for making bread and cookies. Although people made offerings to them, the convent was not entirely open to the public. There was a small area in the front for visitors, but the rest of the convent was closed to the public. Later, feeling that the place no longer suited their needs, the nuns moved to a new place in Santa Barbara. Our opportunity had come. The Master came to take a look and also liked it.

上人：也沒看。我就聽妳講的嘛！在沒有買妥的時候，我沒來看過。

胡果相：差不多搬了這麼多次家，都是我先看的。師父電話裡說可以，就成交了，幾次都是這樣。所以我們很幸運哪！這地方是我們長堤市的一個名勝，因為四十年來這些修女在這兒修道，所以附近的天主教徒對這地方都很認識；若一提這雷當多和海洋大道交叉口，他們都知道這個地方。我們買的時候，外面那尊聖母像，我們想留下來，因為這是我們的觀音菩薩，她們也答應了。

到現在，天天都有人來獻花，外面總有很多鮮花，從前的信眾還常來。原來裡面沒有一個真正大的地方，可以作為佛堂。後來師父看這地方，就是你們現在坐的地方，本來是個花園，我們就設計出來；經過很多程序，還向政府申請，才得到允許加蓋這個佛殿。

上人：長堤聖寺前後的經過，你們都應該知道。這個地方是萬佛聖城掏腰包買的，旁人沒有出過一分錢。每個道場怎麼樣的來歷，怎麼樣的沿革，我都記得很清楚。

我告訴你們。你願意超度，願意復建哪，願意怎麼樣，都可以隨喜功德。因為我現在雖然地方這麼多，開銷這麼大，但是只要單單吃飯、穿衣服，還不至於挨餓、受凍，還可以維持，所以大家都不必替我擔心。

所有我的徒弟，你們要知道，你師父是窮的，你們也都應該跟著我受窮的，不應該有錢，一有錢哪，麻煩就來了，就不修行了。一有錢哪，掛著吃喝玩樂，無所不為了！不像我現在在這兒的時候，一張紙我都用好幾天。我相信我的徒弟，沒有一個是這樣的，他們大約都是自由國家來的，對金錢也不懂得怎麼樣節省。所以我不要對誰一見著人，就錢錢錢的，就說：「天命之謂錢，率性之謂錢。錢也者，不可須臾離也。」不是這樣子的。

今天我也很高興，這裡比我一九七六年在漢廷頓那個地方大得多了；又有花園，又在海邊，空氣也不錯。

**Venerable Master:** I just listened to your description of it. I didn't visit it before we bought it.

**Helen:** In all of these moves, I was always the first one to look at the new place. If the Master okayed it over the phone, we made the deal. We're really lucky to have this place. It's a famous landmark in Long Beach, because the nuns lived and cultivated here for forty years. All the local Catholics know this place. If you just mention that it's at the intersection of Redondo and Ocean Boulevard, people will know it. When we bought the place, we asked them to leave the statue of the Virgin Mary in the front, because we also worship her as Guanyin Bodhisattva. Even now, Catholics still come to pay homage and bring lots of fresh flowers to offer to her every day. Originally, there wasn't an area large enough to serve as a Buddha hall. The Buddha hall we are sitting in now used to be a garden. After we drew up a design and applied for permission from the local government, we converted the garden into the Buddha hall.

**Venerable Master:** You should all know the history of Long Beach Sagely Monastery. It was purchased by the City of Ten Thousand Buddhas; no one else paid a penny. I remember the history of each of our temples very well.

I want to tell you that, from now on, you may make donations according to your ability, whether you wish to perform services to save the deceased, renovate a temple, or whatever. Although we now have so many temples and the expenses are not small, we can still manage to feed and clothe everyone, and no one will have to freeze or go hungry.

Now, you who are my disciples should know that your teacher is poor, and you ought to follow me in poverty. Once you have money, the troubles come and you cannot cultivate. Once you have wealth, you will want to eat, drink, and have fun--and you won't stop at anything. You won't be like your teacher, who uses the same napkin for many days. I don't think any of my disciples do that. You are all from free countries and don't know how to be thrifty. For that reason, I don't want to be like those money-grubbers who say, "What Heaven has conferred is called money; accordance with nature is called money. Money may not be left for an instant."

Today I am very happy. This monastery is much bigger than the one we had on Huntington Drive in 1976. It has a garden and overlooks the ocean, and the air is quite fresh.

# 華嚴聖寺
## 成立的經過及其沿革
# HISTORY OF AVATAMSAKA SAGELY MONASTERY

釋恆佐　　Shi Heng Tso

The Venerable Master Hua
宣公上人

Avatamsaka Monastery was established in 1989 in a small, eighty-some year old, two-story building (about 3,000 square feet) in the Ramsey area of southeast Calgary, Canada. The founders were mostly refugees from Vietnam who needed a place to practice their religion and promote Asian culture. After making a small down payment, this seminal group set out to find Buddhist monks or nuns to live in the temple and conduct the many services and classes traditionally held at Buddhist centers of worship. After some searching, they finally found the Dharma Realm Buddhist Association, whose leader, the Venerable Master Hsuan Hua, agreed to accept and run the new Calgary temple.

華嚴聖寺成立於一九八六年，原是一座屋齡八十多年的二層樓的建築物，有三千平方呎大，座落在加拿大卡格里市東南方的藍塞區。當初創辦的時候，是一些越南人，大部分是難民想成立一座佛教寺廟，也想提倡亞洲文化。在付了頭款之後，這些創始人就尋找佛教僧人來領導膜拜、功課等，及傳統上在佛教寺廟進行的活動。最後終於找到法界佛教總會的領導人——宣公上人，將廟給上人，讓上人來經管這座卡格里的寺廟。

Because the number of devotees attending functions at Avatamsaka Monastery has been increasing yearly, and because the present building is very small, members have been searching for a new, larger location for almost five years. The Association has finally found suitable facilities in the former home of the Mountain Equipment Coop, a one-story building with a full basement and over 21,000 square feet of floor space. This new location will be occupied by the end of July 1996. The address of the new building is: 1009 4th Avenue, South West, Calgary, Alberta T2P OK8, Canada.

因爲上華嚴聖寺的人一年比一年多，寺廟不夠大，所以會員就開始找個大點的地方。找了五年，終於到一個以前是賣登山用品的地方，是一座平房，有地下室。室內面積二萬一千平方呎，一九九六年七月可搬進。新地址是：1009 4th Avenue, South West, Calgary, Alberta T2P OK8, Canada.

# 華嚴精舍
# 成立的經過及其沿革
## HISTORY OF AVATAMSAKA HERMITAGE

華嚴精舍提供
Information provided by Avatamsaka Hermitage

華嚴精舍外景
Avatamsaka Hermitage

一九八九年一月，布希總統就職大典時，邀請了首位來美弘揚佛法的中國高僧——宣化上人，從加州前來觀禮，以示對佛教之敬重。這是上人第一次到華府。

上人抵達華府後，不要住為他所安排的貴賓旅社，卻要求借住佛寺。但當時華府並無佛寺，僅有

When President Bush began his second term in January 1989, he invited the Venerable Master Hua, the first eminent Chinese monk to come to America to spread the Buddha's teachings, to attend his inauguration, thus showing his respect for Buddhism. That was the Venerable Master's first visit to the nation's capital.

When the Master arrived in Washington, D.C., he requested to stay in a Buddhist temple instead of in the hotel arranged for the guests.

一佛教會的組織，會址設於一棟小屋內，僅可供二、三人臨時留宿而已。上人不厭會址簡陋，即借住佛教會，當天並於會址內爲華府佛教信徒們慈悲開示。

有一位葉果金居士和她的家人，都是非常虔誠的佛教徒，且對上人仰慕已久。葉居士聽聞上人蒞臨華府，眞是迫不急待想去晉謁上人，可是當晚無法去晉見，要等到第二天有人開車帶他去。據葉居士說，這一夜在家中等待如坐針氈，心情極爲興奮，竟然夜不能成眠，只盼天亮，就能拜見仰慕已久而人人敬愛的佛教大導師。葉居士在拜見宣化上人時，即懇求上人爲大華府地區開創一個佛教道場，弘揚佛法並教導信眾更爲圓融的佛學知識。但上人認爲華府的佛緣不深，信眾不廣，而且加州及其他多處的道場，又迫切地需要上人常常蒞臨開示、講經，所以未予應允。

在一九八九年的三月，上人應費城信眾邀請，前往費城弘揚佛法，並再次應華府的佛教會之邀，前往舉辦法會、弘揚佛法、利益眾生。

一九九〇年六月，上人應紐約信眾之邀，到美國東岸最大城市——紐約，舉辦法會，開演大乘、弘法利生。同時，上人又應華府各方邀請護持下，第三度到馬里蘭大學舉辦法會，開示大乘佛法，在上人權巧善導下，給迷津中的眾生指出一條光明大道。此時，華府一些信眾也一再請求上人在此處辦道場。

葉居士在華府居住多年，確信在華府設立佛堂是有其必要，所以一次又一次地前往加州萬佛聖城懇求；到第三次去聖城時，上人爲葉居士的誠意感動而應允在大華府地區設立佛堂，以供大眾學佛、習法、修行。

上人多次尋找適當地點，直至一九九〇年下半年看到馬里蘭州，波多瑪河畔的現址，就決定買了下來，定名「華嚴精舍」。那是位於波多瑪克市臨近華盛頓特區的一小叢林內，依小丘而座，前面俯觀溪流，甚爲清靜、稀有，是個修行的好地方。正屋三層，二樓已改爲佛堂及圖書館。另外正屋之左邊原有一獨立房舍，現

However, there was no Buddhist temple in Washington, D.C. at the time. There was only the small house of the Buddhist Association, which could accomodate a couple of people overnight. Not disdaining the simple accomodations, the Master stayed at the Buddhist Association and kindly delivered a talk to the local Buddhists that day.

A layman named Guojin Yeh and his family were extremely sincere Buddhists who had long admired the Venerable Master. When Upasaka Yeh heard the Master was coming to Washington, D.C., he couldn't wait to meet him. Yet he had to wait until the following day before someone could drive him over to meet the Master. Upasaka Yeh relates that he felt like he was sitting on pins and needles that night. He was so excited that he couldn't fall sleep; he could only wait for the day to break, so that he could meet and bow to this great Buddhist teacher whom he had admired for so long. During his visit with the Master, he sincerely requested the Master to start a Buddhist temple in the Washington, D.C. area in order to propagate the Dharma and give the local followers a fuller understanding of Buddhism. Since the Master felt that conditions with Buddhism were not deep there, that there were few followers, and that his numerous other temples already needed him to visit often and give talks and expound Sutras, he did not grant the request.

In March 1989, the Master was invited to go to Philadelphia to propagate Buddhism. At that time, the Washington, D.C. Buddhist Association invited him again, so he visited the capital, held Dharma assemblies, and expounded the Dharma for the benefit of living beings.

In June 1990, the Master responded to an invitation from devotees in New York and went to New York City, the largest city on the East Coast, to hold Dharma assemblies and expound the Great Vehicle Dharma to benefit beings. At the invitation of Buddhists in Washington, D.C., he hosted a Dharma assembly at the University of Maryland and lectured on Mahayana Buddhism. With his expedient and skillful teachings, the Master pointed out a bright path to confused living beings. At that time, some of the Washington Buddhists again requested the Master to start a temple in the Washington area.

Upasaka Yeh had lived in Washington, D.C. for many years and was convinced that Washington needed a Buddhist temple. Therefore he went time and again to the City of Ten Thousand Buddhas in California to beseech the Master to grant his request. On his third visit to the City, the Master, moved by Mr. Yeh's sincerity, promised to establish a temple in Washington, D.C. so the Buddhists there could study and practice the Dharma.

After searching many times for a suitable place, the Master, in the latter half of 1990, decided to buy a house on the bank of the Potomac River in Maryland, which he named the Avatamsaka Hermitage. The house, nestled in the woods of Potomac (a suburb of Washington, D.C.), surrounded by hills and overlooking a creek, was a peaceful place perfect for cultivation. The second story of the main house of three stories was renovated into a Buddha hall and a library. To its left is another house, which has been converted into a three-story Buddha hall over four thousand square feet in area. The large Buddha hall on

也已修建成三層樓的佛堂，全部面積約爲四千多平方英尺，二樓是一大佛堂，法會時可容一百五十餘人，三樓爲打坐靜修之用，一樓尚未正式修繕完畢，暫用作休息及工作室。

道場買下後，上人先派弟子在此閉關進修，並爲道場做一些維修工作。一九九二年四月，上人應邀赴美國總統舉辦的年餐會。在上人攜弟子赴白宮後，又應華府佛教會的邀請，在佛教會舉辦了法會，開演大法，並下榻於華嚴精舍；並舉辦了開光典禮。從此，信眾開始前來進修。

大佛堂已於今年（一九九六年）五月的第一個星期日法會，正式開放使用。來佛堂參拜、禮佛的信眾，日有增加；眞是師父慈悲，爲大華府區的弟子，及信眾開創了這樣完美的佛地。

有一事值得一提，據説上人來尋覓地點時，曾有居士介紹了幾處交通方便、地方又大、又可對外開放的地方，而上人都沒有答應。但當上人一到精舍現址，便一口答應買下此處，並不在乎壹佰萬之高價。後來居士們認爲上人會買此處的原因之一，是因爲此處在一百多年前曾是印地安人，被白人趕盡殺絕，全部退守至此，最後全部都在此處喪命，故冤魂很多……。上人是爲了這些冤魂而買下此處。

the second floor can hold over 150 people for Dharma assemblies. The third floor is for meditation and quiet cultivation, and the first floor, whose renovation has not yet been completed, serves temporarily as a resting and work area.

When the temple was first bought, the Master sent some disciples to practice in seclusion and do some renovation work. In April 1992, the Master accepted President Bush's invitation to an annual dinner at the White House. After attending the dinner with his disciples, the Master held a Dharma assembly and delivered Dharma lectures at the Washington, D.C. Buddhist Association. He also visited the Avatamsaka Hermitage and held a formal ceremony to dedicate the temple. From that time on, people began coming to the temple to cultivate.

On the first Sunday of May this year (1996), the large Buddha hall was used for the first time for a public Dharma assembly. More and more people have been coming to worship and bow to the Buddhas. It was truly kind of the Master to set up such a wonderful Buddhist temple for his disciples and followers in Washington, D.C.

It is worth mentioning that, from what I have heard, although the laypeople showed the Master several places that were spacious, conveniently located, and easily accessible to the public, the Master did not agree to them. Yet as soon as he saw the present location of the Hermitage, he immediately agreed to buy it and did not mind the high price of one million dollars. Later the laypeople figured that one of the reasons the Master chose this place was that over a hundred years ago, when the white men were killing the American Indians and chasing them out of their own territories, the Indians retreated to this final refuge and lost their lives here in the end. The Master must have bought this place in order to help the many resentful spirits that were still around.

華嚴精舍正門
Avatamsaka Hermitage

宣化老和尚追思紀念專集

# 柏克萊佛寺
# 法界宗教研究緣起

# HISTORY OF THE INSTITUTE FOR WORLD RELIGIONS
## AT THE BERKELEY BUDDHIST MONASTERY

釋恆實　Shi Heng Sure

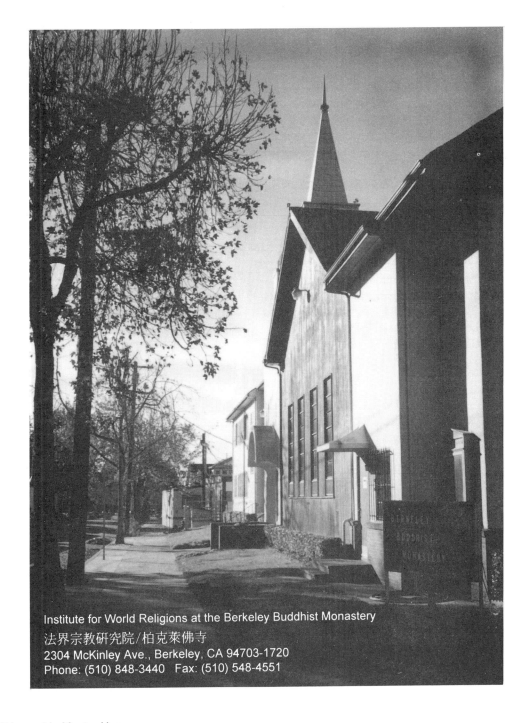

Institute for World Religions at the Berkeley Buddhist Monastery
法界宗教研究院/柏克萊佛寺
2304 McKinley Ave., Berkeley, CA 94703-1720
Phone: (510) 848-3440　Fax: (510) 548-4551

On October 27, 1994, the Dharma Realm Buddhist Association established a Way-place near the University of California at Berkeley. The Venerable Master gave his vision for the new Way-place:

Call it the "Institute for World Religions." I've told you for years about my plans to establish a World Religions Center, and this is it. The purpose of the Institute is to study religions in harmony with other faiths. We do not oppose anyone's religion, nor do we reject anyone's religion. Rather, we investigate the truths of religion together with other creeds and schools. The capacity of our minds should expand to propagate the limitless and boundless spirit of the City of Ten Thousand Buddhas (CTTB). Don't let your mind be too narrow. Use the Six Guidelines of the CTTB as the catalyst for your investigation.

The Master continued,

This temple will include a public forum where we come to deepen our understanding of religion. We will invite other religious individuals in to present their ideas and practices. The important part is to look into the principles of each different idea or custom. If you can reach that level, then people will come spontaneously, by themselves. If you don't investigate principles, then the finest of Buddha images or aesthetic environments won't suffice to bring them in the door.

We were especially inspired by the Master's instructions regarding the programs he wanted set up at Berkeley:

The format can combine a meditation period every morning and evening, followed by a forum for the discussion of religion in the evenings. In the classes when there are more Catholics present, you can learn about Catholicism; when there are more Jews, you can learn Judaism, or Islam, or Confucianism, etc. Invite well-known religious spokesper-

法界佛教總會於一九九四年十月二十七日，在加州柏克萊學區附近，增設一棟道場。上人談及新成立的柏克萊道場時，曾說：

就叫「法界宗教研究院」。幾年來我一直都想成立一個世界宗教中心，現在終於有了這個宗教研究院。研究院就是要讓各宗教在一起和諧地研究宗教。我們不反對任何宗教，也不拒絕任何宗教，我們要和其他各宗教共同來研究宗教的意義。我們要弘揚萬佛城廣大無邊的精神，心量要放大了，不要那麼狹窄。我們研究宗教要以萬佛城的六大宗旨做我們的前導。

上人又說：

這是一個讓我們加深對宗教了解的地方，是開放的。所以我們應該邀請各宗教人士，來談談他們的理想與修持。要緊的是：要深入去研究研究每一個不同宗教的想法和風俗習慣。假如你夠得上程度，人家自然會來；要是你不這麼樣來研究道理，那麼再怎樣莊嚴的佛像，怎麼樣好的環境，也不能夠吸引人來。

上人想在柏克萊道場設立的一些節目，很富啟發性，上人說：

每天早晚可以安排坐禪，晚上舉行宗教座談會。如果來的人，天主教的人多，就可以學習天主教的教義；要是猶太教的人多，就可以學習猶太教的教義；或者是回教、儒教，也都是這

sons to give their presentations. We are the hosts and facilitators, but not the only ones who teach there. Investigate other religions with a whole-hearted, open spirit of cooperation.

Following the tradition of all temples and branches of the Dharma Realm Buddhist Association, the Berkeley Buddhist Monastery maintains a full daily monastic schedule including morning and evening recitation, and the noon meal offering. It offers as well weekly Sutra lectures and meditation classes in English and Mandarin. In its first year of operation the Institute for World Religions, following the letter and the spirit of the Venerable Master's instructions, offered the following public programs and lectures free of charge to the East Bay community:

樣子。我們可以邀請知名的宗教界發言人來演講。我們雖然是主人，但不是只有我們在那裏教，我們要完全把心量放大，和其他的宗教共同來合作。

柏克萊佛寺跟法界佛教總會所屬的道場一樣，每日寺廟功課不停，包括早晚課、上供。每週以中英雙語講經，並開禪坐課。第一年時法界宗教研究院追隨上人精神，開了下列課程，方便舊金山東灣居民參加，不收費。

◆ Two meditation hours daily: open to the public / 每天二小時坐禪，對外開放。

◆ Jewish-Buddhist-Christian trialogue with Dr. Glenn Bucher, President of the Graduate Theological Union, and Prof. Daniel Matt of the Center for Jewish Studies
猶太教、佛教、基督教座談會，與會人有聯合宗教研究院院長布克博士及猶太教研究中心馬教授。

◆ Weekly Chan Meditation Instruction that has taught nearly 1500 students since the first class.
每週之禪坐班自開班以後，已有一千五百人來參加過。

◆ Guest lectures from Ven. Ajahn Sumedho, Ven. Ajahn Sucitto, Ven. Ajahn Amaro and other monks and nuns from the Amaravati Buddhist Centre, England.
客座教授有來自英國永生佛教中心的蘇美度法師、蘇西陀法師，還有阿摩羅法師。

◆ Challenge to Spiritual Traditions: An interfaith dialogue between a Franciscan priest and two Theravadan Buddhist Bhikkhus, Ven. Ajahn Amaro, and Ven. Bhante Madawala Seelawimala, moderated by the Christian theologian Durward Foster.
性靈的交流：天主教神父與南傳比丘阿摩羅及瑪達瓦拉斯法師交談。

◆ Father Kenan Osborne, Franciscan Catholic priest and the late Father John Rogers of Humboldt State University, in conversation with Buddhists. / 天主教奧斯本神父及加州州立漢堡大學的羅吉斯神父（已故）與佛教徒交談。

◆ Weekly gathering of Chochmat Halev, the Movement for Jewish Renewal. / 每週一次的猶太教復興運動聚會。

UC Berkeley Chinese Buddhist Society Practice and Discussion Group
柏克萊加州大學中國佛教學社研習會

- ◆ Science and Spirituality Seminars with quantum physicists from UC Berkeley. / 柏克萊加州大學量子物理學家參與科學與性靈交流座談會。

- ◆ Six evening discussions by Ahimsa, a Vedanta-based Hindu group from the University of California, Berkeley: programs such as "Gandhi and the Principles of Non-violence." / 柏克萊加州大學之印度吠陀團體舉行六次晚間討論會。

- ◆ Buddhist Women's Practice Seminars led by the nuns of the Dharma Realm Buddhist Association. / 婦女佛教座談會，由法界佛教總會尼眾主持。

- ◆ Vipassana Meditation Group led by James Baraz of Spirit Rock Center. 毘婆舍那禪坐社，由靈巖中心之巴拉茲主持。

- ◆ UC Berkeley Chinese Buddhist Society Practice and Discussion Group. 柏克萊加州大學中國佛教學社研習會。

- ◆ Vietnamese Buddhist Community Programs. 越南佛學社節目。

Ribbon-cutting at an art exhibition (right to left: Dr. Glenn Bucher, President of the Graduate Theological Union; Dr. Changlin Tien, Chancellor of UC Berkeley; Professor Songan Ong; Dr. SnjezanaAkpinar, President of Dharma Realm Buddhist University; Dr. Bei, Director of Institute of Buddhist Studies)

書畫展覽會剪綵（自左至右：聯合宗教研究院院長布克校長，柏克萊加州大學校長田長霖博士，翁松安教授，法界佛教大學校長阿比納博士，佛教研究所主任裴博士）

宣化老和尚追思紀念專集

# A CALAMITY IS AVERTED AND THE MOUNTAIN IS INAUGURATED

# 災難化解及山上灑淨結界

編輯部
Editorial Staff

In 1974, the Venerable Master Hsuan Hua, Abbot of Gold Mountain Monastery, was invited by students and teachers at the University of Washington to deliver instructional Dharma talks at the University twice a day for three days, on August 19th, 20th, and 21st. He travelled to Seattle on the 18th of August, and was accompanied while there by five of his Bhikshu disciples, including Heng Ju and Heng Yo, who had just completed their remarkable Three Steps One Bow pilgrimage for world peace.

The Venerable Master took the opportunity of the invitation to speak at the University located in Seattle to travel north to welcome and congratulate his two worthy disciples in the completion of their vows. The Venerable Master also planned to inaugurate the mountain at Marblemount, the future site of Cloud and Dragon Monastery, during his stay in the state of Washington. The new monastery takes its name from a dragon writhing through a cloud in a valley seen from a mountain top one night by Bhikshus Heng Ju, Heng Yo, and Heng Shou.

Because of the busy schedule of lectures at the University, plans were made to travel to Marblemount, Washington, nearly three hours north of Seattle by car, on the day after the lecture series at the University was completed. Early in the week, however, the Venerable Master announced a change in the schedule. On the last day of the lecture series, he announced, we would travel to Marblemount after the morning lecture (which ended at noon), eating our one meal of the day in the car while riding to our destination. When we arrived, we would hold ceremonies to "open the mountain," and then quickly drive back to the University in time for the evening lecture.

Although it seemed like an impossible schedule, everyone followed in accord. On Wednesday afternoon, August 21st, the Master, accompanied by five Bhikshus and three laymen, travelled to Marblemount. The Bhikshus were Heng Ch'ien, Heng Shou, Heng Kuan, Heng Yo, and Heng Ju. The laymen included Upasaka Takping Pong, founder of the Bodhi-Dhamma Center, an affiliate of Dharma Realm Buddhist Accociation, and his wife Gwendolyn Pong.

宣化上人（當時金山寺的住持和尚），應華盛頓大學師生的邀請，於一九七四年八月十九日至二十一日前往講法，一天兩場。宣化上人於八月十八日抵達西雅圖，當時有座下五位比丘弟子陪同上人，包括了剛完成「爲祈禱世界和平，三步一拜」的比丘恆具及恆由。

上人借著這次西雅圖華盛頓大學應邀演講的機會，來到北美地區，一方面也是來歡迎及祝賀他的兩位傑出弟子，完成了他們的誓願；同時上人也計劃，在他停留華盛頓州的期間，到位於大理石山上，也就是未來「雲龍寺」的地點灑淨結界。這新道場的命名是源自於比丘恆具、恆由及恆授，他們在一個晚上，從山頂上看到一條龍穿過雲層盤繞在山谷上。

因爲大學的講法課程緊湊，因此原訂計劃是講完課的第二天，開車前往位於西雅圖北邊，三個小時車程遠的大理石市。然而在這一個星期稍早，上人宣佈變更行程。到了課程的最後一天，上人指示：早上的講經課程結束後，當天就要去大理石山，（當時課程是中午結束）。然後利用去大理石山的路途中，在車內吃我們一天中唯一的一餐。當我們抵達目的地後，舉行灑淨結界儀式；然後很快地回到大學，可以即時趕上晚上的講經課程。

雖然，事先我們大家都認爲這行程不可能辦到。在星期三中午，八月二十一日，上人由五位比丘及三位在家居士陪同，一起前往大理石市。這五位比丘是恆謙、恆授、恆觀、恆由、恆具，三位居士包括龐先生夫婦，龐先生是法總分支道場─菩提達摩中心成立者。

I was one of the Bhikshus accompanying the Master. When we arrived, the second car had not yet appeared, and so I took a walk down the mountain through the dense foliage toward the river...and saw smoke. Upon closer inspection, I found that about 30 square feet of the forest had been consumed, and would soon break out into a raging fire if we didn't do something. A combined effort of Bhikshus and laymen carrying water from the river and turning dirt on the fire, along with support from the local fire department, extinguished the blaze in about an hour.

If we had come to the mountain a day later, as originally planned, instead of a dense green forest we would have found only rocks and dirt. Everyone bowed deeply to the Master and thanked him for saving the forest land.

The Master then inaugurated the mountain, and we returned to Seattle just in time for the evening lecture. The lecture series in Seattle was widely attended, and many people, in spite of their busy schedule, came to all the Master's lectures. Many sought interviews during the day with the Master, and all were delighted to have the opportunity to hear the Dharma.

我是陪伴上人的五個弟子之一，當我們的車抵達目的地後，第二部車還沒有到，所以我就穿過濃密的樹林散步到山下的河邊。然後我看到煙，再走進一點看，我發現了約三十平方呎的森林已被燒燬了，如果我們沒有馬上處理的話，火勢將很快的蔓沿開來。在比丘及居士協力下，從河裡提水，用土倒在火上，接著在當地消防人員的支援下，在將近一個小時內，終於撲滅了這場火災。

如果我們按照原訂計劃，晚一天來到這座山上，那我們看到的將是石頭及灰燼了，而看不見茂盛青翠的森林。我們每個人向上人跪拜頂禮，感謝他救了這片土地，接著上人就為這座山灑淨。

然後我們就回西雅圖去，剛好及時趕上晚上的這堂課。這佛法課程是開放給大眾參加，很多人儘管他們行程多忙碌，還是來參加上人全程的課程。在這一天有很多人想與上人面談，他們都很高興有這個機會來聽上人講法。

# THE BODHI-DHAMMA CENTER
# 菩提達摩中心

On July 21, 1974, at a joint meeting of the general membership of the Sino-American Buddhist Association, Inc., and the Bodhi-Dhamma Center, Inc. of Seattle, a proposal to merge the two organizations was enthusiastically endorsed by a unanimous resolution to affiliate the Bodhi-Dhamma Center with the Sino-American Buddhist Association (later renamed the Dharma Realm Buddhist Association).

The aim of the Center was to provide a place for the study and practice of the Buddhadharma in the Seattle area, including a city center and a mountain meditation center and monastery to be constructed on land on the Skagit River near Marblemount, Washington. The city center and mountain land were the generous donation of Upasaka Takping Pong, founder of the Bodhi-Dhamma Center. A fifteen-member Board of Directors was elected at the joint meeting including Venerable Master Hua as Chairman of the Board.

一九七四年七月二十一日，在中美佛教總會（即法界佛教總會前身）及西雅圖的菩提達摩中心會員聯合會議中，熱烈地同意「兩個組織合併」的提議，全體一致通過「菩提達摩中心成為中美佛教總會的分支道場」。

這中心的目的在提供西雅圖地區，人們研究佛法及修行的場所。他們在市內有一個中心，在山上靠近華盛頓州大理石市的史該吉河旁也將建立一個禪坐中心及一間寺廟。這個市內中心及山上的土地都是龐居士捐贈的，他原是達摩中心的成立者。這次會議選出了十位董事，上人為董事會主席。

屢變土田説大法　從地湧出妙覺山

The repeated transformations of the lands and fields
--expressions of Great Dharma.
Welling up from the earth--Wonderful Enlightenment Mountain!

# 宣演正法萬佛城
## Proclamations of Proper Dharma at
## Ten-Thousand-Buddhas City

滂沱夜雨曉方晴　盡洗人間業障清
三拱山門迎善客　萬佛寶殿響鐘聲
五觀齋苑巍峨立　四眾戒持好放生
寰宇昇平同沐德　拈香參禮一心誠
—宣公上人作—

*Abundant night rains followed by clear skies at sunrise*
*Wash clean the karmic obstacles of all humankind.*
*The triple-arched mountain gate welcomes wholesome guests.*
*In the Ten-Thousand-Buddhas Hall bell sounds reverberate.*
*The Five Contemplations Dining Hall is grand and imposing.*
*The four assemblies hold the precepts and enjoy liberating life.*
*Everyone is bathed in the virtues of a tranquil universe*
*As they light incense and pay homage with single-minded sincerity.*
— by Venerable Master Hua —

✽1979年11月主持啓建山門儀式　November 1979 Hosting the ground-breaking ceremony for the Mountain Gate

屢變土田說大法　　從地湧出妙覺山

The repeated transformations of the lands and fields
--expressions of Great Dharma.
Welling up from the earth--Wonderful Enlightenment Mountain!

# 宣演正法萬佛城
## Proclamations of Proper Dharma at
## Ten-Thousand-Buddhas City

滂沱夜雨曉方晴　盡洗人間業障清
三拱山門迎善客　萬佛寶殿響鐘聲
五觀齋苑巍峨立　四衆戒持好放生
寰宇昇平同沐德　拈香參禮一心誠
—宣公上人作—

*Abundant night rains followed by clear skies at sunrise*
*Wash clean the karmic obstacles of all humankind.*
*The triple-arched mountain gate welcomes wholesome guests.*
*In the Ten-Thousand-Buddhas Hall bell sounds reverberate.*
*The Five Contemplations Dining Hall is grand and imposing.*
*The four assemblies hold the precepts and enjoy liberating life.*
*Everyone is bathed in the virtues of a tranquil universe*
*As they light incense and pay homage with single-minded sincerity.*
*— by Venerable Master Hua —*

❋1979年11月主持啓建山門儀式 November 1979 Hosting the ground-breaking ceremony for the Mountain Gate

❋1979年11月萬佛寶殿開光，於寶殿前，曼都仙諾縣官，及星、馬朝聖團代表剪綵儀式

November 1979 Dedicating the Hall of Ten Thousand Buddhas Ribbon-cutting ceremony in front of the Jeweled Hall joined by Mendocino County officials and representatives from the Singapore and Malaysian delegations

❋1982年10月31日（農曆9月19日）觀世音菩薩出家日，萬佛聖城三拱山門揭幕

October 31, 1982 (19th of the 9th lunar month) Day of Guanshiyin Bodhisattva's Leaving the Home-life. Scene from the Triple-arched Mountain Gate at the City of Ten Thousand Buddhas

❋早期萬佛寶殿　Hall of Ten Thousand Buddhas in the early years

❋1991年於萬佛寶殿　1991 in the Hall of Ten Thousand Buddhas

# 法界眾生皈依處
## The sanctuary where living beings of the ten directions take refuge.

出家披剃豈偶然
How could leaving home and
having one's head shaved be happenstance?

我等盲癡當皈命
We who are deluded should take refuge
for life.

受具隆昌嗣律印
How magnificent to receive the
Complete Precepts and connect with
the Vinaya Seal!

造就良才續傳燈──育良小學、培德中學
Develop wholesome and talented individuals to inherit the transmission
— Instilling Goodness Elementary and Developing Virtue Secondary Schools

振興佛教弘正法
──法界佛教大學畢業
典禮
Disseminating Buddhism
and spreading the Proper
Dharma
— Commencement Exercises
at Dharma Realm Buddhist
University

# 三千世界一念間
## The three-thousand world system encompassed in a single thought

五濁眾生令離垢——1994年浴佛節
May beings in the five turbidities leave defilement!
— 1994 Bathing the Buddha Ceremony

善巧方便化眾生——1992年於萬佛寶殿
Kind and clever expedients change beings
— 1992 in the Jeweled Hall of 10,000 Buddhas

妙覺山頭天外遊
——1990年6月16日
舊金山警局長佐頓（坐
於上人旁邊）造訪聖城
On top of Wonderful
Enlightenment Mountain
roam on beyond the sky!
— June 16, 1990 San Francisco
Police Chief Jordan (seated at
the Master's side) visiting the
Sagely City.

互相勉勵互精進——1989年
Urge each other on; use mutual vigor!
— 1989

同修善法續心印
——1989年於萬佛寶殿

Cultivate good Dharmas together to continue
the Mind Seal. — 1989, Jeweled Hall of 10,000
Buddhas

親近知識修正法
——1994年2月10日於萬佛寶殿

Draw near Good Advisors and cultivate
Proper Dharma. — February 10, 1994, Jeweled
Hall of 10,000 Buddhas

# 小中現大別有天
## The great appears in the small-- another realm entirely!

喜捨無量饒益衆——喜捨院
Joy and Giving have no end in benefiting beings
— Joyous Giving House

佛本不大亦不小——大佛與大香爐
Basically the Buddha isn't big and also isn't small
— Big Buddha and Large Incense Burner

妙語無言空説法
——妙語堂
The speaking of
Dharma is empty;
Wonderful words are
wordless
— Wonderful Words Hall

# 法界歸源萬佛城　從地湧出妙覺山

*The Dharma Realm Returns to Its Source--*
*The City of Ten Thousand Buddhas*
*Wonderful Enlightenment Mountain Wells Forth from the Earth*

宣公上人開示
A talk by the Venerable Master Hua

（編按：沿著一○一號公路北行，越過金門大橋，經過一百一十英里，就到了萬佛聖城。萬佛聖城成立於一九七六年。成立之後，於一九七九年十一月四日，舉行千手千眼觀世音菩薩聖像開光典禮，暨法界佛教大學開幕大典；並於一九八二年十月三十日，舉行三拱山門揭幕、萬佛寶殿開光、五觀堂落成典禮。本書爲紀念上人圓寂一週年，及萬佛聖城成立二十週年，特將上人在添置萬佛聖城前，及在上列典禮中所作之開示講辭刊登出來，作爲對上人的追思紀念，讓聽過的人，重溫上人的教誨；沒聽過的人，也可以分霑法益。）

[Note: The City of Ten Thousand Buddhas, founded in 1976, is located 110 miles north of San Francisco. On November 4, 1979, the Ceremony for Inaugurating the Thousand-Handed Thousand-Eyed Guanshiyin Bodhisattva Image and the Opening Ceremony for Dharma Realm Buddhist University were held. On October 30, 1982, there were ceremonies for dedicating the gate of three arches at the entrance, the Jewelled Hall of Ten Thousand Buddhas, and the newly-completed Dining Hall of Five Contemplations. For the occasion of the first anniversary of the Venerable Master's completion of stillness and the twentieth anniversary of the City's founding, we have compiled the Master's talks from these events and from before the purchase of the City, hoping that those who had heard the Master's teachings can review them and those who have not can also benefit from the Dharma.]

## 一九七六年

我們無論哪一個，是出家人，是在家人，都要認識自己在廟裏頭是做什麼的。我們並不是混光陰，過一天就算一天，我們在廟上住，對廟上有什麼貢獻，這要知道。我們是佛教徒，應該叫佛教一天比一天大起來，不是令佛教活著也不像個活著的樣子，死也不像一個死的樣子。要是這樣子，我們這佛教徒的責任，根本就沒有盡上。我們佛教徒的責任，就是要令佛教發揚光大，要令所有人都明白佛法，依照佛法修行，不是天天就馬馬虎虎地過一天算一天。

所以在深谷這一塊地和房子，現在我們每一個人都應該發願，一定要把這件事情做成了。這個國家是世界最強的，這件事情做成了，那麼我們再把佛教由最強的國家推行到全世界去，令全世界人類都得到佛教的救護，能救度一切眾生，這是我們每一個人的責任。不要盡爲自己做打算，說我一天餓不死就算了，對付一天就算一天，不要有這種消極的主意。若這樣迴光返照，我們一定要做一個佛的眞正好弟子，不要做佛的一個壞弟子。爲佛教來創作、來努力，這是我們應該做的事情，不要什麼也不懂，天天就迷迷糊糊地過，你說這種生活有什麼意義？我們都應該時時刻刻地修行，時時刻刻都把佛教介紹給所有的人類，令全人類都得到佛教的救度，這是我們每一個人應該存的一種思想。所以深谷這個地方，我們一定要有錢就出錢，有力就出力，大家共同把這件事成了。把深谷這個地方做妥了，我們可以創辦佛教的大學，我們可以創辦佛教的安老院，我們可以創辦青年訓導所，我們可以創辦孤兒院，我們可以創辦佛教的醫院，凡是對人類有益的，我們都要做去。所以現在不可以把自己的

## 1975

Every one of us, whether we are left-home people or laypeople, should know what we are doing at the monastery. We aren't here to idly pass the days. We have to be very clear about what we are contributing to the temple as we live here. As Buddhist disciples, our job is to help Buddhism expand and grow. If Buddhism appears to be half dead, how can we be said to have fulfilled our responsibility? Our responsibility is to spread Buddhism and make it flourish so that every person comes to understand the Buddha's teachings and puts them into practice instead of casually letting the days go by.

Now we should all make vows to purchase the buildings and the land in Ukiah Valley. If we are successful in this matter, then, beginning with this most influential nation, we will be able to propagate Buddhism to the rest of the world and use the Buddha's teachings to save the entire human race and all living beings. This is our shared responsibility. We shouldn't pass the days being satisfied as long as we are fed. That's too selfish and defeatist. We should take a good look at ourselves and think, "I definitely want to be the best disciple of the Buddha I can be; I don't want to be a bad disciple." We have to work very hard and be pioneers for Buddhism. Don't pass the days in a muddle, acting as if you didn't understand anything at all. That's totally meaningless. We ought to be cultivating in every moment, working in every second to teach Buddhism to all people and cross them over. As for this piece of land in Ukiah Valley, we should all work together in this matter, contributing whatever money or strength we have to make it a success.

Once this property is purchased, we can start a Buddhist university, a seniors' home, a youth counselling center, an orphanage, a hospital, and any other institution for benefitting people. We shouldn't let our lives go down the drain, without any principles or goals to guide us. We should get serious and do the things we ought to do. Living in this world, we have to be productive and useful to the world; we shouldn't be worthless bums.

萬佛聖城五觀堂
The Dining Hall of
Five Contemplations

光陰都空過去，也沒有一個宗旨，糊糊塗塗地過一天。我們一定要認真了，負起我們自己所應負的責任，這才可以的。我們在世界要做一個有用的人，不要做沒有用的廢人。

我們一定要把深谷那個地方，無論想什麼法子，也要把它買來。我們明年傳戒，就在深谷那個地方，再開一個世界佛教的討論會，請世界各處所有的佛教大德高僧，都到我們這兒，來研究怎麼樣把佛教推行到全世界去，研究這些個問題。等開完會，大約是在九月、十月的樣子，我們再組織一個世界佛教訪問團，到每一個國家去弘揚佛法。我們這個訪問團，白天就各處去參觀訪問，晚間照常講經說法，早晨還照常做早課。這個是從來在佛教歷史上相信也沒有的，沒有人這樣做過。我們現在是開關新天地，在這個世界上，把佛教的種子，種在每一粒微塵裏邊去，我們都要在那兒轉大法輪，弘揚佛法。這個工作，是我們每一個人的責任，不是其他人的責任。我們做佛教徒，就應該做佛教的事情，把佛教推行到每一粒微塵裏，每一個世界去，推而廣之到整個法界裏，這是我們應該做的工作。

No matter what it takes, we have to purchase this piece of land in Ukiah Valley. Then next year (1976) we can hold a transmission of precepts there. We can also convene a World Buddhism Conference and invite all the eminent Buddhist Sangha members to come and study the question of how to spread Buddhism throughout the world. When the conference ends in September or October, we can organize a World Buddhism Delegation and propagate Buddhism to every country. The delegation members can tour and visit various places during the day, but they should continue to hold Sutra lectures at night and do morning recitation in the morning. Such a delegation probably will be the first of its kind in the history of Buddhism. We are now breaking new ground, planting the seeds of Buddhism in every mote of dust as we turn the great Dharma wheel and propagate the Dharma. Each one of us has a share of responsibility in this work. Since we are Buddhists, we should spread Buddhism to every mote of dust in all the worlds of the Dharma Realm.

# 佛教萌芽新大陸　西方重建逍遙園

## Buddhism Sends Forth Shoots in the New Land
## The Garden of Bliss Is Re-Established in the West

### 一九七六年十一月六日

佛教有興的時候，有衰的時候。興和衰，都是一定的，眾生有福的時候，佛教就興盛；眾生福報薄了，沒有福了，佛教就衰了，也沒有佛教了。現在在亞洲，所有的人、一切的眾生，福報都薄了，所以在亞洲佛教就快沒有了。

佛教現在到西方來發揚光大，這是一個新的佛教開始，也是西方人新的生命開始。爲什麼要到西方發展佛教？因爲西方人的福報，還沒有，還很多。因爲福報很多，所以這個福田也就到西方來了。到西方來，這佛教的開始，和東方不同，東方都是每一個小的範圍來發展佛教，在西方必須要有一個大的地方來發展佛教。所以今年才把這個省立醫院買下來，做爲一個佛教的，也就是整個世界的佛教一個發祥地。那麼這樣子，需要每一個人來支持這一件事。有力量的人，必須要盡他的力量來護持佛教，支持萬佛城。

在中國，當初佛教一開始的時候，是皇帝做護法，大臣做護法，所以大興善寺有一個時期，曾經住過二十萬和尚。有一個縣，在一天就有三千多人出家，那時佛教就興盛得那個樣子。現在到西方，佛教剛剛開始，就好像小孩子剛出世一樣，需要母親來照顧，需要其他的人來保護。

爲什麼到西方成立一個萬佛城？這是時勢所趨。現代這個時代，應該出現一個萬佛城。我最初到美國，住在一個basement（地下室），大約方圓有一百五十呎那麼大，既沒有窗戶，又沒有什麼正當的門，只有一個門，一關上，裏邊就變成真空了。我在那兒住了一個時期，以後就搬到 Sacramento（沙加緬度）街；住了一個時期，因爲不願意在 Chinatown（中國城）那個複雜的環境裏頭弘揚佛法，於是乎就搬到Sutter（沙得）街；又住一時期，搬到 Waverly（天后廟）街，中國城天后廟的樓上；這以後，在一九七〇年搬到金山寺。又一九六八年，我們開始翻譯經典。翻譯經典這個工作，在中國幾千年以來，沒有人想到這個工作，沒有人想要做這個工作

### November 6, 1976

Buddhism goes through periods of flourishing and decline. It flourishes when living beings have abundant blessings and declines and disappears as their blessings become scarce. At present Buddhism has virtually disappeared from Asia because the blessings of Asians are becoming fewer and fewer.

The advent of Buddhism in the West marks a new beginning for Buddhism and the start of a new life for Westerners. Because Westerners have abundant blessings, this "field of blessings" has come to the West. The beginning of Buddhism in the West will be different from in the East. Buddhism developed on a small scale in the East, but in the West there needs to be a large place for it to develop. That's why we have purchased the former State Hospital. This place will become the birthplace of Buddhism, the source of world Buddhism. We need everyone's support. Each person should contribute his or her strength and energy to protect Buddhism and support the City of Ten Thousand Buddhas.

When Buddhism started out in China, it was sponsored by the emperor himself and his high ministers. At one point, Chinese Buddhism became so prosperous that Daxingshan (Great Flourishing of Goodness) Monastery housed 200,000 monks and, in one county, over 3,000 people left the home-life in a single day. Buddhism in the West has only just begun and is like a newborn infant who needs his mother's care and the protection of those around him.

Why has the City of Ten Thousand Buddhas been founded in the West? It's because this is exactly the time for such a place to come into existence. When I first arrived in America, I stayed in a windowless basement about 150 square feet in area. It had only one door, and once the door was shut, it was like being in a vacuum. After living there for a while, I moved to Sacramento Street. Later, when I felt it was too complicated to propagate Buddhism in Chinatown, I moved to Sutter Street temporarily, and then to Waverly Street. In 1970 we moved to Gold Mountain Monastery.

We began translating Sutras in 1968. In all these thousands of years, no one in China thought of translating Sutras from Chinese into other languages; no one could conceive of undertaking such an immense project, which would have required the support of the government to be carried out successfully. When Dharma Master Kumarajiva was

，也沒有人敢做這個工作。爲什麼呢？這不是一個小的工作，必須要有國家的力量來支持，才能進行。好像中國鳩摩羅什法師在那兒翻譯經典，有三千多人在一起工作，最少的時候都有八百人。

現在到美國來，只有我一個人，怎麼可以做這個工作呢？在中國歷代大德高僧沒有人敢想像把中國的藏經，完全翻譯成外語文，沒有人敢想的！爲什麼呢？因爲缺乏這種人才。在中國懂外語文的，就是近一百多年比較多一點，一百多年以前，那真是龜毛兔角，好像烏龜身上生毛似的，不可能的！兔子長犄角了，是沒有這個道理。

幾千年以來，沒有人敢做這種工作，我現在不自量力，由一九六八年成立暑假班，有美國三十幾個同學到這兒來學佛法，以後就開始翻譯經典。我們這個翻譯經典，是既無代價，又無報酬，人人都是盡義務。

所以最初一開始翻譯的時候，不錯，好像恆謙所講的，每一天不是翻譯經典，幹什麼呢？每一天就是吵架。「如是我聞」，他說這麼樣翻，那個就說你這樣翻譯不對，應該這麼翻譯；那個說你這個也不對，應該這麼翻譯，各是其是，各非其非。那麼這樣子，進行的速度就很慢。

以後，我就想了一個辦法，每一個人由他自己來翻譯這個經典草創，草創就是「初譯」。初譯以後，再交給一個人「修改」；修改以後，再加上「潤色」；潤色以後，再加「印證」。由這四部推進，以後這個工作就上路了。

所以我們在一九六八年開始翻譯經典，每一部經都要有一百對眼睛來看，一百對就是經過一百個人都看過，認爲沒有什麼大毛病了，我們這些個人的智慧也就是止於此了，再往多的也不能了，所以就拿去印刷。印刷以後，後人認爲還有不滿意的地方，他可以再修改，做好了它。我們現在爲什麼不完全做好再出版呢？要等到完全做好再出版，那就要兩百年以後。我們等不到兩百年以後，所以現在就是有一點毛病，有一點不正確的地方，我們也要出版。等到兩百年以後，他們再去修改去，這是我們翻譯經典的辦法。

translating the Sutras into Chinese, sometimes he had over 3,000 people helping him; at the very least he always had 800 people working on translation.

Now in America, how can I do this work all alone? None of the great monks in Chinese history dared to think of translating the entire Chinese Tripitaka (Buddhist canon) into foreign languages. Why not? Because there was no one who could do it. Although the situation is better now, over a hundred years ago people who understood foreign languages were extremely rare in China.

Not knowing my own limitations, I am now attempting this project which no one in China dared undertake for several thousand years. After the thirty some American students who came to study Buddhadharma completed the 1968 summer session, they began translating the Sutras. Our translators are all volunteers who seek no reward or compensation of any kind.

In the beginning, everyone was arguing instead of translating. They each proposed their own translation for everything, starting from the very first phrase, "Thus have I heard," and criticized everyone else's translation as wrong. Progress was very slow.

Later, I thought of a way. I gave each person his or her own Sutra to translate. After he or she completed his draft of a primary translation, another person would review it. The translation would then be edited and finally, it would be certified as correct. When the work was broken into these four stages, everything proceeded smoothly.

Ever since we began in 1968, I have required that each Sutra translation be examined by one hundred pairs of eyes. That is, one hundred people have to go over the Sutra until they feel there are no major problems with it. That's the best we can do with the wisdom we have, so after that we go ahead and publish the translation. In the future, people can make further revisions. If we waited until we had a perfect translation, two hundred years would pass before we could print anything. Since we can't wait that long, we publish our translations knowing that they are bound to contain minor problems and errors. Two hundred years from now, people can revise them as they see fit. That's our method of translating Sutras.

Since we were translating Sutras, we founded Gold Mountain Monastery. In 1973 Mr. C.T. Shen loaned us a house because we were running out of room. At that time the men and the women were both living at Gold Mountain Monastery, the women on the second floor and the men on the third floor. There were rumors that in Gold Mountain Monastery where the rules were supposedly very strict, the men and women were mixing together in total disregard of the precepts. Many people outside were eager to find fault with us.

In 1975 when our place became too small again, we began to search for another place and came upon what is now the City of

萬佛聖城萬佛寶殿開光
The Opening Ceremony for
the Jewelled Hall of Ten Thousand Buddhas

因為翻譯經典，成立金山寺。到一九七三年，沈家禎借我們一個房子，因為我們房子也不夠用，那時候男男女女都住在金山寺，二樓住女的，三樓住男的，外邊就給造風言風語，說金山寺說是有規矩，男女亂七八糟，是完全不合乎戒律。外邊的人有很多，不要說是誰了，就都想要吹毛求疵。

到了一九七五年，我們地方又不夠用了，所以就找地方，找到現在這個萬佛城；因為地方不夠用，所以發展有萬佛城的出現。我們現在是凡我的皈依弟子，都要發心來護持萬佛城。

你們應該知道萬佛城是怎麼樣成就的？第一次，我來萬佛城看，因為太大了，回去想也不敢想，連這個萬佛城的夢也不敢做。又過了一個時期，又去看那個State Hospital（州立醫院）。第一次我去，沒有看醫院，第二次一看，喔！就這個醫院也就值這麼多錢，這麼多錢也造不下來，也買不下來。好！我那時候就用古來的破釜沉舟，背城一戰。我就說了，我說：「今天開始我們一定要把萬佛城買下來，若不買下來，我把我中國的弟子和美國的弟子，所有出家的弟子、在家的弟子，我完全用這個生死棍都打死，一個也不留，因為留著沒有用了！你們在佛教裏，一點事情也不能做。」由這個，回來把萬佛城才拿下來。

現在萬佛城也還是個小孩子，需要吃奶，需要奶媽子，需要母親來照顧，需要有一切一切的護持，這個小孩子才會長大。誰若怕跟著這個師父吃虧的話，趕快跑到十萬八千里以外；若不怕跟著師父吃虧的話，就要來護持萬佛城。

這是我今天對你們說的最重要的話！誰也不准後退，我們都要勇猛精進。

Ten Thousand Buddhas. You could say the City of Ten Thousand Buddhas appeared because we needed a bigger place. Now all of you who have taken refuge with me should make a resolve to support the City.

You should all know how we came to have the City of Ten Thousand Buddhas. The first time I visited the place, I didn't dare to think of buying it, because it was simply immense! I didn't even dare to dream about the City of Ten Thousand Buddhas. When I came a second time and looked at the hospital, which I hadn't seen the first time, I thought to myself, "This hospital alone is worth much more than the price they're asking for. Even with that much money, we couldn't build such a hospital or buy one like it now." Then I decided to go for broke, to lay it on the line. I said, "We definitely have to buy this place. If we don't, then I'm going to take this 'cane of birth and death' and beat every one of my disciples to death, regardless of whether you are Chinese or American, left-home or lay people. I won't spare a single one. Why should I spare you if you are totally useless and can't do a single thing for Buddhism?" After that, we entered into negotiations and bought the City of Ten Thousand Buddhas.

Right now the City of Ten Thousand Buddhas is still a baby that needs to drink milk and be cared for by its mother and nanny. It needs all kinds of care and protection in order to grow up. If any of you are afraid of taking losses together with your teacher, then you can leave right now and go 108,000 miles away. If you aren't afraid of taking a loss with your teacher, then come and support the City of Ten Thousand Buddhas.

宣化老和尚追思紀念專集

萬佛聖城
千手千眼觀世音菩薩聖像
The Thousand-Handed
Thousand-Eyed Guanshiyin
Bodhisattva image at the
City of Ten Thousand Buddhas

# 上香禮佛心莫貪　心香一瓣敬意長

*Do not harbor greed in offering incense and worshipping the Buddha.*
*Far reaching is the respect in this piece of incense from the mind.*

## 萬佛聖城千手千眼觀世音菩薩聖像開光典禮
## 暨法界佛教大學開幕大典

## The Opening of Light of the Thousand-Handed Thousand-Eyed
## Guanshiyin Bodhisattva image at the City of Ten Thousand Buddhas
## and the Opening Ceremony for the Dharma Realm Buddhist University

### 一九七九年十一月四日

所有的人都在這個法界之內，所有眾生都在這個法界之內。法界大學成立以來，按部就班的，現在是走到上軌道的時候。這一次開光，達摩難陀法師從馬來西亞不遠萬里來，我們法界大學對這位老人是特別歡迎的，所以贈送給這位法師榮譽哲學博士學位。今天你們各位來，在這兒參加這個典禮，大家都要一同向法界大學來學習，也都跟著這位達摩難陀法師來學習，我們共同到這個法界佛國去。想要到法界佛國，先要到萬佛城，萬佛城就是法界佛國所在的辦事處，所以你們每一個人想要成佛，不來萬佛城、不來法界佛教大學讀書，那是去不了的。所以今天這個機會是很好的。現在開始贈送這個榮譽博士學位的典禮。

### November 4, 1979

The Dharma Realm includes all people and all living beings within it. Since its inception, the Dharma Realm Buddhist University has developed step by step and is now ready to get on track. For this opening ceremony, the Dharma Realm Buddhist University is very happy to welcome Dharma Master Dhammananda, who has come all the way from Malaysia to be here, and is presenting him with a honorary Ph.D. degree. All of us in this ceremony today should study from Dharma Realm Buddhist University and Dharma Master Dhammananda, so that we can together go to the Buddhaland of the Dharma Realm. If you want to go there, you must first come to the City of Ten Thousand Buddhas, which is the headquarters for the Dharma Realm Buddhaland. If we want to become Buddhas, but we don't come to the City of Ten Thousand Buddhas and the Dharma Realm Buddhist University to study, we won't be able to reach Buddhahood. And so we all have this fine opportunity today. Now let us begin the ceremony for presenting the honorary Ph.D.

\*　　　\*　　　\*

你們搶著上香，這太迷信了。香爐已經有香了，你到那裏就是叩幾個頭已經表過誠心了，不必搶著燒香。搶著燒香，你香多了，把佛都薰跑了，你自己還不知道呢！你自己將來會變畜生的。

我討厭這種人的，你迷信太厲害了，你太迷信了。用香太多了，你簡直等於是在萬佛的頭上撒你大糞一樣，連你都受不了，何況佛呢？佛呢，你給他那麼多煙幹什麼？他怎麼會抽得那麼多煙？

不可以這樣的！我這兒沒有這麼規矩，這是下流的。我的規矩是不可以搶著來上香的！這是新開的佛教，和其他佛教的道場完全不同的，其他地方那麼迷信，沒有人懂，可以的；我們這兒不許可迷信的。不能到這兒不守規矩，我絕對絕對不歡迎的，你不要來！不是不可以，就根本不歡迎！

有什麼人現在罵我？可以提出來罵。一個人罵我，說：我說你們都這麼上香，這是一種迷信。他不單不懂這個道理，太無知識了！他還罵我，說我出家人不准他上香，我是個什麼東西？我就問我是個什麼東西？你說！我是個什麼東西？那你又是個什麼東西？你根本就不懂東西南北，根本就不是個人了，畜生都不如了。那我現在給你們看看，我是個什麼東西？

這是無父、無君、無老、無少、無佛、無法、無僧的，你到底是上什麼香呢？你上這個香，也一樣下地獄的。你不遵守我的規矩，我就要糾正你們。你罵我什麼都好，你拿把刀來殺我，我都不在乎的，我一樣不准你們犯我的規矩！

你要知道萬佛城是一個正法住世的地方，絕對不許可人迷信的。你想要求佛法，一定要守這個規矩。你不守規矩，你就是地獄種子。你說：「哪有信佛的人去上香，又來罵和尚的？這叫什麼佛教徒！」這若不是畜生？不是地獄種子？他這是什麼？你在這兒造業的嘛！我是寧可無人，不可無法。

Okay! 吃飯要一齊吃，不可以有先後。尤其這個僧人還沒有吃飯，你們在這地方坐著吃飯，能吃得下去嗎？吃東西你都這個樣子，都變成主人了。你先要知道，要是許可你吃才吃，你自己偷偷捧在那地方偷著吃，這叫做什麼？我們這兒不是一個隨隨便便的地方，

It's totally superstitious to insist on personally offering incense to the Buddhas. If there is already incense burning in the censer, you can simply bow a few times to show your sincerity; don't light more incense. If you light too much incense, the smoke chases the Buddhas away without your knowing, and your retribution for causing this is to become an animal.

I am very annoyed by such superstitious people. Burning so much incense amounts to defecating on the heads of ten thousand Buddhas. You wouldn't like such an experience, so how much less would the Buddhas? How do you expect a Buddha to endure so much smoke?

The "rule" that "everyone must light incense" doesn't apply here, because it's too vulgar. My rule is that you cannot fight to offer incense. This is a new beginning for Buddhism; we're different from other Buddhist temples. Such behavior may be acceptable in other places where people don't know any better, but no one is allowed to be so superstitious here. People who don't follow the rules are not welcome here.

If you want to scold me, go ahead. I know someone is scolding me for calling everyone superstitious. Although this person is totally ignorant about the principle, he is scolding me, "Who does this monk think he is, anyway, telling us not to offer incense?" Who do *you* think I am? And who do you think you are? You don't understand anything at all. You're not human; you're not even up to an animal. Tell me, who do you think I am?

In your eyes, there is no father, no national leader, no seniors or juniors, no Buddha, no Dharma, and no Sangha, so to whom are you offering incense, ultimately? Although you offer incense, you will fall into the hells. Because you don't follow my rules, I am obligated to correct you. I don't mind if you scold me or even take a knife and kill me, but I won't allow you to break my rules.

You must realize that the City of Ten Thousand Buddhas is a place that upholds the Proper Dharma. No one is allowed to be superstitious here. If you want to study the Buddhadharma, you must follow the rules. Anyone who does not is headed for the hells. Someone is thinking, "What kind of Buddhist would come here to offer incense and then turn around and scold the Dharma Master?" Now, if that person doesn't become an animal or fall in the hells, what will he become with all the evil karma that he's creating? I would rather that there were no people here than that there be no Dharma; there has to be Dharma.

At mealtime, we should all take our meals together. No one should eat before the others. How can you have the gall to sit

146

宣化老和尚追思紀念專集

there and eat before the members of the Sangha have begun eating? You're basically usurping the host's position. You ought to know better than to begin eating before you're supposed to. How can you sneak off and eat on the sly? People may not casually do as they please here. Everyone must follow the rules. If you don't follow the rules, then you're not welcome here no matter how rich you may be.

I have always looked down on rich people, because their wealth is equal to their offenses. I have to say this. You are welcome to scold me as much as you like, as long as you don't fear the retribution of falling into the Hell of Pulling Tongues.

I'm speaking in this wild way because I'm overjoyed today. I'm not really mad at you. If you're afraid of my getting mad at you, then simply follow the rules well. If you don't fear my temper, then you don't have to follow the rules here.

All of the left-home and lay people at the City of Ten Thousand Buddhas follow the credo:

> *Freezing, we do not scheme.*
> *Starving, we do not beg.*
> *Dying of poverty, we ask for nothing.*
> *According with conditions, we do not change.*
> *Not changing, we accord with conditions.*
> *We adhere firmly to our three great principles.*

At the City of Ten Thousand Buddhas,

> *We renounce our lives to do the Buddha's work.*
> *We take the responsibility to mold our own destinies.*
> *We rectify our lives to fulfill the Sangha's role.*
> *Encountering specific matters, we understand*
>   *the principles.*
> *Understanding the principles, we apply them*
>   *in specific matters.*
> *We carry on the single pulse of the Patriarchs'*
>   *mind-transmission.*

> *We stand facing the wind, not caring if we freeze.*
> *We stick out our bellies and walk, not minding if we starve.*

We will never bow our heads in submission to money.

我們這兒一定要守規矩。不守規矩，任何人你就有多少錢，我也都不歡迎你。

我從來也就是看不起有錢的人，我告訴你。有多少錢，就有都多少罪。我就要這麼說，你們誰願意罵我，我都可以的！我願意接受你們的罵。只要你不怕你那個舌頭將來墮拔舌地獄，誰在罵我，我歡迎的！

我告訴你們各位，我今天因為太高興了，所以對你們說話說大聲一點，並不是對著你們發脾氣，就因為太高興了。你們誰若是怕我發脾氣，就好好地守規矩；若不怕我發脾氣呢，來到這兒不守規矩，我也不管。

萬佛城所有的出家人、在家人，是

　　凍死不攀緣，餓死不化緣，窮死不求緣；
　　隨緣不變，不變隨緣，抱定我們三大宗旨。

萬佛城是

　　捨命為佛事，造命為本事，正命為僧事；
　　即事明理，明理即事，推行祖師一脈心傳。

我們是

　　凍死迎風站，餓死挺肚行

絕對不向金錢去低頭的。

香爐裏，如果有香就叩頭好了，因為人是一口氣，人活著都是一口氣活著，佛是一炷香。不要燒那麼多香，上那麼多香啊，你把佛眼睛薰得睜不開。說：「佛不是像人似的，受煙一薰就睜不開眼睛，流眼淚了。佛什麼都可以受的。」但是你要想一想，我們人受不了的東西，怎麼可以叫佛來受？我們這個人受不了的東西，我們把它來加諸於佛，給佛，這也是一個最最不恭敬的態度。

好像你吃飯，這個人已經吃飽了，你還叫他再吃！再吃！再吃！那把這個人都會撐死了，肚子都漲爆開了。佛就算他受這個香煙，已經有了，他就受了。這個香無論誰裝的，都是等於你裝的一樣，你再誠誠懇懇拜幾拜，這已經夠了。不要像昨天那個人，我說：「你們裝的香太多了！這是一種迷信！」我說得大約口氣也重一點，所以他很不高興了。來，就罵我，其實罵我，沒有關係，但是這的確是對佛一個不恭敬的態度，你到了佛殿裏來，你不守佛教的規矩，你自己願意怎麼樣就怎麼樣，在佛殿就像做土匪了嘛！所以這一點，你們都是皈依我的弟子，應該知道的，應該特別注意這一點。我們大家要共同合作，不要學著一般佛教徒那麼迷信，那麼樣貪心，搶著去上香，你那一搶啊，佛就看你這個人真是 stupid，永遠他都會 stupid，為什麼他永遠都會愚癡呢？就因為他不守規矩，我已經有飯吃了，你給我添了左一碗、右一碗擺著我滿桌子，我怎麼吃得了那麼多？佛這已經有香了，你左一支香、右一支香，把這香爐都裝滿了，那佛怎麼受得了那麼多香煙。

這個香只是表示一個自己的意思，已經有了，就不必再往那兒上香了，尤其現在香很貴的，你浪費這麼多香，這有什麼意思？你們研究，要往深裏一層研究；事情，我們要明白那個真理，那個真正的道理，不要就盲從。說：「他也搶著去上香，我也搶著去上香，這個一定是好的，」其實就是這個，就在佛教裡造罪業了。為什麼你把你的貪心在佛前表露出來，一點都沒有剩。

所以這一點呢，我告訴你們的話，我們信佛的人千萬千萬要真正明白這個道理。我們在佛教裏，不要造一些個罪業，不要在佛教裏，你罵我，我罵你呀！你來也爭著裝香叩頭，我也想搶著裝香叩頭，這個才沒有意思，這真是太迷信了，迷信到極點極點的，太沒有智慧了。因為什麼我們愚癡？就是因為我們盡做一些個愚癡的事情，所以我們就愚癡了。

If there is incense in the censer already, then you should just bow. People live as long as they have a single breath left; likewise, a single stick of incense is enough for the Buddhas. If you light too much incense, the Buddha can't even open his eyes with all the smoke. You may say, "The Buddha isn't like ordinary people. Smoke shouldn't bring tears to his eyes. He should be able to take it." Perhaps, but how can you make the Buddhas endure what people find unendurable? Isn't that too disrespectful?

For example, if you tell someone who is already full, "Eat some more! Eat some more!" you'll make him stuffed to the point of bursting. Likewise, assuming the Buddha does "accept" the offense offered him, then no matter who offered the incense, the Buddha has already accepted it and it's the same as if you offered it yourself. You can simply bow sincerely a few times, and that will suffice. Don't be like the person who scolded me after he heard me say that lighting too much incense is superstitious. I probably put it too strongly, so he was upset and scolded me. I don't mind being scolded, but his attitude was disrespectful to the Buddhas. If you come to the Buddha Hall and act as you please, not abiding by the rules, you are just like a bandit. Those of you who have taken refuge with me should pay close attention to this. We should all work together and not fight to offer incense, being as superstitious and greedy as most Buddhists are. If you insist on fighting to offer incense, the Buddha will think, "This stupid person will always be stupid, because he doesn't follow the rules. He's serving me more food than I need, covering my whole table with dishes of food. How does he expect me to eat so much?" That's an analogy. The Buddha already has incense, yet you light more until the whole censer is filled with incense. How can the Buddha take so much smoke?

The incense is a token of our respect. If there is some in the censer already, we don't need to light more. Incense is very expensive nowadays. Why should we be so wasteful? You should look into this well. In any matter, we want to understand the principle behind it, not just blindly follow others, thinking, "Everyone else is rushing to offer incense, so it must be a good thing." Actually, such people are creating offenses in Buddhism. Why are they so unreserved about showing the Buddha their greedy hearts?

Buddhists should absolutely be sure they understand this principle. We don't want to create offenses in Buddhism by scolding one another and competing to offer incense. Such behavior is pointless. It's utterly superstitious and lacking in wisdom. Why are we still so stupid? It's because we keep doing stupid things like this.

供佛的飯菜也一樣，就是他受的，你也不可以這麼樣子不恭敬的。你左一碗、右一碗擺著滿檯，他怎麼吃得了那麼多？

The same principle of moderation applies to food offerings. It is disrespectful to cover the whole altar with dishes of food. How can we expect the Buddha to eat so much?

極樂世界莫他求
阿彌陀佛在眼前

*Don't seek elsewhere for the Land of Ultimate Bliss;*
*Amitabha Buddha is right before your eyes!*

一九七九年

**1979**

今天給你們講這個極樂世界阿彌陀佛的方法。誰覺得這個世界好，不願意搬家到另外一個世界去的，那你就不需要聽我現在講的。我這個講的，是要你對這個娑婆世界很討厭了，想要生到西方極樂世界，得到永遠的快樂，所以你就注意聽一聽。

Today I'll explain a method for going to the Land of Ultimate Bliss to meet Amitabha Buddha. If you're happy here in this world and have no wish to move to another world, you don't have to listen. However, if you are sick and tired of the Saha world and yearn for the eternal bliss of the Western Land, then listen carefully!

這是說的「一心皈命」：一心，什麼叫一心？就是沒有妄想了，沒有三心二意了，要專一其心。做什麼呢？就皈依「極樂世界阿彌陀佛」：皈依是皈命敬投，就是把自己的身心性命，都歸納到極樂世界去，那兒有一位阿彌陀佛。這阿彌陀佛又是誰呢？他就是在往

The "Vow to Be Reborn in the West" begins: *With one mind I return my life to Amitabha Buddha who is in the Land of Ultimate Bliss.* With a concentrated mind free of discursive or scattered thoughts, I return my body, mind, nature, and life to the Land of Ultimate Bliss, where Amitabha Buddha dwells. In the past, Amitabha Buddha was an ordinary person just like

昔和你我現前的眾生是一樣的人來著，以後他就發心出家修道，修道之後，他就發願，說是：我將來修成佛，那個國土無有眾苦，但受諸樂，沒有三惡道，沒有地獄、餓鬼、畜生這個罪惡的道路。那麼人生在我這個世界，都是快樂的，所以叫極樂。那麼怎麼樣生呢？就是他能念我的名號「南無阿彌陀佛」，乃至十念，最少每天能修十念法，這十念就是由第一口氣到第十口氣，一心念阿彌陀佛，這叫十念法。若不生者，他若不生在我這國土裏頭的，不成正覺，我誓不成佛。

因為他發這個願，所以以後就造成一個極樂世界。我們十方的眾生，無論誰念「南無阿彌陀佛」，都能生在極樂世界去，都能得到無有眾苦，但受諸樂的這種果報。因為這個，所以我們要一心皈命極樂世界阿彌陀佛，「願以淨光照我」：願阿彌陀佛以清淨的光明來照我，「慈誓攝我」：用慈悲的誓願來攝我。「我今正念」：我現在一心正念，「稱如來名，為菩提道」：稱阿彌陀佛這個名號，修這個菩提道，願意「求生淨土」：因為阿彌陀佛往昔的這個誓願，接引一切眾生生極樂世界，所以最少在這個十念之中，若不生極樂世界的，阿彌陀佛也不成佛。

我因為看見阿彌陀佛這麼大的願力，雖然我想把萬佛城造成一個極樂世界，但是現在還沒有正式成就呢，還沒有黃金為地，晝夜六時雨天曼陀羅華。雖然說是沒有成功，將來有一天，一定是成功的。所以我才發一個很笨的願力，說是：「所有跟我出家的弟子，和在家的皈依弟子，他們如果沒有成佛的話，我也不成佛。」皈依我的人，他們做螞蟻，我也跟著做螞蟻；他們做蚊蟲，我也跟著去做蚊蟲去；他們墮地獄，我也跟著墮地獄去；他們變餓鬼，我也跟著做餓鬼去；哪一個做畜生了，我也願意陪著他去做畜生。發這麼一個願力，必須要他們都成佛了之後，然後我若願意成佛，我就成；我若不願意成佛，我還不成。說：「你為什麼不願意成佛呢？」因為我看見還有很多人沒有成佛呢！我還要去拖他們一把，所以就是我的皈依弟子和出家弟子、在家弟子都成佛了，以後我還要看看情形再說。

這是我今天想對你們說的話。所以我說我發這個願是很笨的，不過我這個笨人就有個笨法子，就願意這麼笨。你想教我跑快的路，坐火箭，我不會的。什麼時候在萬佛城裏頭，我都是用兩條腿來走路的，不用那個嘟嘟 car（車）。甚至於今天下雨我也偷偷地就跑來，那個方果悟，左一次要用車接我也接不著，右一次要用車去

us, but after he left the home-life to cultivate the Way, he made a vow. He vowed that when he became a Buddha, the beings in his Buddhaland would endure none of the sufferings but would enjoy every bliss, and that the three evil paths (hells, hungry ghosts, and animals) would not exist in his land. Thus his land is known as the Land of Ultimate Bliss. How can one be reborn there? One can use the "Ten Recitations Method," which is to simply recite "Namo Amitabha Buddha" single-mindedly for at least ten breaths each day. Amitabha Buddha vowed that if beings who did this were not reborn in his land, he would not attain Proper Enlightenment.

By virtue of his vows, he realized the Land of Ultimate Bliss, and any living being in the ten directions can recite "Namo Amitabha Buddha" and be reborn there, where they will endure none of the sufferings but will enjoy every bliss. For this reason, we should with one mind return our life to Amitabha Buddha, *wishing his pure light illumines me and his kind vows gather me in. Now, with proper mindfulness, I praise the Thus Come One's name,* the name of Amitabha Buddha, *in order to take the path of Bodhi and to seek rebirth in the Pure Land.* Amitabha Buddha's past vows gather in all living beings to the Land of Ultimate Bliss. If living beings practice at least ten recitations and are not reborn there, he vowed not to become a Buddha.

Seeing Amitabha Buddha's great vow, I also wanted to turn the City of Ten Thousand Buddhas into a Land of Ultimate Bliss. Even though it hasn't become one yet--the ground isn't yellow gold and a heavenly rain of mandarava flowers doesn't fall in the six periods of the day and night--it will eventually become one. That's why I made a foolish vow, saying, "If any of the disciples who have left home or taken refuge with me have not become Buddhas, I will not become a Buddha either." If my disciples become ants, I will become an ant too; if they turn into mosquitoes, I will become a mosquito and join them; if they fall into the hells, I will follow them right into the hells; if they turn into hungry ghosts, I will turn into a hungry ghost along with them; if one of them becomes an animal, I will become an animal to keep him company. After they have all become Buddhas, then I may or may not become a Buddha. "Why wouldn't you want to become a Buddha?" you ask. It's because I see that so many people still haven't become Buddhas, and I want to give them a helping hand. And so, even when all my left-home and lay disciples have attained Buddhahood, I will wait and see before deciding what to do.

You might think my vow is very stupid, but stupid people have stupid ways of doing things. I don't know how to do things the fast way, at rocket-speed. When I'm at the City of Ten Thousand Buddhas, I always like to walk on my own pick me up，也 empty，也是個空的。另一方面也是沒有那麼大福報，所以願意受一點苦。

你們都被我這句話所迷了，「受苦是了苦，享福是消福。」我們人無論做什麼事，要拿出一個真心來做，不要用虛妄的心去做，不要用攀緣的心去做，要用至誠懇切心來做佛事，來修行。你有一分真心，就有一分的感應；有十分的真心，就有十分的感應；你若有百千萬億分的真心，就有百千萬億分的感應。所以我們信佛，要真看破了，放下，才能得到自在。你不要似是而非的，不要以為這樣是對了，其實是錯了。

那你若真要學佛的人，不貪名，不好好，不攀緣，老老實實地用功修行。你能老老實實用功修行，才能得到真實的感應，才能有所成就。本來我們修行也不希望有什麼感應，也不希望有什麼成就，但是你若對一般人這麼說，說是：「沒有什麼希望，也不需要有什麼成就。」他就好像落了頑空了似的，他就也沒有什麼興趣了。你若對他說修行有什麼好處，將來得到什麼樣的神通，什麼樣的妙用，啊！那他就修行了。其實這樣修行，不是真正為了生死修行，這就為什麼呢？這就為了圖這個虛名，好這個假好，被這個境界所迷倒了，這是很可憐的一件事。

你們這一次從香港來的人，和從馬來西亞來的居士和法師，我覺得非常慚愧，對你們每一個人也覺得好像對不起似的。這話並不是客氣這麼說，真正我自己覺得道不足以感人，德不足以化人，你們這麼多人來了，我要怎麼樣才能對得住你們各位？所以我想我的所長沒有，我的所短呢，是很多，那麼要我教這個所長，等於鳳毛麟角一樣；要我教這個所短的呢，那可就多得很，有牛毛那麼多，有恆河沙那麼多。不管我的短處很多，我的長處很少，我也願意把我認為是長的地方和盤托出，全部教你們。

那麼教你們這個，也是很不容易的，為什麼呢？第一，要有一個信心；第二，要有一個忍耐心；第三，還要有一個長遠的心。

我所長的是什麼呢？方才說沒有什麼所長，不過我雖然沒有所長，觀音菩薩的長處是很多。現在我們是給這個十六吶的觀音菩薩開光，在這個千手千眼觀世音菩薩開光的期間，在這個機會之下，我願意把我所明白的觀世音菩薩的四十二手眼，每一個手眼都教授給你們，傳授

two legs rather than ride in a car. Even on this rainy day, I sneaked over here on my own. Guo Wu keeps trying to pick me up, but she always ends up with an empty car! I know that I don't have that many blessings, so I'm willing to suffer a little hardship.

I have tricked all of you into believing my slogan: "Enduring suffering puts an end to suffering; enjoying blessings uses up blessings." No matter what we are doing, we should do it with a true mind, not with an insincere or opportunistic mind. We have to cultivate the Way and perform the Buddha's work with the utmost sincerity. If you have one part of sincerity, you obtain one part of response; ten parts sincerity yields ten parts response; a million parts sincerity brings a million parts response. Therefore, when we believe in the Buddha, we have to truly give up our attachments before we can obtain freedom and ease. We shouldn't take what is wrong to be right.

To truly study Buddhism, we should not covet fame or advantages, but should honestly work at our practice. Only then can we obtain a true response and have some achievement. Basically, we should not hope for any response or achievement in our cultivation, but if you tell ordinary people that, it makes them feel as if they are in a void and they lose interest in cultivation. On the other hand, if you tell them about the advantages and the wondrous functioning of spiritual powers that can be obtained, they will want to cultivate. Their aim in cultivation is not to end birth and death, but to gain empty fame and benefit. They've been deluded by external states. This is a great pity.

I feel very remorseful towards all the people who have come from Hong Kong and all the laypeople and Dharma Masters from Malaysia. I feel I owe each of you a deep apology. I'm not being polite. I really feel that I lack the virtue to teach and transform people. So many of you have come from so far away, but what do I have to offer you? I have no strengths, but plenty of shortcomings. My strengths are as few as phoenix feathers and unicorn horns, while my shortcomings are as numerous as the hairs on a cow and the sands in the Ganges. Nevertheless, no matter how few my strengths and how many my weaknesses, I would like to impart to you a teaching that I consider a strength. I'm willing to share it entirely with all of you.

This is a very difficult teaching to receive, however, because it requires that you have faith, patience, and perseverance.

What is this strength of mine? Well, as I said before I don't have any strengths, but Guanyin Bodhisattva has plenty of strengths. Now, before we open the light on the sixteen-

給你們。你們信，就信；不信，我也不能勉強你們信。不過你若能以念茲在茲，依這個法修行，將來你們每一個人都可以得到千手千眼。

觀世音菩薩爲什麼有千手千眼？就因爲他修這種法門，所以得到千手千眼。我在馬來西亞曾經說過，我說：「這個四十二手眼是密中之密，玄中之玄，妙中之妙，不可思議，不可揣測的。」這樣子的法門，在佛教裏頭竟然失傳了，現在我想把它繼承起來，傳授給你們各位。所以在每一天一早起，七點半到八點半這個時候，我可以傳授給你們這四十二手眼。在這幾天的時間，我想儘量把這四十二手眼都傳給你們。你們願意學的，早晨七點半到八點半這個期間，我就傳這個法給你們；若不願意學的，就把它忘了。這是我想對你們大家說的話。

foot image of the Thousand-Handed Thousand-Eyed Guanshiyin Bodhisattva, I would like to take this opportunity to transmit Guanshiyin Bodhisattva's Forty-two Hands and Eyes to you, teaching you what I understand of each of the hands and eyes. Whether you believe or not is up to you; I cannot force anyone to believe. But if you can practice this Dharma with total dedication and mindfulness, in the future you will all be able to obtain a thousand hands and a thousand eyes.

Guanshiyin Bodhisattva obtained a thousand hands and a thousand eyes by practicing this Dharma door. In Malaysia I said, "The Forty-two Hands and Eyes are the most secret of secrets, the profoundest of the profound, the wonder of wonders; they are inconceivable and unfathomable." This Dharma door was lost in the past, but now I wish to resume its transmission by teaching it to you. I will be transmitting the Hands and Eyes from seven-thirty to eight-thirty every morning and hopefully will finish in the next several days. All of you are welcome to come and learn. If you do not wish to learn, then simply forget about it.

宣化老和尚追思紀念專集

# TODAY,
# RIDING IN A CAR FLYING BACK TO THE CITY

## 今日飛車回城
## The Master's Unprecedented
## Matching Couplets Class
## 上人空前的對聯課

好古　Oldy But Goody

**The Master with Upasaka Liu Jisheng, his Teaching Assistant.**
上人與助教劉濟生居士合影

"The art of matching couplets is a singularly special style in Chinese literature," commented Upasaka Liu, the Master's Teaching Assistant in his Matching Couplets class. "When the matches are perfect, the metaphorical meanings are deep and far-reaching and the beauty and wonder of the Chinese language is thoroughly revealed. The method by which it is revealed is in matching the upper and lower lines--so they fit together and are related. Particularly, phrases of only a few words are able to communicate many inner feelings."

上人對聯課的助教，劉濟生居士註解，「聯語，是中國文學一種獨特的格調。對稱完整，寓意深遠，充份表現出中國文字的美妙。而其表現的方式，務求上下對稱，恰當貼切。尤以極少數之字句，抒無盡之情懷，更屬難能可貴。」

The Master's Matching Couplets class began back in the l970's at Gold Mountain Dhyana Monastery. A disciple commented:

Of the 84,000 Dharma-doors, one of the most wonderful is completing the second line of a couplet. This practice, a fine art in China, is learned through much study and meditation. Teachers can use this method to inspire and lead students to awaken to their original wisdom. At Gold Mountain Dhyana Monastery, the Master teaches a weekly Couplets class. A good match not only completes the meaning of the first line, but is written so that the meaning, tone, and style are matched character for character. Thus, the first and second lines, although complete in themselves, also are paired to make sense as a whole. This is the first time this Dharma has been taught in the West.

上人的對聯課，開始於一九七〇年代，金山禪寺。一位弟子談論到：

八萬四千法門中，最奇妙的一種就是對對聯。可以經由更多的研究及打坐中，學習這項中國文學藝術。老師使用這種方法來鼓舞、帶領學生去啓發自己原有的智慧。在金山禪寺，上人每週教一堂對聯課。一個好的下聯，不僅是意思與上聯相符合，要在意思、語調、風格上，逐字逐字配合。上聯與下聯雖然能配合了，但在整體上的意義還要能夠通順。在西方，這還是第一次傳授這法門。

宣化老和尚追思紀念專集

**The Master talking to students from the University of California at Berkeley**
上人對柏克萊加州大學學生開示

By 1980, Matching Couplets class was an important event in life at the City of Ten Thousand Buddhas and was a core course in the Dharma Realm Buddhist University curriculum. Upasaka Liu comments, "The method of matching couplets appears to be simple and easy, but actually it's not easy. It's hard to make a good match. If the one composing it lacks scholarship, then the couplet will be too simplistic. If he lacks character, the couplet will be weak. If he lacks feelings, then the couplet will be insubstantial. If he lacks literary skill, then the couplet will be quite ordinary. Without both erudition and lofty character, it is difficult to soar to the sphere of refined literary genius... And so matching couplets is the most exquisite among all of China's exquisite literary forms."

到一九八〇年時，上對聯課成為萬佛聖城生活中一件重要的事情，同時也是法界佛教大學課程裡極重要的一堂課。劉居士註解：「聯語的製作，看似簡單易學，實在頗不容易，更難工整。作者如無學識，便失之淺；如無風格，則失之弱；如無感情，則失之浮；如無辭藻，便失之俗；如無文學修養、則難臻於雅麗之境⋯⋯所以聯語是中國文學精華中之精華。」

"What a shame that currently the art is declining and those who really have talent in making couplets are rarer than phoenix feathers and unicorn horns! And so how fortunate that now the Master is teaching this unprecedented class in which Westerns and Asians can learn about the ancient Chinese art of matching couplets. The Master's ingenious method of teaching is a gradual approach. As an expert, he makes it simple, and Western and Asian students alike have become seriously interested in this art."

「可惜這門學問，近年日漸衰微，後繼乏人，今天在學術界懂得聯語的，真如鳳毛麟角，少之又少。所幸宣化上人，開中西人士學習中國古典文學聯語之先河。上人以獨出心裁的教授法，循循善誘，深入淺出，引起中西學員極濃厚之興趣。」

**Matching Couplets class was held from 6:30-8:00 am at the City.**
對聯課在聖城是從早上六點三十分起至八點結束

And of course Couplets class was more than just study of a literary form. The content of the couplets always contained principles that were proper and timely. Buddhist doctrines, terms, and lists were succinctly expressed in brief phrases of the couplets. Confucian concepts of how to be a good person and how to relate to and benefit the family, society, and all nations were introduced in the brief wording of the couplets.

當然，對聯課不僅只是一種文學形式。對聯的內容還包含了正確的、合時的道理。在簡短對聯句中表達了佛教的教義及名詞。也介紹了儒家思想，如何做一個好人，如何與人建立關係，去利益家庭、社會、及整個國家。

One of the Master's lines, composed in 1980 when he was traveling back and forth between San Francisco's Gold Mountain and the City of Ten Thousand Buddhas at least twice weekly, reveals so well the Master's dedication to education that was so intense that he continually sacrificed his own health and comfort to nurture and support it. The line goes like this:

**Today, riding in a car flying back to the City, I came especially for the sake of tomorrow, to listen attentively to Professor Cheng teach his class, so that later in the future I can establish myself and practice the Way, thus developing a good foundation.**

在上人的句子中，有一上聯是在一九八〇年做的，當時他每週兩次往返舊金山的金山寺及萬佛聖城；在這句中明白地表露出上人對教育的完全奉獻，為了教育他不惜的犧牲自己的健康及舒適。這上聯是這樣寫的：

今日，飛車回城，專為明日，聆聽程夫子授課，以作後日，立身行道，奠定良基礎。

In the couplets below, each word in bold face represents the translation of the Chinese characters in each line of the couplet. The other words are grammatical necessities in English. Analyzing the couplets, the first and second lines' matching words, the parts of speech and grammatical functions in English are shown on the charts.

在下列的英文翻譯對聯句中，特別黑體字是中文對聯的翻譯字；其他的英文字是因為在英文文法解釋上必須有的。另外在英文對聯下面的對聯分析表中，可以看到上下聯逐字如何配對、英文的文法辭類及句中的文法。

**Mountain Gate and mighty oaks at the City.**
聖城的山門及峻偉的橡樹

宣化老和尚追思紀念專集

Proper nouns are matched with proper nouns; common nouns with common nouns; adjectives with adjectives and verbs with verbs. In addition, the grammatical functions in the two sentences of the couplet must match, and no word in the first line can be repeated in the match. Now let's look at some of the Master's own couplets and analyze the grammar. It should be mentioned that the rhyming system involving the sounds and tones used in Chinese couplets is beyond the scope of the discussion that follows.

專有名詞對專有名詞，普通名詞對普通名詞，形容詞配形容詞，動詞對動詞。上下聯中除了文法要相配合以外，上聯的字不能重複出現在下聯。讓我們先看看幾對上人親自做的對聯及文法分析。另外要提的一點，有的對聯要合押韻，對音聲及四聲，但這不在我們下列所討論的範圍內。

## ◆ COUPLET ON THE MOUNTAIN GATE OF THE CITY OF TEN THOUSAND BUDDHAS
### (on the west side－seen upon entering)
### composed by the Master on May 4, 1980

### 萬佛聖城山門正面之對聯 （進山門時可看見）
#### 宣化上人題於一九八〇年五月四日

華嚴境界。楞嚴壇場。四十二手眼。安天立地。

The **expansive scope** of the **Flower Adornment**,
  the **Shurangama's entire platform**,
    and the **forty-two hands and eyes**
      **pinion** the **heavens** and **secure** the **earth**.

妙覺世尊。等覺菩薩。千百億化身。變海爲山。

The **World Honored Ones** with **wonderful enlightenment**,
  **Equal Enlightenment Bodhisattvas**,
    and **hundreds of billions** of **transformation bodies**
      **take seas** and **turn** them **into mountains**.

### Analysis 對聯分析：

| first line 上聯 | matching line 下聯 | part of speech 文法詞類 | grammatical functions 文法 |
|---|---|---|---|
| expansive scope 境界 | World Honored Ones 世尊 | adjective-noun 形容詞・名詞 | 1st subject 第一主詞 |
| Flower Adornment 華嚴 | wonderful enlightenment 妙覺 | noun 名詞 | adjective 形容詞 |
| Shurangama 楞嚴 | Equal Enlightenment 等覺 | proper noun 專有名詞 | adjective 形容詞 |
| entire platform 壇場 | Bodhisattvas 菩薩 | noun 名詞 | 2nd subject 第二主詞 |
| forty-two 四十二 | hundreds of billions 千百億 | adjective 形容詞 | adjective 形容詞 |
| hands and eyes 手眼 | transformation bodies 化身 | noun 名詞 | 3rd subject 第三主詞 |
| pinion 安 | take 變 | verb 動詞 | 1st main verb 第一主要動詞 |
| heavens 天 | seas 海 | noun 名詞 | 1st direct object 第一直接受詞 |
| secure 立 | turn into 爲 | verb 動詞 | 2nd verb 第二動詞 |
| earth 地 | mountains 山 | noun 名詞 | 2nd direct object 第二直接受詞 |

# COUPLET ON THE MOUNTAIN GATE OF THE CITY OF TEN THOUSAND BUDDHAS
## (on the east side－seen upon leaving)
### composed by the Master on May 4, 1980

萬佛聖城山門背面之對聯（出山門時可看見）

宣化上人題於一九八〇年五月四日

慈悲普渡。信者得救。發菩提心。勇猛精進成正覺。

**Kindness** and **compassion universally take** beings **across**－
those who have faith will get saved.
**Bring forth** the **Bodhi resolve**
and with **courage** and **vigor perfect Proper Enlightenment.**

喜捨同修。禮之獲福。立堅固願。忍辱禪定悟眞詮。

**Joy** and **giving together cultivated**－
those who worship will be blessed.
**Make firm vows**
and by means of **patience** and **samadhi awaken** to **genuine truth.**

**Analysis 對聯分析：**

| first line 上聯 | matching line 下聯 | part of speech 文法詞類 | grammatical functions 文法 |
|---|---|---|---|
| kindness 慈 | joy 喜 | noun 名詞 | 1st subject 第一主詞 |
| compassion 悲 | giving 捨 | noun 名詞 | 2st subject 第二主詞 |
| universally take across 普渡 | together cultivated 同修 | adverb-verb 副詞・動詞 | main verb 主要動詞 |
| those who have faith 信者 | those who worship 禮之 | noun 名詞 | subject 主詞 |
| will get saved 得救 | will be blessed 獲福 | passive verb 被動詞 | passive verb 被動詞 |
| bring forth 發 | make 立 | imperative verb 使令動詞 | 1st verb 第一動詞 |
| Bodhi resolve 菩提心 | firm vows 堅固願 | adjective-noun 形容詞・名詞 | 1st direct object 第一直接受詞 |
| courage 勇猛 | patience 忍辱 | noun 名詞 | adverb phrase 副詞片語 |
| vigor 精進 | samadhi 禪定 | noun 名詞 | adverb phrase 副詞片語 |
| perfect 成 | awaken 悟 | imperative verb 使令動詞 | 2nd verb 第二動詞 |
| Proper Enlightenment 正覺 | genuine truth 真詮 | noun 名詞 | 2nd direct object 第二直接受詞 |

# COUPLET AT WESTERN BLISS GARDEN  composed by the Master during the '50's

香港西樂園寺 宣化上人題於五〇年代

念阿彌陀佛　三輩九品從此證

The **three levels** and **nine grades** (of rebirth) **are certified to** by
**being mindful of Amitabha Buddha.**

修波羅蜜法　六度萬行自茲圓

The **six paramitas** and **myriad practices are perfected** from
**cultivating Paramita Dharmas.**

**Analysis　對聯分析：**

| first line 上聯 | matching line 下聯 | part of speech 文法詞類 | grammatical functions 文法 |
|---|---|---|---|
| three levels 三輩 | six paramitas 六度 | adjectives-noun 形容詞・名詞 | subject 主詞 |
| nine grades 九品 | myriad practices 萬行 | adjectives-noun 形容詞・名詞 | subject 主詞 |
| are certified to 從此證 | are perfected 自茲圓 | passive verb 被動詞 | main verb 主要動詞 |
| by being mindful 念 | from cultivating 修 | adverb participle phrase 分詞片語 | participle phrase 分詞片語 |
| Amitabha Buddha 阿彌陀佛 | Paramita Dharmas 波羅蜜法 | proper noun 專有名詞 | participle phrase 分詞片語 |

# ◆ COUPLETS composed by the Master on June 20, 1980

對聯　宣化上人做於一九八〇年六月二十日

諸佛菩薩。神通妙用。移山倒海。難思議。

The **spiritual penetrations** and **wonderful functions**

of **all Buddhas** and **Bodhisattvas**

can **move mountains** and **flip over seas**

—**defying description**!

凡夫眾生。智昧無明。反迷歸覺。證菩提。

The **occluded wisdom** and the **ignorance**

of **the masses of ordinary beings**

can be **turned** from **confusion** and **returned** to **enlightenment**

—**certifying** to Bodhi!

**Analysis 對聯分析：**

| first line 上聯 | matching line 下聯 | part of speech 文法詞類 | grammatical functions 文法 |
| --- | --- | --- | --- |
| spiritual penetrations 神通 | occluded wisdom 智昧 | adjectives-noun 形容詞・名詞 | 1st subject 第一主詞 |
| wonderful functions 妙用 | ignorance 無明 | noun 名詞 | 2nd subject 第二主詞 |
| all Buddhas 諸佛 | the masses 凡夫 | adjectives-noun 形容詞・名詞 | adjective phrase 形容詞片語 |
| Bodhisattvas 菩薩 | ordinary beings 眾生 | noun 名詞 | adjective phrase 形容詞片語 |
| move 移 | turned 反 | verb 動詞 | 1st verb 第一動詞 |
| mountains 山 | confusion 迷 | noun 名詞 | 1st direct object 第一直接受詞 |
| flip over 倒 | returned 歸 | verb 動詞 | 2nd verb 第二動詞 |
| seas 海 | enlightenment 覺 | noun 名詞 | 2nd direct object 第二直接受詞 |
| defying 難 | certifying 證 | verb 動詞 | participle phrase 分詞片語 |
| description 思議 | Bodhi 菩提 | noun 名詞 | participle phrase 分詞片語 |

◆ 文殊大智。諸佛本懷。微塵數三昧。善財成正覺。

**All Buddhas inherently possess** the **great wisdom** of **Manjushri**.

From **samadhis** in **number** like **motes of dust**,

the **Youth Good Wealth realizes Proper Enlightenment**.

普賢宏願。菩薩行為。剎海劫種因。龍女證無生。

**Bodhisattvas actively practice** the **vast vows** of **Samantabhadra**.

From **causes planted** through **eons** equivalent to **seas of lands**,

the **dragon maiden certifies to Non-Production**.

## Analysis 對聯分析：

| first line 上聯 | matching line 下聯 | part of speech 文法詞類 | grammatical functions 文法 |
|---|---|---|---|
| All Buddhas 諸佛 | Bodhisattvas 菩薩 | noun 名詞 | subject 主詞 |
| inherently possess 本懷 | actively practice 行為 | adverb-verb 副詞‧動詞 | verb 動詞 |
| great wisdom 大智 | vast vows 宏願 | adjective-noun 形容詞‧名詞 | direct object 直接受詞 |
| Manjushri 文殊 | Samantabhadra 普賢 | noun 名詞 | adjective phrase 形容詞片語 |
| samadhis 三昧 | causes planted 種因 | noun 名詞 | participle phrase 分詞片語 |
| number 數 | eons 劫 | noun 名詞 | adjective phrase 形容詞片語 |
| motes of dust 微塵 | seas of lands 剎海 | noun 名詞 | adjective phrase 形容詞片語 |
| Youth Good Wealth 善財 | dragon maiden 龍女 | noun 名詞 | subject 主詞 |
| realizes 成 | certifies to 證 | verb 動詞 | verb 動詞 |
| Proper Enlightenment 正覺 | Non-Production 無生 | noun 名詞 | direct object 直接受詞 |

**The drum and bell echo through Deep Valley as the Three Masters are requested to transmit the Precepts.**

當請求三師傳戒時，
鐘鼓聲響遍深谷。

◆ 萬法歸一。深谷聞梵音。有情離苦成正覺。

The **myriad dharmas** return to one.

    **Deep Valley\*** hears Brahma sounds

        and **those with sentience leave suffering**

           and **attain Proper Enlightenment.**   \*Ukiah Valley

千門不二。高峰警迷夢。無緣獲度證菩提。

A **thousand doors** are **non-dual.**

    The **lofty peaks awaken** beings from their **confusing dream**

        and **those without affinities receive rescue**

           and **certify** to **Bodhi.**

| first line 上聯 | matching line 下聯 |
|---|---|
| myriad dharmas 萬法 | thousand doors 千門 |
| return to one 歸一 | non-dual 不二 |
| Deep Valley 深谷 | lofty peaks 高峰 |
| hears 聞 | awaken 警 |
| Brahma sounds 梵音 | confusing dream 迷夢 |
| those with sentience 有情 | those without affinities 無情 |
| leave 離 | receive 獲 |
| suffering 苦 | rescue 度 |
| attain 成 | certify to 證 |
| Proper Enlightenment 正覺 | Bodhi 菩提 |

**The four-fold assembly amid the City's trees--
one of every species that grows in California was
planted on these grounds in the 1950's.**
四眾弟子在聖城的樹下走。早在五○年代，
凡在加州所有的樹都種植一棵在聖城內。

◆ 萬佛城，乃三界導師。演摩訶般若洞天福地處。

**The City of Ten Thousand Buddhas must be** the **Grotto of Heaven** and the **Blessed Abode**
where the **Guiding Masters** of the **Three Realms proclaim Maha Prajna.**

如來寺，是四方眾生。修無上菩提壇場法園林。

**Tathagata Monastery is** the **Way-place** and **Dharma garden**
for **living beings** of the **four directions to cultivate Unsurpassed Bodhi.**

| first line 上聯 | matching line 下聯 |
|---|---|
| City of Ten Thousand Buddhas 萬佛城 | Tathagata Monastery 如來寺 |
| must be 乃 | is 是 |
| Grotto of Heaven 洞天 | Way-place 壇場 |
| Blessed Abode 福地處 | Dharma garden 法園林 |
| Guiding Masters 導師 | living beings 眾生 |
| Three Realms 三界 | four directions 四方 |
| proclaim 演 | cultivate 修 |
| Maha Prajna 摩訶般若 | Unsurpassed Bodhi 無上菩提 |

162

宣化老和尚追思紀念專集

宣化老和尚追思紀念專集

◆ 萬佛慈悲。法輪恒轉。莊嚴道場宣正教。瑞光耀天地。

Through the **kind compassion** of the **Ten Thousand Buddhas**,

    the **Dharma wheel constantly turns**.

      **Adorning** the Way-place and **proclaiming** the **Proper Teaching**

        creates an **auspicious light** that **dazzles heaven and earth**.


三寶普度。有情永化。圓滿德行證菩提。祥雲蔭寰宇。

Relying on **universal rescue** by the **Triple Jewel**,

    **sentient beings** are **eternally transformed**.

      **Perfecting virtuous conduct** and **certifying to Bodhi**,

        forms a **lucky cloud** that **shades** the **entire universe**.


◆ 小人言謊。行紅就綠。換面要充君子。

**Petty people's lies shift from red to blue. Changing** their **countenance**,

    they **pass** themselves **off** as **gentlemen**.


丈夫說話。如白染皂。改口不算英雄。

**A man's phrasing** is like a **stain of black on white. Altering** his **words**,

    he **cannot be counted** a **hero**.

| first line 上聯 | matching line 下聯 |
|---|---|
| petty people 小人 | man 丈夫 |
| lies 言謊 | phrasing 說話 |
| shift from red to blue 行紅就綠 | stain of black on white 如白染皁 |
| changing 換 | altering 改 |
| countenance 面 | words 口 |
| pass off 要充 | cannot be counted 不算 |
| gentlemen 君子 | hero 英雄 |

◆ 莫直爲曲。莫曲爲直。五蘊危城無罣礙。

**Don't mistake the straight for the crooked;**

    **don't mistake the crooked for the straight;**

        and you **won't get hung up** in the **risky city** of the **five skandhas.**


自有化空。自空化有。六道險宅得出離。

When you can **transform existence into emptiness;**

    **transform emptiness into existence;**

        you **can get out** of the **dangerous dwelling** of the **six paths.**


| first line 上聯 | matching line 下聯 |
|---|---|
| don't mistake the straight for crooked 莫直為曲 | transform existence into emptiness 自有化空 |
| don't mistake the crooked for straight 莫曲為直 | transform emptiness into existence 自空化有 |
| won't get hung up 無罣礙 | can get out 得出離 |
| risky city 危城 | dangerous dwelling 險宅 |
| five skandhas 五蘊 | six paths 六道 |


◆ 萬人入信海。普賢行願。華嚴眾妙門。育良五常。國際和平眞基礎。

**Myriad beings enter** the **sea of faith;**

    and then **Universal Worthy's conduct and vows,**

    the **Flower Adornment's multitude of wonderful doors,**

    and **Instilling Goodness's Five Constants**

        form the **true foundation**

            for **peace and harmony** among **all nations.**

這尊唐朝的古觀音像
目前護佑著聖城的戒壇

This ancient Tang dynasty
Guanyin Bodhisattva
now protects and blesses
the Precept Platform
at the City.

一心出迷流。觀音慈悲。楞嚴光明藏。培善八德。法界皈依安樂宮。

**One thought transcends** the **flow of confusion**;

and then **Guanyin's kindness and compassion**,

the **Shurangama's bright-light treasury**,

and **Developing Virtue's Eight Qualities**

become the **pleasant palace**

for our **returning and relying** on the **Dharma Realm**.

| first line 上聯 | matching line 下聯 |
| --- | --- |
| myriad beings 萬人 | one thought 一心 |
| enter 入 | transcends 出 |
| sea of faith 信海 | flow of confusion 迷流 |
| Universal Worthy's 普賢 | Guanyin's 觀音 |
| conduct and vows 行願 | kindness and compassion 慈悲 |
| Flower Adornment's 華嚴 | Shurangama's 楞嚴 |
| multitude of wonderful doors 妙眾門 | bright-light treasury 光明藏 |
| Instilling Goodness's 育良 | Developing Virtue's 培善 |
| Five Constants 五常 | Eight Qualities 八德 |
| true foundation 真基礎 | pleasant palace 安樂宮 |
| peace and harmony 和平 | returning and relying 皈依 |
| all nations 國際 | Dharma Realm 法界 |

This method of matching couplets was an excellent way for the Master to teach people who knew little about Chinese. In the beginning he made the lessons simple. Disciples only had to match a short phrase or a simple sentence. Let's look at some examples of the Master's line and the disciples' matches.

對聯課是上人教只認識一點點中文的人，最好的一個方法。剛開始，他教的很簡單，從最簡單的片語或短句開始。讓我們看一看上人的上聯與弟子的下聯。

❶ 師父的上聯　　　**Master's line:**

幹什麼　　　　　Doing what thing? (What are you doing?)

弟子的下聯　　　**Disciples' matches:**

作對聯　　　　　Matching a couplet.

化眾生　　　　　Transforming living beings.

修正法　　　　　Cultivating Proper Dharma.

為誰忙　　　　　Being busy for whom?

**doing 幹**　　　　　　**what thing 什麼**
matching 作　　　　　a couplet 對聯
transforming 化　　　living beings 眾生
cultivating 修　　　　Proper Dharma 正法
being busy 忙　　　　for whom 為誰

❷ 師父的上聯　　　**Master's line:**

無知錯因果　　　People lacking knowledge make mistakes in cause and effect.

弟子的下聯　　　**Disciples' matches:**

有道受敬仰　　　Those who attain the Way receive respect and admiration.

邪見落空假　　　Those with deviant views fall into emptiness and falseness.

有智了生死　　　Those who are wise end birth and death.

有道出輪迴　　　Those who attain the Way get out of the cycle of rebirth.

多智認黑白　　　Those with sufficient wisdom distinguish between black and white.

有障昧是非　　　Those who have obstacles confuse right and wrong.

有慧作功德　　　Those with wisdom create merit and virtue.

有業作馬牛　　　Those with bad karma have to be horses and cows.

| lacking knowledge 無知 | make mistakes in 錯 | cause and effect 因果 |
|---|---|---|
| attain the Way 有道 | receive 受 | respect and admiration 敬仰 |
| with deviant views 邪見 | fall 落 | emptiness and falseness 空假 |
| are wise 有智 | end 了 | birth and death 生死 |
| attain the Way 有道 | get out of 出 | cycle of rebirth 輪迴 |
| with sufficient wisdom 多智 | distinguish 認 | black and white 黑白 |
| have obstacles 有障 | confuse 昧 | right and wrong 是非 |
| with wisdom 有慧 | create 作 | merit and virtue 功德 |
| with bad karma 有業 | have to be 作 | horses and cows 馬牛 |

**The Master speaking Dharma in Five Contemplations Hall.**
上人在五觀堂開示

❸ 師父的上聯　　**Master's line:**

爲衣食住忙乎！　How busy we are for the sake of clothing, food, and shelter!

弟子的下聯　　**Disciples' matches:**

行仁義孝難嗎！　How difficult it is to practice humaneness, righteousness, and filiality!

滅貪瞋癡善哉！　How fine it would be if we could put an end to greed, hatred, and stupidity!

近佛法僧樂哉！　How happy we are to draw near the Buddha, the Dharma, and the Sangha!

| how busy 忙乎 | for the sake of 爲 | clothing, food, shelter 衣食住 |
|---|---|---|
| how difficult 難嗎 | to practice 行 | humaneness, righteousness, filiality 仁義孝 |
| how fine 善哉 | to put an end to 滅 | greed, hatred, stupidity 貪瞋癡 |
| how happy 樂哉 | to draw near 近 | Buddha, Dharma, Sangha 佛法僧 |

**❹ 師父的上聯**　　　**Master's line:**

志如松柏耐寒暑　Our resolve should resemble a pine tree enduring the winters and summers.

**弟子的下聯**　　　**Disciples' matches:**

願似金剛難動搖　Vows must be like solid vajra resisting shaking and moving.

智似日月透邇邁　Wisdom must be like the sun and moon passing from close to distant.

氣似霓虹貫日月　Energy (*qi*) must be like a rainbow connecting the sun and moon.

修似航舟忍順逆　Cultivation must be like sailing vessels surviving favorable and counter flows.

量似海空容巨細　Our scope must be like the seas and space containing the vast and the minute.

願似蓮華離塵垢　Vows must be like a lotus blossom transcending the mud and mire.

意似江流貫始終　Our intent must be like a flowing river connecting beginnings and ends.

**A resolve like vajra and a mind as strong as a stone.**
志如金剛，心如石

| resolve 志 | should resemble 如 | pine tree 松柏 | enduring 耐 | winters and summers 寒暑 |
|---|---|---|---|---|
| vows 願 | must be like 似 | solid vajra 金剛 | resisting 難 | shaking and moving 動搖 |
| wisdom 智 | must be like 似 | sun and moon 日月 | passing 透 | from close to distant 邇邁 |
| energy 氣 | must be like 似 | rainbow 霓虹 | connecting 貫 | sun and moon 日月 |
| cultivation 修 | must be like 似 | sailing vessels 航舟 | surviving 忍 | favorable and counter flows 順逆 |
| scope 量 | must be like 似 | seas and space 海空 | containing 容 | vast and minute 巨細 |
| vows 願 | must be like 似 | lotus blossom 蓮華 | transcending 離 | mud and mire 塵垢 |
| intent 意 | must be like 似 | flowing river 江流 | connecting 貫 | beginnings and ends 始終 |

**❺ 師父的上聯**　　　**Master's line:**

口是心非偽君子　One whose mouth says "yes" while his mind means "no"
　　　　　　　　　　—a phony "superior person."

　　　　　　　　　　　　　　　　　　　　宣化老和尚追思紀念專集

| 弟子的下聯 | Disciples' matches: |
|---|---|

面從背違眞小人　Someone who to your face is compliant but behind your back opposes
　　　　　　　　— truly a petty man.

言虛行詭小人物　Someone whose words are false and whose actions are cunning
　　　　　　　　— a small-minded individual.

言眞行實大丈夫　Someone whose words are true and whose actions are genuine
　　　　　　　　— a great hero.

事眞意假實老千　Someone whose business is real but whose intentions are deceptive
　　　　　　　　— a first-class cheat.

言正意直眞雅人　Someone whose words are proper and whose mind is straight
　　　　　　　　— truly an exceptional one.

因愼果易實菩薩　Someone whose causes are cautious so his effects are easy
　　　　　　　　— really a Bodhisattva.

外剛內柔眞護法　Someone whose inner stuff is tough but whose outer appearance is soft
　　　　　　　　— a true Dharma protector.

身清意靜眞修者　Someone whose body is pure and whose mind is tranquil
　　　　　　　　— a true cultivator.

意亂情迷糊塗人　Someone whose mind is scattered and whose emotions are confused
　　　　　　　　— a messed-up individual.

| mouth 口 | yes 是 | mind 心 | no 非 | phony 偽 | superior person 君子 |
|---|---|---|---|---|---|
| face 面 | compliant 從 | back 背 | opposes 違 | truly 真 | petty man 小人 |
| words 言 | false 虛 | actions 行 | cunning 詭 | small-minded 小 | individual 人物 |
| words 言 | true 真 | actions 行 | genuine 實 | great 大 | hero 丈夫 |
| business 事 | real 真 | intentions 意 | deceptive 假 | first-class 實 | cheat 老千 |
| words 言 | proper 正 | mind 意 | straight 直 | truly 真 | exceptional one 雅人 |
| causes 因 | cautious 愼 | effects 果 | easy 易 | really 實 | Bodhisattva 菩薩 |
| inner stuff 內 | tough 剛 | outer appearance 外 | soft 柔 | true 真 | Dharma protector 護法 |
| body 身 | pure 清 | mind 意 | tranquil 靜 | true 真 | cultivator 修者 |
| mind 意 | scattered 亂 | emotions 情 | confused 迷 | messed-up 糊塗 | individual 人 |

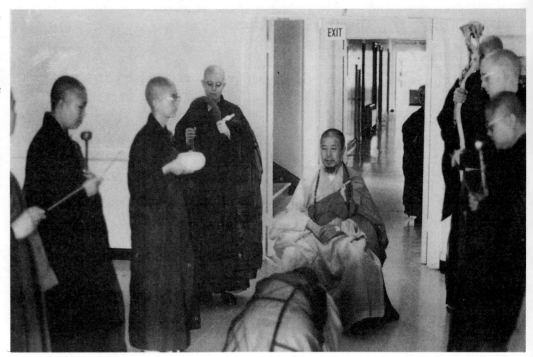

The Master, as Precept-transmitting Master, always reminds preceptees that leaving home is for the sake of ending birth and death.

上人當得戒師時
總是提醒戒子們
出家是為了要了脫生死

**❻ 師父的上聯**     **Master's line:**

生老病死真是苦     Birth, old age, sickness and death— really are suffering!

**弟子的對聯**     **Disciple's matches:**

喜怒哀樂幻如夢     Joy, rage, grief, and happiness— illusory like a dream.

受想行識豈為空     Feeling, thinking, activities, and consciousness— aren't they empty?

常樂我淨永為福     Permanence, bliss, true self, and purity— forever act as blessings.

國城妻子有何戀     Nations, cities, spouses, children— what's there to cling to?

信解行證實為要     Faith, understanding, practice, and certification— absolute essentials!

夢幻泡影原非樂     Dreams, illusions, bubbles, shadows— basically can't be happiness.

地水火風無非蛇     Earth, water, fire, and air— poisonous snakes without exception!

慈悲喜捨能生樂     Kindness, compassion, joy, and giving— begetters of happiness.

行住坐臥原在道     Walking, standing, sitting, and lying down— have the Way as their source.

富貴榮華無非幻     Wealth, honor, glory, and splendor— none is not illusory.

殺盜淫妄實應戒     Killing, stealing, lust, and lying— definite restraints!

父母兄弟一起修     Fathers, mothers, brothers, and sisters— cultivate together!

**❼ 師父的上聯**　　　　**Master's line:**

君子過則勿憚改　　　A superior person does not fear correcting his mistakes.


**弟子的對聯**　　　　**Disciple's matches:**

小人錯而盡掩飾　　　A petty one is always covering her faults.

愚人錯猶不認識　　　A stupid one fails to recognize his faults.

小人咎而好飾非　　　A petty one likes to gloss over her errors.

行者立功勿宣傳　　　A good practitioner won't broadcast his merits.

行者辱即莫起瞋　　　A good practitioner won't get angry over being humiliated.

勇者非而敢承當　　　A courageous individual will take responsibility for his wrong-doing.

達者怒而不輕言　　　An intelligent one won't express her rage.

智者錯而即自新　　　A wise one immediately corrects his faults.

粗漢錯但還固執　　　A coarse fellow insists he's right despite his faults.

凡夫短而復露拙　　　Ordinary people repeatedly display their shortcomings


| **superior person 君子** | **does not fear correcting 勿憚改** | **mistakes 過** |
|---|---|---|
| petty one 小人 | is always covering 盡掩飾 | faults 錯 |
| stupid one 愚人 | fails to recognize 不認識 | faults 錯 |
| petty one 小人 | likes to gloss over 好飾非 | errors 咎 |
| good practitioner 行者 | won't broadcast 勿宣傳 | merits 功 |
| good practitioner 行者 | won't get angry over 莫起瞋 | being humiliated 辱 |
| courageous individual 勇者 | will take responsibility for 敢承當 | wrong-doing 非 |
| intelligent one 達者 | won't express 不輕言 | rage 怒 |
| wise one 智者 | immediately corrects 即自新 | faults 錯 |
| coarse fellow 粗漢 | insists he's right 還固執 | faults 錯 |
| ordinary people 凡夫 | repeatedly display 復露拙 | shortcomings 短 |

**❽ 師父的上聯**　　　**Master's line:**

深谷鐘聲遍法界　　　The sound of the bell in Deep Valley [Ukiah] pervades the Dharma Realm.

**弟子的對聯**　　　**Disciple's matches:**

金山鼓震悟禪心　　　The beating of the drum at Gold Mountain awakens the mind's samadhi.

覺山智光照娑婆　　　The light of wisdom from Enlightenment Mountain illumines the Saha world.

道場淨光照世間　　　The pure light of the Way-place shines on the whole world.

萬佛甘雨潤大地　　　The sweet rain at Ten Thousand Buddhas moistens the great earth.

叢林師吼震寰宇　　　The lion's roar at this big monastery shakes up the universe.

古剎佛音繞耳邊　　　The recitation of the Buddha's name in ancient temples revolves in our ears.

**Heng Lai Shi leads the assembly through Great Compassion House's covered corridors.**
恆來師帶領大眾穿過大悲院的廊簷

| **sound of the bell 鐘聲** | **Deep Valley 深谷** | **pervades 遍** | **Dharma Realm 法界** |
|---|---|---|---|
| beating of the drum 鼓震 | Gold Mountain 金山 | awakens 悟 | mind's samadhi 禪心 |
| light of wisdom 智光 | Enlightenment Mountain 覺山 | illumines 照 | Saha world 娑婆 |
| pure light 淨光 | Way-place 道場 | shines on 照 | whole world 世間 |
| sweet rain 甘雨 | Ten Thousand Buddhas 萬佛 | moistens 潤 | great earth 大地 |
| lion's roar 獅吼 | big monastery 叢林 | shakes up 震 | universe 寰宇 |
| recitation of the Buddha's name 佛音 | ancient temples 古剎 | revolves in 繞 | our ears 耳邊 |

Although the matching line may not repeat any characters (words) in the first line, it is all right for the first line itself to have repeated (words) in it. The following is an example with the repeated Chinese character being translated by the same word and underlined in English.

雖然下聯不能重複上聯的字，但上聯自己可以在句中重複用字。下列是兩個例子，在英文的翻譯句中，若碰到中文是重複字的，就劃底線表示。

**❾ 師父的上聯**

**Master's line:**

做人要有志氣，修道要專誠

In being a person one <u>must</u> have an air of determination;

in cultivating the Way one <u>must</u> be singularly sincere.

**弟子的對聯**

**Disciples' matches:**

習聖當行慈悲，立德當忍辱

In learning to be a sage we <u>should</u> practice compassion;

in doing virtuous deeds we <u>should</u> have patience under insult.

爲僧宜勤惜福，任命宜知足

As a member of the Sangha <u>it is fitting</u> to diligently conserve our blessings;

in accepting our destiny <u>it is fitting</u> to know contentment.

孝子應報慈恩，行善應眞實

As a filial children we <u>ought to</u> repay our parents' kindness;

in doing good deeds we <u>ought to</u> be true and genuine.

成佛必除貪心，行法必懇切

To become a Buddha we <u>have to</u> get rid of greed;

in practicing Dharmas we <u>have to</u> be sincere.

念佛須具恆心，參禪須寂定

Being mindful of the Buddha <u>requires</u> a persevering mind;

investigating Chan <u>requires</u> quiet samadhi.

發心須立誓願，證果須勤進

In bringing forth the resolve, we <u>should</u> make vows;

to certify to the fruition, we <u>should</u> diligently progress.

Sometimes sound plays a part in the match. This line of the Master's has two sets of the same-sounding words— *ru* and *lai*. To make it even harder, one of those same-sounds— *lai*— is also the same character "come." Matches had to use same sounds in those grammatical places and the second same-sound had to be an identical character. Romanized sounds are shown in the English translation to help the reader realize this Chinese sound pattern.

有時候音聲也是對對聯的一部份。在上人的句子中有兩組音聲相同的字——「如」及「汝」，更難的是，另一個字是同一個字——「來」。在對音聲時，第一個字音聲發一樣的音聲，而第二個字要用同一個字。在英文翻譯句中，以羅馬拼音幫助讀者瞭解中文字的同音字的音聲格式。

**❿ 師父的上聯**　　　　**Master's line:**

如來寺中汝來住　　　You come (*ru lai*) and live in Thus Come (*ru lai*) [Tathagata] Monastery.

**弟子的對聯**　　　　**Disciple's matches:**

無言堂內毋言笑　　　Do not speak words (*wu yan*) or laugh in Wordless (*wu yan*) Hall.

喜捨院內悉捨之　　　Everyone's giving (*xi she*) in Joyous Giving (*xi she*) House.

妙覺山上苗覺長　　　Sprouts of enlightenment (*miao jiao*) grow at Wonderful Enlightenment (*miao jiao*) Mountain.

虛雲塔上須雲集　　　There must be clouds (*xu yun*) that billow around Empty Cloud (*xu yun*) Stupa.

極樂國內己樂生　　　It's your bliss (*ji le*) to be born in the Ultimate Bliss (*ji le*) Land.

地藏殿裏滌藏寶　　　Wash the store (*di zang*) of gems in Earth Store (*di zang*) Hall.

萬佛殿裏完佛坐　　　Absolutely all Buddhas (*wan fo*) are seated in the Ten Thousand Buddha (*wan fo*) Hall.

菩提場裏普提心　　　Everyone brings up (*pu ti*) their resolve in the Bodhi (*pu ti*) Way-place.

How many advantages students of the Dharma reaped from the Master's Couplet class! (1) It improved our Chinese vocabulary; (2) it taught us Chinese grammar; (3) we received invaluable lessons in how to cut off afflictions, how to develop our character, how to treat our elders and others, how to create merit and virtue, what our moral obligations were, how to cultivate and perfect our practices, how to expand the measure of our minds, and so forth; (4) we also received timely, direct, personal advice from the Master about correcting our faults through this wonderful expedient in a form we could all accept; (5) we learned to know each others' minds and inclinations by the content of our matching lines. Ah! The good points could never all be listed!

在這一個法門中，學生從上人的對聯課中獲益不淺！第一，增加了我們的中文字彙；第二，學會了中文文法；第三，我們獲得了無價的知識，它教我們如何斷除煩惱、如何改進我們的品性、如何對待我們的長輩及其他的人、如何立功立德、什麼是我們應盡的義務、如何修行圓滿、及如何擴大我們的胸襟等等；第四，上人用我們都可以接受的、不可思議的方便法門，糾正了我們的過錯，給予即時的、直接的、個人的忠告；第五，從我們的下聯含意中，我們知道彼此的心意、思想。種種的好處無法全部在此寫出來！

**You come and live in Tathagata Monastery.**
如來寺中汝來住

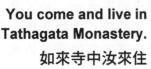

The Master also stressed that in writing our matches on the blackboard, our characters had to be written neatly. The vertical line of characters could not be crooked or lop-sided, nor could the characters be written too large or too small. They had to be properly printed characters— no cursive style was allowed. The Master advised us that a person's character was exposed in his/her writing. Crooked lines meant crooked minds.

上人也強調，在黑板上寫對聯時，字必須工整。直寫時，不可歪七扭八，字也不可太大或太小。一筆一劃要清清楚楚，不可草寫。上人告訴我們，字可看出一個人的個性。寫的彎彎的，表示心也是彎曲的。

A bit of space had to be left between each vertical line of characters— but not too much. We were reminded over and over not to take more than our share of space. I remember one time the Master threatened to charge a young boy "rent" because his line took up too much space on the board!

寫的時候，每一行之間，要留點兒距離，但不要太大。上人總是不斷地提醒，不要超過自己的範圍。記得有一次，上人開玩笑地告訴一個小男生，要向他收租金，因爲他寫得字佔用了太多的黑板。

As a "Chinese-as-a-second-language" disciple, I found that these Couplet classes became the foundation by which I could come to appreciate the exquisite literary style found in the *Shurangama Sutra*, as well as the poetic form of the Master's *Heart Sutra Standless Verses, Shurangama Mantra Verses, Great Compassion Mantra Verses, Patriarch Verses,* and the eloquent language of the Master's *Reflections in Water and Mirrors Turning back the Tide of Destiny.*

對一個中文是第二語言的弟子而言，對聯課是一個基礎課程，從而使我瞭解《楞嚴經》中精美的文學，在師父寫的《心經》非台頌解、〈楞嚴咒〉偈頌、〈大悲咒〉偈頌、歷代祖師偈頌中，體會到詩韻的風格，以及從上人的《水鏡回天錄》裏，領會到動人的詞句。

You may complain that you don't like grammar and that certainly Couplets class would have been too difficult. But not so! Whether we were non-native Chinese speakers or outstanding Chinese scholars, we were encouraged and challenged respectively. For instance the elementary school students— whether Asian or Western—were provided a small stool to stand on so they could reach

**The Master with young students of Instilling Goodness School.**
上人與育良小學學生

the very bottom of the chalkboard to write their matches. The Master gave them their own special line to match. Below is a example.

你可能會抱怨不喜歡文法，而且這對聯課太深了。其實不盡然！不論是非中國籍而說華語的人，或尚未學習完中文的人，我們都受到關心的鼓勵及挑戰。例如，上人爲亞洲或西方的小學生準備一個小板凳，讓他們搆到黑板的下面寫下聯。上人會出一些特別的句子讓他們對，下面就是一個簡單的例子。

▶**師父為小學生出上聯**　**Master's line for young students:**

你我他　　　　　You, me, and others

**學生對聯**　　　**students' matches:**

鬼神魔　　　　　ghosts, spirits, and demons

天地人　　　　　heaven, earth, and people

人鬼畜　　　　　people, ghosts, and animals

老壯幼　　　　　old, middle aged, and young

天人師　　　　　gods, people, and teachers

▶**師父為中學生出上聯**　**Master's line for older students:**

百鳥鳴空　　　　A hundred birds call in space.

**學生的對聯**　　**students' matches:**

萬物説法　　　　The myriad creatures speak the Dharma.

九蓮出水　　　　Nine lotuses grow out of the water.

一石落井　　　　A single stone falls into a well.

萬箭穿心　　　　Ten thousand arrows hit the target.

千流瀉地　　　　A thousand streams purge the earth.

數蝶飛野　　　　A batch of butterflies flutters through the wilds.

And for the most sophisticated couplet scholars, the Master's expedients were also ineffably wonderful. You can find a detailed discussion of that in Volume Two of *In Memory of Venerable Master Hua* in the article "A Bosom Friend for Three Years" where Professor Yang Fusen discusses his experiences in matching couplets with the Master. In perhaps the epitome of scholastic challenges, on the occasion of the Birthday Banquet to Revere the Elderly, Pay Homage to the Worthy, and Honor the Virtuous held in Los Angeles on December 20, 1992, the Master composed a vertical Couplet and horizontal Heading, and then went on to do something that had never been done before: he composed Sub-Couplets for each phrase of the Main Couplet and a Sub-Couplet for the Heading. One wonders how many of the group of distinguished scholars who attended that banquet ever did hand in their matches to the Venerable Master! What follows are the Master's Main Couplet, Heading, Sub-Couplets on each phrase of the main couplet and Sub-Couplet for the Heading.

對博學又專於此道的學者而言，上人的權宜法門，是難以形容的奧妙。《宣化老和尚追思紀念專集》第二冊，楊富森教授「結緣三年獲知音」一文，有很詳細的討論，他與上人對對聯的經驗。一九九二年十二月二十日在洛衫磯的「尊老重賢敬德壽筵」中，上人與與會的老專家學者們鬥機鋒，上人做了一對賀壽聯加橫批，並當場為這對壽聯及橫批寫了從未有人寫過的副聯。不知道當天這麼多卓越的學者中，是否已有人交出卷子了？下列是上人為上下聯及橫批所寫的副聯。

◀ 師父的上聯　Master's line:　尊老重賢。耆年壽考。福慧雙圓。

**Respect elders and honor the worthy,**

　　**for, in their seniority and longevity,**

　　　　**blessings and wisdom are perfected.**

下聯　Master's match:　學佛習聖。耄耋齡高。道德齊臻。

**Learn from the Buddhas and study with the sages,**

　　**so that, at the advanced age of seventy or eighty,**

　　　　**both the Way and virtue will be reached.**

橫聯　Master's title:　松柏長青

**Evergreen like the pine and cedar.**

◀◀ 師父為對聯的第一句所做的副聯

**Master's sub-couplet for the first phrases of his couplet:**

尊老重賢孔孟訓

**To respect elders and honor the worthy**

　　**are the teachings of Confucius and Mencius.**

學佛習聖釋子傳

**Learning from the Buddhas and studying with the sages**

　　**is the transmission of Shakyamuni.**

◀◀ 師父為對聯的第二句所做的副聯

**Master's sub-couplet for the second phrases of his couplet:**

耆年壽考祖師教

**Seniority and longevity:**

　　**the teaching of Patriarchs.**

耄耋齡高天地寬

**At the advanced age of seventy or eighty,**

　　**how vast the universe!**

Master's sub-couplet for the third phrases of his couplet:

福慧雙圓黎民慶

**With blessings and wisdom perfected,**

**all people congratulate you.**

道德齊臻草木歡

**With the Way and virtue both reached,**

**even the grass and trees are delighted.**

◀◀橫聯的副聯

Master's sub-couplet for the title.

竹梅冰雪愧予志

**I am hesitant to admit my resolve**

**to imitate the bamboo and plum tree**

**that endure the ice and snow.**

松柏長青祝君安

**Wishing you superior ones all good health!**

**May you be like the pine and cedar**

**which remain evergreen.**

In the early 1970's a well known leader of Zen Buddhism sent an invitation to Gold Mountain requesting the Master's presence at a Transmission of Dharma ceremony. Although he dressed like a monk and took disciples, this elder religious leader, following the Japanese style, had a wife. We disciples were surprised when the Master said he would accept the invitation. But then he explained why: "The Roshi is doing the right thing. He is in America; he should transmit his lineage to an American. That's the reason I'm willing to go. My presence indicates my agreement with his choice of Dharma heir, not the rest of what he stands for."

一九七〇年早期，一位著名日本禪宗領袖，送了一張請帖到金山禪寺，請上人出席一場傳法典禮。這位年老宗教領袖，雖然他穿著像一位和尚，而且收弟子，但是沿習日本習俗──結婚有太太。當上人說他願接受這邀請時，我們做弟子的都很驚訝。但上人解釋：「這位老師做對一件事。他在美國，應該把他的法傳給美國人，我願意去參加。我的出席就代表我同意他的繼承人選擇，並不是同意其他別的。」

The day came and the Master went, taking some of us disciples with him, of course. The Zendo was full of prosperous laity and we "ascetics" in our patched and unmatched robes and sashes looked quite out of place in the slick, petite, Japanese environment. Actually, the American Dharma heir looked a bit out of place too, in a robe that wrapped his gangling body tightly to the knees only. Perspiring profusely, and trembling enough to be noticed, he took mincing steps in his bare feet as he advanced to the altar to receive the transmission.

到那一天的時候，當然上人帶了幾個弟子隨同參加。當時日本中心擠滿了有錢和有地位的護法。我們這群高大美國的苦行僧，穿著打了補釘而又不合身的長袍及袈裟，與這個華麗而嬌小玲瓏的日本格調，看起來格格不入。實際上，這位美國繼嗣者，看起來也有點不屬於這地方，因爲他不合身的長袍緊緊的包在他修長的身上，又短得只到膝蓋而已。當他打著光腳邁著碎步走向臺上準備接法時，很明顯的看出他正滿身大汗，又全身發抖著。

His elder teacher, who was bedridden with a terminal illness and unable to speak, was barely able to limp valiantly down a long walkway that the Dharma heir at the same time ascended, so that they met halfway, quite a

**Our Master quickly responded with a chuckle and a twinkle in his eye**
上人眼睛蘊著光，笑著很快的回答。

distance from the crowd of spectators. The transmission took place in silence and the Dharma heir descended to bow again at the altar. Tradition had it that as soon as he received the transmission, the Dharma heir was to give a brief inaugural speech before being subjected to a barrage of challenging questions from his inherited followers to test his Dharma prowess.

他年老的老師，因癌症末期已臥病在床，又不能言語。他起身勉強走了幾步，但實在無法走那麼一大段路到臺上去；而同時這位繼嗣者已走到臺上，所以他就走下來到他老師面前，那距離我們這一大群觀眾有一點兒遠。這傳法是在無聲中舉行，稍後這位繼嗣者就再回臺上頂禮。當繼嗣者接到法後，按傳統習俗，必須發表就職演講，然後接受一連串來自他繼承過來的護法們的挑戰性問題，以便測試他的佛法程度。

The Dharma heir's speech was brief: "At the moment of transmission, I received a tremendous communication from our teacher. He pointed up, pointed down, and then drew a circle with his finger. I immediately understood: 'There is no high or low and the circle is empty.'" Then tough questions began to rain down and the new heir did his best to answer them cleverly. I remember one in particular. A young man asked, "This morning when I clipped my toenails, I couldn't find a place to put the clippings. What about that?" The Dharma heir hesitated a moment and then replied, "You work in the kitchen, don't you?" He was hoping, it seemed, to send up a smoke screen. The kitchen worker refused to be distracted. "That's got nothing to do with my question. Answer my question!" Pausing again, the Dharma heir finally replied lamely, "I had the same problem myself (with the toenail clippings)," and passed on to the next question, leaving the kitchen worker and other critics in the crowd dissatisfied.

這位繼嗣者簡單的講：「在傳法的那個時刻，我從我們的老師那兒，得到了一個非常好的訊息。他用手指指天，指指地，然後劃了一個圓圈。我立刻領悟到：『沒有高，沒有低，圓圈就是空。』」

接下來一連串問難，考驗這位繼嗣者，他盡其所能巧妙地回答。我記得有一個特別的問題。一位年輕人問：「今天早上，當我剪完腳指甲，我找不到一個地方放這腳指甲，我該放那裡呢？」這位繼嗣者猶疑了一會兒，然後回答，「你在廚房做事，是不是？」他似乎想用一個障眼法。這位廚房工作者不為所轉地說：「那與我的問題無關，回答我的問題。」這位繼嗣者又停了一下，最後只回答說：「我自己也有同樣的問題（腳指甲）。」他就跳過這問題，繼續其他的問題，讓這位廚房工作者及人群中一些評鑑人很失望。

Back at Gold Mountain after our rare outing, the Master, always vigorously teaching, called us together immediately to discuss our impressions of the experience. The second-American-to-leave-home, Heng Ching, mentioned the poor showing in dealing with the kitchen worker's question. "How would you have answered?" the Master promptly demanded. Heng Ching was stopped short. He had no answer. Our Master quickly responded with a chuckle and a twinkle in his eye. "Had it been me, I would have answered him like this: 'That's easy. Just take your nail clippers and clip a little round hole in your skull. Once that's done, reach inside and clip out a piece of your brain, and then put your toenail clippings there!" We all sat in dead silence for a moment and then broke into delighted laughter. The Master had just exhibited the "principle of bringing dualities back to the Middle Way" taught by the Sixth Patriarch wherein you negate any entity by introducing its opposite, thus canceling out the two extremes and leaving the mind "in the mean between." The top of the head matched with the tips of the toes; the most useless thing about our body— toenail clippings— matched with what we consider the most valuable part of our body— our brain. That was the reason for the initial dead silence after hearing what the Master said— momentarily he brought everyone's mind in balance, focused on the Middle Way.

師父總是不懈怠地教我們，由難得一次的出訪回到金山禪寺後，師父就立刻集會討論這次觀禮的印象。第二個出家的美國人—恆靜，提到這位繼嗣者在與廚房工作人的對答時差勁的表現。師父就問他：「那你會怎麼回答？」恆靜突然呆住了沒有回答。就看見師父眼睛蘊著光，笑著很快的就回答：「如果是我，我會這樣回答：『那很簡單，拿你的指甲刀在你腦殼上剪一圈。剪好後把腦子拿起一塊，然後就把你的腳指甲放進去。』」我們先是一愣，接著哄堂大笑。上人引用了六祖大師的出入不落兩邊，中道了義法。頭頂配腳趾；我們身上最沒有用的東西——腳指甲，配我們所認為身上最有價值的部份——腦袋。那就是為什麼在一聽完師父說的，我們都呆住了；因為在那一剎那間，我們每個人原有的心思都沒有了，都放在一個平衡點上——都集中在中道。

"And as to the gesture the old teacher made in transmitting his Dharma," the Master concluded, "no doubt he was really trying to say, 'Suddenly in the heavens, suddenly in the hells. Here we go again in the cycle of rebirth!'"

上人又做結論說：「再者，這位老師在傳法時所做的手勢，毫無疑問地他真正要表達的是『突然在天上，突然在地獄，我們又要在生死中輪迴。』」

And so finally, we see the Couplet class as much more than a Chinese lesson or a lesson in morality. And we realize that the concept of opposites—inherent in every aspect of this world of dualities we live in—extends far beyond the realm of scholarship. The Sixth Patriarch was illiterate, but his Transmission Dharma contained thirty-six pairs of opposites. He instructs, "Should someone suddenly ask you about a dharma, answer him with its opposite. If you always answer with the opposite, both will be eliminated and nothing will be left, since each depends on the other for existence." The Sixth Patriarch's was the Sudden Enlightenment Dharma door.

所以最後，我們領會到了在對聯課所學到的，遠超過一堂中文課或道德課。我們也瞭解了相對的觀念，遠超過我們在世界上所學的知識領域。六祖大師原是目不識丁，但他所傳的法包含了三十六對相對法。六祖指點：「有人問汝法。出語盡雙。皆取對法。來去相因。究竟二法盡除。更無去處。」六祖是傳頓悟法門。

## ▶ 師父的上聯　Master's line:

今日。飛車回城。專爲明日。聆聽程夫子授課。以作後日。立身行道。奠定良基礎。

**Today** (*jin ri*), **riding in a car flying back to the City,**

I came **especially for the sake of tomorrow** (*ming ri*)

to **listen attentively** to **Professor Cheng teach** his **class**

so that **later in the future** (*hou ri*)

I can **establish myself** and **practice the Way,**

thus **developing** a **good foundation**.

## 弟子的對聯　Disciples' matches:

不對，背覺合塵。如學相對。諦觀老和尚配聯。頃入絕對。悟心見性。可歸中了義。

**Mistakenly** (*bu dui*), **turning from enlightenment** and **getting involved in the world,**

we **should instead study opposites** (*xiang dui*),

**scrutinizing carefully** as **the Master matches couplets,**

so that **instantly** we may perceive **the absolute** (*jue dui*) ,

**awaken to** our **minds** and **see** our **natures,**

and **return** to the **final meaning** of the **Middle**.

---

**today 今日**

riding in a car flying back to the City 飛車回城

especially for the sake of 專爲

tomorrow 明日

listen attentively 聆聽

Professor Cheng 程夫子

teach his class 授課

later 以作

the future 後日

establish myself, practice the Way 立身行道

developing 奠定

good foundation 良基礎

**mistakenly 不對**

turning from enlightenment and getting involved in the world 背覺合塵

should instead study 如學

opposites 相對

scrutinize carefully 諦觀

the Master 老和尚

match couplets 配聯

instantly 頃入

the absolute 絕對

awaken to our minds, see our natures 悟心見性

return 可歸

final meaning of the Middle 中了義

Did you ever experience coming into the Master's presence with a thousand problems in mind and million questions you wanted answered? But then, imperceptibly as you listened to his lecture or instructions— before you ever had a chance to open your mouth— the problems seemed to disappear from your mind and your questions somehow found answers? Or, the more you listened, the less serious your problems seemed and the less important your questions? Do you suppose you were benefiting from the Master's expert use of the expedient of opposites to neutralize your afflictions?

你是否有這樣的經驗，當你到上人面前時，心裡懷著數千個問題想要問；但聽了上人的開示後，你都還沒有機會開口問問題，心裡的疑問似乎不見了，或者問題已經得到答案了？或者再聽了更多一些以後，你重要的問題也隨著變著不重要了？你是否想過，你在上人巧妙的專門對待法中獲益，進而也消除了你的煩惱？

# PINE CONE DHARMA
# 松果的法

釋恆古

Shi Heng Gu

Tonight we have started listening to Venerable Master's commentary on the fifth chapter of the *Dharma Flower Sutra*, "Medicinal Herbs." This has always been my favorite chapter in that Sutra, a beautiful and profoundly moving analogy. Today was also the last day of our DRBU (Dharma Realm Buddhist University) biology class on the trees and shrubs of Mendocino county. Interesting coincidence, but then the Dharma often works in this way. So tonight I'll try to speak some Dharma concerning pine cones. This here is a pine cone from right here in the CTTB (City of Ten Thousand Buddhas): it is rather large, halfway opened, and very pretty.

In the Sutra text the Buddha mentions the three-thousand great-thousand world system. This is a huge concept, and I don't know if our minds can really grapple with the whole idea. But as the Venerable Master always said, the myriad dharmas can just as well be considered in terms of a single dharma. So we don't necessarily need to investigate the whole universe. We can focus just on Mendocino County, or Ukiah Valley, or our environment here at CTTB.

We are all aware that here in the City we have a complex mix of people, languages, and cultural backgrounds. But in addition to people we also have an impressive variety of other life forms: trees, shrubs, herbs, flowers--all kinds of plants from all over the world, coming from places as far apart as the Far East and the Mediterranean, Norway and North Africa. The variety of these plants is just as amazing as the variety of living beings, and the variety of Dharma doors the Buddha has provided for them. The sun and rain benefit every sort of plant according to its kind: from the dry, low-growing chaparral high on the eastern hills to the humid evergreen forests of the coast in the west, every species gets just its right share, just what it needs to grow. Similarly the Buddha provides 84,000 Dharma doors to bring living beings to maturity. The rain of Dharma nourishes living beings according to their roots and capacity, ignoring none, neglecting none.

What does this pine cone contain? Seeds. These seeds can be likened to the seeds of the Buddha nature inside of us, inside all living beings. These seeds need to come out, to be planted in the soil, to be nurtured so that they can grow strong and healthy. Plants have very ingenious and complex ways to transport and plant their seeds. Some seeds have tiny wings to propel them, others have

今晚我們開始聽上人講解的《妙法蓮華經》〈藥草喻品第五〉，這一品一向是我最愛的，這品中的譬喻是優美而且生動。今天同時也是法界佛教大學生物課的最後一天，這門課研究曼多仙諾縣內的樹木，很有意思。那麼巧！而佛法經常是如此的，因此今晚我想談談有關「松果的法」。這是一個產自聖城的松果，蠻大的，半開的樣子，很美麗。

經中，佛提到三千大千世界，這是一個很大的概念，我不知道我們的腦筋是否能夠真正地抓住一個完整的觀念。可是如同上人常說，萬法歸一。所以我們不必去研究整個宇宙，我們可以就專注在曼多仙諾縣裏，或是瑜伽谷，甚至我們萬佛城的四周。

我們都知道，聖城這裏很複雜的，由不同的人、語言、文化組合而成。除了人之外，我們還有不同種類的植物，有樹、灌木、藥草、花等，來自世界，有些遠自亞洲、地中海、挪威、還有北非等。植物種類之繁多，一如眾生，亦如佛陀教化眾生之種種法門，令人驚奇。而陽光及雨水，又根據不同的種類，來普利各種植物；自東邊山坡上乾性低生長的矮橡林，到西邊濕性的長青海岸樹林，各各得到足令其生長的份量。同樣的，佛陀亦提供八萬四千法門給眾生，令其成熟。佛法之雨，根據眾生根基，滋潤了每一個眾生，沒有忽略也沒有遺漏任何一個。

那這個松果包含了什麼呢？種子。就像我們佛性的種子，這些種子需要拿出來，種在土裏加以滋養，才能成長茁壯。植物種子的傳播方法，是極複雜巧妙的。有些種子長有小翅膀做為動力；有些長有毛茸茸的尾巴；又有些長有芒刺或硬殼作來保護它們，以待適當的時機，及因緣的成熟。

hairy tails, still others have spiny burrs or tough nut cases to protect them while the seed waits for the right time, for the conditions to ripen. Often it is not a simple or easy matter for the seed to come out and be planted--it may take a great deal of time. The cones of some trees, especially cypress cones, take several years to open. Nuts of other trees may wait in the ground for years before the seed starts to grow. This is a real lesson in patience for us humans.

In our cultivation we, too, may experience times of waiting, great tests of patience, when nothing much seems to be happening. One may feel like one was stranded on a high desert plateau, engulfed by monotony. With nothing behind us and nothing to look forward to, one wanders as if lost in a wasteland, where all conditions seem inimical to life. One's mind may feel totally parched and arid, totally unable to grow in any direction. The only thing one is able to do is to wait it out, endure the adverse states, and patiently wait for the Dharma rain to rejuvenate the stunted desert vegetation, to moisten one's mind.

Some seeds even seem to resist opening. Some nuts, like those of the black walnut, are incredibly hard. You need to hammer them in order to break the nut case, to get to the part that is sweet and delicious. Similarly, as Buddhist disciples we may be tough nuts to crack: stubborn, opinionated, clinging to our narrow views and bad habits. These kinds of disciples may need hammering, seemingly tough treatment, before their own best qualities emerge from under the tough casing of ingrained habits and faults. But inside it all is the seed that contains all the wonderful potential of growth towards Buddhahood.

Other seeds need a forest fire in order to be planted. The knobcone pine grows in the chaparral, and its cones need to be consumed in a brush fire to open up and release their seeds. A widespread brush fire like the one we had on the hills earlier this month is an impressive, even frightening, sight, and it may be hard to believe that new life and growth can result from this vast destruction. As Buddhist disciples we, too, may sometimes have to pass through ordeals by fire. We may have to suffer intensely, even die to our old selves. There doesn't seem to be any reason why anyone should suffer so much, yet, if we can pass the test, the resulting fruit will be rare and wonderful.

In nature, many animals and plants form symbiotic relationships with each other. In these relationships both life forms benefit each other. For example, some seeds need to pass through an animal's digestive tract before they can open. The benefit is mutual--the animal obtains food and simultaneously helps the plant distribute its seeds. Many factors help out in the distribution and growth of plant seeds: the sun, wind, rain, and soil provide the conditions, and animals and humans contribute, too. When we cultivate the Buddhadharma, we are not doing it alone, either. The Buddhas, Bodhisattvas, and Patriarchs of old are always there to lend us support and inspiration. And our Dharma brothers and fellow cultivators are close at hand, helping us in ways we may not even be aware of.

把這種子拿出來種在土裏，通常不是一件那麼簡單的事。可能需要花很多時間。有些松果，尤其是柏樹的果實，需要數年的時間，才會打開來，而其他樹的堅果，可能要在地下躺好幾年種子才開始生長。對我們人類來說，這真是一堂耐心之課。

我們修行也是如此，在好像毫無進展之時，都有過等待的經驗，經歷過耐心的大考驗。經常我們感覺好像被困在一個高原上，被一片單調的景色所包圍，後無所視，前無可瞻。或者好像迷失在沙漠中，所有的狀況都可危及生命。我們心裏可能整個乾枯，完全無法生長。這時只可等待熬過逆境，耐心地等待法雨，來潤澤我們的心，使發育不良的沙漠蔬菜植物得以恢復活力。

有些種子，甚至似乎不願打開，如黑胡桃樹的堅果就是不可想像地硬，必須要搥開，才能嚐到裏面的甜美。同樣的，我們身為佛的弟子，可能也是難以敲破的堅果：冥頑不靈，自以為是，固執井蛙之見，死守習氣毛病。這樣的弟子，也許需要一翻敲搥，或類似的禮遇，才能使本有的品質，自根深柢固的習氣毛病中，也就是堅硬的外殼裏，脫穎而出；而在殼內的，就是含有成就佛果美妙潛能的種子。

又有一些種子，需要經森林大火，才得以種植。節松長在矮橡叢中，節松果得經由灌木叢火，才會打開，並放出種子。如本月在山丘上一場灌木叢大火，令人驚嚇。在此大破壞中，新生命卻能成長，的確令人難以置信。身為佛弟子，我們有時也必須經過大火的磨煉，經過巨大的痛苦，甚至於死亡，才能從自我解脫出來。受這麼大的苦，似乎沒有什麼道理，但是如果我們能通過這個考驗，其結果會是很殊勝的。

在自然界裏，很多動植物互相共生，彼此互惠。譬如，有些種子必須經過動物的消化器官，才會打開。這種利益是互相的；動物有食物可吃，同時也幫助植物散播種子。在植物種子的散播及成長上，有很多的助緣，如陽光、雨水、土壤等；動物及人類，亦各有貢獻。我們修習佛法，也不是單靠自己一個人的力量，諸佛菩薩及祖師，經常幫助並啟發我們，而我們的師兄弟同修們，亦

So whether we are discussing plant or animal life or life in a human community, we are always connected with others, aided by others in innumerable ways. And the benefits are often mutual: in helping others one finds one is helping oneself.

Still, in nature many seeds or seedlings don't make it. Unlike the Buddha nature which is indestructible, plant seeds are perishable. But in nature nothing gets wasted purposelessly. These seeds don't benefit themselves or their species; instead they give up their life to nourish other living beings, other species. The seeds and plants consumed by other species become "gifts to the food chain"--such is the *dana paramita* [Perfection of Giving] of the plant world. All human and animal life on this planet is sustained by plants, by the vegetation covering this globe. Thus our human life and our possibility to cultivate is supported by the plant world and its Perfection of Giving.

In conclusion, I would like to encourage everybody to keep his or her eyes open while walking around the City. We really don't have to seek far afield. All things speak the Dharma, if we only have the ears to hear, the eyes to see. With an open and appreciative mind we can learn from all species, listen to the Dharma that the redwoods, pines, sycamores, the flowers, or even the grasses speak...  And as the winter rains will soon start, we might keep this chapter on "Medicinal Herbs" and the analogy of the Dharma rain nourishing all plants in mind while sloshing our way to the Buddha Hall.

常在我們身邊，以我們甚至察覺不到方法在幫助我們。因此，不論我們是討論動物、植物，或人的生命，我們總是與別人息息相關，受到他人多方的助益，而幫助別人其實就是幫助自己，這種利益都是互通的。然而在自然界裏，很多種子或幼苗，是沒有機會成長的。不同於佛性的不可壞性，植物的種子是會壞的，可是在大自然中，沒有一樣東西，是毫無目的地浪費掉的。這些種子，無益於自己或其同類，因此放棄了自己的生命，去滋養其他同類或眾生，成為「食物鏈的贈禮」，也就是植物世界的布施波羅蜜。在地球上，人類及動物都是靠蔬植為生，因此我們人類的生命，我們有機會修行，都是植物世界的布施波羅蜜所成就的。

最後，我想要鼓勵大家在聖城裏走路時要注意看看，我們實在不需要去遠處尋求，萬物都在說法，只要我們用心去聽、去看，若能用一個客觀賞識的心態，我們可以自所有的大自然裏學到東西，細聽紅木、松樹、楓樹、花，甚至草所說的法……。冬天雨季即將開始，我們濺著水走向佛殿時，也許可以回想這〈藥草喻品〉滋潤植物的法雨譬喻。

# THE CITY OF TEN THOUSAND BUDDHAS

# 萬佛城寫意

Soohoong Leong

梁素芬

### Springtime at the City of 10,000 Buddhas

春滿萬佛城

*As you enter this Western Pureland,*
*You can feel the serenity pulsing through your spirit.*
*This is a sagely sanctuary*
*For painters, photographers, poets, naturalists,*
*And seekers of Truths!*
*Winter is cold and enchanting,*
*In spring, the flowers are smiling,*
*Deers, mules, sheep and hares,*
*Running, trotting, leaping and hopping...*
  *squirrels perform acrobatic feats,*
*While butterflies dance in midair,*
  *and fish swim merrily in the pond...*
*Exuberant musical sounds come from birds perching on high,*
*Woodpeckers drum on tree trunks with their beaks,*
*And the call of peacocks is like a harsh noise and scream.*
*The stream flows, the winds blow,*
*But, Wonderful Enlightenment Mountain sits in samadhi.*
*This sacred land is a Storehouse of Light!*
*Tread quietly...*
*Don't speculate, don't complicate,*
*Just honestly cultivate.*
*Revert your hearing,*
*Listen to your own self nature,*
*Listen ...*

入此西方淨土中
氣氛寧靜浸心靈
詩人墨客影像師
田園隱士求道人
得其所哉歸故土
寒冬凜冽景色奇
春來百花笑相迎
鹿羊毛驢幷兔子
跳躍追逐嬉戲樂
松鼠上下競技忙
彩蝶翩翩空中舞
游魚穿梭荷花塘
雲鳥枝頭譜新曲
啄木樹上勤擊鼓
孔雀噪聒不落人
蕭蕭風聲急流水
難動定中妙覺山
聖土淨地蘊靈光
春上枝頭已十分
老實修行莫分心
反聞自性不外求

The Sagely City of Ten Thousand Buddhas is a unique and rare sanctuary for all living beings.

When I was young, one of my favorite pastimes was to feed and observe the ants. When I first came to the City in 1990, I was delighted to have arrived at a place where the residents don't deliberately step on ants or kill little creatures that are regarded as pests by most people. The Sagely City is a paradise for anyone who has a sense of appreciation for the plant and animal kingdoms.

The dominant trees in the City of Ten Thousand Buddhas are oak, Douglas fir, and sycamore. Many ancient oak trees are found near the main entrance and in the surrounding meadow and the groves. The huge and imposing valley oak (*Quercus lobata*), in front of the administration office building is said to be several hundred years old. Only oak trees have acorns. Whenever I come across an acorn, I recall what George Bernard Shaw expressed in favor of vegetarianism:

> Think of the fierce energy concentrated in an acorn! You bury it in the ground, and it explodes into a giant oak. Bury a sheep, and nothing happens but decay…

My first encounter with redwood trees was in Yosemite National Park about ten years ago. At that time, their towering height and massive trunks made a deep impression on me. I did not meet up with these giants of the forest again until I came to the Sagely City. Besides oaks and redwoods there are Douglas fir (*Pseudotsuga menziesii*), or Christmas trees. A forest of these grows near the grazing ground. The plant life at the City is amazingly abundant and prolific.

The tree and I have a lot in common. We share the same earth, air and sun--we are both part of the elements that pervade throughout the universe. Due to past causes and conditions, trees have taken the form of trees, whereas I have entered the human realm. While the tree is fixed to its birthplace for life unless man intervenes and transplants it, I am quite free to move around as I please. The tree provides shade, shelter, and inspiration, and, to me, it is a silent poem of endurance and stillness.

The only tree I know of that has a special religious significance is the Bodhi Tree. The Buddha realized Buddhahood when he sat beneath the Bodhi Tree. The Venerable Master explained that as a result of this, the Bodhi Tree gained great merit and virtue. It is also mentioned in a Sutra that the Buddha lay down on his right side in the auspicious position on a couch between twin sala trees when he entered Nirvana.

Several flower gardens that bloom during different seasons adorn the Sagely City. There are also two main vegetable gardens. Many kinds of herbs have been planted in various gardens, while others just grow wild. The leaves of the poison oak turn bright orange or scarlet in the fall and look very beautiful, but they should be avoided. Poison oak teaches us not to be moved when we encounter beautiful forms.

I think the medicinal herbs are a very special category of plants. They have benefited countless living beings. Since ancient times until today,

萬佛聖城是眾生很稀有獨特的一座避難所。

我童年時最喜歡餵螞蟻、觀察螞蟻以爲消遣。所以我一九九〇年第一次來萬佛城時，看到這裡的人特意地不踩螞蟻，對一般人認爲是害蟲的小生物也不殺害，我覺得特別地高興。對能欣賞大自然的動、植物的人，萬佛城的確是一座樂園。

聖城最多的是橡樹、柏樹、大楓樹，在城門進口處、大草原處，還有樹林中，種著許多橡樹。其中有行政大樓前的大橡樹，已有幾百年的樹齡了，只有橡樹會結橡子，每當我看到橡子時，我就想起蕭伯納的贊助素食的話：

> 蘊藏在橡子中的力量多大啊！你埋它在地下，它就會拙長成一顆高大的橡樹。你埋一隻羊，除了腐爛之外什麼也生不出。

我第一次看到紅木，是十年前在優勝美地國家公園。那紅木的高大雄偉給我留下很深刻的印象。之後就是在聖城我才又再看到紅木，還看到橡樹，及松、柏等耶誕樹。聖城的樹木種類繁多。

我跟樹有許多共同點，我們享受著同樣的土地、空氣、陽光，我們都是宇宙裡的組成份子之一。由於過去的因緣，樹現樹形，我則現人形。但樹木一生固定在一個地方，除非有人搬動移植，而我呢？則可自由移動。樹陰可遮陰。樹也是我靈感的泉源，樹也是一首堅忍及靜謐的詩。

菩提樹是我所知道的唯一富有宗教意義的樹，佛陀在菩提樹下證道，上人説菩提樹因此也有了功德。佛經上也説，佛陀在兩棵娑羅樹之間的臥榻上，呈吉祥臥而入涅槃。

聖城中有花圃兩座，又有菜園及藥草園。還有許多種藥草分布在城中各地方，有的還是野生的。小毒橡樹的葉子在秋天時變成橘黃色、深紅色，艷美異常，但我們還是離遠點好，讓我們知道別爲美色所移。

藥草是一種很特別的植物，造福了許多人。自

people have used herbs to maintain health and prevent and cure diseases. The herbs are here to inspire us to quietly cultivate the selfless, magnanimous, and altruistic spirit of the Bodhisattvas.

The Sagely City is like a panoramic, three-dimensional live Sutra, for all the myriad things are indeed speaking the Great Dharma! This dynamic and powerful audio-visual presentation of the Dharma is truly inconceivable, magical, and most wonderful. Peacocks, peahens, and pigeons are a common sight at the City. One can also frequently see grey squirrels scampering about, going up and down the trees, or gnawing away at acorns and nuts.

Not long ago, I was going up a flight of steps when I saw a squirrel coming down. In order to keep from frightening it, I remained still and avoided making any sudden movements. Then I began to recite the Buddha's name so it could hear. When it first saw me, it was obviously terrified, but later it became more relaxed. It started to move slowly down the steps, staring rather curiously at me all the time. When it got close to me it quickly ran down. I turned around to look at it and was very surprised and glad to see the squirrel had decided to come back up the steps to where I stood. It sniffed me a few times before running off again.

If one walks quietly around the more remote areas of the City, one may occasionally meet up with deer and hares. The deer are extremely alert and shy and will run away when they see or hear someone approaching. They are agile and graceful and run in a succession of bounds. They can leap over the fences effortlessly. A flock of sheep and a pair of mules graze in the pastures. In the meadows at the back of the property I have come across many little burrows in the ground, probably the shelters of rodents. During the time that I have been here,

古以來，人類用藥草來保健及治病。城裡的藥草教我們以大公無私的態度安靜修行菩薩道。

聖城的樹是一部巨大的三度空間的經典為眾生轉大法輪。這麼生動有力的法視聽教學是很不可思議，很妙不可言的。孔雀、鴿子到處可見，還有松鼠也不時在樹叢中穿越，啃嚙橡子。

有一次我上台階時看見一隻松鼠向我走來，因恐怕嚇著牠，我停下來，念著佛名，希望這隻松鼠能聽得見。牠剛看見我時，好像很驚嚇的樣子，後來好像不那麼緊張了，就慢慢走下台階，但是還是很注意地看著我。在快靠近我之時，牠忽然快跑而下，我轉身看時，卻發現牠又跑回來，上了台階到我站立之處，聞了我幾下然後才跑開。

走到聖城中僻遠處，常可看到兔子、鹿群。鹿很膽怯，易驚，人若走近，牠就跑了，靈活快速能輕易地跳躍過籬笆。又有羊群、驢子在後山吃草。又有地鼠，地下的穴道恐怕都是它們的居處。每次我去後山，我都看見馬、兔子、狐狸、驢子、蝙蝠、蛇、蚯蚓、青蛙、雉雞、鵪鶉、麻雀、藍鳥、蜂鳥、啄木鳥、貓頭鷹、

The Sagely City is like a panoramic, three-dimensional live Sutra, for all the myriad things are indeed speaking the Great Dharma!

聖城的樹是一部巨大的三度空間的經典為眾生轉大法輪。

I have also seen horses, rabbits, foxes, moles, bats, snakes, lizards, frogs, pheasants, quail, sparrows, bluejays, hummingbirds, woodpeckers, owls, crows, vultures and hawks. Birds are often seen in flight, hovering, parachuting, gliding, soaring, landing or taking off, walking, or perching on fences, branches, or wire lines.

There is a fish pond with aquatic plants next to the Buddha Hall and a waterhole at the pastureland. There is another pond which is located in the midst of the marshes. On this tract of low wetland, cattails grow wild. The marsh provides a habitat for birds and insects. There is a creek that runs through the Sagely City. Certain sections of it are slow-moving, while others are fast. It usually dries up in the summer and fall. The climatic and seasonal changes which can be observed daily, weekly, monthly, or annually are refreshing and instructive...

In the fall, many trees shed their leaves. As one watches the leaves fall, one is reminded of the fact that the only thing that is permanent in this world is change. Due to the dry spell in summer, when autumn comes, the sheep pasture resembles the African savanna. In the early winter, flocks of birds can be seen flying happily about. I wonder if they are a migratory species...When the rainy season begins, green patches of grass sprout up all over the place. Moss covers the trunks of certain kinds of trees, and lichen is seen hanging from other trees. Many plants bloom and bear fruit in the spring and autumn. Butterflies, birds, and insects can be seen visiting flowers.

Mountain ranges can be seen from many parts of the City of Ten Thousand Buddhas. The rising and setting of the sun can have a spectacular effect on those mountains and on the buildings of the Sagely City. During the cold seasons, the fog sometimes covers the mountains partially or completely. When viewed from certain places, the Sagely City appears to be nestled in the mountains. When the sun is hidden behind the clouds, it creates a misty, soothing, and solemn atmosphere--very enchanting.

In the past, I was a member of the Malaysian Nature Society. During that time, I learned something I really liked: We were told that when we go out on field trips, we should not take anything from the areas we pass through. If every visitor or tourist took something back home with him or her, it would eventually upset the ecosystem of that place. What impressed me was the witty manner in which this important message was conveyed. We were seriously advised not to take anything away when we left--except our photographs when we left.

This instruction is in accord with the Buddha's Teaching. In Buddhism, we are exhorted not to take anything that does not belong to us, not even objects as small as a needle or a blade of grass. It would be wonderful if everyone adopted this practice.

I think it would be nice and effective if the students of Instilling Goodness Elementary School and Developing Virtue Secondary School could design some posters or paint a few signboards with the message, "When you leave, please do not take anything except

烏鴉、禿鷹、老鷹，我常看見這些鳥在天空中翱翔，或站在欄柵上或電線上。

在佛殿旁有一塘水，養了金魚，也有水生植物。在後山草原上，在沼澤地上，及水池裡都有香蒲叢生。沼澤地上寄生了許多鳥和昆蟲。聖城中也有一條溪流，流水時急時緩，夏天及秋季溪水乾涸。聖城中每日、每週、每月、每年的氣候變遷及季節變化，都帶給人一種清新感，也蘊有無言之教。

秋天許多樹落下了葉子，看著落葉使人不禁覺得這世界上唯有變易是永恆的。

因為夏天乾旱，所以到秋天時，後山草地看起來就像非洲的大草原。初冬時群鳥優遊天空，不知是否候鳥？雨季開始時，片片綠草茁生。樹幹上、樹枝上覆蓋著青苔，有的樹上長了地衣，成條垂下。春華秋實，那時果實纍纍垂下，蝴蝶、昆蟲、鳥也都繞著樹忙碌異常。

萬佛城中可遠眺山景，山景隨著日出日落而變化不定時，萬佛城也就有著不同的情緒起落。寒冬時霧氣充塞城內，從有的角度看來，萬佛城就像是嵌在山中似的。當霧層遮著陽光時，空中迷迷濛濛一片肅穆安寧。

我以前是馬來西亞自然會社的會員，那時規定我們外出到野外時，不可帶回任何東西，原因是如果遊客可以隨意拾取東西帶走的話，一定會破壞當地自然環境的均衡。這個規矩的表達方式比較特別，是這麼說的：「除了您拍攝的照片之外，離去時，請勿取走任何東西。」這給我留下深刻的印象。

這個規矩很符合佛陀的教化，佛不是說不屬於我們的東西，一針一草都不可以拿走。假如每一個人都能遵守這個規矩，那多好！

我想假如育良小學及培德中學能設計一些海報，或製作一些標語。上面寫著「您離開時，除了您所拍攝的照片之外，請勿帶走任何東西。」這樣的話，每一個人都有機會學習這條規則。要放在明顯的地方，人容易看見。讓小孩子製作，是因為小孩子有一種特別的素質，這也是一種方便法

your photographs with you." That way we can give everyone a chance to practice this principle. We can put them up in places where visitors are most likely to see them. The work of young people has a special childlike quality that makes it especially appealing. This is an expedient way to tell our guests not to pick the fruits or pluck the flowers and leaves while they are here, and not casually remove anything which belongs to the Sagely City.

When the Venerable Master was explaining Chapter Eighteen of the *Wonderful Dharma Lotus Flower Sutra*, he related how he used to study in past:

> When the Dharma Master lectured the Sutras, I listened to the Sutras. When the leture was over, I ran off to the mountains to look at the trees, flowers, and water; I had a lot of fun. My fellow students watched me quite closely. I never said a word all day long, so nobody knew what I was up to. When the time came for the daily review, most of the students read from their notes. I just recited the whole thing from my memory. I repeated everything the Dharma Master had said, not missing a word, not adding a word...I said I was playing in the mountains, but actually I wasn't playing in the mountains, I was in the "studying samadhi." I was up in the mountains, looking at the mountains, but my heart was not in the mountains; it was in the Buddhadharma, going over what the Dharma Master had said during the lecture, reviewing it very thoroughly. That's the real way to study the Buddhadharma.

The Venerable Master explained before,

> Sutras are everyone's breath; without them people are lost. We should step outside of our stuffy rooms to breathe the fresh air of the Sutras.

> *People cannot live without air or Sutras.*

> You ask, "I don't study Sutras or the Dharma, so I don't breathe that air, do I?"

> You breathe that air too, because the Dharma air fills the world, and whether or not you study it, you breathe it all the same. Everyone shares the air. Students of the Buddhadharma exhale Buddhadharma air and non-students breathe it in. You cannot avoid this relationship. Sutras are also food for the spirit, and have many other uses. When you're melancholy or depressed, recite Sutras, for they explain the doctrines in a wonderful way which dispels your gloom and opens your heart.

The pure and tranquil atmosphere that pervades the City of Ten Thousand Buddhas is so inexpressibly wonderful. Its calming effect is profoundly felt. My brother described this "Western

，告訴訪客們不要摘採水果、花朵、葉子，也不要在聖城隨意拿走東西。

上人講解《妙法蓮華經》第十八品時，曾敘述自己以前如何念書，上人說：

> 我記得我學教的時候，是遊山玩水的學教，你們不要學我這個遊山玩水的學教。怎麼樣呢？有法師講經，我就來聽經，聽完經我就跑，跑到山上去看水、看山、看花、看樹，啊！這麼一天悠遊自在的，這麼樣子，覺得很好玩的。我那一班同學，都很注意我的，爲什麼？他們看我一天到晚也不講話，他到底幹什麼呢？這麼樣子！等到複講的時候，他們都要對本子來複講。我把本子合起來，不看本子，眼睛閉上，法師怎麼講，我就講得和法師的一樣，講得一字也不去，一字也不添。因爲我若加，這是我的意思了；我若減，又是妄了。所以也不加也不減……。我說我去遊山玩水，這遊山，我也沒有在山上；玩水也沒有在水裡頭。幹什麼呢？我在那個地方入學習三昧。怎麼樣？看著是看山、遊山，心也沒有在山上。在這個佛法裡。我雖然是在水邊上，但是這個心還是在學佛法裡邊。今天這個法師講的是什麼？是哪一段呢？哪一個字有沒有解釋？他的意思是怎麼樣子啊？自己和自己已經就做了很多的問答。所以到複講的時候，才能很圓滿地講出來。

上人曾經說過：

> 佛經是每個人的呼吸，沒有佛經，人就迷失了，我們應該由沉悶的屋子裡走出，呼吸一下佛經清新的空氣。

人沒有空氣不能生存，同樣地沒有佛經，人也不能生存。有人問：「我既不學佛經，也不學佛法，所以我沒呼吸法的空氣，對不？」其實你也呼吸了，因爲法的空氣瀰漫世界，不論你學不學，你經常都呼吸著法的空氣，每一個人都分享這個法的空氣。佛子呼出佛法的空氣，非佛子則吸入佛法的空氣。你沒有法子避免這種關係。經典不僅是精神的糧食，也還有許多其他用途。你覺得沮喪憂鬱時，可以念經。經書中所開闡的道理，很奇妙地可以將你心中的陰霾一掃而空。

The pure and tranquil atmosphere that pervades the City of Ten Thousand Buddhas is so inexpressibly wonderful. Its calming effect is profoundly felt.

城中寧靜安祥的氣氛妙不可言可以
熨平人的心境

Pureland" most aptly when he wrote,

*A sanctuary and a refuge,*
*truly rare in the Saha world,*
*a Sagely Way-place*
*as conducive and perfect*
*as the earthly plane can allow.*

The Venerable Master, the Founding Patriarch of this "Western Pure-land," often said, "Don't enter the mountain of jewels and return empty-handed." The fauna and flora are the external adornments of the Sagely City. If you wish to uncover its hidden treasures, look deeper...

The Venerable Master once said,

The states which occur at the City of Ten Thousand Buddhas are inconceivable, to the point that all the birds and beasts, all the flowers and grasses, all the trees and herbs exemplify the Dharma, spead the Dharma, and practice the Dharma. Although grasses, trees, and flowers don't actually speak, nonetheless they embody the ineffable wonder of the Buddhadharma. They are,

*Apart from the mark of language and speech,*
*Apart from the mark of the mind's conditions,*
*Apart from the mark of the written word.*

In all four seasons--spring, summer, fall, and winter--they represent the Buddhadharma.

*In the spring hundreds of flowers bloom.*
*In the autumn yellow leaves fall.*

If you can understand the principle behind the myriad transformations of nature, you will become enlightened. That is how

城中寧靜安祥的氣氛妙不可言,可以熨平人的心境。我的哥哥在形容這個西方淨土時,説得好:

聖堂道場避難所,
圓滿利生世稀有。

這位西方淨土的祖師——上人以前常説:「不要入寶山空手而回。」花草樹木只能莊嚴聖城的外貌,假如你想挖掘裡面的寶藏的話,請往深看。

上人曾經説過:

萬佛聖城中所發生的境界是很不可思議的,所有的鳥獸,所有的花草樹木,都在説法、表法、修法。雖然花草樹木不開口講話,但也蘊含了不可思議的佛法,可以説是:

離言説相,離心緣相,離文字相,

春夏秋冬四季,這些花草樹木都代表著佛法。所謂:

春觀百花開,秋睹黄葉落。

白孔雀
White peacocks

Those Enlightened to Conditions awaken to the truth. They contemplate the Twelve Causal Conditions--all of which exemplify the Dharma.

All the creatures here at the City are speaking the Dharma. Black crows caw and white cranes call, each with its own sound. Black crows and white cranes--isn't that a matched couplet? Then there are the bluejays, who are the thieves of the group. They're real bullies. Wherever there is something to eat, they just glare so no other birds dare make the first move. They all have to wait until the bluejays make off with the best of the food and only then are they allowed to pick over the remains. This is speaking the dharma of the "survival of the fittest"--those that are weak are eaten by the powerful ones. Is that taking life? Yes, they are speaking the dharma of taking life. The deer speak the dharma of deer, the rabbits speak the dharma of rabbits, the foxes speak the dharma of foxes...

Isn't it strange that before I made the announcement that everyone should take special care in protecting the wildlife those foxes seldom showed themselves, but now that I've made that announcement, they are seen all the time in most public places and don't seem the least bit afraid of people any more. I you walk past them, they will even parade before you. They'll greet you first! That's why it is said,

> All living beings have the Buddhanature;
> All can become Buddhas.

They are here accompanying us in cultivating the Dharma. In every single dust mote here there are Buddhas and Bodhisattvas cultivating the Way. If you did not have great good roots from past lives, you wouldn't get to come and live here. So don't take it for granted!

如果你能貫穿自然界無窮無盡變化中所蘊藏的道理，你就能開悟。緣覺是這樣證道的，他們觀十二因緣所表的法。

城裡所有的生物都在說法，鳥啼鶴鳴各有聲。烏鴉、白鶴不是副對聯嗎？又有藍鳥——鳥中之賊，盡欺侮別的鳥。只要有好東西吃，藍鳥就橫眉怒眼嚇阻別的鳥不准過來，得等藍鳥吃過，才敢上來吃點剩的，這是說的「適者生存」的法——弱肉強食。這是殺生嗎？不錯，的確是殺生的法。鹿說鹿的法，兔子說兔子的法，狐狸說狐狸的法。

說起來奇怪，在我宣佈大家都得特別小心保護野生物之前，狐狸很少出來，但是在我宣佈之後，牠們全都出來了，到公眾的地方來，一點也不怕人。如果你在旁邊走過，牠還會在你面前遊行，先和你打招呼，所以說

　一切眾生皆有佛性，皆堪作佛。

這些生物是來陪著我們修法的，在每一粒微塵裡都有佛菩薩在修道，如果不是過去你有大善根，你不可能到這兒來住，所以各位不要太輕看了。

我這一生的成就，都是由這六大宗旨走過來的，
你們任何人想修行佛道，必須也要走這六大宗旨。

*Everything I have accomplished in this life came from practicing the Six Guiding Principles.*
*If any of you want to cultivate the path to Buddhahood,*
  *you also must practice the Six Guiding Principles.*

# 禪
## 諸佛的母體
# CHAN
## THE ESSENCE OF ALL BUDDHAS

宣公上人講述
Lectures by Venerable Master Hua

大地春回百物生　　粉碎虛空自在翁
從此不落人我相　　法界雖大盡包容

*When spring returns to the earth, the myriad things are born.*
*Smashing empty space to pieces, one is free and at ease.*
*One will never again become attached to self or others.*
*Although the Dharma Realm is vast, one can encompass it all.*

這幾句偈頌是說，我們現在好像，「大地春回」，春天到了，我們打禪七就是大地春回；「百物生」，就是你有開悟的機會。你自性若光明現出來了，好像春天百物生長的樣子。「粉碎虛空」，虛空本來無形，都沒有了。「自在翁」，這時候你真自在了。從現在「不落人我相」，也沒有人，也沒有我了，人也空，法也空；人相也空，法相也空，人我都沒有了。雖然法界這麼大，但是我把這個法界都包到裏頭了，「盡包容」。你看這個大不大？所以這真正才是大丈夫的所爲。

## 虛空打破明心地

這個「念佛是誰」，就是金剛王寶劍，又是周利槃陀伽所念的「掃帚」兩個字。說：「怎麼叫金剛王寶劍，又叫掃帚？既然是金剛王寶劍，就不會是掃帚、笤掃；既然是笤掃，就不會是金剛王寶劍。」這要看你用哪一頭，這個金剛王寶劍，一頭就是掃帚，一頭就是切金斷玉、斬情斷愛的金剛王寶劍。能把無明斬斷了，煩惱也斬斷了，這樣子就是金剛王寶劍。又是笤掃，你念「念佛是誰？」就好像掃地似的，掃乾淨了一點。「誰？」，又掃一下，又把私欲掃去很多。這個寶劍斬的也是私欲，笤掃，掃的也是私欲；就是你這個欲念，你情情愛愛，這些個問題。這些個不能解決的問題，就用金剛王寶劍來斬它。你參這個「誰」，參到這個「誰」上了，這時候，天魔外道他都沒有辦法了，他無隙可趁，因爲你舉起智慧劍，降伏十大魔軍，這世界上，種種的魔軍都會降伏住了。你就有一個「誰」，什麼魔也沒有辦法的；你若把這個「誰」忘了，那就有窟窿了，魔就會鑽進來，因爲你這金剛王寶劍放下了，你這無明又起來了。

我們參禪參「念佛是誰」，很渺茫的，參來參去，也找不著這個「誰」。找不著這個誰，這時候會生疑情。疑情一生出來，大疑就大悟，小疑就小悟，不疑就不悟，常疑就常悟，短

Springtime is here, and our holding a Chan session is like *when spring comes to the earth. The myriad things are born* means you have the opportunity to become enlightened. The light shining forth from your own nature is compared to the myriad things growing in the spring. *Smashing empty space to pieces,* empty space has no shape or form; it is gone. At that point, *one is free and at ease.* You are truly free and independent. *Never again* will you *become attached to self or others.* There won't be any people and there won't be any dharmas; people and dharmas will both be empty. The attributes of self and others will both be gone. Although the Dharma Realm may be vast, but you can contain it entirely within yourself. *One can encompass it all.*

Now wouldn't you call that great? This is truly the demeanor of a great hero.

## With Empty Space Shattered, the Mind Is Understood

The phrase "Who is mindful of the Buddha" is a regal, precious vajra sword. It is also the phrase "sweeping broom" recited by Kshudrapanthaka. Someone may say, "Why is it called both a regal, precious vajra sword and a sweeping broom? Since it is a regal, precious vajra sword, it can't be a broom. Since it is a broom, it can't be a regal, precious vajra sword." It depends which end you use. One end is a regal, precious vajra sword and the other end is a broom. One end, the regal, precious vajra sword, which can slice through gold and cut through jade, cuts through your emotions and severs your love. Being able to cut off ignorance and afflictions makes it a regal, precious vajra sword. The broom end is like your mindfulness of "Who is mindful of the Buddha?" Just as each time you sweep the floor it gets a little cleaner, so too, sweeping with "who" sweeps away a lot of your lust. What the vajra sword cuts through is lust and what the broom sweeps away is also lust. It's your thoughts of desire, your emotional love, and other such problems. You can use the vajra sword to cut through all these unsolvable problems. As soon as you investigate "who?"— the heavenly demons and externalists cannot do anything to you. There's no crack for them to slip through. That's because you are holding aloft the wisdom sword that subdues the ten great demonic armies. All the various demonic armies in this world will be conquered. None of the demons has any way to deal with your "who?" If you forget to be mindful of "who?" then there is a hole where the demons can wriggle their way in. That can happen because you put down your regal, precious vajra sword and give rise to ignorance.

When you investigate "Who is mindful of the Buddha?" things may get vague. You keep on investigating, but you can't find out "who?" Unable to find the "who," you give rise to a "feeling of doubt." Once this feeling of doubt arises, great doubt will bring great enlightenment. Small doubt will bring small enlightenment. No doubt will bring no enlightenment. Continual doubt will bring continual enlightenment.

疑就短悟。怎麼叫疑情呢？就是找不著這個「誰」了，「哦！這個誰呢？」這一個「誰」字，參幾個鐘頭也不停止，這時候，氣也沒有了，脈也停止了，念也住了，得了湛然大定。這種定，行也是定，坐也是定，站著也是定，躺著也是定都在這個定裏邊，不出不入，所以叫湛然大定。

這時候，上也沒有天了，下也沒有地了，中間也沒有人了，遠處也沒有物了，一切一切都空了。再這空也沒有了，空也粉碎了，虛空粉碎，這時候是個什麼境界？你看一看，想一想，你還有妄想？還有雜念？虛空都沒有，這個妄想、雜念在什麼地方？私欲又在什麼地方？到這個時候，就很容易開悟了，很容易返本還原、明心見性了。到明心的時候，所有的事情都不難了，沒有障礙了；你見了性了，就不知道憂愁。

# 本來面目何處覓

由清朝到現在，多數人是參悟「念佛是誰」，參悟這個「誰」字。要緊的就是「誰」，誰？你不知道是誰；若知道，那就開悟了。要知道是誰念佛，你若說「哦！我念佛嘛！」你？若是你念佛，你死了，用一把火把你燒沒有了，你又到哪兒去？若是你念佛，你不應該死。死了，怎麼用火燒了又沒有了？

參禪的法門，用的話頭很多，有的參悟「如何是父母未生以前的本來面目？」參這個本來面目。還有參「無」字的。無，什麼都能沒有，什麼都是無，那麼什麼又是有呢？參這個「無」和「有」。有的參「怎麼樣是沒有了的？」世界上的東西，都是成住壞空，什麼是不被成住壞空所轉的？參這個。有的又參「狗子有佛性否？」，那狗有沒有佛性，這也是一個話頭。有的又參乾屎橛子；什麼叫乾屎橛子，懂不懂？就是人的大便乾了，叫乾屎橛，參那個東西。你聽得是很好笑的，但是你參悟起來很有味道的。並不是臭味，你不要笑因為它乾了，沒有味了。所以有種種的話頭，但是你用哪一個相應，你就用哪一個。

Brief doubt will bring brief enlightenment. What is meant by a "feeling of doubt"? It's being unable to find out "who?" Hmm. "Who?" Sustained investigation of this word "who" for hours nonstop can bring you to the point that your breath ceases, your pulse stops, your thoughts come to a standstill, and you attain a profoundly great samadhi. With that kind of samadhi, you are in samadhi when you are walking; you are in samadhi when you are sitting; you are in samadhi when you are standing; and you are in samadhi when you are lying down. You neither enter it nor leave it, and so it's called a profoundly great samadhi. At that time, above, there will be no heaven; below, there will be no earth; in between, there will be no people; and afar, there will be no objects. Absolutely everything will be empty. Even emptiness will not exist. Once emptiness is obliterated, what kind of state remains? Take a look. Think about it. Do you still have false thoughts? Do you still have extraneous ideas? When there isn't even any emptiness, where could the false thoughts and extraneous ideas be located? Where could lust be found? At that time, it's very easy to become enlightened. It's very easy to return to the root and go back to the source, to understand your mind and see your nature. When you understand your mind and see your nature, nothing that happens presents any difficulties; there are no obstructions. Once you see your nature, you never worry.

# Where Is the Original Face to Be Found?

From the Qing dynasty on, most people have investigated "Who is mindful of the Buddha?" Investigating the word "who" is the most important part. Who? As long as you don't know, then it's still "who." If you know, then that's enlightenment. You want to find out who it is who's mindful of the Buddha. If you say, "Oh! *I* am mindful of the Buddha!" You? If it's you who is mindful of the Buddha, then suppose you die and are cremated so that you no longer exist--then where have you gone? If it's you who is mindful of the Buddha, then you shouldn't die; but you will die, get cremated, and be gone.

There are many different meditation topics that can be used in investigating Chan. Some people investigate "Who was I before my mother bore me?" Others may investigate the word "Nothing." "Nothing" means there isn't anything at all. Everything is nonexistent. Or does everything exist? They investigate "nothing" and "existence." They investigate how things cease to exist. Everything in the world is subject to coming into being, dwelling, decaying, and becoming empty. What is there that is not subject to coming into being, dwelling, decaying, and becoming empty? That's what they investigate.

Some investigate "Does a dog have the Buddha nature?" Whether or not a dog has the Buddha nature can be a topic too. Others investigate "dried turd." You laugh when you hear that, but when you investigate it, there's a lot of flavor in it! Not smelly, though, so you don't need to laugh. Since it's dry it doesn't smell. There are many different meditation topics. Whichever topic you respond to best is the one for you.

# 行住坐臥細鑽研

　　我們現在打禪七，打禪七最要緊的就是專一，你身、心、意都要專一。身在這兒行就是行，坐就是坐，臥就是臥，一行一坐一臥都要守著規矩。心不打妄想，能心念專一。心念專一，意也要專一。意，沒有貪心，沒有瞋心，沒有癡心，就一心參「念佛是誰」。

　　這個「參」字，好像用一個錐子鑽窟窿一樣。鑽、鑽，把木頭鑽透了。鑽透了，看到那邊去，通了，這就叫開悟。沒有通之前，只是做這個通的功夫；沒有開悟之前，我們現在參這個「念佛是誰」，這也只是做這個開悟的功夫。現在只是做功夫的期間，在做功夫的期間，你不要說：「哦！我鑽不透這個窟窿。」就不鑽了。你不鑽，它就不透。你要今天鑽這個窟窿，明天鑽這個窟窿，後天鑽這個窟窿，鑽來鑽去，你功夫到了，時間久了，就通了。這通了就是開悟了，就是你不明白的，明白了；你不懂的，懂了。

　　這個功夫就好像什麼呢？「如貓撲鼠」，貓在老鼠洞的旁邊，等著老鼠，看老鼠若出來，一爪上去就把老鼠給捉住了。你參「念佛是誰」，也就像貓撲老鼠。什麼是老鼠？你那個妄想就是個老鼠。什麼是個貓？這「念佛是誰」就是貓。這個貓就等老鼠，這是個比喻。

　　「如龍養珠」，又好像龍保護龍珠一樣。龍保護牠的龍珠，是念茲在茲的，時刻都不離這個珠，保護這個珠。

　　「如雞孵卵」，又好像雞想抱小雞子。在那兒就想，想什麼呢？想：「我這個雞仔子，就要生出來了。」所以在雞蛋上趴著，趴著就想：「啊！就快了，就快了，就快有雞仔子生出來了。」所以在這兒，哦！天天想雞仔子，想來想去，卵以想成，哦！就想成了，雞仔子就出來了，雞雛就生出來了。雞雛生出來了，就成功了。我們參禪呢？也像這樣子，也像老母雞在那兒抱雞仔子一樣。母雞在雞蛋上面，熱得不得了，熱得呵呵氣喘也捨不得離開，一定要把雞抱出來才算。

# Carefully Investigate While Walking, Standing, Sitting, and Lying Down

Now we are having a Chan session. Concentration is of vital importance in a Chan session. Your body, mind, and thoughts must be concentrated. Here, your body must walk when it's time to walk, sit when it's time to sit, and lie down when it's time to lie down. Walking, sitting, and reclining, you must follow the rules. Your mind must not give rise to false thinking; then the mind can be concentrated. Your thoughts should be devoid of greed, devoid of hatred, and devoid of stupidity. Single-mindedly investigate "Who is mindful of the Buddha?"

Investigating is like using a drill to drill a hole. You drill and drill until you drill through the piece of wood. Once the drill penetrates, you can see through to the other side. That's what becoming enlightened is like. Prior to penetrating, we are only doing the daily work of drilling. Prior to becoming enlightened, we investigate "Who is mindful of the Buddha?"

Now we are putting in the work that it takes to become enlightened. During the period of working, you don't want to say, "Oh! This drill won't penetrate and make a hole." Then you don't want to drill any more. But if you don't drill, no hole will be made. You must drill the hole today, drill it tomorrow, and drill it the next day— drilling and drilling until your work is realized. After a time, you will penetrate. That penetration is enlightenment. That means what you weren't clear about before, you will be clear about. What you didn't understand, you will understand.

What is this skill like? It's like a cat poised to catch a mouse. The cat waits beside the mouse hole. If the mouse comes out, the cat catches it with one swipe of its claws. Your investigation of "Who is mindful of the Buddha" is like a cat stalking a mouse. Your false thinking is the mouse, and the phrase "Who is mindful of the Buddha" is the cat. The cat is waiting to catch the mouse. That's what this analogy means.

Investigation is also like a dragon guarding its pearl. A dragon is always protecting his dragon pearl. His attention never strays from it.

Again, investigation is like a hen brooding over her eggs. The hen is always concerned about her chicks, thinking, "My little chicks are going to hatch soon." She keeps brooding, "Ah! Hurry up! Hurry up! Little chicks, hurry up and hatch!" Every day she's there thinking about her chicks until they finally hatch. As it is said, "Egg-born come from thought."

When her thinking wins out, the chicks hatch. Once the chicks are hatched, the hen has succeeded. Our investigation of Chan is also like an old mother hen incubating her chicks. While the mother hen is brooding on the eggs, she is extremely hot— so hot she pants. And yet she can't bear to leave the nest. She has to brood until the chicks hatch— that's all there is to it!

# 參破話頭露端倪

我們參禪和這個，是一樣的道理，時時刻刻都
要注意，不打任何的妄想，所謂

> 一念不生全體現
> 六根忽動被雲遮

在一念不生的時候，全體大用都現前了，本有的
智慧也都會現前。六根就是眼耳鼻舌身意。忽動
，忽然間這麼一動，好像天生了浮雲似的，被雲
遮住。一念不生的時候，也就是方才所說的，內
無身心，外無世界。坐禪坐到這種境界上，呼吸
氣也斷了。雖然呼吸氣斷了，但是可不是死，這
時候，一念不生了；你要是忽然間想，我呼吸氣
都斷了，都沒有了，那它又有了。你無心的時候
，呼吸氣斷了；你有心，它又繼續。呼吸氣斷了
還是沒有斷？若一定斷了，就不生存，因為內裏
邊呼吸氣與起來，在裏邊行動起來了，在裏邊有
呼吸氣，所以不需要外邊的呼吸氣。這也叫什麼
呢？這也叫轉大法輪，唱無聲的曲子，唱無聲的
歌，轉無形的法輪。這種境界，也都不要執著。

我們修道就是忽進忽退，有幾天就精進了，精
進一個時期，又懶惰下來，又不精進。在精進期
間，覺得也沒得到什麼益處，於是乎就懶惰下來
，懶惰一個時期，就想要精進了。所以修行也不
要太緊，也不要太慢，要合乎中道，所謂

> 你緊了就繃，慢了就鬆，
> 不緊不慢才成功。

不要緊，就是不要緊張，不要慢，就是不要懶惰
。要很歡喜地來用功，用得行也自在，坐也自在
，站也自在，睡也自在，行住坐臥都是自在；自
在這功夫就上路了。功夫上路了，你真會參禪了
，想停止也不能停止了，行住坐臥都和這個「誰
」離不開了。但是，離不開這個「誰」，還不認
識是「誰」；不認識是「誰」，還要接近這個「
誰」。這個「誰」不能斷了，隨時隨地都是參禪
的功夫打成一片。打成一片的時候，你「終日吃
飯，未吃一粒米」，不是沒有吃飯，但是沒有著
住到飯上，吃而未吃，穿而未穿，「終日穿衣，

# When One Solves the Meditation Topic, A Clue Appears

The same principle applies when we investigate Chan. We must pay attention at all times and not have any discursive thoughts. As the saying goes,

*When not a single thought arises, the entire substance manifests.*
*When the six senses suddenly move, one is covered by clouds.*

When not a single thought arises, the vast functioning of the entire substance is seen. One's inherent wisdom manifests. When the six sense faculties--the eyes, ears, nose, tongue, body, and mind--suddenly move, it is as if the sky were suddenly covered by clouds. When not a single thought arises, then "Inside there is no body or mind, and outside there is no world." When you reach that level in your meditation, your breath stops. Although you stop breathing, you are not dead. When your breath stops, not a single thought arises. But if you suddenly think, "Oh, my breath has stopped. It's gone!" Then it will come back. When you are devoid of thoughts, the breath stops; but as soon as you have a thought, the breath resumes. Actually, your breathing does not completely cease, or else you wouldn't be alive. Rather, an internal breathing begins to function, so you no longer need to rely on external breathing. This is known as turning the great Dharma wheel--singing the soundless song and turning the invisible Dharma wheel. However, you should not become attached to this state.

Cultivators alternately advance and retreat in their practice. We may be vigorous for a few days, but then, feeling that we aren't getting any benefit, we slack off. After being lazy for a while, we become vigorous again. In cultivation, we should follow the Middle Way and be neither too hasty nor too relaxed.

*Go too fast and you'll trip; dally and you'll fall behind.*
*Never rush and never dally, and you'll get there right on time.*

Don't be nervous and don't be lax. Don't go too fast means don't be nervous. Don't dally means don't be lazy. Enjoy developing your skill. Develop it to the point that you are free and at ease when walking, free and at ease when sitting, free and at ease when standing, and free and at ease when sleeping. Walking, standing, sitting and lying down, you have self-mastery. Self-mastery means that your skill is progressing. When your skill progresses, you will be able to truly investigate Chan. Then, even if you consider stopping, there will be no way to do so.

Walking, standing, sitting, and lying down, you won't lose track of "who?" But even though you won't lose track of "who?" you still will not recognize "who?" You want to become familiar with "who?" You can't let the "who?" be cut off. At all times and in all places you investigate Chan until you become one with it. When you become one with it, then "you eat each day but it is as if you hadn't eaten a single grain of rice." It's not that you don't eat, but

未穿一縷紗」。就是行住坐臥都是在用功，把什麼都忘了！吃飯、穿衣服都忘了，何況其他的事情呢！更不成問題了。

## 打破黑筒現本源

打破黑漆筒，也就是開悟。因為本來有一念都是妄想，你參這個誰，也是妄想。用這個妄想，把其餘的妄想就都戰勝了。這是參，時時刻刻都是參這個話頭，不是出氣參，入氣不參；或者入氣參，出氣不參。不是的，你數呼吸氣沒有用的，變成兩個，頭上安頭。真正參禪的話，是一種入門的法，所以我們祖師出氣參，入氣都參；入氣參，出氣都參，應該不斷的，用這個參，參這一念，隨這一念，永遠不斷的，接接連連的，永遠都不斷的。

會用功的人，這個「誰」字總是不能斷的，問一聲：「是誰？」再問一聲：「是誰？」把心意識都參沒有了，心也空了，身也空了，意也空了，識也空了。你打妄想，就是由第六意識生出來的，這第六意識叫你打妄想，叫你知道痛，叫你忍受不住，都是它作怪。你若能把心意識都打破了，參破了，不被它所轉了，這是一個會用功的人。會用功的人，不要說你天天用功相應，就是很少的時間，你這一念相應了，就能開智慧，也就是所說的開悟。

所以古人說：

> 若人靜坐一須臾，
> 勝造恆沙七寶塔。

就一須臾的時候，你真能靜下來，「勝造恆沙七寶塔」，這一須臾的時間，或者一秒鐘的期間，這把你無量劫生死的罪都可以滅了。

用功的人，時時刻刻常在定中，不會用功的人，時時刻刻常在妄中。定能生出智慧，妄就是增長愚癡。怎麼樣才能有定呢？就是要返妄歸真。可是我們人哪，都是跟著這個妄緣來跑，不願意回到定中來。因為這個就常常打妄想，不能歸真，這個真也變成妄了。你若不打那麼多妄想，時時能迴光返照，在自性上用功夫，就會歸真。我們現在打禪七，也就是要返妄歸真，反迷歸覺去

that you are not attached to eating. You eat but it's as if nothing had happened. You wear clothing but you are not attached to it.

"You wear clothes but it is as if you hadn't put on a single thread." This means that whether you are walking, standing, sitting, or lying down, you forget everything. You forget about eating and wearing clothes, how much the more other matters. How much less of a problem will other matters be!

## Smash the Black Barrel and Reveal the Source

Smashing the black lacquer barrel refers to enlightenment. Although the thought of investigating "who" is also a false thought, this one false thought is used to defeat all the other false thoughts. Investigation should be done in every moment; it is not that you investigate on the out-breath, and then don't investigate on the in-breath; or that you investigate on the in-breath and then not on the out-breath. No, counting your breaths is of no use because it creates a duality. It adds a head on top of a head--it is superficial. The true and proper method for investigating chan meditation is the method for entering deeply. Thus, our patriarchs investigated their meditation topic breathing in as well as breathing out; their one thought of investigation continued on forever without interruption.

Those who truly know how to work do not lose track of the topic "who?" Little by little they inquire into "who" until mind, intellect, and consciousness all vanish. The mind becomes empty; the body is also empty; the intellect is empty, and the consciousness is empty. When you strike up false thoughts, it is the sixth consciousness that they come from. The sixth consciousness causes you to strike up false thought, causes you to register pain, and causes you to be unable to bear any more. All of those are distortions of the sixth consciousness. If you are able to smash the mind, intellect and consciousness--if you investigate until you break through them, so that you can't be turned by such thoughts--then you are one who truly knows how to work. Not to mention gaining responses every day in your application of effort, if you gain a response for even the space of a thought, you can open your wisdom, which is another way of saying you can become enlightened.

There's an old proverb that goes,

> *If someone sits quietly for an instant,*
> *Then that is better than building pagodas made*
> *of the seven jewels in number like the Ganges' sands.*

If you can genuinely enter samadhi--stay quiet--for an instant, for just a moment in time, then that in itself can eradicate infinite kalpas of offenses that bind us to birth and death.

Those who know how to practice are always in samadhi, while those who don't are constantly in the midst of falseness. Within samadhi, one produces wisdom, while within falseness one's stupidity increases. How can one obtain samadhi? One must return the false to the true. We, however, are ever eager to pursue false conditions and unwilling to return to a state of samadhi. That's why

妄存真。所以我們把一切一切都放下，在這兒跑香、坐香，行住坐臥不離這個，離了這個就是錯過。這個是什麼？就是提起一句話頭。

## 如是如是觀自在

我告訴你們，跑香你要會跑。不是說跑得快，就是跑香；也不是說跑得慢，就是跑香。要怎麼樣子？要很如法、很自在的。行的時候，還是參「念佛是誰」。一開始只是走，走十五分鐘，或者二十分鐘的時候，才開始跑。只跑一圈或兩圈，最多三圈，就打站板了。跑得時間不能太久，太久，把人累得呵呵氣喘的，又不能用功。只跑一兩轉，或者最多三轉，覺得跑得稍微熱了，身上一熱就打站板。打站板，就停止，就開始坐，因為周身氣血都活起來，活起來再坐著。

坐，什麼時候都要孤炯炯的，像個金剛似的。你沒有任何人有我這樣子有力量的。坐禪就久坐，久坐就有禪。怎麼坐呢？坐要平心靜氣，像一座鐘似的，端然正坐，眼觀鼻，鼻觀口，口問心，時時刻刻都是要這樣子。坐那個地方，要四不靠：前不靠、後不靠、左不靠、右不靠。坐著最好能結雙跏趺座，雙跏趺座，就叫蓮花座。你能結雙跏趺坐，很容易入定，雙跏趺座又叫金剛座。有人說：「我雙跏趺坐，我坐了那麼久，也沒有入定。」就因為你盡打妄想，沒有真正曉得用功，所以你沒有入定。最好的是雙跏趺坐，其次是單跏趺坐，左腿在右腿的上面，單跏趺坐。再坐，不相當了，你可以隨便坐。坐，常常如如不動，了了常明。你坐這兒，舌尖頂上顎，任督二脈在這裏交接，任督二脈通了，氣血也通了，這時候覺得很自在，口裏有口水，把它吞到肚子裏去。時時這樣吞，好像用甘露來滋潤菩提苗一樣的，給它灌水。坐坐，身上會有一股暖氣，很熱的，在這階段裏頭，開始生出一種作用，第一個階段就是熱，熱先從肚子裏熱，以後熱到周身上去，然後再回來，這麼熱幾次，這叫熱的階段。熱了以後，經過一個相當的時間，也就是在這化學工廠裏來化驗，化驗得差不多，接著就到頂位了。覺得頭上好像有一點什麼，又好像沒有，你說有，你也看不見，也摸不著，只是有這個感覺在頭上，總是覺得有一點不可思議的境界，這叫

we constantly indulge in discursive thoughts and cannot return to the truth. As a result, the truth becomes false. If you didn't have so many discursive thoughts, but instead reflected within at all times and worked on your own nature, you would be able to return to the truth. Our Chan session is also for the purpose of turning the false back into the truth, getting rid of the false and keeping the truth. That's why we have set everything aside to come here to walk and sit. Walking, standing, sitting, or lying down, we must not be apart from "this." To separate from this is a mistake. "This" is just the meditation topic, which we must always bring to mind.

## So It Is, So It Is, Contemplate at Ease

I will explain to you about the period of walking. If you know how to walk, you won't race. That is not walking. Nor is that to say that a slow pace is walking. How should you do it? You should be very orderly and yet at ease. During the walks you should still be investigating "Who is mindful of the Buddha?" We first walk for about fifteen to twenty minutes, and then run. The runs should be once or twice around the hall--three times at most--and then the signal to stop should be given. The runs cannot last too long. If the runs last too long, people get tired and winded, and then they won't be able to apply their effort. Just run for one or two laps, three at most. Run until you feel that people are just beginning to get warm. As soon as the body heat rises, hit the fish to stop the run. Then start the sitting period. Once the circulation of blood and *qi* (energy) has come alive, the sit should begin.

While sitting, you must be solid and strong like vajra, so that the strength of your sitting is equal to the best. You have to sit for a long time, and then you will attain Dhyana. What is the method for sitting? In sitting, your mind should be calm, and your breath tranquil. Sit upright like a great bell, your eyes contemplating your nose, your nose contemplating your mouth, and your mouth contemplating the mind at all times. Don't lean to the front, back, left or right. If you can sit in full lotus posture, the vajra posture, that's the very best. It's very easy to enter samadhi when you are in full lotus. "I've sat in full lotus for a long time, but I haven't entered samadhi," someone says. That's because you keep having discursive thoughts and you don't really know how to practice properly. Full lotus is the best posture, and half lotus (with your left foot over your right thigh) is the second best. If you cannot bear that, then you can sit however you like. When sitting, you should be in a state of unmoving suchness and constant clarity. Curl the tip of your tongue upwards so it touches the roof of your mouth, thus connecting the *ren* and *du* energy channels. Once these channels connect, your blood and energy will circulate well and you will feel very comfortable. If you have saliva, you can swallow it down. Your saliva is like sweet dew nourishing your Bodhi sprouts.

After sitting for a while, you will begin to feel a warmth. It begins in your belly, spreads throughout your body, and then returns. The repeated experience of warmth is known as the Level of Heat. After a period of time, in which you experience further changes in your

頂位。頂位以後，就覺得很忍不住，忍不住還要忍，這叫忍位了。在忍的階段，很不容易忍過去，這時覺得頭上很不舒服的，好像有什麼東西，要把頭鑽出個窟窿似的。這時候又忍，久而久之，這個窟窿鑽透了，跑出去了，跑出頭上面，出窟窿外邊去了，就好像小鳥從鳥籠子出去一樣，高興得不得了，這才是世界第一個忍。所以叫世第一，在世界的第一個大丈夫，第一個大豪傑，沒有人可比的，所以叫世第一位。

## 善哉善哉悟誰人

坐禪有初禪、有二禪、有三禪、有四禪。初禪的境界，先得到一種輕安的境界，覺得身上很舒服的，很自在的，很受用的。這種舒服自在，叫法喜，得到一種法喜。你得到法喜充滿的境界，不吃也不餓，不睡也不睏，甚至於不穿衣服也不冷，這就是修行開始的一種感覺，很輕安坐著，覺得像沒有自己似的，走路也像沒有自己似的，不知自己在什麼地方。

在這輕安的境界以後，就會入一點初禪的定，初禪定一入的時候，自己空了，所以覺得脈博也停了。在這時候，盡虛空遍法界都充滿了，這個脈住了，這時你就坐一個鐘頭、兩個鐘頭，也就好像一秒鐘那麼短暫，很快光陰就過去了。到這個境界，也不能說覺得自己不得了，這還是修行的一個前方便，剛剛一個開始，得到定的一點滋味。你脈停止了。第二步，你氣也停止了，鼻孔裏頭也沒有呼吸氣，因為外呼吸斷了，內呼吸活動起來，不需要藉著外呼吸，自己裏邊有這一種真正的呼吸，所以氣也停止了，氣住了。氣住之後再往前用功，用得念住了，這時候，一念也不生了，什麼念頭也沒有了，也沒有妄想了，自己與大自然合而為一了，念慮空。第三步念雖然說是住了，還是有那一念的無明，這個粗的無明。

到第四步，這個念真正斷了，捨了，捨念，把一切的念慮都放下了。參禪參到這個境界上，這還是有漏的四禪，生死還沒有了，也沒有證果。到證初果阿羅漢，要斷八十一品的見惑。什麼叫見惑？見惑就是對境起貪愛，對著境界，你生出貪愛的心，這就叫見惑，見著就迷惑了。證初果是入流，入什麼流呢？就入聖人的法性流，逆凡夫的六塵流。證初果的聖人，是不入色、聲、香

body's "chemical factory," you reach the Level of Summit. There will be a sensation on the crown of your head, which seems to be there and yet not there. It is invisible and intangible, just a feeling, but it seems to be kind of an inconceivable state. After the Level of Summit comes the Level of Patience. During this stage, the sensation on your head becomes very hard to bear, and yet you must bear it. It feels as if a hole were being drilled into your skull. If you can endure the discomfort, then after a while the hole will be drilled all the way through, and you will be able to go out the top of your head, like a bird happily flying out from its cage. This is the Level of Being Foremost in the World. You are the number one hero, unsurpassed in the world.

## Good Indeed, Good Indeed, Awakening to the "Who"

In the course of meditation, one may attain to the First, Second, Third, and Fourth Dhyanas. Prior to attaining the First Dhyana, one first attains a state of lightness and ease, which is quite comfortable and enjoyable. When you attain this state of being filled with Dharma bliss, you can go without food and not feel hungry, go without sleep and not feel tired, and even go naked and not feel cold. This is a state attained in the initial stages of cultivation. Whether you are sitting or walking, you feel as if you have no self. You don't know where your ego went.

After the state of lightness and ease, you enter the samadhi of the First Dhyana. At that time, the self is empty and your pulse appears to stop. You pervade empty space and the Dharma Realm, and one or two hours of sitting seem to go by in only a second's time. However, you should not think of yourself as extraordinary; you have only gotten a tiny taste of samadhi in this initial stage of practice. Your pulse has stopped, and the next step is that your breath stops. When external breathing ceases and you no longer breathe through your nose, an internal "true" breathing begins to function. At that point, you no longer need to rely on external breathing. As you continue to progress in your practice, your thoughts will cease. When not a single thought arises and all discursive thoughts are gone--emptied--you become one with Nature. Although thoughts are said to cease in this third stage, you actually still have a thought of coarse ignorance.

In the fourth stage, thoughts are truly ended; all thoughts are renounced. This state of meditation is the Fourth Dhyana, which is still subject to outflows. You have neither ended birth and death nor realized any fruition (of sagehood). To reach the level of a First Stage Arhat, one has to cut off eighty-one grades of view delusions. View delusions occur when one gives rise to greed and desire when confronted by states. One is confused by what one sees. First Stage Arhats are called Stream-Enterers, for they enter the flow of the Dharma nature of Sages and go against the stream of the six sense objects of ordinary beings. Sages of the first fruition do not enter into forms, sounds, smells, tastes, objects of touch, or dharmas. Forms cannot move them; sounds cannot move them; smells cannot

、味、觸、法；色也不能搖動他，聲也不能搖動他，香也不能搖動他，味也不能搖動他，觸也不能搖動他，法也不能搖動他，他不被六塵境界，所迷惑，證初果阿羅漢是這樣子。我們現在坐禪，連初禪也沒有到呢！你們哪一個覺得自己的脈停止，沒有的。

所以沒有得到這種境界的人，應該時時刻刻特別努力，不要把光陰都空過去，這是很要緊的。這個坐，你能雙跏趺坐更好；不能雙跏趺坐，單跏趺坐也可以的；你雙跏趺、單跏趺都不能，那麼隨便坐也可以。修行不是腿的問題，是心的問題。你心裏沒有妄想，你就怎麼樣坐都會用功的；你心裏有妄想，怎麼樣坐，功夫都不會相應的。所以修道是要修心養性；修心，你常常自己觀察觀察，觀察自己的妄想，哪一種的妄想多，你是貪欲的妄想多？是瞋恚的妄想多？是愚癡的妄想多？要迴光返照審察自己，自己要使這些妄想都清淨了，那你功夫就相應了。不管你是雙跏趺坐、單跏趺坐，隨隨便便坐，都要去除你的妄想，妄想去盡了，真智慧就現前了，妄不盡，真也不現。所以修行就要在心地上用功夫，這叫心地法門，令心裏時時清淨，你一時清淨一時就在靈山；時時清淨，時時都在靈山。無論是念佛是持咒，是修戒律，是講教，是坐禪，都是要把你的心制之一處。心制之一處就是去妄存誠，時時都反求諸己，認識自己的本來面目，這是用功一個開始的方法。

修行不是腿的問題，是心的問題。你心裏沒有妄想，你就怎麼樣坐，都會用功的；你心裏有妄想，怎麼樣坐，功夫都不會相應的。

Cultivation is a matter of the mind, not the legs. If you can be free of discursive thoughts, then you can practice in any posture at all. If your mind is filled with discursive thoughts, then you won't succeed in your practice no matter how you sit.

move them; flavors cannot move them; touches cannot move them; and mental dharmas cannot move them. They are not affected by the states of the six defiling objects. That's at the level of the First Stage of Arhatship. Right now, we have not even reached the First Dhyana in our meditation. None of us have felt our pulses stop beating.

If you haven't attained these states, you should work hard in every minute and second; it's important not to waste time. It's best to sit in full lotus. If you cannot, then you can sit in half lotus. If full lotus and half lotus are both too difficult, then simply sit casually. Cultivation is a matter of the mind, not the legs. If you can be free of discursive thoughts, then you can practice in any posture at all. If your mind is filled with discursive thoughts, then you won't succeed in your practice no matter how you sit. Practice consists of cultivating the mind and nurturing the nature. You must constantly observe your discursive thoughts to see what kind of thoughts are predominant. Are the majority of your thoughts concerning greed and desire? Do your thoughts contain more anger and rage than anything else? Does stupidity dominate your thinking? Reflect inwardly and examine yourself. If you can purify your mind of these discursive thoughts, you are having a response in your work. Whether you sit in full lotus, in half lotus, or casually, the essential thing is to get rid of discursive thoughts so that genuine wisdom can appear. As long as the false is not ended, the true will not manifest. In cultivating we work on the mind-ground. That is called the Mind Ground Dharma door: causing the mind to become pure. If you can be pure for one instant, you are on Magic Mountain in that one instant. If you can be pure at all times, you are always on Magic Mountain. Regardless of whether you recite the Buddha's name, hold mantras, keep the precepts, expound the teachings, or sit in Chan meditation, the goal is to focus the mind on a single point, to cast out the false and retain the true. At all times, look within yourself and recognize your original face.

That is the method to use at the initial stages of practice.

## 性覺靈明原非物

參禪不要有境界，要什麼也沒有就是要空，連空都空了，也不要怕，也不要歡喜。你若有一種恐懼，這也會著魔的；你有一種歡喜，就有歡喜魔來。你看《楞嚴經》五十種陰魔，都是坐禪的境界。你若能明白那種境界，你所見的什麼，就不會被這境界轉。所謂「佛來佛斬，魔來魔斬」，佛來了，不要著住到佛上；魔來了，也不要著住到魔上。不要執著。不要，「哦！這佛來了。」生大歡喜，這也是不得其正。有所恐懼，則不得其正；有所好樂，則不得其正；有所忿懥，則不得其正。所以你要在這個靜中如如不動，遇到什麼境界也不動，也不生分別心，也不追這個境界。境界現前了，隨它現，不要隨著境界轉；不現前，也不要找境界。因為我們無始劫以來，在八識田裏，什麼境界都有的。你這一靜，它就現出來。好像很渾的水，你若是總搖動這個水，它不清；你放到那個地方不動，叫它澄靜下來，它那種渾的東西、那種塵埃，就都到水底下去，這水就清了。這也就好像你一定，心也清了。

心清水現月，意定天無雲。

心裏清了，好像水裏現出月亮似的。所以不要管這個境界是真的、是假的，你用功，這才是真的。不過境界來了，你也不要像一班不明白的人，說：「哎呀！這是不好啊！你著魔。」你因為用功，才有這個境界；你若不用功，根本就沒有，什麼也都沒有的。所以不要怕，真正明白了，要一切無著住，什麼也不著住。

## 智光遍照本來真

我們現在都要學有智慧，學有智慧，就先要受一點苦，在這裏煉一煉，用火來燒一燒。啊！你說你是塊金子，要用火來燒一燒才知道是真的？是假的？若不是金子，就燒沒有了；要是金子呢，真金不怕洪爐火。真的金子你怎樣燒，還是一兩或者 ten ounces（十盎斯），不會減少的。那假的呢？本來是 ten ounces，一燒 ten ounces。所以！我們現在就在這煉，煉！煉什麼呢？煉成金剛不壞身。你金剛不壞身煉成了，無論是原子

---

# With the Nature Bright and Aware, There Is Nothing at All

In investigating Chan, one should not want states to arise. We don't want there to be anything, not even emptiness. Even emptiness is emptied, and yet one feels neither fear nor joy. If you experience fear, then you will be vulnerable to demons. If you experience happiness, then a demon of happiness will come. Look at the fifty skandha demons, which are discussed in the *Shurangama Sutra*. All of those states could be encountered when meditating. If you are clear about those states, then you will not be turned by any state that you may see. There is a saying, "If the Buddha comes, smash him. If a demon comes, beat him away." If a Buddha comes, don't become attached to that Buddha. If a demon comes, don't become attracted to that demon. Do not have any attachments. Don't think: "Wow! A Buddha has come!" and be overjoyed about it, because that's not going about it the proper way. The presence of fear also indicates not going about it the proper way; and the presence of any like or dislike indicates not going about it the proper way. Therefore, you must be able to remain "thus thus unmoving" in stillness; you must remain unmoved no matter what state you encounter so that you do not give rise to discriminations about it and you do not pursue it. If a state appears, let it be. If no state appears, don't look for any. If you perceive a state, don't be turned by it. From limitless kalpas past until the present, we have accumulated all kinds of states of mind within the field of our eighth consciousness. Sitting quietly allows these states to come forth. By analogy, if you keep stirring muddy water, it will not be clear. But if you set the water somewhere and don't disturb it, then all the mud and sediment will sink to the bottom and the water will become clear. It's the same with you. Once you sit quietly, your mind will become clear.

*The mind's clarity is like that of water in which*
   *the moon can reflect.*
*The intellect in samadhi is like a cloudless sky.*

When your mind is pure, then it's like water that reflects the moon. And so pay no attention to whether a state of mind is true or false. Working hard is true. However, you shouldn't be like people who don't understand what's happening, and say, "Ah! This is not good. You are possessed by a demon." In fact it is because you've worked hard that you encounter such a state. If you hadn't worked hard, nothing at all would happen. And so do not be afraid. True understanding is not being attached to anything. Don't be attached to anything at all.

## Wisdom Pervasively Illumines Innate Truth

Now we want to develop wisdom, and in order to do so, we must first go through some suffering. We must be smelted by the fire. Suppose you were a lump of gold, you would have to be smelted to find out if you were true gold or fool's gold. If you were fool's gold, then you would be burned up. If you really were gold, well, true

---

204

宣化老和尚追思紀念專集

彈、氫氣彈，什麼彈都不怕了。為什麼你不怕呢？因為你不壞嘛！沒有任何的東西，可以破壞你的金剛不壞身，但是要先受一點苦。

有的人說：「這個苦我真受不了，太苦了，也太痛了！」誰知道苦？誰知道痛？說：「我知道苦，我知道痛。」你又是誰？說：「我就是我這個身體！」哦！你這個身體就是你，若死了呢？你這個身體還在嗎？怎麼打它，也不知道痛，罵它，也能忍，怎麼樣子苦，也能受了？那時候怎麼就沒有這些問題了？說：「因為死了，所以什麼問題都沒有了。」那你現在也可以就像死了一樣。

若要人不死，須做活死人。

你要想不死嗎？你先要試試看。說「是自殺？」不是的，就好像死了一樣。你現在能看，就好像死了，也不爭了，也不貪了，也不瞋了，也不癡了。歷代祖師、歷代菩薩、歷代諸佛都是從這門裏成就的，一切諸佛從此生，一切菩薩從此生，一切祖師，都是從這個法門生出來的。

我們現在，也不要怕困苦艱難，好好修一修，好好地來認真修一修，把一切的妄想，都放下。不要躲懶，不要偷安，有這口氣，就是跑香的時候，就是坐香的時候。我們藉假修真，要勉為其難，愈不容易，愈要做。我們做的，就是不容易的事。若容易人人都能做了，就因為它不容易，所以我們要做人所不能做，忍人所不能忍的，勇猛精進才能成就你的真正智慧，這叫在大冶洪爐裏煉金剛不壞體。你經過這一鍛鍊，你的身體，就健康了，智慧也現前了。

參禪就是鍛鍊身、鍛鍊心；鍛鍊身沒有殺盜淫，鍛鍊心沒有貪、瞋、癡，這也是勤修戒定慧，息滅貪瞋癡。在禪堂裏頭，你什麼過錯也不會犯，雖然說時時都打妄

gold withstands the foundry's fire. Real gold is not afraid of fire. If you have ten ounces of true gold, it remains ten ounces no matter how much you smelt it. If you start with ten ounces of fool's gold, then there may only be one ounce left after it goes through the fire. Now we are here in this foundry being forged into indestructible vajra bodies. Once you have a vajra body, you won't have to fear atomic bombs, hydrogen bombs, or nuclear weapons of any kind. Why do we experience fear? Because we can be destroyed! Absolutely nothing can destroy your potentially vajra indestructible body, but you must first endure some suffering. Some people say, "It's too much pain and suffering. I can't take it!" Who perceives the pain and suffering? "I perceive it," you say. And just who are you? "I am just this body," you reply. If your body is you, then what about when you die? Where is your body then? If someone hits your body or scolds it then, it will be able to bear it. It will tolerate all sorts of suffering without any difficulty. You say, "That's because I'll be dead, so there won't be any problems." Well, why don't you just play dead right now?

*If a person wants to avoid death,*
*He must first act like a living dead person.*

If you don't want to die, you first have to try out dying. "You mean commit suicide?" you ask. No, I mean act like a dead person. If you regard everything from the perspective of a dead person, you will no longer contend, or be greedy, hateful, or stupid.

All the patriarchs, Bodhisattvas, and Buddhas through the ages succeeded by means of this method. All Buddhas, Bodhisattvas, and patriarchs were born from this Dharma door. So don't be afraid

想，但是你沒有設身處地，實實在在去做，所以身不殺生、不偷盜、不邪淫，令身體一切的習氣都清淨；鍛鍊身，令這個心妄想沒有了，清清淨淨的，恢復本有的智慧，破除所有的無明。

我們的身心，都是不容易返本還原，捨邪歸正。我們執著我們身體，執著我，執著我所，一切都放不下。要是有善根的人，他就能一切不執著，能把我執和法執都看破了。你把身看空了，我執破了；你把心也定了，法執也沒有了。你能沒有我執，沒有法執，這個時候超然物外，不被氣稟所拘，不被物欲所蔽，也就是得到解脫了，沒有執著就是得到解脫了。可是說的是很容易，行起來是很不容易的。有這麼一天，能把我執、法執都沒有了，那也就是盡虛空遍法界，都是你的法身。可惜啊！我們就是不能這樣子，要能這樣子，要經過多少大劫，才能到這種的地步上。

在修道的時候，用這個布施，把自己的身體布施給禪堂；用這個持戒，諸惡不作，眾善奉行；用這個忍辱，忍耐一切的痛來修行，接接連連，不要把這一念的修行心斷了。你時間到了，自然就智慧現前，般若的光明照遍三千大千世界。可是都要經過一番的鍛鍊，就是所說的

不受一番寒徹骨，怎得梅花撲鼻香？

你無論做什麼事情，都要經過一段的時間，然後才能成功的。不是一見到硬就退了，向後轉，這樣子不會有成就的。

## 實相般若在其中

參禪這一法，是無為而無不為。怎麼講呢？你坐這兒參禪，沒有什麼作為，但是在法界裏邊，你一個人能參禪，一個人就幫助，法界這種正氣；人人若都參禪，這個法界就沒有戰爭了。說：參禪，是要坐禪？不錯，坐著才有禪，久坐有禪，你坐的時間久了，就有一種不可思議的境界。可是真正參禪的人，不是單單坐

of difficulty and suffering now. Cultivate well. Diligently apply yourselves to your practice. Cast out all discursive thoughts. Don't be lazy or try to sneak off to rest. As long as you have a breath left, use it to walk and sit in meditation. We borrow the false to cultivate the true. The harder it is, the more you should be determined to overcome the difficulty. Anyone can do easy things. We want to do difficult things that others cannot do; we want to bear what others cannot bear. Only with such vigor and courage can we accomplish true wisdom. That's what's meant by forging indestructible vajra bodies in the red-hot furnace. After this kind of training, your bodies will be healthy and your wisdom will come forth.

Chan meditation disciplines both the body and the mind. The body is restrained from killing, stealing, and sexual misconduct; and the mind is restrained from greed, anger, and stupidity. In this way, we diligently cultivate precepts, samadhi, and wisdom and extinguish greed, anger, and stupidity. It is virtually impossible to commit offenses in the Chan hall. Although we may have idle thoughts, we will not act upon them. Restrained from killing, stealing, and lust, the body is purified of its bad habits. Once the body is disciplined and the mind is pure and concentrated, we can break through ignorance and regain our inherent wisdom. However, due to attachments to the body, the ego, and possessions, it is not easy to return to the origin and to renounce the deviant for the proper; it's difficult to put everything down. Only with good roots can we relinquish all attachments to self and to dharmas. If we can see the body as empty, we destroy the attachment to self. If the mind attains samadhi, the attachment to dharmas will be gone. With no attachments to self or dharmas, we can transcend the material plane and be liberated from the limitations of our inherent disposition and from our materialistic desires. Liberation is simply the absence of attachments. Nevertheless, this is not easy to accomplish. If we can really have no attachments to self or others, our Dharma body will pervasively fill space and the Dharma Realm. What a pity none of us can manage to do that. Who knows how many great eons it will be before we attain that kind of state?

In the course of cultivation, we must "give" our bodies to the Chan hall; we must uphold the precepts by refraining from evil and practicing goodness; we must patiently endure the pain. We must hold on to that single thought of practice and let it continue uninterrupted. When the time comes, after a period of disciplined practice, your wisdom will naturally manifest and Prajna light will illuminate the universe. But that requires a period of smelting.

*Without enduring the bitter cold of winter,*
*How could the plum blossoms smell so sweet?*

To achieve success in any endeavor takes time. Those who retreat as soon as the going gets rough won't achieve anything.

## Within This One Finds the True Appearance of Prajna

The practice of Chan meditation is "nondoing, yet nothing is left undone." What do I mean? As you sit there investigating Chan, you

你痛，痛到極點，
忘然無我了，怎麼會有痛呢？
If you endure the pain to the extreme,
to the point of forgetting yourself,
how can there be any more pain?

那兒參禪，站著也一樣參禪，跑路的時候也一樣參禪，睡覺的時候也一樣參禪，所以行住坐臥沒有一秒鐘不可以參禪的。用功的人不管閒事，時時刻刻就是照顧自己的話頭，參念佛是誰？甚至於吃飯也沒有時間吃飯，喝茶也沒有時間喝茶，睡覺也沒有時間睡覺，行住坐臥都是提起這一句話頭來用功。參到山窮水盡了，啊！到那山的盡頭處，水的盡頭處，這就是說你參到那個極點了。

我們參禪必須要專一，專一到極點，就有辦法了。所謂「物極必反」，無論什麼事情你到極點了，才能有辦法。我們參禪打坐，不要腿一痛就哭起來，因為痛到極點就不痛了，然後就不可思議，妙不可言了。這沒法子講給你聽的，要你自己去試驗。

你痛到極處，就不痛了，痛關過去了，過了一關。但是過了一關不行的，等一等又有一關，等一等又有一關。打破一關是一個鐘頭，等到一個半鐘頭的時候，又開始痛了。為什麼呢？氣血又到這兒，想要打破這個痛的關，又痛了，你還要忍，你忍著不痛，又過去了，你就會得到一種說不出的自在，說不出的快樂，說不出的舒服。這時候覺得地天泰了，把這關打破，才能有好處。如果你像個小孩子似的，就哭起來，那就打不破關了。所以打破這個關需要忍，忍不住也要忍，咬著牙要忍，一定要有忍耐：不怕苦、不怕痛、不怕難，有這三不怕，你就過了三關了。

are not doing much of anything. Yet when you, a single person, investigate Chan, you help the proper energy of the Dharma Realm. If everyone could investigate Chan, there would be no wars in the world. "Do you have to sit to investigate Chan?" you ask. Well, it's said that you must sit to attain Chan (Dhyana), that Chan comes with long sitting. After sitting for a long time, you will experience an inconceivable state. However, true Chan cultivators investigate not only when sitting, but when walking, running, and sleeping. In walking, standing, sitting, and lying down, there is not a moment when they do not investigate. Cultivators are not busybodies; they constantly pay attention to their own topic, "Who is mindful of the Buddha?" to the point that they have no time to eat, drink tea, or sleep. Whether walking, standing, sitting, or lying down, they continue investigating their topic until they "reach the end of the mountains and rivers"--the ultimate point.

Chan investigation requires single-minded concentration. When single-minded concentration reaches its ultimate point, then you will be able to deal with things. It's said, "When things reach their extreme, a change must take place." It doesn't matter what the situation, by pursuing it to it's end, you can deal with it. Now as you sit in meditation, don't cry as soon as your legs start to hurt. After the pain reaches an extreme, it will stop and you will experience an inconceivable and ineffably wonderful state. There is no way I can express that state to you; you have to experiment for yourself. Once you experience pain to the extreme point, you won't have any more pain. You will have broken through the pain barrier. But breaking through one barrier is not enough. After a while there will be another barrier, and then later on another barrier. The first pain barrier was after one hour. But when you have sat for one and a half hours, the pain comes up again. Why does that happen? Your blood and *qi* (energy) reach a certain place, and they want to get through a barrier--another barrier of pain. And so you have to endure the pain again. You endure it until it doesn't hurt any more. Once the pain disappears, you will feel at ease and very happy--an inexpressible bliss, an ineffable comfort. At that time you will feel Earth over Heaven making *Peace*.

在禪堂裏為什麼沒有定力，痛一點也受不了，苦一點也受不了，難一點也受不了，甚至於受不了的時候，就要哭起來了！因為沒有定力，沒打破這個關頭。沒有打破痛關，沒有打破苦關，沒有打破難關。我們現在都要把它打破了；把這關都打破了，就得到自在了。你痛，痛到極點，忘然無我了，怎麼會有痛呢？沒有痛了。無論做什麼事情，一定要做到極點，到那個極處了，就淨極光通達。就是你清淨到極點了，定力到極點，你自然就現出智慧光了，開悟了。每天研究開悟開悟，你連一點痛都忍不了，你開個什麼悟？真是無慚無愧！

有人說：「禪堂裏，很多動靜，有這個人咳，又有那個人打呼，又有人這麼一動彈，這個止單就響了，很多這個動靜。」這個在什麼地方都會有的，你沒有那個動靜，就有那個動靜；沒有那個動靜，又有另一個動靜。你若會用功的人，有動靜，你不為這個動靜所轉，不要聽著一個動靜，你就跟著那個動靜就跑了，說：「他真討厭，令我不能入定。」就是他沒有動靜，你在這時候也不一定入定；你若入定，你就不會知道人有動靜。所以我們在這兒修行，坐禪並不一定要沒有聲音，那聲音愈大，或者你開悟開得更快；沒有聲音，也不能找聲音，有聲音也不要討厭這個聲音，這是修行的一個境界。

你會用功的，就在鬧市裏，也可以修行；你不會用功的，你就鑽到真空的管子裏去，一點空氣都沒有，還是不會用功。在這個地方，想找一個如如法法用功修道的地方，是不可能的。修道就是要能克服環境，無論什麼環境，不要討厭這個環境說：「哦！這個環境不好。」你到另外一個地方，比這個更不好，你再到另外一個地方，更不好，天下就沒有好的地方。你若是克服環境，什麼地方都一樣。佛不擇地而成，佛不是說選擇一個地方成佛，哪個地方都可以成佛的。

你在這時候，要是會用這個忍，不論怎樣不舒服，也能忍得住，不被這種境界，搖動你的心，那也就是有少分的定力。有少分的定力，就會生出少分的慧力。有的人說，想要受戒，我們現在坐禪，這就是受戒。受什麼戒啊？受

You must break through these barriers in order to attain benefits. If you act like a child who cries at the first sign of pain, then you will never be able to break through these barriers. You need to have patience. Endure what is unendurable! Grit your teeth and bear it! But you must be resolute! Don't fear suffering! Don't fear pain! Don't fear difficulty! With these three kinds of fearlessness, you can break through the three barriers.

Why is it that, sitting in the Chan hall, we don't have the samadhi power to endure a little pain, suffering, or difficulty? Why do we find it so unbearable that we feel like crying? It's because we don't have any samadhi power, and we haven't broken through the barriers of pain, suffering, and difficulty. Now, if we can break through these barriers, then we will obtain comfort and ease. If you endure the pain to the extreme, to the point of forgetting yourself, how can there be any more pain? There isn't. In everything you do, you should do it to the ultimate, and then, at the point of extreme purity, the light will penetrate. When your purity and samadhi reach their peak, the light of your wisdom will spontaneously appear and you will become enlightened. Every day you wonder about enlightenment, but what kind of enlightenment do you expect to attain if you can't even take a little pain? Shouldn't you feel ashamed of yourself?

Someone complained, "There's too much noise in the Chan hall. One person keeps coughing; others are snoring; and another person is always wiggling, which causes bench to squeak. The noise is intolerable!" That can happen anywhere. You may try to avoid this noise, but another noise shows up. If you get rid of that noise, you'll become aware of another one. If you know how to apply your effort, then whether it's noisy or quiet, you will not turned by movement or stillness. Not being turned by movement and stillness means that you don't listen to it. Or your eyes may follow the movement and stillness, saying, "He is really irritating! It's impossible for me to enter samadhi!" Even if the other person weren't making noise, you still might not be able to enter samadhi. If you can enter samadhi, then you are not even going to notice his movements. And so in cultivation, while meditating we shouldn't insist on perfect silence. The noisier it is, the greater your enlightenment, perhaps. So don't let sounds aggravate you. On the other hand, if it happens to be quiet, don't go looking for noise. These are all merely states.

If you know how to practice, you can do so right in the bustling city. If you don't, then you won't be able to practice even if you crawl inside a vacuum! There is no such thing as a perfect place for cultivation. You have to overcome the environment. No matter what the situation, don't say: "Ugh, this is a terrible environment." Move somewhere else and it may be worse. Leave that place and go on to another and it may turn out to be worse yet, until there's no place in the universe that suits you. If you can overcome the environment, then everywhere is the same for you. The Buddhas don't choose the place where they realize Buddhahood. It's possible to realize Buddhahood anywhere.

You have to learn to be patient. If you can remain unmoved no matter how uncomfortable you feel, then you have a little samadhi power. That little bit of samadhi will produce a little wisdom. You say you want to hold the precepts? Sitting in Chan is holding the precepts-- the precepts of enduring pain and suffering! As you sit there single-

苦戒；受什麼戒啊？受痛戒。你坐這個地方，一心參禪，參念佛是誰，抱住這個話頭，綿綿不斷，密密不忘，總是念佛是誰？參！這時候你自己說你有沒有罪過？你是不是造了很多業？你在這兒參禪會不會去殺人？會不會打殺人的妄想？「啊！某某人對我最不好，我一定要把他殺了。」你會不會，參這個殺人的禪？不會的。你在這兒參禪，會不會想去偷東西去？不會的啊！你這個不殺人、不偷東西，這就持戒了嘛！在這兒參禪就是持戒，這叫不持之持，不用持戒，自然就持戒了，所以就會生出定力來。

如果你不參禪，盡打其他的妄想，或者殺生、或者偷盜、或者邪淫、或者妄語、或者飲酒，什麼都做出來了。就因為一念之差，所以做了很多罪過的事情。在這兒參禪，這一些個問題都解決了，這叫不持戒而持戒。你就不定而定，雖然你覺得痛，但是你忍著一點，這也就生出定力來。生出定力就會生出慧力來，所以這就是「勤修戒定慧」。勤修戒定慧也就是「息滅貪瞋癡」。我要修行，也不生貪心了；我修行，有人打我，我沒有那麼回事，也不生瞋心了。在這兒參禪，也沒有愚癡的心，沒有那狂心野性，你說這豈不是最大的好處。

所以參禪就是具足一切法，一切法都在這參禪裏包括著。但是我們參禪，是要越參越開悟，越參越聰明、越有智慧，不是參那個死禪啊！愚癡、愚癡、愚癡、愚癡、愚癡，越參越愚癡，那就是參死禪，就是什麼也不懂，就和吃迷魂藥的是一樣的，迷迷糊糊的，也不知東南西北，「這是白天、是晚間呢？」哦！拿著太陽看著是月亮，看著月亮又說是太陽，你說這豈不是顛倒嗎？這就是最愚癡的人的行為。

mindedly investigating "Who is mindful of the Buddha?" without a second's pause, well, you tell me, are you committing offenses? Are you creating a lot of bad karma? While you are sitting in meditation, could you commit murder? Would you have thoughts like, "He's so mean to me, I'm going to kill him"? Would you be investigating the topic of wanting to kill someone? No. Would you think about stealing things? No. And so as you refrain from killing and stealing you are holding the precepts. By investigating Chan, you naturally keep the precepts without even trying, and then based on precepts you develop samadhi power.

If you don't investigate Chan, all the discursive thoughts which arise in your mind may lead you to kill, steal, engage in lust, lie, or take intoxicants. One single wrong thought can lead to many offenses. On the other hand, if you sit in Chan meditation, all these problems disappear as you naturally hold the precepts without trying. If you can be patient with the pain, then the effortless upholding of precepts produces samadhi, and from samadhi there arises wisdom. You are then diligently practicing precepts, samadhi, and wisdom and extinguishing greed, anger, and stupidity. With the resolve to cultivate, you cast out greed and feel no anger if someone hits you. And when you sit in Chan, your stupidity disappears and your mad mind and wild nature vanish. Wouldn't you say these are tremendous advantages? That's why Chan meditation is said to encompass all dharmas. When properly done, the investigation of Chan makes us more awakened, intelligent, and wise. We should avoid a form of "stupefying" Chan which makes us muddled and oblivious, as if we were on drugs, so that we can't tell north from south or day from night.

## 本地風光原如此

你要知道在這個世界上，我們一呼一吸，一舉一動，一言一行，一思一想，都和整個世界、空間、時間有連帶的關係。世界宇宙在這個虛空裏邊，這個善氣、惡氣、清淨的氣和污濁的氣，都和我們通著。如果你想要真正清淨，返本還原，見到你本來面目，你一定要放下身心看破一切，在這個大冶洪爐裏經過一番鍛鍊，你才能清者清，濁者濁。你思想和你的呼吸都變成清淨，沒有染污，你的智慧就會現出來；你有染污，清淨不具足，愚癡就充滿了。所以我們在禪堂裏跑跑坐坐，就好像澄清渾水似的。把它澄清，一點微塵都沒有，微塵都落到底下去了，上邊變清淨的水；你能再把底下那個塵土拿走了，就永遠現出你的清淨法身。怎麼樣拿走這個塵土呢？就要你明心見性，返本還原，就路回家，再見本地的風光，原來如此，那你混濁的塵埃就都撥掉了。

修行要內也清淨，外也清淨；內清淨是不打糊塗妄想，外清淨就是不做糊塗的事情。內要修內聖，外要修外王。內聖就是「栽培心上地，涵養性中天」；外王就是「諸惡不作，眾善奉行」，利益一切眾生。所以你要藉著外功，成就內果，在外邊要立功，在裏邊要存德。立功就是去利益一切眾生，可是利益眾生，你不要有一個利益眾生的想，要行所無事，不要有所執著；你若有所執著，那就是著相了。要立一切功，利益一切人，這都是我們，本分內的事情，我就應該這樣做。不要存一個利益眾生的想，做了之後，沒有這種的執著。外利人，內利己，就是參禪打坐。你坐一分鐘，就有一分鐘的受用，有一分鐘的好處。什麼好處呢？你能靜坐，淨極光通達，坐得內無身心，外無世界。可是你在靜坐的時候，有這種境界，出靜的時候，這種境界，還要繼續存在，這叫動靜一如。也就是說你在靜坐的時候，也沒有妄想；在動的時候，也沒有妄想，動就是靜，靜就是動，動靜沒有兩樣。你功夫到這樣的時候，這就是在定中，這就是常常在三昧裏頭，也就是說：

時時常在定，無有不定時。

## So This Is What Our Original Home Is Like!

Every breath we take, every move we make, every word, every action, every thought, every reflection affects the time and space in the universe. Conversely, the vibrations of good, bad, pure, and turbid energy in the universe affect us as well. If we really want to return to the purity of our original source and discover our true identity, we must break all attachments to body and mind, and see through everything. We must undergo a period of smelting in the blazing furnace before the pure elements can be separated from the dross. Wisdom will appear once our thinking and our breathing are both purified. As long as defilement remains, and the purity is not total, then we are still full of stupidity. When we sit and walk in the Chan hall, we are letting the silt and mud settle to the bottom, so that the water of our mind becomes clear and sparkling. Then if we can remove the sediment on the bottom, our pure Dharma body becomes eternally manifest. Removing the sediment means we come to understand our mind and see our nature. We return to the source, and take the road home to discover what our original home is like.

In cultivation, we should purify ourselves internally and externally. Internal purity refers to not having confused thoughts. External purity means not acting in confused ways. Internally we want to be like sages by cultivating the mind and nature, and externally we want to be like kings by avoiding evil, practicing good deeds, and benefiting all living beings. By means of external merit, we achieve our fruition within. Externally we create merit, and internally we amass virtue. Creating merit means benefiting all beings. When we help others, we should not become attached to the thought that we are helping them. We should do it as if nothing were happening. As soon as there is attachment, then we lend reality to appearances. We create merit and benefit beings because it is what we should be doing anyway; it is our duty to help them. Don't harbor thoughts of having benefited beings so that after you do it all kinds of attachments remain.

Externally benefiting others and internally benefiting oneself is what Chan meditation is all about. There is usefulness and advantage gained every minute that you sit. What are the advantages? When you sit to the point of total stillness, the light will penetrate and you will feel as if there is no body, mind, or world. If you can remain in this state even when you are not sitting, so that when you come out of sitting the experience continues, then that is called movement and stillness becoming one and the same. Another way of putting it is that when you are sitting you don't have any discursive thoughts and when you move about you still don't have any discursive thoughts. Movement is stillness and stillness is movement; they are non-dual.

When you have this kind of skill, you will constantly be in samadhi.

*At all times you are in samadhi;*
*There is no time when you are not.*

一舉一動，都是在定中，一言一行，行住坐臥，都在定裏頭。

眼觀形色內無有，耳聽塵事心不知。

這都是在定中的一種境界。怎麼樣能這樣子？就是要參禪打坐，時間久了，就會這樣子。

你若真是用功用好了，用得相應，餓也不知道餓，渴也不知道渴，冷也不知道冷，熱也不知道熱了，什麼也不知道了。你能到什麼也不知道，這個程度上，你什麼都知道，什麼都能明白了。我們無論做什麼事情，若做到那個極點、做到極處極處，就會有一種變化了。也就是，靜極就動，動極就靜，你動到極點就生出靜來，靜到極點又生出動來。譬如白天和晚間，白天就是動，晚間就是靜；黑到極處，又天光了；天光到極處，又天黑了，這一日一夜也是一動一靜。你若會用功，用得動不礙靜，靜不礙動；動中有靜，靜中有動。你會用功，這裏邊真空就有妙有，妙有又生出真空來了。

我們這參禪的期間，一定要把本份的事情弄清楚了，不要來的時候，糊裏糊塗來的，等到將來死的時候，也不知道怎麼死的，那就太沒有意思了。我們一定要知道怎麼樣生的，將來我們怎麼樣死法，我們死是不是自由自在的？我們要修得來去自由，那是真正的自由，我願意來，我就來；我願意去，我就去，來也沒有煩惱，去也沒有憂愁。我願意去，隨時把腿子盤起來，我要往生西方極樂世界，大家可以隨便談一談，告告假，這就走了。能這樣子，這叫生死真有把握了。要怎麼樣才能這樣子呢？就要「若要人不死，須下死功夫。」你若想了生脫死，就要用一點真正不怕死的功夫。所以不要怕痛，不要怕難，不要怕苦，什麼也不怕，這才行的。

禪這一法，是諸佛的母體，十方諸佛都是從禪定產生出來的。你如果沒有禪定的功夫，是不可以開悟的，是不可以成佛的。所以我們這個無宗無派，我們也不是臨濟宗，也不是曹洞宗，也不是雲門，也不是法眼，也不是溈仰。我們這是整個的，好像這個桌子是全體大用的，不是單單這麼一個角落的，所以我們所行所作，很自然的，沒有一點造作。

Every gesture, every movement comes forth from samadhi; every word, every action--walking, standing, sitting, or lying down--is done in a state of samadhi.

*The eyes see forms, but inside there is nothing.*
*The ears hear sounds, but the mind does not know.*

To attain this state of samadhi, you have to investigate Chan and sit in meditation. After you have done so for a sufficient length of time, you can be this way.

If you really practice well to the point of gaining some response, then you won't know when you are hungry, thirsty, cold, or hot--you won't know anything at all. If you can reach that level of not knowing anything at all, then you will know everything. When we do something, if we can do it thoroughly--to the ultimate point--then a change will occur. When you move to the ultimate extent, stillness manifests. Stillness to the ultimate extent will bring about movement. For example, daytime is movement and night-time is stillness. When stillness reaches an extreme, when the sky grows dark and when that darkness reaches its limit, dawn breaks. When the light of day reaches its extreme, night descends. One day and one night are also one movement and one stillness. If you know how to practice, you can develop your skill to the point that movement does not obstruct stillness, and stillness does not hinder movement--so that within movement there is stillness, and within stillness there is movement. If you know how to apply your skill, then you will find that within true emptiness there is wonderful existence, and from within wonderful existence, true emptiness arises.

We should resolve to meditate until we figure out what we are all about. We were born in a confused way, and life would be meaningless if we also have to die in confusion. We need to find out how we were born and how we will die. Can we be free and independent when we die? The goal of our practice is to attain freedom over birth and death, which is true freedom--the ability to come and go whenever we want, without afflictions or worries. If we wish to go to the Western Land of Ultimate Bliss, we can simply get into full lotus posture, bid farewell to everyone, and go.
That's true freedom over birth and death.

*In order to escape death*
*One must have death-defying skill.*

To gain freedom from birth and death, you must practice without fear of death. You must not be afraid of pain, difficulty, suffering, or anything else.

Chan is the essence of all Buddhas. The Buddhas of the ten directions were born from Chan samadhi. If you lack skill in Chan samadhi, you cannot become enlightened or attain Buddhahood. We do not belong to any sect--we are not of the Linzi, Caodong, Yunmen, Fayan, or Weiyang sects. We encompass the entire substance. For example, if this table represents the vast functioning of the entire substance, then we are like the whole table, not just one corner. That's why we do everything very naturally, without putting on airs.

# 念佛法門
# THE DHARMA-DOOR OF
# MINDFULNESS OF THE BUDDHA

宣公上人講述
Lectures by Venerable Master Hua

宣化老和尚追思紀念專集

# 阿彌陀佛大法王

爲什麼要念南無阿彌陀佛呢？因爲阿彌陀佛和十方一切眾生都有大因緣。在阿彌陀佛因地的時候，就是他沒有成佛以前，也是一個比丘名字叫法藏。這法藏比丘發了四十八個大願，每一願都是要度眾生成佛的。其中他就發了一個願，這樣說的：「所有十方一切眾生，等我成佛的時候，他們若念我這個名字，也一定就要成佛；如果他們不成佛，我也不成佛。」

阿彌陀佛這願力，好像吸鐵石那種吸鐵的力量似的，十方所有的眾生都好像這塊鐵似的，所以把十方的眾生都給吸到極樂世界去。如果吸不到呢？阿彌陀佛也不成佛。所以我們一切眾生，若有稱阿彌陀佛這個名號的，就都有成佛的機會。

# 普攝群機往西方

《彌陀經》是佛不問自說的。爲什麼不問自說呢？沒有人懂這個法門，所以就沒有人問。大智舍利弗，雖然當機，但是也不知道怎麼樣問。

佛可以說是在忍不住之中，把這個最方便、最直接、最了當、最省事又省錢的念佛法門說給大家。只要你每一個人能專心念佛，念得「若一日，若二日，若三日，若四日，若五日，若六日，若七日，一心不亂，其人臨命終時，阿彌陀佛與諸聖眾，現在其前。」就來接引。

所以這個法門是一般人所不能相信的；可是這還是最直接、最了當的法門。這個念佛的法門，是三根普被，利鈍兼收，不論你聰明的人，是愚癡的人，一樣都可以成佛。

生到極樂世界，那是「無有眾苦，但受諸樂」的，從蓮華化生，不像我們人經過胎藏，他那是以蓮華爲胎，在蓮華裏住一個時期，將來就成佛了。

# Amitabha Buddha: The Great King of Dharma

Why do we recite "Namo Amitabha Buddha?" It is because Amitabha Buddha has a great affinity with living beings in the ten directions. Before Amitabha Buddha realized Buddhahood, during his cultivation on the "cause ground," he was a Bhikshu named Dharma Treasury who made forty-eight vows. Among those vows was one that said, "I vow that after I realize Buddhahood, any living beings throughout the ten directions who recite my name will certainly realize Buddhahood. If they will not be able to realize Buddhahood, then I will not realize Buddhahood."

The power of Amitabha Buddha's vows is like a magnet; living beings of the ten directions are like iron filings. That is how he draws beings of the ten directions to the Land of Ultimate Bliss. What if they aren't attracted? Amitabha Buddha vowed that he himself wouldn't realize Buddhahood if they couldn't be! Therefore, all who recite the name of Amitabha Buddha have the opportunity to realize Buddhahood.

# Gathering All Beings into the Western Land

The *Amitabha Sutra* belongs to the category of Sutras that the Buddha "spoke without request." Why was that Sutra spoken without request? No one understood this Dharma-door, and so no one could request the Buddha to speak it. Although the greatly wise Shariputra was an interlocutor in the assembly, even he didn't know how to ask about this Dharma-door. Probably the Buddha couldn't hold back any longer, so he told everyone about this most convenient, most direct, most satisfying, easiest, and most inexpensive Dharma-door of reciting the Buddha's name. If a person can recite Amitabha Buddha's name "whether for one day, two days, three, four, five days, six days, as long as seven days, with one mind unconfused, when this person approaches the end of life, before him will appear Amitabha Buddha and all the assembly of holy ones" to guide him. Although most people find it hard to believe this Dharma-door, it is the most direct and certain practice.

The Dharma-door of reciting the Buddha's name is appropriate for those of all three faculties and beneficial for both the intelligent and the stupid. Whether you are stupid or wise, you can realize Buddhahood. When one is born in the Land of Ultimate Bliss, where beings "endure none of the sufferings, but enjoy every bliss," one will be born transformationally from a lotus. We will not pass through the womb as in the human realm, but will enter a lotus flower, live in it for a while, and then realize Buddhahood.

## 晝夜持名專誠念

一句彌陀萬法王
五時八教盡含藏
行人但能專持念
定入如來不動堂

「一句彌陀萬法王」，這一句彌陀，就是萬法之王。「五時八教盡含藏」，八教：藏、通、別、圓、頓、漸、祕密、不定。五時，是華嚴時、阿含時、方等時、般若時、法華涅槃時。這五時八教合起來，都在這一句彌陀裏頭就包含了。「行人但能專持念」，我們無論哪一個人，能專心念佛，「定入如來不動堂」，一定到常寂光淨土，到極樂世界去。我們末法眾生，就是以念佛得度，我們誰若想得度，誰就念佛。

少說一句話
多念一聲佛
打得念頭死
許汝法身活

我們大家不要忽略這個念佛法門。

## 時刻觀想善思量

這個念佛法門，有四種的念法：有持名念佛，就是念南無阿彌陀佛、南無阿彌陀佛。有觀想念佛，觀想，就觀看，這麼想著，想著：

阿彌陀佛身金色
相好光明無等倫
白毫宛轉五須彌
紺目澄清四大海
光中化佛無數億
化菩薩眾亦無邊
四十八願度眾生
九品咸令登彼岸

這是觀想念佛。

214

---

## Day and Night Hold the Name with Concentrated, Sincere Mindfulness

*The King of All Dharmas is the one word "Amitabha."*
*The five periods and the eight teachings are all contained*
  *within it.*
*One who single-mindedly remembers and recites his name*
*In samadhi will enter the Thus Come Ones' place of quiescence.*

*The King of All Dharmas is the one word "Amitabha."/ The five periods and the eight teachings are all contained within it.* The teachings are arranged in eight categories, four according to the nature of the teaching: the storehouse teaching, the connecting teaching, the special teaching, and the perfect teaching; and four according to the methods of teaching: sudden, gradual, secret, and unfixed. The five periods are: The Avatamsaka, Agama, Vaipulya, Prajna, and Lotus-Nirvana. These eight teachings and five periods are all included in the one word "Amitabha."

*One who single-mindedly remembers and recites his name / In samadhi will enter the Thus Come One's place of quiescence.* Such a one will definitely go to the Pure Land of Eternal Stillness and Light, the Land of Ultimate Bliss. Living beings in the Dharma-ending Age will be saved by reciting the Buddha's name. And so whoever hopes to be saved should be mindful of the Buddha.

*Speak one sentence less;*
*Recite the Buddha's name one time more.*
*Beat your thoughts to death,*
*And let your Dharma-body come alive.*

Don't look lightly on the Dharma-door of reciting the Buddha's name.

## Contemplate at All Times and Reflect Well

There are four types of mindfulness of the Buddha:

1. *Mindfulness of the Buddha through holding the name.* This involves reciting "Namo Amitabha Buddha" over and over.

2. *Mindfulness of the Buddha through contemplative reflection.* This means contemplating that:

*Amitabha's body is the color of gold.*
*The splendor of his hallmarks has no peer.*
*The light of his brow shines 'round five Mount Sumerus.*
*Wide as the seas are his eyes, pure and clear.*
*Shining in his brilliance by transformation*
*Are countless Bodhisattvas and infinite Buddhas.*
*His forty-eight vows will be our liberation.*
*He enables all those in the nine lotus-stages to reach*
  *the farthest shore.*

This is mindfulness of the Buddha through contemplative reflection.

有觀相念佛，觀相，對著一個阿彌陀佛相，來念南無阿彌陀佛，這就是觀相念佛。清清楚楚的，每一聲佛，口裏念得清清楚楚的，耳朵要聽得清清楚楚的，心裏要想得清清楚楚的，這叫觀相念佛。

又有實相念佛，實相念佛就是參禪。你參禪，說「念佛是誰？」找這個念佛的是誰？那麼這兩個禮拜，念南無阿彌陀佛，等這個佛七完了，我們就要找這個念佛的是誰？一定把它找著，不要丟了。你若丟了那就是迷失路徑，回不了家了！回不了家，就見不著阿彌陀佛了。

## 正信正願正行者

信、願、行，這是修行淨土法門的三資糧。什麼叫資糧呢？就好像你要旅行，到一個什麼地方去，你要預備一點吃的東西，這叫糧；又要預備一點錢，這叫資。資糧，就是你所吃的和你所需要用的錢。你想到極樂世界去，也要有三資糧。這三資糧，就是信、願、行。你首先一定要信，你若沒有信心，那你與極樂世界阿彌陀佛也沒有緣；你若有信心，就有緣了。所以首先要有信。你信，要信自己，又要信他；又要信因，又要信果；又要信事，又要信理。

信，什麼叫信自己呢？你要信你自己決定可以生到極樂世界，你有資格生到極樂世界去；你不要把自己看輕了說：「喔！我造了很多罪業，我不可以生到極樂世界去了。」這個是沒信自己。你造的罪業多不是嗎？這回你就遇到好機會了，什麼好機會呢？可以帶業往生。你造的什麼罪業都可以帶到極樂世界去，而生到西方極樂世界，這叫帶業往生。可是帶業，你又要知道，是帶宿業，不帶新業。宿，就是宿世，是前生的罪業可以帶去；新業，就是將來的罪業。帶宿業，不帶新業，就是帶過去的罪業，不帶將來的罪業。你以前所造所行所作，無論你造了什麼罪業，現在你改過自新改惡向善，那麼以前你所造的罪業，可以帶到極樂世界去，不帶將來的業。

信他，你若信真了西方確實有一個極樂世界，離我們這個世界，有十萬億佛土這麼遠。這是當初阿彌陀佛在沒成佛以前，做法藏比丘的時候，他發願將來造成一個極樂世界，十方的眾生發願願意生，他的國土的話，這不用旁的，只念他的

3. *Mindfulness of the Buddha through contemplative visualization.* This means reciting "Namo Amitabha Buddha" while facing an image of that Buddha. One should recite the phrase very clearly, hear it very clearly, and keep it very clearly in mind.

4. *Mindfulness of the Buddha's Real Appearance.* This is just Chan meditation. When we meditate, we investigate the question, "Who is reciting the Buddha's name?" We recite "Namo Amitabha Buddha" for two weeks, and then we try to find out who is reciting the Buddha's name. We have to find out "who" and not lose the "who." If we lose it, then we won't be able to get home. If we can't get home, we won't see Amitabha Buddha.

## One with Proper Faith, Proper Vows, and Proper Practice

Faith, vows, and practice are the three prerequisites of the Pure Land Dharma-door. One who goes on a journey takes along some food and a little money. One who wishes to go to the Land of Ultimate Bliss needs faith, vows, and the practice of holding the Buddha's name.

Faith is the first prerequisite, for without it one will not have an affinity with Amitabha Buddha in the Land of Ultimate Bliss. You must have faith in yourself, faith in the Land of Ultimate Bliss, as well as in cause and effect, noumenon and phenomenon.

What does it mean to believe in oneself? It is to believe that you certainly have the qualifications necessary to be born in the Land of Ultimate Bliss. You should not take yourself lightly and say, "I have committed so many offenses, I can't be born there." Suppose you have created karma involving heavy offenses, well, now you have a good opportunity: you can "take your karma with you into rebirth." That means that regardless of the offenses you have committed in the past, you can still be reborn in the Land of Ultimate Bliss, and that karma goes along with you. However, you need to know that the karma you can take is karma you have already created, not karma that you continue to create. Karma you have already created is the karma from previous lives. Karma you continue to create will ripen in the future. What you can carry is offenses that come from karma created in the past; what you cannot carry is offenses from karma you create now that will ripen in the future. No matter what you have ever done, not withstanding any kind of offenses, you can now change your faults and reform your conduct, stopping evil and becoming wholesome. Then you can take those previously-created offenses with you to the Land of Ultimate Bliss. But continuing to create karma will keep you from being able to go.

Secondly, you must have faith in the Western Land of Ultimate Bliss which is hundreds of thousands of millions of Buddhalands from here. Before he realized Buddhahood, Amitabha Buddha, as the Bhikshu Dharma Treasury, vowed to create the Land of Ultimate Bliss where living beings of the ten directions who vowed to be born there could gain rebirth by reciting his name. There is no need to do anything else; it is easy, simple, convenient, and

名號，就可以生到這個極樂世界上，其他什麼事情都不費。這是又容易，又簡單，又方便，是又圓融，既不費錢，又不費力，可以說這種的法門是最高的法門，最無上的法門，只念「南無阿彌陀佛」，就可以生到極樂世界去。這就是信他。

又要信因，又要信果。信什麼因呢？要信自己在往昔有善根，所以才能遇到這種的法門；你若沒有善根，就遇不著這個念佛的法門，也遇不著佛一切的法門。因為你有善根，在往昔種這個善因，所以今生遇到這個淨土法門，信、願、持名。你要是不繼續地來栽培你這種的善根，你就不會成就將來的菩提果，所以你必須要信因、信果，信你自己在往昔種下這個菩提之因，將來一定會結菩提的果。好像種田似的，你種上了，這個種子種到地裏頭了，你必須要栽培、灌溉，它才能生長。

信事，信理。什麼叫信事呢？什麼叫信理呢？你要知道阿彌陀佛和我們有大因緣，他一定會接我們去成佛，這是事。信理，為什麼說我們和阿彌陀有大因緣呢？若沒有因緣，我們就遇不著這個淨土法門。阿彌陀佛也就是一切眾生，一切眾生也就是阿彌陀佛；阿彌陀佛是念佛成的阿彌陀佛，我們一切眾生如果能念佛，也可以成阿彌陀佛，這是個理。

有這種理，有這種事，那麼我們依照這個事理去修行，所謂《華嚴經》講的「事無礙法界，理無礙法界，理事無礙法界，事事無礙法界」。我們有這種的法界，我們和阿彌陀佛，在自性裏邊來講，根本是一個的，所以我們就有成佛的這種資格。

阿彌陀佛，是眾生心裏的阿彌陀佛；那麼眾生，也是阿彌陀佛心裏頭的眾生。因為這種關係，也就有事有理。但是這個道理，你必須要相信，你也必須要去實行去，你不能懶惰。譬如我念佛，一天比一天要增加，不是一天比一天要減少。

「信」已經講完了，再講那個「願」。什麼叫願呢？願就是你願意的。你所願意的，你意念就所趨；你的心想要怎樣子，就發一個願。這個願，我們都知道有四種，就是：

眾生無邊誓願度　煩惱無盡誓願斷
法門無量誓願學　佛道無上誓願成

interpenetrating--yet it doesn't cost a thing and doesn't waste energy. This Dharma-door can be considered the highest and most supreme, for if you just recite, "Namo Amitabha Buddha," you will be born in the Land of Ultimate Bliss.

It is also necessary to believe in cause and effect. Believing in cause is to believe that in the past you have planted good roots that now enable you to believe in this Dharma-door. Without good roots, no one can encounter this Dharma-door of reciting the Buddha's name, or any other Dharma-door, for that matter. Because of the good roots you planted in the past, you can now encounter the Pure Land Dharma-door of faith, vows, and holding the name. But if you don't continue to nourish the good roots you planted, then you won't be able to reap the fruition of Bodhi in the future. That is why you must believe in cause and effect; believe that in the past you already planted causes for Bodhi and so in the future you will certainly reap the fruition of Bodhi. The principle is the same as planting a field: the seeds must be watered and nourished before they can grow.

Finally, one must have faith in phenomenon and noumenon. The specific phenomenon is this: Amitabha Buddha has a great affinity with us and will certainly guide us to Buddhahood. The noumenal principle is this: We know the great affinity exists because without it we would not have met the Pure Land Dharma-door. Amitabha Buddha is all living beings and all living beings are Amitabha Buddha. Amitabha Buddha became Amitabha Buddha by reciting the Buddha's name, and if we recite the Buddha's name, we, too, can become Amitabha Buddha.

We should cultivate according to the phenomena and the noumenal principle. *The Avatamsaka Sutra* speaks of four Dharma Realms:

1. The Dharma Realm of Unobstructed Phenomena
2. The Dharma Realm of Unobstructed Noumena
3. The Dharma Realm of Noumena and Phenomena Unobstructed
4. The Dharma Realm of All Phenomena Unobstructed

Considering the four Dharma Realms, and speaking from the standpoint of self-nature, we and Amitabha Buddha are united in one, and therefore we have the qualifications to realize Buddhahood.

Amitabha Buddha is the Amitabha Buddha within the minds of all living beings, and living beings are the living beings within the mind of Amitabha Buddha. Due to this interconnection, there are phenomena and the noumenon. However, you must believe in this principle and energetically practice it by reciting the Buddha's name; you cannot get lazy. Your recitation of the Buddha's name should increase day by day, not decrease.

Having discussed faith, we will now discuss vows. What is a vow? When you want something, when your thoughts tend toward a certain thing, your mind has a wish, then you make a vow. In Buddhism there are four vast vows:

*I vow to save the limitless living beings.*
*I vow to cut off the inexhaustible afflictions.*

這是四弘誓願。過去諸佛和過去的菩薩，都依照這四弘誓願，而證得佛的果位，而行菩薩道。現在的佛、菩薩，和未來的佛，也都是依照這四弘誓願而修行證果。但是發願，你要先有這個信心，你首先必須要信「有極樂世界」，第二要信「有阿彌陀佛」，第三要信「我和阿彌陀佛，一定是有大因緣的，我一定可以生到，極樂世界。」因為有這三種，「信」，然後就可以發願，我發願一定要生到極樂世界去，所以才說「願生西方淨土中」，我願意，生到極樂世界去，不是人家勉強叫我去的，不是有人來一定把我牽著去的。雖然說阿彌陀佛來接我，還是要我自己願意去，願意去親近阿彌陀佛，願意生到極樂世界，花開見佛，願意到極樂世界，見佛聞法，要有這種的「願」，然後就要「行」了。怎麼樣行呢？就是念佛嘛！「南無阿彌陀佛、南無阿彌陀佛、南無阿彌陀佛、南無阿彌陀佛……」噢！好像如救頭然，好像這頭要丟了，有人想要把我這頭給割去，就要那麼著急保護自己的頭。

念佛就是實行這信、願、行，這就是往生極樂世界的一個旅費、資糧。資糧就是旅費，就是所用的錢。這信、願、行，是三資糧 holiday travel money，那個旅行支票。到極樂世界，這也好像旅行似的，但是你要有支票，有錢。

## 念佛念法念僧歌

我們現在念南無阿彌陀佛，這就是每一個人造就我們自己的極樂世界，每一個人莊嚴我們自己的極樂世界，每一個人，成就我們自己的極樂世界。這個極樂世界並沒有十萬億佛土那麼遠，這個極樂世界也真是有十萬億佛土那麼樣子遠；雖然有十萬億佛土那麼遠，但是也沒有出去你我現前這一念的心。因為它沒有出去你我現前這一念的心，所以說也就沒有十萬億佛土那麼遠。也就是在我們的心裏面。這個極樂世界，就是你我眾生本來的真心，你得到你本來的真心，你就生在極樂世界；你沒有明白你自己本來的真心，你就沒有生到極樂世界。阿彌陀佛和我們眾生沒有分彼分此，所以我說這個極樂世界並不是那樣遠，我們一念迴光知道本來是佛，本來是佛就是極樂世界。

*I vow to study the immeasurable Dharma-doors.*
*I vow to realize the supreme Buddha Way.*

All Buddhas and Bodhisattvas of the past, present, and future practiced the Bodhisattva conduct and attained Buddhahood by relying on these four great vows.

But in order to make vows you must have faith. First, believe there is a Land of Ultimate Bliss; secondly, have faith in Amitabha Buddha; thirdly, believe that you and Amitabha Buddha have a great affinity, and that you can certainly be born in the Land of Ultimate Bliss. With faith in these three things, you may then make the vow, "I desire to be born in Amitabha's country." There is a saying,

*"I want to be born in the Western Pure Land."*

"I *want* to be born there. Nobody's forcing me to go; nobody's dragging me there. Although Amitabha Buddha has come to guide me, I'm going as a volunteer because I want to be close to him. I want to be born in the Land of Ultimate Bliss and to see Amitabha Buddha when my lotus flower opens. I want to meet the Buddha and hear the Dharma." These are the vows you need.

Then you must practice. How? Recite the Buddha's name, saying "Namo Amitabha Buddha, Namo Amitabha Buddha..." as if you were trying to save your head from the executioner, running ahead to keep your head.

Faith, vows, and practice are the travel expenses for rebirth in the Land of Ultimate Bliss. They are your ticket.

## The Song of Mindfulness of the Buddha, the Dharma, and the Sangha

As we recite "Namo Amitabha Buddha" we each create and adorn our own Land of Ultimate Bliss. We each accomplish our own Land of Ultimate Bliss which is certainly not hundreds of thousands of millions of Buddhalands from here. Now, the Land of Ultimate Bliss really is hundreds of thousands of millions of Buddhalands away; and yet it doesn't go beyond the very thought we are having right now. Since it's right in our hearts, we say it's not hundreds of thousands of millions of Buddhalands from here. The Land of Ultimate Bliss is the original true heart, the true mind, of every one of us. If you obtain this heart, you will be born in the Land of Ultimate Bliss. If you don't understand your own original true heart, you will not. Amitabha Buddha and living beings are not distinct--that's why I say the Land of Ultimate Bliss is not so far away. In one thought, turn the light within. Know that originally you are the Buddha, and your original Buddhahood is just the Land of Ultimate Bliss.

For this reason, you should cast out your defiled thoughts, your lustful desires, your confusion, jealousy, contrariness, selfishness and plots for personal gain. Be like the Bodhisattvas who benefit everyone and enlighten all beings. Just that is the Land of Ultimate Bliss. Don't you agree that the absence of confusion and false thoughts is the Land of Ultimate Bliss? If it isn't, what is? Don't seek outside.

所以你能把你染污的心去了，就是你的私欲雜念沒有了，沒有妒忌心、沒有障礙心、沒有自私心、沒有利己心。你要學菩薩利人，覺悟一切眾生，這就是極樂世界現前了。你沒有雜念也沒有妄想，你說這不是極樂世界嗎？這要不是極樂世界，你說這是個什麼？所以不要向外去找。各位善知識！你們都是有大智大慧的，都比我聰明，將來你們說法都會比我說得更好，現在不過你們不懂中文，我介紹介紹這個老生常談，這個說的，古古老老的，沒有什麼新奇，但是，將來你們神而明之，再變化出來，那就是妙不可言了。

我來給你們唱個歌：

大聖主　阿彌陀　端嚴微妙更無過
七珍池　華四色　湧金波

這是說，這個四色蓮華，大聖主是誰呢？阿彌陀，所以說「大聖主阿彌陀，端嚴微妙更無過。」他坐在那兒端嚴，阿彌陀佛的樣子，啊！那可太妙了！太好了！沒有比阿彌陀佛，這個佛相再好的了，所以說更無過。「七珍池」，這個七寶的池，也就是七珍池，那裏邊的蓮華有四色，所以才說「七珍池華四色」。「湧金波」，啊！那個七珍池的水，波浪都是金色。

## 青黃赤白妙蓮華

我們這兒念「南無阿彌陀佛」，在西方極樂世界那個七寶池、八功德水裏邊，就有蓮華生出來了。我們念佛念得越多，那個蓮華就長得越大，但是它可沒有開，等到我們臨命終的時候，我們自己這個自性，就生到極樂世界，那個蓮華那兒去。所以，你若想知道，你這個品位的高下，是從上品上生啊？是中品中生啊？是下品下生啊？那就看你念佛念得多少？你念佛念得多，那個蓮華就長得大；你念佛念得少，你那蓮華就小。那麼說：「我不念呢？」你若念念佛就不念了，那蓮華就乾了，就枯去了，就死了。所以這全憑你自己去爭取你自己這個果位。

## 風動水靜演摩訶

「心清水現月，意定天無雲。」你念到這一種念佛三昧的時候，你聽這颰風，也是「南無阿彌

Good and Wise Advisors, you are all ones of great wisdom and great intelligence. You are all more clever than I, and in the future you will explain the Dharma better than I do. But now, because you don't know Chinese, I am introducing you to this old-fashioned tradition. In the future you'll transform it and make it unspeakably wonderful.

Let me sing you a song:

*Amita, the Great Sage and Master,*
*Serene, subtle, wonderful*
*beyond all others...*

*Pools of seven gems,*
*Flowers of four colors and*
*waves of shimmering gold.*

It mentions the four shades of lotus blossoms. Who is the great sage and master? Amitabha Buddha is. *Amita, the Great Sage and Master, serene, subtle, wonderful beyond all others.* He is upright, adorned and very wonderful. There is no image as fine as that of Amitabha Buddha. Within the *Pools of seven gems* are *flowers of four colors.* Not only are the pools filled with seven jewels, the water forms *waves of shimmering gold.*

## Wondrous Green, Yellow, Red, and White Lotus Flowers

The response from our reciting "Namo Amitabha Buddha" here where we are is that in the Land of Ultimate Bliss a lotus forms in the pools of the seven jewels, filled with the waters of eight meritorious virtues. The more we recite the bigger it grows, but it doesn't open. When we die, our intrinsic nature is born in that lotus in the Land of Ultimate Bliss. There are nine grades of lotuses, and how high a grade of lotus we are born in is determined by how much we recited the Buddha's name. Reciting more causes our lotus to grow bigger; fewer recitations result in a small lotus. "Well, suppose I don't recite at all?" If we stop reciting altogether, our lotus will wither and die. The grade of lotus depends on our own effort in reciting the Buddha's name.

## The Blowing Wind and the Calm Waters Proclaim the Mahayana

The pure heart is like the moon in water. The mind in samadhi is like a cloudless sky. If you can recite so completely that you enter the Buddha-recitation samadhi, then hearing the wind, it's "Namo Amitabha Buddha," and hearing the rain, it's "Namo Amitabha Buddha." Every sound you hear recites the Buddha's name. *The water flows, the wind blows, proclaiming the Mahayana...* The Chinese poet Su Dongpo said: *Of the colors of the mountain, none is not the vast, long tongue. Of the sounds of the streams, all are the clear, pure sound.* All the mountain's colors are the Buddha's long

佗佛」的聲音；你聽這下雨，也是「南無阿彌陀佛」的聲音，你聽見一切的聲音，都是在那兒念佛呢！所謂「水流風動演摩訶」，水流的聲音也是南無阿彌陀佛，風動的聲音，也是南無阿彌陀佛。水流風動統統都是念南無阿彌陀佛了，所以那蘇東坡說：「山色無非廣長舌」，這個山啊，這個色呀，都是佛廣長舌相來演說妙法，「溪聲無非清淨音」，溪水流的那個聲音，也都是清淨音，這就是得到念佛的三昧。我在以前寫過這麼一首偈頌，講給大家聽一聽：

念佛能念無間斷　口念彌陀打成片
雜念不生得三昧　往生淨土定有盼
終日厭煩娑婆苦　纏將紅塵心念斷
求生極樂意念重　放下染念歸淨念

這說是「念佛能念無間斷」，你念佛，念得無間斷，一天到晚，都是念佛的聲音，沒有停止的時候。「口念彌陀打成片」，口裏念著，南無阿彌陀佛，常常這麼念，打成一片。「雜念不生得三昧」，你沒有其他的妄想雜念，這就得到念佛的三昧，就得到念佛這個定，念佛的這個受用。「往生淨土定有盼」，你往生西方極樂世界，一定有希望會達到你的希望。「終日厭煩娑婆苦」，一天到晚就討厭這個娑婆太痛苦了。「纏將紅塵心念斷」，因為你知道這娑婆世界是苦了，所以把一切塵世間，這種的快樂都斷了，這種念都斷了，也沒有淫欲心，也沒有好好的心，也沒有爭名的心，也沒有奪利的心，把這個世界的外緣都放下了，看這一切就知道它是假的，所以把這紅塵心念斷了。「求生極樂意念重」，求生極樂世界這個意念非常的重要！「放下染念歸淨念」，你放下這染污的念頭，就是得到清淨的念了。那麼這首偈頌，是說明念佛的這種道理。這八句偈頌雖然聽得很淺顯，但是你細翫其味，對於念佛法門上，是很有幫助的。

# 一心不亂成三昧

打佛七天天念佛，這叫做什麼呢？這叫種佛的種子。你念一句佛，就種下一個佛種；念十句佛，就種下十個佛種。我們天天念百千萬聲佛，就種百千萬這麼多佛的種子。你把這種子種下去，

tongue proclaiming the wonderful Dharma. This is the attainment of the Buddha-recitation samadhi. So I wrote this verse:

> *If you recite the Buddha's name, reciting without cease,*
> *The mouth recites "Amita" and makes things of a piece.*
> *Scattered thoughts do not arise, samadhi you attain.*
> *For rebirth in the Pure Land, your hope is not in vain.*
> *If all day you detest the suffering Saha's pain,*
> *Make rebirth in Ultimate Bliss your mind's essential aim.*
> *Cut off the red dust thoughts within your mind.*
> *Put down impure reflections, and pure thoughts you will find.*

Recite the Buddha's name from morning to night and your confused thoughts will not arise. You will naturally attain the Buddha-recitation samadhi and be reborn in the Land of Ultimate Bliss, according to your will. You know that the Saha world is full of pain and suffering; so cut off worldly pleasures and have no thoughts of sexual desire, craving, or struggling for fame and profit. Put down all worldly concerns and view them as false. Seek rebirth, ultimate bliss; this thought of rebirth is extremely important. This verse clearly explains the principles of reciting the Buddha's name, and if you carefully savor its flavor, you'll find it very helpful.

## One Mind Unconfused Is Samadhi

Reciting the Buddha's name every day in a recitation session, we are planting the seeds of Buddhahood. Each recitation sows a seed; ten recitations sow ten seeds. If you recite a million times a day, you plant that many seeds, and one day they will sprout. Just recite; don't worry about having a scattered mind.

> *When the water-clearing pearl is tossed in muddy water,*
>     *the muddy water becomes clear.*
> *When the Buddha's name enters a confused mind,*
>     *the confused mind attains to the Buddha.*

Reciting the Buddha's name is like throwing a pearl into muddy

將來一定會發生的。你也不要管你，念佛是散心念，是定心念。有這麼兩句話說得很好，說：「清珠投於渾水，渾水不得不清；念佛入於亂心，亂心不得不佛。」

「清珠投於濁水」，有一種清水珠，往水裡一放，無論怎樣混濁的水，它也都會清淨了，澄清了。念佛這個佛號，也就好像那個清水珠似的，放到水裡，水裡也清了。「念佛入於亂心」，我們這個心本來都是亂亂糟糟的，妄想紛飛，妄想不知多少，不是這個妄想生出，就是那個妄想來了；這個走了，那個來了；那個走了，那個又來了，這妄想好像那海裡頭的波浪一樣，沒有停息的時候。那麼你這個佛號入於亂心，「亂心不得不佛」，你這個亂心，也就變成佛心了。因為你念一聲佛，你心裡就有一個佛，你念十聲，就有十個佛，念百聲、千聲、萬聲，念得越多這佛就越多。你念一聲「南無阿彌陀佛」，心裡就有一個佛念。你念佛，佛也就念你，也就好像這無線電似的，你這一念阿彌陀佛，那無線電、那個收音機就收去了，就都有一種感應道交。由這兩句話看來，我們念佛這種的功德，不可思議。你在念佛，就不打其他的妄想；不打其他的妄想，這就是你自性的功德。

## 萬慮皆空入蓮邦

你這個心哪，它忙得很，一天到晚要找工作，不會休息的。所以我們這個心，你若不給它一件事情做，它就總不自在，所以就給它找一個「南無阿彌陀佛」。這一句佛號，也就是參禪。你不要以為臨濟坐那個地方，這麼把眼睛一閉，裝模作樣的，這是參禪。你睜著眼睛，也可以參禪，「行也禪，坐也禪，語默動靜體安然。」行住坐臥都是參禪。古人說「有禪有淨土，猶如戴角虎；現世為人師，來生做佛祖。有禪無淨土，十人九錯路。無禪有淨土，萬修萬人去。」淨土法門這是最容易修的一個法門，在過去諸大菩薩都讚歎修行淨土法門。好像文殊菩薩也讚歎念佛，普賢菩薩在《華嚴經》〈普賢菩薩行願品〉也是攝十方眾生，往生淨土，普賢菩薩也一樣念佛求生淨土，觀世音菩薩也是念佛，大勢至菩薩，也是讚歎念佛法

water so that the muddy water becomes clear. This clear-water pearl can purify even the filthiest water. Recitation of the Buddha's name is just like this pearl. Who can count the false thoughts which fill our minds and succeed one another endlessly like waves on the sea? When the Buddha's name enters a confused mind, the confused mind becomes the Buddha. Recite the name once and there is one Buddha in your mind; recite it ten times and there are ten Buddhas; recite it a hundred times and there are a hundred Buddhas. The more you recite, the more Buddhas there are. Say, "Namo Amitabha Buddha," and there's a Buddha-thought in your mind. When you are mindful of the Buddha, the Buddha is mindful of you. It's like communication by radio. You recite here, and it's received there. There is that kind of response. When you recite the Buddha's name, you don't have any other false thoughts, so your inherent nature has inconceivable merit and virtue.

## When All Thoughts Are Empty, One Enters the Lotus Land

Our restless mind is constantly looking for something to keep it busy. To set it at ease, we give it the task of reciting "Namo Amitabha Buddha." This is also a form of Dhyana meditation. You don't have to sit in lotus posture with your eyes closed, like Dhyana Master Linzi, to investigate Dhyana. You can also meditate with your eyes open.

*Walking is Dhyana, sitting is Dhyana.*
*In speech or silence, movement or stillness,*
*One is always at peace.*

One can investigate Dhyana whether moving or still, awake or asleep. An ancient saying goes:

*With Dhyana and Pure Land, one is like a tiger with horns,*
*A teacher of humans in this life, a Patriarch or Buddha in the next.*
*With Dhyana but not Pure Land, nine out of ten go astray.*
*With Pure Land but not Dhyana, ten thousand cultivate and*
*  ten thousand go.*

門。聽過《楞嚴經》的人，應該知道〈大勢至念佛圓通章〉，説這個念佛法門，説得非常之好。這是過去諸大菩薩，統統都讚歎淨土法門，專修淨土法門。在過去的一切祖師都先參禪，而後念佛，參禪開悟了之後，他就專門念佛，他念一句阿彌陀佛，就有一個阿彌陀佛的化身現出來。這是永明壽禪師就是這樣子。最近的，印光老法師專門提倡念佛法門，虛老也是提倡念佛法門。所以這個念佛法門，是最容易修行的一個法門，最方便、最容易、最簡單、最圓融的一個法門。這個法門是十方諸佛所共讚歎的，你看《彌陀經》上六方諸佛，都出廣長舌相，遍覆三千大千世界，來稱讚這一個法門。如果不是正確的話，這六方諸佛，爲什麼都讚歎。由這一點證明，我們修這個念佛法門是最好的；尤其在末法的時候，人人應該修。可是我們現在是正法的時代，你們不修行這念佛法門呢，那就要拼命地來參禪，不要怕苦！

## 頓悟無生佛身現

這持名念佛是末法時代，最重要的一個法門，所以現在普遍一般人，都相信這個念佛法門。這念佛法門不要把它看輕了。永明壽禪師念一聲「南無阿彌陀佛」，在口裡就有一尊化佛出來，當時有五眼六通的人都看得見。他念一句「南無阿彌陀佛」，從他口裡就生出一尊化佛，所以這念佛的功德是不可思議的。並且你這一念佛，你這裡就放光，啊！你這一放光，那個妖魔鬼怪，他就都遠而避之，跑遠遠的。所以這念佛的功德是非常地不可思議的。

## 妙覺果位自承當

這個念佛法門，我告訴你，你不要把它看得真了，也不要把它看得假了。就在真假之間，你用功用得好了，它就變成真的；用功用得不好，它就變成假了。不單念佛法門是這樣，所有一切法門，都是這樣。所以説：「邪人行正法，正法也是邪；正人修邪法，邪法也變成正了。」這是由人那兒而論。所以我們現在修行拜佛的時候，也要作觀想。觀想什麼呢？觀想「我們這個身體也

The Pure Land Dharma-door is the easiest method of practice. All the great Bodhisattvas have praised it. Manjushri Bodhisattva praises it, and Universal Worthy Bodhisattva, in the "Conduct and Vows of Universal Worthy" chapter of the *Flower Adornment Sutra*, exhorts all living beings to seek rebirth in the Pure Land. He himself recites the Buddha's name and seeks rebirth as well. Guanshiyin Bodhisattva is also mindful of the Buddha, and in the *Shurangama Sutra*, Great Strength Bodhisattva praises this Dharma-door of reciting the Buddha's name and describes how he obtained perfect penetration by means of it. Thus, all the great Bodhisattvas of the past have praised and cultivated the Pure Land Dharma-door.The patriarchs of the past all first investigated Dhyana, became enlightened, and then exclusively recited the Buddha's name. There were those who, every time they recited the Buddha's name, would have a transformation Buddha come out of their mouths. Dhyana Master Yong Mingshou was that way. More recently, Elder Master Yinguang exclusively advocated mindfulness of the Buddha and Elder Master Hsu Yun also advocated reciting the Buddha's name. It is the easiest, most convenient, and most perfect Dharma-door, praised by all Buddhas of the ten directions. Doesn't the *Amitabha Sutra* describe how the Buddhas of the six directions each bring forth a vast and long tongue covering the three thousand great thousand worlds to praise this Dharma-door? This is the best practice, and everyone should take it up especially in the Dharma-ending Age. However, since we are upholding the Proper Dharma Age here, if you choose not to recite the Buddha's name, then you should investigate Dhyana (meditate) as if your lives depended on it! Don't fear suffering!

## Suddenly Awakening to Non-production, One Sees the Buddha

In the Dharma-ending Age, recitation of the Buddha's name is a most important Dharma-door. Don't take it lightly. Every time Dhyana Master Yong Mingshou, the Sixth Patriarch of the Pure Land School, recited the Buddha's name, a transformation Buddha came out of his mouth. Those with the Five Eyes and Six Spiritual Penetrations could see it. When you recite the Buddha's name, you emit a light which frightens all weird creatures and strange ghosts away. They run far, far away and leave you alone. So the merit and virtue of holding the Buddha's name is inconceivable.

## Attaining Wonderful Enlightenment Is Our Personal Responsibility

Don't see the Buddha-recitation as true, and don't regard it as false. If you practice skillfully, it becomes true. If you practice poorly, it turns into something false. All Dharma-doors are like this.

*When deviant people practice proper methods,*
*Proper methods become deviant.*
*When proper people practice deviant methods,*
*Deviant methods turn proper.*

遍滿十方無量諸佛國土，在諸佛國土，在諸佛面前，我們向諸佛頂禮。」作這樣的觀想。你能觀想這個法界，你這個身體也就是法界那麼大，所以才說：

> 若人欲了知，三世一切佛；
> 應觀法界性，一切唯心造。

## 切望諸賢齊努力

念佛法門是最容易修行的一個法門，也是人人能修行的一個法門。這個法門你只念南無阿彌陀佛，將來臨命終的時候，生到西方極樂世界，能蓮花化生，天天聽阿彌陀佛說法，將來成佛。本來說是將來臨命終的時候，念佛生西方極樂世界，我們現在，念他做什麼呢？我們現在也沒死，這念佛是預備將來死的時候才有用的。不錯，死的時候有用；但是你活著的時候要栽培。好像你種一棵樹，這樹現在長有十幾丈高。這十幾丈高的樹不是今天長的，是在以前一天一天長的，長到現在才十幾丈高。你念佛也是這樣子，你現在就能念佛，等到臨命終的時候，就沒有病痛，沒有貪心，沒有瞋心，沒有癡心，心也不亂，一心念佛，阿彌陀佛就會接你去了。你若現在不念，等臨命終，四大分張的時候，你就想不起來念佛了。除非有善知識幫著你，提醒你，叫你念佛可以。如果沒有善知識，你自己想不起來念。所以要在生的時候，就天天念佛，念得得到念佛三昧，打成一片了。所以到臨命終的時候，自然而然你就會念南無阿彌陀佛，你就不會忘記南無阿彌陀佛。你不忘記南無阿彌陀佛，阿彌陀佛也就不會忘記你，所以他就乘大願船來接引你，用金臺接

Proper and deviant depend on the person. When we bow to the Buddha, we should make this contemplation: "My body pervades limitless Buddha lands as I bow before each Buddha in each Buddha land." Contemplate your body as expanding to fill the entire Dharma Realm.

*If people wish to understand*
*All Buddhas of the past, present, and future,*
*They should contemplate the nature of the Dharma Realm:*
*Everything is made from mind alone.*

## May All Virtuous Ones Work Hard Together

Everyone can practice the Buddha-recitation Dharma-door. All you have to do is recite "Namo Amitabha Buddha," and at the end of your life you will be born in a lotus in the Land of Ultimate Bliss, where you will hear Amitabha Buddha speak Dharma and eventually attain Buddhahood. "Death is still far off," you say, "why should we recite the Buddha's name now?" You must develop your skill in reciting right now, so that you will remember to recite at the

---

我們這個心，你若不給它一件事情做，
它就總不自在，所以就給它找一個
「南無阿彌陀佛」。

Our restless mind is constantly looking for something to keep it busy. To set it at ease, we give it the task of reciting "Namo Amitabha Buddha."

宣化老和尚追思紀念專集

引你往生西方極樂世界。你念佛，我念佛，你我念佛爲什麼？了生死，化娑婆，處處極樂阿彌陀。無你我，有什麼，萬物靜觀皆自得。煩惱斷，無明破，跳出三界大愛河。

「你念佛，我念佛，你我念佛爲什麼？」你念佛爲的什麼？我念佛爲的什麼？説一説看！有的愚癡的人就念佛，説：「求佛幫助我，我明天吃點好東西。」有的人念佛，念説：「南無阿彌陀佛、南無阿彌陀佛，你快幫著我，不要這麼冷囉！」這是一種。有的人念南無阿彌陀佛，「我希望沒有一切的麻煩，如意吉祥，平安快樂。」也是爲了這個來念佛。有的人爲了念佛就再不受苦了，那麼這是一種，種種的不同。主要不是爲的這個，爲的什麼呢？爲的「了生死」呀！你們要把這種不一定的生死要了了它。沒有自己、沒有主宰的這種生了死、死了生，要有了主宰。有什麼主宰呢？我們願意活著就活著，願意死就死。願意活著的時候，我天天念南無阿彌陀佛，我不願意，捨我這個壽命，就永遠都活著。願意死，我念著，南無阿彌陀佛，阿彌陀佛就來接我去，生極樂世界。一點問題都沒有，身無病苦，沒有病；心不貪戀，心也不貪什麼；意不顛倒，這個意也不顛倒；如入禪定，就好像入禪定似的，就生到極樂世界去。主要是爲這個。「化娑婆」，把這娑婆世界，也化成極樂世界，變成極樂世界，沒有一切苦，但受一切樂。所以説「處處極樂阿彌陀」：處處都是極樂世界，沒有苦惱的世界。阿彌陀，處處是極樂世界，處處都是阿彌陀佛。「無你我」你念佛念得你也沒有了，我也沒有了，佛也沒有了，什麼也沒有了！説：「那這個太危險了！念得，什麼也沒有了，那不完了嗎？」就怕你完不了，你若真完了那就是解脱了。你沒有真完，所以，就不會完的。你若真完了怎樣呢？「萬物靜觀皆自得」：所有的世間一切一切，你都明白了，皆自得。甚至於烏鴉爲什麼牠黑？白鶴牠爲什麼白？松樹它爲什麼直？荊棘它爲什麼彎？你都明白了。所以叫萬物靜觀皆自得，你都明白了。這時候你都明白就「煩惱斷」了，無明也破了，「跳出三界大愛河」：你跳出去這個欲界、色界、無色界這三界大愛河。這個三界裏邊是個什麼？就是一個好像大愛河似的喔！顛顛倒倒，你又講愛我，我又講愛你，愛來愛去地，愛死了，還不知道醒悟，又等到來生，還是跟著這條路走，總也出不去。現在就要跳出三界大愛河，把這個大愛河跳出去。有的人説：「那我不願跳出去這個愛河。」那你就再等一等囉！這個地方，你停留下來，就是在這

time of death. Just as a tree must grow for many years before it becomes a hundred feet tall, you must begin practicing reciting the Buddha's name now so that when it comes time to die, you will be able to recite single-mindedly, without sickness, greed, hatred, stupidity, or confusion, and Amitabha Buddha will come to guide you. If you don't recite now, you won't remember to when your body starts to fall apart at the time of death, unless a Good and Wise Advisor is there to remind you and help you. Therefore, it's important to recite the Buddha's name every day and enter the Buddha-recitation samadhi, so that reciting will come naturally at the time of death and you won't forget. Or if you are unable to recite Namo Amitabha Buddha, Amitabha Buddha won't forget you and so he will come riding the ship of his great vows, receive you onto a golden dais, and take you to the Land of Ultimate Bliss. He won't forget about you.

*You are mindful of the Buddha,*
*I am mindful of the Buddha;*
*Why are we mindful of the Buddha?*
*To end birth and death, to transform the Saha,*
*So that everywhere is ultimate bliss, everywhere Amitabha.*
*With no you and no me, what is there?*
*In still contemplation, the myriad things are understood.*
*Cut off afflictions, smash through ignorance;*
*Leap out of the Triple Realm's great river of love.*

Foolish people recite the Buddha's name, hoping the Buddha will give them some good food to eat. Some recite, "Namo Amitabha Buddha, Namo Amitabha Buddha, please give us some warmer weather!" Other people recite hoping to obtain good luck and happiness, or to escape problems and suffering. The primary purpose of reciting the Buddha's name is to end birth and death, that is, to have control over our own births and deaths. If we want to live, we can recite Amitabha Buddha's name day after day and live forever. If we want to die, then we recite "Namo Amitabha Buddha" and the Buddha will come to receive us. We will be free of illness, greed, and delusion, as if entering samadhi, and we will be reborn in the Land of Ultimate Bliss with no problem at all. Secondly, if we recite the Buddha's name, we can transform the Saha world itself into the Land of Ultimate Bliss, where beings endure none of the sufferings and enjoy every happiness.Recite to the point that you, me, the Buddha, and everything else disappears. "That's too dangerous! If everything is gone, won't we all be finished?" you say. It's only to be feared that you won't be finished. If you are truly "finished," then you are free. At that time, you will understand the myriad phenomena of the world, such as why crows are black and cranes are white, why pines are straight and brambles are twisted. Since you understand everything, afflictions are cut off, ignorance is smashed, and you leap out of the great river of love that courses through the Desire, Form, and Formless Realms. In the Triple Realm, we are so deluded by love, loving each other until we die, and

個地方，生了又死，死了又生，生死輪迴，一生不如一生，一死不如一死。所以就往下跑，跑來跑去，就跑到河底下，就上不來了，就淹得更死了。眞是淹死了！這個淹死是什麼呢？就是墮落到極點，就性化靈殘了。或者變一個小蟲子，或者變一個小螞蟻，或者變一個蚊蟲，變這個小小的東西，這智慧也小了，福報也沒有了，也很容易死，又很容易生。所以這叫一生不如一生，一死不如一死。

## 西方極樂是君家

你要明白世界無論什麼事情，都不是一定的，若有一定的，那是已經做成的；沒有成事實的，就不會有一定，就可以有轉變的。好像我們每一個人本來沒有生西方極樂世界的資格，但是你一念「南無阿彌陀佛」，每一個人都有生西方極樂世界的資格了，就看你念不念。你若念，做不到的也能做得到，就是生西方極樂世界本來很困難的，但是也能做到；你若不念呢？做到的也做不到了。你若不念「南無阿彌陀佛」，本來可以生極樂世界，你一念就生了，但是你不念，就不生了，就做不到了。所以這世間的事情是無有定法的，《金剛經》上說的，沒有定法，是名阿耨多羅三藐三菩提，這就是無上正等正覺一個方法。我們要發大勇猛心，不怕苦、不怕難、不怕凍、不怕餓，勇猛向前，走到極樂世界爲止。我們念「南無阿彌陀佛」，這才是眞的。我們念「南無阿彌陀佛」，了生死是最要緊的。

then coming back for another round, never waking up enough to escape. Now, however, we want to leap out of the river of love. "I don't want to," someone says. Then you can undergo a few more rounds of birth and death. With each round, you sink lower and lower, until you sink to the very bottom of the river of love! Drowning represents your soul being split into many small creatures, such as mosquitoes and ants. These insects have low intelligence, few blessings, and very short lives.

## The Western Land of Ultimate Bliss Is Your Home

In this world, nothing is fixed before it happens. The future can always be changed. For example, before we recited "Namo Amitabha Buddha," we didn't have the qualifications to be reborn in the Land of Ultimate Bliss. Once we recite, we become qualified. Even if originally it would have been difficult for you to be reborn in the West, once you recite it becomes possible. On the other hand, even if you could be reborn in the West with a single recitation, if you don't recite once, you won't get there. So nothing is fixed. The *Vajra Sutra* says, "There are no fixed dharmas. This is called Anuttarasamyaksambodhi." That is the method for attaining unsurpassed, proper and equal, right enlightenment. We should advance courageously, undaunted by suffering, difficulty, cold, and hunger, until we arrive at the Land of Ultimate Bliss. Reciting "Namo Amitabha Buddha" is what really counts. In reciting, the most important thing is to end birth and death.

我們念「南無阿彌陀佛」，
　　這才是眞的。
我們念「南無阿彌陀佛」，
　　了生死是最要緊的。

Reciting "Namo Amitabha Buddha" is what really counts. In reciting, the most important thing is to end birth and death.

宣化老和尚追思紀念專集

# 觀音 觀音 觀世音
# GUANYIN, GUANYIN, GUANSHIYIN

宣公上人講述
Lectures by Venerable Master Hua

# 娑婆有幸聞觀音

觀世音菩薩和這個娑婆世界的眾生，有大因緣，在中國有句俗話說：「家家觀世音，處處阿彌陀。」爲什麼有這句俗話呢？就因爲觀世音菩薩和阿彌陀他們這種慈悲，深入到一般人的心裏去了，所以人人都知道有觀世音菩薩，人人都知道有阿彌陀佛。（觀就是觀察，世是世間，音是音聲；觀世音就是觀察世間所有的音聲。）

觀世音菩薩在佛教裏頭，他是佔很重要的地位，觀世音菩薩有的人說他是中國人，有的人又說他是外國人，有的人又說他是男人，有的人又說他是女人。現在我告訴各位，觀世音菩薩他也不是中國人，也不是外國人，他是哪會兒的人呢？他是盡虛空遍法界，哪個地方都是他，哪個地方也都不是他，他是隨類應現，應該以什麼身得度的，它就現什麼身而爲眾生說法，所以他沒有一定的。這觀世音菩薩他也現佛身來度一切應該成佛的眾生，他也現菩薩身來度一切應該成菩薩的眾生，他也現天上的天王身來度一切眾生；總而言之這個眾生應該以什麼身得度的，觀世音菩薩就是現什麼身，來給這一類的眾生說法。在佛教裏頭觀世音菩薩，他各處去教化眾生，要度一切眾生發菩提心，他就先看這個眾生歡喜什麼，他先先就投其所好；他一投其所好，那麼這個人就歡喜了，所以他說什麼法，這個人也都歡喜聽，於是乎就把這個眾生度了。所以說觀世音菩薩，他也不一定是男身，也不一定是女身，他也是男身，也是女身，不過都是變化的。那麼觀世音菩薩的本體呢，他是如如不動的，和佛是一樣的；並且觀世音菩薩在很久以前，他已經成佛了，他的名字叫正法明如來，所以現在他化菩薩身來教化眾生。

在佛教裏，他現菩薩身，在外道裏邊，他也現外道的身，所以往往有一個穿著白衣服的，在耶穌教裏就說他是聖母。其實這個聖母是誰？也就是觀世音菩薩去教化那一類的眾生，他去現那麼一個穿白衣服的人的樣子，那麼一般的耶穌教就說這是聖母其實也就是觀世音菩薩，去顯現令這個眾生來發心，無論早晚都會令他明白佛法；明白佛法之後就發菩提心，這是觀世音菩薩他這種妙用無窮的一種不可思議的境界。

觀音菩薩他是慈悲喜捨的觀世音菩薩，他是要普度眾生的，觀世音菩薩有七難二求、十四無畏、十九說法、三十二應身。那麼你若是沒有小孩子，你願意求男孩子，就會得到男孩子；願意求女孩子，就得到女孩子，這叫二求，求男、求女，都會遂心滿願的。所以在這個，觀音七的期間，無論誰要發什麼願，求什麼果報，這一

# How Lucky We Are to Hear Guanyin's Name in the Saha World

Guanshiyin (Avalokiteshvara) Bodhisattva has a great affinity with living beings in the Saha world. There is a saying in China, "Guanshiyin in every household, Amitabha in every place." This shows that everyone knows Guanshiyin Bodhisattva and Amitabha (the name means "Limitless Light" and "Limitless Life") Buddha, that their compassion has deeply entered people's hearts. *Guan* means "Contemplate"; *shi* means "world"; *yin* means "sounds." Thus the name means "Contemplating the World's Sounds."

Within Buddhism, Guanshiyin Bodhisattva holds a very important position. Some people say that Guanshiyin Bodhisattva is Chinese and some say he is a Westerner; some say the Bodhisattva is male and some say female. But now I am informing all of you that Guanshiyin Bodhisattva is neither Chinese nor Western, neither male nor female. Well, then, where does he come from? He fills empty space and pervades the Dharma Realm; he is in every place and yet not in any place. He appears according to what kind of body is needed to save each particular category of beings. He manifests in whatever physical form is appropriate to speak Dharma for beings; thus his identity is flexible. Guanshiyin Bodhisattva appears in the form of a Buddha to save those who are ready to become Buddhas. He appears as a Bodhisattva to save those who should become Bodhisattvas. He appears as a heavenly king to speak Dharma for beings in the heavens.

Within Buddhism, Guanshiyin Bodhisattva is one who goes about everywhere teaching and transforming living beings, inspiring them to bring forth the Bodhi mind. He first sees what a particular being likes and then makes them happy with what they like. Once they are happy, they will like to listen to the Dharma he speaks and gradually he will be able to rescue them. That's why I say that Guanshiyin Bodhisattva is not necessarily male or female; he could be male or he could be female. In any case those are just transformations. As to Guanshiyin Bodhisattva's own body, he is in a state of unmoving Suchness—he is just like the Buddhas. Anyway, Guanshiyin Bodhisattva already became a Buddha a long time ago, by the name of Right Dharma Brightness. He simply appears as a Bodhisattva in order to teach and transform living beings.

In Buddhism, he appears as a Bodhisattva; in other religions he often appears clad in white robes. In Christianity, he is the Holy Mother; he appears as the Holy Mother to teach and transform a certain category of beings. He appears in white robes and Christians call her Mother Mary, but actually she is Guanshiyin Bodhisattva manifesting in that form to inspire beings to bring forth a resolve that will lead them sooner or later to understand the Buddhadharma.

定會成功的。因為觀世音菩薩他是有求必應，誰求他他
就答應誰。你願意求他出家也可以，你願意求他不出家
又可以，你願意求他成佛還可以，所以觀世音菩薩是大
慈大悲的。你向他面前求什麼事情，他都不會令你失望
的，一定使你遂心滿願。所以我們舉行這個觀音七，你
門誰願意求什麼都可以，你就是求男得男，求女得女，
求富貴得富貴，求長命得長命。不過話又說回來，這些
個都是有漏的快樂，你要找一個無漏的快樂是好的。無
漏的快樂是什麼？就是成佛。世間的富貴榮華都是有漏
的，有漏的都是有盡的、有了的；無漏的是無窮盡、沒
有了的。所以我們現在想要得到沒有了的這種果，就是
念多幾聲觀世音菩薩。

## 勇猛精進一心念

念觀音菩薩要不停止地念，要接接連連地念，好像那
個流水一樣，流水沒有停止的時候，我們念觀音菩薩也
要這樣，念得打成一片，行也是念觀世音菩薩，坐也是
念觀音菩薩，臥也是念觀音菩薩，站那個地方，還是
念觀音菩薩。要特別注意，不要忘了觀世音菩薩這個名
號，念茲在茲的，念念不忘，念念還要明明白白，清清
楚楚，不是說一邊念一邊睡覺，或者一邊念一邊打妄想
，不是那樣子。要專一其心來念觀世音菩薩，旁的什麼
也不想了，只是念「南無觀世音菩薩」這一句菩薩的名
號，行住坐臥都不離開這觀世音菩薩的名號。

你念觀世音菩薩，觀世音菩薩就會念你。你念觀世音
菩薩，希望觀世音菩薩，慈悲普度；那麼觀世音菩薩念
你，是要你離苦得樂，要你災消病散，罪滅福生，要你
菩提增長，道心圓成，這是觀世音菩薩的希望。我們應
該不辜負，觀世音菩薩慈悲護念我們的這種恩澤，我們
應該，把什麼都擺脫開，只是念觀世音菩薩。你若能這
樣念觀世音菩薩，那觀世音菩薩和你一定在一起，行住
坐臥都跟著你，都來加持你，令你業障消除，善根增長
。我們得到觀世音菩薩加被，我們必須要更發菩提心，
更存一種堅固的心，勇猛精進，一時一刻也不可以馬虎
。所以不要講那麼多話，你們不講話也可以，不吃飯也
可以，不睡覺更好，但是不能不修行，人人都要修行。
我們希望天天打觀音七，我們希望時時刻刻都打觀音七
，我們希望年年月月，甚至於在每一個大劫裏邊，都是
在念觀世音菩薩，修這種不可思議的法門，那才對了。
不要以為這個七打完就得到解放了，我們一天沒有開悟
，一天也得不到真正的自由；一天你得不到真正的自由

Once they understand the Buddhadharma, they will bring forth the resolve for Bodhi. These are the endless miraculous functions and inconceivable states of Guanshiyin Bodhisattva.

Guanshiyin Bodhisattva uses kindness, compassion, joy, and giving to save all living beings. He saves beings from the seven difficulties, responds to two kinds of seeking, has fourteen kinds of fearlessness, speaks Dharma in nineteen ways, and has thirty-two response bodies. If childless people seek sons or daughters, their wishes will be granted. These are the two kinds of seeking. Therefore, in a Guanyin recitation session, any vow can be fulfilled and any result can be obtained, because Guanyin Bodhisattva responds to all requests. You may seek to leave the home-life, to remain a layperson, or to become a Buddha. Guanshiyin Bodhisattva has great kindness and compassion, and will not disappoint you no matter what you ask for. He'll definitely fulfill your wishes. Therefore, during the Guanyin session, you may seek whatever you like. Whether you seek a son, a daughter, wealth, or long life, you will be able to obtain them. But these are forms of happiness subject to "outflows"; you ought to seek the nonoutflow happiness of Buddhahood. Worldly riches, honor, and glory all come to an end, but nonoutflow happiness is endless and infinite. Let's recite Guanshiyin Bodhisattva's name more in order to realize an everlasting fruition.

## With Vigor and Courage, Recite with One Heart

Our recitation of Guanyin Bodhisattva's name should continue nonstop, like an ever flowing stream, until everything becomes one. Walking, standing, sitting, and lying down, we recite the name of Guanyin. We must pay close attention and not forget Guanyin's name in thought after thought. Each recitation must be clear and distinct; and we certainly shouldn't fall asleep or have idle thoughts while reciting. We must recite single-mindedly, thinking of nothing but the words "Namo Bodhisattva Guanshiyin," not leaving the name whether we are walking, standing, sitting, or lying down.

If you are mindful of Guanshiyin Bodhisattva, he will be mindful of you. You recite Guanshiyin Bodhisattva's name hoping that he will compassionately save all beings; he recites your name hoping that you can leave suffering and attain bliss, be free from disasters and sickness, cancel offenses and create blessings. He hopes you will increase in Bodhi and perfect your mind for the Way. We shouldn't let Guanshiyin Bodhisattva down. He is so compassionate and mindful of us, we ought to set everything else aside and concentrate on reciting his name. If we can do that, he will

，你就不能發退悔的心。人人要記得、要想，想什麼？「趕快再打觀音七，打觀音七我好可以用用功。」

我們天天念觀世音菩薩，就好像我們要穿衣服，你必須要用你的手，把那個衣服拿起來穿上，這「觀世音菩薩」就等於你兩隻手拿著，穿衣服一樣。你吃飯的時候，也必須要用筷子，或者用刀叉，或者用碗，你要張開口來吃才能飽；那麼念觀音菩薩也像這個一樣的，你若不念，你這法身也不會飽；念觀音菩薩，在你這個法身裏邊也會飽了，不會饑餓了。你念觀音菩薩，也就好像你要進房間裏頭去休息，你要用鑰匙對這個鎖，一開，把房門就開了，你就能進去休息；那麼觀音菩薩也就好像這個鎖和鑰匙是一樣的，我們每一個人都好像在監獄裏頭，那個監獄的鎖就是觀世音菩薩。你念一聲觀世音菩薩，把你那無明鎖就開開一點，你越念，這個鎖就越有開的機會。這個鎖就是我們的無明，你用觀世音菩薩來開這個鎖，這就是智慧，用這個觀世音菩薩的智慧鑰匙，來開我們自己這個無明的鎖，無明鎖一開了，你豁然開悟了。在儒教裏頭叫豁然貫通焉！這貫通焉還沒有完全開悟，他只是開一部份。那麼佛豁然開悟，從無始劫以來的生死根本就會斷了，這無明會破了。

觀音菩薩會尋聲救苦，他和我們娑婆世界所有的眾生都特別有緣，這個緣非常地深，所以有的人常常得到觀世音菩薩的加被，放光攝受，我們為什麼沒有得到呢？就因為我們心裏不誠，雜念很多，雖然你在這兒念觀音菩薩，你的心各處跑去了，各處隨著這個境界轉，打這種種不清淨的妄想，所以把光陰也都空過去了。你要知道我們人生是有限的，在這個這麼好的機會，再若不好好用功，把這個好機會錯過去了，你再想用功更不容易了。

所以各位要珍惜這個時間，不要把光陰都空過了，不要那麼隨幫唱影，不要那麼樣子一點也不注意，這個道場成就，你們各人來用功修行，就是希望你們能誠心來念觀音菩薩。你念觀音菩薩，念得風也吹不透了，雨也打不漏了，那時候得到念佛三昧，念觀音三昧，得到這種正定正受，那才是我們的本份盡了，所以這一點各位不要忽略了。

## 千手千眼大慈悲

我們在這兒朝拜，觀世音菩薩萬聖之尊，我們要對觀世音菩薩認識，觀世音菩薩現在這個相，是一個千手千眼的法相，那麼觀世音菩薩是不是只有千手千眼呢？不是的。觀世音菩薩有無量手、無量眼。因為他

definitely be with us whether we are moving or still, awake or asleep. He will aid us, destroy our karmic obstacles, and make our good roots grow. Having received Guanshiyin Bodhisattva's aid, we should strengthen our resolve for Bodhi and advance vigorously without slacking off for a moment. We shouldn't chatter so much. If you decide not to talk, eat, or sleep, that's fine; but don't fail to cultivate. Everyone has to cultivate. We should regard every moment and every day as a Guanyin session. In fact, we should wish to cultivate the inconceivable Dharma door of reciting Guanyin Bodhisattva's name every month, every year, and every great eon. Don't think that you're free once the session is over, because you are not truly free unless you become enlightened. So don't entertain the thought of retreating. We should all be wishing for another Guanyin session so we can continue to develop our skill.

The function of reciting Guanyin's name can be compared to using our hands in getting dressed and when eating. The name "Guanshiyin Bodhisattva" is equivalent to your hands, which you use to put on clothes. When you eat, you must use chopsticks or a fork to bring the food to your mouth; likewise, you must recite Guanyin Bodhisattva's name in order to feed your Dharma body.

Reciting Guanshiyin Bodhisattva's name is also analogous unlocking a door. We are locked up in the prison of our ignorance, and Guanyin's name is the key to the prison's door. Each time we recite it, the lock of ignorance opens up a little. The more we recite, the more the lock opens. We use Guanyin Bodhisattva's key of wisdom to open our lock of ignorance. The moment it opens, we gain sudden enlightenment. Confucianism speaks of a state of sudden comprehension, but that is only a partial, not a total, enlightenment. With sudden enlightenment, one breaks through ignorance and cuts off the very source of births and deaths without beginning.

Guanyin Bodhisattva listens to the sounds of living beings and rescues them from suffering. He has particularly deep affinities with the living beings in our Saha world. There are many cases in which Guanyin Bodhisattva has protected people and shined his light upon them. Why haven't we obtained such a response? Our minds are not sincere. We have too many scattered thoughts. On the one hand we recite his name, but on the other hand our mind chases after external states and strikes up all kinds of impure thoughts, so we waste all our time. We should realize that life is short. If we don't cultivate seriously right now, we might not have another chance.

Cherish the time and don't let it go by in vain. Don't just mindlessly follow the crowd. You ought to take advantage of this opportunity to cultivate at a monastery by sincerely reciting Guanyin's name. You will have completed your work only when you attain the Guanyin Recitation Samadhi, the state of proper concentration which cannot be disturbed by the gusty winds or the driving rain. Don't overlook that point.

有無量手，所以能用他無量手把眾生從苦海裏邊拉出來，接引到一個快樂的彼岸上；他用萬眼、無量眼來看所有的一切眾生。誰若有苦難對於他有緣的眾生，他一定不會不管這個閒事的，一定會救助這個眾生。

觀世音菩薩，是最勤的一個菩薩，最精進的一位菩薩，不願意休息的一位菩薩。他願意一天到晚都救度眾生，他不怕工作多，不怕眾生困難多。所以可以說是一個最忙的菩薩，最勤的菩薩，不是一個懶菩薩，不是一個歡喜休息的菩薩。他一個手救人救得少；二個手救人呢，也救得有限，所以他就要千手千眼——千手，可以救大千世界的眾生；千眼，可以照顧大千世界的眾生——他所照顧的眾生，都是受苦的眾生；他所救度的眾生，也是有災難的眾生。一切眾生在困苦艱難的時候就想起來了，想起誰來了？想起這個大慈悲父來了，想起這大慈悲母來了。大慈悲父是誰？觀世音菩薩；大慈悲母是誰？觀世音菩薩。想起來怎麼樣呢？他就念了「南無觀世音菩薩，南無觀世音菩薩，……」，眾生有災難的時候，一念「南無觀世音菩薩」，觀世音菩薩就用千眼看見了，就用這個智慧眼看見了，用這個智慧耳聽見了，於是乎就用智慧手救眾生來了。因為眾生不是分開不同的時候有災難，在同時有百千萬億眾生都有災難，所以在同時有百千萬億眾生稱念「觀世音菩薩」，這百千萬億眾生同時都得到解脫，同時都得到快樂。

有一些個難民，今天拿來一個觀世音菩薩的法相，據說這些難民在難民船上，船長從虛空裏頭攝這個相。他這個照觀世音菩薩在那兒清清楚楚地在雲端裏頭現出一個法相來。那麼由這個就知道觀世音菩薩是「千處祈求千處應，苦海常作渡人舟。」不過我們人對觀世音菩薩還沒有深深地認識，深深地信，生一種信心。所以有的時候，我們對觀世音菩薩敷衍不生信，那麼當我們在七難之中，觀音菩薩也就不管我們的閒事。我們如果拿出真心來，信仰觀世音菩薩，觀世音菩薩，對我們一切的問題，一定不會袖手旁觀的。

## 解三毒苦化眾難

為什麼要念觀音菩薩呢？因為觀音菩薩，以前發過願，發過什麼願？他說：若人多瞋、若人多貪、若人多癡，你無論有貪心也好，有瞋心也好，有癡心也好，你若能常常念觀世音菩薩，恭敬觀世音菩薩，把你的貪心不知不覺也會丟了，把你的瞋心不知不覺也會沒有了，把你的癡心在不知不覺之中也會忘了，想起來什麼呢？想起來定力了，想起來戒力了。我們人人

## A Thousand Hands and A Thousand Eyes Bestow Great Compassion

Let us get to know Guanshiyin Bodhisattva, the most venerated of sages, as we pay homage to him. The Bodhisattva's image shows a thousand hands and a thousand eyes, but actually, Guanshiyin Bodhisattva's hands and eyes are infinite. With his infinite hands, he pulls living beings out of the sea of suffering and sets them on the blissful other shore. With his infinite eyes, he beholds all living beings and rescues those who are in difficulty or danger. He will not ignore any living being with whom he has an affinity.

Guanshiyin Bodhisattva is a most diligent Bodhisattva. He is extremely vigorous and doesn't ever rest. He rescues living beings all day long. No matter how much trouble living beings get into, he doesn't mind the work of saving them. He is a tremendously busy and energetic Bodhisattva, not a lazy one who likes to rest. One or two hands can't save very many people, so he has a thousand hands to rescue living beings from disasters and a thousand eyes to take care of suffering living beings in the great thousand world system.

When living beings are in trouble, they think of their greatly compassionate father and mother, Guanshiyin Bodhisattva. Then they start reciting, "Namo Guanshiyin Bodhisattva, Namo Guanshiyin Bodhisattva." When living beings who are in difficulty recite "Namo Guanshiyin Bodhisattva," the Bodhisattva sees them with his thousand eyes. He beholds them with his wisdom eyes, hears them with his wisdom ears, and uses his wisdom hands to save them. Even if millions of living beings who are in difficulty call out to Guanshiyin Bodhisattva at the same time, the Bodhisattva can rescue them and make them all happy.

Today some refugees brought a photograph which they say was taken when they were on the refugee boat. In this shot of the sky, taken by the boat captain, a distinct image of Guanshiyin Bodhisattva appears at the fringe of the clouds. From this, we know that Guanshiyin Bodhisattva responds to prayers everywhere, sailing the sea of suffering and crossing people over. However, if we have not yet deeply recognized Guanshiyin Bodhisattva and produced a deep and sincere faith in him, Guanshiyin Bodhisattva may not be aware of us when we are in trouble. If we bring forth true faith, then Guanshiyin Bodhisattva certainly won't ignore us when we are in trouble.

## He Neutralizes the Three Poisons and Resolves All Difficulties

Why should we recite Guanshiyin Bodhisattva's name? It's because he made vows in the past that if people have much greed, much anger, or much stupidity, and if they constantly

應該常常念恭敬觀世音菩薩，那麼不單能去你的貪瞋癡，又能把你真正的災難也免去了。所以能常念恭敬觀世音菩薩，設入大火火不能燒；設入大水水不能淹，你看這個力量有多大！所以這七天念觀世音菩薩，無論哪一個若能參加圓滿的七天，那個功德不可思議的，你一切不如意的事情都會沒有了。

觀世音菩薩雖然能令你入火不燒，入水不溺，可是你若有一種信心，真真地信觀世音菩薩，沒有頭髮絲那麼多疑惑心，就能得到靈感；你若有一種疑惑心：「他講是這樣講，是不是真的？」真的也變成假的；你若沒有疑惑心，假的也會真，這個靈感還是在你的心裏，不是在觀世音菩薩那裏。你有了麻煩就念「南無觀世音菩薩」，那個麻煩就跑了。麻煩就怕觀世音菩薩，因為觀世音菩薩就能觀那個麻煩的因，一看見這個麻煩因，麻煩因就跑了，所以這是一個最好的方法，也是一個最妙的方法。我講這方法，一講出來你說：「哦！那我也知道念觀世音菩薩。」但是你到時候麻煩來了，你就不會用，就忘了。麻煩一來，你就知道憂愁了：「啊！怎麼辦呢？」就沒有法子了。

《法華經》〈觀世音菩薩普門品〉說得很明明白白：「若多貪欲」這個欲也就是淫欲，你若是淫欲心太重，就要常念恭敬觀世音菩薩。你這種情感太重了，麻煩一來，不知道怎麼好？甚至於要發顛發狂的樣子。那你就不要著急，慢慢等一等，你念南無觀世音菩薩，南無觀世音菩薩⋯⋯，不要大喊著念，要在你裏頭念，心裏頭有個南無觀世音菩薩。你這個心的聲音，觀世音菩薩的耳朵已經可以聽見了，你心裏沒有說出口來，他能知道，說：「哦！這個可憐的孩子，現在自己情感這麼重，沒有法子控制情感，現在找我幫忙啦！好了，我幫幫他的忙囉！」把他情感的這種麻煩就給減去一點就輕了。「若多瞋恚」，說這個人脾氣太大了，你要發脾氣的時候，你千萬先等一等再發脾氣，先念幾聲觀世音菩薩，然後再發脾氣。你念「南無觀世音菩薩⋯⋯」，在心裏念了幾聲，脾氣不知道跑到什麼地方去了？再找也找不著了，沒有了。你說這是妙法、不是妙法？但是妙法可是妙法，你聽這麼多經，還沒有領會這個意思。現在我對你一講，你覺得很清楚：「哦！這個有這麼大的靈感。」豈止這麼大靈感，比這個還大。「若多愚癡」，愚癡的病誰都有，常念觀世音菩薩，便得離癡。

《法華經》是釋迦牟尼佛說的，讚歎觀世音菩薩，如果觀世音菩薩，沒有這種的大威神力，佛怎麼會讚歎他呢？佛怎麼會隨隨便便說：某一個菩薩有什麼功

recite his name and worship him, their greed, anger, and stupidity will disappear even before they realize it. They will forget about these poisons and think instead of samadhi and precepts. And so, if we constantly recite and venerate Guanshiyin Bodhisattva, not only will our greed, anger, and stupidity vanish, but we will be safe from all disasters. If we enter a blazing fire, we will not be burned. If we fall into deep waters, we won't drown. That's how incredibly powerful his name is! If we can recite Guanshiyin Bodhisattva's name for a full seven days, we will gain inconceivable merit and escape all misfortunes.

Even though Guanshiyin Bodhisattva can protect you from being burned by fire or drowned by water, you must have total faith in him to obtain such a response. If you have doubts: "That's what they say, but is it for real?" then even the true will become false. If you have no doubts, then the false can become true. The response occurs in your own mind, not on Guanshiyin Bodhisattva's side.

If you encounter something troublesome, just recite "Namo Guanshiyin Bodhisattva" and the trouble will go away. Troubles fear Guanshiyin Bodhisattva, because he can contemplate them and find their cause; as soon as he discovers their cause, the troubles go away. This is a most wonderful method, the best way to solve problems. You say, "Okay, I'll recite Guanyin's name next time." But when the time comes and you are faced with a problem, you fret and worry and forget all about this method.

The chapter on "Guanshiyin Bodhisattva's Universal Door" in the *Lotus Sutra* says very clearly that "Those with much greed and desire," people who have heavy sexual desire, should constantly and reverently recite the Bodhisattva's name. Emotional people are easily flustered by problems. When you encounter trouble, don't get nervous. Calm down and recite "Namo Guanshiyin Bodhisattva, Namo Guanshiyin Bodhisattva." You don't have to shout the name, just recite it in your mind. Guanshiyin Bodhisattva's ear can pick up the voice in your mind. He'll hear you and say, "This poor child can't control his emotions and he's asking me for help." Then he helps you to calm your emotions.

The Sutra also says "Those with much anger and hatred," people with big tempers, should recite. If you are about to lose your temper, hold on! Before you explode, first recite "Namo Guanshiyin Bodhisattva" in your mind a few times. When you have done so, you won't be able to find your anger anymore. It'll be gone. Now wouldn't you say this is wonderful Dharma? Wonderful it may be, but you didn't understand it before. Now that I've told you, you think, "These are great responses!" Actually, there are even greater ones. "Those with much stupidity" can get rid of it by constantly reciting Guanshiyin Bodhisattva's name.

Shakyamuni Buddha spoke this chapter of the *Lotus Sutra* to praise Guanshiyin Bodhisattva. Now, would the Buddha

德，有什麼道業，有什麼本領。佛不會隨便講的，一定是有這種的本領，有這種的感應，所以佛才向我們所有的眾生來介紹，就是你有什麼困難的問題不能解決了，給你找出來一個方法。

那麼我今天對你們所講的方法，以前講過很多次了，不過沒有講得這麼明顯，沒有講得這麼淺白，現在講給你們聽，你們就會用了。有人這樣講說是：「我就歡喜這個貪欲，所以我不念觀世音菩薩；我就歡喜發脾氣，我也不歡喜念觀世音菩薩；我就歡喜愚癡，所以我也不歡喜念觀世音菩薩。」那你可以念念你自己啊！看看你自己是個什麼？只要能認識你自己了，那也就會認識觀世音菩薩。你為什麼要念觀世音菩薩？就因為你沒有認識你自己。那麼你自己有這個貪欲也覺得不是麻煩，有這個瞋恨也覺得不是麻煩，有這個愚癡也覺得不是麻煩，所以不願念觀世音菩薩。你不願意念這是個什麼？這就是個麻煩，就是你的麻煩。你因為有麻煩，所以你不願意念觀世音菩薩。

講到這個地方，你要是不怕麻煩的話，什麼也不要學；你若怕麻煩就要學佛法；學佛法，就要學念觀世音菩薩。所以你若不想認識你自己說：「我自己不是個人，所以我不需要念佛、念法、念僧。」那就很快會變鬼了，因為你不想做人嘛！就變鬼了！那時候你若想念觀世音菩薩，還可以的。不是變鬼了，觀世音菩薩就離你很遠了，變鬼也可以念觀世音菩薩，只要你願意念的話。甚至於你現在就是個鬼，鬼也可以念觀世音菩薩；你現在是個畜生，畜生也可以念觀世音菩薩。說：「我現在在地獄裏。」在地獄也可以念觀世音菩薩。所以地獄、餓鬼、畜生這三惡道裏都可以念觀世音菩薩，你不要認為自己在三惡道裏，就沒有法子。這個為什麼叫妙法呢？為什麼觀世音菩薩的境界不可思議？就是在這兒。你在三惡道裏，也可以念觀世音菩薩，就可以離苦得樂了。我們每一個回到家裏，去度一度你地獄的眾生，去度一度你這個餓鬼的眾生，去度一度你這個畜生的眾生。你能把你自己家裏的三惡道眾生度出來，那這就是行菩薩道。有人就問了，說：「我家裏還有這三惡道的眾生？」你家裏沒有，你心裏有，你有貪心、有瞋心、有癡心，這就是三惡道的眾生啊！

## 常念自性觀世音

我們學佛法也不要在什麼高深的地方去學，平常心是道，直心是道場，用你直心來修行，你念觀音菩薩不要有一個貪心，念觀音菩薩就要平平常常這個心來念，沒有一切的所求。你真念觀音菩薩，怎麼還會想吃好的、

praise him if he didn't possess such awesome spiritual powers? No, the Buddha wouldn't casually say, "Such and such a Bodhisattva has such merit and virtue, such practices, such powers," unless it were true. Because Guanshiyin Bodhisattva really does have such powers and bestows such responses, the Buddha introduced him to us, giving us this method to handle the problems we cannot solve on our own.

Now I've explained this method to you so clearly and simply that you should be able to apply it. "But I'm pretty fond of my greed, anger, and stupidity," you say, "so I don't want to recite Guanshiyin Bodhisattva's name." Then you can recite your own name. Figure out who you are, and then you'll recognize Guanshiyin Bodhisattva. We recite Guanshiyin Bodhisattva's name simply because we don't recognize ourselves. We are not troubled by our greed, anger, and stupidity, so we don't want to recite. But our very unwillingness to recite is itself trouble.

Now, if you're not afraid of trouble, then you don't have to learn anything. If you fear trouble, then you should study the Buddhadharma and learn to recite Guanyin's name. If you don't want to recognize yourself and you say, "I'm a nobody, so I don't need to be mindful of the Buddha, the Dharma, and the Sangha," then you'll soon turn into a ghost, since you don't want to be a person. At that time you can still recite Guanyin's name. Guanyin Bodhisattva doesn't abandon you when you become a ghost. Ghosts can recite Guanyin's name, and so can animals. If you're in the hells, you can recite his name as well. You can recite in any of the three evil paths, so don't think you'll be doomed. That's why it's called the Wonderful Dharma. Guanshiyin Bodhisattva's state is inconceivable. If you recite his name in the three evil paths, you will leave suffering and attain bliss. All of you should go home and cross over your own hell-beings, hungry ghosts, and animals. If you can cross over the suffering beings in your own home, you are practicing the Bodhisattva Way. "Do such beings exist in my home?" you ask. By your home, I mean your own mind. Your greedy thoughts, angry thoughts, and stupid thoughts are living beings in the three evil paths.

## Constantly Be Mindful of the Guanshiyin in Your Own Nature

In studying Buddhism, we should not seek for what is lofty or profound. The ordinary mind is the Way. The straight mind is the Way-place. Cultivation must be done with an honest mind. Don't use a greedy mind to recite Guanyin's name. Recite with an ordinary mind, without seeking anything. If you truly recite Guanyin's name, how could you think of eating good food, wearing nice clothes, or living in a fine place? You would forget everything else and become one with Guanyin Bodhisattva. There is a Guanyin Bod-

穿好的、住好的，什麼都忘了。什麼都忘了，那你和觀音菩薩才能合而為一。我們每一個眾生的心裏頭都有一位觀音菩薩，因為有一位觀音菩薩在你的心裏，所以你現在才能念，你這一念，就是念你心裏頭的觀音菩薩。觀音菩薩什麼都不想，一切無著一切不求，他所做的就是度眾生，他願意令一切眾生都離苦得樂，了生脫死，早成佛道。所以觀世音菩薩是這樣子，無所求於眾生，就要眾生真正明白，也沒有貪心了，這是觀世音菩薩對我們一切人的希望。我們現在念觀世音菩薩不要一天到晚盡打妄想。

念觀世音菩薩，拜觀世音菩薩，觀世音菩薩來現身見你，你又不認識觀世音菩薩，所以我們眾生這是很苦惱的。什麼叫做觀世音菩薩現身你不認識？就是你這個當面關，也就是你那個考驗。你念觀世音菩薩，要學觀世音菩薩那個樣子，觀世音菩薩是大慈大悲大願大力的，我們念觀世音菩薩要學觀世音菩薩的大慈大悲大願大力。無論誰對我們有不好的地方，我們應該不動心。也就是說誰罵我們，我們要忍；誰打我們，我們要忍；甚至於有人想要殺了我們，我們也要忍。要忍，並且要認賬，為什麼要認賬呢？假如我往昔沒有殺過這個人，他不會來殺我；我往昔若沒有罵過這個人，他也不會來罵我；我在往昔沒有打過人，人也不會打我。為什麼有人罵我、打我、殺我？就因為我往昔在愚癡的時候，也罵過人，也打過人，也殺過人，所以今生我們遇著這個境界，這只是把我們往昔所欠的這種債務還了它。以前不明白的時候，就好像扛債不還似的，借人的錢也不願意還人家；那麼現在我們明白了，我們就應該老老實實承認這種的債務。我們若能承認這種的債務，這就是見著觀世音菩薩了，就和觀世音菩薩有真正法眷屬的關係了。

## 慈觀悲觀喜捨觀

怎麼樣叫認識觀世音菩薩？我們就要知道觀世音菩薩他的宗旨是什麼？他的宗旨就是「慈悲喜捨」四個字。我們要學觀世音菩薩的慈，慈運無緣，對我們沒有緣的人，都要用一種慈悲心來對他，慈是給眾生樂，既然給眾生樂，是把我們自己的樂給一切眾生，我們不要自己就顧自己，要沒有自私心，這叫慈，慈能予樂。悲就能拔苦，拔眾生的一切苦難，我們也幫著把它拔出來，拔一切眾生苦。那麼喜就是無論眾生對你怎麼樣發脾氣，你也要歡喜的，要不發脾氣。捨，就是把我們所有一切珍貴的物質，一切捨不得的東西，我們都要捨給眾生。我們要有慈悲喜捨這四無量心

hisattva in every person's mind. That's why you are able to be mindful. You are being mindful of the Guanyin Bodhisattva in your mind.

Guanyin Bodhisattva has no thoughts, no attachments, and nothing that he seeks. His work is to cross over living beings, to help living beings leave suffering and attain bliss, end birth and death, and quickly become Buddhas. He doesn't seek anything from living beings; he simply wants them to gain true understanding and put down all their greed. That's his hope for each of us. And so, as we recite Guanshiyin Bodhisattva's name, we should not constantly indulge in idle thoughts.

We recite Guanyin Bodhisattva's name and bow to him, but when he manifests before us we don't recognize him. We are truly pathetic. Not recognizing Guanyin Bodhisattva when he manifests, we fail the test. When we recite his name, we should learn to have Guanyin Bodhisattva's great kindness, compassion, vows, and power. When people treat us badly, scold us, beat us, or try to kill us, we should remain unmoved and endure it, paying back the debts we owe. If we hadn't killed, scolded, or beaten others in past lives, they wouldn't be treating us that way now. They want to hurt us now, because in the past when we were stupid and deluded, we also hurt them. In the past when we didn't understand this principle, we refused to pay our debts. Now that we understand, we should honestly acknowledge our debts. To acknowledge and pay our debts is to truly see Guanyin Bodhisattva and become a true member of his Dharma family.

## He Contemplates with Kindness, Compassion, Joy and Giving

How can we recognize Guanshiyin Bodhisattva? We have to know his principles. His principles are kindness, compassion, joy, and giving. We should learn Guanyin Bodhisattva's kindness and be kind towards those with whom we have no affinities. Kindness means making living beings happy. It means sharing our own happiness with living beings, not being selfish. Compassion pulls beings out of suffering. We should help those who are suffering or in difficulty. Joy means being happy and not feeling anger even when others get angry at us. Giving means taking our most prized possessions and giving them to living beings. If we can base our practice on the four limitless minds of kindness, compassion, joy, and giving, then we are true Buddhists. Those who lack the four limitless minds are not qualified to be Buddhists. We should never be selfish, seek personal gain, tell lies, or covet what is not ours. If we wish to win a fortune at a casino so we can do meritorious deeds, we are seeking beyond our rightful due and Guanyin Bodhisattva will not help us out. We should follow the Six Guiding Principles that are advocated every day at the City of Ten Thousand Buddhas: no fighting, no greed, no

，你若能本照慈悲喜捨四無量心向前去奉行佛教，這是眞正的一個佛教徒。你佛教徒若沒有，慈悲喜捨這四無量心，那不配做佛教徒，所以我們一定要把自私心割除了，自利的心也不要了，也不要打妄語，也不要份外貪求。好像我們本來不應該去賭錢，我們偏偏想要賭錢贏錢，來做功德，那就是份外的要求，所以觀世音菩薩不會保護這一類的人，不會滿這一類人的願。所以也不要爭，也不要貪，這是萬佛城天天所講的六大宗旨：不爭、不貪、不求、不自私、不自利、不打妄語，這六個條件你要能實實在在去做去，以四無量心爲體，以六大宗旨爲用，互相來幫助。這樣子就是你認識佛教、認識觀世音菩薩的本來面目了。

念觀世音菩薩，可是觀世音菩薩是什麼意思？我們不知道，尤其在西方人念中文，若懂得中文的人會明白一點，不懂中文的就和念咒是一樣的，就和密宗念這個「嗡嘛呢叭彌吽」一樣的，因爲不明白它的意思。觀就是觀察，觀察世間所有的音聲，這一位菩薩他就是沒有事情做，要找一點事情來做。這個觀也就是看，不是看外邊，是看眾生的心，看你哪一個心裏沒有妄想了，空了，就開悟了。所以才說：「十方同聚會」，十方的善男信女大家聚會到一起。「皆共學無爲」，在一起幹什麼呢？修這個無爲法。我們這念觀世音菩薩也是一種無爲法，無爲而無不爲，這種無爲法就叫你不要打妄想。

## 菩薩哥哥法王父

你念「南無觀世音菩薩」，觀世音菩薩也念你，彼此互念；就好像你想你的親戚，你親戚也就想你。我們和觀世音菩薩是無量劫以來，是法眷屬，是法親。從什麼地方論呢？從阿彌陀佛那兒論。阿彌陀佛是西方極樂世界的教主，也就是觀世音菩薩的師父，觀世音菩薩就是幫助阿彌陀佛來弘揚淨土法門的一位菩薩，大勢至菩薩也是其中的一位菩薩。我們念「南無阿彌陀佛」就會往生到極樂世界，以阿彌陀佛做我們的師父做我們接引的導師。觀世音菩薩是阿彌陀佛的弟子，因爲這種關係，我們和觀世音菩薩都是法兄弟，觀音菩薩就是我們沒有生到極樂世界一切眾生的一個哥哥，我們是他一個弟弟。這樣說起來，我們這是很近的親戚，所以想我們這個親兄弟，這哥哥在那兒也就想弟弟，我們就是觀世音菩薩的弟弟，觀世音菩薩就是我們的哥哥。說：「觀世音菩薩，怎麼會是我們的哥哥，那我們不是太高攀了嗎？」不是的，觀世音菩薩不單拿我們當弟弟，拿所有的一切眾生都當他的

seeking, no selfishness, no pursuit of self-benefit, and no lying. If we can honestly apply the six guidelines as our function and take the four limitless minds as our substance, so that function and substance assist each other, then we will recognize what Buddhism and Guanshiyin Bodhisattva are all about.

We recite "Guanshiyin Bodhisattva," but do we know what it means? Those who know Chinese might understand a little, but for Westerners who don't know Chinese, it's just like reciting a mantra. For example, people recite "Om mani padme hum" but they don't know what it means. *Guan* means to contemplate, to observe the sounds *(yin)* of the world *(shi)*. That's what this Bodhisattva does, because he has nothing better to do. He looks, not outside, but inside living beings' minds, to see whose mind is free of idle thoughts. Once the mind is empty, then one can become enlightened. A verse says, "People flock from the ten directions / To study the unconditioned." All the faithful men and women come together to cultivate the unconditioned dharma. Reciting Guanyin's name is an unconditioned dharma for stopping our idle thoughts. It is unconditioned, and yet nothing is not conditioned by it.

## We Have a Bodhisattva for a Brother and a Dharma King for a Father

When you recite "Namo Guanshiyin Bodhisattva," Guanshiyin Bodhisattva is mindful of you. It's just as when you think of your relative, your relative thinks of you. We have been relatives in the Dharma with Guanshiyin Bodhisattva for countless ages. It all began with Amitabha Buddha, the teaching host of the Western Land of Ultimate Bliss and the teacher of Guanyin Bodhisattva. Guanyin Bodhisattva and Great Strength Bodhisattva help Amitabha Buddha to propagate the Pure Land Dharma door. If we recite "Namo Amitabha Buddha," we will be reborn in the Land of Ultimate Bliss and Amitabha Buddha will be our guide and teacher. Since Guanshiyin Bodhisattva is Amitabha Buddha's disciple, he is our elder Dharma brother. In fact, he is the elder brother of all living beings who have not yet been born in the Land of Ultimate Bliss. If I explain it this way, we become very close relatives. So we are mindful of our brother, and our brother also keeps us in mind. We are Guanshiyin Bodhisattva's younger brothers, and Guanyin Bodhisattva is our elder brother.

Someone is saying, "How can Guanshiyin Bodhisattva be my elder brother? Doesn't that make me too exalted?" Not only does Guanyin Bodhisattva regard us as his younger brothers, he treats all living beings as his younger brothers. Otherwise, why would he listen to our sounds and come rescue us from our suffering? When we get ourselves into trouble, why would he want to help us out? He sees that all

233

弟弟；要不然的時候，他爲什麼要尋聲救苦呢？爲什麼所有的眾生有什麼困難，他就幫助呢？他就看一切眾生是他的手足一樣，是他的骨肉，所以他才這樣不怕一切的困苦艱難，而來救度我們在娑婆世界這個苦眾生。所以各位不要忘了自己這個法兄弟，我們這兒一念觀世音菩薩，觀世音菩薩也就念我們了。我們叫一聲觀世音菩薩，裏邊包含就是哥哥，觀世音菩薩就叫一聲我們這個未來的菩薩、未來的佛，這個小弟弟。你若能這樣看，念觀世音菩薩更應該誠心，更應該親切，念得就像念我們自己的兄弟一樣。所以我們遇著念觀世音菩薩這種法門，我們不要空過，要特別懇切至誠念觀音菩薩。不過我們念觀音菩薩的時候，不要盡低著頭念，要把頭抬起來，要有一種勇猛精進的精神。這個時候，觀音菩薩一看你這麼精神，就拉著你的手，說：「快跟著我走啦！」就一步一步的，將來就會到西方極樂世界。

我方才講的話，有人打了妄想了，打什麼妄想呢？他說：「觀世音菩薩都 look, look, too much look，爲什麼不叫我 look, look, too much look？我怎麼就不可以 look 呢？」你要知道，你看的和觀音菩薩的看法不同。觀音菩薩是看裏邊，你是看外邊，觀音菩薩他看自己的自性，他自性和每一個眾生都有個電波，都有個雷達，那麼他看他自己這個電波和雷達，就知道一切眾生的若干種心，這個眾生打什麼妄想他都知道。因爲眾生有的離他很遠，雖然是千手千眼，但是看無量無邊的眾生也不夠用，也看不過來，那麼他迴光返照，反聞聞自性，看自己的自性，自性的眾生，哪一個受什麼苦了，他就去救度這個眾生。你看你是向外看，把自己根本的智慧就忘了，所以你這個看和他那個看不同的。這是我答覆你這個妄想。

## 慈悲即是觀世音

什麼是觀世音菩薩？觀世音菩薩，是觀世音，不是觀己音，不是觀自己的音，是觀世界的音，所謂「無我無人觀自在」，沒有我也沒有人了，這就是觀自在。觀自在也就是觀世音，觀世音就要無人無我，你能無人無我，你就是觀世音；我能無人無我，我就是觀世音。你能以無人無我，沒有貢高我慢，嫉妒障礙，你就是觀世音；你若有貢高我慢，嫉妒障礙，你就不是觀世音。所以觀世音菩薩不是向外找的，向自己這兒找的。所以沒有妒忌，沒有障礙，才能和觀世音菩薩合而爲一。

人人要學觀世音，不要有脾氣，不要有貪心，不要

living beings are just the same as his own hands and feet, his own flesh and bones. That's why he fears neither trouble nor difficulty, and comes to rescue all the beings who are suffering in this Saha world. None of us should forget our Dharma brother. When we recite "Namo Guanshiyin Bodhisattva," Guanshiyin Bodhisattva is also mindful of us. When we call out to Guanshiyin Bodhisattva, we're calling our elder brother. He then calls out to his younger brothers, who are future Bodhisattvas and future Buddhas. If we contemplate in this way, we'll recite Guanshiyin Bodhisattva's name even more sincerely, as if we were reciting our own brother's name. Now that we have encountered the Dharma door of reciting Guanyin Bodhisattva's name, we shouldn't miss our chance. We should recite as sincerely as we can. But as we recite, we shouldn't let our heads droop. We should lift our heads up and recite with courage and vigor. When Guanyin Bodhisattva sees our vigorous spirit, he'll take us by the hand and say, "Quickly come with me!" Then he'll lead us step by step towards the Western Land of Ultimate Bliss.

Someone else is wondering, "Why does Guanshiyin Bodhisattva do so much looking, while I am not allowed to look at anything at all?" You should know that your looking and Guanyin Bodhisattva's looking are not the same. Guanyin Bodhisattva looks inside, but you look outside. Guanyin Bodhisattva looks at his own nature. He has every living being on his radar screen, and he knows all the thoughts in their minds. Because some living beings are far away from him, even a thousand hands and a thousand eyes are not enough. He wants to look at infinite living beings, but he cannot see them all. That's why he turns his attention inward to look at and listen to his own nature. He looks at the living beings in his own nature and saves those who are in suffering. You, on the other hand, look outside and forget all about your inherent wisdom. That's why, in response to your idle thought, I said your looking and his looking are different.

## Kindness and Compassion Are Guanshiyin

Guanshiyin Bodhisattva contemplates not his own sound, but all the sounds of the world. There's a saying, "With no self and no others, he contemplates at ease." "He Who Contemplates at Ease" is another name for Guanshiyin, so Guanshiyin is also devoid of self and others. Anyone who is devoid of self and others is Guanshiyin. If you are free of arrogance, jealousy, contrariness, and attachment to self and others, then you are Guanshiyin. If you have these faults, then you are not. Seek within yourself, not outside, for Guanshiyin. If you wish to become one with Guanshiyin, then you cannot be jealous of or wish to obstruct others.

Learn to be like Guanshiyin by getting rid of your bad temper, greed, anger, and stupidity. If you can get rid of the three poisons and cultivate precepts, concentration, and wisdom, you are Guanshiyin Bodhisattva. Are you Guanshiyin

有瞋心，不要有癡心，把三毒去了，你要修戒、修定、修慧，那就是觀世音菩薩。所以這觀世音菩薩，你就問問你自己，我有沒有觀世音菩薩？我要是觀世音菩薩，就不應該發脾氣，就不應該動無明，就應該要修慈悲，要修忍辱，要修精進，要修布施，要修持戒，要修禪定，要修般若。你有般若你就是觀世音，我有般若我就是觀世音；你沒有般若你就不是觀世音，我沒有般若我也不是觀世音，你看那小孩子會點頭那就是般若嘛！他若沒有般若他就不會點頭。每個人自己心裏都有一個觀世音菩薩，不過你沒有看見他，就以爲沒有了，現在我給你介紹，你知道有一個觀世音菩薩在你的心裏邊，你就應該時時聽觀世音菩薩的話，聽觀世音菩薩的教化，聽觀世音菩薩的指導。「什麼是觀世音菩薩？」你問我，我也不知道，不過現在我們六祖大師在這兒坐著，他早就說過：「慈悲即是觀音，喜捨名爲勢至。」什麼是觀世音菩薩呢？你能做慈悲的事情，就是觀世音菩薩。你能布施，歡喜布施，這就是大勢至菩薩。這兩位菩薩離你都不遠，天天都跟著你走。不過你對他盡發脾氣，一天到晚見到觀世音菩薩，你也不認識，你就發脾氣。見到大勢至菩薩，你也不認識，對他生一種瞋恨。見到阿彌陀佛，你口念「南無阿彌陀佛，南無阿彌陀佛……」，南無阿彌陀佛現在你的前邊，你看都不看他。所以啊！對面不認識觀世音，對面不認識大勢至，對面不認識阿彌陀佛。這西方三聖，常常和你在一起，你就離他們遠遠的，觀世音菩薩雖然那麼慈悲，也沒有辦法；大勢至菩薩雖然那麼喜捨，也是沒有辦法了，阿彌陀佛也說等一等啦，慢慢地，慢慢地他就發菩提心了。

## 更能迴光觀自在

「觀自在菩薩。行深般若波羅蜜多時。照見五蘊皆空。度一切苦厄。」《心經》這幾句講什麼呢？就講這個觀世音菩薩。觀世音菩薩他證得耳根圓通，怎麼樣證得耳根圓通呢？他就能「反聞聞自性，性成無上道。」反聞聞自性，這個反聞就是反聽，又可以說是反觀，就是迴光返照。返照就是一個參禪的參，你若能參，那個不思議的境界在你那兒，不是我能夠告訴你的，要你自己用功修行，才能夠得到那種眞實的味道。所以返照也可以說是想，也可以說是思，也可以說是那個參，也可以說是觀照般若那個觀照。爲什麼用一個返？返就是在他那個地方，這種不可思議的境界，要你自己去眞實用功修行，才能領會得到，才能得到。你迴光返照，用你般若的智慧來把它照一照，照破一切的黑暗，這也叫反聞聞自性。你自性是一個清淨無染的，你那個心有染污，

Bodhisattva? If so, then you should not give rise to anger or ignorance, but instead should cultivate compassion, patience, vigor, giving, morality, Chan samadhi, and Prajna. Whoever has Prajna is Guanshiyin; whoever doesn't, is not. The little child who knows how to nod his head is also demonstrating that he has Prajna. We all have a Guanshiyin Bodhisattva in our hearts, but we haven't seen him so we don't know that he's there. Now that I've introduced him to you, you should always listen to the Guanshiyin Bodhisattva in your mind.

"Who is Guanshiyin Bodhisattva?" you ask. I don't know. But the Sixth Patriarch long ago said, "Kindness and compassion are Guanyin; joy and giving are Great Strength." If you do kind and compassionate things, you are Guanshiyin Bodhisattva. If you joyfully give to others, you are Great Strength Bodhisattva. Not recognizing these two Bodhisattvas who are right beside you every day, you get mad at them all the time. And you recite "Namo Amitabha Buddha" all day long, but you don't even look at Amitabha Buddha when he appears before you. You fail to recognize Guanshiyin, Great Strength, and Amitabha when coming face to face with them. The Three Sages of the Western Land are constantly right next to you, but you insist on putting them at a distance. And so although Guanshiyin Bodhisattva is so kind and compassionate, he cannot help you. Great Strength Bodhisattva is joyous and giving, but he has no way either. Amitabha Buddha thinks, "Let's wait a little longer. Gradually, one of these days, he will bring forth the Bodhi mind."

## Turn the Light Around and Contemplate at Ease

"When Bodhisattva Avalokiteshvara was practicing the profound Prajna Paramita, he illuminated the five skandhas and saw that they are all empty, and he crossed beyond all suffering and difficulty." This line from the *Heart Sutra* speaks of Guanshiyin (whose name in Sanskrit is Avalokiteshvara) Bodhisattva, who realized perfect penetration by means of the faculty of hearing. He "turned the hearing back to listen to his own nature, so his nature attained the unsurpassed Way." To turn the hearing back means to "turn the light around and reflect within," and to "investigate." If you investigate, you will discover an inconceivable state. I cannot describe this state to you; if you want to taste its flavor, you have to work at your own practice. Turning the light around means to reflect, to investigate, to illuminate. You have to truly practice if you want to experience that inconceivable state. You turn the light around and reflect within, using your Prajna wisdom to illuminate it and dispel all the darkness. This is also known as turning the hearing back to listen to your own

這個心不是講的真心，是人這個緣利心，攀緣私利的心。這個心它很不老實，就像那個猴子一樣跳上跳下的，一天到晚都蹦蹦跳跳的，我們人心也就是這個。現在反聞聞自性，就靠一個人看著你這個心，看著你這個性。看著你這個心要歸到這個性上，性是不動的，心是動的；性是靜的，淨極就光通達，你淨到極點就有光明現出來了。你反聞聞自性，等到你光通達了，那就是性成無上道。這個反聞聞自性是觀世音菩薩所修的。迴光返照的功夫，要反求諸己，你聞聞你自性裏頭有沒有貪心？有沒有瞋心？有沒有癡心？若有，這是三毒；若沒有，這就是三無漏學，變成戒定慧了。這是反聞聞自性大概的意思。

因為他能反聞聞自性，所以他才自在，才得到觀自在。所謂自在，就是一種無人、無我、無眾生、無壽者的境界。那說：「自在，在什麼地方自在？在什麼地方不自在？」在聖人的地位上就是自在，在凡夫的地位上就不自在。為什麼在聖人的地位上，他就會自在？因為聖人他就是無人相、無我相、無眾生相、無壽者相，所以他能得到自在。凡夫為什麼沒有自在？因為凡夫又有人相，又有我相，又有眾生相，啊！壽者相那更不用提了。學佛法的人，學來學去，也是有人相，也是有我相，也是有眾生相，也是有壽者相，因為這四相不能空，所以始終得不到自在。你想要自在，一定要掃三心、非四相。所謂掃三心，「過去心不可得」，為什麼不可得？已經過去了，過去就過去了，所以過去心不可得。「現在心不可得」，現在心為什麼不可得呢？說我現在在這兒呢！可是現在，你說這個是現在，喔！這個又過去了。這現在不存在，現在也是虛妄的。「未來心不可得」，怎麼說未來心不可得？還沒有來嘛！沒有來，你想他幹什麼？所以這三心了不可得，四相也空了。你能三心不可得，空四相，你就是觀自在菩薩。

我們現在打禪七幹什麼？就是要觀自在啊！人人都要觀自在不是說：「喔！觀世音菩薩是觀自在菩薩，那在《心經》上說的。」不是的，你誰自在了，誰就是觀自在；你誰不自在，誰就不是觀自在，這觀自在菩薩，沒有一定的名，所謂一切眾生都是觀自在。我們現在開始坐禪，就是觀一觀你自在不自在？啊！你若自在了，那你就能照見五蘊皆空了，也就是行深般若波羅蜜了。行深般若波羅蜜，才能照見五蘊皆空；你照見五蘊皆空，這才是行深般若波羅蜜。你能這樣子了，才能度一切苦厄，一切苦都了了，所以得到自在了。那麼不單觀世音菩薩和我們是一個，十方諸佛、十方的菩薩和我們都是一個的。

nature. Your inherent nature is pure and undefiled, but your mind--not the true mind, but the human mind which exploits for selfish benefit--is defiled. That mind is very unreliable, like a monkey that bounces up and down all day long. Turning the hearing back to listen to the nature means watching over the mind until the mind returns to the nature. The mind moves, but the nature is still and unmoving. When the stillness reaches an extreme, the light becomes penetrating. When you are still to the utmost point, the light appears and your nature attains to the unsurpassed Way. This is the method that Guanshiyin Bodhisattva cultivated. Reflecting within means seeking inside yourself, listening to your nature to see if you have thoughts of greed, anger, or stupidity. If the three poisons are not present, then you have the three nonoutflow studies: precepts, concentration, and wisdom. This is the general meaning of turning the hearing around to listen to the nature.

Because he turned the hearing back to listen to his own nature, he was able to contemplate at ease. Being at ease is a state of being without others, self, living beings, or a life span. "At what level is one at ease?" you ask. One is at ease at the level of sagehood. Ordinary people are not at ease. Sages have no mark of others, self, living beings, or life span, so they can be at ease. Ordinary people are attached to these four marks, so they are never at ease. People study the Buddhadharma but cannot see the four marks as empty, so they cannot obtain ease. To be at ease, you must sweep away the three minds and annul the four marks. "The mind of the past cannot be got at," because it has already passed. "The mind of the present cannot be got at. "You may say "this" is the present, but by then it has already become the past. There is no such thing as "the present"; it is false. "The mind of the future cannot be got at," because it is not here yet. Since the future hasn't arrived, why think about it? If you know that the three minds cannot be obtained and the four marks are empty, then you are the Bodhisattva Who Contemplates at Ease.

We are holding a Chan session so we can contemplate at ease. Everyone should contemplate at ease. Don't say, "Guanshiyin Bodhisattva is the Bodhisattva Who Contemplates at Ease; it says so in the *Heart Sutra*." Whoever is at ease is the Bodhisattva Who Contemplates at Ease. This Bodhisattva doesn't have a fixed identity. All living beings can be the Bodhisattva Who Contemplates at Ease. As you begin to sit in Chan, contemplate yourself to see if you are at ease. If you are, you'll be able to "illuminate the five skandhas and see that they are all empty." That is what is meant by "practicing the profound Prajna Paramita." If you can do that, then you'll be able to "cross beyond all suffering and difficulty." Having ended all suffering, you are at ease. Not only will Guanshiyin Bodhisattva become one with us, all the Buddhas and Bodhisattvas in the ten directions will become on͏ ͏ ͏us.

# 天地靈文楞嚴咒

## THE SHURANGAMA MANTRA--
## THE EFFICACIOUS LANGUAGE OF HEAVEN AND EARTH

宣公上人講述
Lectures by the Venerable Master Hua

我現在給你們講〈楞嚴咒〉，這〈楞嚴咒〉百千萬劫也沒有人講一次，也不容易講一次。這麼一個法會是很稀有的，難遭難遇的。在我給各位講時，我知道沒有人聽得懂。就是有人自以為懂得，也不是真懂。有人自以為懂了，所以不注意，那也等於不懂。在佛教裏頭，〈楞嚴咒〉是最重要的一部咒，是咒中的王，也是咒裏邊最長的一個咒，這個咒關係整個佛教的興衰。〈楞嚴咒〉是支持天地沒有毀滅的靈文，〈楞嚴咒〉是支持世界不到末日的靈文。所以我常說，世界上若有一人會念〈楞嚴咒〉，這世界就不會毀滅，佛法也不會毀滅的。等到世上沒有人會念〈楞嚴咒〉時，這世界就快毀滅了，因為正法不存在了。

現在便有一些天魔外道說，《楞嚴經》和〈楞嚴咒〉都是假的，這是天魔外道派出魔子魔孫來造出這些謠言，令人不相信《楞嚴經》和〈楞嚴咒〉。《楞嚴經》和〈楞嚴咒〉，這是正法最要緊的一部經和一部咒，《楞嚴經》就是為〈楞嚴咒〉而說的，這《楞嚴經》就是解釋〈楞嚴咒〉的一部經。《楞嚴經》和〈楞嚴咒〉的重要性是沒有法子能說得完的，盡未來際也說不完它的這種功德和妙用，所以是不可思議。說來說去，歸納起來，《楞嚴經》就是讚歎〈楞嚴咒〉的。如果有一個人能在世界上念〈楞嚴咒〉，這妖魔鬼怪都不敢公然出現於世，因為他們所怕的就是〈楞嚴咒〉。如果一個人也不會背〈楞嚴咒〉了，這時候妖魔鬼怪就都出現於世。他們在世界上為非作歹，一般人也不認識他們了。現在因為有人會念〈楞嚴咒〉，妖魔鬼怪就不敢公然出現於世。所以若想世界不滅，就趕快念〈楞嚴咒〉、讀《楞嚴

Now I am explaining the Shurangama Mantra for you and it is extremely difficult to encounter such a rare Dharma assembly as this. Billions of eons pass and no one explains the Shurangama Mantra even once. Nor is it easy to explain even once. When I am explaining, I know full well that no one understands what's being said. Even if there are those who think they do, they don't really understand. Some think they already understand and so they don't pay attention, but that's also failing to understood.

Among the Buddha's teachings, the Shurangama Mantra is considered to be the king of mantras because it is the longest and most important. The flourish or demise of Buddhism rests entirely with the Shurangama Mantra. It is the efficacious phrases of the Shurangama Mantra that keep heaven and earth from being destroyed. It is the efficacious phrases of the Shurangama Mantra that keep the world from coming to an end. That is why I often tell you that as long as a single person can recite the Shurangama Mantra, the world cannot be destroyed, nor can Buddhism. But when there is no longer anyone who can recite the Shurangama Mantra, then very quickly the world will be destroyed, because the Proper Dharma no longer abides.

Now there are even heavenly demons and externalists who claim that the *Shurangama Sutra* and the Shurangama Mantra are false. These heaven demons and externalists send their demon sons and grandsons to stir up rumors that cause people to not believe in the *Shurangama Sutra* and the Shurangama Mantra. This sutra and mantra are critically important to the preservation of the Proper Dharma. The *Shurangama Sutra* was spoken for the sake of the Shurangama Mantra. There's no way to ever finish expressing the importance of the *Shurangama Sutra* and the Shurangama Mantra; to the ends of all time their merits, virtues, and wonderful functions could never be told--so absolutely inconceivable and ineffable are they! When all is said and done, the *Shurangama Sutra* is an ode to the Shurangama Mantra. As long as there is even one person who can recite the Shurangama Mantra, the demons, ghosts, and strange entities don't dare show themselves in this world. They fear the mantra. But when not even one person can recite the Shurangama Mantra by heart, then those weird entities, those demons and ghosts will come out of hiding. Depraved and up to no good, they will not be recognized by most people. At this point in time, since there are still those who can recite the mantra from memory, those malevolent beings haven't made their appearance yet. And so, if you want to keep the world from being destroyed, quickly

經》，這就是正法住世。

今天開始講〈楞嚴咒〉，〈楞嚴咒〉的「楞嚴」兩個字，就翻譯成「究竟堅固」。

這〈楞嚴咒〉的名字叫「摩訶薩怛多般怛囉陀羅尼」，又叫「佛頂光明摩訶薩怛多般怛囉無上神咒」。佛頂就是佛的頂上化佛，所以這〈楞嚴咒〉是微妙不可思議的。〈楞嚴咒〉裏邊所說的，都是降伏天魔、制諸外道的，從一開始到終了，每一句都是諸佛的心地法門，每一句有每一句的用途，每一個字有每一個字的奧妙，都具足不可思議的力量。即使只念一字、一句、一會，或念全咒，都是驚天動地，所謂驚天地，泣鬼神，妖魔遠避，魑魅遁形。所以佛頂光明，這光明也就是表示咒的力量，是能破除一切黑暗，能成就人一切功德。你若能受持〈楞嚴咒〉，將來一定是成佛的，一定得到無上正等正覺的。你若常常誦念〈楞嚴咒〉，就能消除你宿世的業障，往昔的罪業都可以消除。這是〈楞嚴咒〉的妙用。

摩訶是梵語，翻譯中文叫「大」，英文叫big。那麼什麼叫大？就是體、相、用都是大的。體遍十方，所以叫大；這個用是盡虛空遍法界的；相，它是沒有相的，可是無相無不相。這個用也可以說它沒什麼用，盡虛空遍法界無所不用。這用是大用，這個相是大相，這個體也是大體，周遍十方，盡虛空、遍法界，這是摩訶的意思。薩怛多也是梵語，翻譯過來叫「白」，就是清淨的意思，也就是沒有污染的意思。所謂白淨法，清淨沒有染污的法，這〈楞嚴咒〉是白淨法。

般怛囉也是梵語，翻譯中文叫「傘蓋」。傘蓋是譬喻，這個傘蓋它是用陰萬德，這傘蓋的用，就是保護一切有德的人，誰有德行，誰就能遇到這種白淨法；沒有德行的人，是遇不到這種法的。所以才說：

　　三光普照透三才
　　閻浮世界你不來
　　大德大善能於得
　　無德無善不明白

learn the Shurangama Mantra and read the *Shurangama Sutra* to keep the Proper Dharma in the world.

Today the explanation of the Shurangama Mantra is beginning. The word "Shurangama" translates as "Ultimately firm and strong."

The entire title of the Shurangama Mantra is "Great White Canopy of Light Dharani Mantra" (*mo he sa dan tuo bo da la tuo lo ni zhou*). It is also called "Brilliant Buddha's Crown, Great White Canopy of Light, Unsurpassed Spiritual Mantra." The Buddha's Crown refers to the transformation Buddha atop the Buddha's crown. There is no way to conceive the subtle wonder of the mantra. The content of the Shurangama Mantra subdues heavenly demons and controls externalists. Every line, from beginning to end, is the Buddhas' mind-ground Dharma-door. Each line has its own function; each possesses its own esoteric wonder; and each is endowed with incredible power. The recitation of a single word, a single line, a single assembly, or the recitation of the entire mantra causes the heavens to vibrate and the earth to tremble; it's said that heaven and earth are shocked, the ghosts and spirits wail, the demons keep a wide distance, and mountain and river sprites hide away. That brilliance at the Buddha's crown represents the power of the mantra that can dispel every sort of darkness and that enables people to amass all kinds of merit and virtue. If you can accept and uphold the Shurangama Mantra, then you will definitely become a Buddha in the future. You will certainly attain the Unsurpassed Proper and Equal Right Enlightenment. If you continually recite the Shurangama Mantra, then you can get rid of your karmic obstacles from last life and all past lives. That's the incredible function of the Shurangama Mantra!

*Mo he* is Sanskrit and means "Great." The substance, appearance and function are all great. The substance is said to be great because it pervades the ten directions; the function fills up empty space and reaches throughout the Dharma Realm; and the appearance--well, there isn't any appearance. You can say that it neither has any appearance nor lacks any appearance. The function also doesn't really exist, yet there isn't any place its function doesn't reach in all of space and the Dharma Realm. That's a great function, a great appearance, and a great substance. Pervading the ten directions, exhausting the limits of space, and filling the Dharma Realm is the meaning of "mo he."

*Sa dan tuo*, also Sanskrit, means "white" and represents purity and lack of defilement. Pure white Dharma is devoid of filth. The Shurangama Mantra is pure white Dharma.

*Bo da la* is also Sanskrit and translates as "canopy." Canopy is an analogy. This canopy provides shelter for those with myriad virtues. The function of this canopy is to protect those endowed with virtue and those practicing virtuous conduct, meaning anyone who encounters this mantra. Those lacking virtuous conduct won't have an opportunity to meet with this Dharma. It's said:

*The three lights universally illumine, permeating the three forces.*
*In all this world of Jambudvipa you may not come upon it.*
*Only those with great virtue and great goodness will attain it.*
*Those lacking virtue and goodness just won't understand it.*

「三光普照透三才」，這三光不是日、月、星，是你誦持〈楞嚴咒〉，身上有身光，口裏有口光，你心裏頭有心光，身、口、意這三業都放光。三才，就是天、地、人。「閻浮世界你不來」，在閻浮界你找不著，你各處找不著，你一定要受持〈楞嚴咒〉才能得到這種光。「大德大善能於得」，你若有大的德行、大的善，才能得到這種法門。「無德無善不明白」，你若沒有德行，沒有善功德來栽培著，你就是當面也會錯過，交臂也會失之。見到黃金你以為是銅，見到鑽石你以為是玻璃，都會不認識。你見到〈楞嚴咒〉了，以為這是很普通的，沒有什麼，所以就不知道寶其所寶，不知道妙其所妙！不知道〈楞嚴咒〉這種的功德，是不可思議的。

這方才說三光，還不只這個身、口、意三業放出清淨的光明，還有紅光繚繞。你誦〈楞嚴咒〉，自然就有紅光繚繞。所以才說：

千朵紅蓮護住身
坐駒騎著墨麒麟
萬妖一見往遠躲
濟公法師有妙音

「千朵紅蓮護住身」，有千朵的紅蓮來護持你的身，紅蓮華放出紅光。你一念〈楞嚴咒〉最前面二十九句咒文，就會現出這個境界。「坐駒騎著墨麒麟」，一念這〈楞嚴咒〉，這持咒的人是坐在一個麒麟的身上。「萬妖一見往遠躲」，什麼妖魔鬼怪一見都跑了，他不敢面對這種大威德的相。我們人人都知道佛教裏有一位濟公，當初濟公就是專用這一段咒文來降伏天魔、制諸外道，很靈感的，所以說「濟公法師有妙音」。這一段咒文是教我們「皈依盡虛空、遍法界，一切諸佛、一切菩薩、一切聲聞緣覺、一切諸天。」這也是護持三寶的一段，所以念這一段咒的時候，一切的妖魔鬼怪都要退避三舍；不止退避三舍，要退到他所不能退的地方去，他們都不敢作怪，都老實了。

這是說這一段咒文大概的意思，至於若詳細說，這〈楞嚴咒〉是妙不可言的，所以又說：

*The three lights universally illumine, permeating the three forces.* Here, the three lights do not refer to the sun, moon, and stars. Rather, it means that when you recite the Shurangama Mantra, your body emits light, your mouth emits light, and your mind emits light. It is talking about the light of the three karmas. The three forces refer to heaven, earth, and people. *In all this world of Jambudvipa you may not come upon it.* Throughout our world, Jambudvipa, you may seek but not find it. You absolutely must uphold the Shurangama Mantra in order to attain this light. If you have amassed virtuous conduct and have magnanimous virtue, then you will be able to attain the Dharma-door. *Those lacking virtue and goodness just won't understand it.* If you don't have sufficient virtue and haven't done enough good deeds, then even if you come face-to-face with it, you'll miss your chance. Right within arms' reach, you'll lose it. Having come upon gold you'll mistake it for copper; having found a diamond, you'll think it's a piece of glass. You'll fail to recognize it. You'll look upon the Shurangama Mantra as nothing at all out of the ordinary, and as a consequence won't realize it's the gem of gems, the wonder of wonders! You won't have any concept of the Shurangama Mantra's unfathomable merit and virtue.

Besides the three lights emitted when the three karmas of body, mouth, and mind are pure, there is also a swirling red light. Recitation of the Shurangama Mantra generates a swirling red light. It's described this way:

*A thousand petaled red lotus supports one's body.*
*As one sits firmly mounted on a black unicorn.*
*Seeing this, the hordes of monsters go far away to hide.*
*Dharma Master Ji, the Venerable,*
    *mastered these wonderful sounds.*

*A thousand petaled red lotus supports one's body.* When you recite the first twenty-nine lines of the Shurangama Mantra a state occurs wherein a red lotus with a thousand petals manifests and emits red light. *As one sits firmly mounted on a black unicorn.* Upon reciting the Mantra, the person chanting finds himself sitting astride a unicorn. *Seeing this, the hordes of monsters go far away to hide.* No matter what kind of weird creature or demon or ghost it might be, they all flee, not daring to face such a magnificent and awesome manifestation. The Venerable Ji is a well-known High Master in Buddhism. His expert use of this passage of the mantra to subdue heavenly demons and control externalists was extremely efficacious. And so the last line says: *Dharma Master Ji, the Venerable, mastered these wonderful sounds.* This passage of the mantra instructs us to "take refuge with all the Buddhas, all the Bodhisattvas, all the Hearers and Condition-Enlightened Ones, and all the gods throughout empty space and the Dharma Realm." It's a passage that protects the Triple Jewel, and so when you recite it the demons flee and the ghosts don't stop running until they're ten miles away. Not just ten miles, they back off until there's no more room to retreat. They don't dare make trouble; they are forced to behave themselves.

That's a general description of what this passage of mantra is about; the details are even more wonderful.

奧妙無窮實難猜
金剛密語本性來
楞嚴咒裏有靈妙
五眼六通道凡開

*Unendingly miraculous and mysterious,*
  *it's extremely hard to fathom.*
*This vajra secret language wells forth from your own nature.*
*Inside the Shurangama Mantra is marvelous magic!*
*Then come five eyes and six penetrations and the Way opens up.*

「奧妙無窮實難猜」，這個〈楞嚴咒〉非常奧妙，它的變化也不可思議，很不容易測度的。「金剛密語本性來」，〈楞嚴咒〉是密中之密，這是金剛來護持這個咒。本性來，它是從自己那個佛性中生出來的。「楞嚴咒裏有靈妙」，〈楞嚴咒〉也叫做靈文，因為他特別靈，特別有力量，所以說〈楞嚴咒〉裏有靈妙。「五眼六通道凡開」，你若能常持〈楞嚴咒〉，專心一致，心不旁騖，你可以得到五眼六通，可以有不可思議的那種境界來變化莫測，所以不是一般凡夫俗子可能知道的。因為這個，所以希望大家都能讀誦《楞嚴經》，背誦〈楞嚴咒〉。你一誦〈楞嚴咒〉，為什麼妖魔鬼怪不敢出來？因為力量太大了，盡虛空遍法界沒有一個地方，不是有這種祥光瑞氣彌漫著。所以有人誦〈楞嚴咒〉，就是補天地正氣的不足。你一個人念〈楞嚴咒〉，就有一個人的力量；百人念〈楞嚴咒〉，就有百人的力量，這世界妖魔鬼怪都會老老實實的。所以多一點人念〈楞嚴咒〉是好的。

無上神咒，什麼叫「無」呢？這個無，就是高明無極，也光明到極點了，沒有再超過這種高和光明的，這叫無。「上」呢？是沒有再比這更尊貴、更高尚了，這叫上。神就是不可思議，也就是威靈叵測，這叫神。咒就是感應道交，有一種力量，你念這咒就有感應。「佛頂光明摩訶薩怛多般怛囉無上神咒」，這是說佛頂的光明，猶如大白傘蓋來陰罩我們一切持咒的人。

這個咒是沒有人明白的，也不能一句一句、一個字一個字去講，不過你如果想要明白它，我可以勉強講給你聽。單這〈楞嚴咒〉，一年也講不完，三年也講不完，甚至於十年也講不完。現在我把這個咒的大意講一講，它有五會，這五會就表示五方，五方就是東、西、南、北、中。東方就是金剛部，阿閦佛為教主；南方就是寶生部，寶生佛做教主；中央就是佛部

*Unendingly miraculous and mysterious, it's extremely hard to fathom.* The Shurangama Mantra is quite esoteric and its changes and transformations are inexplicable; it's not easy to figure out. *This vajra secret language wells forth from your own nature.* The Shurangama Mantra is the secret within the secret. That's the vajras who come to protect the mantra. Your own nature--it is born from your own Buddha nature. *Inside the Shurangama Mantra is marvelous magic!* The Shurangama Mantra is called an efficacious language because of its spell-binding power. That's what "marvelous magic" is referring to. *Then come five eyes and six penetrations and the Way opens up.* If you can continually uphold the Shurangama Mantra--single-mindedly without entertaining other thoughts--then you can attain the Five Eyes and Six Spiritual Penetrations. You will then experience the inconceivable, unfathomable changes and transformations that occur which ordinary people are totally unaware of. And that's the reason why I hope everyone will learn to read the Shurangama Mantra and memorize it. Why is it that the demons, ghosts, and goblins don't dare show themselves when you recite the Shurangama Mantra? It's so powerful that there isn't a place in all of space or the entirety of the Dharma Realm that isn't flooded with auspicious light. Recitation of the Shurangama Mantra patches up the imperfections in the heavens and the earth. One person reciting the Shurangama Mantra creates power equivalent to one person. A hundred people reciting create power equivalent to a hundred people. And the weird beings here in this world become very well-behaved. So it's better if more people recite.

It's an unsurpassed spiritual mantra. The negating prefix "un-" actually means "lofty to the utmost; brilliant to the extreme." Peerless radiant illumination piercing the heights is the meaning of "un-". And "surpassed"? Well, there's nothing more esteemed, nothing more venerated. "Spiritual" is what is inconceivable and ineffable, what is awe-inspiring, efficacious and unfathomable. The power of mantras brings a response with the Way. When you recite mantras, something happens. "Brilliant Buddha's Crown, Great White Canopy of Light, Unsurpassed Spiritual Mantra." This means that the light at the crown of the Buddha's head is like a great white canopy that comes to shelter and protect all of us who recite the mantra.

No one understands this mantra, nor can they explain line by line and word by word. But if you want to understand it, I can try my best to explain it to you. The Shurangama Mantra can't be explained in a year's time, or three years' time, or even ten years' time. Now I will explain the general intent of this mantra. This mantra is composed of five assemblies which represent the five directions of east, west, south, north, and center. The east is the vajra division with Akshobhya Buddha as the teaching host. The south is the welling up of jewels division with Welling Up of Jewels Buddha as the teaching host. The center is the Buddha division with Shakyamuni Buddha as the teaching host. The west is the lotus division with Amitabha Buddha as the

，釋迦牟尼佛做教主；西方就是蓮華部，阿彌陀佛做教主；北方叫羯磨部，成就佛做教主，共有這五部。這五部就是管理這世界五方的五大魔軍，因為有這五魔，所以佛也分開五方，鎮壓這個魔。如果沒有佛，那魔就會出現於世了。所以你一誦〈楞嚴咒〉，這五方的五大魔軍就都俯首低頭，老老實實，不敢違犯〈楞嚴咒〉的這種威力。〈楞嚴咒〉具足這五部，所以這個〈楞嚴咒〉是最妙不過了；可是你要沒有執著，若有所執著，就不會太妙了。

〈楞嚴咒〉有五會，其中分出來有三十幾部法。我過去在東北的時候，能對治一切人的病痛，都因為〈楞嚴咒〉的這種力量。可是這〈楞嚴咒〉不是隨隨便便人人都可以使用的，若使用也不是全面的，因為分出來有三十幾部法。這是大概，若往詳細了說，有一百多種。

這個法，有成就法：就是一誦這〈楞嚴咒〉，你無論修什麼法門，求什麼事情，求什麼願，都會成就的，這是一種。又有增益法：就是譬如你修道，道心不夠，你一誦這個咒，能增益你的智慧，增益你的菩提心，增益你的願力，一切一切都會增加。你誦這個咒，對你自己有所求，也可以增益；對於旁人也可以增益，這是增益法。

息災法：就是你有什麼災難，你一誦這個咒就沒有了，消災了。譬如本來這個人應該掉海裡淹死，一念這個〈楞嚴咒〉，就把他解過去了，掉到海裡也淹不死了。或者你搭船，這個船應該會沉了，念這個咒，這個船也不沉了。或者坐飛機，這個飛機在空中應該爆炸，你一念這個咒，它也不爆炸了。但是你還要靠自己，把你自己心裡的災，也要消除出去。你心裡有什麼災呢？譬如你單靠著念咒，你心裡還是亂打妄想，盡想一些不好的念頭，你有這些不清淨的雜念、欲念，那你心裡頭那根本的災沒有除去，你念什麼咒也沒有用。所以想要息你的災，你必須要心裡先清淨；心裡清淨了，那是真息災。你心裡要是貪、瞋、癡裝滿肚子，你念什麼咒都不靈的。所以這心是最要緊的，心一定要慈悲良善，願意幫助其他人，要有一種好心。

勾召法：就是遇著天魔外道，你想要把他抓

teaching host. The north is the karma division with Accomplishment Buddha as the teaching host. Altogether these five divisions watch over the five demonic armies that abide in this world. Because of these five demons, the Buddhas split up in five directions to repress these demons. Without the Buddhas, these demons would show themselves here in our world. And so, when you recite the Shurangama Mantra, the five demonic armies in the five directions submit and surrender. They behave themselves and don't dare try to oppose the power of the Shurangama Mantra. The five divisions in the mantra are what make it so fine. But you shouldn't be attached. Your becoming attached won't be so fine.

Within the five assemblies of the Shurangama Mantra are more than thirty sections of Dharmas. Before, when I was in Manchuria, the reason I was able to cure people's illnesses was all because of the power of the Shurangama Mantra. But the Shurangama Mantra cannot be used casually. If used, it's not the entire thing that's used, because within it are, in general, more than thirty different Dharmas. If looked at in detail there are over a hundred.

As to these Dharmas, there's the Dharma of Accomplishment. That means by reciting the Shurangama Mantra, whatever method you are practicing will be perfected; whatever thing you want to do will get done. There's also the Dharma of Increasing Benefits. That means, for example, if you don't have enough resolve for the Way in your practice, by reciting the mantra you can increase your wisdom; increase your Bodhi mind; increase the power of your vows; everything will get better. When you recite the mantra, everything you hope increases will surely do so! It will increase for others, too.

The Dharma of Quelling Disasters means that if a calamity is due, reciting the mantra will make it disappear. The disaster will be quelled. Suppose someone is due to drown in the ocean. Reciting the mantra can change the situation so that he doesn't get drowned. Or you're on a boat that's supposed to sink. Recitation of the mantra can keep the boat from sinking. Or the airplane is supposed to crash, but you are reciting the mantra and so it doesn't. Nonetheless, you have to take responsibility for dispelling the calamities in your own mind. What calamities are there in your mind? Well, if you merely rely on the mantra, but inside you are a bundle of false and malevolent thoughts, scattered and impure thoughts, lustful thoughts, then you certainly haven't expelled the calamities in your own mind. In that case, no mantra is going to work. And so if you want to avoid disasters you must first purify your own mind. The purity of your mind is what really dispels calamities. If you are full of greed, hatred, and stupidity, no mantra is going to be efficacious. Our frame of mind is extremely important. We must be kindhearted and filled with goodness, wishing to help others. Our mind should be wholesome.

The Dharma for Hooking and Summoning is for use when you meet up with heavenly demons and externalists and want to catch them. Just as law enforcement officers catch criminals, so too, the Hooking and Summoning Dharma catches weird creatures, demons, and ghosts. They do something here to harm others or do some bad thing that causes people to get sick and then they run away. But you want to catch them and so you recite the mantra, using the Hooking and Summoning Dharma. Well, no matter how far away from you

來的時候用。舉個例子，就像世間的警察，把那犯罪的人抓來了；勾召法也是這樣子的，這妖魔鬼怪，他在這個地方害人，做不對的事情，令人生病，或者生災難，然後他跑了。你想要把他抓來，一誦這咒，用這個勾召法，他就相離多遠，這一切的護法善神、天龍八部、八萬四千金剛藏菩薩，即刻就能把妖魔鬼怪抓來。但是抓是抓來，他有時還是不服的，你必須用種種的方法來教化他。你單強壓迫他，來降伏他，是下品法，不是一種好的方法。好的方法，不用任何的勢力來壓迫，也不壓迫他，也不和他鬥爭，不要好像修羅似的，鬥爭堅固，不要學那樣。你明明有力量可以降伏他，也不要用降伏法，要用德行來感化他，來教化他。

又有降伏法：魔它也有神通，他也有咒，你念咒，他也念咒。但是你用這個〈楞嚴咒〉，就把他所有的咒，都給破了，把他降伏了。用這勢力把他折伏了，令他老實了。我以前對你們大家都講過，〈楞嚴咒〉其中有幾句是破魔羅網的一種咒，也是破魔咒術的。為什麼這個〈楞嚴咒〉一念，那個先梵天咒就沒有效驗了呢？就因為有這個五大心咒。這五大心咒是破天魔外道一切咒術的根本的咒。無論他有什麼咒，你一念這幾句，就都給他破了，他的咒就沒有功效了。我這個法如果要賣錢，幾百萬我也不賣。不過我看你們都有點誠心，我一個 cent（分）也不要，傳授給你們。

這就是降伏法。總而言之，無論你修什麼法，你必須要有無上的菩提道心，大慈大悲、大喜大捨。不可以用你的道力，來壓迫任何的人，或來壓迫任何的妖魔鬼怪。

又有吉祥法：你念這個咒，一切的事情都隨心如意，很吉祥的。這是有這種種的法，我把這幾種法的意思給你們講一講。

這個咒如果要說它的好處，那就是說幾年也說不完的，太多了。所有十方一切諸佛都是從〈楞嚴咒〉裡邊生出來的，所以〈楞嚴咒〉可以說是佛的母親。十方如來就是藉著〈楞嚴咒〉，得成無上正遍知覺。十方如來能應身到微塵數那麼多國家，去轉法輪教化

they are, the Dharma-protecting good spirits, or members of the eightfold division, or some of the eighty-four thousand Vajra Treasury Bodhisattvas will immediately snatch them and bring those demonic beings back. Even then, sometimes they won't give in and you have to use all kinds of expedients to teach and transform them. If you use brute force to subdue them, then that's the lowest grade of dharma, it's not a good method. The best methods don't use any sort of power plays to oppress beings. Don't oppress them and don't contend with them. Don't be like an asura--tough and looking for a fight. Even when you clearly have the power to do so, don't use the dharmas to subdue them. You should use virtuous conduct to influence beings and then teach and transform them.

And finally, there is the Dharma of Subduing. Demons have spiritual penetrations and they also have mantras. You recite your mantra and they recite theirs. But when you use the Shurangama Mantra, you break through all their mantras and subdue them. You use the power to quell them and make them behave. I've told you all before that the Shurangama Mantra has within it a few lines of mantra that rends the nets of demons. Why was the mantra from the Brahma Heavens rendered useless? It was because of the Five Great Hearts Mantra. The Five Great Hearts Mantra destroys the mantras underlying the demons' and externalists' spells and incantations. It doesn't matter what mantra they use, when you recite these lines, their spells are smashed and their mantras become ineffectual. If I wanted to market this Dharma, a million dollars wouldn't even touch my asking price! But I can see that you have a bit of sincerity and so I am transmitting it to you absolutely free. To sum it up, no matter what Dharma you cultivate, you must have the unsurpassed resolve for Bodhi; you must have great kindness and compassion; you must practice great giving and great renunciation. You must not use the powers you gain in practicing the Way to oppress any other person or to squelch any demon, monster, goblin, or ghost.

Furthermore, the Dharma of Auspiciousness enables things to go your way when you recite the mantra. Good fortune prevails. Now I've given you an explanation of these Dharmas.

I could talk for several years and never finish describing the good points of this mantra. All Buddhas of the ten directions come forth from the Shurangama Mantra. The Shurangama Mantra is the mother of all Buddhas. It was by means of the Shurangama Mantra that all Buddhas perfected Unsurpassed Proper and Pervasive Enlightened Knowledge. The ability of the Buddhas of the ten directions to create response bodies and go throughout the ten directions turning the Dharma wheel to teach and transform living beings; to rub the crowns of those beings and bestow predictions upon them; to rescue beings from their complex sufferings; to enable beings to escape both large disasters and small calamities--their ability to do all that comes from the power of the Shurangama Mantra Heart. If you want to attain the fruition of Arhatship, you absolutely must recite this mantra to keep demonic things from happening. During the Dharma-ending Age if people can memorize the Shurangama Mantra or encourage others to memorize it, well, fire cannot burn such people and water cannot drown them. No matter how potent a poison, it cannot harm them. For those who recite the Shurangama Mantra, poison turns to sweet dew as soon as it enters their mouths. People who recite the Shurangama Mantra will never get born in bad places, even if they want to. Why is that so? It's because the Shurangama Mantra pulls you back and won't

眾生，在十方給眾生摩頂授記，拔濟眾生的群苦，令眾生一切大小諸橫同時得到解脫，都是憑著這個〈楞嚴咒〉心的力量。假設想得阿羅漢果，你一定要誦這個咒，才能沒有魔事。末法的時候，如果有人能背誦〈楞嚴咒〉，或者叫他人誦讀〈楞嚴咒〉，這樣的人火也不能燒他，水也不能淹死他，無論大毒小毒，都害不了他。一切的毒入到誦持〈楞嚴咒〉這個人的口裡，都會變成甘露味。受持〈楞嚴咒〉的人不會生到不好的地方，就是你想去也不行。為什麼呢？這個〈楞嚴咒〉拉著你，叫你不要去！不要去！誦持〈楞嚴咒〉的眾生縱然他自己不做什麼福德，十方如來所有的功德都給這個人。你說這便宜不便宜！只念念〈楞嚴咒〉而已。你念〈楞嚴咒〉，就能常常生在佛出世的時候，和佛在一起熏修。

假設你心念非常散亂，沒能專一，而且沒有定力。可是你心裡想佛所說的〈楞嚴咒〉，口裡就誦持。金剛藏王菩薩就用很精真的這種心，跟著你這個散亂心持〈楞嚴咒〉的人，暗暗來催速，一點一點令你這個散亂心就沒有了，一點一點就可以得到定力。就是在默默中幫助你，令你開智慧，心念專一，從前八萬四千恆河沙劫這麼長時間的事情，你就一切一切都明瞭了。

你若能把〈楞嚴咒〉讀會了，能背得出，就像由你自己心裡流出來的，〈楞嚴咒〉也就是你一個心，你的心也就是〈楞嚴咒〉，得到持咒三昧，誦得猶如流水似的，源源不斷。這樣子，你最低限度也可以七生都像美國煤油大王那麼有錢，七世都做員外，做有錢的人。說：「這麼好，我趕快學〈楞嚴咒〉，好做七世員外。」你要是境界這麼小，那就不要學〈楞嚴咒〉了，七世員外也是一眨眼的期間。那麼念會〈楞嚴咒〉要希望什麼呢？要希望究竟作佛，得到無上正等正覺。不要境界那麼小，實際上學〈楞嚴咒〉，就是佛的化身；不但是佛的化身，還是佛的頂上化佛，化佛中的化佛，所以〈楞嚴咒〉的妙處是不可思議的。有人真能持〈楞嚴咒〉，在這個地方，虛空裡頭就有一個大白傘蓋。你的功夫若大、若高，你一念這個傘蓋，甚至於幾千里地以內，都無災無難了。

allow you to go. Someone who recites the Shurangama Mantra may never have amassed any blessings or virtue, but, simply because he recites the mantra, the Thus Come Ones of the ten directions will bestow their own merit and virtue upon that person. Wouldn't you call that a bargain? That happens based on the recitation of the Mantra alone. If you recite the Shurangama Mantra, you will continually get to be born at a time when a Buddha is in the world and will be able to immerse yourself in cultivation under that Buddha's guidance.

If your mind is terribly scattered so that you can't concentrate and don't have any samadhi-power, but you think about the Shurangama Mantra and recite it with your lips, the Vajra Treasury King Bodhisattvas will very attentively watch for ways to invisibly help you gradually until your confusion has disappeared and you develop samadhi. They will imperceptibly help you open your wisdom and concentrate your mind to the point that you become crystal clear about all the events spanning the previous eighty-four thousand Ganges' sands of eons.

If you can learn the Shurangama Mantra until you have memorized it fluently--so that you become one with the mantra--then you attain the mantra's samadhi and your recitation will be like flowing water, welling up uninterrupted. If you can do that, then at the very least for seven lives to come you will be as wealthy as America's richest oil magnates. And you say, "That's great! I'm going to learn the mantra right away! I wouldn't mind being a magnate of some kind!" Well, if you are that selfish, then don't even bother learning the mantra. Seven lives pass in the blink of an eye anyway. What should those who learn the Shurangama Mantra be hoping for? You should hope for ultimate Buddhahood; hope to attain the Unsurpassed Proper and Equal Right Enlightenment. Don't be so petty! Actually those who are really dedicated in reciting the Shurangama Mantra are transformation bodies of Buddhas. Not just any transformation bodies, but those atop the Buddha's crown--transformation bodies of that transformation body! And so you see that the wonderful aspects of the Shurangama Mantra are difficult to express, difficult to conceptualize. Wherever someone is seriously reciting the Shurangama Mantra, a great white canopy will be there in the space above him. If your skill in reciting the mantra is high-level and far-reaching, then when you recite, the canopy will extend for thousands of miles, preventing any disasters or difficulties. If you only have a little skill, then the canopy will be right above your own head protecting you. If you have virtue in the Way, if you are a High Sanghan, then when you recite, the entire nation will be benefitted and no calamities will occur. Or if disasters are unavoidable, big ones will turn into little ones, and the little ones won't even happen.

It doesn't matter if it's a nationwide famine, plague, war, or plunder, all those kinds of disasters will be alleviated. Suppose you were to write out the Shurangama spiritual mantra and place it at the main entrances to the city, or in its watchtowers or other lookout places; suppose you could inspire the nation's inhabitants to show interest in the Shurangama Mantra, so that they bow to and revere it and single-mindedly make offerings to it as if they were offering to the Buddhas themselves; suppose you could get every single citizen to wear the mantra on their person or to keep it in their place of

；你功夫若小，那麼這個傘蓋在你自己的頭上，也保護著你。你要是有道德，是一個大德高僧，你這一念，甚至於整個國家都得到好處了，都沒有什麼災難了。就有災難，大的災難也就化小了，小的災難就化沒有了。

無論哪一個國家飢荒、瘟疫傳染病，或者有打仗、賊難，所有一切的災難。你若能寫楞嚴神咒，放到城的四門上，或者有砲臺、堡壘那個看崗的地方，使令這個國家所有的眾生都迎接這個〈楞嚴咒〉，叩頭頂禮恭敬，一心供養這個〈楞嚴咒〉，就像供養佛那麼樣恭敬。使令這個國家的人民，每個人身上都佩帶一卷〈楞嚴咒〉，或者每個人把它放到自己所住的宅子裡邊。這樣，這些災難的事情都消滅了。如果有〈楞嚴咒〉在這個地方，天龍就都歡喜，也沒有狂風暴雨這種災害了，所有的五穀也都豐收，一般老百姓都很平安的。所以〈楞嚴咒〉這個功德是不可思議的，你想也想不到，思也思不到的，它妙的地方也在這個地方。

本來破戒是不可補救的，但是你若能念〈楞嚴咒〉，還能恢復你戒根清淨。但是能念，不是就念一念，一定要得到誦咒三昧。這個咒就是從你心裡念出來的，這個咒又能回來到你心裡。所謂咒心心咒，這個心和咒成一個了，沒有分別，你想要忘，也忘不了了，這叫不念而念，念而無念。你把一切妄想雜念都念沒有了，就是一個誦持〈楞嚴咒〉的心，這叫打成一團，成一個了，團結起來了。你這思想念頭團結起來了，沒有第二念了，就像流水源源而來，前浪推後浪，浪浪不斷，這樣子水流風動演摩訶，水流的聲音，和風動的聲音，都是〈楞嚴咒〉的咒心。你能念到這個樣子，那時候你就是破戒了，也還能得到戒根清淨；你沒有受戒，就得到受戒。本來你不向前進步，不研究佛法，一念〈楞嚴咒〉，念得時間久了，也自然生出一種精進心來；沒有智慧的人，也會開智慧。如果你修行不得清淨，開齋破戒，但是因為你不忘〈楞嚴咒〉，所以很快又恢復清淨了。如果你在沒持咒、沒受戒以前，犯過禁戒，那麼持咒之後，所有一切破齋犯戒，這一些個罪，不管是輕、是重，甚至於不通懺悔的四波羅夷罪、五逆、四棄八棄，你一念〈楞嚴

residence; well, if you could do that, all disasters would disappear. Whenever the Shurangama Mantra can be found in a place, the gods and dragons are delighted, and so that place will be free from devastating storms; the crops will produce in abundance; and the populace will be peaceful and happy. That is why I say that the merit and virtue of the Shurangama Mantra is inexpressible; it can't be reckoned in the mind; it can't be cognized in our thoughts. That's the wonder of it!

Basically broken precepts cannot be mended. But if you recite the Shurangama Mantra, you can return to purity. But when I say recite, I don't mean you can just do it casually. You have to attain the mantra-recitation samadhi. The recitation of the mantra must flow forth from your mind and the mantra must flow back into your mind. That's called "the mantra is the mind and the mind is the mantra." Your mind and the mantra become united. There isn't any distinction. It reaches the point where you couldn't forget it if you wanted to. That's called even when not reciting, the recitation continues; when reciting there really isn't any recitation. You recite until there aren't any idle thoughts remaining. The only function of the mind is the recitation of the Shurangama Mantra. That's called meshing with the mind. There are no second thoughts. The flow of the mantra's recitation is like water that flows on in uninterrupted waves. At that point, everything expresses the Mahayana--the sounds of the breezes blowing and the water flowing are all the Shurangama Mantra's Heart Mantra. If you can reach that level, then if you have broken precepts, you will be able to return to pure precepts. You will be endowed with the precepts without going through the formal transmission. If you are someone who doesn't want to progress in your practice, who doesn't want to investigate the Buddhadharma, but you recite the Shurangama Mantra for a period of time, quite naturally you will be inspired to be vigorous; those who lack wisdom can open their wisdom. If you are not pure in your cultivation so that you break your vegetarian practices and violate the precepts, but you have not forgotten the Shurangama Mantra, you will be able to quickly return to purity. If you violated precepts before you began upholding the mantra and prior to receiving the precepts, then once you start reciting the mantra you can completely wipe out all those former offenses, no matter how serious they were, including even the Four Parajikas, the Five Rebellious Acts, the Four or Eight Offenses warranting dismissal from the Sangha, which are basically unpardonable. Not even a hair's breadth of an offense will remain. And so I say that the power of the Shurangama Mantra is beyond all conception or description!

Some people who learn how efficacious the Shurangama Mantra is decide to exclusively recite it and ignore all other aspects of cultivation. That's going overboard. In cultivation, no matter what Dharma it is, you have to keep to the Middle Way. Don't do too much and don't fail to do enough. Although the mantra is definitely efficacious, still, you have to develop samadhi. The Shurangama Sutra describes how efficacious this mantra is, but it also explains the method of returning the hearing to listen to your own nature by cultivating perfect penetration of the ear organ. That's also extremely important. While you are reciting the mantra you should be returning your hearing to listen to your own nature. You must reflect within. Didn't I explain earlier how the mantra becomes the mind and the mind becomes the mantra? The

咒〉，無論怎麼樣重的罪都消滅了，連一個頭髮那麼多都沒有了，所以〈楞嚴咒〉的力量是不可思議。

有的人聽見〈楞嚴咒〉這麼靈，他就單單念咒，也不修行了，這也是一種太過的行為。因為修道，無論修哪一種法，要求中道，不要太過，也不要不及。這個咒固然是靈，但是定力也要修的。《楞嚴經》說這個咒是靈的，但是反聞聞自性，修耳根圓通這個法門，也是最要緊的。你就誦咒的時候，也應該反聞聞自性，要自己迴光返照。前邊不是說嗎？誦這個咒，咒就是心，心也就是咒，心和咒分不開了，心、咒，二而不二。你能到這個樣子上了，你求什麼就都能隨心如意，一定會成就的。那麼你能心和咒都合到一起，這也正是你得到禪定三昧了，得到真正的定力了。所以這一點，我們每一個人要知道的。

〈楞嚴咒〉每一句都有無量意義，每一義都有無量功能。要明白〈楞嚴咒〉是天地間的靈文，靈文中之靈文，秘中之秘，無上法寶，是一切眾生救命之寶。它包羅萬有，上自十方諸佛，下至阿鼻地獄，四聖六凡都要遵從〈楞嚴咒〉的法，十法界中，無論哪一個法界都沒有超出這個範圍；所有一切鬼種類、神種類、一切護法諸天的種類、聲聞、緣覺、佛乘都在〈楞嚴咒〉內。〈楞嚴咒〉所說的都是鬼神王的名字，一念這鬼神王的名字，其餘鬼眷屬和神眷屬就都服服貼貼，循規蹈矩，不敢放肆了。天天念〈楞嚴咒〉，能令世上的妖魔鬼怪都老實一點，不敢出來害人。〈楞嚴咒〉是全體大用的，可以說是包括佛教所有的教義，若能明白〈楞嚴咒〉，就能將佛教秘密精華都明白。天地間的奧妙、天地間不可思議的事情，也是在〈楞嚴咒〉內。若會〈楞嚴咒〉，則不必學密宗，白教、黑教、黃教、紅教，什麼教也不需要學。這是根本的三昧法，最究竟的密法。不過這種密法沒有人懂得，也沒有人認識。一般人都是學而不化，只知道念，卻不知它的意義。本來咒不必知道意義，只要知道它是不可思議的靈文就夠了。

能念〈楞嚴咒〉就是利益眾生，不能念就不能利益眾生。各位趕快把〈楞嚴咒〉學會，背

mind and the mantra cannot be separated; they are non-dual. When you get there, then you can attain whatever you seek; everything will go the way you want it to; and you will have success in whatever you undertake. When the mind and the mantra merge into one, then you have actually attained the samadhi of Chan meditation and have acquired real samadhi-power. That is something you should know.

Every line of the Shurangama Mantra contains infinite meanings as well as infinite functions. You should realize that the Shurangama Mantra is the most efficacious language in the world--the efficacious within the efficacious, the esoteric within the esoteric! It is an unsurpassed Dharma Treasure--the gem that can save living beings' lives. It embraces all that exists. From the Buddhas of the ten directions to the Avichi Hell, all the four kinds of sages and six sorts of common realms pay homage to the Shurangama Mantra. None of the ten Dharma realms transcends its scope. All categories of ghosts, spirits, Dharma-protecting deities, Hearers, Condition-enlightened Ones, up to the Buddha Vehicle are contained within the Shurangama Mantra. The Shurangama Mantra contains the names of ghost and spirit kings. When the names of those leaders are recited, all the ghosts and spirits in their retinues become very obedient and behave themselves. They don't dare to make trouble. Reciting the Shurangama Mantra every day can cause demonic beings and weird ghosts throughout the world to settle down and stop harming people. The substance and function of the Shurangama Mantra are all-encompassing. It can be said that within the mantra can be found the entirety of Buddhism's teachings and meanings. If you can understand the Shurangama Mantra, then you have understood the essence of Buddhism's esoteric teachings. All the inconceivable wonders and esoteric phenomena in the universe are contained in the Shurangama Mantra. If you master the Shurangama Mantra, then you don't need to study the esoteric school's white teaching, black teaching, yellow teaching, red teaching or any other teaching. This is the ultimate method of samadhi and the most esoteric Dharma. Unfortunately no one really understands this esoteric Dharma; no one even recognizes it. Most people study it but cannot absorb it; they can only recite it but don't know its meanings. Basically it's not necessary to know the meanings of mantras, you need only realize that they are an ineffable efficacious language.

Being able to recite the Shurangama Mantra is a benefit to all beings. Not being able to recite it, you cannot offer that benefit to beings. Quickly learn it, memorize it, investigate and understand it! Then you will be doing what Buddhist disciples should do. The very best is for those who want to recite the Shurangama Mantra to do it for the sake of the entire world; transfer all the merit to the whole world. There isn't anything more important in Buddhism than the Shurangama Mantra. The Shurangama Mantra is a sure sign of the Proper Dharma. The existence of the Shurangama Mantra ensures the existence of the Proper Dharma. When the Shurangama Mantra is gone, the Proper Dharma is gone. Those who cannot recite this mantra are not worthy of being Buddhist disciples. The Shurangama Mantra is nicknamed "six months' stupor" because for most people it takes a half year of diligent recitation to get it memorized. Those of us who can recite the Shurangama Mantra have been planting and

得出，再研究明白了，才是佛教徒所應有的行爲。想學〈楞嚴咒〉，持誦〈楞嚴咒〉的人最好能發大心，爲全世界誦持，把所有的功德迴向給全世界。在佛教裡再沒有比〈楞嚴咒〉更重要了，〈楞嚴咒〉是正法的代表，有〈楞嚴咒〉就有正法，沒有〈楞嚴咒〉就沒有正法，不會背〈楞嚴咒〉不配做佛教徒。〈楞嚴咒〉叫楞半年，天天念，要念半年才會背。我們能誦〈楞嚴咒〉的人，都是在無量劫以來培植大善根的人，才能把〈楞嚴咒〉讀得熟，背出來，永遠也不忘，這就是善根的表現。若你沒有善根，不但不能念，就連〈楞嚴咒〉的名字也遇不著；就算遇著了也不懂，不會念。所以我們現在能念能背，都是有大善根。

楞嚴法是百千萬劫難遭遇的法門，我們學得一句，明白一句的力量，便要照著去實行。但也不是聽說法有大靈感妙用及力量，就去用它。你用法，但不持戒，好像一般人什麼都不懂，隨便殺生、偷盜、邪淫、妄語、飲酒，而在緊要關頭時念五大心咒，這是污蔑法；沒有功德，卻要支配鬼神及護法，那只有增加自己的罪業，自己會遭受飛災橫禍之事。所以修法的人首先要守持戒律，要注重德行，必須要不爭、不貪、不求、不自私、不自利、不打妄語。你道德不夠，就像假傳聖旨，冒充國王，這是行不通的。現在人只注重念咒靈驗有功力，但不注重自己的品德，即使念也沒有功力。

所以學〈楞嚴咒〉法，所行必須要正，存心要正，不打不清淨的妄想，不做不清淨的事，要念茲在茲修清淨的行門。如果一方面修〈楞嚴咒〉法門，一方面不好好守規矩，就會有很大的問題發生，這一點大家必須明白。若是你不存正念，不行正行，便會令金剛藏菩薩不佩服你，不保護你，佛菩薩是慈悲的，他不會損害眾生，不會瞋害人；可是所有的侍從，一切的護法、天龍、鬼神，都是有很大的脾氣。這種惡鬼、惡神，他見到你這修道持咒的人有過錯了，他就給你一點災害，或者令你不自在，令你有很大的麻煩，你便會發生種種災難，受種種的果報，這是絲毫不可以開玩笑的。所以必須要齋戒沐浴，要心裡也清淨，不打染污的念頭；身上也清淨，不行染污的法門，時時刻

nurturing good roots for countless eons. Being able to memorize it perfectly and never forget it is evidence of those good roots. Without good roots, not only will you not be able to recite it, you will never even hear of the existence of the Shurangama Mantra; or if you hear of it you won't understand it and won't be able to recite it. Truly, then, those who can recite it by heart do have great good roots!

The Shurangama Mantra is a Dharma-door difficult to encounter in billions of eons. For every line we learn and understand, we activate one part of its power. But, then, we must actually put it into practice. However it's not that you try to make use of the mantra's vast efficacy and tremendous power. If you use this Dharma but you don't hold the precepts--like most people who aren't clear about anything and casually kill, steal, are lustful, lie, and indulge in intoxicants, and who only recite the Five Great Hearts Mantra when some crisis happens--then you are defiling the Dharma and there is no merit in that. If you insist on trying to control the ghosts and order the Dharma protectors around, then you're just going to be increasing your own karmic offenses. You will bring calamities down upon yourself. Therefore, the first criterion for people who want to cultivate a Dharma is to hold the precepts and place emphasis on developing virtuous conduct. You must not fight, be greedy, seek, be selfish, pursue your own advantages, or lie. If your virtue in the Way is insufficient but you pretend to be a sage who can transmit teachings, or pass yourself off as the leader of a nation, then your behavior is unacceptable. Nowadays everyone is interested in getting the most magic out of mantras, but they are not attentive to their own moral character. And so in fact their recitation will be ineffectual.

Therefore those who study the Shurangama Mantra Dharma must be proper in their behavior, proper in their intent; must not have defiled thoughts, and must not do impure deeds. They should be very attentive to cultivating purity. If on the one hand they cultivate the Shurangama Mantra and on the other hand they don't follow the rules, then they will get themselves into deep trouble. Everyone should pay close attention to this point. If your intent is not proper and your conduct is not proper, then the Vajra Treasury Bodhisattvas will lose their respect for you and won't protect you. The Buddhas and Bodhisattvas are compassionate and would not hurt any living being or harm beings out of anger. But their attendants--the Dharma-protectors, gods, dragons, ghosts, and spirits will become enraged. Those evil ghosts and evil spirits, upon seeing you cultivating the mantra while committing offenses, will bring disaster and harm down upon you; will make you feel very uncomfortable; will cause you to get in grave trouble; or make you have to undergo a series of misfortunes or a series of retributions. This is really no joking matter! Therefore you must eat vegetarian food and purify yourself. Most of all your mind must be pure. Don't have defiled false thoughts. Maintain physical purity and don't practice defiling dharmas. At all times guard your purity. Don't commit even the slightest infractions of the rules.

Reciting the Shurangama Mantra is more valuable than any amount of gold. Reciting the mantra once is equivalent to tons of gold! But your recitation shouldn't be motivated by greed! If you hold the precepts, then you won't be jealous or obstructive; you won't be greedy or angry and your recitation of the mantra will generate

刻要保持清淨，不可以有絲毫不守規矩的行爲
。

誦持〈楞嚴咒〉比買賣黃金更賺得多，誦〈楞嚴咒〉一遍，就等於幾萬萬盎斯的黃金那麼有價值，不過不能用貪心來誦持。若能持戒律，無嫉妒障礙，無貪瞋癡，那麼誦持〈楞嚴咒〉就有大感應、大利益；若你有不守規矩的行爲，修這個法便沒有大的感應力量。並不是咒沒有靈驗，而是因爲你不守規矩，護法善神離得你遠遠的，有什麼事情他也不管。所以凡是讀誦〈楞嚴咒〉的人，不要有一種詭譎的心，不要有一種盡造罪業的行爲。任何時候都要正大光明，只知利他，不知利己，存菩薩心腸，行菩薩行門。

修楞嚴法是很靈感的，但也不是那麼容易，首先要沒有自私心，其次要沒有自利心，要存大公無私的心，要存至中不偏的心，要存捨己爲人的心，要存普度一切眾生的心。有以上所說這樣的心，便能很快成就。各位要很注意，你一定要守五戒，奉行十善，這是最低限度要遵守的規則。修這個法不守規矩是不行的，你不守戒律，或心裏盡打染污的妄想，不單修法沒有感應，不能成就，而且會有奇禍。所以修楞嚴法的時候，要特別注意，要身、口、意三業清淨，才可以相應。不可以隨隨便便講是講非，挑撥離間，或令大家在道場住得不安樂。你一定要舉動行爲管自己，行住坐臥不離家，不可以盡給旁人洗衣服，要自己好好把自己照顧一下，迴光返照。

〈楞嚴咒〉是靈文，每一句有每一句的效力，你不必想：「我持〈楞嚴咒〉怎麼沒有什麼效驗？」不管有沒有功效，你就去念，好像打功夫，天天去打拳，不管功夫如何，鍛鍊就有功夫，不可說不鍛鍊就有功夫。同理，受持法要天天不間斷，在任何情形下，在百忙中都要修法。不要時間久了就生懈怠，對〈楞嚴咒〉不再有興趣。這不是說你一念，就見到什麼功效，就見、不見什麼功效，你也要天天受持讀誦。這必須要日久功深，不是一朝一夕就能成就，就有感應的。好像讀書要讀十年、二十年、三十年，才能真正有學問，修行亦復如是。持誦這個咒，你要念茲在茲的，時時刻刻都誦持這個咒，不要間斷，也就像穿衣、吃飯、睡

pervasive responses and massive benefits. But if your behavior doesn't accord with the rules, the Dharma protecting good spirits will stay far away from you and when something happens to you they won't pay any attention. Therefore, those who recite the Shurangama Mantra shouldn't be cunning or behave in ways that continually create offenses. At all times they should be open and public-spirited; they should strive to benefit others, not themselves; they should cherish the ideals of Bodhisattvas; and cultivate the practices of Bodhisattvas.

The Shurangama Mantra is extremely efficacious, but it is not that easy to master. First of all you cannot be selfish; next you cannot be out to get your own private gains. You have to be magnanimous and devoid of selfish thoughts. You have to be impartial and not prejudiced. You have to be willing to sacrifice yourself for the sake of others. You have to have the resolve to universally save all living beings. If you can embody the above-listed qualities, then you will have swift success. Pay close attention: you must hold the five precepts and practice the ten good deeds. That's the very least you should do.

It won't work to practice this Dharma if you are not following the rules. If you cultivate this Dharma but you don't behave yourself; if you don't guard the precepts or if you are always having defiled thoughts, then not only will there be no response, not only will you have no success, you will in fact bring disaster down upon yourself. And so when you are cultivating the Shurangama Mantra you must be very attentive to maintain purity with your body, your mouth, and your mind. That's the only way you're going to get a response. You cannot say things that cause schisms or make people in the Way-place uneasy. You must pay attention to all aspects of your behavior, whether walking, standing, sitting, or lying down. It's not all right to always be "washing other peoples' clothes" as it were. Take care of yourself. Look into yourself.

The Shurangama Mantra is an efficacious language. Every line has its own particular efficacy. But you don't need to think: Why don't I get any responses from holding the Shurangama Mantra. Don't pay any attention to whether there are responses or not, just keep reciting it. It's like practicing martial arts, every day you have to practice your punches, regardless of what your skill is like. Skill comes through training. It's impossible to have skill without training. By the same principle, you should cultivate your Dharmas every day, no matter what happens, no matter how busy you are. Don't slack off after you've been at it for a while, losing interest in the Shurangama Mantra. It's certainly not the case that you will have some efficacious response as soon as you begin reciting it. Regardless of whether you perceive any response, you should continue reciting it every day. You must deepen your skill day by day. Success doesn't happen overnight. For instance you have to study for ten, twenty, or even thirty years before you gain real scholarship. It's the same with cultivation. You must keep your mind on your recitation of the mantra, continuing your recitation without ever letting it get cut off. It should be just as important as putting on clothes, eating food, and going to sleep; you shouldn't be able to be without it for a single day. It doesn't matter whether there's any response, because by reciting every day you will gradually have a foundation and quite naturally the mantra will

覺那樣要緊，一天都不可以少的。不管它有沒有功效，你天天受持讀誦，時間久了就有基礎，自然就有它的功用。

你想成就妙行，得到不可思議的力量，你不要心裏總打妄想，想入非非，總是妙想天開。你誦咒若間斷了，你三昧就不會成就的。修習楞嚴法門要拿出真心、誠心來修習。什麼叫真心？就是為修持〈楞嚴咒〉，把時間也忘了，空間也沒有了。是日、是夜都不知道，吃飯、沒吃飯也不知道，睡覺、沒睡覺不知道。什麼都忘了，什麼都沒有了，一念像無量劫那麼長，無量劫又為一念。要有這種精神，吃飯、睡覺什麼都忘了，只一心來修行〈楞嚴咒〉，一定成就楞嚴三昧的。不能這樣，就談不到真正修楞嚴法門。不只修楞嚴法是如此，修其他的法門都要如此，行不知行，坐不知坐，渴不知渴，餓不知餓。說：「那不是變成最愚癡的人了嗎？」就是要如此，這才叫

### 養成大拙方為巧　　學到如愚始見奇

你若能學愚癡到這個樣子，無論你修那個法門，都能得到三昧，都會有所成就的。就因為你沒能愚癡，沒能真正深入三昧的境界，所以修來修去也不相應。

你用功持誦〈楞嚴咒〉的時候，或者會夢見拜佛，或者夢見佛放光，或者夢見佛來摩頂，或者夢見佛和你講經說法，或者夢見菩薩、緣覺、聲聞、聖僧，或天上的天將，或者夢見自己騰身虛空，或者夢見會飛了，這都是好境界；或者騎馬，或者渡江，種種祥瑞的光，或者有種種非常出奇的異相。假設得到這樣的應驗，你更應該很小心的，你要發菩提心，身、口、意三業要清淨，更加緊你的功夫來持誦這個咒。可是你不可以對人去宣說，你有什麼感應了，有什麼靈驗，叫人相信你，對你有好感。你有什麼感應，自己知道就得了，你盡炫示自己的功德，各處賣廣告，滿街賣修行，這是不對的。你如果這樣，便有了漏洞，魔就得其便。就好像你有了財寶，不把它放在保險箱裏，你把它放在門口，一定會被人偷去。所以修佛法要很小心，不要讓天魔外道得便。可是和你同道的，就是一同修行，你不是為了名利，或

function.

If you hope for its wonderful functions and inconceivable power, then you must not keep having false thoughts, always day-dreaming and fantasizing. If you cut off your recitation of the mantra, then you will not be able to attain samadhi. You must use your true mind and practice the Shurangama Mantra with sincerity. What's a true mind? It means that for the sake of reciting the Shurangama Mantra you can forget all about time and even space disappears. You don't know if it's day or night; you don't know if you've eaten or not; you don't know if you've slept or not. You forget everything else. Everything disappears and one thought extends for infinite eons, while infinite eons is one thought. That's the kind of spirit you should have--forgetting to eat and sleep for the sake of cultivating the Shurangama Mantra. In that way you certainly can attain the Shurangama Samadhi. If you cannot be that way, then you aren't really cultivating the Shurangama Dharma-door. You should be that way not only in cultivating the Shurangama Mantra, but in the cultivation of any Dharma door-- walking without realizing you are walking; sitting with being aware you are sitting; being unaware that you are thirsty or hungry. "Well," you say, "isn't that just turning into a stupid person?" That's right. It's said,

*When you learn to be a big idiot, then you start to have some skill; Studying until you are as if stupid is the beginning of real insight.*

If you can learn to be as if stupid, then no matter what Dharma door you cultivate you will attain samadhi and gain some realization. It's just because you are unable to be stupid that you cannot properly enter into samadhi and don't get any response from your cultivation.

When you are developing your skill in reciting the Shurangama Mantra, you may dream of yourself bowing to the Buddhas; or in a dream see the Buddhas emitting light; or dream that you see the Buddha come as rub the crown of your head; or dream that the Buddhas speak Dharma for you; or dream that you see the Bodhisattvas, or Condition-enlightened Ones, or Hearers, or Sagely Sanghans or gods and heavenly generals; or in a dream see yourself ascending into space; or dream that you can fly. All of these are good experiences. Or you may be riding a horse or crossing a river and encounter all sorts of auspicious lights; or there may be other extremely rare appearances that manifest. If you do attain responses such as these, then you should be very careful. You should bring forth the resolve for Bodhi; guard the purity of the karma created by your body, mouth, and mind; and increase your efforts and tighten your skill in reciting the mantra. You should not tell others what kinds of responses you've had in order to get others to believe in you or to think highly of you. It's enough for you yourself to know what responses you've had. If you keep advertising your own merits and selling your cultivation out on the streets, then you are wrong. If you act like that, you leave yourself open and the demons will attack. That's like failing to put your jewels in a safebox. If you leave them at the doorway, then someone is certainly going to steal them. Therefore, we must be very careful in our cultivation of the Buddhadharma. Don't let the heavenly demons and externalists have their way with you. But you can report

宣化老和尚追思紀念專集

者爲了令人恭敬我、讚歎我，你可以説的。

在《楞嚴經》上説：你要是誦持〈楞嚴咒〉，有了功夫，有了受用，那麼八萬四千金剛藏菩薩和他的徒眾眷屬，就都常常隨從保護著你，令你遂心滿願。縱然魔王想找一個漏洞，想來找你的麻煩也沒法子。在過去五祖弘忍大師在湖北東山那個地方修行，他戒行精嚴，修行也特別認真。

有一次土匪把湖北這個城給圍上，弘忍大師忍不住了，就想要救這個城裏頭的老百姓，於是乎他就下山了，從東山那個地方到湖北城裏去。土匪一見弘忍大師來了，就嚇得丟盔卸甲望影而逃，爲什麼這樣子呢？因爲弘忍大師雖然是一個人下山來的，可是土匪就看到完全是穿金盔金甲的天兵天將，好像從天上下來的天神一樣，都穿著金盔金甲，手拿著寶劍威武奇揚的。土匪一見到這樣的情形就嚇得望影而逃，不用一刀、一鎗、一箭，他們就撤退了。這是因爲弘忍大師他誦持〈楞嚴咒〉，所以土匪一見著弘忍大師就嚇得跑了。這也可以説是金剛藏菩薩顯聖，也可以説是弘忍大師修行的威德把他們都懾服了。那麼一個修道的人能不用一兵一卒，把這個土匪給嚇跑了，這就是有眞正的功夫才能這樣子，若沒有眞正的功夫，怎麼會有這樣的感應道交。

因爲釋迦牟尼佛爲了保護我們現在所有一切初發心的學道人，所以宣示〈楞嚴咒〉，來幫助我們得到定力，令我們身心泰然，沒有什麼麻煩。所以我們時時刻刻不要忘了這個法，我們若能誠心專一誦持〈楞嚴咒〉，就是紹隆佛法，就是正法住世。

your experiences to your fellow-cultivators if you are not doing it in order to get famous or rich or to make people respect and praise you.

The *Shurangama Sutra* says, "If you recite and uphold the Shurangama Mantra until you gain skill and can make it function, then eighty-four thousand Vajra Treasury Bodhisattvas and their retinue of followers will always stay near you and protect you, so that everything you hope for will come true." But the demon kings never give up searching for a hole so they can give you more trouble than you can handle.

In the past, Great Master Hongren, the Fifth Patriarch, was cultivating in Hubei at East Mountain. He upheld the precepts strictly and cultivated with unusual intensity. Once when a group of bandits surrounded the city of Hubei, Great Mater Hongren could bear it no longer and decided to try to save the people in that city. He came down the mountain and walked into that city. As soon as the bandits saw Great Master Hongren coming, they were terrified, dropped their armor and weapons, and fled. Why? Because although Great Master Hongren came alone into the city, the bandits saw an army of heavenly generals and heavenly troops clad in golden armour. It was as if the gods themselves had come down to earth--all donning golden armour and carrying jeweled swords and other awesome weapons. That's what caused the bandits to retreat in such haste. And so, without the use of a single knife, spear, or arrow, he routed the bandits. It was because Great Master Hongren recited the Shurangama Mantra that the bandits found him to be so terrifying. You could say that was a manifestation created by the Vajra Treasury Bodhisattvas or you could say it was the awesome virtue of Great Master Hongren that frightened them. That a cultivator was able to frighten the bandits into retreat without the use of a single soldier or weapon is verification of his genuine skill. How else could there have been such a response in the Way?

Shakyamuni Buddha proclaimed the Shurangama Mantra in order to protect of all of us who have brought forth the initial resolve to study the Way; to aid us in attaining samadhi; to help us be at peace in body and mind; and to keep us out of trouble. Therefore we should never forget this Dharma. We should recite and uphold the Shurangama Mantra with single-minded sincerity. By doing so we are helping to perpetuate the Buddhadharma, to keep the Proper Dharma long in the world.

# 宣公上人語錄
## QUOTATIONS OF THE
## VENERABLE MASTER HUA

◇ 我們大家要發願：
「我們不要末法，我們就要正法！我們走到什麼地方，什麼地方就要變成正法！」
We should all make this vow: "We don't want the Dharma to come to an end.
Wherever we go, we want the Proper Dharma to exist there."

◇ 翻譯經典都要特別謹慎小心，不是隨便就把經的某一段就取消了。
We should be very scrupulous in translating the Sutras, and we should not casually delete
passages.

◇ 聽法是特別能增長人善根的，特別能開人智慧的。有機會聽法，
那比你賺多少錢都有價值。你們各位不要認為這是一件很平常的事情，
你們現在能來聽經，來學習佛法，這都是有大善根、大德行的。
Listening to the Dharma is an especially good way to increase our good roots and open our
wisdom. An opportunity to listen to the Dharma is worth more than any amount of money you
could earn. You all shouldn't think it is a simple matter to be able to come and listen to the
Sutras and study the Dharma. You are able to do so only because you have amassed a lot of
good roots and virtuous conduct.

◇ 往前進，精進！精進！精進！就是菩薩了，就是這樣子，沒有旁的巧妙的。
A Bodhisattva is simply someone who advances with great vigor. That's all there is to it.
There's no other secret.

◇ 古來的聖人，是自己責罰自己，
不是像現在的人，什麼事情不說自己的不對，就找人家的不是。
The ancient sages always blamed themselves. Modern people, however, look for faults in others
instead of acknowledging their own faults.

◇ 愁一愁，就地獄遊一遊；
笑一笑，就老還少；
哭一哭，就地獄有個小黑屋。
Depressed and melancholy, you roam through the hells.
Happy and smiling, you enjoy eternal youth.
Weeping and woe make a small dark room in the hells.

◇ 忍辱就是人家罵我，我也忍；人家打我，我也忍；
人家對我怎麼樣不好，我也要忍。
Patience means: "If people scold me, I can bear it. If they hit me, I can take it.
No matter how badly they treat me, I can endure it."

宣化老和尚追思紀念專集

◈ 錢是最邋遢的一個東西，你要是和它接近得太多了，那就是塵埃。
Money is the filthiest thing around. If you stay around it very long, you'll be defiled.

◈ 你做的好事，願意教人知道，那不是真的好事。
你做的壞事，怕人知道，那才是壞事。
If you wish others to know about your good deeds, they are not truly good deeds.
If you fear others will find out about your bad deeds, those are truly bad deeds.

◈ 修道，能增益你的智慧，增益你的菩提心，增益你的願力，一切一切都會增加。
Through cultivating the Way, you can increase your wisdom, your resolve for Bodhi,
the power of your vows, and everything else.

◈ 各位善知識，不要做釋迦牟尼佛一個不孝順的弟子，我們不要常常自己搗亂，
自己骨肉殘傷，自己給自己麻煩，這是我對現代佛教的期望。
All Good and Wise Advisors, we should not be unfilial disciples of Shakyamuni Buddha.
We fellow Buddhists should not stir up trouble among ourselves and try to hurt each other.
This is my hope for modern Buddhism.

◈ 時時刻刻都要精進勇猛，向前去邁進，不要向後退，不要懶惰。
At all times we should vigorously and courageously advance. We must never retreat or
become lazy.

◈ 佛教裏頭，沒有什麼不能解決的問題。
There aren't any problems that can't be solved in Buddhism.

◈ 地獄沒有門，地獄這個門是自己開的。
There are no doors to the hells; you yourself make the doors.

◈ 要柔和善順，不應該暴躁，心裏面對於一切事情也不驚恐。
Be gentle and agreeable. Avoid a hot temper. Don't be frightened under any circumstances.

◈ 做人一定要循規蹈矩，你不循規蹈矩，將來受的果報也就是不正常、不正當的。
Be someone who abides by the rules. If you don't follow the rules, you will have to under go
the retribution of being abnormal in the future.

◈ 若不到隨緣不變、不變隨緣的境界，一定要小心謹慎，時時刻刻都不要打妄想。
If you have not reached the state of being able to accord with conditions without changing,
you must be very careful not to indulge in idle thoughts at any time.

◈ 任何的境界來了，任何魔障來了，我也一定要學佛法。
我不會變易我這種的思想，我絕對要有這個堅固的心，真心來學佛法。
No matter what circumstances or demonic obstacles we encounter, we are determined not
to waver in our resolve to study the Buddhadharma. This is the kind of resoluteness and
sincerity we must have in studying Buddhism.

◆ 父母就是堂上的活佛，我不能捨近求遠。
Parents are living Buddhas right in your own home, so don't neglect what is near to seek afar.

◆ 你這個身體是應該給這個世界有一點貢獻，做一點工作。
With this body of yours, you ought to do some work and make a contribution to the world.

◆ 修道要有一種恆心，要有一種誠心，又要有一種堅固心。
Practice of the Way requires perseverance, sincerity, and determination.

◆ 學佛法就是想要了生死。
The purpose of studying Buddhadharma is to put an end to birth and death.

◆ 要一天比一天有進步，就必須要自己一天比一天管自己，自己要收攝身心。
收攝身心，就是不打妄想。
If we want to make daily progress, we must become more strict with ourselves each day.
We must become more collected and focused by not indulging in discursive thoughts.

◆ 佛所說的法是觀機逗教，應人說法，
應病予藥的法門，沒有什麼地方是一個對，也沒有什麼地方是一個非。
When the Buddha spoke Dharma and taught people according to their needs, he was like a physician dispensing the right medicine to each patient. Therefore, one cannot say of any part of his teachings that they are right or wrong per se.

◆ 你不說人好，不說人壞，也不怨嫌人家，
你心裏就安樂了，就沒有貪瞋癡在你心裏了。
If you avoid praising, criticizing, and bearing grudges against others, your mind will be peaceful and free from greed, anger, and delusion.

◆ 你內裏沒有障礙了，外邊障礙也就障礙不了你，也就沒有憂愁了。
If you have no obstacles in your own mind, then outer obstacles will not hinder you or cause you worry.

◆ 不可以隨隨便便地罵學佛法的人、修佛道的人。
One may not carelessly scold those who study and practice the Buddha's teachings.

◆ 不應該拿著佛法來講笑話，來隨隨便便地談論。
Don't joke about the Dharma, and don't talk about it frivolously.

◆ 常常應該深心，恭恭敬敬地禮拜十方的諸大菩薩，要常常存這種的心。
你有一分的恭敬心，
就得到一分這種感應的好處；你有十分的恭敬，就得到十分這感應的好處。
You should always maintain an attitude of deep respect and make obeisance to the great Bodhisattvas of the ten directions. For every bit of respect you have, you will gain a bit of response. If you are one hundred percent respectful, you will gain the benefit of a response of one hundred percent.

宣化老和尚追思紀念專集

◆ 這種種的戒律，無非教人守規矩。能守規矩，能以令社會安定秩序，
能以令人群沒有一切的麻煩。所以這個戒律，是安定世界的一個基礎。

All the various kinds of precepts are aimed at helping people follow the rules. People who follow the rules can help maintain order in society and resolve the problems faced by humankind. Thus, the moral precepts are the basis for world peace.

◆ 學佛法的人，一天比一天要精進，一天比一天要誠心，
一天比一天要守規矩，一天比一天要聰明。

Students of the Buddhadharma should become more energetic, more earnest, more disciplined, and more intelligent each day.

◆ 想要有真正的智慧，必須要循規蹈矩來用功夫，
才能得到這種真正的智慧。

To obtain genuine wisdom, we must work hard in our practice and be in accord with the rules.

◆ 我希望各位，以後都自己要照顧自己，自己要管著自己。
自己能管自己，終究有一天，你就會成功的。

In the future, I hope all of you will look after yourselves and supervise yourselves. With such self-supervision, you will certainly succeed one day.

◆ 佛的智慧和光明，就好像太陽普照大地似的。
他是無微不照，沒有一個黑暗的地方他照不到的，所以好像如日之照。

The Buddha's wisdom and radiance are like the sun, because they shine upon the entire earth, lighting up even the remotest corners of darkness.

◆ 立功，譬如你建造廟宇，修補橋樑、道路，為所有的人來謀幸福，
令所有的人都得到利益了，這叫立功。德，就是自己沒有虧心的事情，
你做事情做得仰不愧於天，俯不怍於人，外不欺人，內不欺己。

Merit is created through deeds that benefit society, such as building temples and repairing bridges and roads. Virtue means having a good conscience and not being ashamed before Heaven or people because one has neither deceived others nor cheated oneself.

◆ 我注重的是真功實行，不注重那些個虛偽的宣傳。

What I stress is genuine merit and real practice, not false publicity.

◆ 常常要修行這種直言直行，對於任何的人，
也沒有彎曲心，所謂「直心是道場」。

Always be honest and open in your speech and actions. Don't be sneaky or evasive with anyone. A straight mind is the Bodhimanda.

◆ 你研究佛法，比你把金錢放到銀行裏去更有價值！
對你這個法身慧命是更重要，所以不要以為世間的財那是真的。

Studying Buddhism is worth more than any amount of money you save up in the bank! In terms of your Dharma body and wisdom life, the Dharma is far more important than money. Don't take worldly wealth so seriously.

◆ 學佛法，這個是功德法財，不可以把它看輕了！不可以馬馬虎虎的！
When you study the Dharma, you amass a wealth of Dharma and meritorous virtue. So, don't look lightly upon this and act in a careless manner.

◆ 說的是法，行的才是道，你要躬行實踐去修行，依照法修行，這才能得到受用。
The Dharma is spoken; the Way has to be practiced. In order to derive benefit, you have to actually practice according to the Dharma.

◆ 世界愈昌明，昌明到極點，就又該黑暗了。
這世界上，大同小異，什麼事情，都有一個循環的道理。
No matter how flourishing the world becomes, when it reaches the height of its glory, it will become dark again. All things in the world, great and small, are pretty much the same; they all go through cycles.

◆ 我們人怎麼樣生的呢？就是從無明生的，就是糊糊塗塗就生出來了。
How were we born? We were born from ignorance; we came into the world in a muddled fashion.

◆ 無明就是煩惱的一個根本，也是生死的一個根本，
也是所有麻煩的一個根本，也是所有問題的一個根本。
Ignorance is the root of afflictions, the root of birth and death, and the root of all troubles and problems.

◆ 虛妄的名、虛妄的利，令自己的心裏頭時時都有很多的煩惱、很多的打擊，
這是我們人和佛不同的地方。
Because of desires for illusory fame and profit, our minds are constantly being traumatized and afflicted. This is where we differ from the Buddhas.

◆ 我們學佛的人，所以不能與道相應的，就因為疑心太多了。
The reason we haven't obtained a response in our practice of Buddhism is that we have too many doubts.

◆ 我們要給世人做一個榜樣，
真正地令人佩服我們佛教徒的一種品行，一種思想，那才能感化動人呢！
The only way we can influence people is to set a good example for them and win their respect for our integrity and values.

◆ 自古神仙無別法，廣生歡喜不生愁。這是修道人的座右銘。
"The spirits and immortals of old had no special tricks; they were simply happy as could be, and they never worried." This should be the motto of all cultivators.

◆ 要知道世間的事，沒有不勞而獲的，
沒有出力，而想得到代價，哪有這樣容易的事？
We should know that nothing in the world comes easily; how can we expect a reward when we haven't put in the work?

254

◈ 聽經、念經，我們都要有一種忍耐心，不要生疲厭的心。

In listening to Sutra lectures and reciting Sutras, we must be patient and not grow weary.

◈ 如果你不爭了、不貪、不求、不自私、不自利，什麼脾氣都會沒有了。

If we did not fight, were not greedy, did not seek anything, were not selfish, and did not want to benefit ourselves, we would have no anger.

◈ 正法就是不爭、不貪、不求、不自私、不自利、不打妄語。
這是修道人的六大宗旨。無論什麼法，都可以用這六大宗旨做爲尺度，
來衡量、來觀察，合者是正法，不合者是邪法。

The proper dharmas are: not fighting, not being greedy, not seeking, not being selfish, not wanting personal advantages, and not telling lies. These are known as the Six Great Guidelines. No matter what dharma it is, you may use the Six Guidelines as a yardstick to measure, judge, and contemplate it. If it accords with the six rules, it can be called a proper dharma. If it goes against them, it is a deviant dharma.

◈ 人的眼睛都是很雪亮的，
會認識你的這好處，不需要自己讚歎自己。

People have sharp eyes and will see your good points. You don't need to praise yourself.

◈ 我們現在做人的時候，和魔王是很接近的，和佛是很遠的。
我們若願意做魔王，隨時都可以做；若願意成佛，
就要破除種種的惡見稠林，沒有邪知邪見，常修正知正見，才能出魔這個羅網。

As human beings, we are close to the demons and far from the Buddhas. We can become a demon king any time we want. If we wish to become a Buddha, however, we must cut through dense thickets of evil views. We have to cast out deviant views and constantly cultivate proper views before we can escape the demons' nets.

◈ 我們研究佛法一定要令大家心服口服，
心裏沒有一點疑惑才可以。

In studying the Dharma, we should investigate the principles until we are completely convinced of them, without the slightest doubt in our minds.

◈ 眞正沒有妄想了，就是往生極樂世界；
你眞正沒有欲念了，那就是教化眾生了。

If you really have no deluded thoughts, then you have already been born in the Land of Ultimate Bliss. If you are truly free of desire, then you have already taught and transformed living beings.

◈ 我們人要把因果認清楚了，不要錯因果。尤其我們到寺院裏頭來拜佛的人，
不應該跑到廟裏頭來想找便宜，總怕自己吃了虧。甚至於到廟上來偷，
偷這個飲食、偷財物、偷一切的一切，這將來一定會墮落三惡道的。

We must be clear about cause and effect and not make mistakes in cause and effect. When we come to the temple to bow to the Buddhas, we should not try to gain something for ourselves. We should not be afraid to take a loss. People who come to the temple to steal food, money, or other things will certainly fall into the three evil paths.

◆ 不說一些個讓人家起淫欲心的這種話，或者開不正當的玩笑，
講一些個沒有意義、無聊的話。這些不該講的話都不講了。
We should not say things that cause people to entertain thoughts of lust. We should not tell improper jokes or engage in frivolous or idle chatter. In general, we should not say the things we are not supposed to say.

◆ 我們學佛法的人，要看這佛法比任何事情都重要，
比每一天所學到的東西還重要，比我們做生意賺錢更重要。
Students of Buddhist should treat the study of the Dharma as more important than anything--more important than their studies at school, more important than their business and livelihood.

◆ 現在這個佛法傳到西方來，西方的佛法剛開始，那我們絕對是要提倡正法，
主持正法，弘揚正法。我們一舉一動都是爲正法來做標準，來做我們一個目標，
這是我一向的宗旨。各位聽了之後，都要來發大菩提心，擁護這個正法眼藏。
Buddhism has just come to the West, and we must staunchly support and propagate the Proper Dharma; we must take the Proper Dharma as our standard in all we do; the Proper Dharma is our goal and purpose. We should all make a great Bodhi resolve and protect the Treasury of the Proper Dharma Eye.

◆ 所有的煩惱，都因爲自私在後邊那兒支持著，所以就有很多脾氣、很多煩惱。
All afflictions are based on selfishness. That's why we have so much anger and so many afflictions.

◆ 只要你有個真心，有個誠心，你不上香，
那菩薩也一樣來護持你。
If you are truly sincere, the Bodhisattvas will protect you even if you don't offer incense.

◆ 你自己應該把那個邋遢的思想，
那一些個垃圾，在腦裏頭都清理出去。
Clean out the garbage and defiled thoughts in your own mind.

◆ 這個嫉妒，是一種惡心所，這種惡它是在裏邊藏著，
在意念裏頭，生一種嫉妒的意念。
Jealousy is an evil mental state which is hidden in one's thoughts.

◆ 我們要有擇法眼，我們要自己拿出真正智慧，
來分析這個法的是法、非法，才沒有白學佛。
If you don't develop Dharma-selecting vision--the genuine wisdom to distinguish between the Dharma and what is not the Dharma--you will have studied the Dharma in vain.

◆ 學佛是要愈學愈明白，不是愈學愈糊塗，
要認識真理，這就是開開智慧礦。
The more you study Buddhism, the more you should understand. You shouldn't become more confused. Recognize the truth and open up your "mine of wisdom."

◈ 一般人所最執著的，就是男女的愛情。
愛之，就欲其生；惡之，就欲其死。
What ordinary people are most attached to is the love between men and women. They hope their loved ones will live and their enemies will die.

◈ 在你修道用功，魔境現前，
但你稍微有不合乎正知正見，就會落到邪見去。
When you are cultivating the Way and a demonic state appears, if you are the slightest bit not in accord with proper knowledge and views, you will be caught up in deviant views.

◈ 什麼是你的寶啊？就是你自己本有的如來藏性。
你若是要恢復你的如來藏性，首先就要保持你的精、氣、神。
What are your treasures? They are your very own Treasury of the Tathagata. If you want to regain your Treasury of the Tathagata, you first have to protect your essence, energy, and spirit.

◈ 我們學佛的人，要倒過來；
倒過來，就是要利益其他人，這才是夠上一個學佛的人。
In studying Buddhism, we should "turn it around" and benefit others. Only then do we deserve to be called Buddhists.

◈ 在修道中，你就是不著魔，也要有真正的智慧，要有擇法眼。
In cultivation, even if you do not become possessed by a demon, you must still have genuine wisdom and Dharma-selecting vision.

◈ 你要是想認識，是真的、是假的？是不是菩薩，還是魔？
你就可以在這個地方來看。第一，看看他有沒有淫欲心；第二，看他有沒有貪欲心。
If you want to determine whether a person is genuine or phony, whether he is a Bodhisattva or a demon, you can look for the following things: First, see whether he has any desire for sex; and second, see whether he is greedy for money.

◈ 把以前所學的，所明白的，用以普渡眾生，匡扶世俗。
Let's use what we have learned and what we understand to universally save living beings in the world.

◈ 你們要記得，受戒之後，不要信這種迷信的境界，
這個說法的人，無論有什麼大神通，你要觀察他。
要是有貪心，到處斂財，或者有淫欲心，那就不是真的，就是假的。
You should all remember: After you take the precepts, never be deceived by such states of confused belief. Even if a Dharma-speaker displays mighty spiritual powers, you should look him over carefully and see if he is greedy. If he is out for money or if he has lust, then he's not genuine. He's a phony.

◈ 你能以把這個聽經的時間，認為是特別重要，那你做佛教徒，是再沒有什麼可說的了。
If you can regard the Sutra lectures as being especially important, then you have pretty much fulfilled your duties as a Buddhist.

◆ 你要是能返本還原，那時候你也沒有無明，也沒有淫欲，
也沒有貪欲，也沒有這個癡心妄想，什麼都沒有了，乾而潔淨。

If you can return to the origin, then you will be free of ignorance, lust, greed, stupidity and false thinking--you will have none of them. It is an absolute and total purity.

◆ 爲什麼你有生死呢？就因爲你妄想太多了，前念滅、後念生；
後念滅、後念又生，生生不已，如水波浪，川流不息。

Why do you undergo births and deaths? Simply because you have too many false thoughts. When one thought ceases, the next one arises. When that thought ceases, another one arises. Like waves on water, thoughts arise in endless succession.

◆ 你、我都在一切眾生之內，他也沒有跑到眾生之外去，
你想跑到外邊去，也跑不了的。

We are all included in the definition of living beings. You cannot exclude yourself even if you want to.

◆ 人修道，無論什麼也不要貪，好的也不貪，壞的也不貪，
你就平常心是道，要平平常常的，不要生一種貪心，你貪什麼都是不對的。

In cultivation, people should not be greedy. Don't be greedy for good things, and don't be greedy for bad things. The ordinary mind is the Way. Just act ordinary, and don't be greedy. No matter what you may be greedy for, it's not right.

◆ 《楞嚴經》這個哲理，講得是最徹底了，這是究竟的哲學，究竟的真理。

The philosophical doctrines discussed in the *Shurangama Sutra* are ultimate. This is the summit of philosophy, the ultimate truth.

◆ 我們一定要養氣，不要生氣，你要修養你這個氣，所謂「栽培心上地，
涵養性中天」，這都是養氣。你若想養氣嘛，就不要講那麼多的話。

It is essential that we nurture our energy; we should not lose our temper. You should cultivate your energy, as in the saying, "Foster the ground of your mind, and nurture the sky of your nature." If you want to nurture your energy, then don't talk so much.

◆ 這個魔的境界現到你前面，你能認識這個境界，知道這是魔或者是佛。
這個境界有的是外魔，有的是內魔。外魔容易降伏，內魔很難降伏了。

You have to be able to recognize a demonic state when it appears before you, and be able to tell whether it is a demon or a Buddha. Some states come from demons external to you and some come from your own mind. The external demons are easy to subdue. The internal demons of the mind are very difficult to subdue.

◆ 要守規矩，做事要光明正大，這才有定力。

Don't break the rules. You should accord with propriety and be open and upright in your conduct; only then will you attain samadhi.

◆ 在修道中，你就是不著魔，也要有真正的智慧，要有擇法眼。

In cultivation, even if you do not become possessed by a demon, you must still have genuine wisdom and Dharma-selecting vision.

◆ 你若能沒有貪、瞋、癡，也就把這陰魔都降伏了。
沒有自私、自利、有所求、有貪、有爭這五種的毛病，什麼魔也沒有辦法你。

If you are without greed, anger, and stupidity, then you will subdue these *skandha*-demons. If you do not have the faults of being selfish, wanting personal profit, seeking, being greedy, or contending, then no demon will be able to do anything to you.

◆ 你修行有魔現出了，那個魔的現出也正是因為你自性裏頭那個陰念、
陰氣所幻化出來的。雖幻化出來，你能不為它所搖動，也就沒有事了。

The demons that you encounter in cultivation are illusory transformations produced from the yin thoughts and yin energy in your own nature. If you can remain unmoved by these illusory transformations, then there's no problem.

◆ 你用功修行無論修到什麼程度上，也不要生歡喜，
也不要生恐懼心，這是修道人最要緊的一個根本解決魔障的辦法。

No matter what level you reach in your cultivation, do not become happy or afraid. This is a most essential and basic way for cultivators to resolve demonic obstacles.

◆ 魔是我們修道人的一種考試，也是來試驗試驗，
所以各位不要有一種恐懼心，你若有恐懼心，
你就不想叫這魔來，他也會來了；你若沒有恐懼心，他要來也來不了了。

You need not fear demons; they are just testing you, trying out your skill in cultivation. If you're afraid, then they will come even if you don't want them to. If you are not afraid, then they will not be able to come.

◆ 魔，他所怕的就是「正大光明」這四個字。
你若能有正大光明，魔他也就循規蹈矩，也就向你叩頭頂禮了。

Demons fear those who are proper, great, and bright. If you can be that way, then the demons will behave themselves and will even bow to you.

◆ 我們修行人，也不用念什麼咒，也不必用什麼法，
就老老實實的，不爭、不貪、不求、不自私、不自利，
埋頭苦幹，好好修行，什麼魔也沒有辦法你。

Cultivators don't need to recite any particular mantra or practice any particular dharma. Just be honest and true; don't contend, don't be greedy, don't seek, don't be selfish, and don't pursue personal gain. If you put your shoulder to the grindstone and cultivate diligently, no demon can bother you.

◆ 我們若能沒有貪欲了，什麼麻煩也沒有了；
你有貪欲，什麼事情都發生出來了。

If we had no greed or desires, then we would have no trouble. If you have greed and desire, then all sorts of things will happen.

◆ 所以最要緊的地方，就是有一個淫欲，他有淫欲心，
盡行不淨行，這就是魔；他不貪錢，沒有淫欲，那就是真的。

The most important thing is lust: If someone has lust and indulges in impure conduct all the time, then he's a demon. If he is not greedy for money and he is free of lust, then he is genuine.

◈ 所以這是不殺生、不偷盜、不邪淫、不打妄語、不飲酒。
佛教徒對於這五種的戒律，一定要特別特別注意，
要守著它，絲毫不可毀犯，這樣才是夠得上一個佛教徒。

These are the precepts of not killing, not stealing, not engaging in sexual misconduct, not lying, and not taking intoxicants. Buddhists should pay close attention to these five precepts and avoid committing the slightest transgression; only then are they qualified to be called Buddhists.

◈ 我們不可借外緣，要自強不息，
用自己的毅力，來克服不如意的境界。

We cannot rely on external conditions. We have to renew ourselves continuously without rest. We must use our will power to overcome unfavorable circumstances.

◈ 能夠迴光反照，把貪心降伏，世界自然會轉好，災難戰爭也自然消滅。

If we can reflect upon ourselves and overcome our greed, the world will become a better place and wars will naturally cease.

◈ 有邪知邪見的人，將來受果報，也受沒有眼睛的果報。
他都是瞎人的眼目，令人找不著正路。所以這一點各位要特別特別注意的。

People who hold to wrong knowledge and views undergo the retribution of having no eyes, because they have blinded others and led others astray. Pay close attention to this.

◈ 這因果是特別厲害，絲毫都不爽的。就由我這一生的經驗，
我就知道你不能做錯一點事情，你稍微做錯一點事情，那個果報就來了。

The law of cause and effect is very serious; it is not off by a bit. From my experience, I know that we cannot do even the slightest wrong deed, for if we do, we will soon have to undergo the retribution.

◈ 不思善、不思惡，你也不要貪好境界，也不要怕壞境界；
就是遇到境界，還若無其事似的，不生一種執著心。

Think of neither good nor bad. Don't crave good states, and don't be afraid of bad states. When you encounter a state, just act as if it didn't exist. Don't get attached to it.

◈ 所有的眾生都是我的家人，宇宙是我的身體，
虛空是我的大學，我的名字了無形相，慈悲喜捨是我的功用。

All living beings are my family; the universe is my body; all of space is my university; my name is "Empty and Formless"; kindness, compassion, joy and giving are my functions.

◈ 我們修道的人，一定要自勵，不靠任何人，不靠任何事，
不靠任何物，一定要做得非常的堅強，一定要心如鐵石。

We who practice the Way must stand on our own and not rely on other people, matters, or things. We must be extremely strong in caliber, with an iron will.

◈ 道德是為人的根本，有了道德，我們才能立得住腳。

Moral virtue is our basis as human beings. Only with virtue will we be able to establish ourselves.

◆ 道是要行的，不行則要道何用？德是要修的，不修則德從何來？
The Way must be walked; if it is not walked, of what use is the Way? Virtue must be cultivated; if we don't cultivate, where does virtue come from?

◆ 我們應該躬行實踐，常把「生死」二字掛在眉梢，把「道德」二字放在腳下。
We should honestly practice with the words "birth and death" constantly before our eyes and the words "Way and virtue" beneath our feet.

◆ 有了道德，我們才能立得住腳；
反之，腳下無根，則無處可立，不能有所作為了。
Only with virtue can we establish ourselves. If we have no basis upon which to stand, then we cannot accomplish anything.

◆ 妄想是修道的絆腳石，障礙你成就道業。
False thoughts are the stumbling block to cultivation of the Way.

◆ 在我們修行人的眼中，一寸光陰簡直就是我們的一寸命；
少了一寸光陰，就等於我們短了一寸命一樣。
An instant of time, in the eyes of cultivators, is an instant of life. With each passing moment, our life is that much shorter.

◆ 無論在誰的面前懺悔，要把話說得清楚，
不要說些模稜兩可的話。應該在佛前至誠懇切地懺悔。
No matter whom we repent in front of, we should confess our wrongs clearly and not be ambivalent. We should repent with utmost sincerity before the Buddhas.

◆ 佛法是絲毫也不能馬虎的。
We cannot be the least bit careless with regard to the Buddhadharma.

◆ 如果能真正生出懺悔心，也未嘗沒有商量之處。
If we are truly repentant, there is nothing that cannot be pardoned.

◆ 我們都要懇切地懺悔，否則會如入泥沼，愈陷愈深，
罪業愈來愈重，把我們壓得喘不過氣，無能自拔。
If we do not repent sincerely, we will sink deeper and deeper in the quicksand, dragged down by ever heavier offenses until we can no longer breathe or pull ourselves out.

◆ 只要肯下真心與決心，精進勇猛地一步一步做去，也是可以成功的，努力吧！
As long as we can be sincere in our resolve and advance step by step with brave vigor, we will surely succeed. Work hard!

◆ 凡是想成功的，便會不由自主地要「朝起早，夜眠遲」了，
既不是為利忙，也不是為名忙，而是為「法」忙。
If we wish to succeed, we will naturally rise early and retire late. We are busy not for the sake of fame or profit, but for the sake of Dharma.

◆ 我們學佛，處處要真誠，不然便是虛偽，
虛偽便會「開謊花，不結果」，所以學佛切記不要自己騙自己。
In studying Buddhism, we must be sincere in everything we do. Otherwise, we will be phony, like sterile flowers that do not bear fruit. Buddhists should never, ever cheat themselves.

◆ 如果你自己不打電話，又有誰來接你的電話？所以念佛也是這個道理。
If you don't make the call, then no one will receive your call. The same principle applies to recitation of the Buddha's name.

◆ 我們修行要仗自力，打起精神，鼓起勇氣，勇猛精進。
In cultivation we must rely on our own strength, strike up our spirits, and bring forth a vigorous and courageous spirit.

◆ 誰叫你自己在沒病的時候，任作胡為，不好好地珍惜自己。
Who told you to behave so recklessly and fail to cherish yourself when you were still healthy?

◆ 平時不加檢點，等到見了閻王時，才知自己生前所行所事及存心都不正當。
If you don't engage in self-reflection on a regular basis, you won't realize how crooked all your intentions were until you meet King Yama [the Lord of Death].

◆ 修行要下苦功。
Cultivation requires bitter effort.

◆ 要常聽善知識的開導，這就是修道的要訣。
The secret to cultivation is to constantly listen to the instructions of a wise teacher.

◆ 人若是不經過一番的病苦，是絕不肯發心修行的。
Those who have never undergone the suffering of sickness will not wish to cultivate the Way.

◆ 皈依那天，看作我們的生日，把我們修行的階段從那時候算起。
The day we took refuge can be considered our birthday, the day when we began to cultivate.

◆ 眾生的心性，本來也是磊落光明，只是被無數的罪障、妄念遮蔽罷了。
Living beings' minds and natures are originally pure and bright; it is just that they have been obscured by numberless offenses and discursive thoughts.

◆ 世界上誘人的罪惡多得很，若是一不小心，
掉進了罪惡的深淵，失掉了人身，那便是萬劫不復，千古遺恨了。
There are plenty of temptations to commit offenses in the world. If we are not careful, we will fall into the abyss of evil. Once we lose our human body, we may not regain it for tens of thousands of eons. How endless our regret will be then!

◆ 缺乏定力、道心不堅的緣故，很容易受到外來的引誘而墮落。
When we lack samadhi and our resolve is weak, it is easy for us to be influenced by external circumstances and end up falling.

◈　雜念叢生，奔波勞碌，又怎能冷靜地判別是非、明白眞理呢？
If our scattered thoughts arise in profusion and we are always
busy running around, how can we make clear judgments and understand the truth?

◈　修道的祕訣是「定力」，有了定力，便能產生智慧，更能進一步地了道，成佛。
The secret to cultivation is samadhi power. With the power of samadhi, one can develop
wisdom and then enlighten to the Way and become a Buddha.

◈　我勸在座各位，都能把「戒定慧」這三個字，作爲修道的座右銘，常常拿來警惕自己。
I exhort all of you to always caution yourselves with the motto of "precepts, samadhi, and
wisdom."

◈　休息的時間，不可以隨便亂講話，不可以隨便打妄想，
更不可躲懶偷安，就是一分一秒的時間，也要愛惜。
During the rest periods, one is not allowed to chatter, to indulge in idle thoughts, or to be lazy.
Every second and every minute should be cherished.

◈　學佛法要拿出眞心，一舉一動，一言一行都要往眞的做。
We should study Buddhism with a true heart. In everything we do and everything we say, we
should try to be true.

◈　爲什麼學佛法學得很久，卻沒有相應呢？
就因爲保護著我們的過錯，不肯拿出眞心修行。
Why haven't we had any response after studying Buddhism for so long? It's because we cover
up our mistakes and aren't sincere in our cultivation.

◈　在道場裏，要節省一切物質，若不小心，不知惜福，就把功德都漏掉了。
所修的，不如所造的；所得的，不如所丟的。
We should be frugal with all the material things in the temple. If we are careless and don't
know to cherish our blessings, then all our merit and virtue will be lost. Our cultivation will
not measure up to our offenses, and what we gain will not be able to make up for what we
throw away.

◈　一舉一動，一言一行都不要傷害到其他的人。
In every word and every move, we should take care not to hurt others.

◈　情愛也要把它看空了，才能遂心滿願，成就你的菩提道果。
We must see emotional love as empty. Then we will be able to fulfill our wishes and
accomplish the fruit of Bodhi.

◈　你要行所無事，做出來了，還要不執著你有麼功德。
You have to do things without being attached to the merit created.

◈　我們應該把慧炬的火焰，播散到世界的每一個角落去。
We should spread the flames of the torch of wisdom to every corner of the world.

◎　貧、病都是我們修道的助緣。
Poverty and sickness are both factors that aid us in cultivating the Way.

◎　若是有了欲念，好像常被土匪打劫，財寶被搶去了。無漏是修行人所求之瑰寶。
Having thoughts of desire is like allowing thieves to plunder your treasures. The treasure sought by cultivators is freedom from outflows.

◎　一天到晚，要靠講是非、打妄想來生存，你們說怪不怪？真令人費解。
Some people can only survive if they gossip and indulge in idle thinking from morning to night. Strange, isn't it? I don't understand them.

◎　不修行的人，戴著假面具，昧心厚顏，
專做些不守規矩、不光明正大的事，自己還不承認。
There are people who don't cultivate, but wear the disguise of cultivators. With no conscience and no shame, they sneak around doing things that break the rules, but refuse to acknowledge their deeds when questioned.

◎　我們應該覺悟世界所有一切的聲音，皆在說法。
善人給你說善法，惡人給你說惡法。
We should realize that all the sounds in the world are speaking the Dharma. Good people speak wholesome Dharma for you, while evil people speak evil dharmas.

◎　人做事情要正大光明、大公無私，不可處處想佔便宜，不肯吃虧。
We should do things in an upright, open, public-spirited and unselfish manner. We shouldn't be constantly hunting for bargains and unwilling to take losses.

◎　我們還有這口氣在，就要對人好，可是不應有情愛的思想摻在內。
As long as we have a breath left, we should be good to others, but without having thoughts of emotional love.

◎　佛教是勸人向善，瞭解因果，多做善功德，
也就是不爭、不貪、不求、不自私、不自利、不打妄語。
Buddhism teaches people to become good, to understand the law of cause and effect, and to create wholesome merit. In other words, it teaches: no fighting, no greed, no seeking, no selfishness, no pursuit of personal gain, and no lying.

◎　各位！要從「心」著手，改造世界，化干戈為玉帛，令世界平安。
To create a better world and transform war into peace, we must begin by changing our minds.

◎　怎樣令世界安穩？唯一辦法，來正法道場學佛法，悔過自新。
人人改惡向善，世界就沒有三災八難，人人和睦相處，無爭無貪，成為大同世界。
How can we make the world peaceful? There's only one way: Come to a Way-place of the Proper Dharma to study Buddhism, repent of your mistakes, and begin anew. If everyone can change their evil and go towards the good, the three disasters and eight difficulties will disappear. Then people will dwell in harmony without fighting or coveting others' possessions, and peace and justice will prevail in the world.

所有的眾生都是我的家人，
宇宙是我的身體，
虛空是我的大學，
慈悲喜捨是我的功用，
我的名字了無形相。

*All living beings are my family;*

*The universe is my body;*

*All of space is my university;*

*Kindness, compassion, joy and giving are my functions.*

*My name is "Empty and Formless".*

髙風亮節無倫比　大志偉願有誰全

His lofty reputation and clear principles are matchless!
Who else possesses such great resolve and extraordinary vows?

# 來去解脫離罣礙
## Free to come and go--beyond all hindrances

於臺灣臺北縣板橋市市立體育館
In the Banqiao Auditorium, City of Banqiao, Taipei County, Taiwan.

✳ 禮佛拜懺 Bowing to the Buddhas in repentance

✳ 追思法會 Memorial Services

三千界內同瞻仰　流芳古今照地天
—宣公上人作—

*All alike throughout three-thousand realms pay homage!*
*Such glorious renown spans past and present illumining heaven and earth!*
*— by Venerable Master Hua —*

✴慈濟代表 Representative from Compassionate Rescue Society

✴瞻仰舍利 Revering the Sharira

✴傳供大典 Everyone joins in passing the Offerings during the High Meal Ceremony

# 生死真如更弗拘
## Neither birth and death nor True Suchness can be grasped.

續佛心燈光無盡　萬劫千秋永緬懷
—宣公上人作—

*In perpetuating the Buddha's mind-lamp
with its infinite light,
It must be embraced forever through
thousands of years and myriads of eons!*
— by Venerable Master Hua —

✻瞻仰舍利——於澳門綜藝大會堂
Revering the Sharira - Macao

✻香港北角大會堂
Beijiao Auditorium,
Hong Kong

✻澳門綜藝大會堂
Performing Arts Theater,
Macao

✳長老致詞——於香港北角大會堂
Speeches by Elder Sanghans
Beijiao Auditorium, Hong Kong

✳瞻仰舍利——於香港北角大會堂
Paying Homage to the Sharira –
Beijiao Auditorium, Hong Kong

✳讚頌法會——於澳門綜藝大會堂
Commemorative Dharma Assembly
Performing Arts Theater, Macao

# 般若智果化三千

## The fruition of Prajna wisdom can transform the triple-thousand worlds!

五色繽紛堅固子　萬德鍛鍊滿月圓
—宣公上人作—

*From those hard seeds*
*five colors radiate in multiplicities!*
*Myriad virtues are smelted*
*and perfected like the full moon.*
— by Venerable Master Hua —

✹法師、貴賓與義工合影
Dharma Masters, Honored Guests, and
Volunteer Staff join for a photo

※法師、貴賓與義工合影
Dharma Masters, Honored Guests, and
Volunteer Staff join for a photo

# 化緣已畢吾當行

## When my conditions for teaching are finished, I shall leave.

大聖化物無方隅　千秋後世莫徘徊
—宣公上人作—

*Great sages teach creatures regardless of location.*
*For thousands of years to come, don't hesitate.*
— by Venerable Master Hua —

✳板橋市市立體育館會場涅槃堂
Nirvana Hall in Banqiao Auditorium,
City of Banqiao, Taiwan

✳香港大嶼山慈興禪寺放生法會
Ceremony for Liberating the Living, Flourishing
Compassion (Cixing) Monastery, Lanto Island,
Hong Kong

✳香港佛教講堂涅槃堂
Nirvana Hall at the Buddhist Lecture Hall,
Hong Kong

# 臺港追思法會記實
## MEMORIAL CEREMONIES IN
## TAIWAN AND HONG KONG

宣公上人於一九九五年六月七日圓寂，荼毗後，留下上萬顆舍利。
臺灣、香港的四眾弟子們發起舉行追思，
由美國追思團迎請舍利至臺港共同主持追思法會。

**The Venerable Master Hua passed into stillness on June 7, 1995.
About ten thousand sharira (relics) remained after his body was cremated.
When disciples in Taiwan and Hong Kong decided to hold memorial ceremonies
for the Venerable Master, an American delegation went to help host the ceremonies
and took the Master's sharira with them.**

仁德　Ren De

# 臺灣

　　追思團於一九九五年十一月九日晚間抵達桃園中正國際機場，百餘位四眾弟子著法服合掌誦念佛號恭候，當恆佐師及恆實師分別捧著上人德相及舍利率先出現時，大眾匍匐頂禮。

　　「宣公上人圓寂追思大法會」是由臺北法界佛教印經會與追思團聯合主辦。於十一月十一日至十三日，假板橋體育館舉行。前二日的法會內容為：誦《普賢行願品》、傳供、拜《華嚴懺》、念佛和讚頌報恩，以及觀看幻燈片等。數百張幻燈片，分為六個單元，在兩天內向大眾簡介上人由東北到香港、美國弘法、翻譯經典、提倡教育、提倡中國文化與義務教學、振興佛教、建立如法僧團，及在世界各地弘法利生、涅槃、荼毗等事蹟。

　　十一月十三日是追思法會正日。法會於上午九點開始。大會主席為恆實師。蒞臨貴賓有：證嚴法師弟子代表、曉雲法師弟子代表，及中華民國總統府資政：林洋港先生、黃尊秋先生夫婦、梁肅戎先生，省政府林議員、楊英風教授、花蓮縣政府邱主任等卅餘人，及近百位慈濟功德會代表。

　　由兩位法師代表，分別以中、英文宣讀讚頌報恩文。接著大眾合唱上人所作的兩首歌曲：〈盡虛空〉及〈轉法輪〉。傳供儀式分四區進行，共有一百零八道供品，從大眾手中傳遞至佛前，歷時約八十分鐘，與會追悼者有四千餘人。

　　下午會場陳列上人舍利，供大眾瞻仰。全體來賓與信眾首先禮拜上人的十八大願，法師並介紹十八大願的意義。

　　上人的舍利有多種顏色，有許多凝結在骨頭上，呈翠綠色，晶瑩潤澤，彷彿古玉。有數百朵各式形狀的舍利花，及十二顆牙齒舍利。

　　整個法會辦得甚為隆重和周詳。會場工作共劃分為十一組，有五百多位義工參與籌備。及一百名香積組義工，負責準備法會期間的三餐。並備有結緣品：《宣化老和尚追思紀念專集》第一冊與第二冊、上人法相、墨寶、舍利相片，及佛書等。

　　大會主席恆實師於十三日致詞時，讚揚上人

# Taiwan

The delegation arrived at the Zhongzheng International Airport in Taoyuan, Taiwan, in the evening of November 9, 1995. More than one hundred disciples were waiting at the airport, dressed in their ceremonial gowns and reciting the Buddha's name with joined palms. They bowed when they saw Dharma Masters Heng Sure and Heng Tso appear, carrying the Venerable Master's sharira and portrait.

The Memorial Ceremony for the Venerable Master Hua's Nirvana, which was jointly organized by the Dharma Realm Buddhist Books Distribution Association (DRBBDA) in Taipei and the memorial delegation from America, was held from November 11 to 13 at the Banqiao Auditorium. The program for the first two days included recitation of the chapter "Universal Worthy Bodhisattva's Conduct and Vows," the Ceremony for Passing Offerings, the Flower Adornment Repentance, recitation of the Buddha's name, speeches in praise and recognition of the Venerable Master, and slide presentations. Several hundred slides were shown in six parts during the two days, covering the Venerable Master's journey from Manchuria to Hong Kong, and then to America, where he propagated the Dharma, directed the translation of Sutras, promoted education, advocated Chinese culture and volunteer teaching, caused Buddhism to flourish, set up an orthodox Sangha, and spread the Dharma to living beings around the globe. The slides also covered the Venerable Master's Nirvana and cremation ceremonies.

The memorial ceremony proper began on November 13 at 9:00 a.m. Dharma Master Heng Sure presided over the ceremony. There were more than thirty guests of honor, including representatives of Dharma Masters Cheng Yen and Xiao Yun; several advisors to the President of the Republic of China, including Mr. Lin Yanggang, Mr. Huang Zunqiu and his wife, and Mr. Liang Surong; Councilmember Ling of Taiwan provincial government; Professor Yang Yingfeng; Director Qiu and over thirty members of the Hualien County government, and nearly one hundred representatives from the Tzu-chi Foundation.

An article in praise and appreciation of the Venerable Master was read in Chinese and English by two Dharma Masters. Then the assembly sang two songs by the Venerable Master: "To the Ends of Space" and "Turning the Dharma Wheel." In the Ceremony for Passing Offerings, which lasted for an hour and twenty minutes, 108 kinds of offerings were passed in four lines from the back of the assembly up to the front. Around four thousand people attended the memorial ceremony.

In the afternoon, the public was allowed to view and pay respect to the Venerable Master's sharira. The guests and disciples first bowed to the Venerable Master's eighteen vows and listened to a Dharma Master explain the meaning of the vows. The Venerable Master's sharira are of many colors. Many of them are crystallized onto the bones and are a lustrous bluish green, resembling ancient jade. There are several hundred sharira clusters of various shapes and twelve sharira from the teeth.

The preparatory work for the well-organized memorial ceremony was divided into eleven areas and carried out by more than five hundred volunteers. About a hundred volunteers worked in the kitchen

preparing three meals a day for the duration of the event.

Free souvenirs and gifts, such as the two volumes of *In Memory of the Venerable Master Hsuan Hua*; photographs of the Venerable Master, his calligraphy, and his sharira; and Sutras and other printed material were distributed.

Dharma Master Heng Sure, the host of the ceremony, praised the Venerable Master for his lifelong practice of altruism and the Bodhisattva path. The Venerable Master offered to living beings the treasury of the Buddhadharma as well as twenty-seven Way-places--including the City of Ten Thousand Buddhas, Dharma Realm Buddhist University, and the International Translation Institute. The Master also gave his disciples their Dharma bodies and wisdom lives, the pure precept substance, the resolve for enlightenment, and the Dharma-selecting Vision. He taught them to esteem their own spiritual natures and to apply the six guiding principles in their minds. Dharma Master Sure urged everyone to live up to the Venerable Master's expectations by bringing forth a great resolve for Bodhi.

Presidential Advisor Lin Yanggang spoke of how the Venerable Master had encouraged and instructed him on two special occasions. He praised the Venerable Master's lifelong contributions to the development of Buddhism and to the culture of humankind, saying that the Venerable Master set a good example for generations to come.

Presidential Advisor Huang Zunqiu, who is also the Chairman of the World Religions Fellowship, called the Venerable Master's passing into stillness a tremendous loss to Buddhism and to the human race as a whole. There were two things that Advisor Huang particularly respected about the Venerable Master: (1) The Master's advocacy of Chinese culture and ethics in his Dharma lectures, in the hope of saving humankind. (2) The Master's great loyalty to his country and his refusal to change his citizenship despite the inconveniences that it brought. Advisor Huang said that in order to restore today's contaminated society to a pure and simple state, everyone must follow the six guiding principles and the eight virtues.

Presidential Advisor Liang Surong praised the Venerable Master for his pioneering efforts in propagating the Buddhadharma in China, Southeast Asia, Hong Kong, and America. The Venerable Master had twice invited him to serve as the Chancellor of Dharma Realm Buddhist University, and after he declined, the Venerable Master still appointed him as the Chairman of the University Board

一生廣行布施，行菩薩道。把萬佛聖城、法界佛教大學、國際譯經學院等二十七座道場，及佛法寶藏布施給一切眾生。弟子們的法身慧命、清淨戒體、大菩提心、擇法眼，都是上人所賜。上人也使弟子們懂得尊重自己的靈性。又教導六大宗旨的心地法門。法師希望大家都能發大菩提心，這樣才不會辜負上人。

總統府資政林洋港先生致詞時，提到上人對他個人兩次的指點與勉勵。並讚揚上人一生對佛教以及人類文化發展的貢獻，並為後來學者的楷模與指標。

總統府資政也是世界宗教徒聯誼會會長的黃尊秋先生說：「上人圓寂，為佛教界及全世界人類莫大的損失。」黃資政特別敬重上人，因為：一、上人弘法時必定同時闡揚中國文化，及倫理道德，以拯救人類。二、上人具強烈的愛國情操，不願放棄國籍。黃資政並認為要淨化污染的現代社會，使之恢復純樸，大家必須實踐「六大宗旨」與固有的「八德」。

總統府資政梁肅戎先生讚揚上人，在大陸各地、南洋、香港、美國大開佛法的路，傳揚佛教有成。梁資政曾先後兩次受邀為法大校長；辭讓後，上人仍請他擔任理事主席。梁資政說：「上人圓寂後，弘揚佛法以及改良教育的責任，應由弟子們和有心人士繼續發揚，特別是法界佛教大學要充實擴大。承繼上人的遺志，才是對上人最好的追思紀念。」

＊　　　＊　　　＊

一位女居士經營素食館，因為生意不好，想要到美國改做葷菜館。一夜夢到宣公上人告訴她：「妳不要去美國啦！十一月十一日、十二日、十三日，我在板橋體育館有個法會，妳去幫幫忙！」經向朋友打聽，她才知道真地有追思大法會，於是她前往法界佛教印經會報名，擔任香積組義工。

由臺灣飛抵香港，追思團一行於入境檢查時，海關人員問一位團員所捧的可是哪尊佛像？他一邊就自動用手去揭開罩布，團員告訴他是師父的德相。他瞻仰後說：「你們師父這麼莊嚴，一定是位有道的高僧。我也結了佛緣！」

上人圓寂數日後，在夢中安慰一位弟子：「如果你相信我去了，我就去了；如果你相信我還在，我就在！」誠如上人所說的：「人生如戲，是一場度生的戲。」

# 香港

訪問團於十四日清晨轉往香港。追思讚頌報恩法會是由香港佛教講堂主辦，於十一月十四日至十六日假北角大會堂舉行。

前兩晚的法會以〈香讚〉開始，誦《阿彌陀經》和念佛；接著由弟子們敘述上人的教化與感召，及觀賞幻燈片。法會由多位老弟子及義工們著手籌備，各界人士皆期待瞻仰上人的舍利。

十一月十六日為追思法會的正日。法會於上午九點三十分開始，由西方寺住持永惺老和尚主持，當地法師擔任維那與悅眾。蒞場的諸山長老有十二位：初慧、融靈、智開、道海、旭林、意昭、宣揚、暢懷、法雲、淨真等。法會於大眾念佛聲中開始。先舉〈香讚〉，接著由永惺長老致詞，惺老對上人真修實證的成就推崇備至。

of Directors. Advisor Liang stressed that after the Venerable Master's passing, his disciples and devoted followers must continue the work of propagating the Dharma and improving education--in particular the expansion and development of Dharma Realm Buddhist University. The best way to remember the Venerable Master is to carry on his mission.

＊　　　＊　　　＊

One laywoman whose vegetarian restaurant in Taiwan was not doing well had thought of going to America to open a nonvegetarian restaurant. One night she had a dream in which the Venerable Master told her, "Don't go to America. On the eleventh, twelfth, and thirteenth of November, I'll be having a Dharma assembly at the Banquiao Auditorium. You should go and help out!" She later found out from her friends that there was indeed going to be a Memorial Ceremony there, and so she went to Dharma Realm Buddhist Books Distribution Association to volunteer her help in the food service group.

When the delegation was going through customs in Hong Kong, a customs officer asked a delegation member what Buddha was depicted on the portrait he was carrying. As the officer lifted the cloth that covered the portrait, the delegation member told him it was the Venerable Master's image. The officer gazed at it and remarked, "Your teacher has such a dignified air; he must be a great and virtuous master. And now I have some affinities with Buddhism!"

Several days after the Venerable Master passed into stillness, he comforted a disciple in a dream, saying, "If you believe that I'm gone, then I'm gone. If you believe that I'm still around, then I'm still around!" As the Venerable Master said, "Life is like a play in which living beings are crossed over."

# Hong Kong

The memorial delegation left for Hong Kong in the early morning of November 14. The Memorial Ceremony in Hong Kong was organized by the Buddhist Lecture Hall. It was held at the Beijiao Auditorium from the fourteenth through the sixteenth of November.

During the first two evenings, the program began with the Incense Praise and recitation of the *Amitabha Sutra* and the Buddha's name. Then disciples spoke of the teachings and inspiration that the Venerable Master had given them. Finally there was a slide presentation. Many old disciples and volunteers organized the program. People from all walks of life came eagerly to view the Venerable Master's sharira.

The Memorial Ceremony proper began at 9:30 a.m. on November 16. Elder Master Yongxing from Western Monastery presided, and local Dharma Masters played the Dharma instruments and led the ceremony. Twelve Elder Masters from various monasteries attended, including Chuhui, Yongling, Zhikai, Daohai, Xulin, Yizhao, Xuanyang, Changhuai, Fayun, and Jingzhen. Following the Incense Praise and recitation of the Buddha's name, Elder Master Yongxing eulogized the Venerable Master's accomplishments in cultivation.

The Ceremony of Passing Offerings was performed by the Elder

慈興寺是上人四十年前在香港所興建的道場。
Cixing Monastery was established by the Venerable Master in Hong Kong more than forty years ago.

Masters and other Sangha members. One hundred and eight dishes of delicacies, incense, fruits, and jewels were passed one by one to the altar in the front. Dharma Master Sure then read the eulogy. The meal offering ceremony began with the Lotus Pool Praise, the recitation of *Amitabha Sutra*, and the Sangha Jewel Praise. After the transference of merit, Dharma Master Sure thanked the Elder Masters on behalf of the four-fold assembly. After the guests had lunch at a restaurant, the Dharma Masters in the delegation returned to the Buddhist Lecture Hall to speak Dharma for the laity and to do their evening recitation.

The Ceremony in Praise and Recognition of the Venerable Master's Kindness was held at the Beijiao Auditorium in the evening. The program included a slide presentation and an exhibition of the Venerable Master's sharira. The disciples in Hong Kong, who had been away from the Venerable Master for over thirty years, could not help but shed tears as they viewed the slides and sharira.

On the first day of the memorial ceremony, Elder Master Yongxing from the Bodhi Association gave a speech. He recalled meeting the Venerable Master at Nanhua Monastery in Canton in 1948 and spending about a month together. Although they were both from Manchuria, they had not met each other before. In Hong Kong they began to see each other more often. He said that the numerous sharira remaining after cremation are a result of the Venerable Master's cultivation of precepts, concentration, and wisdom. He also expressed concern that there might be no one to carry on the lineage in the Dharma-ending Age after the Venerable Master's passing into stillness. He hoped that more laypeople would bring forth the Bodhi resolve, leave the home-life, and protect the Buddhadharma. Left-home people protect Buddhism internally. Without left-home people, Buddhism would become extinct. After studying the Dharma, one should put it into practice; practice and theory should go hand in hand. The Elder Master spoke very sincerely and became choked by sobs several times during his speech.

During the memorial ceremony proper on November 16, Dharma Master Yongxing said, "It is with tremendous sadness that I host this grand Ceremony of Passing Offerings for the Venerable Master Hua. I knew him for many years. He was truly outstanding in propagating the Dharma and in his own cultivation. In this day and age, the Venerable Master was able to truly practice the precepts; he always wore his precept sash, took one meal a day, and set a good example for the rest of us. He went through many hardships in order to

傳供大典由長老們，與上人的出家弟子們代表進行，一百零八道精美上味，及香果珍寶，一盤盤傳遞至佛前；接著恆實師代表讀誦祭文。上供的儀軌是先舉〈蓮池讚〉、誦《阿彌陀經》和〈僧寶讚〉；迴向功德後，恆實師代表四眾弟子們禮謝諸山長老。全體來賓於餐館用午齋；結齋後，追思團的法師返佛教講堂為善信們開示和作晚課。

讚頌報恩法會於晚上在北角大會堂舉行，並觀看幻燈片與瞻仰上人舍利。香港弟子們與上人闊別三十餘年，如今觀影片、見舍利，許多信眾難免感傷，頻頻落淚。

追思法會第一日，菩提學會永惺長老致詞時說，與上人認識是在一九四八年廣東南華寺，相處一個多月。在東北與上人是同鄉，可是沒有機會見面，到香港後才常見面。

上人茶毗後有許多舍利，足證上人的修持功夫，這是戒定慧的薰修。上人圓寂，末法時代後繼無人，實在是一大隱憂。並希望居士們發心出家，護持佛教；出家人為內護，沒有出家人佛法就消滅了。學法後要實行，要解行相應。老法師言出至誠，數度哽咽揮淚。

十一月十六日追思大典正日，永惺法師致詞時說：「本人爲宣公長老主持傳供大典感到非常難過。我與上人相熟多年，感到上人在弘法、實修方面都是傑出人才。在這個時代，能真正行持戒律嚴謹，衣不離體，日中一食，爲我們的模範。上人數十年來艱苦奮鬥，創辦道場多處，講經不息，轉末法爲正法。上人的圓寂是佛教界的大損失，今日請諸山長老來舉行傳供，大家齊集追思，希望大家不要忘了老和尚的志願，承擔起弘揚佛法，堅持戒律的修行工作！」

恆佐師在香港北角大會堂時，以〈盡虛空〉中的一句歌詞「要大公，除自私，直心最好」，做爲上人救眾生而忘自己的寫照。追思法會中宣讀了上人一封信，上人當年爲何要在美國建立萬佛聖城，從信中可略見一二：

……我相信中國能以倫理道德爲基礎，以聖人來領導世界。……我欲把中國文化、佛教道理，推行至全世界，令全世界人類得救。…中國數千年所以未亡國者，因爲中國人有孝悌忠信、禮義廉恥得天獨厚之德行文化基礎；而中國文化，又以佛教文化爲基礎。……佛教乃中國之固有文化傳統，……在中國建立千萬廟宇，不如在海外建立一所基本廟宇。美國本無佛教，……若能在此地建立中國寺院，以中國道德文化領導世界，……。

追思團全部團員由法總所屬香港分支道場負責人恆益師陪同下，於第二日，一行四十五人搭早晨七點的渡船，前往參觀座落於大嶼山的慈興寺。這是上人四十年前在香港所興建的三座道場（西樂園寺、佛教講堂、慈興寺）之一。下午一點，慈興寺與香港佛教講堂信眾聯合舉行放生，由恆佐師主持放生儀式。將近一千隻鳥，早上隨團由港過江，在〈大悲神咒〉與諸佛菩薩加被的慈光中，獲得了新生。

追思團部份團員於十一月十七日上午七時，前往志蓮淨苑拜訪果禮（九十二歲）及果良（九十一歲）二位比丘尼。這兩位老法師是上人早年在香港的出家弟子。志蓮淨苑安老院內住有二百多位女眾，平均年齡八十七歲。院內生活環境舒適，照顧周到。

establish a large number of temples and centers. He lectured on the Sutras without rest, determined to turn the Dharma-Ending Age into the Proper Dharma Age. His passing is indeed a great loss to Buddhism. On this occasion, all of you Elders are invited to join in the passing of offerings; we are gathered here to commemorate the Venerable Master. I hope you will not forget the Venerable Master's wishes, and will take up the responsibility to propagate the Buddhadharma and strictly uphold the precepts in your cultivation.

At the Beijiao Auditorium, Dharma Master Heng Tso recited the lyrics of "To the Ends of Space"--"Be open and fair, unselfish, and straightforward"--to describe the Venerable Master's selfless efforts to save living beings. A letter written by the Venerable Master and stating the reasons for establishing the City of Ten Thousand Buddhas in America was read during the memorial ceremony. Excerpts are given below:

...I believe that with China's foundation in moral principles and ethical values, it can produce a sage to lead the world... I wish to spread Chinese culture and the principles of Buddhism throughout the world in order to save mankind... China has survived for thousands of years, because it has a unique cultural foundation based on the virtues of filial piety, fraternal respect, loyalty, trustworthiness, propriety, righteousness, incorruptibility, and a sense of shame. And Chinese culture takes Buddhist culture as its foundation... Buddhism is part of the Chinese cultural tradition. Instead of building tens of thousands of temples in China, it would be better to build one temple to serve as a base overseas. Buddhism is virtually unknown in America... If a Chinese temple could be built here and Chinese ethics could play a leading role in the world...

On the second day, Dharma Master Heng Yi, the head nun of Hong Kong Buddhist Lecture Hall, led forty-five people, including the members of the delegation, to take the 7:00 a.m. ferry and visit Cixing (Flourishing Kindness) Monastery on Lantao Island. Cixing Monastery is one of the three Way-places set up by the Venerable Master in Hong Kong more than forty years ago. At 1:00 p.m., disciples from Cixing Monastery and the Buddhist Lecture Hall held a ceremony for liberating lives. The ceremony was led by Dharma Master Heng Tso. Nearly a thousand birds, ferried across the straits from Hong Kong in the morning, were set free in the protective light of the Buddhas and Bodhisattvas as people recited the Great Compassion Mantra.

At seven o'clock in the morning on November 17, some of the members of the delegation visited two elderly nuns, Guo Li (92 years old) and Guo Liang (91 years old) at the Zhilian Hermitage. Both of them had left home with the Venerable Master many years ago in Hong Kong. The old folks' home at the hermitage accommodates more than two hundred women averaging eighty-seven years of age. The living environment is comfortable, and the elderly are well taken care of.

# 澳門

澳門是追思團臺港之行的最後一站。由澳門地藏殿的同修居士們主辦。

追思法會於十一月十七日假綜藝館青年中心舉行。法會以舉〈香讚〉、誦《阿彌陀經》，及念佛號開始。接著司儀報告地藏殿成立緣起等。恆實師應邀開示說，老和尚曾囑咐在美國弘揚佛法，不可用神通，因為西方人受的是科學教育，而要用道德感化。恆實師並勉勵在座青年佛友應該多在德行上用功夫，養成吃素的習慣與實踐孝道的理念。

由法師以廣東話簡報上人的生平事略，接著大眾列隊依序瞻仰上人舍利。迴向功德後，繼續幻燈片的介紹，其中放映了許多古老的、未曾放映過的記錄資料。約有五百餘人齊聚在會場中，觀看上人的事蹟，重溫上人的教誨。

# Macao

The delegation's last stop was Macao, where a memorial ceremony was organized by laypeople from the Earth Store Temple.

The memorial ceremony was held at the Youth Center Performing Arts Theater on November 17. The program began with the Incense Praise and recitation of the *Amitabha Sutra* and the Buddha's name. The Master of Ceremonies recounted the history of the establishment of Earth Store Temple. Dharma Master Sure mentioned in his speech that the Venerable Master had advocated using ethics and virtue, rather than spiritual powers, to propagate Buddhism to Westerners, because Westerners are scientifically oriented. Dharma Master Sure encouraged the young Buddhists at the temple to emphasize virtue, to adopt a vegetarian diet, and to practice filial piety.

Another Dharma Master gave a brief account of the Venerable Master's life in Cantonese, after which the assembly lined up to view the Venerable Master's sharira. After the transference of merit, there was a slide show that presented many old, documentary materials to the public for the first time. More than five hundred people gathered at the theater to watch the show and to reflect on the Venerable Master's teachings.

## 港澳輓聯三則
## Three Elegies from Hong Kong and Macao

宣化上人示寂
On the manifestation of stillness by the Venerable Master Hua

數十載弘法中外　艱苦備嘗　建寺興學留單接眾　世緣已了歸西去
剎那間莊嚴坐化　人天同敬　守戒傳經開覺啓迷　大願無窮望再來

*Over the decades, he propagated the Dharma in China and abroad.*
*Experiencing all kinds of suffering and hardship,*
*He established temples and schools, supported the Sangha, and received living beings.*
*Now his conditions with the world are over, and he has gone back to the West.*

*In an instant, he left in dignity.*
*Respected by humans and gods alike,*
*He observed the precepts and transmitted the scriptures, enlightening the confused ones.*
*Inexhaustible are his vows; we hope he will come back again.*

西方寺住持
菩提學會會長　永惺暨兩序大眾頂禮

Yongxing, the Abbot of Western Monastery and the President of the Bodhi Association, leads the assembly in bowing respectfully

---

宣揚佛法　普令眾生皆得度
化導有情　堪於苦海作舟輪

*Proclaiming and propagating the Buddhadharma, he universally rescued living beings.*
*Teaching and guiding sentient beings, he was a worthy vessel in the sea of suffering.*

香港佛經流通處　智開暨同人敬輓
In respectful mourning,
Zhikai and others from the Hong Kong Sutra Distribution Center

---

五眼六通除有情俗苦　世世修行本不去
三身四智與眾生淨樂　生生乘願再重來

*With the Five Eyes and Six Spiritual Powers, he casts out the mundane sufferings of sentient beings.*
*In life after life, he cultivates and fundamentally does not depart.*
*With the Three Bodies and Four Wisdoms, he bestows pure joy upon living beings.*
*In life after life, he comes back riding on his vows.*

（澳門地藏殿的輓聯）
(An elegy from the Earth Store Temple in Macao)

# 痛失英才
# THE LOSS OF A NOBLE HERO

無論是自己一個人，他也照樣地行持；
只有一個人，他也照樣講，多個人也是這樣。

**Even if he was all alone, he continued with his cultivation.**
**Whether many people came or only one, he still lectured in the same way.**

釋永惺　Shi Yongxing

我跟宣化上人認識很久了，一九四八年在廣東韶關南華寺，大家都在逃難，來到廣東，住在南華寺裡，相處有一個多月。他住在藏經樓，得到虛雲老和尚非常的器重。

宣化上人也是我們一個大同鄉，在東北已經知道他的名，但是沒有機會見面，所以到了南華寺見到之後，感到相見恨晚。那個時候，大家都在逃難期間，心情也不定，所以都是短暫的一個居住而已。輾轉到了香港之後，也是常常見面，常常在一起，知道宣化上人是一個非常用功修行的人，他不怕吃苦，在諸多的行持方面，他是一個很務實而不華的人，所以我們也就非常敬重他的。

而且到了美國之後，度了很多外國的徒弟，因為他不懂英文，而竟能夠跟外國人交談，這也是他的長處。他有過目成誦之才，他記憶力非常地好，看過之後就能記得。所以在美國這麼多年來，大弘道法度了很多的信眾，這是非常值得人敬佩的地方。

他志在修持，沒有道場，自己怎麼樣堅苦地奮鬥，在修持方面是毫無懈怠，無論是自己一個人，他也照樣地行持；只有一個人，他也照樣講，多個人也是這樣，所以他這種堅苦毅力使人非常地敬佩。他能夠有今天的成就，在世界到處弘法，非常受人歡迎，這都是他有一定的實修，所以才有今天。大家非常敬仰他的修持，所以走到哪裡，都是人山人海的歡迎、皈依，所以這都是宣化上人一種務實修行的感應。

聽到他火化之後，燒出很多的舍利，這也足以證明他修持有功夫，有戒定慧的成就、薰習力，才有很多的舍利，所以這也就證明他修行的成就。同時他在美國弘法利生，印很多的經書，翻譯了很多中

I met the Venerable Master Hua way back in 1948 at Nanhua Monastery in Shaoguan, Guangdong. Everyone had gone there to escape the war. The Master and I were together there for over a month. He was living in the Tripitaka Hall. Venerable Master Hsu Yun thought very highly of him.

The Master and I were from the same part of China. I had only heard of him in Manchuria, and when I finally met him at Nanhua Monastery, I wished I could have met him earlier. At that time everyone was feeling very insecure, because we were fleeing from the war and were staying there only temporarily. Later, in Hong Kong, the Master and I often saw each other and were together. I discovered that the Venerable Master was an extremely diligent cultivator who was not afraid of suffering. His cultivation was realistic and genuine, not at all frivolous or superficial. Thus, we all respected him very much.

After going to America, he received many Western disciples; one of his great strengths was that he could communicate with Westerners even though he didn't know English. He had an extremely good memory and could remember anything after reading it once. His many years of propagating Dharma and the large following he came to have in America are very admirable indeed.

He was determined to cultivate even in the most difficult situations when there was no Way-place. He was never the least bit lax in his practice. Even if he was all alone, he continued with his cultivation. Whether many people came or only one, he still lectured in the same way. This spirit of perseverance won him great respect. No matter where he went in the world to propagate the Dharma, the multitudes flocked to welcome him and take refuge. This was a response to his honest cultivation.

I heard that many sharira (relics) were found after his cremation. This is proof of his skill in cultivation. It is through his accomplishment in the practice of precepts, concentration, and wisdom that he was able to have such a great amount of sharira. At the same time, he did everything he could to propagate the Dharma for the benefit of people in America. He had many Sutras printed and many volumes translated from Chinese into English. This is not an easy thing to do.

文成英文的書籍，也是相當豐富。在弘法利生方面，他也是盡其所能，能做到這一步，也不是容易的事情。

所以我們聽到宣化上人往生之後，也感覺到佛教少了一位法將，少了一位德高望重的長者，所以我們也感到很可惜。尤其現在末法時代，有道有德的法師，一個一個這樣去了，後繼無人，這是我們一個很大的隱憂。就是後來的人追不上，同時出家人在行持方面、在修持方面也是追不上，所以我們感到擔心的是後繼無人，大德一個個往生了，這是佛教的隱憂。

我們很希望在座各位大居士們，能夠發心出家，要護持佛教。我們出家人是內護，是傳持佛法的人，如果沒有僧寶，佛法就滅了，所以出家非常地重要。出家之後，不是出了家就完了，還要去學法，學法後還要實行、實修。不是懂點佛法，就靠嘴巴皮，還是不行的，所以必須解行相應，才能有所成就，你光靠一面都是不行的。所以我們最敬佩宣化上人，他解行相應，在這方面他真實做到了，所以他今天才這樣地受人尊敬。

When we heard of the Venerable Master's passing, we felt that Buddhism had lost a great leader in the Dharma, a virtuous and esteemed elder, and we felt it was a great pity. In the present Dharma-ending Age, the virtuous Dharma Masters who have attained the Way are passing away, one by one, with no one to succeed them. This is our great worry. Those of later generations cannot measure up to them. In terms of cultivation, most left-home people cannot match them either. As the virtuous leaders pass away, we worry that there will be no successors. This is a hidden concern in Buddhism.

We hope that you laypeople will bring forth the resolve to leave the home-life and support Buddhism. Left-home people protect Buddhism from within by devoting themselves to the practice of the Dharma. If the Sangha Jewel didn't exist, Buddhism would also die out. Therefore, it is essential to have left-home people. Leaving home is not enough; one must also study the Dharma and then put it into practice. It's not enough to just learn a little Dharma and then rely on your mouth to do all the work. Understanding must be paired with practice in order for there to be some achievement. If you have one but not the other, you won't get anywhere. What we admire most about the Venerable Master Hua was that his understanding matched his practice. He was really able to do this, and that's why so many people look up to him today.

# 偉大的師父
## MY EXTRAORDINARY TEACHER

釋果忠 十八歲　Shramanera Gwo Jung, age 18

在我這一生中，從來沒有跟師父談過一句話，也沒有被師父的枴杖打過，更沒有為師父做過任何事，但是我對師父的生平事蹟卻知道不少。因為每當我聽到有人說他們和師父的因緣時，我一定是專心地聆聽，惟恐有所遺漏。

每當我看《宣化上人事蹟》時，總是不忍釋手，欲罷不能。而且每次讀師父開示錄，或聽到與師父有關的事蹟時，就不自覺地感到師父的偉大。因此我認為師父不只是一位大菩薩而已，而是佛的化身。因為師父的德行和願力真地是太偉大了，不是筆墨所能形容的。

I have never had the opportunity to either talk with the Venerable Master or directly serve him. However, I know a lot about him through his biography. Also whenever I heard anyone start talking about their affinity with the Venerable Master, I would pay full attention, afraid to miss any part of the story.

Whenever I started to read "The Biography of the Venerable Master Hua," I was unable to stop and put the book down. Because, within myself, I strongly feel the greatness of the Venerable Master, and the hardship that he has undergone. Sometimes, I felt that the Venerable Master is not just a great Bodhisattva, as people have always thought, but something more like the transformation body of a Buddha. The Venerable Master's conduct and vows are just unbelievably great. There isn't any scripture that can describe them.

# 上人給我的訓誨
# THE VENERABLE MASTER'S TEACHINGS TO ME

## 爲政者，必須愛民像愛自己的子女一樣
## Those in government should love the people as their own children.

總統府資政林洋港先生
Presidential Advisor Yanggang Lin

今天是宣化大法師圓寂追思大法會，國內各界在這裡集會，紀念這位一代大師，我想最重要的意義，應該是回顧老和尚一生對佛法、對佛教、對人類、社會、文化發展的偉大貢獻，做爲後來繼起者追隨學習的楷模和指標。

關於宣化上人一生的事蹟，今天在座的各位，比我瞭解得更清楚，我就不再多說。佛法是從印度東來的，而把佛法再傳往西方去，是宣化上人一生最大的貢獻。他傳承了虛雲老和尚的法脈，成了爲仰宗第九代接法人以後，就開始在香港建寺弘法；十餘年後，他單身赴美，在舊金山收徒宣揚佛法，爲第一批美國青年剃度出家，並率團赴各大學及世界各國弘法。

我第一次有幸見到宣化上人，是在一九九二年七月，在我訪問美國，考察司法制度以後。七月四日，我先抵達瑜珈鎮萬佛城參觀，在那裡有人告訴我說，當初要建萬佛城的時候，是一片荒地，尤其最傷腦筋的是飲水的問題，可是上人看了一個地方，用手杖指點說：「在這裡造井。」果然找到非常清澈良好品質的泉水。然後他們又帶我看所有的設施，並且以午餐款待我。

當天下午我抵達舊金山灣區，在國際譯經學院會晤上人。見到上人，我第一句話說：「我對佛法一點也沒有研究，請上人您多指導、多開示。」上人對我說：「我們兩個人雖然初次見面，可是我聽說你是孔孟儒家思想的信奉者和實踐者。……」他說：「實際上，佛法的道理和儒家思想的道理是一樣的。」所以他就以如何正心誠意、修身齊家的道理來訓勉我。並且提到美國的福利制度，我們不要太迷信它，美國過份的福利，使美國國民墮落了，好逸惡勞，並且破壞了家庭的觀念。他又告訴我說，

Today many people have gathered here for the Memorial Ceremony for the Venerable Master Hua's Completion of Stillness to remember this Great Master of our time. I think the most important purpose is to memorialize the Venerable Master's great contributions to Buddhism, humankind, society, and cultural development, so that future generations will be able to learn from and follow his guidance and example.

I will not say too much about the Master's life, since all of you know more than I do. The Venerable Master's greatest contribution was to take Buddhism, which had come eastwards from India to China, to the West again. Upon receiving the Dharma transmission from the Venerable Master Hsu Yun and becoming the ninth generation patriarch of the Weiyang Sect, he went to Hong Kong where he built temples and spread the Dharma. Over ten years later, he went alone to the United States and, in San Francisco, began propagating the Buddha's teachings and receiving disciples, including the first group of young Americans who left home with him. He also led delegations to various universities and countries to spread the Dharma.

The first time I had the honor of meeting the Venerable Master was in July 1992, after I came to America to study the legal system. On July 4, I went to visit the City of Ten Thousand Buddhas in Ukiah. I was told that there had been an insufficient water supply when the City was first established, but that the Master told them to dig a well at a certain spot and a source of clear, good quality spring water was found. I was given a tour of the City's facilities and also treated to lunch there.

That afternoon I went to the San Francisco Bay Area and met with the Venerable Master at the International Translation Institute. The first thing I said was, "I have not studied Buddhism at all, so I hope the Venerable Master will kindly instruct me." The Master said, "Although we are meeting for the first time, I have heard that you are a faithful follower of the teachings of Confucius and Mencius...Actually, the principles of Buddhism and Confucianism are the same." Then he instructed me on how to rectify the mind, make the intent sincere, cultivate one's mind, and manage the household. He warned against the American welfare system, saying that excessive welfare has spoiled Americans and made them lazy, and that it has also undermined the

中國大陸現在的制度、方向是錯誤的，是行不通的。這是我們第一次見面的時候，我憑我的日記所寫下的，向各位報告。

我第二次和上人見面，是一九九三年一月間，上人回臺弘法的時候。那一天，上人事先約好中午與黃資政尊秋先生、梁資政肅戎先生和我三人一起吃飯；不過他特別交待我：「你能不能提早四十分鐘，或者一個小時，到這裡來。」

我遵照指示到華懋大飯店，去覲見上人。上人那一天給我指示很多：

第一，人人都有求利益的欲望，政治是很現實的，要注意合理公平地給每一個人民滿足。

第二，己欲立而立人，己欲達而達人，推心置腹才是團結的真正基礎。做人不要鬥爭，不要貪求名位。

第三，為政者，必須愛民像愛自己的子女一樣。

第四，他說看臺灣一切的現象，很像南宋的臨安一樣，偏安不知道奮發，他說：「希望林院長（那時我還沒辭掉司法院院長），你要為國家同胞多做努力！」

這樣子勉勵我，這是我翻開日記，憑我日記的記述來向各位報告。

我家裡也有上人的開示錄，我只有二冊。宣化上人常常說的一些話，對於現代人具有極大的啟示意義。例如說，「不要對面不識觀世音，觀世音其實就在每個人的心裡頭。」上人又說：「做佛事就是佛，做菩薩事就是菩薩，做鬼事就是鬼，做佛、做鬼都在於我們自己，只看自己怎麼做。」我想這段話實在是發人深省。

除了廣譯佛經、弘揚佛法於世界之外，更難能可貴的是，宣化上人具有寬闊的胸襟與深遠的世界觀，他開放萬佛聖城做為一個國際性的宗教中心，提倡團結世界宗教，互相溝通合作，共同追求真理，為世界和平而努力。這早已超出一個宗教家的境界，實在令人感佩不已。

今天我參加這個追思法會，心裡很後悔！很難過！上人在去年六月間，託一個人告訴我，希望我能不能在去年十月間，再到美國去訪問，同他再見面。可是我因為事情忙，我想上人一定會活到一百歲，我就沒有去，又失掉了一次聆聽他對我開示指導的機會。

family. He also told me that the government in mainland China is presently taking the wrong direction and that their policies will not work. This is what I recorded in my diary from my first meeting with the Master.

The second time I saw the Venerable Master was in January of 1993 when he came to Taiwan to propagate the Dharma. That day, Advisors Zhunqiu Huang and Surong Liang and I were scheduled to have lunch with the Master. However the Master had asked me to arrive forty minutes or an hour early. Accordingly, I went to Huamao Restaurant to see the Master. He gave me much advice that day:

1. Everyone seeks benefit. Politics is very realistic. Make sure to satisfy every citizen's needs in a fair and reasonable way.

2. If you want to become established, you should help other people become established. If you want to understand, you should help other people understand. Honesty is the basis for unity. People should not fight, nor should they covet fame and position.

3. Those in government should love the people as their own children.

4. The situation of Taiwan is similar to that of the Southern Song dynasty, when the government was confined to Ling An, enjoying a partial peace and neglecting to work hard. The Master said, "Director Lin (I had not yet resigned as the Director of the Legislative Assembly then), I hope you work extra hard on behalf of your country and fellow citizens!"

These are the exhortations the Master gave me, based on what I recorded in my diary.

I have two volumes of the Venerable Master's instructional talks at home. The Master's teachings are extremely meaningful to the people of today, for example, "Don't face Guanshiyin and fail to recognize him. Guanshiyin is right in everyone's heart." The Master also said, "If you do what a Buddha does, you are a Buddha. Doing a Bodhisattva's deeds, you're a Bodhisattva; and doing a ghost's deeds, you are a ghost. Whether you are a Buddha or a ghost depends on yourself, on what you do." Everyone should reflect deeply on this teaching. Aside from translating many Buddhist scriptures and propagating Buddhism in various parts of the world, what is even more remarkable is that the Venerable Master, with his expansive and far-reaching view of the world, opened the City of Ten Thousand Buddhas as an international religious center where all religions are encouraged to communicate and work together in the pursuit of truth and world peace. His admirable spirit far surpassed that of an ordinary religious leader.

As I take part in this memorial ceremony today, I am filled with regret, because in June of last year, the Master told someone to ask me if I could visit him again in America that October. Because I was very busy and assumed the Master would live to be a hundred, I didn't go, thus missing the opportunity to hear personal instructions from the Master again.

# 我所尊敬的上人

## THE VENERABLE MASTER WHOM I MOST REVERED

### 他不但是一位苦修的高僧，同時是最有愛國心的一個國民。

**He was not only a great monk of ascetic practice, but also a most patriotic citizen.**

世界宗教徒聯誼會會長
總統府資政黃尊秋先生
President of the World Religions Fellowship
Presidential Advisor Zhunqiu Huang

宣化上人圓寂的惡耗傳來，我們大家都是非常地悲悼，上人的圓寂是我們佛教界，而且也是世界人類一個莫大的損失。

上人一生從事於弘法、苦修、譯經，特別把大乘佛經，如《法華經》、《華嚴經》、《阿彌陀經》、《地藏經》等等，譯成英文、西班牙文、越南文、日文等等幾個國家的文字，把佛教的教義傳播到世界各地，對於佛教的貢獻，以及人心的影響非常之大。

今天我僅就幾點我對上人的敬重，提出來向各位報告。第一點：上人令我最尊敬的，他在弘法的時候，一定同時闡揚我們中華文化，也就是說他同時弘揚佛教和我們中華文化、倫理道德，讓佛教跟儒教溶為一體，相輔相成，來拯救人類的陷溺，這種尊重中華文化的寫照，實在是令我非常地敬佩他。

第二點：我認為上人是一個很強烈的愛國者，他從一九六二年到美國弘法，三十幾年的時間，在美國沒有國籍有多少不方便；但是他堅持他是中國人，絕不變更中華民國的國籍。所以我認為他不但是一位苦修的高僧，同時是最有愛國心的一個國民。

第三點：上人提倡六大宗旨，而且自己身體力行，他的六大宗旨就是「不爭、不貪、不求、不自私、不自利、不妄打語」，這個跟我們中華文化「忠、孝、仁、愛、信、義、和、平」固有八德的傳統，是一致的。

今天看看我們的社會，大家很有錢，生活很富裕，但是我們的心靈是怎麼樣？我們的心裡頭實在很貧窮，不少的人只顧自己，自私自利，爭權奪利；到處是金錢掛帥，功利第一，使我們的社會受到嚴重的污染。今天我們要把這個被污染的社會，讓它重回很乾淨、很淳樸的這種境地，我認為大家就應該實現這六大

We were all terribly grieved by the news of the Venerable Master Hua's completion of stillness. His passing is the greatest loss to Buddhists and to the world at large.

The Master's life was devoted to the propagation of Dharma, ascetic cultivation, and the translation of the Buddhist canon. He directed the translation of Mahayana Sutras such as the *Lotus Sutra*, the *Avatamsaka Sutra*, the *Amitabha Sutra*, and the *Earth Store Sutra* into English and other languages such as Spanish, Vietnamese and Japanese, thus disseminating the Buddha's teachings throughout the world. His contributions to Buddhism and his influence on humankind were extremely great.

Today I shall only mention a few points which I particularly respected about the Master .

First of all, the Master was able to propagate Chinese culture and ethics simultaneously with the Buddhadharma. He was able to merge Buddhism with Confucianism so that they complemented and supported each other, and propagate them together to rescue humankind. His respect for Chinese culture won my deep admiration.

Secondly, the Venerable Master loved his country fervently. Although he went to America in 1962 and lived there for over thirty years, he insisted on maintaining his Chinese identity and refused to give up his Chinese citizenship, despite the inconvenience that this caused him in the U.S. In my view, he was not only a great monk of ascetic practice, but also a most patriotic citizen.

Thirdly, the Venerable Master not only preached, but also practiced, the six guiding principles--no fighting, no greed, no seeking, no selfishness, no pursuit of personal gain, and no lying. These principles are in complete accord with the eight virtues of Chinese cultural tradition: loyalty, filiality, humaneness, universal love, trustworthiness, righteousness, harmony, and peace.

If you take a look at our society today, people enjoy wealth and luxury, but their souls are actually impoverished. Most people selfishly fight for fame, power, and profit. Our society has been seriously corrupted by the emphasis on money and

宗旨，以及固有的傳統八德。

上人已經圓寂了，但是他還是留給我們很多的法語，很多的教訓，願大家一起來遵循他這種教導，並且把它弘揚光大，讓我們的社會更為乾淨，大家可以過著很快樂、很充實的生活。

utilitarian concerns. I believe that if we want to make society clean and honest again, we must all follow the six guiding principles and the eight traditional virtues.

Although the Master has passed into stillness, he has left many teachings for us, and I hope we will all follow them, spread them, and make them flourish, so that we will have a cleaner society and everyone will lead a happier and richer life.

謹按：先師離欲上人，坐化三年。偶於遺稿中，發現師於一九八五年農曆五月十七日，有「讚萬佛城」偈一首，表達其對萬佛聖城欣慕讚嘆之一片赤忱。謹錄出作為供養。

妙首釋昌臻謹誌於中國四川樂至報國寺
一九九五年六月六日

Note: It has been three years since our teacher, Venerable Master Liyu, left the world sitting in full lotus posture. We accidentally came upon a verse named "Praise to the City of Ten Thousand Buddhas" composed by the Master on the seventeenth day of the fifth month in 1985. The verse expresses his sincere admiration for the City, and we present it to you as an offering.

--Miaoshou, aka Shi Changzhen of Baoguo Monastery, Lezhi, Sichuan Province, China
June 6, 1995

# 讚萬佛城
## Praise to the City of Ten Thousand Buddhas

萬佛城中萬佛生　萬丈光明萬戶燈
萬代一心萬代業　萬邦共仰萬佛城

*In the City of Ten Thousand Buddhas, ten thousand Buddhas are born.*
*Ten thousand miles of bright light shine from the lamps of ten thousand households.*
*Ten thousand generations with one mind do the great work*
　　*that will last ten thousand generations.*
*Ten thousand nations together admire the City of Ten Thousand Buddhas.*

宣化老和尚追思紀念專集

# 發揚上人的精神

## GLORIFYING THE VENERABLE MASTER'S SPIRIT

### 他的精神永遠留在人間，留在我們的心裏。

**His spirit will remain in the world and in our hearts forever.**

總統府資政梁肅戎先生
Presidential Advisor Surong Liang

我同上人是東北同鄉。上人是出生在松遼平原的吉林省雙城縣，自幼出家，可以說是一位非常偉大的苦行僧。上人在大陸各地學佛修行，又到香港、到南洋，最後到美國，把佛教的思想，傳到西方社會。西方社會是天主教和基督教的範圍，上人打開這一條佛法的路，可以說是非常偉大，而且已經有了成果。

我曾兩度到萬佛城和舊金山探望上人，記得一九九二年我從立法院院長退職之後，到美國美東華人學會講演，然後到萬佛城，同上人有一次很長時間的懇談。上人邀請我做法界佛教大學的校長。

各位知道，上人在萬佛城除了弘揚佛法之外，在柏林根市有一個非常完美的譯經處，把佛經翻譯成英文；另外他也要建立法界大學——一所綜合的大學，目前已經成立了二個研究所。那麼他希望能用法界大學，自己親自弘揚佛法，而且在學術界更能發揚光大。

但是我個人在美國沒有那麼多的深厚關係，我是到日本留學的，所以語言條件對我也不適合。後來他說：「好了！我本來是法界大學的理事主席，我讓給你做好了，你來幫我推動。」當時我也接受了。但是很遺憾的，我回到臺灣之後，沒能脫身去幫他推動這個學校的建立，自己覺得很對不起上人。

今天上人雖然圓寂了，但是他這種精神，所有他的弟子們，或者他的信徒，以及社會各方面的朋友們，將會繼續發揚光大。

我倒是希望，在弘揚佛法之外，法界大學能夠在一個適當時期建立，同時把學術和實際的研究，自己加以訓練，這是非常重要的。今天我們追思上人，我想他的精神已經永遠留在人間，留在我們的心裏。

The Venerable Master and I are both natives of Manchuria. The Master was born in Shuangcheng County of Jilin Province, which is situated on the plain where the Song and Liao Rivers meet. He left the home-life in youth and was an admirable ascetic monk. After studying Buddhism and cultivating in various parts of mainland China, he went to Hong Kong, the South Pacific, and finally to America. He introduced the Buddhist teachings to the West, opening up a path for Buddhism in a society that is predominantly Christian. This is an admirable feat, and his efforts have already borne fruit.

I paid two visits to the Venerable Master at the City of Ten Thousand Buddhas and in San Francisco. In 1992, after resigning as Director of the Legislative Assembly, I went to America to deliver a talk at the Eastern American Chinese Academy, and then I went to the City of Ten Thousand Buddhas, where I had a long conversation with the Master. The Master asked me to be the Chancellor of Dharma Realm Buddhist University. As you all know, aside from propagating Dharma at the City of Ten Thousand Buddhas, the Master also established a fine Translation Institute in Burlingame to translate the Buddhist canon into English, and he founded the Dharma Realm Buddhist University, a general university with two graduate institutes. He hoped, through this university, to disseminate the Buddha's teachings and cause Buddhism to flourish in the academic world.

However, I told him that I didn't have close ties with America (I had studied in Japan), so due to the language barrier I was not a suitable choice. Finally the Master said, "Okay. Originally I was the Executive Chairman of Dharma Realm University, but now I'll let you have the position so you can help me develop the university." I accepted then, but I regret to say that after returning to Taiwan, I wasn't able to devote myself to help him establish the university. I feel I have let the Master down in this respect.

Although the Master has passed into stillness, all of his disciples, followers, and friends in various circles will continue to glorify his spirit. I hope that, in addition to disseminating the Buddhadharma, the Dharma Realm Buddhist University will be able to set itself up within a suitable time frame, and will increase its training in both scholarship and practical research. This is extremely important. In remembering the Master today, I believe that his spirit will remain in the world and in our hearts forever.

# 緬懷禪師宣化上人

## IN MEMORY OF THE VENERABLE MASTER HSUAN HUA

一九四五年，東北光復。師父來我家與父親商量。
師父因為仰慕虛雲老和尚為宗門泰斗，擬前往參禮，要弘揚佛法，爺爺也贊成。
父親送師父到小穗，直奔平房。
師父開始普度眾生，踏上他十八大願的菩提道。

When the Japanese returned Manchuria to China in 1945, the Master wished to make a journey to pay respects to the Great Master Hsu Yun, whom he admired greatly, and to propagate the Buddhadharma. He came to my home to consult with my father. My grandfather supported the Master's decision. Father accompanied the Master all the way to Xiaosui to see him off, and from there the Master headed for the Pingfang Region. The Master was setting off on the Bodhi path to fulfill his eighteen great vows to save all beings.

潘秀珉　Pan Xiumin

師父的原籍，在中國吉林省（現今黑龍江省）雙城縣，屬長白山脈，張廣才嶺餘脈的東北松花江平原上。一九一八年農曆三月十六日，師父聖誕於滿族居住地，西鑲黃旗一個偏僻小村。

師父八、九歲時，因太師母患病求醫，慕名來到離家二十多里的劉正崴屯找我爺爺。我爺爺是雙城方圓百里有名的老中醫，布施窮人，仗義疏財，鄉親們稱我爺爺為「潘善人」，他老人家也是當時我們潘家三十二族的掌櫃。爺爺與道德會會長王鳳儀（俗稱王善人）是好友。

師父到我家後，和小他一歲的家父潘義振成了知交。我有三個伯父，父親行四，下邊是三個叔叔。我爺爺有兩個兒子；大伯和我父親；二爺有我五叔；我老爺有二大伯父、三大伯父、六叔、七叔。師父是我父親那時的孩子王。只要有師父在，幾個叔伯就不敢欺負我父親。只要師父一來我家，父親就不讓師父走。時間長了，師父和我爺爺成了忘年交。我爺爺當時很願意讓孩子們認字，就請私塾先生教，別人都不願意學，父親就留師父一起去聽講。不長時間，師父的「千字文」、「百家姓」就會背。師父的天資聰慧

The Venerable Master was a native of Shuangcheng County, near the city of Harbin in the Heilongjiang Province. His hometown is on the Songhuajiang Plain, below the Zhangkuangcai Ridge of the Manchurian Changbaishan Range. The Master was born on the sixteenth day of the third month in 1918, in a rural village of the western section of the Huangqi district in Manchuria. At the age of eight or nine, the Venerable Master's mother became ill and needed to see a doctor. Upon hearing of my grandfather's reputation, the Master came all the way to Liuzhengwei Village, over twenty Chinese miles away from his home. My grandfather was a herb doctor who was well-known within the hundred miles radius of Shuangcheng County. He helped poor people, devoted himself to public service, and gave generous support to charity. Friends and relatives called my grandfather "Good Man Pan." He was the head of the entire Pan family of thirty-two households at that time. He was a good friend of the chairman of the Virtue Society, Wang Fengyi (commonly known as Good Man Wang.)

After the Master came to my home, he became good friends with my father, Pan Yizhen, who was a year younger than he. I have six uncles, three of them older than my father and three younger. My grandfather had two sons--my father and my first uncle; my second grand uncle had one son--my fifth uncle; and my first grand uncle had four sons--my second, third, sixth, and seventh uncles. The Master was the leader of the children at that time. As long as the Master was there, my uncles would not dare to bully my father. So, whenever the Master came to my home, my father would not let him leave. After some time, the Master and my grandfather became confidants. My grandfather wanted the children to learn to read and write, so he hired a private tutor. No one wanted to study except my father, and he invited the Master to join him. Before long, the Master had memorized the Chinese classics, the *Thousand Character Essay* and the *Hundred Surnames*. The Master was endowed with exceptional intelligence and wisdom. He was tall and polite. My

、智力超人、個子高、懂禮貌；爺爺待如上賓，行針、開方、都不瞞著師父。師父也佩服我爺爺的人品——仁、義、禮、智、信，管家才能，和我們家的家規。師父說男人種地、女人料理家務、輪流煮飯、燒茶挑水、養雞養鴨，各有份工，各負其責。

師父和父親經常在一起對對子，寫毛筆字。他們讀《四書五經》、《史記》。那時我爺爺對師父越來越器重。師父到十四、五歲時，孔、孟等子書過目不忘；而且當時最難懂的《康熙大字典》也會用，誰家孩子取名字都來找師父。

我家屬旗人，按滿族風俗，孩子沒出世就取名、封地，當時我大伯父已結婚，我爺爺求師父給取名字，我們這一輩是「范宏」字，師父當時寫下了：

　　男孩：林、森、岩、濤、國、耀、亮
　　女孩：珍、芬、華、玲、珉、坤、麗

所以，當師父知道我就是秀珉，相當高興，這是後話。

師父對我父親的影響是相當的大。師父和父親會吹簫，最愛的是中國的民歌「蘇武牧羊」，說的是每一個人不能忘國。師父還會拉二胡，對象棋也通，下象棋必第一。

爺爺對師父的話，言者必從。我家不但供祖宗，還供佛，尊敬師長，有禮有貌，犯錯誤還要罰跪的。

師父逢年過節更忙，別人求寫春聯，師父是有求必應的。爺爺好客，是一位老修行，也是一位善人，所以親朋好友來，師父也都必幫陪契。爺爺非常讚歎師父的聰慧，以及孝敬父母。有時師父當天就往返二十餘里地，回家向母親請安，噓寒問暖，給母親叩頭，因此鄉親們稱之為「白孝子」。

師父領著父親，開始給比他小的叔姪、甥女認字，後來就開始辦義學教書了。這時族人反對說：「家有三年糧，不當孩子王」，爺爺不管族人反對，支持師父和父親，每次從雙城縣哈爾濱市看病回村，一定買來很多的書、字帖等教材，很支持師父。

有一天，師父陪著爺爺趕著大車，送小米

grandfather treated him as an honored guest and allowed the Master to watch as he treated patients with acupuncture or wrote prescriptions. The Master also admired my grandfather's character--his humaneness, righteousness, propriety, wisdom, trustworthiness--and his skill in managing the family, as well as our house rules. The Master often said that men should till the fields while women take care of the household chores and take turns cooking, making tea, carrying water, and feeding the chickens and ducks. Every one has his or her share of duties, and each is responsible for himself or herself.

The Master often got together with my father to match couplets or to write calligraphy. They studied the *Four Books*, the *Five Classics*, and the *Historical Records*. My grandfather came to respect the Master more and more. At the age of fourteen or fifteen, the Master demonstrated a remarkable ability to memorize such texts as the works of Confucius and Mencius. He also learned to use the most difficult dictionary, the *Great Kangxi*. People who wanted to find names for their children would come to the Master. My family is Manchurian. According to the Manchurian custom, a child would be given a name and a piece of land before birth. My first uncle was already married at that time, and my grandfather asked the Master to give names for my generation. The Master wrote:

Boys:　Lin, Sen, Yan, Tao, Guo, Yao, Liang
Girls:　Zhen, Fen, Hua, Ling, Min, Kun, Li

When the Master learned that I was named Xiumin, he was quite pleased.

The Master had considerable influence on my father. They both knew how to play the flute. Their favorite piece was a Chinese folk song called "The Shepherd Su Wu," a song that urged people to be faithful to their country. The Master could also play the two-stringed Chinese violin, and he was so proficient at Chinese chess that he never lost a game.

My grandfather always listened to and followed the Master's advice. Our family worshipped the Buddhas as well as our ancestors. We were taught to respect our teachers and the elderly, and to be proper and polite. As punishment for making mistakes, we were made to kneel.

The Master was especially busy during the Chinese New Year. People would ask him to write spring couplets, and he never disappointed them. Grandfather, an old cultivator and a good man, was very hospitable. When friends and relatives came by, he would ask the Master to be there to receive them. Grandfather admired the Master not only for his intelligence and wisdom, but also for his filial piety toward his parents. Sometimes, the Master would travel over twenty Chinese miles in one day just to go home to greet his mother and bow to her. His relatives and neighbors called him "Filial Son Bai." The Master guided my father to teach the younger nieces and nephews Chinese. Later they started a free school. The family objected to this, saying, "When we have sufficient grain to support the family for three years, there's no need for you to make a living by teaching." Nevertheless, my grandfather supported the Master and my father. When he went to Harbin to treat patients, he would buy a lot of books and notebooks for the school.

One day, the Master accompanied my grandfather as he drove an oxcart loaded with millet and newly harvested rice to make offerings to the Abbot of Sanyuan (Three Conditions) Monastery, Dharma Master Changren. When the Master went into the monastery, he chatted with the Abbot as if they were old friends. It seemed that they knew each other

子和新伐的大黃米，去供養三緣寺方丈和尚常仁大師時，師父和常仁大師一見如故，似乎往昔早已熟識，說些爺爺都不懂的禪話。

師父遍覽釋、儒、道，三教經典，不但有畫畫的天賦，而且懂音律，還領著我父親給別人看地理。後來師父和我父親一起參加道德會，當時還有我父親的胞姊一起參加道德會，師父經常問到我這位姑姑。

師父也幫助父親度過很多難關。最使爺爺感動的是，師父十二歲那年，正好來我家時，家裡抬來一位心臟病人，人已經不行了，還跪著求爺爺救命。爺爺心軟了，死人當活人醫，剛一行針，人就斷氣了。這家人不念我爺爺平日周濟之恩，卻大哭大鬧，要我爺爺償命。爺爺只好給買了棺材，我們全家親朋好友共四十餘口披麻戴孝給送葬；族人怨聲載道，爺爺心灰意冷，一宿頭髮都白了，大病。這時候，師父安慰我爺爺，並開導與送藥。爺爺病好之後，作主讓師父和父親供佛，成了叩頭生死情同手足的弟兄。師父十二歲以前，不知天高地厚；十二歲以後，知人命關天，生死事大。

師父的《易學》也很精湛，但他不輕易使用的。一天，我們有個鄉親把豬丟了，那時失主尋死尋活，百般求師父，師父給算了，說：「在西邊有一戶鄉親的柴火垛裡邊。」但西邊那家又不讓動，鄰里勸說看準不準，過了晌午才讓動。由於東西太多，下午三點才搬動好。那豬頭朝裡面，被卡在板的夾縫裡，身上還有血道子二劃，豬都叫不出來了。師父還有很多神機妙算的故事。

在一九三六年秋，太師母不幸病故，師父借三百吊錢為太師母買了棺材厚葬。當時的情況使人很震驚、佩服。師父在廬墓守孝時，父親往返幾十里地給師父送飯，還一起守孝。師父到哈爾濱平房區的三家子鄉三緣寺正式出家，拜常智老和尚為師。師父出家後，仍去太師母墓守孝、送燈。我父親去墳上看師父，師父說：「你回去吧！每天都有人給我送飯。」沒想師父是靠著涼水、誦《華嚴經》，在太師母墓前度過的。師父修禪定、禮佛拜懺，在聖母墓前風雨不動，發十八大弘願。

from past lives. They engaged in some Chan banter that Grandfather could not understand.

The Master was well-versed in the scriptures of Buddhism, Confucianism, and Taoism. He was talented at painting, and he also understood the theory of music. He even took my father with him to investigate geomancy. Later the Master and my father joined the Virtue Society of Manchuria. My father's sister also joined with them. The Master often asked about this aunt of mine. The Master helped Father in overcoming many difficulties. What touched my grandfather most was an incident that happened when the Master was twelve years old. The Master was at our home when a family brought over a patient who had suffered a heart attack. The chances of the patient recovering were nil, but the family knelt down and pleaded with my grandfather to do something. Finally, my grandfather gave in tenderheartedly and treated the patient as best he could. The patient died just as my grandfather finished placing the acupuncture needles. Forgetting about how my grandfather had helped them before, the patient's relatives wailed bitterly and raised a ruckus. They demanded that my grandfather make restitution for the life lost. My grandfather had to buy a coffin for them, and our entire family plus friends--over forty people in all--had to put on mourning clothes and attend the funeral. Complaints could be heard throughout the family. My grandfather was so frustrated that his hair turned gray overnight and he became seriously ill. The Master consoled him by talking to him and bringing him medicine. After he got well, he allowed the Master and my father to worship the Buddha. The two had since become companions in life and death, and they were just like blood brothers. The Master had been very naive before he turned twelve, but when he was twelve, he learned about the grave matter of birth and death.

The Master was well-versed in the *Book of Changes*, but he would not use it casually. Once, a relative of ours lost a pig. The owner threatened to commit suicide as he pleaded repeatedly for the Master's help. Finally, the Master used divination to determine that the pig was hidden in a pile of firewood at another relative's house on the west side of the village. However, that household refused to let people do anything at their house. The household finally granted their permission after noontime, since neighbors urged them to see if the Master's words were accurate. Since there were great piles of things all over the place, the people did not finish sorting through them until three o'clock in the afternoon. The missing pig was stuck in a crack between boards, facing inward. It had several bloody cuts on its body and could not even squeal. There were many stories like this about the Master's magical divinings.

In the autumn of 1936, the Master's mother passed away. The Master borrowed three hundred dollars to buy a coffin, and he gave his mother a very decent funeral. Many surprising things happened at that time, which caused people to admire the Master greatly. During the time the Master was practicing filial piety by his mother's grave, my father would walk some ten Chinese miles to bring food to the Master. Sometimes, my father would stay and keep the Master company.

The Master went to Three Conditions Monastery in the Pingfang region in Harbin to shave his head and bow to the Venerable Changzhi as his teacher. After the Master left the home-life, he continued his filial practice by his mother's grave. Once when my father went to see him, the Master said, "Please go home. I have people bringing me food every day." Who would have guessed that the Master lived only on icy water and the *Avatamsaka Sutra* by his mother's grave? He cultivated samadhi,

斷三障緣　除五怖畏
行菩薩道　廣化一切

師父出家皈依三寶後，受沙彌戒，寵辱不驚，本著

多認不是少爭理
安然清淨智慧生

的原則。爺爺往三緣寺送糧，就會把師父接回來。師父給爺爺講的第一部經是《金剛經》，接著講《地藏菩薩本願功德經》、《因果經》等，使我爺爺大徹大悟要出家。爺爺經過一年多的考慮，於一九四二年給族裡開會：

（一）修精舍；
（二）掌櫃的傳我堂二伯父；
（三）素灶，由我母親送飯；
（四）我奶也信佛，和我四奶住一起。

一九四三年秋，精舍蓋好。師父幫助請佛，師父給我爺爺剃度。我們老家開始都信佛，禮敬諸佛，廣修供養。這時師父在我家和我爺爺在一起講經說法，多時半年，少時半月，和我爺爺無所不談。師父在我家這麼長的時間裡，從沒與我母親說一句話，也說母親的人品好。爺爺出家時已五十八歲，爺爺腿硬不會坐禪。師父用什麼功夫幫助爺爺坐禪呢？我母親也不清楚。去年（一九九四年），我問師父，師父說：是爺爺自身修慧得來的。

一九四五年，東北光復，師父來我家與父親商量，我媽也和父親談了看法。師父因為仰慕虛雲老和尚為宗門泰斗，擬前往參禮，要弘揚佛法，爺爺也贊成。父親送師父到小穗，直奔平房。師父開始普度眾生，踏上他十八大願的菩提道。

worshipped the Buddha, and bowed in repentance. Not moved by wind or rain, the Master made his eighteen great vows in front of his mother's grave.

*Sever the conditions of the three obstacles;*
*Dispel the fear of the five terrors.*
*Practice the Bodhisattva's path*
*And extensively transform all.*

After the Master took refuge, left the home-life, and received the novice precepts, he was moved by neither slander nor praise. His personal motto was:

*Admit your faults more, and argue less.*
*Peaceful, pure, and at ease, you give rise to wisdom.*

When my grandfather brought grain over to Three Conditions Monastery, he invited the Master home. The first Sutra the Master explained to my grandfather was the *Vajra Sutra*. It was followed by the *Sutra of the Past Vows of Earth Store Bodhisattva*, the *Sutra of Cause and Effect*, and others. As a result, my grandfather had an awakening and wanted to leave the home-life. After considering it for over a year, he called a family meeting in 1942. Several decisions were made:

1. a hermitage was to be constructed;
2. the family business would be passed on to my second uncle;
3. a vegetarian kitchen would be set up, and my mother would be responsible for delivering food; and
4. my grandmother would live with my fourth grand aunt and practice Buddhism.

In the fall of 1943, the hermitage was constructed. The Master helped to invite the Buddhas. He also shaved my grandfather's head. The entire family became Buddhist and began worshipping the Buddhas and making extensive offerings. During this period, the Master lived with my grandfather in my home. Together, they would speak the Dharma and lecture on Sutras for at least half a month straight, and sometimes for half a year. My grandfather could discuss everything with the Master. During the time when the Master lived in my home, he never spoke a word to my mother. However, he often praised my mother's good character. My grandfather was fifty-eight years old when he left the home life. His legs were rather stiff, and he could not sit in meditation. My mother could not give a clear account of how the Master helped him to sit in meditation. Last year (1994) when I asked the Master about it, the Master simply replied that it was due to my grandfather's own cultivation of wisdom.

When the Japanese returned Manchuria to China in 1945, the Master wished to make a journey to pay respects to the Great Master Hsu Yun, whom he admired greatly, and to propagate the Buddhadharma. He came to my home to consult with my father. My parents both approved. My grandfather also supported the Master's decision. My father accompanied the Master all the way to Xiaosui to see him off, and from there the Master headed for the Pingfang Region. The Master was setting off on the Bodhi path to fulfill his eighteen great vows to save all beings.

# 緬懷上人

## IN REMEMBRANCE OF THE VENERABLE MASTER

### 上人過去的教導，我一點都不馬虎。
### I have followed the Master's teachings
### very seriously and diligently.

楊英風　Yingfeng Yang

今天參加這個追思大會，本人內心感覺到非常地難過。我曾經在十幾年前，有三年的期間在宣化上人身邊，能夠受到他老人家的教導和照顧，並且能夠在萬佛城、法界佛教大學，參加各種苦修、聽經，給我一生中很大的一個感動。我曾看到上人的偉大，他在苦修中教導所有的信眾，這種情況實在令我受益良多，對我一生的前途及各方面，都有很大的鼓勵。由於上人過去的教導，我一點都不馬虎，遵守他的教導，所以能夠努力到今天，這都是上人給我的鼓勵。

上人把佛教傳到美國，但是並不因此忽略對中國的關心；特別是對臺灣，上人來過臺灣好幾次，主持護國息災法會，關心我們社會未來的發展，這是大家都深深體會到的。今天雖然上人圓寂了，我們還是沒有離開他，他也是一直在關心我們整個人類、整個社會。我們應該要團結一致，以上人的為人做一個領導，為整個社會共同來努力，造就一個更好的國家社會。這是我個人感覺，我們必須要這樣去做。

I feel very sad to take part in this memorial ceremony today. Over a decade ago, for a three year period I was able to be at the side of Venerable Master Hua, receiving his teaching and care, and to take part in the ascetic cultivation and Sutra lectures at the City of Ten Thousand Buddhas and Dharma Realm Buddhist University. That was a very touching period of my life, during which I witnessed the Master's greatness in ascetic cultivation and in teaching his disciples. That experience has benefitted and encouraged me greatly in my life. That is why, up to today, I have followed the Master's teachings very seriously and diligently.

The Venerable Master took Buddhism to America, and yet he did not forget about China. He returned to Taiwan several times and held Dharma sessions to protect the nation and avert disasters. Everyone is aware of how concerned he was about Taiwan's future.

Although the Master has completed the stillness, he has not left us. He is still mindful of the human race and of the entire society. We should unite and work hard together, guided by the Master's example, to build a better nation and society. This is what I feel we must do.

---

若有見正覺　解脫離諸漏　不著一切世　彼非證道眼
若有知如來　體相無所有　修習得明了　此人疾作佛
　　　——《大方廣佛華嚴經》〈光明覺品第九〉

*If someone sees the one of Proper Enlightenment*
*As liberated and free from all outflows,*
*And as not being attached to all worlds,*
*That person still has not certified to the Way-Eye.*

*If someone knows the Thus Come One's*
*Body and marks do not exist,*
*And cultivates and attains this understanding,*
*Then that person will quickly become a Buddha.*

Flower Adornment Sutra, Chapter Nine, Light Enlightenment

---

# 有利於民　盡心盡力

## DO YOUR BEST TO BENEFIT THE PEOPLE

### 要做個好公務員，在自己職責範圍之內，
### 只要對人民有利益的事情，就應該努力放心地去做。

**You should be a good public servant.
Do everything in your power to benefit the people.**

陳吉雄　Jixiong Chen

一代高僧宣公上人，在美國洛杉磯圓寂的消息，傳抵臺灣的時候，帶給弟子們陣陣的震驚與無限的哀痛。弟子們懷著悲傷與追思的心情，相互一一地走告這不幸的消息，紛紛組團前往美國萬佛聖城，參加荼毗與追思大典。雖然很多人趕去美國萬佛聖城，但是師父在臺灣的弟子數以萬計，為了讓未能趕赴美國參加荼毗大典的弟子們，以及許多崇敬師父的大德們，能有機會緬懷師恩，向他們敬愛的師父致敬起見，特別請美國萬佛聖城的法師，前來臺灣共同主持「紀念宣公上人圓寂追思法會」，並且以此功德迴向臺灣安定及世界和平。

我在多年以前就敬仰師父他老人家長年苦行修持的聲名，但是苦無機會見到老人家。直到一九八九年，師父返臺弘法時，我得到一個機緣，終於見到了師父。我因為工作上的關係，有機緣得以接近佛法，認識法師，也獲得一些佛教界的資訊，也瞭解了臺灣佛教今後需要努力精進的方向，因此當我聆聽師父的開示之後，我內心非常地歡喜，如獲至寶似的，因為我找到了尋覓已久的名師。

皈依宣公上人之後，我每年都到美國觀見師父，蒙師父親切慈祥的開示，心中均有所感應，受益良多，使我在工作上，以及進德修業上，都得到很多的啟示，同時有很多的進步。師父曾經告訴我說：

要做個好公務員，在自己職責範圍之內，只要對人民有利益的事情，就應該努力放心地去做，多為國家社會大眾盡心盡力。不要發脾氣，因為脾氣發多了，人與人之間將充滿了戾氣，衝突跟糾紛就跟著來了。萬一遇上令人生氣的情況，那就念〈忍耐咒〉：『忍耐，忍耐，多多忍耐，不要生氣，娑婆訶。』

The news of the completion of stillness of the Venerable Master Hua, an eminent monk of our time, brought shock and boundless grief to his disciples in Taiwan. Disciples mournfully spread the sad news and organized groups to attend the Cremation and Memorial Ceremonies at the City of Ten Thousand Buddhas in America. Although many were able to attend the ceremonies in America, not all of the Master's over ten thousand disciples in Taiwan could go. In order to give those disciples who could not go and others who esteemed the Master the opportunity to express their remembrance, gratitude, and respect for the Master, we have invited Dharma Masters from the City of Ten Thousand Buddhas to come to Taiwan to hold the Memorial Ceremony for the Venerable Master Hua's Nirvana, the merit of which will be dedicated to stability in Taiwan and world peace.

For many years I admired the Master's ascetic cultivation, but unfortunately did not have the opportunity to meet him until 1989, when the Master came to Taiwan to spread the Dharma. Through my work, I was able to draw near to Buddhism, to meet Dharma Masters, to receive news of Buddhist affairs, and to understand the direction that Buddhism in Taiwan needs to take. After listening to the Master's lectures, I felt as ecstatic as if I had discovered a treasure, for he was the great teacher I had been searching for.

After I took refuge with the Venerable Master, I went to visit him in America every year, and each time he would kindly instruct me. I responded to and benefitted immensely from these instructions, which allowed me to gain insight and make progress both in my work and in my cultivation. The Master once told me,

Be a good public servant. Do everything in your power to benefit the people. Do your best for the nation and society. Don't get angry. When there is much anger, there will be enmity and conflict among people. In trying circumstances, recite the Patience Mantra: 'Gotta be patient, gotta be patient, don't get angry, suo po he!'

師父也告訴我：

> 不要生煩惱，要以靜心養性，
> 要多念佛以消業障。

我始終牢牢記住師父對我的告誡，因此使我在許多困難的境遇中，都能化險為夷，轉危為安，更加使我感覺到師父的這些教訓彌足珍貴。

師父經常以「不爭、不貪、不求、不自私、不自利、不妄語」六大宗旨，諄諄告誡眾生。他老人家悲天憫人的精神，和一生無我無私、篤踐勵行弘揚佛法的風範，令人肅然起敬。多年來我也確實恪遵師父的六大宗旨，使我在言行修持方面都有所依循，不至於迷失了方向。

師父雖長年在美國弘法，但他老人家卻關懷臺灣社會眾生的一切。一九八九年師父返臺弘法，見到臺灣社會流於奢侈虛榮，人們沉迷功利、耽於聲色，生活腐化，不禁發出誠摯的呼籲，不顧自己孱弱的身體，斷食三週，以消弭眾生貪瞋癡的念頭，期使眾生在茫茫人生苦海中，迷途知返，同登彼岸。

師父多年來一直保留著中華民國的國籍，並且始終珍藏著一面青天白日滿地紅的國旗。師父他老人家熱愛國家、熱愛同胞的精神，是多麼令人感動。而今師父已圓寂了，巨星遽殞，世人同悲，為了不負師父的教誨與期望，我們應該記取師父的訓示與風範，「勤修戒定慧，息滅貪瞋癡。」只要我們能真誠發心，師父他老人家都將與我們同在。

師父！您將是弘揚佛法、拯救愚迷眾生的一顆救星，永遠指引眾生度向光明。

The Master also said to me,

> Avoid affliction. Keep a calm mind and nurture the nature. Recite the Buddha's name frequently to dissolve karmic hindrances.

The Master's instructions are truly precious. I have successfully resolved many difficult crises as a result of keeping them in mind.

The Master often exhorted people to follow the Six Principles: no fighting, no greed, no seeking, no selfishness, no pursuit of personal advantage, and no lying. His selfless compassion and active propagation of the Dharma have won the respect of many people. For many years the Six Principles have given me guidance in my daily conduct and my cultivation, preventing me from going astray.

Although the Master lived in America for many years propagating the Dharma, he never failed to show the greatest concern for the people of Taiwan. When the Master came to Taiwan in 1989 to propagate the Dharma, he sincerely spoke out against the extravagance, corruption, and infatuation with fame and position that he saw. He also embarked on a three-week fast despite his own weak condition, hoping to quell people's greed, anger, and delusion and to guide them out of the boundless sea of human suffering to the bliss of the other shore.

The Master always maintained his Chinese citizenship and kept a flag of the Republic of China. Many have been touched by the Master's fervent loyalty to his country and his fellow countrymen. The Master's passing is like the fall of a great star, and is mourned by people around the world. In order to live up to the Master's teachings and expectations, we ought to follow the Master's example by diligently practicing the precepts, concentration, and wisdom and by extinguishing greed, anger, and delusion. If we sincerely make a resolve to do this, the Master will always be with us.

Master! You are a star of deliverance, disseminating the Buddha's teachings to save the deluded masses, eternally guiding living beings towards the light.

---

若於佛及法　其心了平等　二念不現前　當踐難思位
若見佛及身　平等而安住　無住無所入　當成難遇者
　　　　　——《大方廣佛華嚴經》〈光明覺品第九〉

*If with regard to the Buddha and the Dharma*
*One's mind is completely level and equal*
*And the two thoughts do not manifest,*
*Then one will realize the position which is hard to conceive of.*

*If there is someone who sees the Buddha and living beings*
*As level and equal, and peacefully dwelling,*
*Yet without dwelling and without a place of entering,*
*Then that person will become one who is difficult to encounter.*

Flower Adornment Sutra, Chapter Nine, Light Enlightenment

# 讚頌宣公上人德澤

## IN PRAISE OF THE VENERABLE MASTER HUA'S VIRTUE AND KINDNESS

上人認爲「教育是做人的根本，也是世界的根本。」
所以倡導教育，不遺餘力。

**The Master regarded "education as the foundation for being
a good person and the foundation for the world."
That's why he spared no energy when it came to education.**

何伯超
Pai-cho Ho

宣公上人示寂，已經一週年。萬佛聖城舉行涅槃紀念法會，追思上人德澤法貌，宛在目前；聖城中一切日常儀規，遵守上人遺訓，奉行如昔，懷念往日勝況，實感無盡哀思。

追憶上人在世時，正值國步維艱，民族多難，上人遠渡重洋，來美弘法，建立道場，教化弟子，曾多次率團巡迴南洋各地，並親赴國內及歐洲各國，舉行消災護國和平法會，不辭勞瘁，弘法忘身，拯救世人苦難，消弭戰禍，其慈悲喜捨與無畏濟世精神，爲世人造福，四海同欽。

現代社會，由於科技發達，道德日趨淪喪，上人認爲挽救之道，在於發展教育，認爲「教育是做人的根本，也是世界的根本。」所以倡導教育，不遺餘力。又主張弘揚佛法，應以發展教育爲基礎，因爲「佛法不離世間法」，教人爲善，能修成佛道。在萬佛聖城中，創辦大、中、小學校，教導青少年，培養人才，其苦心孤詣，真知灼見，至爲深遠。

上人提倡六大宗旨：「不爭、不貪、不求、不自私、不自利、不妄語」，此不僅應爲佛門信守戒律，其意義涵概各宗教之義理。如道教主張「清靜無爲」，無私、

It has already been one year since the Venerable Master Hua manifested entry into stillness. The Memorial Nirvana Assembly held at the Sagely City of Ten Thousand Buddhas, in which the Master's kindness was remembered, still appears clearly in my mind. The ceremonies and traditions continue as usual in the Sagely City; following the Master's final instructions, everyone continues to practice as in the past. Remembering the wonderful times of bygone days, I am filled with boundless sorrow.

The Master lived at a time when China was in great crisis and its people suffered many hardships. The Master brought the Dharma across the ocean to America, establishing Way-places and teaching disciples here. He also led many delegations to various parts of the United States and to countries in Southeast Asia and Europe, where he hosted Dharma gatherings to avert disasters, protect nations, and pray for peace. With tireless zeal and self-sacrifice, he propagated the Dharma hoping to relieve human suffering and put an end to wars. With kindness, compassion, joy, and giving, he fearlessly worked to rescue the world and to bestow blessings on all. Thus he came to be respected throughout the world.

In today's society with its advanced technology, virtue and ethics have been forgotten. The Master thought that the way to save the situation is to develop good education, for he regarded "education as the foundation for being a good person and the foundation for the world." That's why he spared no energy when it came to education. He felt that the propagation of Buddhism should be founded on the development of education, because "The Buddhadharma is not apart from the world." If people are taught to be good, they will be able to cultivate the path to Buddhahood. At the City of Ten Thousand Buddhas he founded a university and secondary and elementary schools to educate and nurture young people. His painstaking efforts and clear vision were truly profound and far reaching.

The Master set forth the Six Guiding Principles--no fighting, no greed, no seeking, no selfishness, no pursuit of personal benefit, and no lying--which not only reflect Buddhism's emphasis on the precepts, but encompass the doctrines of all other religions. For example, these Six Principles include the Taoist ideas of purity, nonaction, egolessness, and noncontention, as well as the Confucian doctrine of "restraining oneself in accord with propriety" and

無爭。儒家主張「克己復禮」；非禮勿視
、勿聽、勿言、勿動，皆已融會其中要義
，實爲明心養性與修己安人之無上箴言。

上人出家立誓十八大願，精勤苦修，嚴
守戒規，日中一食，夜不倒單，履行惟恐
不逮；主持翻譯佛藏經典，爲各國語言經
書，採用現代語文淺釋，廣爲流傳，其功
德普被眾生，澤及法界，皆爲上人之睿智
卓行。其他弘法利生之偉蹟，不可足述。
謹撰偈頌一篇，敬表哀思。

not looking at, listening to, speaking about, or practicing improper things. The Six Principles are truly an excellent formula for understanding the mind and nurturing the nature, for cultivating oneself and dwelling peacefully with others.

After leaving the home-life, the Master made eighteen great vows and applied himself vigorously to his practice. He held the precepts strictly, took only one meal a day, and did not lie down to sleep; his only worry was that he was not practicing zealously enough. He gave modern language explanations of the major Buddhist scriptures and directed their translation into various languages and their publication and circulation around the world. His massive merit and virtue benefits living beings and his grace pervades the Dharma Realm. These are all due to the Master's wisdom and peerless conduct. His monumental contributions in propagating Dharma to help living beings are too numerous to relate. I can only compose a verse to express my sadness.

## 宣化上人讚頌

## A Verse in Praise of the Venerable Master Hsuan Hua

（一）
長白山麓有高僧，
一襲破衲禦寒冬；
廬墓三年報親恩，
鄉里盛傳孝子名。
出家立誓十八願，
普度法界濟眾生；
鬩墻戰火遍神州，
參訪大德萬里行。

I.
*At the foot of the Eternally White Mountains was a noble monk;*
*A single tattered robe was all he had to ward off the bitter winter cold.*
*Living by his mother's grave for three years to repay her kindness,*
*He won renown as a Filial Son among the village folk.*
*Upon leaving the home-life, he made eighteen vows*
*To universally save the living beings of the Dharma Realm.*
*As civil war spread throughout the land of China,*
*He embarked on a ten thousand mile journey to visit great virtuous ones.*

（二）
精修禪學朝南華，
親謁雲老拜祖庭；
授命戒壇嚴律法，
嗣承潙仰九代宗。
世局動亂難平息，
艱赴香江演佛乘；
巡迴海外弘教化，
輾轉北美續星燈。

II.
*To pursue his intense study of Chan, he personally visited Nanhua*
*And bowed to the Venerable Yun in the patriarch's court.*
*Assigned to the precepts platform, he sternly upheld the rules of Vinaya.*
*And later became the ninth generation heir of the Weiyang sect.*
*As the situation in China became ever more chaotic,*
*He went to Hong Kong and lived in poverty, expounding the Buddha Vehicle.*
*Travelling to foreign lands to preach Dharma and teach beings,*
*Eventually he came to North America to light up the stellar lamp.*

宣化老和尚追思紀念專集

（三）

（三）

佛陀文化隆世運，
自古仁者遠傳經；
玄奘跋涉南天竺，
鑑眞浮海泛東瀛。
宣公西渡建法幢，
媲美先賢化有情；
廣譯三藏揚獅吼，
光被異域覺無生。

III.

*The Buddha's teaching can bring prosperity to the world.*

*Since ancient times, the sages have transmitted it afar.*

*Venerable Hsuan Tsang scaled mountains and forded rivers to reach southern India.*

*Venerable Jianzhen sailed eastwards across the sea to Japan.*

*Venerable Hua crossed the Pacific and raised the Dharma banner in the West.*

*In teaching living beings, he did not fall behind the ancient worthies.*

*Extensively translating the Tripitaka, he gave forth the Lion's Roar.*

*His light illumines foreign lands, causing people to awaken to nonproduction.*

（四）

日中一食不倒單，
苦行持戒履梵行；
皈依弟子遍寰宇，
參禪悟道繼宗風。
提倡道德興教育，
孝親愛國護和平；
示寂舍利照大千，
荼毗靈灰撒虛空。

IV.

*Taking only one meal a day and not lying down to sleep,*

*He upheld the precepts and was pure and ascetic in his practice.*

*Living beings around the world took refuge and became his disciples.*

*After awakening to the Way through meditation, he carried on the Chan tradition.*

*Promoting ethics and virtue and working to make education flourish,*

*He was a filial child and a loyal citizen who protected the cause of peace.*

*After his manifestation of stillness, his precious relics illumine the universe.*

*After cremation, his holy ashes were sprinkled high up in the air.*

師弟：「師兄！妳要不要寫一篇文章登在上人紀念專集裡面？」

師兄：「寫什麼文章？我寫：師父！我怎麼想您、怎麼想您。

師父會說：『我叫妳修的法，妳都沒修！想我做什麼？不想法
想人，真是顛倒！』」

Younger Dharma brother: "Elder Dharma brother, would you like to write an essay for the Master's memorial book?"

Elder Dharma brother: "Write what? I'd write: 'Shr Fu, I'm thinking of you, I miss you so much.' Shr Fu would say, 'You haven't practiced any of the Dharmas I taught you to practice. What are you thinking of me for? Thinking of a person instead of the Dharma--truly deluded!'"

# 上人的大願——辦教育
# THE VENERABLE MASTER'S GREAT VOW--EDUCATION

**人人以身作則，清廉自許，把所懷的抱負和智慧教給下一代。**

**Everyone should be a good model of integrity who will pass his or her aspirations and wisdom on to the next generation.**

陳威宏　Weixiong Chen

上人有三大願：

第一，將佛教在西方紮根；
第二，翻譯經典；
第三，辦教育。

上人非常關心教育的問題，上人說：

教育是根本，是最徹底的國防。

在現在這個社會，全世界每天都發生許多事情，我想起上人這句話，不禁感觸良深，也覺得非常有意義。一個國家如果沒有優秀的青年，光有最先進的武器，那就算沒有外面的敵人來侵略，這個國家也要從內部開始衰弱下去。

一九七六年，上人在三藩市金山寺創立了育良小學。一九八〇年左右，育良小學就移到了萬佛聖城，並且開設了培德中學。上人希望我們教導學生「忠孝」的道理，要學生學習愛身，愛護自己的身體、生命；愛家，愛護自己的家庭；愛國，愛護自己的國家。在育良小學、培德中學裏面，我們首先教小學生注重孝道。孝道是我們中國自古以來非常優秀的一個傳統，但是在今天這個世界裏，就不像以前有那麼好的發揚，所以在我們學校裏面開有道德課，教導小孩子《孝經》、《弟子規》，簡單的《四書》、《五經》，灌輸他們孝順的重要，孝順父母。我們灌輸他們，就算你念佛念得再好，如果不孝順父母，這也是沒有用的。

中學生呢？上人要我們教導他們愛護國家、忠於國家。國家是保護我們人民的，我們要忠於它。另外很重要的，要愛惜生命，上人教導學生，不可以太早結交異性朋友。因為小孩子生理沒有成熟的時候，就開始找對象，在生理或心理上都會吃虧的。上人曾經說：

The Venerable Master's three great vows are:

1. To firmly implant Buddhism in Western soil
2. To translate the Buddhist canon
3. To promote education

The Venerable Master was deeply concerned about education. He said,

Education is the most fundamental form of national defense.

In today's troubled society, the Master's statement has great meaning. If a nation has the most advanced weaponry, but no promising young people, then even in the absence of foreign invasions, an internal decline is inevitable.

The Master founded Instilling Goodness Elementary School at Gold Mountain Monastery in San Francisco in 1976. Around 1980, the school moved to the City of Ten Thousand Buddhas, where Developing Virtue Secondary School was also founded. The Master encouraged us to teach students to be loyal and filial, and to cherish themselves, their families, and their country.

The schools emphasize filial piety, an ancient Chinese virtue which is unfortunately neglected in today's world. In ethics class, children are taught such texts as the *Classic of Filiality*, *Standards for Students*, and simplified versions of the *Four Books* and *Five Classics*. We tell them if they are not filial to their parents, then no matter how well they recite the Buddha's name, it's useless.

The Master instructed us to teach secondary students to love their country and loyally serve it, because the country protects the people. The Master also exhorted students to respect themselves and not start dating too early. Premature romantic involvements result in psychological as well as physiological harm. The Master said,

宣化老和尚追思紀念專集

女孩子在二十歲以後才交男朋友，男孩子在二十五歲以後才交女朋友，這樣子他們在年輕的時候，可以專心在課業上研究，有好的學問，將來才會成為好的人才，我們的國家社會也才有希望。

今年暑假我們面試了一些聖城附近的美國學生，在面談中我們了解到，在美國就算達摩鎮那麼偏僻的地方，一般學校也會發生小孩子帶槍，互相在學校射擊、幫派、毒品這些問題。這在大城市尤其是非常地盛行，還有交男女朋友，這在西方都是司空見慣的事情。所以現在有不少當地的美國父母，他們也不滿意美國這種教育系統，當他們知道聖城有這樣一個小學，都有這種意願把他們的小孩送到這裏來試試看，看是不是能夠對他們的小孩子有所幫助。

另外上人也曾經指出：

我們身為父母的，
要對小孩子負起最大的責任。

現在這個社會離婚率非常高，在美國尤其地高。以我個人的經驗，我教一班初級的中文班，班上有五個美國小朋友，其中四個的父母都已經離婚了，還有一、二個學生他們的父母已經是二婚或三婚的，這對他們幼小的心靈，都有很大很大的影響。所以我們身為父母的，如果能盡好責任，學校也負責好好地教導學生，那麼我相信可以培養出很好的人才。

上人為了樹立老師清廉崇高的形象，所以在幾年前，也建立了義務老師的制度，歡迎所有有抱負，有崇高理想，能夠遵行六大宗旨的善知識、居士，來到聖城的學校，貢獻他們的所長，教導下一代。上人說：

希望老師們人人以身作則，清廉自許，把所懷的抱負和智慧教給下一代，不爭薪水，不罷工。

這是上人辦教育的一些原則，和我們學校現在大概的情形，希望大家能共同努力，培養出良好的人才，也不負上人的期望。

Girls should not start dating before the age of twenty, and boys should wait until after twenty-five. Young people should concentrate on their studies so that they can become productive citizens in the future. Then there will be some hope for society.

Through interviewing some local American students this past summer, we found out that even in such small towns as Talmage, there are shootings, kidnappings, and drug dealing in the schools--problems that used to be common only in big city schools. Of course, casual dating among students has already become the norm in Western society. Some American parents, dissatisfied with the public school system, hope to give their children a better education by sending them to school at the City of Ten Thousand Buddhas.

The Master said,

Parents bear the greatest responsibility towards their children.

The divorce rate is extremely high today, especially in America. Of the five American children in my Beginning Chinese class, four had divorced parents and the fifth one had parents in their second and third marriages. Children suffer serious psychological stress when their parents are separated. If we, as parents, can fulfill our role, and the schools can do a good job of teaching, I believe we can raise the young generation well.

In order to promote integrity in the teaching profession, several years ago the Master established a volunteer teachers program at the City of Ten Thousand Buddhas, giving aspiring teachers who agree to live by the six guiding principles the opportunity to contribute their skills and teach the next generation. The Master said,

I hope every teacher will be a good model of integrity who does not go on strike for the sake of salary, but will pass his or her aspirations and wisdom on to the next generation.

This has been a summary of the Master's guidelines for education and a brief description of our schools. I hope everyone will work together to bring out the best of the next generation, so that we will not disappoint the Master.

---

能見此世界　其心不搖動　於佛身亦然　當成勝智者
——《大方廣佛華嚴經》〈光明覺品第九〉

*If one can look upon this world*
*With a mind that is unmoving,*
*And see Buddhas and living beings as the same,*
*Then such a one will accomplish supreme wisdom.*

Flower Adornment Sutra, Chapter Nine, Light Enlightenment

# IN GRATITUDE AND REMEMBRANCE
# 感恩與懷念

Guowei Shang
商果維（音譯）

I must admit that my husband and I are most fortunate to be able to encounter the Proper Buddhadharma in this lifetime. We are both most grateful to all the Buddhas, Bodhisattvas, Patriarchs, and Sages in the world systems of the ten directions and the three periods of time. Our gratitude also extends to the Venerable Master Hsuan Hua for his great works and to his disciples for translating the Buddhist Sutras into English for people like us.

We are both Buddhists by birth. However, it was only in 1994 that we read some very interesting books on Dharma talks given by the Venerable Master Hua. Later, we started to investigate Buddhism in depth and to try to get more books from the Sagely City of Ten Thousand Buddhas in the U.S.A. We were greatly shaken and much awakened by the simple messages the Venerable Master gave as he tirelessly spoke the Dharma despite his advanced age and deteriorating health. We began to see and realize that all these years, we had been living our lives in vain and wasting all our valuable days away just like fish in evaporating water... Where is the joy?

We would like to let the whole world know that we are indeed fortunate to be among the rare few who have visited the Sagely City of Ten Thousand Buddhas. We also participated in and completed the Ten Thousand Buddhas Jewelled Repentance from April 17 to May 10, 1995. When we first heard of the repentance ceremony from our Dharma friends, we were very excited but did not know the true significance of the ceremony. Only after the first day of bowing about 400 times to the Buddhas and reciting their names with each bow did we realize how compassionate the Buddhas are in using every means to save sentient beings. By doing this ceremony, we became more mindful of the Buddhas and had the chance to reflect upon ourselves directly.

Always remember: the Buddha shows us the way, but it is we ourselves who need to hurry up to walk the middle path; nobody can do it on our behalf. Do no evil, practice all good deeds, and purify the mind; this is the Teaching of the Buddha. As human beings who have the ability to read and write, we must not casually waste our precious time away and fail to heed the Buddha--the Greatest Teacher on earth. We should give ourselves a chance to increase our knowledge and find out more about his Teachings with an open mind. "One's greatest enemy is oneself." This is absolutely true indeed. We hardly ever find faults with ourselves, but instead we usually criticize others and find a scapegoat whenever problems arise. It is very rare to find someone who is willing to admit his own mistakes readily and

我得承認我及我先生兩人，能在這一生中遇到正法是最幸運的一件事。我們非常感激十方三世一切諸佛、菩薩、祖師、聖人。對於宣化上人座下弟子所做的偉大工作，也同樣地感激；他們為我們這些不懂中文的人，把佛經翻譯成英文。

我們一出生就是佛教徒。但是直到一九九四年，年中的時候，才得以拜讀宣公上人的開示錄。那幾本書真地非常有意義，使我們開始深入探討佛法，也從萬佛聖城請了更多的書。這簡單的法語，是上人不顧自己這麼大把年紀和日漸衰弱的身體，不厭倦地開示。既震撼我們、啟發了我們，令我們瞭解到這幾十年來的生活是不實際、空虛的，亦浪費了不少寶貴的生命。誠如經上說的「如少水魚，斯有何樂？」

我們希望讓全世界的人知道，我們真地是少數能到美國加州萬佛聖城的幸運者。我們也參加一九九五年四月十七到五月十日的萬佛寶懺。當我們從佛友處聽到這萬佛寶懺時，我們非常地興奮，然而當時我們並不完全瞭解這法會的意義。但在第一天禮佛四百拜（每稱一佛號名就禮佛一拜）後，我們才瞭解到，佛是如何地慈悲，用各種方法去救度一切有情眾生。因為參加了此次法會，我們常憶念佛，有機會就反省自己。我們一直牢記，佛指引我們這一條道路，但是要我們自己趕快邁向這中央大道，別人替不了我們。佛教導我們要「諸惡莫作，眾善奉行，自淨其意。」

生為人類，我們有讀跟寫的能力，所以我們不要再在懈怠中浪費我們寶貴的時間，不注意世界上最偉大的導師——佛。也不給我們自己一個機會去增加知識，用開放的心胸去發覺更多佛的訓示及教義。「我們最大的敵人就是自己」，這的確是非常正確。我們從來看不見自己的錯誤，總是批評別人；有問題時，我們就找個代罪羔羊。要找到一個人願意坦白承認自己錯誤，是極不容易的。

openly. Before encountering Buddhism, I was a very hot-tempered and temperamental woman. There was never a peaceful moment in the family. I was always finding faults with everyone except myself. Life was miserable for the whole family, and I was unable to find any peace and happiness.

Finally, my husband realized that he was unable to tame me on his own and decided to turn to Buddhism for help. With the aid of two very valuable Buddhist books--*Herein Lies the Treasure Trove*, Volumes I and II, both my husband and I gained tremendous insight on how to cope with our lives. Very quickly, we realized our mistakes and awakened to the principle of impermanence. We continued to read and investigate, and we ordered more books from the City of Ten Thousand Buddhas. After much reading over a period of about nine months, much to the amazement of my mother, in-laws, relatives, and friends, I totally reformed--I have become a more patient, calm, tolerant, understanding, and cheerful woman.

In my personal experience, reading and right understanding of the true principles of the Buddha's fundamental teachings is very important. Reciting the Great Compassion Mantra in the morning and evening helps a lot, too. Also, mentally reciting Amitabha Buddha's name helps us to be more patient with ourselves and others. By practicing these methods, my husband and I have become more mindful and blissful than ever before. We have discovered that true peace and happiness is priceless, and the wonderful thing is that you do not need any money to experience it. It's free! We are still doing this every day. This is just our little encouragement to readers--we hope everybody will find peace within themselves. Please do not seek outside for comfort, which is not as reliable as the bliss found within oneself. By writing this article, we hope to encourage more people to quickly seek the light of wisdom within themselves, just as we have done, instead of blindly following hearsay and being led astray, sometimes unknowingly, by unethical people or circumstances.

Our only regret is that we did not have enough good blessings to personally meet the Venerable Master Hsuan Hua, but we are most content to be able to learn the true principles of Buddhism through his teachings. Although the Venerable Master has completed the stillness, we feel he is still very patiently looking after us. Therefore we should strive on to find happiness and to end our own sufferings quickly. We are deeply indebted to him, and mere words cannot express our gratitude and admiration for his great works and the example he set in this lifetime to educate the world with selflessness and unsurpassed wisdom. Shifu, being able to address you in this way means so much to me. I vow that in all my lives to come, I shall follow you and your teaching. In life after life I shall adhere to your Six Principles of not fighting, not being greedy, not seeking, not being selfish, not benefitting oneself, and not lying. Only in this way can we repay the Venerable Master's great compassion.

May all living beings resolve themselves on the Bodhi Way and attain rebirth in the Western Pure Land in this life time. Namo Amitabha Buddha!

在遇到佛法以前，我是一個非常暴躁、情緒變化多端的女人。家中沒有一刻安寧，除了自己，每一個人的毛病我都挑。整個家庭的日子，過得很痛苦，我自己也一點都不安寧、不快樂。最後，我先生知道他再怎麼努力也沒法改變我，於是決定轉向佛教求助。看了《人生要義》一、二冊佛書之後，我和我先生兩人，在如何應付我們自己的生活方面，得到非常大的啟蒙。我們很快就認識了自己的錯誤，也覺醒到無常的道理。我們繼續進一步去研討，又從萬佛聖城訂了許多的書。讀了這些書以後，在將近九個月的時間，我完全變了一個人，使我的母親、婆家、親戚及朋友很驚訝，我變得很有耐性，很冷靜，又能包容諒解，而又開朗的一個人。

以我個人的經驗來說，看佛書、瞭解佛陀教導的基本道理是非常重要。另外，早晚誦持大悲咒也有很大的助益。默念阿彌陀佛名號，也可以幫助我們在待人待己時更有耐心。在修習了這些方法後，我和我先生從此精神也比較集中，也比較安樂。我們也發覺這真正的寧靜及快樂是無價的，而且這絕妙的感覺，是不需要花錢就可以得到的，絕對免費！現在我們每天仍然繼續做這些。講這些是我們給讀者一點的激勵，希望每個人都能在自己那兒找到安寧。不要向外找尋安慰，那都不如自己內心的快樂來得可靠。藉著這篇文章，我希望鼓勵更多的人，就像我們一樣，能夠很快地找到自己的光明及智慧，不要盲目聽從，以免不知不覺聽人道聽塗說，或碰上不道德的人和環境而墮落了。我們唯一的遺憾是，我們沒有足夠的福報，能親自見到宣化上人。但是能夠藉著上人的教導，聽到了佛法的真實道理，我們也很滿足了。

雖然上人已經圓寂，但是對我們而言，他還是很有耐性地為我們謀幸福。所以我們應該努力早日離苦得樂。我們欠上人太多了，上人這一生以無我、高超的智慧來教育眾生，我們實在是無法用文字來表達對他的感激，及由衷的敬佩。

師父，我能稱您師父，對我們有很重大的意義，我願生生世世跟隨您及您的教導。我願堅守您的六大宗旨：「不爭、不貪、不求、不自私、不自利、不打妄語。」只有這樣，我們才能報答上人您的大慈悲。

願一切眾生發菩提心，今生即可生到西方極樂淨土中。南無阿彌陀佛！

# 老和尚心血的布施

## THE VENERABLE MASTER'S GIFTS FROM THE HEART

我願意做一條道路，讓一切衆生在我背上

走到無上菩提，走到極樂世界。

**I'm like a road that all living beings can walk on
to reach supreme Bodhi and the Land of Ultimate Bliss.**

釋恆實　Shi Heng Sure

今天各位來參加「宣公上人追思讚頌報恩大典」，大約是老和尚的十八大願吸引來的，就像吸鐵石吸鐵似的。有的人說老和尚是菩薩乘願再來，老和尚否認這種說法，老和尚說：

我像個小螞蟻、小蚊蟲，像一匹馬，我願意做一條道路，讓各位佛教徒和各宗教的信徒，乃至一切衆生，在我背上走到無上菩提，走到極樂世界。

這種話可以表現出來老和尚的精神。各位想想看：如果老和尚是個菩薩，我們怎麼知道呢？

菩薩是修六度萬行的，六度第一個，大家很清楚，就是「布施」。有三種布施：財施、無畏施，最高是法布施。我們研究看看老和尚的行爲，從我本身第一天認識老和尚到他最後離開世間，老和尚一直都是在行布施。他看學生沒有學費，就補他們的學費；看圖書館需要經書，老和尚就送他們經書；學生沒有機會讀書，老和尚建立學校給他們機會讀書，送他們一個教育的機會。這也是布施波羅蜜到彼岸。

其實老和尚是修布施行，他把福田布施給我們每一個弟子，每一個信徒。怎麼說呢？老和尚創立了萬佛聖城、法界佛教大學、國際譯經學院，及二十七座道場，又留給我們佛法的寶藏、救我們法身慧命的清淨戒律，還有各位的大菩提心，完全是老和尚布施給我們的。這也是布施到彼岸。

「擇法眼」能辨別邪正，也是老和尚送給我們的。這個擇法眼能令我們一生都跟著佛的中道了義來走，不會走邪，不會遇著魔障或者業障。出家人從

All of you who have come to attend the Memorial Ceremony in Praise and Recognition of the Venerable Master Hua's Kindness have probably been drawn here by the Master's eighteen great vows, just as iron filings are drawn to a magnet.

Some people say the Master was a Bodhisattva who came to the world on his vows, but the Master firmly denied this. He said,

I'm just like a tiny ant, mosquito, or a horse. I'm like a road that all Buddhists, the followers of all religions, and all living beings can walk on to reach supreme Bodhi and the Land of Ultimate Bliss.

This statement reveals the Master's spirit. Everyone think for a moment: If the Master really is a Bodhisattva, how can we tell?

Bodhisattvas practice the six perfections and the myriad conducts. The first perfection, as you all know, is giving. There are three kinds: the giving of wealth, of fearlessness, and, the highest kind, of Dharma. Let's take a look at the Master's conduct. From the very first day I met him until he finally left the world, the Master gave constantly. He paid tuition for students who couldn't afford it, donated Sutras to libraries lacking them, and started schools for people who had no opportunity to study. He practiced giving to perfection.

He gave blessings to every disciple and every faithful follower. In what way? The Master founded the City of Ten Thousand Buddhas, the International Translation Institute, and twenty-seven branch temples. He gave us the precious storehouse of Buddhadharma, the pure precepts that protect our Dharma body and wisdom life, and our great resolves for Bodhi.

He also gave us Dharma-selecting vision, the ability to distinguish between proper and deviant, so that we would be able to follow the ultimate truth of the Middle Way and not go astray, or encounter demonic or karmic obstacles. The Venerable Master transmitted the path of the ancients, the "ultimate truth of the Middle Way," to us, and yet he never expected anyone to thank him.

上人受到傳統以來古人的道路，所謂中道了義，但是老和尚從來不要人說一句「謝謝」。

我們跟隨老和尚出家，在他法座下修行的弟子，上人把我們的心改成清淨無染污；上人把六大宗旨送給全世界，不爭、不貪、不求、不自私、不自利、不打妄語，這六大宗旨是心地法門，令我們的心又清淨，又有光明。這種布施就是菩薩所行的布施波羅蜜，上人給我們每一個人所願意行的法門，令我們在福田上建功立德，這只看各位是否願意雙手全心接受。

有一次，在一個空檔的時間，我趁機會請老和尚開示一下。老和尚很驚奇說：

你也要來求開示囉？你不要往外求，絲毫也不要向外馳求，你什麼時候能不求，什麼時候得到解脫，到無求處便無憂，夠了！

老和尚是這麼說的。然後上人就微笑，又加一句，今天把最後這句和各位分享。上人說：

我到這個國家來，可以說到這個世界來，
就是等哪一位發大菩提心，我就可以說成功了。

各位哪一天發大菩提心，那就沒有辜負老和尚心血的布施。

\*       \*       \*

# 以德服人　弘法西方

上人比較吸引大家的注意，是老和尚的一些感應，一些可以說是與眾不同的那方面，特別功能這些故事。不過老和尚吩咐過，說：

在西方，不准講神通這一套，為什麼呢？在西方一般的人受過科學教育，你如果講一些眼睛看不到，耳朵聽不到的事情，大家很不相信的。在西方要注重什麼呢？要講德行，要講道德，大家心裡才能感動，然後才能感應道交，才能有相應處。

所以在美國很少很少講到特別功能那方面去。本人有一次體會到這些德行感化眾生的例子，想在今天晚上跟各位分享一下。

For those of us who left the home-life and practiced under his guidance, the Master purified our minds of defilement. The Master gave to the world the six guiding principles--no fighting, no greed, no seeking, no selfishness, no pursuit of personal gain, and no lying. These principles are the Mind Ground Dharma-door; they can make our minds pure and bright. Such is the perfection of giving practiced by Bodhi-sattvas. The Master gave to each of us the Dharma-door we like to practice, enabling us to plant blessings, merit, and virtue. All we have to do is accept this gift with open arms.

Once, taking advantage of a spare moment, I requested instruction from the Master. The Master said in surprise,

You're seeking instruction too? Don't seek outside, not even the slightest bit. When you can finally stop seeking, you'll be liberated. 'When you reach the place of no seeking, there are no worries.' That's enough!

Then he smiled and added,

I have come to this country, or you could say to this world, hoping that someone will bring forth a great Bodhi resolve. When that happens, I will have achieved my aim.

On the day that each of you brings forth a great Bodhi resolve, you will have fulfilled the Master's aim in giving from his heart.

# Using Virtue to Convert People and Propagate the Dharma in the West

Most people are drawn by the stories of the Venerable Master's miraculous responses and extraordinary powers. But the Master told us,

In the West, we should not speak of spiritual powers, because most people are educated in the scientific tradition and if you tell them about things that they cannot see or hear, they won't believe you. What should the emphasis be on? Virtue. We have to teach virtue in the West, and there were be a response in their hearts.

And so in America, the subject of superhuman spiritual powers is seldom discussed. Tonight I'd like to share an experience which shows how virtue can influence people.

I was on the road for nearly three years, making a pilgrimage to the City of Ten Thousand Buddhas. When I reached the City, I continued to hold a vow of silence. Since I did not

有一段時間，本人在朝拜萬佛城的時候，快到三年，是在外邊用功。然後到了萬佛城之後，那個時候還是保持止語的願，就不講話，已經三年。那個期間，跟父母親、親戚就完全斷絕了關係了，因為不講話，也不看信，也不寫信什麼的。所以那個時候，就怕我老母親在家裡，不知道她的兒子是不是被什麼旁門左道給洗腦過的，會不會？或者有的人就傳謠言說，老和尚是給這些美國弟子吃毒藥了，就把他們給偷了，這些個謠言滿天飛的。豈不知這是一個人因為感動了，看見老和尚修行，就願意削髮，向一個方向而努力，所以止語了。母親在家裡也不知道是不是丟了一個兒子了？什麼叫出家了，做了僧寶了，根本不知道，沒看過，沒聽過！

所以就說到了萬佛城之後，母親怎麼樣也一定要來，親自看看她的兒子，到底變成什麼樣的怪物。

記得很清楚，那天晚上老母親也是比較晚到，天已經黑了。那天本人就到辦公室，在北加州萬佛聖城辦公室裡面，有人說：「嘿！你不知道嘛！你母親也在這裡了。」我還不可以講話，所以到裡面去看看。一進去就看到老和尚，師父上人就在那邊，我母親就在旁邊。可以看得出母親流過眼淚，淚痕還在她的臉上，不過老和尚在和她講話，也是握著她的手，藉著她的手安慰安慰她，叫她不要哭了，「don't cry!」師父用英文跟她講，不會講英文的一個老師父，也是用英文來跟她講話，也不用任何人來翻譯。老和尚看我進來，他說：「不用你在這兒，我會處理這個事情，回去了！」奇怪了，看見母親的表情上雖然有一點好像害怕，不過眼睛裡面另外有一種表情，是什麼？好像有一種恭敬的心態在裡面。好了，我就走了。過幾天有法會什麼的，就不見母親，她回去了。

再過一、二年，止語期滿了，我就開始講話。那個時候母親怎麼樣呢？老和尚請我母親到萬佛城來過她五十歲生日，他說第一次在美國有一個比丘的母親到廟上來過生日。很奇怪，就這樣歡迎母親來過五十歲生日，老和尚叫所有育良小學的女生，給我母親做一個觀音菩薩聖誕節的生日卡，每個小孩都要畫觀音菩薩像。她那天收了三十多張生日卡，都是有關觀音菩薩的對子或者小詩，或者慶祝的話，當然母親非常感動，說到底觀世音菩薩我也認識了，然後老和尚請她跟大家講話，母親上來說：「你們這裡的出家人要注意了，你們的老師父是很有智慧的一個人，他給我這串念珠了，然後他拿出來念珠，教我念『南無觀世音

speak, or read or write letters, I completely cut off all contact with my parents and relatives. I feared that my mother was at home worrying that her son had been brainwashed by some cult, for there were rumors going around that the Master had kidnapped his American disciples and was giving them drugs. Little did she know that I had shaved my head and stopped speaking because I had been touched by the Venerable Master's cultivation and wanted to diligently work on my practice. My mother probably thought she'd lost her son; she had no idea of what leaving the home-life to join the Sangha was all about.

So, when I reached the City of Ten Thousand Buddhas, my mother was determined to visit me and see what kind of freak her son had become.

I remember very clearly that my mother came quite late in the evening, when it was already dark. When I went to the office (of the City of Ten Thousand Buddhas), someone said, "Hey, guess what? Your mother's here!" Still holding a vow of silence, I went in to take a look. My mother had been crying, judging from her tear-streaked face. The Master was speaking to her and holding her hand, consoling her and telling her in English, "Don't cry." Although he didn't know English, he was speaking to her in English, without relying on a translator. When he saw me, he said, "There's no need for you to be here. I can take care of this." Strange! Although my mother looked slightly scared, there was something else on her face--an expression of reverence. I left the office. Since I was involved in a Dharma session a few days later, I didn't get to see my mother again, and she went home.

After a couple of years, when my vow of silence was over, I began to speak again. At that time, the Master invited my mother to come celebrate her fiftieth birthday at the City of Ten Thousand Buddhas. He said it was the first time a Bhikshu's mother had been invited to celebrate her birthday in a monastery. The Master asked all the girls in Instilling Goodness Elementary School to make cards for Guanyin Bodhisattva's Birthday for my mother. That day, my mother received over thirty birthday cards with pictures, couplets, and short verses of Guanyin Bodhisattva drawn and written by the little girls. She was very touched and said, "Why, I know who Guanyin Bodhisattva is!" When the Master invited her to speak to the assembly, she said, "All of you monks and nuns should know that your elderly Master is a very wise person. He gave me a string of recitation beads and told me to recite, 'Namo Guanshiyin Bodhisattva,' and that's what I've done."

Afterwards, my mother related what had happened the first day. "You know, I was very scared the first time I came to the City. I thought they might have drugged my tea, and that if I drank it I might also become bald like you. When I got here, I just started crying. Then your Master came out and shook hands with me. Although I was very nervous, deep down in my heart I seemed to understand what the Master was saying to me. Then the Master invited me to sit in his golfcart (which

雖然母親還是一個信耶穌的基督教徒，
可是那天她的腳步，已經走到佛教的道路上了。

My mother, a Christian, had already stepped
onto the Buddha path that day.

菩薩』，我也會念……。」過後，母親跟我講當
天的事情，她說：「你知道嗎？第一天我到了萬
佛聖城，我非常的害怕！我都不知道我喝一杯茶
，會不會給放毒了，我喝了以後是不是也會像你
這樣也沒頭髮了。我雖然怕，但是我一到了，我
什麼都說不出來，我就哭了，哭了一大場。你的
師父也出來了，他就跟我握握手。雖然我心非常
著急，他說的話好像我心裡也懂了，我就好像在
心深深的地方，老和尚的意思，我會覺察到了……。
」她說奇怪了，「然後老和尚叫我上他那個小高爾夫
球車……」，你們大家知道萬佛城地方大，老和尚是
開那個小噗噗車，那個高爾夫球車，是開來開去，老
和尚請她坐那個高爾夫球車。在那個晚上，他是正眼
看著我說：

You should be happy you have a Bhikshu for a son. Your
son has followed me for life after life. You haven't lost a
son; you've gained a monk. You should be grateful. Your son
will have many things to do. （妳應該生歡喜心，妳的
兒子是一個比丘，妳的兒子是生生世世跟隨著我
。妳沒有少一個兒子，妳是多了一個比丘，妳應
該感激，妳的兒子有很多事情要做。）

她說老和尚是這麼跟我說的，她說：「你到底覺得他
是什麼意思？」

老母親問我，我也不懂。不過可以看得出那天晚上
，老和尚若不是用德行感化一個弟子的母親，那是用
的什麼呢？並不是神通，並不是什麼特別功能，用一
顆真誠的心腸，雖然母親還是一個信耶穌的基督教徒
，可是那天她的腳步，已經走到佛教的道路上了，也
會念「南無觀世音菩薩」，還是帶著念珠念。

所以，老和尚有個對聯，是說這種精神，說老和尚
怎麼樣在香港、在臺灣、在美國弘法利生：

上聯是「慈悲普度信者得救成正覺」
下聯是「過化存神禮之獲福悟無生」

he drove around the City of Ten Thousand Buddhas because
the place was so big). That evening, he looked straight at me
and said,

You should be happy you have a Bhikshu for a son.
Your son has followed me for life after life. You haven't
lost a son; you've gained a monk. You should be grateful.
Your son will have many things to do.

What do you think he meant by this?"

I didn't understand either. But if the Master wasn't using
virtue to influence my mother, then what was he using? Not
spiritual powers, that's for sure. He was using plain sincerity.
My mother, a Christian, had already stepped onto the Buddha
path that day. She even recited "Namo Guanshiyin Bodhisattva" and had recitation beads.

There's a couplet about the Venerable Master which describes his spirit in propagating the Dharma to benefit living
beings, be it in Hong Kong, Taiwan, or America. It goes:

*His kindness and compassion cross over all;*
*Believers are liberated and perfect*
  *the Right Enlightenment.*
*Transforming beings wherever he goes,*
  *his spirit remains intact;*
*Those who venerate him obtain blessings and awaken*
  *to the Unproduced.*

# 歷久彌新的教誨
## TIMELESS TEACHINGS

他老人家身教、言教，點點滴滴的教誨，
猶如海浪般一波一波地襲擊腦海。

**His teachings, by personal example and by words,
reverberated through my mind.**

柯果誠　Gwo-Cherng Ko

六月七日傍晚，接到一位佛友來電，告知師父圓寂了。我第一個反應是「怎麼會呢？」頓時，思緒一片混亂。當晚十一點，與幾位佛友趕到殯儀館，瞻仰遺容。在繞佛、念佛之際，回想自一九八九年皈依上人之後，受到他老人家身教、言教的點點滴滴教誨，猶如海浪般一波一波地襲擊腦海，不由淚下沾襟。

每一位接觸過師父上人的人，都對上人肅然起敬，即使不是佛教徒也都可感受到他的威儀及德行。我常想師父的威儀不是造作出來的，而是，由於持戒精嚴，自然流露出來的一位修行人的本色。

上人最令人敬佩之處在於他的身教——「以身作則」，如日中一食，衣不離體及夜不倒單等修行方式，都讓四眾弟子奉為圭臬。上人以他的智慧，將佛制五戒詮釋為六大宗旨，深得戒律的精髓，令現代人易懂易接受。六大宗旨為「不爭、不貪、不求、不自私、不自利、不打妄語」，痛指時病。如今世界戰亂不休、生靈塗炭，都是因為主政者的貪瞋癡所致。如果主政者能聽聞上人的法語，或許能免除一場浩劫。

上人每次的演講或開示，都有如春風化雨。個人有幸幫忙打字謄稿，看到上人的答覆，字字珠璣，令人欽佩。有時候上人的對答，又如禪門公案，讓人深思。

有一次，外子學業不順利，我請示上人，他老人家的一句話令我畢生難忘，他說：

因為你脾氣太大所造成的。

On June 7, at dusk, I got a call from a Buddhist friend informing me of the Master's completion of stillness. My first reaction was, "How could it be possible?" Suddenly, my mind was thrown into confusion. That night, several Buddhist friends and I rushed to the mortuary to pay our last respects to the Master. While walking and reciting Amitabha Buddha's name, I recollected bits and pieces of what I had learned from the Master since I took refuge with him in 1989. His teachings, by personal example and by words, reverberated through my mind. I could not stop my tears.

Anyone who encountered the Master had a great deal of respect for him. Even non-Buddhists could feel the Master's awesome deportment and virtuous conduct. The Master's dignity was not pretentious. Rather, it came naturally as a result of his strict observance of precepts. The most admirable thing about the Master was that he always taught by example. He set an example with his own actions, such as eating one meal a day, always wearing the precept sash, and not lying down to sleep. All his disciples look upon him as their model. Through his infinite wisdom, he reconstituted the five precepts into the Six Guiding Principles, thus capturing the essence of the precepts and making them easier to understand and accept in this modern age. The Six Guiding Principles (no fighting, no greed, no seeking, no selfishness, no pursuit of personal advantages, and no lying) point directly to the maladies of the current time. The endless wars in eastern Europe and the sufferings of extreme deprivation are due to the greed, anger, and stupidity of key political leaders. If they could have heard the Master's teachings, such catastrophes might have been avoided.

The Master's every speech and lecture could be likened to the spring breeze and the nourishing drizzle. I have had the good fortune of helping with the typing and editing of the Gold Wheel Monastery Newsletter. Each word of the Master's replies to questions was awesome and admirable. Sometimes, his dialogues resembled the Chan stories of old, leaving people to ponder deeply.

Once, when my husband was doing poorly in his studies, I went to ask the Master for advice. I will never forget his reply. He said,

It's because of your big temper.

我當時不能接受他的教誨，我執很重的我，認爲個人的脾氣大，對家人又有何影響呢？殊不知，家和萬事興，天天發脾氣，家裡怎麼會順利、平安呢？這是很普通的道理，卻讓我參了好久，幾年後才悟出其中的道理。我所欠缺的就是迴光返照、反求諸己的功夫。

上人一生不攀緣、不化緣、不求緣，他唯一「化緣」的是弟子們的壞脾氣與壞習性。他要我們將壞的習氣毛病都布施給他，目的要我們早成佛道，這是何等地慈悲啊！然而沉迷執著的我們，還是硬抱著自己的習氣毛病不放，枉費上人的一番苦心。上人常警惕弟子們：

一把無明火，燒盡功德林。

就是要我們忍讓，與世無爭，如此在修行上才有進步。

雖然上人圓寂了，但他留下了豐富的智慧寶藏，令吾等生生世世受益不盡。在緬懷感恩之際，吾等應該發大菩提心，效法上人的十八大願，爲弘法利生盡一份心力，願以與眾生共成佛道自勉。

At the time, I wasn't ready to accept his admonition. Being very egoistic, I questioned how a person's temper could affect other family members. Many people overlook the fact that goodnaturedness leads to prosperity. How could things go smoothly at home if we lose our temper every day? This is common sense, yet it took me several years to realize it. What I lacked were the skills of inner reflection and self-examination.

Throughout his life, the Master never exploited conditions, solicited alms, or asked for anything. The only alms he solicited were his disciples' bad tempers and habits. He wanted us to give them up so that we could attain Buddhahood earlier. Yet, despite his vast compassion, we deludedly held fast to our habits and shortcomings, and the Master's strenuous efforts to help us might have seemed in vain. The Master often admonished us,

*The fire of ignorance easily burns down*
*An entire forest of merit and virtue.*

He wanted us to be patient and yielding, to be in harmony with the rest of the world, for only then can we make progress in our cultivation.

Though the Master has completed the stillness, he has left us an abundant treasury of wisdom, which will benefit us endlessly in life after life. In grateful remembrance of the Master, we should bring forth the Bodhi mind. Taking his eighteen great vows as our model, we should work to propagate the Dharma for the benefit of all beings, and urge each other on so that we can all realize Buddhahood together.

---

宣華嚴境界　啓楞嚴壇場　守戒律傳後學
千載宗風從此續　素衣緇子萬佛堂上莊嚴萬佛

化智度精神　敷濟度法會　興叢林結眾緣
一生辛苦有誰知　碩德豐功十方界中普度十方

*Proclaiming the Avatamsaka state, opening the Shurangama Platform,*
*and upholding the precepts, he transmitted them to students of the future.*

*The thousand-year tradition is thus perpetuated; the Sangha and the laity adorn*
*the ten thousand Buddhas in the Hall of Ten Thousand Buddhas.*

*Transforming in the spirit of wisdom, hosting assemblies of salvation,*
*and establishing Bodhimandas, he created affinities with the multitudes.*

*Who can know the hardships that he underwent? His merit and virtue are monumental;*
*he rescued beings throughout the worlds of the ten directions.*

乙亥閏八月杪不肖弟子孫果秀追懷於萬佛聖城麒麟精舍
By unworthy disciple Sun Guoxiu in the Unicorn House at the City of Ten Thousand Buddhas,
on the last day of the eighth intercalary lunar month, 1995

# 普應群心解眾難

## RESPONDING TO AND SAVING BEINGS EVERYWHERE

**只要你眞地很誠心，師父上人是有求必應的。**

**If you are truly sincere, the Master will not fail to respond.**

釋恆茂　Shi Heng Mao

一九八九年，臺灣社會投機風氣瀰漫，很多人都在玩股票，玩大家樂。師父上人應邀回國主持「護國息災大悲觀音法會」，當他一下飛機時，就表示：

我準備餓死在臺灣，我願將我所有的福報，悉皆迴向給臺灣眾生；願將臺灣眾生所有的苦難，由我一人代受。

師父他老人家是說得到就做得到的。

當時我有幸在服務台擔任義工，整個法會期間所見所聞都令我終生難忘。那時有弟子就說：「爲什麼我們自己所造的業，要讓師父一人代受，我們自己也應該要盡上一份責任。」於是就有很多人紛紛發心，一天、三天、五天、七天，也不願吃飯，大家同心協力想要挽救臺灣的情勢。原本我只持六齋日，當時我想爲什麼我就做不到，所以我也就改成只吃早餐、午餐，整個法會結束以後，我已經學會了日中一食。

師父上人的願力說：

只要我在舊金山一天，我就不准舊金山大地震。

可是就在當時舊金山大地震了，美國的信眾非常地緊張，紛紛打電報回來，請求師父上人慈悲。於是上人悲心切切，不辭勞苦，馬上搭機飛回美西息災。這樣一來，臺灣信眾就非常惶恐，因爲有一個大颱風來了，所以他們又請求上人趕快回來，因此第二天、第三天，上人又馬上搭飛機回來，繼續主持法會直到結束。在臺灣一個月的期間，上人眞地是一粒米飯都沒進，只喝白開水。這種不爲自己求安樂，但願眾生得離苦，大慈悲普度，流血汗、不休息的精神，令我感動得五體投地。這個就是我要找的善知識，就是我要深深依止的善知識。

法會期間，有一天晚上師父上人說：「有誰想要出家，就趕快上台來。」我的同伴推著我說：「你不是

In 1989, many people in Taiwan were speculating in the stock market and playing the lottery. When the Venerable Master stepped off the plane after arriving in Taiwan to hold a Great Compassion Guanyin Dharma Session for Protecting the Nation and Quelling Disasters, he said,

I'm prepared to starve to death in Taiwan. I wish to dedicate all my blessings to the people of Taiwan, and to take all their sufferings upon myself.

The Master never spoke in vain.

I will never forget what I saw and heard as a volunteer at the front desk during the Dharma Session. Some of the Master's disciples said, "Why should we let the Master suffer alone for the karma we have created? We should do our part, too." Many people fasted for one, three, five, or seven days, hoping to rescue Taiwan from its critical situation. I had been observing six days of vegetarian fasting a month, but during the session I began skipping dinner; and by the end of the session I was eating only one meal a day.

The Master had vowed,

As long as I am in San Francisco, I will not allow San Francisco to have an earthquake.

When the great earthquake occurred in San Francisco (while he was in Taiwan), many worried American disciples sent telegrams asking the Master for help. The Master immediately flew back to the United States. But then a great typhoon hit Taiwan, and the disciples in Taiwan beseeched the Master to quickly return. Only two or three days later, the Master flew back to Taiwan to continue hosting the Dharma session to its end. During that month in Taiwan, the Master only drank water and didn't ingest so much as a single grain of rice. I feel the deepest respect and admiration for the Master's spirit of forgetting himself to deliver beings from suffering, of "saving all with great compassion, sparing neither blood nor sweat, and never pausing to rest." He is the Good and Wise Advisor I have sought and hope to rely upon in life after life.

One evening in the Dharma session, the Master said, "If

想要出家嗎？這個大好機會，你趕快上台，去表明心聲。」我鼓起勇氣上台去，師父上人看了我一眼說：「你想出家呀！」「是的！我想出家。」「好吧！那你就來講一講話。」我帶著顫抖的聲音，鼓起勇氣把話講完了。師父上人說：「不容易呀！」「是的！弟子知道不容易，業障深重，習氣毛病那麼多。」我下台以後，就一直不斷地跟師父上人叩頭頂禮，請求師父上人幫助我，今生我如果沒辦法出家，我希望來生也能夠出家。

只要你真地很誠心，師父上人是有求必應的。上人給我的力量，使我在整個法會結束之後，當我再度回到工作崗位時，整個人就一百八十度的轉變，不但日中一食，而且也學做早、晚課，晚上又加一部《地藏經》，也把我的習氣毛病一點一點地改了。二個多月以後，當我準備到美國在台協會辦簽證的前一、二個晚上，我就夢見自己已經來到萬佛聖城，上人在大殿坐著，等著我，笑著對我說話；整個夢境顯示上人要我多加忍耐。到了萬佛聖城，不到十天左右，我就出家了。

一九九三年，就是師父上人最後一次回臺灣時，在法界佛教印經會，上人對大眾開示說：

我這一生凍死不攀緣，餓死不化緣，窮死不求緣，但是今天我要向在座各位化一個大緣，就是把你們的無明煩惱、脾氣，一切一切都布施給我，不能捨也要能捨。

大家想一想，煩惱、脾氣，誰都不要，就是師父上人敢要！雖然師父上人現在色身已經不在了，可是他留給我們的法寶是無窮無盡的，只要我們跟著師父上人去修行，一句話都受用無窮的。上人圓寂以後，很多信眾都紛紛問我們說；「誰是師父上人的傳法人？」那就是真正在日常生活中身體力行萬佛聖城的六大宗旨：不爭、不貪、不求、不自私、不自利、不打妄語，那就是師父上人的傳法人。

you want to leave home, come up to the stage right now." My friend gave me a push and said, "Don't you want to leave home? This is your big chance! Quickly go and tell the Master." I bravely went forward, and the Master said, "So you want to leave home?"

"Yes!"

"Okay, why don't you say a few words to everyone?"

After I spoke in a quavering voice, the Master said, "It's not easy!"

"Yes, I know I have such heavy karmic obstacles and so many bad habits."

After walking off the stage, I bowed many times to the Master and prayed that he would help me leave home, if not in this life, then hopefully in the next life.

If you are truly sincere, the Master will not fail to respond. The strength I received from the Master enabled me to turn my life around. I began eating only one meal a day, learned to chant the morning and evening recitations and the *Earth Store Sutra*, and gradually changed my bad habits and faults. Two months later, one or two nights before I was to go to AIT to apply for a visa, I dreamed that I was already in the City of Ten Thousand Buddhas. In my dream, the Master was seated in the Buddha hall waiting for me, and he smiled and spoke to me. I interpreted the dream as a message that the Master wanted me to be patient. I left the home-life less than ten days after arriving at the City.

When the Master returned to Taiwan for the last time in 1993, he said to everyone at the Dharma Realm Buddhist Books Distribution Society,

All my life, my credo has been: 'Freezing, I will not scheme. Starving, I will not beg. Dying of poverty, I will ask for nothing.' However, today I want to ask for a great donation from all of you. Please give me all your ignorance, afflictions, and tempers, no matter how dearly you cherish them!

No one wants ignorance, afflictions, or a temper, but the Master dared to ask for them.

Although the Master is no longer physically with us, he has given us an inexhaustible treasury of Dharma. Each sentence of the Master's teaching, if truly practiced, yields infinite benefits. Many people have asked, "Who received the Master's Dharma transmission?" Whoever truly practices the Six Guiding Principles of the City of Ten Thousand Buddhas (no fighting, no greed, no seeking, no selfishness, no self-benefit, and no lying) has received the Master's Dharma transmission.

---

色受無有數　想行識亦然　若能如是知　當作大牟尼
——《大方廣佛華嚴經》〈光明覺品第九〉

*Forms and feelings are without number;*
*Thinking, process and consciousness are also like this.*
*If one is able to know this*
*Then one can become a great Muni.*

Flower Adornment Sutra, Chapter Nine, Light Enlightenment

---

# In Memory of the Venerable Master Hsuan Hua

# 緬懷宣公上人

## The beneficial shade from his tree of teaching extended thousands of miles and comforted my restlessness and uncertainty.

## 上人的教化，猶如大樹，福蔭廣延數千里之遠，安撫了我的焦慮與不安。

Gary McMillen　佳瑞

*Deep roots make a tall and sturdy tree.*
*The cool shade is all-encompassing.*

It was my good fortune to receive the guidance and protection of Master Hua even though I never met him personally. The beneficial shade from his tree of teaching extended thousands of miles and comforted my restlessness and uncertainty.

My story is small and insignificant. I am an American layperson who is at the Beginner-Kindergarten level of Buddhism. Living in New Orleans, Louisiana, I attend services in a Chinese home-temple. The Sangha is very friendly, patient, and helpful to me. It was through this spirit of giving in the association that I began to receive newsletters, magazines, and tapes from the Dharma Realm Buddhist Association in the City of Ten Thousand Buddhas.

I was touched immediately by the clarity and directness of Master Hua. Even though he could not see me, I felt he was able to see through me. Constant and perpetual--Master Hua's wisdom-message caught my attention and kept knocking on the door of my muddled and unsettled mind. Even in death he does not go away.

The monk who cultivated by his mother's grave taught me three universal lessons:

1. There is no more time to waste. To delay one day is to delay one year. Keep death on both eyebrows, and my life will not be wasted.

2. Leave the academic and intellectual discussion of Buddhism to others who are better suited or more inclined. What counts is action. Bodhi resolve and lofty aspirations are good-sounding terms but somebody better be cooking the rice and sweeping the floor. A cultivator's practice is not some

根深樹大　涼蔭遍覆

雖然我未曾見過上人，但是我很幸運的能得到上人的教導及保護。上人的教化，猶如大樹，福蔭廣延數千里，安撫了我的焦慮與不安。

我的故事是微不足道的。我是一個美國在家人，在佛教裡，是屬於幼稚園程度的初學者，我住在路易斯安那州的紐奧良市，平時去一個家庭式的中國寺廟參加法事，那裡的出家人很友善，很有耐心，而且很照顧我。在他們這種布施的精神裡，我開始收到萬佛聖城法界佛教總會的活動通訊雜誌、及錄音帶等。

宣公上人明確而直接的話語，立即感動了我，雖然他沒見到我，可是我覺得他看透了我。宣公的智慧之語，恆長而永久地吸引了我的注意，而且不停的扣著我顛倒而不安的心門。即使上人圓寂之後，也沒有離開過。

在母親之墓旁結廬修行的這位和尚，教了我三件大事：

（一）無時間可浪費，一天的拖延，等於一年的拖延。要將死字掛在眉梢上，才不至於浪費我的一生。

（二）讓那些比較合適亦歡喜做佛學學術討論的人去討論。實際行動才是眞的。菩提心及崇高的抱負，是很好聽的名辭，可是還要有人來煮飯掃地才行。修行是不帶有什麼神秘的色彩。修行是平常的，例行的、

mysterious quality. Practice is normal, routine, direct, pragmatic, and uncomplicated. Good practice means that your knees hurt. Master Hua opened my understanding to the importance of staying grounded on Earth and not flying, unnecessarily, off to Heaven.

3. The contemporary world today is upside-down and totally unbalanced. The only way we can remain undistracted and stay on the path is to have rules that we believe will work for us. There are ancient solutions to modern problems. The way to see our way through this "new age" modern mess is to respect, preserve, and honor the ancient and traditional teachings. Master Hua clearly gave us those rules to live by. That was his effort. Our job is to follow and obey the rules.

The Master's death should not alarming. Actually you could say that he died many times for us during the course of his lifetime. Each time he let go of some attachment, or seeking, or some piece of selfishness, he died a little. Think of how many small deaths he incurred that brought him closer, each time, to the root of his tranquility. From this deep, natural peacefulness the seeds of his teaching could sprout, flourish, and propagate. Everything arises, returns, and is returned.

直接的、實際的,而且是不複雜的。修行好就是膝蓋疼痛。上人讓我們了解腳踏實地,不好高騖遠的重要性。

(三)現代這個世界是顛倒的,完全不平衡的。真正能讓我們繼續行在正道上,而不走上旁門左道的唯一的方法,就是守有用的規矩。

古老的辦法可以解決現代的問題。要想看透這個新時代的摩登混亂,就要尊敬並保存那些古老傳統的教導。上人很明確地給了我們這些規矩,那正是他的教化。我們的職責只是去遵守這些規矩。我們毋須爲上人的圓寂而驚惶。其實你可以說,在這一生他已爲我們死過很多次了。每次上人放下一些執著、欲求,或一些些自我,他就死了一點。想想看:多少這種小小的死,把上人一點一點地帶近終點,直至最後的圓寂。上人教導之種子,就在這甚深而自然的寧靜中發芽、茁壯、成長。所有的事物皆昇起又回復,而至於回歸。

# 宣化老和尚　慈悲度有情

## THE ELDER MONK HSUAN HUA,
## WITH GREAT KINDNESS AND COMPASSION RESCUES SENTIENT BEINGS

宣法大道眾所歸　　　*Proclaiming the Dharma of the Great Way which the multitudes return to,*
化緣無數法無邊　　　*Transforming countless ones with affinities, with boundless Dharma,*
老師佛法無生滅　　　*Teaching the Buddha Dharma of non-production and extinction,*
和順一切同道化　　　*Harmoniously complying with all and assimilating into the same path.*
尚心本妙應即至　　　*The original wonderful mind of the Monk immediately responds to calls.*
慈光普照遍法界　　　*The light of compassion universally illumines throughout the Dharma Realm.*
悲智雙運常光明　　　*Exercising his kindness and wisdom which are constantly bright,*
度化三界同大道　　　*Crossing and transforming the three realms into the same Great Way,*
有道理覺歸正法　　　*Abiding in the Way, the enlightened substance returns to the Proper Dharma.*
情了佛種因地生　　　*Sentient beings with Buddha's seeds sprout in the causal ground.*

方廣普供合十
美國達拉斯　甲戌年六月廿九日/一九九四年八月六日
Means Expansive universally offers with joined palms
August 6, 1994  Dallas, USA

# 緬懷師父上人
# LINGERING MEMORIES OF THE VENERABLE MASTER

## 痛失良師，正如痛失慈父
## With the Venerable Master's completion of stillness, I am as pained as if I had lost a compassionate father.

朱果霞　Gwo-shia Chu

由於自己緣慳福薄，認識師父上人只有短短五年的時間，一九六三年自港移民來美，一連搬了數次家，直到一九八九年搬到金輪聖寺附近，才安定了下來。那時因洛市之中文電視台每天中午播五分鐘的佛法講座，由金輪聖寺的法師們主講，所以才知道有個金輪聖寺。

因自己業障深重，從一九八五年開始，每天念誦《地藏經》一遍，誦了三年，而師父上人曾說過，金輪聖寺是地藏王菩薩的道場，所以我相信，由於誦念《地藏經》而得逢善知識及正法道場。並且在九一年，我七十歲的時候，有幸於萬佛聖城皈依上人。

雖然親聆上人教誨次數不多，但是，從上人精湛幽默且詳盡開示的書籍和錄音帶中，增加不少智慧，令我這愚癡無智者茅塞頓開。同時個性也變得比以前開朗，忍耐力更增強，所以脾氣也不斷地有所改善，然每思及上人所發的十八大願，時刻為利益眾生著想，以抱病之軀，流血流汗不休息，如此無人無我的行菩薩道，總令我感動淚下，慶幸得遇明師，得聞正法，如此偉大的修行者，當今世上能有幾人。

我嬰兒時期染患小兒痲痺，遍訪名醫無效，到四、五歲仍無法站立，後幸<sup>上</sup>虛<sup>下</sup>雲老和尚慈悲加持，癒我右腿，而能站立，然因自己業障深重，半途而廢，故左腿仍無力。直到九二年在萬佛聖城，眾人於祖師殿頂禮師父上人，我對上人說：「師父，請您原諒弟子，因為我的左腿有小兒痲痺症，跪下去就站不起來，所以無法向您叩頭頂禮。」上人一聽，便拿起他的杖在我腿上打了三下，從此以後，我走路走得比以前好，也比以前快，不像以前總是一拐一拐地走路，感覺到左

Owing to my lack of blessings, I knew the Master for only five short years. After immigrating from Hong Kong in 1963, I moved several times until I finally settled near Gold Wheel Monastery in 1989. At that time, there was a five-minute Buddhist lecture program hosted by Dharma Masters from Gold Wheel Monastery shown on the Chinese T.V. channel in L.A. at noon every day. That was how I learned about the monastery. Because of my heavy karma, I had been reciting the *Earth Store Sutra* daily for three years, starting in 1985. After hearing the Master say that Gold Wheel Monastery is a Way-place of Earth Store Bodhisattva, I was convinced that my recitation had led me to encounter wise teachers and a Way-place of the Proper Dharma.

In 1991, at the age of seventy, I was fortunate enough to take refuge with the Venerable Master in the City of Ten Thousand Buddhas. Although I received personal teachings from the Master only a few times, I learned a lot by reading and listening to the Master's lectures in books and on tape. I was like an ignorant fool waking up. I became more open-minded and patient, and my temperament improved. Whenever I recall the Master's eighteen great vows, his constant concern for the welfare of living beings, his incessant work in spite of physical sickness--sparing no blood or sweat and never pausing to rest, and his utterly selfless Bodhisattva conduct, I am moved to tears. How fortunate I am to encounter such a wise teacher and to listen to the Proper Dharma! How many great cultivators like him are left in the world?

I contracted an incurable case of polio in early childhood, and I still could not stand up by the time I was four or five. Later, through the compassionate aid of the Noble Hsu Venerable Yun, my right leg was healed and I could stand. However, due to my heavy karma, I was unable to continue the healing and my left leg was still debilitated. Then, in 1992, when everyone was bowing to the Venerable Master Hua in the Patriarchs' Hall at the City of Ten Thousand Buddhas, I said, "Master, please forgive this disciple of yours, who is unable to bow to you. My left leg has polio and I cannot get up after kneeling down." The moment the Master heard my words, he took his cane and struck my leg three times. From then on, I could walk faster and better than before, without limping. My left leg became stronger, and I was able to get up on my own after kneeling and bowing to the Buddhas, something I

宣化老和尚追思紀念專集

腿比以前更有力了些，而且禮佛跪拜之後，也能自己從地上站起來，這是過去七十多年來一直都不能做到的事情。同時，人老體衰乃自然定律，而我現在卻老當益壯，病痛減少，視力較以前更好，也不像以前常摔跤，這種種不可思議的改變，皆因師父上人慈悲加持所賜，令我能在這風燭殘年，隨心所願，學佛修行。

而今上人圓寂，弟子痛失良師，正如痛失慈父，蒙師賜我法身慧命，由腿宿疾，因禍得福，種下善根因緣，大恩大德，難報萬一，唯有依教奉行，並願往後生生世世常隨師父上人修行，於菩提道上永不退轉。

had not been able to do for the past seventy years. Although the laws of nature dictate that our body will weaken as we grow older, I feel more energetic now and have less sickness and pain. My eyesight has improved, and I don't stumble as often. These inconceivable changes are due to the Master's compassionate aid; he has fulfilled my wish and enabled me to cultivate at my advanced age.

With the Venerable Master's completion of stillness, I am as pained as if I had lost a compassionate father. The Master gave me my Dharma body and wisdom life. Through the conditions of my crippled leg, I gained blessings and planted good roots. Such great benevolence is infinitely difficult to repay. The only thing I can do is to conduct myself in accord with his teachings, and resolve to follow him in cultivation in life after life, never retreating from the Bodhi path.

# 懷念師恩
## REMEMBERING THE MASTER'S KINDNESS

釋果誠 十二歲
Shramanera Gwo Cheng, age 11

我對師父的教誨永遠難忘。記得在我剃度當天，師父曾對我們說：

師父引進門，修行在個人。
你們今天出家發菩提心，是為了要修菩薩道，利益眾生，
你們不要把光陰空過了。

這幾句話一直牢記在心中，尤其令我感動的是，
當時上人病得很重，還特地來為我們主持剃度大典，甚至抱病還到各地方去說法。

師父他老人家教化眾生卻無休無息，令很多人發菩提心，師父在我的心目中是一位大菩薩。

The Venerable Master's teachings are very hard for me to forget. On the day I left home, the Venerable Master said to us:

The Master can lead you to the door, but you cultivate on your own.
Today you left home, and you have brought forth the Bodhi-mind to cultivate the Bodhisattva Way
and benefit all living beings. Don't waste time.

These few words have stayed in my mind. I was very moved by the fact that, although the Master was very sick, he still shaved our heads. Even though he was very sick, he went to many places to speak Dharma.

He taught living beings without weariness and made a lot of people bring forth the Bodhi Mind. In my mind he is a great Bodhisattva.

# 上人是不休息的

# THE VENERABLE MASTER NEVER PAUSES TO REST

黃文彥
Wenyan Huang

師父入涅槃的時候，我一直在師父的旁邊。師父這一生，從一九九〇年開始示現病相；但是他示現病相以後，一直不為自己的病去療養或是做什麼，他還是照樣地度化眾生。也到美國各大學，及各分支道場演講，一九九三年又再度回到臺灣。只要他能站起來，他就出來演講，除非那天他真正不能起來了，他才沒有上來；不然的話，他在萬佛聖城，或是國際譯經學院、洛杉磯，或是各大學演講都是一樣。他是以大菩薩那種大慈悲心來度化眾生，也就是上人作的〈宇宙白〉所說的：「流血汗，不休息。」他是以這樣的精神來度化眾生。尤其上人在他的十八大願裏說，如有一眾生未成佛的話，他也誓不成佛。

師父曾經講過，在佛教裏辦教育，所以現在教育方面，在美國洛杉磯、舊金山、萬佛城，或是柏克萊的道場都有成就了。譯經方面，三藏十二部經現在也正進行翻譯成英文、越南文、西班牙文、法文和日文。而且上人在病中也一直都在關心這些事。

以前師父在的時候，師父像大傘蓋一樣，蓋著我們，我們不用去煩惱很多事情。現在師父走了，我們怎樣來完成師父所留下來的很多很多事情，需要我們大家去共同完成，所以大家要發菩提心，來護持正法，護持萬佛聖城。

I was with the Master right up to the time when he entered Nirvana. Although the Master began manifesting illness as early as 1990, he didn't seek any kind of treatment but continued to teach and save living beings, giving lectures at various American universities and at temples, and even coming to Taiwan in 1993. He would never fail to show up for a lecture unless he was so sick that he could not even stand up. If he had the strength to stand up, he would lecture as usual, whether it was at the City of Ten Thousand Buddhas, the International Translation Institute, other branch temples, or various universities. He rescued and taught people with the great compassionate heart of a great Bodhisattva, "not sparing blood or sweat, and never pausing to rest" (a line from his poem, "White Universe"). He made eighteen great vows to the effect that, if there is a single being who has not attained Buddhahood, he will not become a Buddha.

The Venerable Master said that Buddhism should promote education and establish schools. Now, his wish has been realized at the City of Ten Thousand Buddhas, as well as at the branch temples in Los Angeles, San Francisco, and Berkeley. As for his vow to translate the Buddhist scriptures, the Three Treasuries and Twelve Divisions of the Canon are now being translated into English, Vietnamese, Spanish, and French. The Master expressed concern about this work even when he was seriously ill.

When the Master was alive, he was like a great canopy sheltering all of us, taking care of things so we wouldn't have to worry about them. Now that he is gone, we must all work together to carry out the many projects and affairs that he has left behind. Let us all make a great Bodhi resolve to support the Proper Dharma and the City of Ten Thousand Buddhas.

---

眾生無有生　亦復無有壞　若得如是智　當成無上道
——《大方廣佛華嚴經》〈光明覺品第九〉

*Living beings are without production*
*And also without extinction.*
*If one is able to obtain this kind of wisdom*
*Then one will accomplish the Unsurpassed Way.*

Flower Adornment Sutra, Chapter Nine, Light Enlightenment

宣化老和尚追思紀念專集

# 懷念恩師感言

## IN REMEMBRANCE OF MY KIND TEACHER

### 佛力無邊，師慈無量

**The Buddhas' boundless power,
my Teacher's infinite kindness...**

羅果英
Guoying Luo

由臺灣來美國，已有十五餘年；在這段時日中，我有很大的轉變，由一個有病的身體，變成健康無病，由喜愛吃葷菜而變成素食者，由一個自私心很強的思想變成喜歡做利他的事，由一個好勝驕傲的性格轉變成謙讓和容忍。雖然不能做得很完滿，但亦是我個人的大轉變和大突破；這一切的良好轉變，均是由於依止師父上人，皈依三寶，聽聞佛法後而顯現。

十年前，經過醫師的診斷，我患了子宮良性腫瘤，形如雞蛋，定期大量出血，必須開刀切除方能根治。但念「佛力無邊，師慈無量」，故每次去萬佛聖城參加法會，均虔誠拜佛，懇請師父上人加持，以除病根和業障；自己並從此發心吃素，不沾葷腥、虔拜懺文、除惡習氣、放生修福、廣結善緣。

半年後，經醫生複診，證實腫瘤已消失於無形，不須開刀。此奇蹟般的現象，均是萬佛及師父上人的慈悲威力救拔所致，使弟子脫胎換骨成為一個新生之人，並賜我慧命，走上修行之道。

為報佛及師恩，發願在有生之年，將為弘揚佛法之事業盡一份力量，並守持五戒使六根清淨；勤修戒、定、慧，息滅貪、瞋、癡；以上報四重恩，下濟三途苦為己任。

期法界一切眾生均能種下成佛的種子，開菩提花，結菩提果，以圓成佛道，達到了生脫死，涅槃清淨的境地，才不辜負佛陀出生於世，度化眾生的悲願，和師父上人宣揚佛教的期望。

I have changed a great deal in the fifteen or so years since I came to America from Taiwan. From being a chronically ill person who loved meat, I have become a healthy vegetarian. From being very selfish, I have come to enjoy helping others. From being competitive and proud, I have become humble and tolerant. This character transformation and breakthrough, though not perfect, has happened as a result of studying from the Venerable Master, taking refuge in the Triple Jewel, and listening to the Buddhadharma.

Ten years ago, the doctor told me I had a tumor in my uterus the size of a chicken egg. Because it bled profusely at regular intervals, it was necessary to remove it surgically. But knowing of the Buddhas' boundless power and my Teacher's infinite kindness, I bowed faithfully to the Buddhas and sincerely prayed to the Master to heal my illness and dispel my karmic obstacles whenever I went to the City of Ten Thousand Buddhas to attend a Dharma session. I also resolved to become vegetarian, to avoid meat and pungent plants, to sincerely bow various repentances, to change my bad habits, to set creatures free and nurture blessings, and to create extensive wholesome affinities. Half a year later, a second medical check-up showed no trace of the tumor, and surgery was no longer needed. This miraculous recovery, which gave me a new life of wisdom and set me on the path of spiritual practice, was brought about by the Buddhas' and the Venerable Master's compassionate and awesome strength.

In order to repay the Buddhas and my Teacher, I vow to help spread the Dharma, uphold the five precepts, and purify my six sense faculties. I shall diligently practice morality, concentration, and wisdom, and extinguish greed, hatred, and stupidity. I shall regard it as my duty to repay the four kinds of kindness above and save those suffering in the three paths below. May all living beings plant the seeds of Buddhahood; may their Bodhi flowers bloom and bear Bodhi fruit; may they perfect the Buddha Way, end birth and death, and attain the purity of Nirvana. Then they will be repaying the Buddha's compassionate vows to come to the world and teach living beings, and they will be fulfilling the Venerable Master's expectations in propagating Buddhism.

# HOW DOES THE MASTER CROSS OVER WESTERNERS?

# 上人如何教化西方人

Shi Heng Liang
釋恒良

Amitabha! To talk about the Master in ten minutes is actually impossible. But I was given a topic--"How is it that the Venerable Master can cross over Westerners and how is it that he can educate people?" The Master, wherever he went, any place in the world or beyond the world, whenever he encountered a living being, he could fully understand that living being. He could recognize each and every one of us. He could know our past causes and conditions and our future Buddhahood. He could know the best and the worst of each one of us. The wonderful thing about drawing near to the Master was that he helped us to recognize our worst, but at the same time he was able to bring out the very best in each of us. He did this in many ways. He did this by his adorned, pure appearance; by the words he said, which were always true; and through his deeds of virtue, which were uncountable.

He taught and transformed living beings with his every breath, with every pulse of his blood and every beat of his heart. Yet he never sought a reward of any kind--not only fame or money--he never even sought for anyone to recognize how much he was doing for living beings. He called himself an ant and a mosquito and the stupidest of people. Now, our first impression might be, "Well, an ant or a mosquito is just a very tiny, insignificant living being. That must be what the Master means." Actually, ants are very hard workers, and the Master was a very hard worker. Ants keep the earth clean of impure things; they clean away all the messes that other living beings leave. The Master cleaned up the karma of many, many living beings. An ant takes that mess on his own back and carries it away; and the Master took on the karma of many living beings. He actually took upon himself the sicknesses of many living beings. When you think of a mosquito, you think of the mosquito's never-ending sound. And that's how the Master was--he constantly spoke the Dharma; he never stopped speaking the Dharma. And he called himself the stupidest of people, because in a world where we all know how to cheat and to lie, the Master only knew how to tell the truth and how to take a loss. And just by being this way, he was able to cross over countless living beings.

阿彌陀佛！在十分鐘之內要來談上人是不可能的。但是我有一個題目「上人如何度西方人，如何教化眾生？」上人不管到什麼地方，此世界、他世界，不論何時，凡遇到一個眾生他都能悉知悉見。上人都認識我們每一個人。上人知道我們往昔的因緣，也知道我們未來成佛，上人也知道我們每個人的優點與缺點。親近上人最好的一點，就是上人會用各種方法幫助我們認識自己的弱點，也會將我們的優點發掘出來；有時上人用清淨莊嚴的外表，有時用真實的語言，有時用無邊的德行。

上人只要有一口氣在就會教化眾生，但卻從來不求名聞利養，也不要人知道他為眾生做了多少事。上人自稱小螞蟻、小蚊蟲，是最愚癡的人。有人聽了以後可能會直覺地認為「小螞蟻、小蚊蟲是微不足道的小生物，上人大概就指的這個意思吧！」事實上螞蟻工作很勤奮，上人工作也很勤奮；小螞蟻為保持地面清潔，清理其他眾生留下的垃圾，上人也清理了許多許多眾生的業；小螞蟻把垃圾背在身上帶走，上人也是一樣背負許多眾生的業。上人事實上承擔了許多眾生的病痛。我們想到小蚊蟲時，就會想起小蚊蟲嗡嗡不斷的響聲；上人也就像這樣子，永遠持續不斷的說法。上人自稱是人類中最愚癡的一個，因為在這個世界上大家都只會互相詐騙，上人則只懂得講真話，願意吃虧。就是這樣子，上人才度了無數眾生。

\* \* \*

318

People often ask how it was that the Master was able to cross over Westerners. Today I was thinking of the causes and conditions of why I left the home-life. I remember the time when I was still working in Berkeley. I had a very good job and was in a good situation. Once I went into a store to buy a pair of socks. I started writing out a check, and the salesperson told me that in order to cash my check, she needed my fingerprints. At that point I decided the world was becoming too complicated. That was around the time when I started thinking that I wanted to do something else. That was also around the time when I met the Master. The Master, compared to this modern world of asphalt and steel and computers and atomic bombs, is an oasis of compassion. He is a forest of humaneness, and he emphasizes simply being human. He emphasizes the human qualities, and he teaches us that to become a Buddha and to become fully enlightened, we need to perfect ourselves as people.

Now, the Master didn't go to the U.S. to become famous as a Dharma Master who crosses over Americans. He simply took up his responsibility. Because the Master was a very responsible person and a very responsible cultivator, when people take refuge with the Master, he takes complete responsibility for them and for their future as potential Buddhas. And he takes on a lot of karma. I remember, as an example of this, once in the City of Ten Thousand Buddhas, a Bhikshuni had made a mistake, and she broke the precepts. She was taught by the Master, as we all were, to confess her mistake and to repent and reform. She knelt in the Buddha hall in the midst of the great assembly and before the Master, and she repented, and then the Master, sitting on the high seat, looked down at her and said sternly, "What you have done will cause you to fall in the hells." Because this Bhikshuni truly believed in the Master, she was very afraid. She asked, "What can I do to save myself?" The Master said, with a very broad smile on his face, "I have a way to save you. I can go to the hells myself in your place and undergo the retribution for you." She couldn't accept that, of course, but the Master had already said that he would do it.

Another time, another Bhikshuni told me that one night she was very, very sick and couldn't stop vomiting. She very much believed in the Master, and so she bowed before his picture and prayed to the Master and asked him to bless her and take away her suffering. Then suddenly she felt well, and that night she had a good rest. The next morning she went to a refuge ceremony where the Master was transmitting the three refuges and the five precepts. After he had transmitted the refuges, he turned to the Bhikshuni and said, "This morning has been very difficult for me, because last night I suddenly became very ill and I vomited all night long, and so today I have no strength." That Bhikshuni knew very clearly that the Master had simply taken her suffering onto himself.

Many people wonder how was it that the Master could become so ill and how could he have left us the way he did. But many of us who have been with him through the years know, and we know what a great debt of kindness we have to pay the Master. And the only way to do that is to try our very best to cultivate.

常常有人問及上人怎麼能夠度西方人。現在我就談一談我爲什麼出家，我記得我還住柏克萊時，我的工作蠻不錯，環境也不錯。有一天我到店裡去買一雙襪子，正開支票時，店員跟我説她要我的手指紋才能兌現我的支票。就在那時，我覺得這個世界真是太複雜了，我想脱離這樣的環境，也就是這個時候我剛好遇到了上人。上人跟這個由瀝青、鋼鐵、電腦和原子彈組成的世界比較起來，真像是一片慈悲的綠洲。上人就像仁慈的森林，他所注重的就是人道。他重視人性，並且教導我們要成就佛道必得先圓滿人道。

上人到美國來，不是來做一個以度美國人而聞名的法師，他只是來盡他的責任而已。因爲上人是很有責任感的人，也是非常負責的修行人，他來美國就是來盡他的責任。有人來皈依上人時，上人對皈依弟子及他們日後成就佛道負起了全部的責任。上人也擔負了許多的業。

舉例來說我記得有一次在萬佛城有一位比丘尼犯了過錯，破了戒。上人平常教我們犯了錯要發露懺悔。所以這位比丘尼在佛殿大眾中跪在上人面前發露懺悔。上人坐在臺上往下看著她，很嚴肅地說：「妳做的事會讓妳墮地獄。」這位比丘尼很相信上人，所以很害怕，便問上人：「我該怎麼辦呢？」上人面帶令人寬慰的笑容說：「我可以救妳，我到地獄裡去代妳受報。」這位比丘尼當然不能接受，但是上人已經說他會到地獄去代她受罪。

又有一次，另外一位比丘尼跟我說，有一天晚上她病得很厲害，嘔吐不止。她很相信上人，所以就對上人的照片叩頭，祈求上人加持，幫她解除痛苦。忽然她就好了，那晚睡得很好。第二天早上她去參加上人打皈依傳五戒的儀式。在上人打完皈依後，轉身對她說：「今天早上我很難過，因爲昨晚我忽然病了，吐了一個晚上，所以今天我沒有力氣。」那位比丘尼很明白，上人替她受罪了。

很多人猜疑上人怎麼會病得這麼嚴重，怎麼會這樣走的。跟隨上人多年的人都知道，我們虧欠上人太多了，唯一報答上人的方法，便是努力修行。

# 懷念上宣下化師父上人
# REMINISCING ABOUT THE VENERABLE MASTER

我一直覺得他老人家，
無時無刻不是在關心著弟子們的一言一行。

**I feel that the Master was conscientiously mindful of us
in everything we did and said.**

于果龍　Gwo-Lung Yu

一九九五年的五月要比往常來得涼爽，以前在這個季節上課的時候，熱得汗流浹背，意味著炎夏將來之兆。今年則相反，常常陰天，還偶而下毛毛雨。有一次從學校駕車回家，一路上只覺得氣候非常清涼，望著天上讓人納悶的烏雲，心裏想著：「大概是因爲師父在洛杉磯養病，所以龍天護法都來護持吧！？」沒想到在這年的春季學期將結束的最後一個禮拜，竟驚聞師父圓寂的消息，心中非常悲痛我們失去了一位好導師了。回想自從皈依師父以來，自己從沒有好好遵守師父的教誨，盡是在胡混過日子，心裏很是慚愧。

記得剛皈依師父的時候，有一次師父回臺灣弘法，我和母親、二姐趕著去機場送機。但因爲有事耽延了時間，深怕趕不上送師父上飛機，因此一路上車子開得飛快，同時也希望飛機不要太快起飛才好。我那時心中有許多問題要請問師父，因此急著要早點到機場。皇天不負苦心人，趕到機門的時候，師父剛好要進去，我急急忙忙地給師父頂了禮，只說了句：「師父..」就再也講不下去了，滿腔的疑難，在那個時候竟一個字兒也說不出來。師父那時用英文跟我說：「Do your best！」這一句話解決了我當時一切的問題，我幾乎不敢相信自己聽到的話，整個人呆在那兒。恒實法師看我這般情景，就重複了一遍師父的話，我這才明白師父已經曉得了我心裏的疑問。這簡短有力的一句話，帶給了我一股莫名的信心，使我勇於面對許多過去所不敢面對的困難，同時也證明了師父的修行與智慧，是多麼不可思議。

我個人因爲福報淺、業障重，因此沒能多親近師父，以增長善根。也沒能奉行師父教誨，以培養德行。但是一直覺得他老人家，無時無刻不是在關心著弟子們的一言一行，深怕我們走錯路，相信大家都有這樣

In 1995, the month of May was colder than in other years. In the past, when I went to school around this time of year, my sweat would be a sign of the hot summer soon to come. This year, however, it was always cloudy and sometimes there was a light drizzle. Once when I was driving home from school, I looked up at the cloudy sky and thought, "Maybe it's so cool because the Master is recuperating in Los Angeles and the dragons have come to protect him!" However, I never would have known that during the last week of the spring quarter, I would hear the shocking news of the Master's passing into stillness. My heart painfully laments the loss of our great teacher. With deep regret I think of how I squandered my life and didn't follow the Master's teachings well after I had taken refuge with him.

Soon after I took refuge, the Master was going to Taiwan to propagate Dharma. My mom, second eldest sister, and I rushed to the airport to bid him farewell. But as we got delayed, I drove as fast as I could, hoping the plane would be delayed so we wouldn't miss the Master. I had a lot of questions to ask the Master, so I was anxious to get to the airport sooner. When I arrived, the Master was just about to step into the boarding gate. I hurriedly bowed to him and only got out the words, "Shifu (Master)..." I couldn't continue, because there were so many things in my mind and on the tip of my tongue. Then the Master said to me in English, "Do your best." That answered all the questions I had wanted to ask. I just couldn't believe what I heard. As I stood in awe, Dharma Master Heng Sure noticed and repeated the Master's words. It then dawned upon me that the Master already knew what my questions were. His words gave me the confidence to courageously confront all my problems. This goes to show how inconceivable the Master's practice and wisdom were.

Possessing few blessings and heavy karma, I did not have the chance to draw near to the Master to cultivate good roots, nor was I able to follow his teachings to foster virtue. Nevertheless, I feel that the Master was conscientiously mindful of us in everything we did and said, fearing that we would step in the wrong direction. I think others have similar experiences.

的經驗。在聽師父說法時，師父常指出為佛弟子所不應犯的過錯，有時聽了自己會嚇一跳，這不是自己才犯的錯誤嗎？應該只有自己心知肚明，怎麼師父會知道？有一、二次實在是講得太符合自己的毛病了，使我不得不感激和信服。

我曾和母親談到這不可思議的事時，母親告訴我，早年我們家剛來美國時，我自己還小，尚未皈依，母親和二姐就已是師父的皈依弟子了。那時家中十分困難，父親的生意不是很好，母親曾為了一筆生意去求過師父，師父當時叫母親念觀世音菩薩聖號，那時母親回答：「已經在念了。」師父就說：「叫你念，你就念。」母親回家後就很誠心地每天念觀世音菩薩聖號，結果那筆生意真地很順利地接洽成了。這件事，母親至今仍十分感念師父。

諸如此類的事蹟，多得不勝枚舉。而事實上師父他老人家對弟子們的恩德，尚不止此，他老人家更是弟子們法身慧命的恩人。想到他老人家在世時，常抱重病為弟子們說法，心裏甚感難過。有時細思他老人家如此辛苦地以捨身命的精神，在末法時代為宣揚正法而努力，如此以不屈撓的精神為末法眾生立一龍象榜樣，自己除了感慨與佩服之外，更應該對自己的無明愚癡痛下針砭，以報師恩，不能一天到晚躲懶偷安地度日，白白辜負了師父的苦心。

師父他老人家慈悲和藹，毫無罣礙的風範；直言無諱，剛正不阿的氣節；以及誨人不倦的精神，和平時所教導的修行及做人的道理，我謹當銘記於心，永遠不敢或忘。

The Master, in his talks, always pointed out the offenses that Buddhists should take care not to commit. Sometimes I am stunned to hear it, because I think, "Didn't I just do that not too long ago? No one but myself knows about it. How did the Master find out?" That has already happened twice, leaving me feeling both thankful and faithful.

When I related these incredible occurrences to my mother, she told me that many years ago, when we had just moved to America (I had not yet taken refuge, but she and my second sister had), our family had financial difficulties because my father's business was not doing well. When my mother asked the Master to bless the business, he told her to recite the name of Guanshiyin (Avalokitesvara) Bodhisattva. My mother said, "But I'm already reciting it." The Master replied, "I told you to recite it, so just recite it." After my mother went home, she recited Guanshiyin's name every day, and as a result the business went smoothly and successfully. To this day, my mother is very grateful for the Master's compassion.

Incidents such as this are too numerous to mention. The Master's kindness to his disciples goes beyond such events, for he is the savior of our wisdom and spiritual lives. I grieve to think of how he continuously gave talks and lectures even when he was ill. The Master's spirit of sacrificing his body and life to spread the teachings in the Dharma-ending Age makes me reflect deeply. Such indefatigable vigor sets an example for all beings. Besides feeling gratitude and admiration, I shall endeavor to eliminate my own ignorance. I can't be lazy if I want to repay the Master for all his hard work.

I shall never forget the Master as a model of kindness, compassion, and total spontaneity. His frankness enabled him to be direct without fear of offending others. He followed the principles without bending them. He taught us incessantly about the Way to a proper practice and life. I shall always remember this in my heart and not dare to forget it.

# 痛念師父上人
## IN MEMORY OF THE VENERABLE MASTER

夏果周　Gwo-chou Hsia

師父上人來虛空　今朝示寂復歸空
何奈弟子道未成　淚眼望天無所從

*The Venerable Master came from empty space,*
*And to empty space he returned.*
*Alas! This disciple has not accomplished the Way;*
*His teary eyes gazing at the skies, he's bereft of his mentor.*

# A TEACHING BY THE VENERABLE MASTER

# 上人的教誨

## That amazing teaching eventually will lead to a kind of strength to fulfill an "impossible" vow--not with arrogance but with humility and gratitude.

### 這不可思議的教誨，一定會帶給我一些力量來完成，我那「不可能做到」的願──不是用驕慢，而是謙虛及感激來完成。

Shi Heng Hsien
釋恒賢

When I first left home I was very arrogant about my ability to stay awake when meditating while others fell asleep. Then my retribution came, and I got so that I fell asleep as soon as I sat down. It became a big problem. In those days, we could ask the Venerable Master about all sorts of things, and because I was very concerned about my sleeping problem, I pleaded with the Venerable Master to help me with it. Of course, skill in meditation is something one has to develop oneself, and there are no magic formulas to make things easy. However, the Venerable Master employed an unusual method to aid me. It was the L.A. bus.

I had become so desperate to find some way out of my dilemma that I had even made a vow before the great assembly that I would not fall asleep during meditation. Right away a fellow-cultivator planted a doubt in my mind by saying to me and others that I should not have made a vow I could not keep. And I didn't manage to keep the vow. Because I didn't keep it, many things in my life and cultivation started to go wrong. It's hard to interpret what that means when such things happen. One starts to doubt in various ways when right in the midst of such states; but in retrospect they might just be part of a change that will lead in time to progress out of a difficult impasse.

In any case, my turn came to be sent to Los Angeles. In those days, the nuns used to take turns going to live in Gold Wheel Temple in Los Angeles. The Venerable Master went to L.A. every month, and that's when we would go down or come back. Fortunately, the month I went down it was not by car. That month our big bus drove there, and a lot of people went. I believe it was in the early 1980's, although without research I don't know the exact date; and we were staying at the third Gold Wheel which was on 6th Street in downtown L.A. When my turn was completed, I was also fortunate. I say fortunate, because I always carry a lot of things with me when I travel, so I also needed to take many things back with me. But the bus had come down again, so I thought there would be no problem.

剛出家時對自己在打坐時仍能保持清醒而別人卻昏睡，頗覺自豪。可是後來業障來了，我變得一坐下來就立刻睡著。這成了一個大問題。在那時，我們有問題都有機會問上人。因為我很關心打坐睡覺的問題，我就向上人求助。打坐的功夫是要每個人自己去磨練出來的，沒有什麼仙丹妙藥可使過程變得較輕鬆容易。可是上人卻用了一個不尋常的方法來幫我。那就是用洛杉磯的巴士，我因為很急切地想自這個困境脫身出來，就在大眾前發了一個願，說我再也不在打坐時睡覺。說完，一個同修立刻就在我心裏種了一個令我信心動搖的因，她說，對自己、對他人，我都不該發一個我做不到的願。而我確實也沒有做到。因為我沒有做到，在我的生活上及修行上就開始出了很多問題。在開始出狀況時，自己很難判斷到底是怎麼回事，人在面對境界時會產生很多疑問。可是回想起來，那也可能只不過是種種脫離困境時必經的一個轉換過程。

那時，女眾輪流駐守在洛杉磯的金輪寺。上人每個月都到金輪寺一次，我們就在那時換班。輪到我去金輪寺時很幸運的，我下去的那個月開的是我們的大巴士，很多人跟著一起下去。那時大約是一九八○年代的早期，我沒有詳細去查，確實的日子不記得。我們住在當時在第六街的金輪寺。我留守期滿時，得幸運的，開的又是大巴士。我說幸運的原因是因為我每次出門都帶很多東西，所以我也很多東西要帶回去。可是因為開的是大巴士，我想就沒問題了。

322

However, on Monday morning when it was time to board the bus, the Venerable Master unexpectedly announced, in a loud and displeased voice for all to hear, that I was not allowed to get on the bus. His reason? He told me and all the people who had come to see him off, along with all the people who were going back on the bus, that the bus was not for someone as lazy as I who fell asleep as soon as she sat down! With that, the bus drove away without me, and I was left very astonished and remorseful in L.A.

Actually, it was a beautiful, sunny morning in Los Angeles, and Gold Wheel Temple was filled with joyous light and wholesome energy from the Venerable Master's visit. But I just felt deeply ashamed and repentant. I didn't even try to think of what to do. I just went into what had been my room for the past month and meditated. You can imagine I didn't fall asleep that time! I just reviewed my spinelessness and lack of resolve, and was profoundly sorry. Then after about half an hour we heard noise in the parking lot. The bus had returned and I was allowed to get on it after all! Other nuns told me later that the bus had driven off, and after awhile on the highway the Venerable Master had told the driver to turn around and go back to Gold Wheel--to get me.

I think it's hard for people who did not experience it to realize the amount of energy and resourcefulness the Venerable Master put into teaching his disciples. When I received that teaching, I was, as with many similar teachings, intensely focused on the immediate situation. But looking back I can see the Venerable Master's incredible compassion and how much he helped me get through a very difficult period--by having a bus travel so far with all those people and then come back, pushing me to the brink of remorse, and then giving me the joy of being forgiven and the underlying assurance that the Venerable Master cared that much about whether I cultivated or not. He had responded to my repeated pleas for help in a most dramatic way, with a lesson that went very deep. How much others might have learned from it as well is also hard to estimate, but certainly must have been part of the teaching.

I'm slow, and it will probably be a long time before I never fall asleep in meditation. But I did improve after that amazing teaching. And remembering it now, I feel that there must have been something planted by it which may take a lot of time to grow, but which eventually will lead to a kind of strength to fulfill an "impossible" vow--not with arrogance but with humility and gratitude.

可是星期一早上，上車的時候，上人卻帶著不悅的口氣很大聲地宣布我不能上車。原因呢？上人對所有來送他，還有所有要同車走的人說，這巴士不能載一個像我那麼懶，一坐下來就睡著的人。然後巴士就開走了，把一個又驚愕又羞慚的我留在洛杉磯。

那天早上陽光燦爛很美的，金輪寺裏也洋溢著上人來訪而昇起的愉悅正氣。可是我深感慚愧也沒去想該怎麼辦，只是回到我住了一個月的房間裏去打坐。可想而知的，我這次可是沒睡著，我不斷地反省自己的軟弱，缺乏決心，覺得很難過，約半小時後，我們聽到停車場有聲音，巴士回來，讓我上車了！別的同修事後告訴我，巴士上了高速公路不久，上人就叫司機回頭，到金輪寺接我。

對於沒有親身體驗過的人來說，可能很難了解上人是用多少的心力在教導弟子與其他我所受到的類似教誨一樣，當我上了這一課時，我對當前狀況的注意力是很強的。

回想起來，我了解到上人那想像不出的慈悲，還有為幫我度過那一個困難的時期，他是幫了我多少——讓一輛載滿人的巴士，開出那麼遠再回來；把我逼到羞愧交加的盡頭，又回過頭來讓我感到被原諒的喜悅，及其背後上人對我們有修行與否都關懷備至的保證。上人用最戲劇化的方式來回答我不斷的求助，同時也給我上了一個難以忘懷的一課，其他人是否也從中學到一樣多，是很難說的，但可肯定的是，他們也是這次教誨的一部份。

我是很慢的，也許要過很長的一段時間，我才學會不在打坐時睡著，可是在這不可思議的教誨後，我確實是有進步。現在想起來一定有什麼種子已經種下了，也許要很多時間才能成長，可是它一定會帶給我一些力量來完成，我那「不可能做到」的願——不是用驕慢，而是謙虛及感激來完成。

---

諸佛如虛空　究竟常清淨　憶念生歡喜　彼諸願具足
——《大方廣佛華嚴經》〈光明覺品第九〉

*All Buddhas are like empty space,*
*Ultimately and eternally pure.*
*By always remembering to bring forth happiness,*
*All of one's vows are completed.*

Flower Adornment Sutra, Chapter Nine, Light Enlightenment

# My Personal Experiences

# 我個人的經驗

林柏利
Randolph Lum

I came to Buddhism in December 1984. Previous to that time, I had been reading many books on Christianity and always had a deep desire to learn more about religion and spirituality. I always had an innate desire to know more about myself and what happens to our souls after death and the meaning of our earthly existence. I did not pursue religion because I was caught up in the desire to complete my professional education and develop a career.

In 1984, I was satisfied with the level of my career and decided that it was a good time to pursue the study of religion again. My uncle asked if I might be interested in Buddhism. He said he had met the Venerable Master through a family friend. My uncle said this high monk was very special and many people spoke very highly of him. Please understand, my uncle always studied martial arts and qi gong. He was always fascinated with anyone who had those types of skills, and he believed high monks should always possess such skills. He said there was a temple in Los Angeles, Gold Wheel Monastery, which the Venerable Master had established, and suggested I go there and investigate for myself. I went to Gold Wheel Monastery in December 1984 and was immediately over-whelmed by the aura of the monastery. It was very simple, but had an air about it which is difficult to explain but instilled faith and trust. I immediately bought some beginners' books on Buddhism and read them. I read the life history of the Master and was profoundly impressed. At that moment, I knew this was the religion I was looking for. It is difficult to explain. I knew without a doubt that I should be a Buddhist disciple.

Within a month, I became a vegetarian and took refuge with the Master. I remember once when I was going to ask the Venerable Master a question, and a Dharma Master was translating for those of us who did not speak Chinese. The Master answered my question before I could ask it, and the answer was perfect. It was precise and very accurate. I was amazed the Master knew my thoughts before I had the opportunity to speak to him.

I know the Master is gone from our current time, but I do not believe he is entirely gone. Occasionally I dream

我於一九八四年成爲佛教徒。在這之前,我看過很多基督教的書,對宗教和形上學,有著強烈的欲望,想多了解一點。在我內心深處,總想知道更多關於我自己、人死後靈魂的歸處,以及這個世界存在的意義。最後我沒有訴求於宗教,因爲我被完成職業訓諫和事業發展的欲望圈限住了。

在一九八四年,我對事業的發展感到滿意,因而決定這是一個很好的機會,再一次追求宗教方面的知識。開始尋找、研究宗教。我舅舅問我是否對佛教有興趣。他說透過家人的朋友,他見到了師父。舅舅說這位高僧非常地特別,並且很多人對他有很高的評價。你要知道,我舅舅常常研究功夫和氣功,他總是很迷那些有這種功夫的人,也相信高僧都應該會有這些功夫。舅舅告訴我,在洛杉磯有一師父建立的金輪聖寺,並建議我去那裡研究。一九八四年,我一來到金輪聖寺,立刻不可抗拒於寺中的靈氣。簡單的寺,但是有一種無法言說的氣氛,滲透著信心和信任。我立刻買了些初級的佛教書籍來讀。讀了師父的事蹟之後,我深深地受感動。立刻我知道,這是我在找尋的宗教。這是無法解釋的,但我知道,毫無疑問地我應是一個佛弟子。

在一個月內,我開始吃素,也皈依了師父。記得一次,去問師父一個問題,有一位法師,爲我們不會說中文的弟子翻譯。上人在我發問之前,就回答我的問題,並且答得很圓滿,既仔細又正確。我很驚訝,在我有機會和師父說話之前,師父就知道我的想法。

這些年來,我都儘量參加金輪聖寺和萬佛聖城的聽經和法會活動。我必須承認,在我自己了生的路上,並沒有多大的進步。然而,我偶爾會讀當時所買的初機佛書。上人也仍然一直是我最大的啓迪者,我也一直尊敬他的獻身於大眾。上人離開了,一切都有些困難。修行的路上,有位老師帶著我們是比較順利的。我想我還沒有準備好,來接受他給我的贈與。我會想念他的。

about him. I remember in one dream the Master was riding around the City of Ten Thousand Buddhas and, as in the old days, he was bidding farewell to us before we left to return home by bus. The Master used to give some additional instructions on cultivation, such as to leave our greed, anger, and stupidity behind with him. In this dream, there was no one around except me. He spoke to me in Chinese and gave me very specific and special instructions, but to this day I do not know what he said, because I do not understand Chinese. These thoughts are still perplexing me to this day.

上人現在是離開了，但我不相信他是眞正地走了。偶爾地，我夢到他。記得在一個夢裡，像往常一樣，上人在萬佛城裡開著車，在我們要離開準備上車回家之前，他囑咐著我們一路平安。在修行上，師父總是給我們額外的教導，例如，要我布施貪瞋癡給他。在這個夢裡，除了我沒有別人，上人用中文給我做了非常特別的開示。但是到今天，我還不知道他說什麼，因爲我不懂中文。直至今日，這些想法仍然令我困窘著。

# 懷念師恩

## IN REMEMBRANCE OF OUR MASTER'S KINDNESS

釋果安　十一歲
Shramanera Gwo An, age 11

一九九四年六月，上人在洛杉磯傳四十二手眼。
當時上人爲了滿眾生的願，不辭勞苦，
輪流在兩個道場傳四十二手眼，一次在金輪寺，一次在長堤聖寺。

有一次在長堤聖寺傳四十二手眼，時間是在早上，而且太陽很大。
上人發著燒抱病前來。

四十二手眼的法會結束之後，上人即將離開時，
我看見上人的背上都是汗，可是上人一句話也沒有說。

此情此景常在我腦海中浮現，
這豈不正是上人「流血汗，不休息」的感人寫照嗎？

In June 1994, in order to fulfill the wishes of living beings, the Venerable Master endured a lot of suffering to transmit the Forty-Two Hands and Eyes at both Long Beach Monastery and Gold Wheel Monastery in Los Angeles.

One morning, despite being sick with a high temperature, the Venerable Master came to Long Beach Monastery to transmit the Forty-Two Hands and Eyes.

After the transmission ceremony, when the Venerable Master was leaving, I saw that his back was covered with sweat, but he did not even say a word about it.

I kept on thinking about this scene. Isn't this an example of the Venerable Master's verse:

"Spare neither blood nor sweat, And never pause to rest."

# 憶師父——宣公上人

## IN MEMORY OF MY TEACHER--
## THE VENERABLE MASTER HUA

師父以身教導了我們，我們應該自己動手清除內心裏面的垃圾。

**With the Master's personal practice as our example,
we should make an effort to get rid of the trash in our own minds.**

王果雪　Guoxue Wang

願將法界眾生所有一切苦難，
悉皆與我一人代受。

我現在就好像兩個人，一個人到處去救人，
我這一個人，我是不會管他的，
即使一根手指頭的力量，我也不會幫助他的。

師父啊！師父！您老人家是如此地慈悲，如此地無緣大慈，同體大悲。

眾生啊！眾生！我們又是如此地自私自利，從來沒有體會到師父是如何承受了一切的苦難，我們只想到自己，把所有的災難丟給了師父。

回想一九九四年初，舍弟突然身患惡疾，送往長庚醫院開刀，開刀過程中，我一直在心裏求師父救救我的小弟。爾後小弟也一直很順利眶復原，九個月之中的追蹤檢查也都無事。但因家庭環境因素，小弟無法放下心中的執著，內心的貪、瞋、癡一直在循環作怪，終而在十月初併發了一個腫瘤。先是查不到病因，只見全身黃疸，繼而發現膽管阻塞，到了年底終於在肚臍上看到了一個東西長出來，醫生判定無法開刀。眼看它慢慢長大，終至長成像火龍果一樣大小的東西，家人這時都極擔心「它」如果破裂，真不知小弟會被折磨成什麼樣子？

一九九五年三月，師父派了兩位弟子回國，在法界印經會打皈依，我們也在這時替小弟代受皈依於師父座下。六月八日師父上人圓寂。從沒有去過萬佛聖城的我，終於在這個因緣下，促成我往萬佛聖城的心願。就在七月二十日要出國的前三天，突然接到小弟入院抽肺積水的電話，此後二天小弟就無法進食。而在聽到我已回到嘉義火車站的消息時溘然去世，走時身

I vow to fully take upon myself all sufferings and hardships of all living beings in the Dharma Realm.

Right now I'm like two people. One is still saving living beings everywhere. As for this person who is me, I don't care about him. I won't lift even a finger to help him.

Teacher, teacher, how kind you are, even to those with whom you have no affinity! How compassionate you are, regarding everyone as being the same as yourself!

Living beings, living beings--how selfish we are, never realizing all the suffering the Master undergoes for us. Thinking only of ourselves, we throw all our troubles to the Master.

In early 1994 when my younger brother suddenly fell ill and was hospitalized for surgery, I kept praying to the Master during the operation, asking him to save my brother. Afterwards my brother had a smooth recovery and his checkups were normal for the next nine months. However, his family situation prevented him from being able to let go of his attachments. Greed, hatred, and stupidity continued to trouble him, and finally in October a tumor broke out. There had been no sign of it earlier, but his body became yellowish with jaundice, his bile-duct was blocked, and a protrusion grew above his navel. Since the doctor ruled out surgery, we watched as it grew to the size of a "fire dragon fruit" and wondered whether my brother would be able to sustain the trauma in the event that it burst open.

In March 1995 when the Master sent two disciples to Taiwan to transmit the Three Refuges, I took refuge with the Master on behalf of my brother. On June 8 the Master entered the stillness, and that was how I decided to go to the City of Ten Thousand Buddhas, which I had never visited before. On July 20, three days before I was to leave, I was notified that my brother had been hospitalized to remove water from his lungs. He was unable to eat anything for the next two days. Unfortunately, he passed away by the time I reached the Jiayi train station. Although the tumor was still present, he did not suffer

上火龍果似的腫瘤依然存在，也沒有末期腫瘤病人臨終時的那種痛苦。病中最大的不適，就是脊椎骨酸痛及去世前二天不能進食。小弟在我出發的前一天撒手人寰，給我的強烈感受，就是他要跟我一起去萬佛聖城，參加師父的荼毗大典。

在萬佛聖城七天所體會到的，更是難以形容，總之師父的慈悲及設想的週到，並不因師父肉身的入滅而有所減少！真是如人寒冬飲冰水，點滴在心頭。

師父圓寂已快滿週年了！這期間我所聽到的，看到的，讓我深深地感受到他老人家是如此地慈悲，也深深地體會到我又是如此地自私，只為了手足情深，心想師父是聖人，他會幫助我們。那想到師父上人的救助眾生，是把眾生的業障扛起來，由老人家去承受，每想到此，我真是無限追悔。愚癡的我們只想師父常住於世教導我們，而又把一切垃圾丟給了師父。如今師父以身教導了我們，我們應該自己動手清除內心裏面的垃圾，不要再有丟給人的癡想了！畢竟師父能扛的是眾生的業報，眾生心裏面的三毒，貪、瞋、癡，是我們自己得清除的。

師父啊！師父！願您老人家慈悲，乘願再來教導我們，弟子願生生世世追隨您。阿彌陀佛！

the severe pain typical of those at his advanced stage of illness. The greatest discomfort he experienced were an aching spine and the inability to ingest food two days before his death. Because he died before the day of my trip, I am strongly convinced that he wanted to go with me to the City of Ten Thousand Buddhas to attend the Master's Cremation Ceremony.

It would be difficult to describe my feelings during my seven days at the City. In general, I realized the Master's compassion and considerate care were not lessened despite his physical passing. I could feel this deeply in my heart.

It's been almost a year since the Master's passing, and what I have seen and heard in this time has made me aware of his great compassion and my selfishness in thinking that the Master was a Sage and could help my brother. Little did I know that the Master's way of saving people was to take their karmic hindrances upon himself. Every time I think of this, I am filled with regret. I foolishly assumed the Master would always be around to guide us, and I dumped all my garbage on him. With the Master's personal practice as our example, we should make an effort to get rid of our own trash instead of passing it to others. While the Master may take on our karmic retributions, we ourselves must clean out the three poisons of greed, hatred, and stupidity in our own minds.

Teacher! Please compassionately return on the power of your vows to teach us. Your disciple vows to follow you in life after life. Amitabha!

---

# 我們的師父——宣化上人
## OUR VENERABLE MASTER

釋果志　十四歲　　Shramanera Gwo Jr, age 14

我媽媽的心中一直覺得師父是她的法身父母。
自從在高雄第一次聽到師父開示後，媽媽就覺得師父把她從無明海中救出來了。

師父圓寂以後，媽媽告訴我：

師父是一位大慈大悲的菩薩，他不會把我們放下不管；
他只是肉體往生，他的法身是無所不在的。

My mother feels that the Venerable Master is the parent of her Dharma body. Ever since she first heard the Venerable Master lecturing in Kaoshiung, she has felt that the Venerable Master has saved her from the sea of ignorance.

When the Venerable Master passed away, she told me,

The Venerable Master is a great compassionate Bodhisattva. He won't leave us uncared for. Only his body passed away; his Dharma body is still with us.

# 高山仰止　感懷師恩

## LOOKING UP TO HIS AWESOME VIRTUE--
## IN MEMORY OF THE GRACE OF OUR TEACHER

他的精神與教化是永遠不會磨滅的。

**His energy, his spirit and his teachings will never, ever disappear.**

黃果君
Guojun (Hector) Wong

在師父眾多的皈依弟子中，身受各式各樣感應的人很多。但我自從十一歲（一九五〇年）皈依師父以來，並沒有像一般人那麼多采多姿，似乎沒有什麼靈異的感應。但對我來說，沒有感應本身就是最好的感應，所謂「默默感應默默中」，並不是一定要有明顯的禍福吉凶等波動才是感應。不過這四十多年以來，有幾件事卻是我常常銘記於心的。

記得我剛皈依時，師父曾就我的個性作了兩句評語：「性格剛強，有脾氣。」當時我只知道有脾氣不好，需要改。假如說我現在的脾氣不算太壞的話，這完全要歸功於師父及時的訓誨。至於「性格剛強」，當時我還以為有性格，是一種優點。後來讀《地藏經》至「南閻浮提眾生，其性剛強，難調難伏」時，才知道性格剛強，正是婆婆世界眾生，所以不能出離惡世的一大原因。也因此我才真正明白師父當時的用意，是教我凡事都要隨緣，不要我相太重，固執己見。師父自己不也常常說：「Everything is OK！」嗎？

因為大家都知道師父有預知的能力，所以我在十五、六歲的時候，也曾問過師父：「以後我會怎麼樣？」他看著我，只短短地答了我一句：「只要心慈。」他沒有再往下說，我也沒有追問。這短短的四個字，就這樣成了我一生的座右銘。待人處世只要心存慈悲，即是福田，命運自然會好，不必去求神問卜。

過後不久，我學人畫了一幅達摩祖師像，並蛇足一番，題了幾句偈贊說：「你看這是誰？人道達摩老祖；自西天來東土，面壁一坐九年，明心

Many of the Venerable Master's disciples have experienced various kinds of responses. Personally, I haven't had any unusual experiences or spiritual responses ever since I took refuge with the Master in 1950, at the age of eleven. But as far as I'm concerned, no response is the best response, for "imperceptible responses occur in imperceptible ways." Responses don't have to be as obvious as disasters turning into blessings or misfortunes melting into windfalls of good luck. However, there have been several incidents over the past forty years that I remember especially well.

I remember just after I'd taken refuge, the Master wrote a sentence describing my personality: "a stubborn character with a big temper." At that time, I knew I would have to change my big temper. If my temper is smaller now, all the credit goes to the Master for his frequent teachings on the topic. At that time, I thought that having such a stubborn character was an asset. It was only when I read the *Earth Store Sutra* to the place where it says, "The beings of Southern Jambudvipa have natures which are stubborn and obstinate, difficult to tame, difficult to subdue," that I realized having a "stubborn character" is the main reason we cannot escape the Saha world. That realization enabled me to really understand the Master's intent--he wanted me to be more mellow and not so egotistic and opinionated. Doesn't the Master himself always say, "Everything is OK"?

Because everyone knows that the Master had foreknowledge, I, too, asked him one time when I was fifteen or sixteen, "What does the future hold for me?" He looked at me and answered with one short sentence, "Just be kind and compassionate." He didn't say any more; and I didn't ask any more. Those few words, however, have served as a lifelong reminder. In dealing with people, we need only be kindhearted. Just that is the field of blessings that will quite naturally bring us good destiny. There's no need to consult the spirits or the hexagrams. Not long after, like many other people, I, too, painted a portrait of Patriarch Bodhidharma, and even went so far as add some totally unnecessary words of praise: *"Who does this look like to you? / People say its Old Patriarch Dharma, / Who came on his own from west to east / And sat nine years facing a wall. / He understood his mind and also saw his nature. / Having nothing to do, he found something to do."* The Master looked it and said, "It sounds a little like Chan banter, but shows you are still an

而又見性，原來沒事找事做。」師父看了説：「頗有禪機，但是外行，因爲明心就是見性，並不是兩回事。」自此以後，我就不敢再耍嘴皮了。

師父於一九六二年離開香港到美國來，而我也於一九六六年去了非洲。時光荏苒，此後的十多年我沒有再親近師父。

一九八六年，我移民來美國。一九八八年師父命我在金山聖寺講《金剛經》。在這之前，我本來是非洲、美國兩地來回跑，一年來美國兩趟，每趟停留兩、三個星期；每次來，我都到金山聖寺去拜見師父。有次剛好碰到師父在講經，師父就叫我替他翻譯粵語。之後，師父説：「在你沒有回非洲之前，可以來對他們講講話。」當時我因在美國的時間有限，所以只能和大家隨便地談談。這次回來，突然要我講《金剛經》，我心裡就想：「講經是一件很鄭重的事，不能講講停停。」經過一番考慮，終於決定辭去非洲的工作，專心地學習講經。

在我開始講《金剛經》的時候，師父就對我説：「不必要求講得好。」又説：「也不要講得太容易了。」當我講經時，師父常常坐在門口聽。有次我問師父：「師父，弟子不知道有沒有講錯的地方？」師父説：「你仔細地玩味經文的道理，就這樣講就對了。」我説：「我當然是認爲對的才講，不過不知道是真的對或假的對？」師父答：「你不是一步就跨進去了嗎？」

師父這幾番的教誨，對我一生影響很大。經過多年來的體認，心常慈悲就是修福；不發脾氣、減少我執及研讀經典就是修慧。修福、修慧正是學佛者最重要的兩個課題，除此之外，都是末梢支節。佛在《二夜經》裡曾説：「我從成道夜，迄至泥洹夜，時常説般若。」般若，就是妙智慧。佛説法四十九年，五時八教，三藏十二部，翻來覆去地講，無非是要告訴我們解脫的智慧法門；一切佛菩薩的讚頌，最後也都以「摩訶般若波羅蜜」——以智慧到彼岸，作爲總結，可見智慧在佛教中的重要性！

所謂佛教，就是要人覺悟的教；所以修福也是爲了要養慧。因爲若福報不夠，不但自身修行會多所障礙，在弘法利生時，也會因缺乏福報，而與眾生無緣。因此行善積福的目的，也只是爲了

outsider, because understanding the mind is itself seeing the nature. They certainly aren't two different things."After that I never dared sound off again!

In 1962 the Master left Hong Kong and came to America, and in 1966 I moved to Africa. Time took its course and for more than a decade I didn't draw near the Master. Then in 1986 I moved to America. In 1988, the Master directed me to lecture on the *Vajra Sutra* at Gold Mountain Monastery. Prior to that, I had divided my time between Africa and America. I would come to the U.S. twice a year, staying two to three weeks each time. Every time I came I would go to Gold Mountain Monastery to pay my respects to the Master. One time I arrived while the Master was in the middle of a Sutra lecture, and the Master asked me to translate into Cantonese. Afterwards, the Master said, "Before you go back to Africa, you can come here and lecture for us." Since the amount of time I was to be in America was limited, all I could do was give some informal talks. The next time I came back, the Master suddenly told me to lecture on the *Vajra Sutra.* I thought to myself, "lecturing on a Sutra is a very serious matter. I can't just lecture for a while and then stop." After some careful consideration. I retired from the work I was doing in Africa and began to concentrate single-mindedly on learning how to lecture on the Sutras.

When I began lecturing on the *Vajra Sutra,* the Master told me, "It's not necessary to seek to be an excellent lecturer." He also said, "On the other hand, don't make your explanations too simple." When I was giving my lectures, the Master was often sitting outside the door of the hall listening. One time I asked him, "Teacher, this disciple doesn't know if he's made any mistakes in his lectures." The Master replied, "When you have savored the flavor of a Sutra's principles, then however you explain them will be right." I said, "Of course I think I'm right before I explain something, but I don't know if I am truly correct or if what I think is right is really phony." The Master answered, "Well, haven't you jumped over the hurdle?"

Those several instances of instruction from the Master have had a great influence on me. After many years of experience, what I have realized is that keeping our minds compassionate is the cultivation of blessings; not losing our temper, diminishing our attachment to self-image, and reading and investigation the Sutras is the cultivation of wisdom. Cultivating blessings and cultivating wisdom are the two essential topics in the study of Buddhism. Everything else is superfluous. In the *Two Nights Sutra* the Buddha said, "From the night I realized the Way to the night I passed into Nirvana, I always spoke Prajna. "Prajna means wonderful wisdom. The Buddha spoke the Dharma for forty-nine years and as we review the five periods and eight teachings and the three treasuries and twelve divisions, absolutely all of them are telling us about the Dharma-door of wisdom through which liberation is attained. All the different praises to the Buddhas and Bodhisattvas end with the same phrase: "maha prajna paramita"--using wisdom to reach the other shore. From this we can see how important wisdom is within Buddhism.

Buddhism is the teaching of enlightenment. The cultivation of blessings is done in order to nurture wisdom. That's because if our blessings are insufficient, then not only will we run into many obstacles in our own cultivation, but we will lack affinities with

要自覺覺他，而不是爲了求神通感應，或人天福報。我們一定要認清目標來兼修福慧，千萬不要本末倒置，自誤誤他。福慧具足圓滿時，才能圓成佛果。「眾生皆有佛性，皆堪作佛；但以妄想執著不能證得。」諸佛已經告訴我們學佛是爲了明自本心，見自本性；師父也已經把方法都教我們了，雖然各人的體會不盡相同，但以智慧來破除無明執著，藉修福來養慧，應該是一條人人可行的正確道路。語云：

師父領進門， 修行在個人。

如今師父的色身雖已不在，但他的精神與教化卻是永遠不會磨滅的。願大家在菩提道上一起勇猛精進，以不負恩師的教誨。

beings when we try to propagate the Dharma and benefit beings. And so the goal of practicing good deeds and accumulating blessings is only for the sake of enlightening ourselves and others; it is not in order to seek spiritual powers and responses or blessed rewards in the human realm or among gods. We should clearly recognize our aim in cultivating blessings and wisdom. We should definitely not confuse the fundamentals with the superficials, or else we will end up misleading ourselves and others. When blessings and wisdom are both perfected, then we can realize Buddhahood."All living beings have the Buddha nature; all can become Buddhas. It is only because of false thinking and attachments that they have not yet done so." All the Buddhas have told us that we study Buddhism in order to understand our own minds and see our own natures; the Venerable Master has taught us the method. Although each person's conception is not exactly the same, still, using wisdom to break through ignorance and attachments and cultivating blessings in order to nurture wisdom should be a proper path that everyone can travel. It's said: "The teacher leads us in the door; cultivation is up to each of us."

Although now the Master is not physically with us, his energy, his spirit and his teachings will never, ever disappear. I hope we can travel the path to Bodhi together with courageous vigor, never failing to uphold the instructions of our kind Master.

# 師恩浩蕩 德被十方
## THE GREAT KINDNESS OF THE VENERABLE MASTER AND HIS VIRTUE WHICH PERVADES THE TEN DIRECTIONS

釋果展 十二歲　Shramanera Gwo Jan, age 12

出家後，兩年半前，我和果維、果榮、果羅、果青第一次搬到長堤聖寺時，當時師父也在寺裡。他老人家幾乎每天都會下來看我們，有時叫我們背〈證道歌〉，有時對我們開示幾句話，有時教我們四十二手眼，並且常用手打我們的頭，消我們的業障，這段時間可以說是我和師父最親近的時候。

如今，雖然師父已經涅槃了，但他的法身卻無所不在，他的言行教化，深植在我們的心中。因此只要我們能時時刻刻記得師父的教示，效法他的行爲，遵守六大宗旨，以

凍死不攀緣， 餓死不化緣， 窮死不求緣。

的精神來學習佛法，如此才不辜負師父教導的一片苦心。

About two and a half years ago, after leaving home, Gwo Wei, Gwo Rong, Gwo Lwo, Gwo Ching and I first came to Long Beach Monastery. The Venerable Master was also living in the temple. At that time, almost every day, the Master would come down and check on us. Sometimes he would tell us to memorize the "Song of Enlightenment"; sometimes he would give a lecture, or teach us the Forty-two Hands and Eyes. He always smacked our heads with his hand to eradicate our karma. My closest relationship with him was during this period at Long Beach.

Now, although the Venerable Master has entered Nirvana, his Dharma body is still everywhere. His words and teaching are already planted deeply in our minds. I feel as if he is here. We should always remember the Venerable Master's teaching, follow his conduct, practice the Six Great Principles and, to learn the Buddhadharma, use the spirit of the Three Guidelines.

*Freezing, we do not scheme; starving we do not beg; dying of poverty, we ask for nothing.*

In this way we will not let the Venerable Master down.

# 給師父上人的一封信
## A LETTER TO THE VENERABLE MASTER

### 驚風雨、泣鬼神——憶上人十八大願
### Stirring Up Storms and Causing Ghosts and Spirits to Weep--
### In Memory of the Master's Eighteen Great Vows

王盈今　Yingjin Wang

師父上人慈鑑：

　　上人您雖然已經走了，可是在昨夜裏，您還在夢中保護我，不知您人在哪裏，似乎遙不可及，可是我在夢中呼喚您，您又呼之欲出。我知您身雖不在我們身邊，可是您的慈心，卻是時時刻刻，片刻不離。上人，您知道嗎？雖然我學了很久的音樂，讀過許多的古詩，可是我一直覺得，您說得話美得賽過一首首的歌，美得賽過一首首的詩，因爲您的話語，無一句不是出自心扉，至誠懇切，智慧深重，語帶機鋒，如此種種，無不是美過一首首的流行歌曲。杜甫的詩句中有句形容他的心志，他說：「筆落驚風雨，詩成泣鬼神。」上人，如此的神來之筆，比起您卻只是小兒科，因爲您筆不落風雨先驚，詩未成，鬼神已泣。諸如您的十八大願，願願驚天動地，而其中兩大願，即其十一願

　　　將我所應享受一切福樂，
　　　悉皆迴向，普施法界眾生。

及十二願

　　　將法界眾生所有一切苦難，
　　　悉皆予我一人代受。

每念及此二願，我皆暗自飲泣，眾生之苦何其苦，何其多！上人，您太苦了。我一想及此即起心動念，我縱然不能身代其苦，起碼也要分擔憂勞，但是您在何處？您的憂勞，我又何從分起？我只能常常以淚相待，淚眼汪汪望著觀世音菩薩，希望能報答您的恩情於萬一。

　　上人，除了父親之外，您是世界上唯一能感動我的人，只願上人師父在另一時空裏，一切安好。

　　　　　　　　　　　不肖弟子盈今頂禮

Dear Venerable Master:

Venerable Master, although you are gone, you were there to protect me in last night's dream. I don't know where you are, probably somewhere very far away, but when I called to you in my dream, you seemed to appear. I know that even though you are no longer physically with us, your compassionate heart is with us at all times. Venerable Master, do you know that even though I have studied music for many years and have read many poems written by classical authors, I find that your words surpass all other songs and poems in beauty? Because your words come straight from the heart and are full of sincerity, deep wisdom, and clever wit, they are more beautiful than all those popular songs. The poet Tu Fu once described his aspiration in a poem: "Where the brush falls, it stirs up a storm; when the poem is completed, it moves the ghosts and spirits to tears." Yet his divine poems are mere childsplay compared to yours, because your brush stirs up a storm even before it touches the paper, and the ghosts and spirits start weeping even before you have finished your poem. Every one of your eighteen great vows startles heaven and quakes the earth. Two of those vows are:

*Eleventh Vow:* I vow to dedicate all the blessings and bliss which I myself ought to receive and enjoy to all living beings of the Dharma Realm.

*Twelfth Vow:* I vow to fully take upon myself all sufferings and hardships of all living beings in the Dharma Realm.

Every time I read these two vows, I cry inside, thinking of manifold and immense sufferings of living beings.

Venerable Master, you suffer too much. Every time I think of it, I figure that even if I cannot physically take your suffering, at least I can lessen your burden a bit by sharing your worries. But how can I begin to share your worries? I can only use my tears. With tear-filled eyes I gaze at Guanshiyin Bodhisattva, hoping to be able to repay a tiny part of your kindness.

Venerable Master, aside from my father you are the only person in the world who can move me. I hope that, in whatever time and space system you are, everything is well.

Your unworthy disciple, Yingjin, bows in respect.

# 捨己爲人帶病度衆生
## SELF-SACRIFICE:
## SAVING LIVING BEINGS EVEN IN ILLNESS

爲了廣度衆生，
正在忍受極大極大的痛苦與折磨。

**The extreme agony and pain the Master was undergoing
for the sake of saving living beings.**

陳果財　Guo-cai Chen

一九九五年夏天，上人在洛杉磯養病期間，他仍然是不辭辛勞，特別爲弟子傳授〈四十二手眼〉。非常幸運有這個法緣，親自聆聽上人傳授〈四十二手眼〉。那個時候，我們都不很清楚師父上人的身體病況，但是我記得師父每次來上課，或在法會中，偶爾會用顫抖的手，很困難地舉杯飲水，也常常用毛巾擦臉上的汗水，但是我們都不知道，師父爲了廣度衆生，正在忍受極大極大的痛苦與折磨，就算是再大的困難，也不能阻攔師父上人振興佛教的大志。

有一次上課上人來晚了，到達以後，只是輕描淡寫地告訴大家，因爲傷風感冒，當天吃過中飯以後，嘔吐了很多次。上人爲了教化衆生，不顧自己的身體健康，依然不眠不休宣揚佛法，到處提倡教育，創立道場，吃盡了非常非常多的苦痛，也沒一點怨言。我聽一位晚期在師父身邊服侍的居士說，像師父這樣擁有這麼多的道場、這麼龐大組織的法總創辦人，連一張餐巾紙，都捨不得丟棄，一天就擦一個角落，一點一點地擦，擦到第八天，才不得已丟棄。這樣子地惜福，這樣子高尚的情操，眞是令人非常感動。師父說過的話，說得出，就做得到。師父說過

大慈悲普度，流血汗，不休息。

的確，上人這一生中，度化的衆生，何止千千萬萬，上人對每一位求見的人士，以及參加法會的每一位居士，都滿他們的願，給予加持，給予幫助。但是他自己在病勢最嚴重的時候，還對身旁的人說，他對自己是連一根指頭都不會用的；就是再大的苦，再大的責

When the Venerable Master was convalescing in Los Angeles in the summer of 1995, he continued to explain and transmit the Forty-two Hands and Eyes to disciples, disregarding the toll it took on him. We were extremely fortunate to have the Master personally teach us this Dharma. Although we were not very clear about the Master's health condition at the time, I remember how Master's hands trembled as he struggled to raise a glass of water to his lips and how he constantly wiped the sweat from his face. We didn't realize the extreme agony and pain the Master was undergoing for the sake of saving living beings. No difficulty, no matter how great, could deter his great resolve to cause Buddhism to flourish.

The Master once casually told everyone that he was late for class because he had vomited several times after lunch. He totally disregarded his own health when it came to teaching living beings. He never rested as he propagated the Dharma, promoted education, and established temples everywhere. He never uttered a word of complaint despite the tremendous suffering he endured.

The Master was able to live up to every word he spoke. He said,

With great compassion rescue all, sparing neither blood nor sweat, and never pause to rest.

And indeed, throughout his whole life, he taught limitless numbers of beings. He fulfilled the wishes and bestowed blessings and aid on every person who sought from him or took part in the Dharma sessions. Yet when his illness was at its most critical, he said to those beside him that he would not use a finger's strength to help himself. He was willing to bear and suffer any amount of pain.

One of the eighteen great vows the Master made was to

難，他都忍下來了，他都承受下來了。

上人有十八大願，其中之一，就是願代眾生受苦。上人就這樣默默地不讓我們知道，實踐他的大願，承擔了我們的罪業。這種聖潔無私、爲法忘軀的無我精神，也不知道感動了多少頑愚眾生。

我們有幸身爲上人的弟子，我們身受上人的恩惠，數也數不盡。甚至有一位開眼的居士，曾經說過，上人這樣高風亮節的德行，所到之處，路的兩旁都有龍天護法在跟師父頂禮，跟師父致敬。

我記得一九九四年十一月的時候，上人在長堤聖寺舉行剃度儀式和傳授三皈五戒。在法會結束之前，上人說了一段勉勵大家的話：

師父領進門，修行在個人，今天就是釋迦牟尼佛親自前來傳授佛法，如果我們不知道珍惜，不知道自己好好修行，也是沒有用的，望你們好自爲之！否則以後還有很多苦日子要過。

我是一個無明很重又愚癡的人，當時也不明白師父的意思，我一直以爲師父在百歲燃身供佛之前，我們還可以依賴著上人混日子。哪裏知道上人爲了度化眾生的大因緣，竟然捨壽乘願而去。

爲了報答師恩，我們應該在此互相勉勵，依著佛法，承續上人留下來給我們的無數無數的智慧法寶，勤修奉行，只要認眞修行，持戒精進，相信上人的法身也將與我們常在。

我願在此再引用上人的一句話，與大家共勉：

將軍不下馬，各自奔前程。

讓我們在成佛的道路上一起努力，奮力前進。師父在等著我們成佛，讓我們在佛的國土裏再相見。

take the sufferings of living beings upon himself. He silently practiced his vows, taking our offenses and karma upon himself without our knowing. His selfless spirit of forsaking himself for the Dharma touched the hearts of countless stubborn living beings.

Those of us who are fortunate enough to be the Master's disciples received immeasurable kindnesses from the Master. One layperson who has opened his spiritual eyes reported that due to the Master's lofty virtue, wherever he went there were Dharma-protecting gods and dragons lined up on both sides of the road making obeisance to him.

I remember that in November 1994, the Master held a Leaving Home Ceremony and transmitted the Three Refuges and Five Precepts at Long Beach Monastery. Before the ceremonies were over, the Master told everyone,

The teacher leads you in the door, but you yourselves must cultivate. If you don't cherish the teaching and cultivate well, then even if Shakyamuni Buddha personally transmitted the Dharma to you, it would be of no use. I hope you all will try your best! Otherwise, there will be a lot of hard times in store for you.

Being a very ignorant and dull-witted person, I didn't understand the Master's meaning. I thought I could take it easy and rely on the Master up to the Master's 100th birthday, when he would burn his body as an offering to the Buddha. I hardly expected that the Master would, for the sake of teaching living beings, renounce his life so soon and depart by the power of his vows.

In order to repay the Master's kindness, let us urge one another to respectfully study and diligently practice the innumerable Dharma treasures of wisdom the Master has given us. If we cultivate seriously and vigorously uphold the precepts, I believe that the Master's Dharma body will always be with us. Let me share one last sentence of the Master's with everyone:

The generals do not dismount, but hasten forth on their respective journeys.

Let's go forward together on the path to Buddhahood. The Master is waiting for us to become Buddhas. May we all meet again in the land of the Buddhas.

---

不可思議劫　精進修諸行　爲度諸眾生　此是大仙力
——《大方廣佛華嚴經》〈光明覺品第九〉

*Throughout inconceivable kalpas*
*Vigorously cultivate all practices*
*In order to cross over all living beings.*
*This is the Great Immortal's strength.*

Flower Adornment Sutra, Chapter Nine, Light Enlightenment

# 上人弘願——造活佛

## THE MASTER'S GREAT VOW--
## TO CREATE LIVING BUDDHAS

釋恒哲
Shi Heng Je

這一次代表團回到臺灣，很多人恭迎上人的舍利子，非常地悲痛，掉下傷心的眼淚。今天我們也因為這個因緣，聚集在這裏，本人不量力，想要在這短短的時間，表達我做弟子對上人的緬懷與追思。上人這一生，為了弘法利生，真地是不遺餘力，流血汗、不休息。他告訴我們：

> 這個世界上懂得佛法的人太少了，知道「非法」的人太少了，我們如果懂得佛法，就要去照著佛法做，我們若真地懂得佛法，我們就要做那些「不合法」的事情。

上人去西方之前，立下了宏願，要到西方，在世界上造活佛、造活祖師、活菩薩、活羅漢。我們也聽過上人說，就是聲聞、緣覺、菩薩，也不懂得他的境界。我想一位菩薩，絕對沒有辦法令別人成為一個活佛的。所以我們今天聚集在一起，不管親近上人已經很久的，或者今天因仰慕上人德行來到的，我們都不要難過。只要發心修行，只要發心深入經藏，只要發心改變習氣毛病，師父永遠都不會離開我們的。每一個人的心，上人悉知悉見。只要你發了願，要成一個聖賢，你就必然成為聖賢。如果今天哪一個人的心裏頭，還在那裡滋長自己的五欲，不讓自己的無明減少，我們就是不認識善知識。

上人一生辛苦辦教育，興建道場，弘揚佛法，就是為了幫助我們走上了生脫死、成佛的道路，他為法忘軀。我們有幸成為上人座下的佛弟子，每一個人都要記得，上人所告訴我們的，每個人都有走的時候，我們要發心用功，就和他在一樣。

一九六二年上人到西方弘揚佛法的這個種子，今天都已經在萌芽、結果。佛法要興，要靠我們每一個人把佛法用在日常生活，要靠我們每一個人在自己的身

During this delegation's visit to Taiwan, many people were extremely sad and tearful as they respectfully welcomed the Venerable Master's sharira. As we are gathered here today under these circumstances, I would like to very briefly express my own feelings in remembrance of the Master.

The Venerable Master gave his entire life to propagating the Dharma for the sake of living beings, not sparing blood or sweat and never pausing to rest. He told us,

> In this world, there are too few who understand the Buddhadharma and too few who understand "non-Dharma." If we truly understand the Buddhadharma, then we should not act in a worldly way.

Before he went to the West, the Master made great vows to go the West and to create living Buddhas, living Patriarchs, living Bodhisattvas, and living Arhats. We have heard the Master say that even Hearers, Pratyekabuddhas, and Bodhisattvas cannot comprehend his realm of being. And I think it would be impossible for a mere Bodhisattva to make a living Buddha out of someone.

Therefore, whether we have drawn near the Master for a long time or have only heard of and admired the Master's virtue, we should not be sad. As long as we resolve to cultivate the Way, to deeply enter the Sutra treasury, and to change our faults, we will never be apart from the Master. The Master completely knows every person's heart. If you vow to become a sage, you will certainly achieve your vow. But if you indulge in the five desires and cannot decrease your ignorance, then you still haven't recognized a wise teacher.

The Master labored all his life to promote education, establish temples, and propagate Buddhism, all because he wanted to lead us onto the path to ending birth and death and becoming Buddhas. He renounced himself for the sake of the Dharma. Each of us who is fortunate enough to be the Master's disciple should remember what the Master told us: Everyone must go some day; if we are resolved in our practice, then it will be as if he is still here.

The seeds of Buddhism that the Master planted in the West

上轉法輪。我們現在如果還有脾氣，還有煩惱，還有很多很多要追求的事情，就是我們不明白佛法，就是我們不能夠依教奉行。我自己跟著上人，從上人身上看到一切一切的境界都是考驗，都是虛妄不實的，都是在考驗我們每一個佛弟子，有沒有「依教奉行」？是不是做如法的事情？只要有一絲絲善惡夾雜的心，我們得到的果就是不真。

師父上人走到哪裏，都是說真法，都是說成佛的法，都是希望出家人依照佛制。所以不願意依照佛制修行的人，看他都是非常不順眼的。今天我們聚在這裏，很多人排除了工作的忙碌、家庭的忙碌到這裏，但也有很多人不願意來。只要我們把上人的教誨，把上人的精神，牢牢記得放在心裏頭，我們就能得到好處。不願意依照正法來做的，就是在苦海裏頭沉淪了。

我希望我們都能好好恭聆上人留下來的法音，因為現在不能親自親近上人，我們就靠聆聽這些法音。上人每一次講法，心懷太虛的胸懷，希望大家都能明白佛法的慈悲心。希望每一個人都好好照著上人的法來修行，雖然今天上人的色身不在，可是我們永遠都跟上人在一起。虛空是無所不在，無論你今天在這個體育館裏，或者在家裏，在公司，在擁擠的馬路上，上人永遠都跟你在一起。上人跟你在一起，他用慈眼看著你，是不是依照不爭、不貪、不求、不自私、不自利、不打妄語來做事。他告訴我們：「一切的境界都是假的！」看我們的心是不是佛的心？還是魔鬼的心？還是餓鬼的心？

in 1962 have already sprouted and borne fruit. The flourishing of Buddhism depends on each and every one of us. We must integrate the Dharma into our daily lives and turn the Dharma wheel in our own selves.

If we still have a bad temper, afflictions, and many desires, then we don't understand the Buddhadharma and we cannot practice it. From following the Master, I have learned that everything is an illusory state, a test to see if we are able to practice the teachings and conduct ourselves properly. If we have the tiniest bit of evil within the good that we do, then the outcome will not be true.

Wherever he went, the Master spoke the true Dharma--the Dharma for becoming a Buddha, in the hope that left-home people would follow the Buddha's rules. Those who didn't follow the Buddha's rules found this completely unacceptable. Many people have made time in their busy schedules at work and at home to come here today; but there are also many people who did not come. If we can remember the Master's teachings and the spirit he conveyed, we will benefit by it. Those who cannot accept the Proper Dharma can only flounder in the sea of suffering.

I hope everyone will listen well to the sounds of the Master's Dharma. We must listen to his Dharma sounds on tape since we can no longer hear him in person. The Master's every lecture is so all-encompassing in spirit; he hoped everyone would understand the ideal of compassion in Buddhism. I hope each of us will earnestly practice the Dharma that the Master introduced to us. Even though his body is gone, the Master is always with us, for empty space is everywhere. Whether you are in this auditorium, in your home, at your office, or on the crowded street, the Master is always with you, watching you with kindly eyes to see if you are fighting, greedy, seeking, selfish, wanting to benefit yourself, or lying. He has told us that all states are false. It all depends on whether we have the mind of a Buddha, a demon, or a hungry ghost.

---

導師降眾魔　勇健無能勝　光中演妙義　慈悲故如是
——《大方廣佛華嚴經》〈光明覺品第九〉

*The Guiding Master subdues the multitudes of demons,*
*He is courageous, strong, and invincible.*
*Within the light he proclaims the wonderful meaning.*
*He is this way because of his kindness and compassion.*

Flower Adornment Sutra, Chapter Nine, Light Enlightenment

# 迷途知返猶未晚

## IF YOU KNOW TO TURN BACK FROM CONFUSION, IT'S NOT TOO LATE

念阿彌陀佛聖號的時候，我的淚一直流個不停。
我在想，我就是一個迷途的孩子，惹得這麼髒，背覺合塵。

**I kept crying as I recited Amitabha Buddha's holy name.
I thought, I'm just a lost child who has gotten himself into a mess,
turning his back on enlightenment to join with the dust.**

劉果福　Guofu Liu

本人能夠在這一生遇到師父，是我很大的榮幸，也是在我這一生中得到最大的寶貝。

遇到師父的時候，師父講了一句話，可以說好像給了我一粒石頭。我好像是蚌，他就放了一粒石頭在裏面，給我去磨，好在我還會去磨，今天還可以跟大家見面，學習佛法。

他給我什麼石頭呢？皈依之後，有人叫我去見上人，我說：「我沒有東西問。」「你可以叫上人加持呀！」所以就寫了名字，上三樓，見了師父就說：「請師父加持！」師父在我頭上打了三下，說：「業障很重！」

這一句話呢，我一下樓，就很不服氣，我又沒有殺人放火，怎麼師父說我業障很重呢？就很不服氣，可是又不知道這是我吃喝玩樂所造的業，今天想起來非常可怕。

後來，一九八八年去美國旅行，跟太太一起去。順道就去聖城。到了城門，不太想要進去，又覺得到了城門又不可能不進去，就逼著自己進去了；因為如果我走的話，太太沒機會見上人，所以就一起進去。

進去之後，在禮佛時，以前所做的惡事，那些愚癡的事情，一直在我腦子裏不停地現出來，沒有一分鐘停止。我在這種無法控制的情況下，就想到：「咦！我今天是來參加萬佛寶懺的，就順便懺悔啊！」我就跟佛菩薩懺悔，還是不行，那沒辦法了，就拿出一本小簿子，寫我過去的惡習，第一我要改這個這個……，第二就是說回去之後好好地做人……。寫完了，心

Meeting the Venerable Master has been the greatest honor of my life. It's also the greatest treasure I have gained.

When I met the Master, he said one sentence that acted like a tiny piece of stone put inside an oyster's shell. I was the oyster, and he put that tiny piece of stone inside for me to polish. Fortunately I was able to polish it, and so now I am able to see all of you and study Buddhism with you.

What stone did he give me to polish? After I took refuge, someone suggested that I meet the Master. I replied that I didn't have any questions to ask. "You can ask the Master for a blessing," he said. So I signed up and went up to the third floor to see the Master. When I asked for a blessing, the Master hit me on the head three times and said, "What heavy karmic obstacles!" As I went downstairs, I thought, "I haven't committed murder or arson, why did the Master say my karmic obstacles are heavy?" I was totally unaware of the karma I was creating by indulging in a life of eating, drinking, and partying. It's truly frightening when I think of it now.

In 1988 my wife and I travelled to the United States and stopped by the City of Ten Thousand Buddhas. When we reached the front gate of the City, I didn't feel like entering, but since I had already gotten that far, I forced myself to go in. Also, my wife would have missed seeing the Master if I didn't go in, so we went in together.

When we were bowing to the Buddhas, all the bad and stupid things I had done in the past kept surfacing in my mind, and there was no way I could stop them. In that instant, I thought, "Since I've come for the Jewelled Repentance of Ten Thousand Buddhas, I might as well repent of them all!" However, even though I repented before the Buddhas and Bodhisattvas, it still didn't work. Finally, I took out a small pad and wrote a list of my bad habits: "First, I must change this and that... Second, I must go home and become a good

平靜了。

去聖城之前，我還帶了八個問題去，沒有機會問。很奇怪的，就在聽經或看書的時候，那八個問題統統都有答案了，也不用問了，我都很滿意。

之後，念阿彌陀佛聖號的時候，我的淚一直流個不停。我在想，我就是一個迷途的孩子，惹得這麼髒，背覺合塵。阿彌陀佛就好像我的父親，在那邊歡迎著我，叫我去，可是這個孩子走錯路了，把身體也弄得很髒了，感覺到一直遠離自己的父親，就開始哭了起來。

由於萬佛聖城給我很大的好處，我從來沒有這樣清淨的心，所以我每一年都要到聖城一次。我又想，在這個社會上，你欺我詐，爭名奪利，你貪我貪這麼樣，就決定把生意統統放下，於是就求師父，禮拜師父跟觀世音菩薩，滿我的願，能夠去聖城。終於在一九九四年，我們全家去聖城當義工，直到現在。

我覺得師父相片兩旁所寫的那兩行字，是非常真實不虛的：

慈悲普度信者得救成正覺，
過化存神禮之獲福悟無生。

雖然我是那麼地污穢，那麼地骯髒，師父都能不嫌棄我，還會來度我，這是很慈悲的一種做法。那麼信者得救，為什麼我能得救呢？為什麼我從迷途能走向上呢？也是因為我相信他，所以才能得救。成正覺；就還沒有成正覺，不過每一個眾生都有佛性，都能夠成佛。

過化存神，師父無所不在，都在度眾生。禮之獲福，我得到滿願，也就是因為禮拜師父，得到的果報。悟無生，能夠了生死，我覺得我這個人過去我慢心很大，因果也不怕；自從明白了因果，我覺得這個要很注意，尤其是這個我慢。我覺得在我一生中，其他的都是小聰明，也沒有什麼東西值得了不起的，除非能夠了這個生死。

希望大家能夠一起跟著師父的法，讓我們一起終生奉行，諸惡莫作。

person..." By the time I finished, my mind had settled down.

I had prepared eight questions before coming to the City, but strangely enough, even though I didn't have a chance to ask them, the answers came either when I was listening to the Sutra lectures or when I was reading, and they fully satisfied me.

Later, I kept crying as I recited Amitabha Buddha's holy name. I thought, I'm just a lost child who has gotten himself into a mess, turning his back on enlightenment to join with the dust. Amitabha Buddha is like my father, welcoming me with open arms, but I got lost and now I'm all filthy. The realization that I'd been away from my father for a long time made me cry.

Because I had never experienced such purity of mind as I did at the City of Ten Thousand Buddhas, I began visiting the City every year. Seeing the greed, fraudulence, and struggle for fame and profit in our society, I wanted to give up my business and move to the City. I prayed to the Master and to Guanyin Bodhisattva to grant me this wish. In 1994, my whole family moved to the City, where we have lived and worked as volunteers up to today.

I feel that the couplet written below the Master's picture is totally true:

*His kindness and compassion cross over all;*
*Believers are liberated and perfect the Right*
*    Enlightenment.*
*Transforming beings wherever he goes,*
*    his spirit remains intact;*
*Those who venerate him obtain blessings and*
*    awaken to the Unproduced.*

Even though I am so defiled and messed up, the Master still wants to save me; he is very compassionate and hasn't given up on me. I have been saved and I have been able to turn back from confusion because I believe in him. Although we haven't attained Right Enlightenment yet, all living beings have the Buddha nature and can become Buddhas.

The Master is present everywhere, crossing over living beings. My wish was granted as a result of paying homage to the Master. To awaken to the Unproduced means to end birth and death. I used to be very conceited and unafraid of cause and effect. Now that I understand the law of cause and effect, however, I think we must be very careful, especially about becoming conceited. I feel the only important thing in this life is to end birth and death; anything else would be just a product of petty cleverness, nothing special.

I hope we can all follow the Master's teachings and refrain from all evil for our whole lives.

# 名利場中　急流勇退

## BRAVELY GIVING UP THE RAT RACE

師父爲了讓我遠離名和利，
所以才把我留下來掃地。

**The Master had asked to me stay and sweep leaves
because he wanted me to distance myself from
the pursuit of fame and profit.**

陳淑滿
Shu-man Chen

我很榮幸能隨萬佛城的追思團來香港，參加師父上人的追思法會，今天我想說一說，我住在萬佛城的一點感應。

在兩年多以前的一個秋天，我到萬佛城時，師父對我很慈悲。他有一天就問我說：「妳幾時要回臺灣哪？」我就告訴師父。師父說：「怎麼不多住幾天呢？」當時我覺得非常奇怪，師父怎麼會留我？但是後來我想一想，我還是聽師父的話，就住下來了。

剛剛住在萬佛城的時候，我不知道要做些什麼事情，所以每天就在萬佛城裡的馬路上掃掃樹葉，而且掃得非常歡喜，我也不知道爲什麼掃地的時候會這麼高興。有一天我正在掃地，師父的三哥，我們在萬佛城都叫他三爺的，他今年九十二歲，也住在萬佛城裏，他走過來就跟我說：

'師父說，
把你留下來掃地，
不讓妳回臺灣。

喔！我才恍然大悟，師父原來把我留下來掃地的！後來我在萬佛城的萬佛殿前面看到一首掃地的歌，就是師父作的，他說：

掃地掃地掃心地

是說要掃除我們心裏骯髒污濁的心，當時我才明白，哦！我們生活在這五濁惡世裏面，是被這個五慾財、名、利、食、睡弄的顛顛倒倒的，師父爲了讓我遠離名和利，所以才把我留下來掃地。今天，我利用這個機會，表示一下感謝師父給我的教誨。

I feel very honored to come to Hong Kong to participate in the Venerable Master's Memorial Ceremony with the delegation from the City of Ten Thousand Buddhas. Today I would like to share some of my feelings about the City with everyone.

When I went to the City in the fall over two years ago, the Master was very kind to me. One day he asked me when I was returning to Taiwan. When I told him, he said, "Why don't you stay a little longer?" I thought it strange that the Master would want me to stay, but after some consideration, I decided to listen to his advice and stay at the City.

When I first started living at the City, I didn't know what work to do, so I swept the leaves on the streets of the City. I don't know why, but sweeping leaves made me feel extremely happy. One day as I was sweeping, the Master's third eldest brother, who is ninety-two this year, walked over and said,

The Master says we should keep you here to sweep leaves and not let you return to Taiwan.

"Oh," I thought, "so that's why the Master wanted me to stay--to help sweep leaves."

Later I saw in front of the Buddha hall a "Sweeping Song" composed by the Master. It goes,

Sweep, sweep, sweep the mind ground

Telling us to sweep the filth and defilement from our minds. It suddenly dawned on me that we live in this evil world of five turbidities, deluded by the desires for wealth, form, fame, food, and sleep. The Master had asked to me stay and sweep leaves because he wanted me to distance myself from the pursuit of fame and profit. Today I just wanted to take the opportunity to express my gratitude to the Master for what he taught me.

# 在生活中實現佛法
## APPLYING THE BUDDHADHARMA IN DAILY LIFE

師父最重視的，就是在一個人的本份上，
我們應該怎麼樣刻苦自待，
怎麼樣忘掉自己，怎麼樣去利益旁人。

**What the Master emphasized most was that
we should be able to take suffering and
forget about ourselves in order to help others.**

釋恒是
Shi Heng Shi

我個人在道場的時間非常地短淺，雖然有這個因緣，可以在上人座下出家學習，但是個人在學習方面，沒有什麼用心。今天我想談幾椿很平常的事情，從上人非常耐心教導我們弟子的身上，來體會上人的教化。

記得有一次，弟子請問上人說：「師父！弟子實在很想向上人懺悔，但是弟子知道不能跟上人求懺悔，為什麼呢？因為弟子覺得，如果一個人真心要改過的時候，他懺悔，他就不會再犯第二次，這才有資格來請求懺悔，但是如果弟子覺得，不能夠不再重複犯第二次的錯誤的話，那麼就沒有這個資格來請求上人懺悔，所以弟子雖然想懺悔，但覺得沒資格懺悔。」講完這些話，上人就默默地聽，然後就說了一句話：

都怪我沒有把你教好！

所以當時心裏覺得非常非常地慚愧。

上人教化弟子可以說是非常非常有耐心，每一次上人都是風塵僕僕地奔波於各個道場，他對於每一個弟子都是一樣地關心。常常在晚上聽經的時候，在妙語堂上人每一次一定比大眾早到，可是大家一定沒有想到，上人不是先坐在自己的法座上，那上人在什麼地方呢？上人站在妙語堂的門口。冬天在萬佛聖城是非常非常地寒冷，夏天的太陽是非常非常地炎熱，上人都是站在門口，等著我們大眾念佛到妙語堂，上人就站在妙語堂門口的地方，一個一個看著我們進去。那聽完經的時候怎麼樣呢？上人比我們早出來，早出來做什麼？還是一樣站在門口，一個一個看著我們，送著我們大眾一個一個都離開了。最後也不曉得上人要站到多久他才離開。我們每

Although I have had the opportunity to leave the home-life and study under the Venerable Master, I have been in the temple for only a short time and have not studied very well. Today I would like to discuss a few very common-place incidents which illustrate the patience with which the Venerable Master taught his disciples.

I remember once saying to the Venerable Master, "Teacher, I really wish to repent to you, but I know that I cannot. Why? I feel that a person is qualified to repent only if he sincerely wants to change and will not repeat his offense after repenting. If I know that I can't refrain from repeating my mistake, then I'm not qualified to seek repentance. So, although I wish to repent, I don't feel I deserve to."

The Master listened quietly, and then said,

It's my fault that I didn't teach you well.

His words made me feel terribly ashamed and remorseful. The Master taught his disciples with tremendous patience. He constantly travelled from temple to temple, caring for every disciple with equal concern. In the evenings when we had Sutra lectures at Wonderful Words Hall, the Master always arrived before the assembly did. But instead of taking his seat at the front of the hall, what did he do? He stood by the door.

Whether it was freezing winter or blazing hot summer, he stood looking at each of us as we filed into Wonderful Words Hall reciting the Buddha's name. After the lecture, the Master would leave the hall before the assembly, and again, he would stand by the door, watching us as we walked out one by one, as if to send us off. No one knows how long the Master continued to stand there after we had all gone, for he was the last to leave.

一次排隊要去聽經的時候，心裏面都非常地期盼著，可是也非常地惶恐，又很想見到上人，又很怕見到上人，為什麼有這樣子的矛盾呢？想見上人的想法，就是好像見到自己的父親那樣，雖然不能夠天天見面，可是知道晚上聽經的時候只要上人在，上人一定陪大家一起聽經的。那很怕見到上人，就覺得自己也沒有好好地盡自己的本份，也沒有教自己，所以覺得沒有顏面可以對上人。這是我們一般上人的弟子大家心裏面的矛盾。

上人除了苦心教我們之外，他常常希望我們學習聖賢人，上人很歡喜讚歎的就是顏回，他常常說：

你們知道嗎？顏回，顏子他真是一位聖人中的賢德的人，為什麼呢？因為他從來不犯第二次的錯誤。那大禹他是個聖德的人，因為他聽到人家做善，他就禮拜。子路他也是一個有德行的人，他聽到人家說他的過錯，他就非常的歡喜。

所以常常上人最歡喜我們去學習的，就是改自己，改變自己，改惡向善，做什麼事情，都要用我們的誠心，要很認真。

說到認真，想到上人在做沙彌的時候，可能很多人知道這故事，也許很多人不知道，但是知道也好，不知道也好，我們最重要的是要學習上人的風範，怎麼樣在日常生活當中勉勵自己去學習。上人在做沙彌時，每天在東北這麼嚴寒的氣候，冬天很冷，大雪天的，上人很早就起身，大眾都還沒有起身，都還沒有打板，他已經起來了。他起來之後做什麼，他不是自己起來趕快做自己的功課，自己用功。他起來之後，趕快把大眾要上殿的那個路上，把那個雪鏟乾淨，方便大眾上殿的時候不會滑倒，那冬天那個毛坑大便小便都要掏。有一次，他就跟弟子們說：

我相信，你們今天一定不敢吃這一頓飯，為什麼呢？因為這一頓飯是我今天用手煮的。那你們知道我這雙手，今天做了什麼事情嗎？我用我的手去洗了三十間的馬桶廁所，所以我相信你們一定不敢吃這個飯，因為洗了廁所的這個手，髒髒的，臭臭的，去煮出來這個飯，我相信你們一定覺得不要吃。

從這些點點滴滴，上人所教導我們的是人格自然偉大，不是談玄說妙。師父最重視的，就是在一個人的本份上，我們應該怎麼樣刻苦自待，怎麼樣忘掉自己，怎麼樣去利益旁人，可以說是真正的佛教精神，慈悲喜捨。所以我們學很高深的佛法，很高深的理論，不如從我們的

Every time we lined up to go to hear the Sutra lecture, we were both extremely anxious and extremely afraid to see the Master. Why did we have such contradictory feelings? We hoped to see the Master because it was just like seeing our own father. Even though we couldn't see him every day, we knew that if he was in the City, he would join the assembly for the evening lecture.

On the other hand, we were afraid because we knew we hadn't done a good job of cultivating and teaching ourselves, and so we felt couldn't face the Master. This was the contradiction that arose in the hearts of many of the Master's disciples.

In addition to remonstrating sincerely with us, the Master often encouraged us to emulate the sages and worthy ones. He especially praised Yan Hui, saying,

Yan Hui was a worthy and virtuous sage, because he never made the same mistake twice. The Great Yu was also a virtuous sage, for he would make obeisance whenever he heard about a person's good deeds. Zi Lu was also a virtuous man, for he rejoiced when others pointed out his faults to him.

The Master wanted us to learn to change ourselves, to transform our evil into goodness, and to be sincere and diligent in everything we do.

Speaking of diligence, I thought of a story concerning the Master when he was a novice monk. Many of you may know this story, but it doesn't hurt listen to the Master's exemplary deeds again; it will encourage us to imitate him in our daily lives.

When the Master was a novice monk in Manchuria, in the bitterly cold winters when it snowed, he would get up long before anyone else, before the morning boards were hit. He didn't get up so early so he could do his own practice, but to clear the snow from the walkways so everyone would be able to walk safely to the Buddha hall without slipping. He also cleaned the filth from the pit toilets. One day he said to his disciples,

If you knew what I did with my hands today, I bet none of you would dare to eat the food I cooked today. I got my hands all messy and stinky scrubbing thirty toilets, and then I cooked this meal. I bet nobody dares to eat it.

From these small incidents, we can see that the Master taught us that having a noble character was more important than being able to discuss lofty theories. What the Master emphasized most was that we should be able to take suffering and forget about ourselves in order to help others. This is the true Buddhist spirit of kindness, compassion, joy, and equanimity.

We may study the most profound doctrines, but it would

生活當中去真正的體會，去實踐一點一滴，這個才是真正的勉勵自己依教奉行。

這是很多年來，我想要提供給大家一點點的經驗，希望我們可以從上人日常生活當中所教導我們的，一個字也好，一句話也好，我們勉勵自己去實行。

be better to truly understand and practice even a little bit of it in our own lives. Then we are truly putting the teaching into practice.

This is the little bit of personal experience gained through the years that I would like to share with everyone. I hope that we can all urge ourselves to apply even just a single word or sentence of what the Venerable Master taught us in daily life.

# 修行要忍耐
# WE HAVE TO BE PATIENT WHILE WE ARE CULTIVATING

釋果定 十一歲
Shramanera Gwo Ding, age 11

我們修行一定要忍耐，
如果不能忍，遇到魔障就無路可走了。
師父宣公上人曾經說過：
修行的時候要忍耐，

忍耐，多多忍耐，
不怕痛，娑婆訶。

師父說這一句話就是希望我們修行的時候要忍耐，
不然，遇到魔障來考我們的時候，
我們就會忍不住而還俗，有時候甚至於自殺。

總之，修行一定要忍，忍是修行人不可缺少的大助手。

When we are cultivating we have to be patient. If we cannot be patient, we will have nowhere to go when we meet the demons. Our Teacher, Venerable Master Hsuan Hua, has said that when we are cultivating we have to be patient. He gave a "mantra":

Patience, patience, got to have patience, don't get angry, Swo Pe He.

The reason our Master said this mantra is that he hoped we would have patience when cultivating and when facing demons. Otherwise we will fail the test and maybe return to lay-life, or perhaps even commit suicide.

Remember: we have to be patient. Patience is a cultivator's great helper.

# 無限感恩與追思

## IN BOUNDLESS GRATITUDE AND REMEMBRANCE

林果信　Guoxin Lin

上人涅槃近週年了，身為弟子，覺得如同孤兒似地，在過去的日子裡，每當憶起上人德相，眼淚不禁奪眶而出。嘆眾生福薄，菩薩示現人間如此短暫，娑婆世界眾生失導航明燈。

《金剛經》云：「凡所有相，皆是虛妄，若見諸相非相，即見如來。」故我們修行千萬不可執著於相，色身總是會壞的。最重要的是，學上人崇高之精神及生前所留下來的法寶，取之不盡，用之不絕，這都是真正的法。

雖然上人色身不在，但法身、精神依然還在。上人曾說：

> 如果你們不精進用功修行，
> 就算釋迦牟尼佛在你身邊，也救不了你。

的確如此，所以我們四眾弟子，應牢記在心，化悲痛為力量，遵守上人一生堅守之六大宗旨「不爭、不貪、不求、不自私、不自利、不打妄語」，時時迴光返照，我們是否依教奉行呢？還是每天唸歸唸，聽歸聽，行歸行呢？

上人一生崇高之德行，偉大之精神，慈悲教化眾生，又在末法時期，出現於世，如亂世中之清流，為佛教立下千秋大業，流芳萬古。

上人講經說法，自性流露，上人可以一日不吃飯，但不可一日不說法，只要有一口氣在，就要說法，就要講真話，做真事，使愚癡顛倒的眾生，開啟大智慧，走向未來成佛之大道。末學今能踏入佛門，也是從上人開示中，而親近三寶。

上人悲憫法界眾生，發十八大願，就算善根如頭髮那麼細的人，也都得滿願。

上人更是個大醫王，代一切眾生受苦受難，治好無法計數，眾生疑難怪病，使其離苦得樂。弟子深感懺悔，把百病悉給上人，而自己得樂，常感自己太自私了。

The first anniversary of the Venerable Master's Nirvana is almost here. This disciple feels like an orphan. Every time the Master's visage appears in my mind's eye, I can't stop my tears from falling. Alas, how paltry our blessings are, that a Bodhisattva appeared for so short a time in the world. The living beings of the Saha world have lost their teacher, who served as a guiding ferry and a bright lamp in the darkness.

The *Vajra Sutra* says, "All appearances are false. If one sees appearances as nonappearances, one sees the Thus Come One." In cultivation care should be taken not to become attached to appearances. The physical body is subject to decay. The crucial thing is to emulate the Master's noble spirit and to study the Dharma treasures the Master left for us. They are endless for the taking and inexhaustible in their use; these are the true Dharma. The Master's physical body may be gone, but his Dharma body and his spirit remain. The Master once said,

> If you fail to cultivate vigorously, even if Shakyamuni Buddha were beside you, he wouldn't be able to save you.

It's really true. Therefore, we disciples of the fourfold assembly should clearly remember this, transform our grief into strength, and follow the Six Guiding Principles that the Master upheld throughout his life: no fighting, no greed, no seeking, no selfishness, no pursuit of personal advantage, and no lying. At all times we should reflect: "Have we put the teachings into practice? Or is what we recite and listen to one thing, and what we do another?"

With the Venerable Master's lifelong virtuous conduct, his noble spirit, and his compassionate teaching of living beings, he appeared in the Dharma-ending Age like a clear stream in the turbid world, and his contributions to Buddhism will endure for countless generations. When the Master expounded the Sutras and spoke the Dharma, it came straight from his inherent nature. He could skip eating for a day, but he would not miss a day of speaking Dharma. As long as he had a single breath in his body, he would explain the Dharma, speak the truth, and do true deeds to bring forth wisdom in foolish and deluded beings and lead them on the path to Buddhahood. I myself became a Buddhist as a result of reading the Master's Dharma talks.

Out of pity for the living beings of the Dharma Realm, the Master made eighteen great vows. By virtue of these vows, even people with only a hairsbreadth of good roots can have their wishes fulfilled. The Venerable Master is the greatest of doctors; he took the suffering and hardships of all living beings upon

師恩浩瀚永難報，弟子虧欠師父太多，太多了，上人過去最喜歡看到弟子用功修行，我若不用功修行，怎能對得起上人呢？

上人一生精持戒律，修苦行，致力弘法，辦義務教育，翻譯經典，無私無我，改造無數眾生，今後四眾弟子，更應以懺悔感恩之心，同心協力，各盡職責，來完成上人生前未完成之大業。發揚上人的慈悲教化，以身作則，以「流血汗、不休息」之精神，流傳下去，這才是師父的真弟子，弟子真誠相信上人定會早日乘願再來。

himself and healed countless strange illnesses, allowing beings to leave suffering and attain bliss. I feel very ashamed and selfish, for I gave all my sicknesses to the Master and enjoyed happiness myself. The Master's kindness is so immense and difficult to repay, and I fear my debt is entirely too great. In the past, the Master was always most pleased to see his disciples cultivating diligently. If I don't cultivate well now, how will I ever face him?

Throughout his life, the Master strictly kept the precepts and practiced austerities. He devoted his energy to propagating the Dharma, promoting free education and volunteer teaching, and translating the scriptures. With total selflessness, he transformed the lives of innumerable people. We, his disciples, should, in repentance and gratitude, work together to carry on the great work that the Master began. We should spread the Master's compassionate teachings by serving as personal examples, perpetuating the spirit of "sparing neither blood nor sweat and never pausing to rest." Then we will be the Master's true disciples. I sincerely believe that the Master will soon return on the power of his vows.

# 懷念宣公上人頌
# IN PRAISE OF THE VENERABLE MASTER

釋果豪　十五歲
Shramanera Gwo Hao, age 15

宣揚大乘化眾生，
*Proclaiming the Mahayana, he crosses over all.*

開啓華嚴之玄門，
*Opening the door of the Flower Adornment and*

揭示楞嚴之奧密，
*revealing the secrets of the Shurangama, he teaches all.*

教化一切諸群萌。
*Transmitting the sacred hands of Gwan Yin, he rescues all.*

親傳四十二手眼。
*Day and night he's always busy teaching and transforming living beings.*

廣度一切諸眾生，
*Observing the sounds of the world he listens to*

夙夜匪懈化有情，
*the cries of suffering and those in need of help.*

尋聲救苦娑婆世，
*Out of great kindness and compassion he sails the prajna boat,*

慈悲普渡到彼岸。
*taking living beings aboard and crossing them over to the other shore.*

爲法忘軀化群倫，
*Forgetting his own self, he benefits living beings in whichever way he can.*

代眾受苦不疲厭。
*Even when his body is ill and frail, he never gives up.*

一息尚存猶説法，
*As long as he has a breath of air he will speak the Dharma.*

法輪常轉濟含識，
*As long as he has a bit of energy he will lend a hand to help those who need it.*

利益眾生不爲己，
*Everything that he does is not for himself but for others.*

流血流汗不休息。
*Sparing neither blood nor sweat he never stops to rest.*

# 冥護眾生的上人

## THE VENERABLE MASTER, WHO INVISIBLY PROTECTS LIVING BEINGS

張果祺
Guoqi Zhang

一九八一年，師父上人返臺於臺北濟南路民眾服務處弘法，我有幸參加此盛會，第一次恭聞上人開示。上人講法淺顯易懂，生動活潑，給我印象深刻，尤其對於誦持〈楞嚴咒〉之開示，令我五體投地。此外，法會中尚有一特色是在臺灣從沒見到的，就是上人開示完，又叫隨從出家弟子輪流向大眾講法。後來才知道這是上人用心良苦，為了培育弘法僧寶，不惜以一代祖師之尊，向出家弟子下跪造就出來的！在此次法會結束前，我也隨眾皈依上人。

慚愧的是：我當時並沒有依照上人之教誨修行，直到一九九四年隨果昌師兄到臺北法界佛教印經會，見到上人法相，頂禮時，不知不覺流下眼淚，感覺像離家出走很久的小孩，回到家裡見到父母親一樣，那時似乎聽到上人慈悲地說：「回來就好了！」自此以後，我開始參加法界佛教印經會每星期日的共修，也閱讀師父上人之佛經淺釋及開示錄等，慢慢地瞭解到上人之大慈、大悲、大智、大願及大行。由於上人之德行及法師們身教之薰習，我不久即斷葷茹素。正當慶幸遇到明眼善知識，誰知福薄一九九五年六月七日上人圓寂，開始心裡很難過也很徬徨，好像大海中之船失去導航，幸而在法師們的教導下，瞭解「依法不依人」，上人之色身雖不在，其留傳下來之正法仍在，更何況上人之法身遍法界無所不在。為了感謝上人對我們的大恩大德，代我們受苦，將福給我們，尤其教導我們了生脫死之正法。

在上人圓寂後，我到法界參加義工及共修的時間增加，也曾至美國萬佛聖城參加上人荼毗大典，及在臺灣舉行追思法會擔任義工。表面上我似乎付出不少心力、時間及金錢，卻學到許多，而這些不是世間錢財所能購得。在這一年裡，《華嚴經》八十一卷我雖尚未全部誦到，卻愈誦愈法喜；〈楞嚴咒

In 1981 I had the fortune of hearing the Venerable Master's instructional talk for the first time when he lectured at the Public Welfare Center in Taipei. I found his talk lively, moving, and easy to understand. I was especially impressed by his instructions on reciting the Shurangama Mantra. Another unique feature of his Dharma lecture which was unprecedented in Taiwan was that he asked his left-home disciples to take turns speaking Dharma after him. Later I learned that this eminent Patriarch had actually knelt before his disciples to beg them to speak, for the sake of nurturing the Sangha's abilities to propagate Dharma. At the conclusion of the lecture, I took refuge with the Master along with the assembly.

I am ashamed to say that I didn't follow the Master's teachings at the time. When I went with a colleague to the Dharma Realm Buddhist Books Distribution Society in 1994, tears came to my eyes as I bowed to the Master's picture. I felt like a child coming home and seeing his parents after a long absence. The Master seemed to kindly say to me, "It's okay, now you're back."

I began to attend Dharma events at the Society every Sunday, and I read the Master's explanations of the Sutras and his instructional talks. I gradually began to comprehend the immense magnitude of the Master's kindness, compassion, wisdom, vows, and conduct. Influenced by the Venerable Master's virtue and the practice of his disciples, I soon became a vegetarian. Just as I was congratulating myself for meeting a Clear-eyed Good Advisor, the Venerable Master entered the stillness on June 7, 1995. I felt sad and lost, like a boat that has lost its navigator. Fortunately, the Dharma Masters helped us to understand that we should "rely on the Dharma, not on a person"; that although the Master's body is gone, he left us the Proper Dharma, and his Dharma body pervades the entire Dharma Realm.

In gratitude to the Master's tremendous kindness and virtue in undertaking suffering on our behalf, transferring his blessings to us, and teaching us the Proper Dharma, which is for ending birth and death, I increased my hours of volunteer work and cultivation at the Society, travelled to the City of Ten Thousand Buddhas in America for the Master's Cremation Ceremony, and worked as a volunteer during the Memorial Ceremony in Taiwan. It may appear that I expended a great deal of energy, time, and money to do all of this, but the priceless things I learned and gained far surpass what I spent. In the past year, though I didn't

）雖尚未背誦，看本子已經誦得很熟。我可以肯定地說，若沒有上人，我此生是無緣無福讀誦《華嚴經》及《楞嚴經》此兩部大乘經典之無上法寶。此外，也體認到守戒的必要性，以前雖然知道，但因業障重，當被蚊蟲叮咬時，仍會隨手將其打死，後來聽錄音帶恭聞上人開示說：

若要打死一隻螞蟻，那先殺死我好了。

使我慚愧得無地自容，自此以後不僅不會打蚊蟲，若遭其叮咬時，也會懷著慚愧心及還債心將血施捨給牠們。

另一方面值得一提的，是我的同修及兩個小孩，一個十歲，一個十一歲，這一年來也隨我到法界佛教印經會當義工及共修。同樣地很快即斷葷茹素。現在我的同修從初學者已進步了許多，其發心及精進，個人自嘆不如。兩個小孩從剛開始之勉強至法界共修，到現在把它當第二個家。

他們不僅會背《永嘉大師證道歌》，現在也開始背誦〈楞嚴咒〉。我認為若不是上人德行之感召及加被，他們怎麼會改變如此大。

尤其去年底發生的兩件事情更印證我的想法。一件是某晚我的同修在法界當義工，當我去買晚餐過馬路時，突然冒出一輛機車撞過來，結果機車倒地，騎士及我卻都平安無事。另一件是我的同修在去年底某天因疏忽忘了關瓦斯爐，屋子因天氣冷，窗戶幾乎全部關著，結果瓦斯漏出，家人皆無察覺，這時恰有一通電話，她出去辦事情，約一小時後她回來，從外面新鮮空氣進入屋內即被漏出之瓦斯嗆到，才警覺瓦斯漏出，忙去查看，才知忘了關。若無此電話請她出去辦事，後果真不開堪設想。此外，去年十一月在臺灣板橋舉行上人圓寂追思法會時，一位師姊身體不適卻發心參加，在第一天拜《華嚴懺》時，幾乎要昏倒，這時看到師父上人給她加持，使她以後二天法會皆能順利參加。

由此可見，只要我們知道修行、精進，依照師父上人教導的正法奉持，師父上人隨時隨地會加被我們的，令我們業障消除，智慧增長，早證菩提。

get to recite the entire *Avatamsaka Sutra*, I was filled with Dharma joy each time I did recite. Though I didn't memorize the Shurangama Mantra, I became quite familiar with it following along in the book. If it hadn't been for the Master, I would never have had the blessings to read and recite the *Avatamsaka* and *Shurangama Sutras*, two supreme treasures of Mahayana Buddhism. I have also learned how important it is to hold the precepts. Although I knew this before, my karmic hindrances were heavy and I would involuntarily slap biting mosquitoes. Later I was filled with remorse upon hearing the Venerable Master say on tape,

If you want to slap an ant, you might as well kill me first.

Now not only do I refrain from killing insects, I gladly and remorsefully offer them my blood when they bite me.

It's also worth mentioning that my wife and my eleven and twelve year old children have joined me in volunteering and attending Dharma events at the Dharma Realm Buddhist Books Distribution Society this past year. They have quickly become vegetarians as well. My wife has learned a lot since she began, and she is even more vigorous and resolved in her practice than I am. My two children were reluctant to come to the Society at first, but now they regard it as their second home.

They have memorized Great Master Yongjia's "Song of Enlightenment" and are now memorizing the Shurangama Mantra. How could they have made such great progress were it not for the Venerable Master's virtue and blessing? Two incidents at the end of last year confirm this. One evening when my wife was working at the Society, as I was crossing the street to buy supper, a motorcycle suddenly came careening by. The motorcycle fell to the ground, but neither its rider nor I were injured. On another day, my wife forgot to turn off the gas stove at home. The gas could not escape, since the windows were all closed in the cold weather. None of the family noticed that the gas was leaking, however. Just then someone happened to telephone and ask my wife to go out. About an hour later, when she walked in from the fresh air outside, she choked on the gas-filled air and realized she had forgotten to turn the stove off. I can hardly imagine what would have happened if that phone call had not come.

Last year one of my colleagues decided to attend the Venerable Master's Memorial Ceremony in November despite her poor health. When she was on the verge of passing out while bowing the Avatamsaka Repentance on the first day, she saw the Master give her aid and she felt better on the second day of the ceremony.

As long as we are willing to vigorously practice in accord with the Proper Dharma, the Master will always aid us, eradicate our karmic hindrances, increase our wisdom, and help us to quickly realize Bodhi.

# 感懷師恩　當勤精進
## TO REPAY THE MASTER'S KINDNESS, WE MUST BE VIGOROUS

一切的事情，皆看我們以怎樣的心境去體悟與領納。

**It all depends on our ability to appreciate and understand it with our minds.**

鄭果崑
Guo-kun Zheng

有時，生活上之體驗，帶給我們很大的改變。雖然，師父上人的色身不在，但是他的法身卻永遠常存，遊步於娑婆世界中。記得九年前剛來美國，由於語言、環境，以及種種人、事、等各方面的問題，使學人感覺壓力很大；而師父他常常給予學人各方面的鼓勵與支持。他慈祥的眼神與句句如實的勵人法語，幫助學人度過了難忍需忍、難行需行的日子。每當學人在工作或生活上受到挫折，師父上人的法相便立刻呈現於眼前，為學人說法。

有一天，大概是深夜十一點鐘。學人在大雪紛飛的路上開車，因剛下班，急著回家，又礙於時間有限；便懶得打開暖氣和把車上覆蓋的積雪消除，只在前車的窗上撥了一個小洞，就發動引擎開車上路。開車後，不到幾分鐘，忽然覺得霞光萬道；學人心想，大概是沿途上持〈大悲咒〉的緣故！霞光持續了一陣子，忽然移至學人眼前，仔細一看，哇！原來是一部警車。因整條路積雪，學人看不見前面的方向，於是便緊跟著警車，停在它的後面，警察人員說：「他從來沒有看過這樣開車的人，能在視線約兩個手掌大的範圍內駕駛；看不見背面，也看不見兩側。」在這樣子的情況下，開了一張罰單給學人。

當時，學人深感不服與冤枉，很委屈地坐在車內而不想動彈。警察人員等了半天，覺得不耐煩，便下車幫學人把車上的積雪除去，讓學人先離開。車子上路了，但學人仍抱怨不停，為何持〈大悲咒〉還被開罰單呢？心中一直感覺得納悶。後來，師父說：「就是因為你持〈大悲咒〉，所以觀世音菩薩來救你，若不是那位警察的出現，你可能掉到左側的湖底或右邊的溝裏。不論你掉到那一邊，其後果比一張罰單更為嚴重與不堪設想。」

Sometimes we are greatly transformed by the experiences in our life. Although the Venerable Master's physical body is gone, his Dharma body exists forever, roaming through the Saha world.

Nine years ago when I first arrived in the United States, I was under a lot of pressure as I tried to adjust to the new environment, language, and people. The Master gave me a lot of encouragement and support. His kind eyes and precious words of Dharma helped me through those hard times. Whenever I encounter difficulties, the Master's image appears in front of me to speak Dharma to me.

One night I was driving in the snow at around eleven o'clock. I had just gotten off work and wanted to rush home. In order to save time, I didn't bother to turn on the heater to clear the snow from the windshield. Instead, I just cleared a hole on my side of the windshield and started driving. Within a few minutes, I saw bright lights ahead of me and thought it might be a response from holding the Great Compassion Mnatra. The light then moved right in front of me. Upon a closer look, I realized it was coming from a police car. As the road was covered with snow and there was no way to tell where I was, I followed the police car and parked behind it. The police officer said, "I've never seen anyone driving under such circumstances--your front view is limited to a small hole, and you can't see to the sides or to the rear at all." He gave me a ticket for reckless driving. I sat there in the car, feeling frustrated, and didn't feel like driving away. The policeman waited for me for awhile, and then got out of his car impatiently and cleared all the snow off my car so I could leave.

As I pulled onto the road again, I couldn't help grumbling: "How could I get a ticket when I was reciting the Great Compassion Mantra?" I was very upset. Later the Master told me, "Because you were reciting the Great Compassion Mantra, Guanyin Bodhisattva came to rescue you. Had the policeman not found you, you could have fallen into the lake

第二天，當學人上班時，特別把師父的話印證了一下，才有恍然大悟之感。於是對那位警察，不再心存抱怨；相反的，轉爲感激，並深深的懺悔自己不該怪罪於菩薩。一般人，常以爲學佛、誦經、持咒，就像是投保一般，一切都必須是平安如意。自從這次事故後，學人深自體會；無論任何事情，都有它的好與壞，我們必須從這兩方面，去衡量整個事件的情形過程中之輕重與得失，不再爲自己增添無明煩惱。

幾年後，學人又經歷了一場大車禍。當時，正是學人載著家母看牙醫後在回程的路上。一部卡車，飛快地從學人的左方衝撞而來，在千鈞一髮之際，撞上了左車頭，車子被拖了幾尺遠，車頭像爆炸了一般，碎片滿天飛，整個車子前頭一片稀爛，依照當時情形，我們應可能被撞得粉碎，但母子二人卻毫無傷，當時，學人摯誠鎮定的持念觀世音菩薩聖號，希望一切能平安。現在回想起來，餘悸猶存。那次的車禍，令學人再也不埋怨，並心存感謝，感謝師父和菩薩的慈悲，於冥冥之中，加被弟子。

學人以前很怕事，但皈依師父後，因時常聽師父的開示，便不再對於逆境感到恐懼。經云：「一切爲心造。」不論是世間法還是出世間法，一切的事情，皆看我們以怎樣的心境去體悟與領納。師父常說：「惡知識也就是善知識。」又說：「一切是考驗，看爾怎麼辦？覿面若不識，須再從頭煉。」

記得有一次，是在溫哥華的金佛寺；一天，師父突然說他要獨自出去走走，不准任何人跟。當時，學人心想，師父怎麼也貪玩，他是到外面散步，還是看熱鬧呢？後來才明白，是學人無知。師父爲了減輕眾生罪孽，特意在附近的街頭、店面走一走，與眾生結緣，令菩提種子撒在人們的心中，使菩提樹王之善根成長。

當學人處於逆境時，師父他幫助學人站了起來；當學人悲傷沮喪時，他令學人改變了人生觀。深願弟子能像師父一樣的心包太虛，能同師父一般的慈、悲、喜、捨，能於師父的教誨下，常常領納在心，且精進不懈；並願藉師父的慈悲願力與法身慧命，引導我們邁向菩提大道。

on the left side or the ditch on the right side of the road. Either case would have been worse than getting a ticket."

I confirmed the Master's words on my way to work the next day. That really inspired me, and my resentment towards the policeman was replaced by gratitude. I felt deeply repentant for having blamed the Bodhisattva.

People often feel that practicing Buddhism, reciting Sutras, and holding mantras is simply a way to buy insurance--to make sure nothing goes wrong in our lives. After this incident I realized that everything can be looked at in a positive and a negative light. We need to evaluate the overall situation instead of giving rise to ignorance and affliction.

Several years later I was in another car accident while taking my mother home from the dentist. A truck hit the left side of my car and dragged it for several feet. My car was totalled, and we could have been seriously injured. However, my mother and I were both safe and sound. I had been sincerely reciting Guanyin Bodhisattva's name and praying that everything would be all right. I also recall that I was very scared. I didn't complain about that accident, but instead felt grateful to the Master and to Guanyin Bodhisattva for protecting us from danger.

I used to be very passive and timid, but after taking refuge with the Master and listening to his Dharma talks, I was no longer afraid of adverse situations. The Sutras say, "Everything is a creation of the mind." Whether it is a mundane affair or the Buddhadharma, it all depends on our ability to appreciate and understand it with our minds. The Master always said, "A bad teacher is also a good teacher." "Everything is a test to see what you will do. If you don't recognize what's before you, you'll have to start anew."

I remember once when, at Gold Buddha Monastery in Vancouver, the Master said he would like to take a walk by himself. I thought to myself, "Does the Master want to go amuse himself? Is he planning to take a walk or go window shopping?" Later I realized how ignorant it was to think that way. The Master walked around the block in order to create affinities with living beings and to alleviate their bad karma and plant Bodhi seeds in their minds--seeds that would eventually grow into Bodhi trees.

When I found myself in adversity, the Master helped me to stand on my own feet; when I was sad and frustrated, the Master changed my perspective on life. I hope the Master's disciples will have the Master's all-encompassing spirit and his kindness, compassion, happiness, and giving. I hope they will bear the Master's teachings in mind and practice them. Last but not least, may the Master's compassionate vows and the wisdom of his Dharma-body guide us towards the great Bodhi Way.

# 家庭和樂　忍讓爲要

## THE ABILITY TO YIELD IS THE KEY
## TO A HAPPY FAMILY

### 忍與反求諸己，拉近了人與人之間的距離。
### Patience and self-examination shortened
### the distance between others and ourselves.

張果助　Guozhu Zhang

弟子皈依三寶雖已十年，卻一直荒廢功課，在業海中沉淪多年。去年十月聽說師父宣公上人已圓寂，在懺悔之餘，喚醒了我這個難調又糊塗的浪子。吳聯輝師兄一再鼓勵我，將我的遭遇寫出來，希望能藉此與一些與我遭遇類似的朋友共勉，也藉此聊表不肖弟子對恩師的感懷於憶萬分之一。

一九八五年暑假，一個巧合的機會下，我與友人參加金輪聖寺的朝山團到萬佛聖城。三天的法會除了洗滌身心，法喜充滿外，爲自己有幸得遇高僧，有緣來此聖城感到榮幸，更是折服於聖城內這些修苦行、勤研佛學經典的法師。家母與我都是教師，深知若非住持宣公上人的德行與身教，無法攝服這麼多弟子身體力行嚴守家規！

法會的第三天舉行皈依儀式，雖然很想當下皈依，但單身在外求學的我，很想有個伴攜手同遊浩瀚的學海，於是心中默默的求上人爲我找個理想伴侶，爾後再來皈依。奇妙的是開學第一天就遇上了我的同修，家庭背景相似，都是學數學的，同是佛教徒。一年後，在回臺結婚的路上經過三藩市，想到皈依上人這個願，於是打電話與金山寺聯絡，師父當下叫我次日九時來，當時無知的，我只覺自己好幸運，今日才知師父上人是如此的慈悲！

師父出來並贈送一張名片（這張名片我粘在觀世音菩薩聖像反面隨身攜帶，這十年來多遇貴人相助，逢凶化吉，大概源於此）。師父開示社會亂象的原因，教育與家庭的重要等等，要我們先答應他「決不離婚」，他才肯爲我打皈依。我不

Although I took refuge with the Triple Jewel ten years ago, I have been lax in my cultivation, and thus I have been floundering in the sea of karma for many years. Last October, I heard that the Master had entered Nirvana. Aside from making me feel repentant, the news shook me up in the depths of my obstinate and confused soul. My Dharma brother Wu always encouraged me to write down my experiences with the Master. Hopefully, this story of mine will encourage friends who have similar experiences. With this story, I would also like to express a tiny part of my gratitude to the Master.

In the summer of 1985, I joined a three-day pilgrimage to the City of Ten Thousand Buddhas organized by Gold Wheel Monastery. Aside from feeling purified and filled with joy for the Dharma, I felt extremely lucky to visit the holy city and meet the Venerable Master. I deeply admired the Dharma Masters for their ascetic practice and diligent study of Buddhist scriptures. My mother and I are both teachers, and we recognized that only the Master's virtue and personal example could inspire so many disciples to uphold the City's strict tradition.

There was a Refuge Ceremony on the third day, and although I really wanted to take refuge, I was hoping to have a companion in cultivation, since I was by myself and away from home. Silently, I promised the Master that if he helped me find a good companion, I would come back and take refuge. Miraculously, I met my husband on the first day of college. We were both math majors and Buddhists, and we had similar family backgrounds.

A year later, we passed by San Francisco on our way back to Taipei to get married. Remembering my vow to take refuge with the Master, I called Gold Mountain Monastery. When the Master learned that I wanted to take refuge, he told me to return at nine o'clock the next morning. I rejoiced at my good luck! Only now do I realize how compassionate the Master was! The Master came out to meet us and gave us one of his cards. (I glued this card on the back of a picture of Guanshiyin Bodhisattva that I carry with me. That's probably why I have always received timely help in difficult situations.) The Master talked about the causes of our society being so chaotic and the importance of education and the family,

假思索一口答應，師父笑笑問我們的生辰八字，雖然我們説得不齊全，只見師父屈指在算，眼睛盯著同修（他小時已皈依三寶），我有些吃味，後來想師父可能在爲他「打預防針」，因爲我這個女子非常難養！師父爲我取名果助，並賦予我四個任務，先齊家後助弘法！

長子出生後不久，課業繁重，身體欠佳，孩子難帶，爭執吵架接踵而至，都認爲自己最辛苦，對方不夠盡責。吵到不耐煩時，「離婚」二字，就成了最簡單的解決之道。我想如果這孩子是我一人的，我一定會「毫無怨言」的克盡責任作一切事，但是現在是「兩人共有的」，你也要像我一樣認真照顧他！這般計較，恣意的發無名火，直到對方很認真的回答，如果你不怕違抗師命的話，立刻離婚！這才決定先忍一口氣冷靜一下，這才警覺到自己長久以來的矛盾想法是這麼的不合邏輯學了，這麼多年的數學、科學訓練、邏輯推理能力的訓練，幫我解決了許多難題。但若理智不清，又不能忍時，這些是破除不了無明的障礙的。

其實動怒的前一剎那，理智與無明在比高下時，我常懶得思考而放縱自己，任由那無名的火焰盡情燃燒，傷人傷己。其實當初吸口氣、喝口水、忍口氣、少説一句，不就沒事了嗎？這也就是師父上人一再教誨我們的，要忍要反求諸己的道理。「決不離婚」成就了一個和樂的家，忍與反求諸己，拉近了人與之間的距離。

十年間，我們完成了學業，也順利的在同一所大學任教，一家人的健康，也因善知識的治療及持〈大悲咒〉而改善。一切都平順的時候，卻得知師父上人圓寂。我們既無助、悲傷又悔恨錯失十年命光，荒廢功課，真是無顏面對恩師，至今每當頂禮恩師時，我的心好難過，喊一聲師父原諒弟子不肖，熱淚盈眶。

師父圓寂，喚回了我這個糊塗浪子，師父賦予我的工作還沒作呢？趕快努力吧！師父知道我們生性懶惰，沒有恆心毅力，易受環境牽引，慈悲的讓我們認識多位善知識，時時提醒、教導我們，提供寶貴意見，解我們的迷惑。師父宣公上人雖回到虛空，但仍時時刻刻護衛著我們。從師父的法音、開示錄、經典淺釋、萬佛城月刊、智慧之源等等刊物，可以知道在菩提道上，師父時時

etc. Before allowing us to take refuge, he wanted us to promise that we would "never divorce." I gave him my word without hesitation. He smiled and asked for the hours and dates of our birthdays. We could not give him the complete information, but he went ahead and calculated with his fingers while gazing at my husband, who had taken refuge as a child. I was a little jealous. Later I thought that the Master was probably giving him a "prophylactic shot" since I was a very difficult woman. The Master gave me the Dharma name Guozhu along with four tasks. He said that I must first help in establishing the family and then propagate the Dharma. Shortly after my first son was born, my schoolwork became burdensome, my health deteriorated, and the child was difficult to raise. Fights and quarrels ensued. We each felt that we were doing more than our share. When we fought to the point that we were disgusted with each other, divorcing seemed the easiest way out. I reasoned: if the child were mine alone, I would do everything I could to care for him without complaint; however, since the child belonged to both of us, my husband should work as hard as I did to take care of him. In this way, I let my ignorance get the better of me until my husband seriously told me, "If you have no concern about violating the Master's instruction, we can get a divorce immediately." I decided to cool down and be a little more patient. Only then did I realize how illogical and contradictory I was being. The power of deductive reasoning gained from so many years of studying science and mathematics had helped me solve many problems before. However, ignorance can hardly be overcome with a lack of clarity and patience.

In fact, in the split second prior to losing my temper, while reason was competing with ignorance, I often indulged myself and let the fire of ignorance blaze unchecked. Behaving this way, I hurt both of us. If I could have held back a little, said a few words less, things would have been all right. That is the principle of patience and self-examination the Master had been teaching us over and over again. "Never divorce" made a happy family; patience and self-examination shortened the distance between others and ourselves.

During the past ten years, my husband and I finished our studies and found teaching posts in the same university. The health of our family has improved as a result of treatment from a good and wise advisor, as well as upholding of the Great Compassion Mantra. When everything seemed to go smoothly, the Master entered Nirvana. We were much saddened, and felt helpless and remorseful over having wasted ten years of our lives. We had been neglecting our cultivation. How could we ever face our kind teacher? To this day, every time I bow to the Master my heart is filled with sorrow. Tears fill my eyes: "Master, please forgive this unfilial disciple!" The Master's entry into Nirvana has caused this confused drifter to turn around. I have not completed the tasks the Master gave me. I must hurry up! The Master knew that our natures are lazy, that we have no perseverance and are easily influenced by the surrounding environment. He kindly provided us with many good and wise advisors who constantly give us precious instructions to dispel our confusion. Though the Master has returned to empty space, he is still protecting us as always. From

伴著我們，拉拔我們，只要我們有心，用心，任何難題師父都能用最淺顯易懂的智慧之語，一語道破我們的無明。

　　師父宣公上人的大恩大德，不肖弟子實難以言喻，無法言盡，僅以拙文聊表我內心的感念於億萬分之一。

his taped and printed Dharma talks and explanations of the Sutras, as well as from the monthly *Vajra Bodhi Sea* magazine and the newsletter "Source of Wisdom," we know that the Master accompanies and helps us all the time along the path of Bodhi. As long as we are truthful and sincere, the Master will always zero in on our ignorance with the simplest words of wisdom.

The great kindness and virtue of our teacher can hardly be expressed by such an unfilial disciple as me. No words can adequately describe these qualities. With this article, I would like to express one billionth of my gratitude and feelings.

# 師父的恩德
# THE KINDNESS OF THE VENERABLE MASTER

每次看到師父，都覺得他很威嚴；
聽他說話，更覺得他慈悲、和藹可親。

**Every time I saw the Venerable Master,
I felt he is very awesome. Every time I heard the way he talked,
I felt he is very kind and compassionate and affable.**

釋果榮　十三歲
Shramanera Gwo Rong, age 13

我出家三年了。在以前並沒有機會常常跟師父說話。雖然如此，可是每次看到師父都覺得他很威嚴；聽他說話，更覺得他慈悲、和藹可親。

每次翻開師父的《開示錄》，或聽師父開示的錄音帶時，常令我法喜充滿。我覺得師父的開示都很實際，很生活化，能夠讓我了解應該怎麼做，才是正確的，也幫助我解除心中的疑惑。

譬如說有一次我聽師父的開示，教我們要跟大家一樣，不能任性，要聽別人的教導，如果不聽教導的話，果報就會不可思議的。

我聽了之後，就想到我平時常不聽師長的教導，不聽同學的勸告，我覺得我應該要虛心接受他人的勸告，不能再那麼傲慢任性，一方面有損自己的道業，再方面這也要背負因果的。

In the three years since I have left home, I did not have much chance to talk with the Venerable Master. However, every time I saw the Venerable Master, I felt he is very awesome.

Every time I heard the way he talked, I felt he is very kind and compassionate and affable. Every time I hear the Venerable Master's Dharma talks, I feel happy, because they are very useful. They show me how I should act; they also help me solve problems that I do not understand.

For example, once I heard the Venerable Master tell us to be of the same substance with others; we should not just do whatever we want. We should listen to people when they try to teach us, for if we do not, our retribution will be inconceivable.

After I heard that, I reflected that in my daily life I never listened to the advice of my teachers and classmates. I decided to change and listen to others' instructions. I should not be so arrogant and follow my own wishes. Otherwise I will have to suffer the retribution.

# 迷時師度
## WHEN CONFUSED, OUR TEACHER SAVES US

普光　Universal Light

（一）

喜聞道友互精進
叢林勤修戒定慧
持戒嚴謹相莊嚴
口意清淨身與心
參禪雖未悟本性
修行皆靠金剛志
持之以恆爲中道
精進接勵現般若
六度萬行菩薩道
廣度群倫本佛誓
恭敬三寶賴僧傳
綿綿無期眾生度
虛空有盡願無盡
同登蓮臺返娑婆

（二）

回首前塵入雲霧
紅塵昔日女嬋娟
天地靈秀一釵裙
六塵六識不清淨
重重業海煩惱慾
業障現前關難度
燒盡釵裙平靜心
妄念皆是魔來考
煩惱慾海皆自找
活該自受因境轉
慚愧考驗得零字
還須重頭再煉起
感恩菩薩夢中度
又蒙恩師來開示
心中清淨如靜湖
收拾經本更精進
不負菩薩與祖師
恆心中道來自度

**I.**

I'm delighted to hear that my Dharma friends
Are vigorously cultivating precepts, samadhi, and wisdom,
Urging each other on in the monastery.
Holding the precepts strictly, their features are adorned;
And they are pure in body, mouth, and mind.
Before one has awakened to one's basic nature,
One must rely on a vajra resolve in one's practice.
Holding to it with constancy is the Middle Way.
With vigorous perseverance, Prajna can come forth.
With the six perfections and myriad practices of the Bodhisattva Way,
Vastly take across the multitudes by relying on the Buddha's vows.
Revere the Triple Jewel; the Dharma relies on the Sangha to transmit it.
Constantly and ceaselessly, cross over living beings.
Space has a boundary, but our vows have no end.
Let us together ascend the lotus dais and then return to the Saha.

**II.**

Entering the fog of the hazy past,
I remember that there was a lady in the world
Who was excellent and refined in her ways.
With the impurity of the sense objects and consciousnesses,
The multi-layered sea of karma surges with afflictions and desires.
When karmic obstructions arise, it's hard to pass the test.
Burning her feminine clothing and adornments,
She sought to achieve peace and tranquility of mind.
False thoughts are demons coming to test us.
The sea of afflictions and desires is created by ourselves.
We deserve the consequences for being swayed by states.
Flunking the test, we are filled with shame.
We have to start all over again.
Thankfully, a Bodhisattva came in a dream to save me.
And a kind teacher also bestowed instruction.
With a mind as calm and clear as a placid lake,
I pick up the Sutra text with increased vigor.
Not wishing to let down the Bodhisattvas and Patriarchs,
I shall steadfastly walk the Middle Way to take myself across.

（三）

何須言謝又悵然
人生無常已難逢
只因提筆三四次
境界現前無明障
無明不除心不靜
何忍堪擾師勤修

六根六塵和六識
齊來考驗吾之志
財色名睡尤重色
汗顏汗顏又慚愧
誰知修道是容易
難關不破皆是障
非得降伏自心魔
調伏自心柔軟性
一日下班閨房至
恍然悟到擲虛陰
生生死死又死生
不出輪迴六道生
一掃妄想與執著
懺悔慟哭於佛前
感恩大悲大慈父
故而書寫成偈誦

師問近日何事忙
上班族人忙俗事
朝九晚五行路忙
夜幕誠心來懺悔
輾磨吾之劣根性
不發脾氣瞋與癡

一日自知又懺悔
哭訴吾師道難行
吾之短處歷歷現
令我心驚又膽顫
識得吾面真恐怖
不覺毛骨皆悚然
耽心害怕墮地獄
故求師來指迷津

*III.*

*What need is there to say thanks when I am disappointed with myself?*
*Human life, fleeting as it is, is difficult to encounter.*
*I pick up my pen three or four times, trying to write.*
*When states appear, I am impeded by ignorance.*
*If ignorance is not removed, the mind cannot be still.*
*How could I disturb my teacher's diligent cultivation?*

*The six organs, six dusts, and six consciousnesses*
*All at once come to test my resolve.*
*Desires for wealth, form, fame, and sleep--especially form--*
*Cause shame and remorse as I break out in a sweat.*
*Who thinks that cultivation is easy?*
*Every hurdle we fail to cross becomes an obstacle.*
*There is no other way but to subdue the demons of our mind.*
*We must subdue the mind until it is mild and gentle.*
*One day upon returning home after work,*
*I suddenly realize I have thrown my time away.*
*Birth after birth, death after death,*
*I have not known to escape the six paths of transmigration.*
*Sweeping away deluded thoughts and attachments,*
*I repent and weep bitterly in front of the Buddhas.*
*In gratitude to my kind and compassionate father,*
*I write these lines of verse.*

*My Teacher asks me what I have been doing recently.*
*Just going to work and keeping busy with worldly matters,*
*Running about here and there, from nine until five each day.*
*When night falls I sincerely come to repent.*
*I shall crush my bad habits and imperfections;*
*I shall not lose my temper or give rise to anger or stupidity.*

*One day, I reflect upon myself and again repent.*
*Crying, I tell my Teacher that the Way was difficult to practice.*
*My weaknesses appear clearly in my mind's eye.*
*Causing me to shudder with fright.*
*Seeing how terrible I really am,*
*My hairs all stand on end.*
*Worried and afraid of falling into the hells,*
*I beseech my Teacher to show me the way out.*

宣化老和尚追思紀念專輯

師曰
墮三惡道之易耶
汝應學行菩薩道

吾覆曰
不願墮落三惡道
唯菩薩道更難行
嗟嘆修行道難行
又嘆人生是苦海
反觀自我業重重
何時除卻汙垢盡
自形慚穢不如人
自度不了何曰道


再閱行者之日記
痛哭流涕華嚴意
重重無盡世界海
真如本性一念心
恍如夙昔讀此經
不容許我自了漢
強行捕捉宿世憶
卻道似有又似無
昔是佛門修行者
苦為我今仍俗子


師曰
世尊修行億萬劫
劫劫修行無止盡
汝應往前勿自棄
掃除妄想勿執著
改過向善學聖賢
衝破難關更精進
閱讀壇經須自悟
金剛般若波羅蜜

一九九四年元月
書於宛廬

My Teacher's reply:

*It is indeed easy to fall into the three evil paths.*
*You should learn to practice the Bodhisattva Way.*

My response:

*It's not that I want to fall into the three evil paths,*
*But the Bodhisattva Way is so hard to practice.*
*Alas! While the path of cultivation is difficult to walk,*
*Human life is nothing but a sea of suffering!*
*Taking a look at myself, weighed down with karma,*
*I wonder when I shall ever get rid of all that filth.*
*I'm ashamed that I don't match up to others.*
*If I don't save myself, how can it be called the Way?*


*Re-reading the diary of the bowing monks,*
*I am moved to tears by the Bodhisattva's intent in the Flower Adornment Sutra.*
*Layer upon layer, the seas of worlds are endless.*
*Yet the basic nature of True Suchness is but a single thought.*
*I seem to have read this Sutra somewhere before.*
*It prevents me from caring only about my own salvation.*
*Striving vigorously to remember my intent in past lives,*
*I must say that it is intangible and vague.*
*In the past I was a Buddhist cultivator;*
*What a pity I am now a worldly person.*


My Teacher says:

*The World Honored One cultivated for tens of thousands of eons,*
*Practicing without cease in eon after eon.*
*You ought to advance and not give up on yourself.*
*Sweep away your false thoughts and don't get attached.*
*Change your faults, go towards goodness, and learn from sages.*
*Smash through barriers and be ever more vigorous.*
*Read the Platform Sutra: it says you must enlighten yourself.*
*Vajra Prajna Paramita!*

*Written at Wanlu in January 1994*

# REMINISCING ON LIFE AND SESSIONS
## AT THE CITY OF TEN THOUSAND BUDDHAS

# 回想萬佛城的生活及法會

Shi Heng Tso
釋恆佐

The Master said,

> The most important thing in cultivation is
> to benefit living beings.

That exemplifies what the City of Ten Thousand Buddhas has always been about. Ever since its establishment in 1976, the spirit of the City has been to benefit living beings.

When we first came here, we didn't even have clothespins to hang up our clothes in the monastery. Everything was very basic. The food, clothing, bedding, and everything was much more basic then than it is now. The Master used this as a method to teach all of us who came and studied with him. It didn't matter what we had; we all worked hard. There was a certain spirit--camaraderie--among the people who were cultivating and trying to follow the Master's example. One of the points he taught us was that

> In benefiting living beings
> we should learn as much as we can.

The *Avatamsaka Sutra* talks about how a Bodhisattva can do just about anything, from being a very skilled and wise teacher who can lecture Sutras to being a carpenter, a sculptor, a farmer, and so on. A Bodhisattva knows all these skills. Why? Because he has to teach all different kinds of living beings.

The Master also emphasized education. All of us took part in learning many things. We didn't specialize in one thing. The Master taught us to learn everything we could. He taught each person according to their propensities--according to what they were best at. When it came time for recitation and meditation sessions; because everyone was working together and working vigorously, the attitude carried on to the sessions. Months before we would have a session, we would be arranging our schedules so that we could attend it as much as possible.

In the past we used to have Chan sessions at least three or four times a year, and they would last three, five, six weeks...up to 108 days. Everyone was always very excited to have the opportunity to cultivate this dharma. It was almost like a vacation from all the work. Why would you think suffering from 2:30 in the morning till 12 midnight would be a vacation? It's because we really worked hard, and this was a chance to single-mindedly practice one Dharma-door.

上人説：

修行最重要的事情就是利益眾生。

這是聖城成立的宗旨。自從一九七六年成立以來，聖城的一貫的精神就是爲了利益眾生。

當我們初次來到這裡，在寺院裡，甚至沒有衣夾子可以把衣服掛起來。一切都很簡陋。衣、食、臥具，所有的一切都比現在簡單得多。師父用這種方法來教導所有向他學習的弟子。不管我們缺什麼，我們都很用功。在這些追隨師父修行，及學習上人的風範的人當中，有種精神存在——同參道友間的友愛及互助。上人教導我們的一件事情是：

爲了利益眾生，
我們必須竭盡所能去學習一切。

《華嚴經》中描述，菩薩幾乎能做所有的事情，從善於講經説法的老師到木匠、雕刻師、農夫等等。菩薩善知一切工巧技術。爲什麼呢？因爲菩薩必須教化所有各類不同的眾生。

上人也注重教育。我們每個人都參與多方面的學習，並沒有專學某一樣東西。上人教導我們盡力地去學習每一件事情。上人因材施教，依各人最會做的而教。當念佛法會及禪七時，由於各人平日一起精進辦道，把這種態度和氣氛也帶入法會。早在法會開始前數月，各人都已安排好自己的時間表，以儘量爭取多一些參加法會的時間。

過去，我們一年之中最少會打三至四次禪七。禪七有爲期三週、四週、五週、六週，乃至一百零八天的。每個人都很興奮，能有機會修學這個法門，差不多像是從所有的工作中休假。爲什麼

During a session, all you have to do is follow the schedule. The session is such that you will gain a lot of benefit just by following the schedule. People who live in the monastery or the Joyous Giving House (nuns' quarters) are required to come to the lectures every evening. You can't run off to sleep or visit friends or chat or whatever. You have to come to the lectures. The lectures are the bread and butter--the food. If you live at the City of Ten Thousand Buddhas and you don't come to lectures, other people will say, "Well, this person doesn't go to lectures, so I don't have to go either. I can rest in my room or go talk to people." You're not only being lazy yourself, but you're creating an offense by influencing other people not to attend.

The Master's lectures--even though they were spoken twenty, fifteen, or ten years ago--are very pertinent to our life right now. Just because it's a taped lecture doesn't mean it's not equally as important. I remember one time at Gold Summit Monastery, we were all listening to his taped lecture and he came to visit. He walked downstairs and sat in the Buddha Hall, and he used his hand to bless everybody. The way I took it was: This is what he does whether he's there in the flesh or not. He told us that time: "If you attend my (taped) lectures, then I'll try my best to benefit you." The way I understand it is, it doesn't matter whether or not he is physically present at the lecture; he's still there, and he's still helping us.

Once a laywoman said after attending a session: "Well, nothing special happened to me."

I asked her, "Well, did you get angry?"

She said, "No."

"Did you feel bad in any way?"

She said, "No."

"Well, that's already a really good thing." Think of all the people in the world, especially in the West, who pay thousands of dollars to doctors just so they can feel good for a little while. Being peaceful and happy is already a big benefit.

During the sessions, we go to the Buddha Hall for morning recitation at four o'clock in the morning and stay in the Buddha Hall cultivating all day long until the end of the Great Transference at nine-thirty at night. The only time we leave the hall is during lunchtime.

The style of the recitation session is quite simple--usually we use only one slow tune and one fast tune. When we recite one way the whole time, we can actually hear the Buddha's name recited even when we are not reciting.

I remember once during a Guanyin Session in the summertime, there were fans in the Buddha Hall, and after a few days of reciting, people were hearing Guanyin's name coming out of the fans. When you're quiet or even when you go to sleep, you can also hear the Buddha's name, because you keep repeating the sound over and over throughout the day.

The Master emphasized that reciting the Buddha's name is something everyone can practice. He would have heaters in the Buddha Hall so the old people wouldn't be cold. Young people don't mind the cold, but old people are very bothered if they are

你會認爲從早晨兩點半至午夜十二點的受苦,是假期呢?這是因爲我們眞用功。這是一個一心專修一個法門的機會。

法會期間,你要按照時間表作息。這些法會的性質是,只要你能夠依照時間表作息,便會獲得很大的利益。寺裡或喜捨院(出家女眾寮房)所有的住眾,每晚必須去聽經。不能溜去睡覺、找朋友或閒談等等。必須去聽經。聽經是我們的生計:麵包和奶油──食物。假如你住在萬佛城而不去聽經,其他的人會説「既然這個人可以不去聽經,我也不必去。我可以在房間休息,或找人談話去。」這樣,你不但自己懶惰,也因爲影響人不去聽經而造業。

上人所講的經,雖然是在二十、十五、十年前講的,與我們現在的生活是很契機且恰當的。不要因爲這是錄音講經,就不把它看得同樣重要。我記得有一次在金峰寺,在聽上人的錄音講經時,上人來看我們。上人走下台階,坐在佛殿當中,用手加持每一個人。我對這件事的看法是:不管上人的肉身在與否,這是上人所做的事情。那一次上人告訴我們:「假如你來聽我講經(或錄音講經),我會盡全力來幫助你。」據我所瞭解,不管上人是否親身在講經,上人還是在那裡,上人還是在幫助我們。

有一次,一位女居士在法會結束後説:「並沒有什麼特別的事情,發生在我身上。」我問她:「你是否發了脾氣?」她説沒有。「你覺得有什麼不妥嗎?」她説沒有。「那麼,這已經是件很好的事情了。」試想想,世間上所有的人,尤其是在西方,他們爲了可以暫時感覺好一些,花了上千塊錢去看醫生。能平平安安、快快樂樂,已經是很大的利益了。

佛七期間,我們從早晨四點到大殿做早課,一整天都留在大殿修行,直到晚上九點半大回向結束。唯一離開大殿的時間,是在用午齋的時候。

法會的格式非常簡單──通常我們會用一個慢調,和一個快調。當我們整天都用同一種念法,即使是在不念的時候,的的確確還是會聽到念佛的聲音。

記得有一年夏天的觀音法會,當時佛殿裡有風扇,經過數天念佛,有人聽到觀音聖號從風扇中發出來。當你靜下來,或去睡覺時,還是會聽到念佛的聲音,因爲一整天你一直重覆地在念佛。

上人強調,持名念佛是人人可行的。上人在佛殿安置暖爐,使老人家不會覺得冷。年輕人雖不介意

cold or they can't relax as they are reciting the Buddha's name.

The method that the Venerable Master taught us was to recite half an hour walking, recite half an hour sitting, and recite half an hour in silence. That gives people a lot of time to concentrate and to meditate.

冷，但是老人家冷的話，會起很大的煩惱，或者在念佛時，不能放鬆自己。

上人教導我們的方法是：半小時繞念、半小時坐念、半小時止靜默念。這個方法給予我們足夠的時間專心靜坐。

# OUR MASTER IS ALWAYS WITH US
# 師父永遠與我們同在
## I am always with you.
## 我會永遠和你在一起

釋果羅　十三歲
Shramanera Gwo Lwo, age 13

Our Master is always with us. His light leads us on the right Path, and his compassion teaches us all. There shall never be a time when the Master is not with us.

He once said to me, "I am always with you." I knew that the Master did not just mean me, he meant all living beings. Our Master is always there to help us, 24 hours a day.

Almost everyone knows about how he prevented earthquakes in San Francisco, but how about wars? I think not too many people knew about this. During the Persian Gulf War, the Master spiritually protected the soldiers' and peoples' lives. That is why not too many people were killed. The Master compassionately saved all of those living beings, how much more the rest of the beings in the Dharma Realm!

Our Master is always with us. His wisdom crosses over all, and his kindness moves all living beings. There shall never be a time when the Master is not with us.

師父，總是不時地用他的光，在正道上引導我們，用他的慈悲教導我們，他沒有一刻不和我們同在。他曾向我說過：

　　我會永遠和你在一起。

我知道，師父不僅僅指我，還包括了所有的眾生。師父，總是在那兒幫助我們，一天二十四小時毫不休息。例如，幾乎每一個人都知道師父如何去防止三藩市大地震的發生，但是我想很少有人知道他如何去防止戰爭。在波斯灣戰爭中，師父以其高超的精神，保護作戰的士兵和人民的生命，因此沒有太多人傷亡。師父慈悲不僅救度了這些眾生，甚至包含更多的法界眾生啊！

師父總是和我們同在。他的智慧救度一切，他的慈悲感化所有的眾生，他無時不刻不和我們同在。

# 最沒有架子的老僧人
## THE MOST GENUINE ELDER MONK

釋恆泰
Shi Hengtai

何其慶幸這一生能有機會踏入萬佛城的山門，更慶幸能在聖城之中，在一位德高望重、嚴持戒律，善巧方便，或現怒目金剛、大威猛力，或現談笑風生、慈祥和藹的善知識座下剃度出家。

正慶幸得到善知識接引指導，走上正確路途時，哪知善知識走得太快了，使我半途失明燈，留下無限的遺憾及後悔。遺憾沒有福報再承受善識的聖教，後悔沒更早放下財色名食睡及兒女之情，來得太遲了。

上人有時現怒目金剛，當四眾前指責你的錯處，不容覆藏，使你即時返光回照，懺悔惡行，消除我慢，訓練忍耐，精進、禪定，如果考不過，須從頭再煉。

上人是一位大慈悲父，無論老、少、出家、在家弟子，都一視同仁，細心關懷教導。記得為求出家，上人在辦公室接見，談完後，要離開時，外面正好下毛毛雨，上人詢問「是否用了晚餐？要到那兒去？」「我們已練習不吃晚餐了，但是要回齋堂去，因剛好是我們值日料理晚餐。」師父便起來邀我們坐他的小車子，送到齋堂去。我們受寵若驚，怎麼好意思讓師父送，但師父堅持要我們上車，恭敬不如遵命，真是「迷時師度！」只可惜至今還是在迷中，師父便已離我們而去，只好戰戰兢兢地堅守師父上人的三大宗旨：凍死不攀緣、餓死不化緣、窮死不求緣、隨緣不變，不變隨緣。嚴持六大條款：不爭、不貪、不求、不自私、不自利、不打妄語，及衣不離體、日中一食，以期自度。相信上人的法身是遍虛空盡法界，只要我們真心向道，上人無時不在照顧我們的。

念念真誠念念通，默默感應默默中。

願與大家共勉之。

How fortunate I am to have been able to set foot inside the City of Ten Thousand Buddhas! I have been even more fortunate, for I was able to leave the home-life under a greatly virtuous monk who upheld the precepts sternly and taught with skillful expedients, sometimes with awesome fury, sometimes with friendly smiles and gentle kindness.

Just as I was rejoicing in my good fortune for having found a wise teacher who could guide me in the proper direction, my teacher walked too fast, leaving me in the dark without a lamp, leaving me filled with regrets. I regret that I didn't have the blessings to receive further teachings from my wise teacher. I regret that I didn't let go of my attachments to wealth, lust, fame, food, and sleep, and to my children, earlier--I was too late.

The Master was a compassionate father who regarded all his disciples--old and young, left-home and at-home--with equal kindness, teaching and caring for them with careful attentiveness. I remember when I met with the Master in his office in order to seek his permission to leave the home-life. When I was about to leave after the meeting, it was drizzling outside. The Master asked, "Have you taken dinner yet? Where are you going?" "We are practicing not taking dinner, but we're going to the dining hall because it's our turn to cook dinner." The Master rose and invited us to ride in his little car back to the dining hall. We could hardly imagine accepting the Master's offer, but he insisted that we get in the car. Out of respect, we obeyed--it was truly a case of "the teacher saving you when you are confused." What a pity--we are still confused, but our teacher has already left! We can only be very cautious and stick closely to the Master's Three Great Principles: "Freezing, we do not scheme; starving, we do not beg; dying of poverty, we ask for nothing. According with conditions, we do not change; not changing, we accord with conditions." We should also observe the Six Guidelines: no fighting, no greed, no seeking, no selfishness, no self-benefiting, and no lying. We should always wear our precept sashes and take only one meal a day, so that we can take ourselves across. I believe the Master's Dharma body is all-pervasive throughout space and the Dharma Realm. As long as we sincerely practice the Way, the Master will always protect us.

*With every thought sincere, every thought penetrates;*
*There's an imperceptible and silent response.*

I would just like to share these thoughts and offer encouragement to everyone.

# 沒有感應就是最大的感應

## THE GREATEST RESPONSE IS NO RESPONSE AT ALL

朱翠霞
Cuixia Zhu

以前我是一個不願意爲他人付出，貪小便宜，且愛吃葷的佛教徒；現在我是一個癌症末期，法界義工，吃素的虔誠佛教徒，這之間的轉變，並不是突然地開了智慧，而是慢慢的轉移變化。

嚴格說來，我真正親眼見到上人，只有一次，但他卻是改變我觀念的第一人。談起上人，這要回溯到一九八一年，那時我在郵局上班，當時雖對佛法有相當的興趣，但並沒有因讀佛經而開智慧，反而依舊吃葷殺生，一直認爲佛菩薩會原諒我，實在是大錯特錯。

當時的郵局提供郵局工作人員佛法訊息的「普門文庫」，剛好有一則小小的消息說：「聽到宣化上人法音之人，都可在他之前成佛」，且普門文庫發行了三卷上人法音錄音帶，共台幣一百元，內容包括上人親自唸的楞嚴咒及講述佛法。當時，我想那麼便宜，就毫不考慮買了。老實說，初見上人的照片，就不太喜歡上人的模樣，所以不是很恭敬，但仍興高采烈帶著三卷錄音帶回家，晚上家人吃飯時，拿出來放給大家聽，沒想到一放錄音帶，別說是我這不是佛教徒的佛教徒聽了很難受，我先生馬上大喊「關掉！關掉！」一分一秒都再也聽不下去。上人的聲音實在是太震撼了，爲何如此難聽，如果要形容得真實點，我們是一群妖魔鬼怪。聽到正法之咒，而渾身難過，所以放錄音帶不到一分鐘就關掉了。

往後的日子，我都是在半夜聽上人的錄音帶，漸漸地，我愈喜歡聽，尤其當我身體不舒服，心情煩悶，都會聽聽上人的法音。那三卷錄音帶，也變成我的寶貝，裏頭提到如何開智慧，都是其它上人法音錄音帶所聽不到的，我也越發愛聽上人講佛法，常與同事相偕跑去當時在林森北路的法界佛教印經會，討價還價地買上人的書及錄音帶。將近十年的時間，我雖沒見過上人，但他的聲音，他的脾氣，他的智慧，無不令我相當的佩服。直到一九九○年，上人來臺弘法，我也趁便

I used to be a "Buddhist" who craved petty bargains, didn't like to do anything for others, and loved to eat meat. Now that I am in the advanced stages of cancer, I have become a devoted Buddhist who is vegetarian and volunteers at the Dharma Realm Buddhist Books Distribution Society (Taipei, Taiwan). This change was a gradual one; my wisdom didn't develop all at once.

Although I saw the Venerable Master in person only once, he played a primary role in changing my views. In 1981 when I was working at the post office, although I was quite interested in Buddhism and read the Sutras, I continued to eat meat, assuming the Buddhas and Bodhisattvas would forgive me for taking creatures' lives. Actually, I was making a great mistake.

In a Buddhist newsletter distributed to the post office employees, there was a small item saying that "those who heard the Dharma spoken by the Venerable Master Hua would be able to attain Buddhahood before he did." The Universal Door Bookstore sold a set of three tapes of the Venerable Master's Dharma talks and recitation of the Shurangama Manra for NT$100. Since it was so convenient, I bought a set without thinking. To be honest, the first time I saw the Master's picture, I did not like the Master's appearance and was not very respectful. Nevertheless, I enthusiastically took the three tapes home, thinking to play them for the family at dinnertime. But when I turned on the tape player, not only did I find it hard to listen to, my husband couldn't stand it and shouted, "Turn it off! Turn it off!" The sound of the Master's voice really shook us up. Hearing the mantra of the Proper Dharma, we were like a bunch of ghosts, feeling so uncomfortable that we turned it off before a minute had passed.

Later on, I began listening to those three tapes in the middle of the night. The more I listened, the more I liked what I heard. Whenever I felt physically unwell or depressed, I would listen to the Master's Dharma sound. I treasured those three tapes, for in them the Master talked about how to open wisdom, something I didn't hear in most of his other tapes. I become very fond of listening to the Master's Dharma talks and often went with my colleagues to the Dharma Realm Buddhist Books Distribution Society to buy tapes. For nearly a decade I admired the Master's sound, his righteousness, and his wisdom, before I actually met the Master and took refuge with him in 1990, receiving the Dharma name Guo Xia. Unfortunately, not realizing my first meeting with the Master would also be the last, I didn't cherish my opportunity.

When I discovered in 1993 that I had advanced stomach cancer, my life, work, and family were turned topsy-turvy. Having cancer

皈依上人，法名果霞。也就只有那一次，是第一次，也是最後一次見到上人，但那時並沒有好好把握住機會。

一九九三年，發現得到胃癌，且已末期，這對我的生活、工作、家庭，都產生重大改變。生了癌就好像掉入了人間地獄一樣，斷斷續續的開刀住院，化學治療，胃鏡，腸鏡....各種人間刑具都嘗過了。一直苦求諸佛菩薩加持，幾乎一點感應都沒有，病痛不但沒減輕，反而越加嚴重。

一九九五年三月，在臺大腫瘤病房難過得受不了，無意想起往昔所聽錄音帶，有人唸上人名號而病好起，便唸起上人名號，病有些許好轉。當晚做了一個夢，夢到三個僧人在天上飛，似乎暗示著我某些事。半年後又住院，巧遇同病房的趙老師，介紹我在臺北市忠孝東路的法界佛教印經會，雖我早已知道法界搬新家了，但未曾接觸。出院後便開始接觸上人的道場，蒙各法師的慈悲照顧，便決定吃素，做義工，使我的心靈得到了從所未有的祥和。

雖然以前我嫌上人的容貌不好看，聲音不好聽，但上人仍不計前嫌地指引我，更可見上人的慈悲大度。

上人走了，我沒好好把握機會，覺得好難過。我常在法界佛教印經會，摸畫中上人的手，真希望他能用他的枴杖敲我這不精進的弟子的頭。

was like falling into the hells. I was hospitalized, operated on, given chemotherapy, examined by gastroscopes and entero-scopes...in short, given every form of torture. My desperate prayers to the Buddhas and Bodhisattvas seemed fruitless as my cancer grew ever more serious.

In March 1995, I was wracked with pain as I lay in the cancer ward of the National Taiwan University Hospital. Suddenly remembering hearing a tape of how someone had recited the Master's name and recovered, I began reciting the Master's name, and I *did* feel a better. I recited more and there were further signs of improvement. That night I dreamed of three monks flying in the sky who seemed to give me some hints regarding certain matters. Half a year later when I was hospitalized again, I happened to share a room with Ms. Zhao, who told me about the new location of the Dharma Realm Buddhist Books Distribution Society. Although I knew it had moved, I had not been to its new location. After being discharged, I began going to the Master's Way-place and, under the kindly concern of the Dharma Masters there, I decided to become vegetarian and start doing volunteer work. I experienced an inner peace that I had never known before.

Even though I had disliked the Master's appearance and the sound of his voice, the Master guided me without holding any grudge, showing me his measureless compassion.

Now that the Master is gone, how I regret not cherishing the opportunity I had! I often touch the Master's hand in his picture, wishing that he would hit this lax disciple on the head with his cane.

以彼智慧心　破諸煩惱障　一念見一切　此是佛神力
擊于正法鼓　覺悟十方剎　咸令向菩提　自在力能爾
——《大方廣佛華嚴經》〈光明覺品第九〉

*Using the mind of wisdom*
*To smash all afflictions and obstacles,*
*In one thought he could see all.*
*This is the spiritual power of the Buddha.*

*He beats the Proper Dharma drum*
*To enlighten those in the lands of the ten directions,*
*So all are caused to go towards Bodhi.*
*The power of self-mastery can achieve this.*

Flower Adornment Sutra, Chapter Nine, Light Enlightenment

# 超時空的法語

## DHARMA THAT TRANSCENDS TIME AND SPACE

師父上人的説法是華嚴境界，是不可思議的，
過去可以變成現在，現在可以成爲未來，
是超時空的，沒有一定的限制。

**I knew that the Venerable Master's speaking of Dharma
is in an inconceivable realm, the realm of the Flower Adornment,
in which the past can become present and the present can turn into future.
It surpasses time and space and has no fixed limitation.**

釋恆頤
Shi Hengyi

十一月八日，訪問團從三藩市飛往臺北的途中，在飛機上，我就開始複聽人家所謄的稿，那裏面是上人所講解的《華嚴經》。當我按下錄音機時，感到很驚奇，上人説：

這個焰光明城所住的居民，因爲往昔所造的業，所以現在他們都有神足通。他們乘空而來，不用飛機，喜歡到哪裏，就到哪裏去，喜歡去哪裏旅行，就到哪裏旅行，都不需要買飛機票。

我聽了覺得很驚奇，所以師父上人的説法是華嚴境界，是不可思議的，過去可以變成現在，現在可以成爲未來，是超時空的，沒有一定的限制。

這種不可思議的境界，不是一次、二次，很多時候在聖城發生了一些事情，或者是關係整個聖城的，或者是個人的問題，很奇怪的是，當我在午餐負責播放錄音帶時，很多人聽到上人的法音，他們的問題都可以得到解決。然後他們都會很驚奇地問我：是不是我故意開？我説我不知道。只有一、二次，我是故意開，但是大部分時候，不是故意的，所以上人説法就是那麼不可思議。

我記得當師父的法體，從長堤聖寺移靈回萬佛聖城的時候，有三天的大法會。因爲師父剛剛入滅，大家心情非常沉痛，很難過。就在那天午餐的時候，我又拿起上人的法音播放給大家聽，可是當我的手指按下錄音帶之後，我幾乎忘了拿起來，我的眼睛發愣看著錄音帶很驚奇，因爲錄音帶那邊傳出來上人的話：

While on the plane flying from San Francisco to Taipei on November 8 with the delegation, I began listening to a tape of the Venerable Master's lecture on the *Flower Adornment Sutra*, in order to check the transcription. When I pressed the PLAY button, I was surprised to hear the Master's voice:

The residents of the City of Flaming Light, due to their past karma, all possess the power of spiritual travel. They can travel through the air, going sightseeing wherever they wish, without having to buy a ticket and ride on a plane.

So I knew that the Venerable Master's speaking of Dharma is in an inconceivable realm, the realm of the Flower Adornment, in which the past can become present and the present can turn into future. It surpasses time and space and has no fixed limitation.

Such inconceivable states are very common at the City of Ten Thousand Buddhas. When I play the Master's taped lecture during the noon meal, it often speaks directly to problems concerning the whole City or to personal problems. Many people, upon hearing the tape and discovering the solution to their problem, ask me in surprise, "Did you play that tape on purpose?" I tell them that I did not. I have deliberately played a tape only once or twice; most of the time I do not intentionally play a particular tape. Thus, the Venerable Master's speaking of Dharma is inconceivable.

I remember that when the Venerable Master's body was transported from Long Beach Monastery to the City of Ten Thousand Buddhas, there were three days of memorial services, and everyone was extremely sad. On that day when I pressed the button to play the Master's tape for the assembly at lunchtime, I was shocked to hear the Master say,

當佛入滅的時候，你們這些比丘、比丘尼、優婆塞、優婆夷，應當以戒爲師，以波羅提木叉爲師……。

當時因爲我們剛剛失去師父，我們的心情是非常非常非常難過，但是就在那一刹那，師父的這一句話，師父的心是那麼地慈悲，那麼溫和，令我們沉痛的心情，都得到了安慰，我們覺得非常非常感謝師父。

從三藩市搭機，經過很長的旅途，當十一月九日晚上來到臺灣，我們抵達機場時，看見一條很大的布條，上面寫著：「歡迎法界佛教會訪問團」。當時我看了覺得很有親切感，但是很快地我的鼻子一酸，眼睛也合起來了。我覺得很難過，我替別人難過，也替自己難過，我可以想像當師父在的時候，來到臺灣，大家看到師父，都會圍過來，好像見到爺爺、見到慈父一樣，師父前、師父後地跟著。但是這次來，大家沒有看到師父，只是看到師父的照片和舍利子，痛失師父的難過是可以想像的。但是在痛失良師之餘，我們應該痛下針砭，痛改前非，以戒爲師，行師所師，學師所學。希望大家能夠更努力，能夠抖擻精神，勇猛向道，然後我們大家一起努力復興聖教，這樣才能報答師父上人的恩德。

When the Buddha entered Nirvana, he said, 'You Bhikshus, Bhikshunis, Upasakas, and Upasikas should take the precepts, the Pratimoksha, as your teacher.'

Having just lost our Master, all of us were extremely grieved. However, in that instant, we could sense the compassion and gentleness with which the Master spoke that sentence, and we were consoled and extremely grateful.

When we arrived at the airport in Taiwan on the evening of November 9 after the long trip from San Francisco, we were greeted with a banner: "Welcome to the Visiting Delegation of Dharma Realm Buddhist Association." It gave me a very warm feeling, but then I felt bad, because I remembered that when the Master came to Taiwan, everyone would gather around him as if he were their elderly grandfather or kindly father. This time, instead of seeing the Master, everyone only saw his photographs and his sharira. I can imagine how much they missed the Master. However, beyond missing the Master, we ought to painfully change our own faults and take the precepts as our teacher, practicing what our Master practiced and studying what he studied. I hope everyone will advance with increased vigor on the Path, so that we can together make Buddhism flourish and repay our Master's kindness.

---

不壞無邊境　　而遊諸億刹　　於有無所著　　彼自在如佛
諸佛如虛空　　究竟常清淨　　憶念生歡喜　　彼諸願具足

——《大方廣佛華嚴經》〈光明覺品第九〉

*His state is indestructible and has no boundary,*
*And he can roam throughout billions of lands.*
*Towards existence he has no attachment*
*And he is comfortable like the Buddha.*

*All Buddhas are like empty space,*
*Ultimately and eternally pure.*
*By always remembering to bring forth happiness,*
*All of one's vows are completed.*

Flower Adornment Sutra, Chapter Nine, Light Enlightenment

# 凡事總是謹慎點好
## IT'S ALWAYS BETTER TO BE CAUTIOUS

雖然只是區區幾個字，但已涵蓋了全部的重要性，
如今已永烙我心，成了我的座右銘。

**Those few short words conveyed the importance
of the project to me. They remain engraved in my mind
to this day and serve as my motto.**

張麗美
Limei Zhang

一九九四年四月，在王珠慶居士的推薦下，抱著戰戰兢兢的心，隨臺灣法務團至美國法界聖城，參加上人的壽誕，並將籌辦上人十二月份於臺灣舉辦的佛學講座及護國息災大法會的企劃書，呈給上人過目。

當我第一次面見上人時，他慈祥、悲憫的容顏，感動得我猶如失散多年的孩子，剎那間見著自己親人似的，多麼溫馨。慈父般的關懷，湧現瀝瀝，頓時我嚎啕大哭，欲言又止，數度哽咽無法報告。數日後，於洛杉磯再度晉見上人，針對企劃書內容，請上人指示修改，上人手握整疊的資料，面帶微笑的說：

凡事總是謹慎點好。

雖然只是區區幾個字，但已涵蓋了全部的重要性，如今已永烙我心，成了我的座右銘。

一九九五年六月七日，上人圓寂，我心中的慈父離開了我們。一年多來的期盼，瞬間落空，真是不能接受這事實，只有埋怨自己如此沒福報。在臺灣眾多緬懷上人德行的四眾弟子，希望能舉行追思法會，這個提議得到美國法界佛教總會的支持。承蒙法師及王珠慶居士再次推薦，我當下承擔下此次籌劃的工作。以下是我籌劃過程中，一些不可思議的感應事蹟：

（一）上人夢中指示：上人在我身旁就如生前一般無異，訝異的是，竟然很直接的答應我，會滿

In April 1994 at the urging of Upasika Zhuqing Wang, I joined a Dharma delegation from Taiwan to participate in the Venerable Master's birthday celebration at the City of the Dharma Realm, and to show the Master the plans for his trip to Taiwan in December to deliver lectures and to hold the Dharma Assembly for Protecting the Nation and Quelling Disasters. The first time I saw the Master, I was deeply touched by his gentleness and compassion. I felt like a lost orphan who had suddenly found his parent. He was as warm and caring as a father. I became choked with sobs and could hardly give my report. Several days later, when I again met with the Master in Los Angeles and asked for instructions regarding the overall preparation for the event, the Master touched the pile of materials with his hand and said with a smile,

It's always better to be cautious.

Those few short words conveyed the importance of the project to me. They remain engraved in my mind to this day and serve as my motto.

The Master passed into stillness on June 7, 1995. Our compassionate father departed from us, and over a year's worth of preparation instantly went down the drain. I could hardly bring myself to accept this fact, and lamented my own lack of blessings. The Master's many disciples in Taiwan hoped to hold a memorial Dharma assembly, and their suggestion was supported by the Sangha in America. At the urging of the Dharma Masters and of Upasika Zhuqing Wang, I accepted responsibility for organizing the event. Under the guidance of the Sangha, I humbly sought advice, eagerly assumed responsibility, seriously carried out the work, and did not stray from the Master's Three Great Principles. The following inconceivable responses occurred during the time I was planning the memorial ceremony.

(1) *The Master came to instruct me in my dream.* When I was taking up the task of organizing the event, I dreamed of the Master. He appeared beside me just the way he had been when alive, and he immediately promised to give me the help that I asked for.

我的願。有許多居士經過他身旁，怎麼都沒有看見上人呢？我相當訝異！這不就是提示著「上人從虛空來，回到虛空去」，只要你有心求助於上人，上人就如同觀世音菩薩，千處祈求千處見，為眾生解難。

（二）確訂法會日期、地點及內容之擬定：日期擇訂於十一月十一日至十三日，十一、十二日舉行追思法會，十三日是追思大會並供眾瞻仰上人舍利。十一日（農曆九月十九日）是觀世音菩薩出家日，銜接著是連續假日，在這大日子裏，承租場地是個大問題。適用於大型法會的場地，在臺北唯有板橋體育館，但報備承租須在一年前，如同一日期以先登記者優先。於今事出突然，經過協調，我與公關組長果雄居士，拜見大觀寺⊥悟⊤修法師，法師慈悲地說：「你們眼前最重要是：如何將追思法會圓滿的辦好。其他不是問題，上人是一代高僧，如今我未能幫上什麼忙，實在很慚愧。」他將自己籌劃已久，且已陸續發出萬份通告的法會延後，來成就我們，到現在我還感激不已。

（三）場地的使用限制：已有數十次使用的經驗，板橋體育館場地對我而言熟悉無比，只隔數月，為何在使用上的限制會如此之多。數次溝通均無商量的餘地，造成很大的不方便。但是又不得不取得館方同意，能恢復香積組「大寮」使用的地方，為了衛生、方便製作每日數千個便當。另外，舞台背景突出物的拆除，因有礙安置佛像及安全問題等等，且又要秉持我們的三大宗旨，我幾乎被考倒。沮喪多天，求助上人加持，賜給我智慧與好的助緣，職之所在，決不能洩氣。冷靜數日後，突然想出另一種方法，一切如原先計劃圓滿達成，有些更是物超所值。

（四）義工感應事蹟：此次法會時間由每日上午九時至晚上九時，連續三天。從事先準備工作、佈置，及圓滿後場地的整理等，時間相當長。在上人德行感召下，登記發心的義工近六百位。在此忙碌的工業社會裏，居士們如此發心，實屬難得。其中有位居士早已報名，在期間中發生車禍，以前縱使小傷皮膚也很難復原，但她意志堅定，抱定參加的決心，往後奇蹟似的快速恢復，終於滿她的願。還有

However, I was surprised because none of the other laypeople who passed by the Master saw him. This was testimony to the fact that the Master came from empty space, and he returned to empty space. If we seek his help, he is just like the Bodhisattva Observer of the World's Sounds (Guanshiyin), who appears simultaneously in thousands of places in response to living beings' pleas for aid.

(2) *The fixing of the dates, place, and program of the Dharma assembly.* The dates were set to be from November 11-13, with the memorial ceremony on all three days and the exhibition of the Master's sharira on the 13th. The 11th (lunar date 9/9) was the Anniversary of Guanshiyin Bodhisattva's Leaving the Home-life, and the next two days were holidays. It was very difficult to rent a large hall on such dates. The only place in Taipei suitable for a large Dharma gathering was the Banqiao Auditorium, but it required signing up a year in advance, and those who signed up first were given first choice of dates. Due to the suddenness of our event, I negotiated with Mr. Guoxiong, leader of the Public Affairs Committee, and we visited Dharma Master Wu Xiu of Daguan Monastery. The Dharma Master kindly told us, "Your most important concern right now is to organize the memorial ceremony well. Nothing else matters. The Master was a pre-eminent monk of his time, and I'm ashamed that I cannot be of any help." In order to accommodate our event, he postponed his own Dharma assembly, which had been planned long in advance and for which he had distributed 10,000 announcements. I am still deeply grateful for his kindness.

(3) *Restrictions on the use of the place.* I had rented the Banqiao Auditorium several dozen times before and was extremely familiar with the place. It was strange because many new restrictions had been placed on its use in the last few months. All attempts to negotiate failed, and as a result there were many inconveniences. Yet I needed to obtain the Auditorium's agreement on several points, such as (a) to use part of the facility as a kitchen, as that would be the only hygienic and convenient way to prepare several thousand meals daily; (b) to remove objects protruding from the background of the stage, in order to install Buddha images and for safety reasons. At the same time, I had to uphold the Three Great Principles. I nearly gave up. After several days of despair, I prayed to the Master to give me wisdom and to let the conditions be favorable. I could not give up on my duty. After several days of calm reflection, I suddenly thought of another way (the details of which will not be given here). Everything was able to go through as planned, and some aspects even surpassed my expectations.

(4) *The response of the volunteers.* The schedule of the Dharma assembly ran from 9 a.m. to 9 p.m. for three successive days. Considerable time was spent setting up, decorating, and cleaning up the auditorium before and after each day's events. Drawn by the Venerable Master's virtue, nearly six hundred volunteers signed up. For laypeople to be so willing to contribute their time and energy is truly remarkable in this busy society. One of the volunteers who had signed up early on was injured in a car

裱貝上人法語的老闆，他家中香爐突然發火，他告訴文宣組長顏居士，菩薩指示他一定要接此工作，同時也只能拿一萬二仟元的工本費，雖然費時最少一個月的工作天，但他欣然接受。

（五）殊勝的傳供：在此次追思法會中，每日午供均安排佛前傳供大典，以香、燈、花、果、齋菜等，共一百零八道供品，以分區方式輪流傳供。由四十多位法師引導之下，在莊嚴肅穆的供養真言中，供養佛、上人。與會數千信眾，無不法喜充滿。在臺灣大型法會中，如此殊勝之極，此乃創先例。

（六）瞻仰舍利：追思大典當天下午，請出上人數千來顆不同色澤，晶瑩剔透的舍利子、舍利花，供大眾瞻仰。前來瞻仰的信眾，早已把會場擠得水洩不通，數百名義工各就自己崗位，讓數千信眾魚貫進入，在「阿彌陀佛」佛號聲中依序瞻仰。有少數來不及瞻仰者，當眾大哭，經法師開緣後，滿他們的願。

在籌劃請臺灣佛教界長老參加追思大典過程中，有一次在臺中，已晚上六點多了，告辭了法師，欲回臺北時，想找個地方充飢。但我人生地不熟的，只好借問雜貨店老闆，素食店在那兒。結果問到的那一家已打烊了。正想打消念頭，在背後突然有位太太說：「到我家來吃，我也吃素，只要妳不嫌棄，今晚我菜還很多。」我嚇了一跳，轉身一看，她站在街的對面，差我尚有一段距離，奇怪！怎麼會聽到呢？她面帶笑容，牽著我的手，當時真是不好意思，我說：「我只想喝碗湯而已」，再三婉拒她的好意，她說：「那這樣！我不常住這裏，我女兒在拐彎處開皮包店，問她較清楚。」說著到了她女兒店裏。眼看她動作迅速地往裏走，馬上兩手端出四盤菜，接著湯、飯擺滿了收銀台。我想這下子不吃，對不起人家好意，要吃，真是不好意思。她女兒說：「我們全家茹素，我母親已三十年了，我們都是一家人，今日才如此有緣。」是！真是有緣！有位組長義工知道這經過後說：「上人處處都關照妳，怕妳渴，怕妳餓，妳真有福報。」我的同修賴居士也說：「連上人都捨不得妳煮飯，洗碗。」他們

accident. Nevertheless, she was determined to participate in the memorial ceremony. Although it had always taken a long time for even minor scrapes to heal in the past, this time she recovered with miraculous speed and was able to fulfill her wish. Also, the man who was to frame the Venerable Master's calligraphy saw a sudden burst of fire in his incense burner at home. He told Upasaka Yan, the leader of the Publicity Committee, that a Bodhisattva had told him he had to accept the job, but could only accept NT $12,000 in payment, even though the work required at least a month's time. He happily accepted these conditions.

(5) *The supreme Ceremony for Passing Offerings.* For the daily meal offering ceremony at noon, under the guidance of forty-some Dharma Masters, 108 items including incense, lamps, flowers, fruits, and vegetarian dishes were passed from person to person to the front to offer to the Buddha and the Venerable Master. This was done as the assembly solemnly chanted the True Words for Making Offerings. Everyone was filled with the joy of the Dharma. Such a sublime effect was unprecedented in large-scale Dharma assemblies in Taiwan.

(6) *Beholding the sharira.* On the afternoon of the final day, the Venerable Master's several thousand sharira and sharira clusters of different colors, some as transparent as crystal, were taken out for the assembly to behold. The auditorium was packed, and the several hundred volunteers had to form several levels of "human walls," allowing the thousands of devotees to line up and behold the sharira as everyone recited the name of Amitabha Buddha. When several people who missed the event began to cry, the Dharma Masters gave them a special chance to see the sharira.

Once when I was in the process of inviting elders of Taiwan Buddhism to participate in the memorial ceremony, I was in Taichung and it was already past six o'clock in the evening. I took my leave from the Dharma Masters, thinking to return to Taipei. My stomach was rumbling and I needed to satisfy my hunger. Being in an unfamiliar place, I asked a local shopkeeper where the vegetarian restaurant was. Unfortunately, the one I asked about was already closed. Just when I was about to give up, a woman behind me said, "Why don't you come eat at my house. I'm vegetarian, and if you're not too picky, I still have a lot of food left from supper." Startled, I turned around and saw her standing on the other side of the street. Strange! How could she have heard my conversation? Smiling, she took me by the hand. I felt embarrassed and said, "I just wanted a bowl of soup, that's all," trying to decline her invitation. She said, "Come on! I'm not here very often, but my daughter has a dress shop around the corner, let's ask her." Then she went into her daughter's shop. I watched as she quickly went to the back and came out carrying four dishes of food, followed by soup. She covered the entire counter with food. I thought that it would be too impolite not to eat, but I also felt embarrassed to eat. Her daughter said, "Our family is vegetarian, my mom for thirty years now. We're all one family. That's why we have such affinities." Indeed, we truly had affinities. When another volunteer heard what happened, he said, "How blessed you are! The Master watches over

以上的一番話，帶給我無限的鼓勵。

一場法會的圓滿，要有多種因緣的具足，每個人都是顆小小螺絲釘，需要緊密結合，鬆動一顆都會影響大局。三天的活動，我與多位組長在臨圓滿之際，無不熱淚盈眶。其中一位組長有感而發，她這輩子均無因緣親近上人，此次參與義工，是她追隨上人法緣的開始。又有一位組長說：「有一晚，他夢見上人身著黃色祖衣，有許多位法師圍繞在他身旁誦經，場面相當隆重。他不知道發生何事，就問身旁的人，有人告訴他，上人圓寂了，快去板橋體育館誦經。」事隔幾天，就接到我電話請她發心。雖然在數天的護法工作下，但他們個個無倦容，將會後的場地，裏裏外外整理就緒，就連館方管理員也說，是有始以來的大掃除，她們才圓滿卸下此番義工的責任。

我十多年來，參與相當多次的法會籌劃工作，唯獨此次，面臨前所未有的考驗。其外在因素，讓自己不得不以毅力、恆心、用心逐一克服，諸如場地佈置的克服，人事方面的協調……等。又許多的過程，我均未有經驗，傳供大典、舍利瞻仰。在區區有限的館內，從事動態的進行方式，必須要事先週詳的計劃，嚴密的組織。團隊的默契，到臨場經驗的掌控，是非常機動性的。上人告訴我「凡事總是謹慎點好！」我是馬虎不得，承蒙僧團的指導，我全力能達到最圓滿的程度。

「上人捨命爲佛事」他願生生世世爲佛教奮鬥，爲佛教努力，甚至犧牲性命，在所不辭，我的發心只是冰山一角。上人的弘願，是我效法的目標，往後應該更加精進，懈怠不得。

you constantly, worrying that you might be hungry or thirsty." My fellow cultivator said, "Even the Master didn't want you to be troubled by cooking or washing dishes." I was greatly encouraged by their observations.

Various conditions are needed to bring about the successful completion of a Dharma assembly. Each person is like a small screw that needs to be screwed on tight. If even one screw comes loose, it will affect the whole structure. By the end of the three-day event, I and many of the group leaders were moved to tears. One of them told me that although she had not had been able to meet the Venerable Master, being a volunteer had given her the chance to follow the Master's Dharma. Another group leader said one night she dreamed of the Master wearing his yellow host sash, surrounded by many Dharma Masters who were reciting a Sutra. The scene was solemn. When she asked what was happening, she was told that the Master had perfected the stillness and she ought to hurry to the Banqiao Auditorium to recite Sutras. A few days later she received my phone call asking her to volunteer. Despite toiling for several days in a row to protect the Dharma, none of the volunteers looked tired. After the Dharma assembly was over, they cleaned up the entire auditorium, inside and out, thus completing their duties. Even the auditorium management admitted it was the first time the facility had received such an overall cleanup.

I have organized many Dharma assemblies for more than ten years, but this was the first time I faced so many challenges. Under the circumstances, dogged determination and careful diligence were required to overcome difficulties in decorating the place, coordinating personnel, and so on. I had no prior experience with certain items of the program, such as the passing of offerings and the display of the sharira. To allow several thousand people to move in line and view the sharira in the limited space required detailed advance planning, careful organization, and close teamwork. Keeping the crowd under control was quite a nerve-wracking experience. Having been told by the Master that "it's always better to be cautious," there was no way I could be careless. With the guidance of the Sangha, I put my full efforts into making the Dharma assembly as successful as possible.

The Venerable Master renounced his life to do the Buddha's work. He vowed to work zealously for Buddhism in life after life, and was perfectly willing to sacrifice his own life to do this. My own resolve is only the tip of the iceberg. Taking the Master's great vows as my model, I must be even more vigorous and never slack off.

---

佛了法如幻　通達無障礙　心淨離眾著　調伏諸群生
——《大方廣佛華嚴經》〈光明覺品第九〉

*The Buddhas understand that dharmas are like an illusion,*
*And have penetrated them without obstruction.*
*Their minds are pure, apart from the multitude of attachments,*
*And they are able to subdue all beings.*

Flower Adornment Sutra, Chapter Nine, Light Enlightenment

# A GENTLE REMINDER
# FROM THE VENERABLE MASTER

# 上人的一個輕輕提示

## At times of real need, this (outline of a heel) is a tangible and very gentle reminder of where I should be going.

## 我真正需要時，這個有形的腳印，輕輕提醒我，該往哪裡走。

Lee Eagleson (Kuo Li)
果璃

Recently, I have developed a minor skin condition on the skin of my right foot wherein the skin is dyed red from hemoglobin from ruptured capillaries. On the top of my foot is a distinct outline of the heel of a shoe, about the size of an Arhat shoe heel. To find out how this happened, I will take you back nineteen years to the summer of 1976 at the City of Ten Thousand Buddhas ("CTTB").

It was a few days before the first ordination at CTTB, and I was working on an electrical problem at Great Compassion Quad using a ladder with a smooth metal skid on the smooth concrete sidewalk. The bottom of the ladder slipped out, causing me to fall about six feet and end up with my ankle mashed between the sidewalk, the ladder, and my body weight. I was taken to the hospital for X-rays and there was no fractures, but the ankle was swollen and hurt badly. A few days after that, I was sitting in a chair in the Buddha hall when Shrfu returned from San Francisco with a few guests. Shrfu came straight away over to me carrying his White Whisk. I put my palms together as he whisked me from head to foot, whisking everything into my right leg and foot; then he gave a gentle kick to my shin and stepped on my foot with a gentle and firm pressure; as I remember, the heel of his shoe was right where the mark is now, nineteen years later.

Shrfu told me that because of my temper, Weitou Bodhisattva had given me a whack, as a warning. Though the ankle was not healed (some lessons should be painful), the work that Shrfu did on me was far deeper and more profound than I have been able to understand. In the *Dharani Sutra* the White Whisk is used to eradicate karmic obstacles and difficulties resulting from evil killing karma.

Though I continue to dream of Shrfu occasionally, at times of real need, this is a tangible and very gentle reminder where I should be going, and a warning to always change for the better.

最近，我右腳的皮膚開始有輕微的毛病出現，從破裂的毛細管滲出的血紅素將那部分的皮膚染成紅色，在腳背上出現了一個很明顯的腳印，大小如一隻羅漢鞋的鞋跟。要知道這是怎麼一回事，我就要把你帶到十九年前，一九七六年的萬佛城。

那時正是第一次傳三壇大戒的前幾天，我在大悲院修理電氣。我用的梯子底部有金屬的墊底，而走道的水泥地又很滑。梯子的底部打滑，我自大約六尺的高度摔下來，右腳踝正好被壓在走道、梯子、及我自己的體重間。我到醫院去照X光，沒發現骨折，但是腳踝是腫的，而且疼得厲害。幾天後，我正坐在大殿的一張椅子上時，師父帶了幾個客人自舊金山回來。他手持白拂塵，直接向著我來。當師父幫我加持時，我雙手合十；師父的白拂塵將我從頭拂到腳，將所有的一切都拂進了我的右腿及右腳，然後輕輕地踢了我的小腿一下，並在我的腳背上輕踏一下。我記得師父踏的地方，正是十九年後鞋印出現的地方。

師父告訴我，韋陀菩薩給我一個教訓，因為我脾氣太壞。雖然腳踝沒有立刻完全復元（有些教訓是很痛的），但是師父給我的加持，遠比我所能了解的還要深遠。《陀羅尼經》裡說，「白拂手」是用來消除由殺業所造成的業障。

雖然，我還是偶爾夢到師父，可是在我真正需要時，這個有形的腳印，輕輕提醒我該往哪裡走，那也同時警告，我要往好的做去。

# 宇宙白作曲心得

## THOUGHTS ON COMPOSING THE MUSIC FOR "WHITE UNIVERSE"

〈宇宙白〉是一位大菩薩的悲願以盡虛空微塵法界爲責任，
捨命拔濟衆生，頑冥難度猶不放棄，
誠懇爲法獻身。

**"White Universe" describes a great Bodhisattva who takes every mote of dust to the ends of space and throughout the Dharma Realm as his own responsibility, and whose compassionate vows are to renounce his own life to save living beings--not giving up on them no matter how obstinate and wayward they are--and to sincerely dedicate his life to the Dharma.**

F 小調　F Minor

猶記爲〈宇宙白〉作曲當兒，曾請教上人，上人說：

啊…，這〈宇宙白〉是按照岳飛〈滿江紅〉之氣勢而做的。

一般佛教歌曲，調子大多較爲平和。宣公上人作〈宇宙白〉，雖謙稱仿效〈滿江紅〉古調而塡詞，但氣魄精神已遠勝於〈滿江紅〉。爲了配合〈宇宙白〉詞句之多番變化，不同凡響，所以唱法難度提高，音域亦廣。事實上〈宇宙白〉曲子，比〈滿江紅〉只高兩個音階度；若唱得起〈滿江紅〉，唱〈宇宙白〉並不是問題。

〈宇宙白〉是一位大菩薩的悲願以盡虛空微塵法界爲責任，捨命拔濟衆生，頑冥難度猶不放棄，誠懇爲法獻身。由至極的寂靜中，緩緩甦醒，刹那間，便幻化出無限生機，但靜不礙動，從定中把動態在電光石火中示現，而卻動不礙靜。

在〈宇宙白〉之作曲過程中，不禁驚歎於文詞之絕妙。短短未足百字的詞句中，竟涵藏多番變化，流露出數不盡的意思，表白了說不盡的感懷。這是心思言語之外所難述的境界，是上人一生之精神之寫照，十八大願之精髓。

When I sought the Venerable Master's advice as I was composing the music for "White Universe," the Master said,

Ah...'White Universe' was written after the style of Yue Fei's 'Red River.'

Most Buddhist tunes are relatively mellow. Although the Master's poem "White Universe" is humbly said to emulate "Red River" in style and meter, its magnificent spirit far surpasses that of "Red River." The need to accomodate the myriad transformations and unusual sound of "White Universe" makes the melody more difficult to sing and requires a wider range of pitch. Actually, the tune to "White Universe" is only two notes higher than the original tune for "Red River"; anyone who can sing "Red River" will have no difficulty with "White Universe."

"White Universe" describes a great Bodhisattva who takes every mote of dust to the ends of space and throughout the Dharma Realm as his own responsibility, and whose compassionate vows are to renounce his own life to save living beings--not giving up on them no matter how obstinate and wayward they are--and to sincerely dedicate his life to the Dharma. Slowly coming alive from the utmost stillness, in an instant, he can create infinite life potentials, yet stillness does not obstruct movement; from within samadhi he can manifest instantaneous movement, yet that movement does not hinder stillness.

While composing the music for "White Universe," I could not help marvelling at its awesome wonder. In fewer than a hundred characters, it embraces so many transformations, reveals meanings beyond reckoning, and expresses infinite feelings. This is a realm of being beyond words and thought; a portrayal of the Venerable Master's spirit; the essence of his eighteen great vows.

今試以凡夫淺識，配上曲調，並將詞意分三段
詮釋：

第一段，「冰天雪地」，浮現起一幅清雅畫面，
引人沉思，孰不知幻想之外，此景並不可愛，畫
之細處竟把「無數條小蟲」冷得「凍斃且蟄眠」
。定的起點「靜裡觀察」，動靜同現，「動中審
諦」，攝念不失。緊隨著卻是激烈的場面：「龍
爭虎鬥」常遊戲，「鬼哭神嚎」……急勢忽收，
動靜的演變，歸回三字「幻化奇」。

第二段，是實相的演述，佛法之精華。「眞實義
絕言」；但無言欲說，待止再進，「不思議，當
進趨。」詞意深廣表露，從小現大，從內到外，
從微塵至法界，調子從低漸高，最後大、小、內
、外、微塵、法界，皆同歸一體，圓融無礙。「
大小泯，內外非，微塵遍，法界周，團團個圓融
。」再度高潮，又歸回「互相無礙」。

第三段，完全是上人大悲愍懷的激動感慨，悲願
難述以「雙拳打破虛空蓋，一口吞進剎海源」，
形容艱辛大志。因「大慈悲」，故猶在五濁惡世
中「普度」，以至「流血汗，不休息。」

Having attempted to set the poem to music based upon my shallow understanding, I shall now give a brief explanation in three parts:

The first section *"Ice in the sky, snow on the ground"* presents an sublime vision that invites deep reflection. The scene is not endearing, however, for a closer look reveals that *"Numberless tiny bugs die in the cold or sleep in hibernation."* Samadhi begins with the next phrase: *"In the midst of stillness you should contemplate,"* this is stillness and movement appearing simultaneously, *"and within movement you should investigate,"* collecting your thoughts without cease. An exciting scene follows: *"Dragons spar and tigers wrestle in continual playful sport; / Ghosts and spirits wail."* The transformations of movement and stillness are summarized in the words, *"their illusory transformations strange."*

The second section describes the state of reality, the essence of the Buddhadharma. *"Ultimate truth transcends words."* Although there are no words, one wishes to speak. Having stopped, one advances again. *"Not thought about or talked about, you ought to advance with haste."* As the poem's vast and profound meaning progresses from small to great, from inside to out, from a mote of dust to the Dharma Realm, the pitch rises from low to high. Finally, great and small, inside and out, a dust mote and the Dharma Realm all return to a single substance. *"With great and small destroyed, with no inside or out, / It pervades every mote of dust and encompasses the Dharma Realm, / Complete, whole, and perfectly fused."* This second climax ends with the words *"interpenetrating without obstruction."*

The third section is full of the Venerable Master's overwhelming compassion and pity for living beings. The next lines describe his compassionate vows: *"With two clenched fists, shatter the covering of empty space. / In one mouthful swallow the source of seas of Buddhalands. With great compassion rescue all."* With his great kindness and compassion, he rescues all of us in the evil world of the five turbidities, *"sparing no blood or sweat, and never pause to rest!"*

---

一一地獄中　經於無量劫　爲度眾生故　而能忍是苦
不惜於身命　常護諸佛法　無我心調柔　能得如來道
　　　　　　——《大方廣佛華嚴經》〈光明覺品第九〉

*Within each hell*
*One passes through limitless kalpas.*
*In order to cross over living beings,*
*One can endure all that suffering.*

*He has no regard for his body or life,*
*As he constantly protects all Buddhadharmas.*
*His mind has no self and so he is compliant.*
*And so he is able to obtain the Way of the Thus Come One.*

Flower Adornment Sutra, Chapter Nine, Light Enlightenment

宇宙白

# 提燈的老人
## AN OLD MAN CARRYING A LANTERN

王果容
Guorong Ong

苦海中一片茫茫，人生像個盲者迷失在路中央。
沒有智者的引導，沒有明眼善知識的教導，徘徊在路中央，無有去處。
隨著業風，忽天忽地，在六道輪迴中輪轉不息。

*In the vast and boundless sea of suffering, human life is like a blind man lost on the road.*
*With no wise one to guide him, with no enlightened teacher to instruct him,*
*He paces back and forth on the road, not knowing where to go.*
*Blown by the wind of karma, suddenly up to the heavens and then back to earth,*
*We turn forever in the wheel of the six paths.*

正當盲者感到沮喪、失落、失去自我時，
提燈的老人出現了，為人世間帶來了光明。
點燃眾生的心燈，救療眾生的心病，引導眾生走向光明大道。
大家不再迷茫，不再徬徨。
法雨的滋潤帶來了多少新生命的重生，多少浪子的依怙。

*Just when the blind man is about to give up in despair,*
*An old man carrying a lantern appears, bringing light to the world.*
*Lighting up the lamps of our minds, healing the illnesses of our minds,*
*Leading living beings onto the broad and brightly-lit road.*
*No one will be lost and flustered again.*
*The nourishing moisture of the Dharma rain:*
*To how many has it brought new life?*
*To how many wandering sons has it provided refuge?*

智者的法雨，洗滌眾生內心的污垢與塵埃。
眾生都沐浴在一片法雨中，
時時得到法雨的灌溉，
菩提苗也日愈增長，
心靈中一片光明與寧靜。

*The Dharma rain of the wise one*
*Washes away the dust and defilement in living beings' minds.*
*Living beings bathe in the rain of Dharma,*
*Constantly receiving its moisture.*
*Their Bodhi sprouts grow day by day,*
*Their hearts and souls become bright and peaceful.*

眾生對這位大慈悲父充滿了無限的感激，
他的大恩大德永世也難以報答，
為末法的我們帶來了幸福與希望，
對人生充滿了無限的憧憬。

Infinite is our gratitude towards our compassionate father.
In endless lifetimes it would be difficult to repay his kindness and virtue.
Bringing blessings and hope to us in the Dharma-ending Age,
He inspired boundless dreams and aspirations in our lives.


世間的無常，歲月的無情。
大慈悲父示現病態捨我們而去，
這無情的打擊，使幼小的我們不願接受這殘酷的事實。
只有默默地等待，希望重見慈父的慈顏。
然而這一切的等待，換來的只有失落與痛苦。

Impermanent is the world; merciless is time.
Manifesting illness, our compassionate father left us.
Merciless trauma! We are too young and cannot accept this cruel reality.
Silently we wait, hoping to see our father's compassionate face once more.
But waiting all this time has only brought pain and disappointment.


老人色身確已離去，留下的是那無盡的法藏。
大家唯有重拾希望，重新整頓，從悲傷中回到現實，
繼續奮鬥，重提老人所燃起的明燈。
傳承老人的三大願：弘法、教育、翻譯經典。
為挽救末法的眾生，繼續努力。

Although our elder one is gone in body, he has left behind an infinite treasury of Dhama.
We must all pick up our hopes, repair our spirits, and turn from grief to face the reality.
With continuing zeal, let's raise up the bright lamps he lit,
Carrying on the elder's three great vows--
Dharma propagation, education, translation of Sutras--
And working hard to save beings in the Dharma-ending Age.


\*       \*       \*


苦海中一片茫茫，人生像一片小舟，漂泊在海中央。
沒有明燈的導引，沒有指南針的指示。
迎著風，踩著浪，前程茫茫，
在業海中，浮浮沉沉找不到出路。

In the vast and boundless sea of suffering, human life is like a little boat floating on the sea.
Without the guidance of a bright light or a compass,
It breaks the waves and heads into the wind, following its vague course.
Bobbing up and down on the sea of karma, we cannot find a way out.

正當掌舵的人兒感到無助、徬徨、恐慌時，
在海島上呈現一道光芒，
爲險難的眾生帶來了一線生機；
燃起眾生心靈的燈光。
從此人生有了目標，有了方向，不再迷茫。

*Just when the boat captain is feeling helpless and frightened,*
*A ray of light shines forth from an island,*
*Bringing the hope of life to living beings in danger,*
*Lighting up the lamps in our hearts.*
*With new purpose and direction in our lives,*
*We are no longer lost and confused.*

挺著胸，抬起頭，再也不怕澎湃洶湧的巨浪。
提起勇氣面對一重一重的危機，
爲人生點綴了亮麗的色彩。

*Standing tall, lifting our heads, we fear no more the huge, surging waves.*
*Plucking up our courage, we face one danger after another,*
*Painting bright colors on the canvas of life.*

眾生對這位提燈的老人所帶來的幸福與希望，
心裡充滿著無盡的感恩。
時時得到善知識的指引，
一步一步走向光明大道，
迎接著晨曦的陽光。

*Thinking of the old man with a lantern,*
*Who brought us hope and blessings,*
*Our hearts are filled with deep gratitude.*
*Under the constant guidance of our good teacher,*
*We walk step by step on the great bright path,*
*Going forward to greet the sunrise.*

正當大家沉浸在歡樂與法喜的歲月中，
不幸的事情隨著這歡樂的腳步來臨了。
提燈的老人決定回到虛空去了，
他希望我們不要依賴他，
要靠自己點燃自己的心燈。

*Everyone was intoxicated with the bliss of Dharma in those happy days,*
*But right on the footsteps of our happiness came the sorrowful news.*
*The lantern-bearing old man decided to return to empty space.*
*He hopes that we will not depend on him,*
*But will light up our mind lamps by ourselves.*

宣化老和尚追思紀念專集

老人的一片苦心，
期望徒兒們能自己長大，自強不息，
爲苦海中的眾生，
把佛教發揚光大。

*The elder one's earnest wish*
*Was that his disciples would grow up*
*And become strong and self-reliant,*
*So that we could make Buddhism flourish*
*For the sake of beings in the sea of suffering.*

大家收起悲哀與傷痛。
承繼老人的遺教，
爲末法的眾生盡上各人的心力。
維護正法永住於世。

*Let us all put aside our sorrow and pain,*
*And carry on the elder one's final teachings.*
*Let us do our best to help living beings in the Dharma-ending Age*
*By supporting the Proper Dharma and keeping it alive forever.*

In Memory of Venerable Master Hua

# 善用其心
# PUT YOUR MIND TO GOOD USE

釋恆貴
Shi Heng Gwei

在我沒有出家以前，有一次在金佛聖寺，有人請求師父給他寫一首《金剛經》偈誦，師父滿了他的願。當時我在旁邊，我沒有求，但是上人不求自寫，寫了一張墨寶，上面寫著某某留念，「勤修戒定慧，息滅貪瞋癡」。雖然我不是很懂，但我很高興，裱了之後把它掛起來。有一天，我的教授看見這一幅字畫，就問我「你的師父是方外人，為什麼還像世俗人一樣，什麼留念，這樣子呢？」當時我懂的佛法不多，雖然我知道上人並不是像世俗人一樣有感情的，但是我卻不會回答他。

過了幾年我出家了，出家的第一天，用完齋後，到方丈室，上人對我講：「妳看妳想出家想了這麼多年，今天是心想事成了。」上人又說：「我們的心好像猴子似的，東跑西跑，你不管著它，它就沒有控制了，所以你心信什麼、想什麼，終有一天，會成就什麼。」

我就想起幾年前師父寫給我的墨寶上有「某某留念」，所以我們念念都要注意自己的念頭，不要打那些不清淨的念頭，不要善惡交雜，要純一清淨。修行學法，就是要用師父的六大宗旨，用我們的真心來修學，這樣子才能夠成就聖果的。假如我們的心，是善惡交雜的，將來的果，也是善惡交雜的。

上人的教化，我體會最深的，就是「善用其心」。無論什麼時候，我們常常要迴光返照——我這個念頭對不對呢？我現在想的是什麼呢？我要成佛、要學聖賢，我將來必定能夠心想事成。如果打一些無聊的妄想，口是誦經，心想那些不正當的事情，善惡交雜，將來也不會成就，如我所想的得到聖果。所以今天我把這寶貴的經驗寫出來跟各位共勉。

我們一定要多多留念，善用其心。

Once when I was at Gold Buddha Monastery before I had left the home-life, someone asked the Master to write in calligraphy a verse from the *Vajra Sutra*. The Master did as requested, and I watched from the side. Then, without my asking, the Master wrote for me in calligraphy "For So-and-so to remember me by: Diligently cultivate precepts, samadhi, and wisdom; and put to rest greed, anger, and stupidity." I didn't really understand, but I was very happy to have it, and so I framed it and hung it up. One day my professor saw it and asked me, "Your Master is a cultivator, why would he want someone to remember him the way worldly people do?" Although I knew the Master was not sentimental the way worldly people were, I didn't understand much Buddhadharma and couldn't answer him. Several years later, on the day I left home, I went to the Abbot's quarters after lunch. The Master told me, "You see, you wanted to leave home for so many years, and now your wish has finally come true." He also said, "The mind is like a wild monkey running here and there. If you don't pay attention to it, it will go out of control. Whatever your mind believes in and thinks about will one day come true."

That reminded me of the words "For So-and-so to remember me by" which the Master had written several years back. The meaning is that we must pay attention to our thoughts. We must keep our mind pure and avoid impure thoughts, not let our thoughts be a confused mixture of good and evil. In studying and practicing the Dharma, we have to use the Master's Six Guiding Principles. Only by cultivating with a true mind will we be able to realize the fruition sagehood. If our mind is a mixture of good and evil thoughts, our future attainment will also be a mixture of good and evil.

I deeply feel that the essence of the Master's teaching is to use the mind well. We should constantly reflect upon ourselves and ask: "Is my thought proper? What am I thinking about?" If we want to become Buddhas or sages, we will certainly be able to accomplish our aim as long as we are mindful of it. On the other hand, if we indulge in idle thoughts and daydream about improper things as we are reciting the Sutras, we will not achieve sagehood. I have set down this personal experience as an encouragement to others.

We must always remember to put our mind to good use.

# 懷念師父上人
## IN MEMORIAM OF THE VENERABLE MASTER

師父這種爲法忘軀的精神，令我生出無比的敬佩與感動。

**I am deeply touched by, and feel the highest admiration for, his spirit of sacrificing himself for the sake of the Dharma.**

林聖婷
Shengting Lin

我很喜歡看到出家人，每當我走在街頭，有出家人從我身旁越過，我就滿心歡喜。

在一九九三年時，有這個機緣能夠見到上人，同時皈依受戒。當時上人應邀至一所技術學院演講。

演講會那一天，我提早半小時到會場，坐在最前座，結果沒想到我坐到了貴賓座，之後覺得很難爲情。過沒多久，法師帶領大眾念誦觀音菩薩聖號，上人就在這聖號中一步步走進會場。當上人從我面前走過，我心就喊著：「我終於見到上人了！」當時淚水不知爲何就像泉水般地湧了出來。之後，上人就到板橋體育館弘法，那時我正好在服務台結緣書處當義工。法會告一段落，人群紛紛湧出，從體育館裏傳出觀音菩薩聖號，於是大家知道上人要出來了，所有的義工都跪了下來，合著掌念聖號。我抬著頭望著上人走過，但當上人走不遠時，頭稍微往我的方向望一下，我嚇的馬上閉上眼睛，低下頭，有好幾分鐘不敢抬頭，心想自己是否做錯什麼事，要不然爲什麼那麼害怕。

傳三皈五戒的日子來了，當天師父上了臺，就先頂禮佛菩薩。我第一次看到一位高僧頂禮佛菩薩，覺得非常不可思議，因爲以往所見到的高僧大德都是直接上臺就開始講法了，上人是如此的恭敬佛菩薩。三皈五戒結束後，上人就開示：

受完五戒，就是成佛的第一步，
接下來就靠個人的努力了。

我很天眞地想著：太好了，受戒就可以成佛了，但是之後要靠自己努力，不知努力到何時？最後

I really like to see left-home people. Whenever a left-home person passes me as I walk on the street, my heart is filled with joy.

In 1993, I had the opportunity to meet the Venerable Master, take refuge, and receive the precepts from him. The Master had accepted an invitation to give a lecture at an institute of technology.

On the day of the lecture, I went half an hour early so that I could sit in the front row. By accident, I sat in the seats reserved for honored guests, and was very embarrassed. After a little while, as the Dharma Masters led the audience in reciting the name of Guanyin Bodhisattva, the Venerable Master walked slowly into the auditorium. As the Master passed in front me, I cried out in my heart, "I've finally seen the Master!" I started crying without knowing why. Afterwards, when the Master went to the Banqiao Auditorium to speak Dharma, I was working as a volunteer at the reception desk, where free books were being distributed. At some point in the Dharma assembly, the crowd in the auditorium began reciting Guanyin Bodhisattva's name. Knowing that the Master was about to come out, all the volunteers knelt down and recited along with joined palms. I was looking up at the Master as he walked in my direction, but when the Master directed his glance slightly in my direction, I was so frightened I immediately closed my eyes and lowered my head, not daring to look up for several minutes. I wondered if I had done something wrong to cause me to feel so afraid.

On the day when the three refuges and five precepts were to be transmitted, the Master ascended the stage and first bowed to the Buddhas and Bodhisattvas. That was the first time I saw an eminent monk make obeisance to the Buddhas and Bodhisattvas, and it was extremely inconceivable to me. In the past, I had always seen other high monks and virtuous ones go on stage and begin lecturing right away. Only the Venerable Master was so respectful to the Buddhas and Bodhisattvas. After transmitting the refuges and precepts, the Master gave a Dharma talk:

Receiving the five precepts is the only first step towards becoming a Buddha. The rest depends on your own hard work.

I naively thought to myself, "It's great that receiving the precepts means we can achieve Buddhahood, but I wonder how long we'll have to "work hard" before we succeed." Finally, as the Master

師父坐著念觀音菩薩聖號，我就在這聖號中，頂禮師父三拜後，離開會場。

上人給我的感覺，就像一位慈祥的佛菩薩，他的願力廣大無邊，將佛法傳至西方國家，及將佛經翻譯成各國的語言，讓世界各國的人，能夠分享法益。辦教育是上人的心願，讓未來的主人翁，將來能成為一個奉公守法的好公民。同時陸續在世界各地開闢新道場，讓每一個人能夠見聞佛法，同時有機會參與修行的行列。

師父對佛法的貢獻，行人所不能行，忍人所不能忍，受人所不能受，流血汗，不休息，這種為法忘軀的精神，令我生出無比的敬佩與感動。

上人已在一九九五年六月圓寂，雖然上人法身不在，但法師們，仍然不畏艱辛困難，繼續宣揚佛法，將正法流傳於世間，永住於世。

remained seated and recited Guanyin Bodhisattva's name along with the assembly, I bowed three times to the Master and left.

To me, the Master seems like a compassionate Buddha or Bodhisattva. His vows are vast and boundless: to bring the Buddha's teachings to the West, to translate the Buddhist canon into the world's languages so that all people can benefit from the Dharma. Another of the Master's vows was to promote education, in order to teach the future leaders of the world how to be good, law-abiding citizens. He opened new temples and monasteries in various places around the world, giving people the opportunity to see and hear the Buddhadharma and join the ranks of those who practice it.

I am deeply touched by, and feel the highest admiration for, the Master's contributions to Buddhism, and his spirit of sacrificing himself for the sake of the Dharma. He practiced what ordinary people could not practice, endured what others could not endure, and underwent what most people could not undergo. Sparing no blood or sweat, he never paused to rest.

Although the Master passed into stillness in June of 1995 and his physical body is no longer here, his disciples, undeterred by the hardships, continue to propagate Buddhism in order to cause the Proper Dharma to dwell forever in the world.

---

或有見初生　妙色如金山　住是最後身　永作人中月
或見經行時　具無量功德　念慧皆善巧　丈夫師子步
或見紺青目　觀察於十方　有時現戲笑　為順眾生欲

——《大方廣佛華嚴經》〈光明覺品第九〉

*Perhaps someone sees him first being born,*
*His wonderful form like a golden mountain.*
*Dwelling in his final body,*
*He eternally acts as a moon among people.*

*Perhaps someone sees the Buddha walking,*
*Replete with limitless merit and virtue.*
*His mindfulness and wisdom are wholesome and skillful,*
*As he steps like a heroic lion.*

*Perhaps someone sees his purple-blue eyes*
*Which contemplate the ten directions.*
*Sometimes they appear as laughing*
*In order to accord with living beings' desires.*

Flower Adornment Sutra, Chapter Nine, Light Enlightenment

# 大慈悲父
## OUR GREATLY COMPASSIONATE FATHER

上人是一個以身作則、慈祥的長者，
凡事以身作則，身教重於言教。

**The Master was a kind elder
who often taught by personal example.**

陳秀菁　Xiuqing Chen

所謂「有眼不識盧舍那，有耳不聞圓頓教。」不知是福薄緣淺，或是業重障深，上人幾次返臺弘法都因故不能前往拜見，聆聽法音，和宣公上人始終緣慳一面，此一大憾事也。

學佛十餘年，哪裡有講經或法會；就往哪裡跑，打了十餘年的游擊。在接觸法界佛教印經會（以下簡稱法界）前，對上人的事蹟略有所聞，知道上人是位旅美得道高僧，神通廣大，法力無邊，常有信眾前往要求加持。舉凡各種疑難雜症，也都不藥而癒，這是接觸法界前對上人的所知所聞。因緣際會得以進入法界，得知法界為美國法界佛教總會在臺灣的分支道場，負責弘揚宣公上人的法音與經書之流通，使其法音遍佈世界各地。對法界的第一印象是，簡單而不失莊嚴，法師行佛制：「衣不離體，日中一食，夜不倒單。」為一清淨道場，更是修福修慧的好地方。到法界後，常利用假日前往參加法會共修或當義工，對佛法也有了初步的了解。

在一九九四年時，得知要恭請上人返臺舉辦護國息災大法會的消息後，終於可以見到上人了，那時心裡很高興，認為機不可失，這次無論如何一定要去見上人，心裡這麼盤算著。但是，經過幾次開會後，得知上人不能返臺，希望落了空，心裡感到很失望。就自我安慰地想：「這次見不著就等下次；再不然，反正上人在美國，去美國不就看得見了。」想到這裡，心裡就釋懷了些。抱著一絲希望渴望得見上人，這是那時候的心境。

對上人的法有較深入的了解，是始於一九九四年，當時在法界參與電腦中文輸入，有《妙法蓮華經淺釋》、《大方廣佛華嚴經經疏淺釋》。所謂「無

There's a saying, "One has eyes, but does not recognize Nishyanda Buddha; one has ears, but does not hear the perfect and sudden teaching." I do not know whether it was due to scanty blessings and superficial affinity or heavy karmic obstacles on my part that I was not able to pay my respect to the Venerable Master when he came to Taiwan several times for Dharma propagation. I felt gravely sorry that I could not go and listen to him speak the Dharma.

I have been a Buddhist for more than ten years, and during that time I went around to all the temples wherever there was Sutra lecture or Dharma session. I had already heard of the Venerable Master before I visited the Dharma Realm Buddhist Books Distribution Society. I knew that the Master was a lofty monk living in America, who had attained the Way and had great spiritual power. Many faithful Buddhists often went and sought help from him, and their various difficult illnesses would be cured without taking medicine. That was what I knew of the Society before I visited it. When I had the chance to visit the Society, I learned that it is one of the branch temples of Dharma Realm Buddhist Association in Taiwan, and its duty is to publish and distribute the Master's Dharma talks and Sutras. My first impression of the place was that it was simple and yet adorned. The Dharma Masters there honor the Buddha's teachings, always wearing the sash, eating only one meal a day, and sleeping sitting up. It is a pure monastery and an ideal place for one to cultivate blessings and wisdom. After joining the Society, I have often participated in sessions and worked as a volunteer on holidays. I have also gained an initial understanding of the Buddhism.

In 1994, when I learned that the Master had been invited to come to Taiwan to host a Dharma Session for Protecting the Nation and Quelling Disasters, I was delighted and thought that I could meet the Master at last. I told myself I could not let this chance slip by and that no matter what I must see the Master this time. However, after a few more meetings, it became clear that the Master could not come to Taiwan. I was disappointed but comforted myself thinking, "I just have to wait for the next chance then, or perhaps I can go to America to see him." I felt a little better and still harbored a slim hope of seeing the Master.

I obtained a deeper understanding of the Master's Dharma in

上甚深微妙法，百千萬劫難遭遇。」因為中文輸入工作的緣故，有幸得聞上人所說的無上甚深微妙法，這是最大的收獲。有道是「人身難得，佛法難聞。」感謝諸佛菩薩慈悲加護，今生得獲人身，得聞佛法，得遇明眼善知識，得以一償夙願。

上人很重視講經說法，其所講的都是大部的經典，都是大乘的經典，成佛的經典。《華嚴經》、《妙法蓮華經》、《楞嚴經》，乃至於〈楞嚴咒〉，都是到法界後才有機會研讀。在此之前，經是經，咒是咒。生平第一次持〈楞嚴咒〉、誦《華嚴經》是在一九九五年，法界連續幾星期的持誦〈楞嚴咒〉與《華嚴經》，請明眼善知識常住於世。那時持誦得法喜充滿，天真地以為如此可以使上人的身體好轉。現在回想起來，以上人的修持又何須我們誦什麼給他，那不過是給眾生種成佛的因。

對於上人圓寂的消息，有的人說是入定，有的人以為是上人在考驗弟子們，眾說云云，後來才知道原來是替眾生扛太多的業力而走的。記得上人說：

人家一天吃三餐，活五十歲；
我們一天吃一餐，可以活一百五十歲。

言猶在耳，卻不得不面對此一殘酷的事實。要大家持〈楞嚴咒〉，是因為只要世上有人會背誦〈楞嚴咒〉，妖魔鬼怪就不敢亂來，天地就增加一分正氣，又可以化暴戾之氣為祥和。《華嚴經》是經王之王，誦《華嚴經》可以對治我們的習氣毛病，種成佛的因。上人之用心良苦，又豈是眾生所能領悟！

上人講經說法深入淺出，生動活潑，對於人性之剖析是一針見血。對於講經說法人才的培養，更是不遺餘力，他說：

只要有一口氣在，就要講經說法。

足見其為法忘軀的精神。

記得在一九九四年，要在四、五天內打完十篇《華嚴經疏》稿件（平時上班利用空餘時間打，大概二天打一篇），好讓法師帶回美國。十篇稿件要在短時間內趕完，確有困難，只能儘量趕，能打幾篇是幾篇。在那四天中，從早打到晚，孩子的中餐、晚餐皆由其父代勞，就這麼樣趕著，皇天不負苦心人，總算如期完成，就興沖沖地將打完的磁片送到法界，一如往常般的先禮佛，就在第三拜將起身時

1994 when I helped type the Master's explanation of the *Lotus Sutra* and the *Prologue* to the *Flower Adornment Sutra* into the computer at the Society. It is said, "The profound and wonderful Dharma is hard to encounter in hundreds and thousands of eons." I derived incredible benefit from the typing, for it gave me the chance to learn the profound and wonderful Dharma spoken by the Master. It is said, A human body is hard to come by, and the Buddhadharma is hard to hear.

I am grateful to the Buddhas and Bodhisattvas for their compassionate protection and aid, enabling me to obtain a human body in this life, hear the Dharma, meet a bright-eyed Good and Wise Advisor, and fulfill my wish.

The Master put great emphasis on lecturing Sutras and speaking Dharma. The Master lectured almost exclusively on Great Vehicle Sutras, which teach people how to achieve Buddhahood. After coming to the Society, I had the chance to study the *Flower Adornment Sutra*, the *Wonderful Lotus Flower Sutra,* the *Shurangama Sutra*, and the Shurangama Mantra. Before, I had been quite a stranger to Sutras and Mantras. The first time I recited the Shurangama Mantra and the *Flower Adornment Sutra* was in 1995 when the Society held a several week long session for reciting that mantra and Sutra as a way of requesting the Master to remain in the world. The recitation filled me with the joy of Dharma, and I naively thought it would help the Master get better. Now in reflection, I know the Master did not need us to recite anything for him; he was just giving living beings a chance to plant the seed of Buddhahood.

As for the news of the Master's entering perfect stillness, some people said the Master had entered samadhi while others thought the Master was giving his disciples a test. There were various opinions. Later, we learned that the Master left the world because he had undertaken too much karma for the living beings. I remember the Master once said,

People who eat three meals a day live to be 50 years old;
we who eat one meal a day can live to be 150 years old.

His words were still ringing in my ears, and yet I was forced to face the cruel fact (of his passing). The Master wanted us to recite Shurangama Mantra because as long as the Mantra is recited, the demons and strange creatures dare not to cause mischief and the world's righteous energy will be increased and violent energy transformed into auspiciousness. The *Flower Adornment Sutra* is the king of Sutras. Reciting it enables us to correct our bad habits and faults while planting the cause of Buddhahood. How can living beings understand the pains the Master took in teaching us?

When explaining the Sutras, the Master always used simple words to express profound principles. His lectures were always lively, and his analysis of human nature was always right to the point. The Master spared no effort in training people to propagate Buddhism. His statement,

As long as I still have a breath, I will not stop speaking the Dharma and explaining the Sutras.

Clearly shows his spirit of sacrifice for the Dharma.

，看見上人兩眼炯炯有神開心地笑著，突如其來愣住了，卻也更堅定信念，決心要把《華嚴經疏》完成。再者，左手腕上突出的骨頭也不知道何時變平了，我想這大概是上人慈悲加護的力量吧！記得上人曾說：

有誠心就可以看得見你想看的。

這佛教就講的一個「誠心」，心誠則靈，心誠則自然感應道交。未能皈依上人，一大憾事也，不免耿耿於懷，久久不能釋懷。但見上人在《華嚴經疏》上說：

皈依，只要一次就可以。有的法師為了怕信徒跑了，供養少了，所以都不據實以告。皈依兩次、三次那是佛教的敗類。

心裡釋然得到解脫。上人慈悲愍念眾生的精神，由此可見一斑。上人不貪圖名聞利養，不爭、不貪、不求、不自私、不自利、不妄語，六大宗旨更是為人所津津樂道。

在打稿件時，常聽上人叫果寧、果護、果修、果地……那時只知道皈依上人的弟子法名是果字輩，直覺地以為「果」字是在家居士，「恒」字是上人的出家弟子。所以，由字裡行間看見上人都是叫果什麼的，而不是恒什麼的，心裡不免納悶；「為什麼上人都是叫果什麼的，而不是恒什麼的，難道上人的身旁都是在家居士嗎？」一肚狐疑又得不到解答，納悶不已，如此日復一日，總見上人這麼叫著，終於忍不住問同修，同修也說不知道。就在幾天後，有一天打字打到上人說：

果什麼是皈依時取的法名，出家後又取個別號叫，恒什麼的。

這才恍然大悟，原來是這樣哦，陰霾一掃而空，心裡頓時欣喜若狂，久久不能自己，那時第一個感覺就是：「上人真是太厲害了，我心裡在想什麼他都知道。」真是太不可思議了！對上人更是佩服得五

I remember once in 1994 I had to finish typing ten manuscripts of the *Flower Adornment Sutra Prologue* in four or five days so that a Dharma Master could bring them to the United States. (Normally, it took me two working days to type one manuscript.) To rush out ten manuscripts in such a short time would be hard, but I tried my best. For four days, I typed from morning to night. My husband prepared lunch and dinner for the children. My effort was rewarded and I finished the job on time. Happily, I brought the diskette to the Society. As usual, I bowed to the Buddha first. Just when I was about to rise from the third bow, I saw the Master smiling happily, his eyes bright and sparkling. I was astonished but my faith was deepened, and I resolved to finish typing the *Prologue*. Also, a small bone protrusion on my left wrist disappeared without my realizing it, and I believe it was due to the Master's compassionate aid. I remember the Master once said,

> If you are sincere, you will be able to see
> what you like to see.

Buddhism emphasizes sincerity, for sincerity brings efficacious responses. It was my greatest regret that I could not take refuge with the Master and become his disciple. I was quite distressed by this, but then I read in the Master's commentary to the *Prologue*,

> One needs to take refuge but once. Some Dharma Masters are afraid to lose followers and thus offerings, so they do not tell people the truth. Instead, they encourage people to take refuge twice or three times. These people are the "black sheep" of Buddhism.

I was relieved to read the Master's words, which showed his compassion for living beings. The Master never coveted fame or benefit. Many people like to quote his Six Guiding Principles: no fighting, no greed, no seeking, no selfishness, no pursuit of personal benefit, and no lying.

When typing the manuscripts, I often read the Master addressing his disciples: Guo Ning, Guo Hu, Guo Xiu, Guo Di... I knew that the Dharma names of the Master's disciples all began with "Guo" and I intuitively assumed that Dharma names beginning with "Guo" belonged to lay disciples, while those beginning with "Heng" belonged to left-home disciples. Since all I read in the manuscripts was the Master calling "Guo such and such" and never "Heng such and such," I could not help wondering, "Does the Master always have only lay disciples around him? How come he never calls anyone by the name of 'Heng'?" I was filled with doubt but could not find an answer. Day in and day out, I never saw the Master call his disciples by any other way. Finally, I could bear it no more and asked my fellow cultivator. He said he did not know either. A few days later when I was typing the manuscript, I came to a part where the Master explained,

> The Dharma name beginning with "Guo" is given when people take refuge, and another Dharma name beginning with " Heng" is given when they leave the home-life.

So that's how it is. All my doubts were wiped away, and I felt

體投地。這就好像佛對眾生說法，眾生總以為佛是對自己講的一樣，我亦如是。雖知上人不是針對我講的，但當時的感覺卻好像是針對我講的。套句上人的話：

我是一個很愚癡的人！

由講經的稿件中，得知上人是一個以身作則、慈祥的長者，凡事以身作則，身教重於言教。例如在東北時，參加道德會，那時的物質不是很豐裕，吃馬鈴薯時，上人叫大家要連皮一起吃下去，很多人偷偷地把皮吐掉，上人知道後也不多說，就將丟棄的馬鈴薯皮撿起來吃，那些人看了都很難為情，也就不敢再扔掉皮了。上人闡述佛法，為將正法發揚光大，敢說真話，不怕得罪人，不怕斷了財源，不怕沒人供養。上人說：

我最瞧不起有錢的人！

聽了不禁為其捏把冷汗。有錢者財神也，人人爭相巴結惟恐不及，又豈敢輕易罪之，其氣節乃現。上人又說：

萬佛聖城有很多博士、碩士、學士，
而我是無士。

我倒覺得上人的學問高深，見識廣博，由自性所流露出來的智慧光更是無與倫比。譬如《妙法蓮華經》的「蓮華」二字，「華」通「花」，「蓮華」是譬喻，以蓮花作譬喻。為什麼取蓮花為喻？一般人一定以為蓮花出污泥而不染，所以殊貴，故而雀屏中選。上人卻有其獨到的見解，上人說：

蓮花是花果同時，花開就蓮現，花落蓮成。」根在泥土表示一般凡夫，花梗表示二乘。凡夫著到「有」上，所以在泥土裡，這就譬喻「有」，凡夫著於「有」。二乘就著到「空」上，所以這個莖在水裡面，這表示「空」。蓮花超出空、有，表示是一種中道了義，既不落於空，又不落於有，就是中道、了

exuberant for a long time. All I could think was, "The Master is really out of the world; he knows exactly what's on my mind." It is inconceivable! I admired the Master even more. When the Buddha spoke Dharma, each living being thought the Buddha was speaking to him. I felt the same way. I know the Master did not say it for me in particular, but at that moment it seemed that he was speaking to me. The Master often said,

I am a stupid person.

From the Master's Dharma talks, I learned that the Master was a kind elder who often taught by personal example. For instance, when the Master was in Manchuria working in the Virtue Society during hard times, he told students to eat the skins of their potatoes as well. Many stealthily spit out the skin. When the Master found out, he said nothing but picked up the skins and ate them himself. Those who did not eat the skin were embarrassed and did not dare to throw it away again.

In order to promote Proper Dharma, the Master fearlessly spoke the truth even when he knew it might offend people, cut off the source of financial support, or cause people to stop making offerings. When he said,

I despise rich people more than anything,

Those who heard it broke out in a cold sweat. Because rich people give large contributions, most people are only afraid they have not flattered them enough and would never dare to offend them. This shows the Master's integrity.

The Master also said,

Many people at the City of Ten Thousand Buddhas hold Ph.D.s, Master's, and Bachelor's degrees. I am the only one without a degree.

Yet in my opinion the Master was extremely erudite, knowledgeable, open-minded, and an incomparable wisdom shined forth from his intrinsic nature. For example, let us consider the question of why the lotus is used as an analogy in the *Lotus Sutra*. Most people say it is because a lotus grows in mud and yet remains undefiled, thus symbolizing its nobility and supremacy. The Master gave a unique explanation. He said,

The lotus seeds appear when the lotus blooms, and by the time the flower withers, the seeds are ripe." The lotus root buried in the mud represents ordinary people. The stem represents sages of the Two Vehicles. Ordinary people are attached to "existence," which is represented by the mud. Sages of the Two Vehicles are attached to "emptiness," which is represented by the hollow stem in the water. The lotus flower rises above both "existence" and "emptiness" and represents the Middle Way, which is attached neither to existence nor to emptiness. The simultaneous appearance of the flower and the fruit represents the nonduality of cause and effect. The cause is just the effect, and the effect is just the cause. As is the cause, so will be the effect. One who sows the seed of Buddhahood will reap Buddha fruit. The simultaneity of flower and fruit also represents "opening the

義。而花果同時表示因果不二，因也就是果，果也就是因，如是因，如是果。因是種佛的因，果就成了佛果，花果同時也表示開「權」顯「實」。這花又有種種不同，有「謊花無果」──外道、「一花多果」──凡夫、「多花一果」──聲聞乘、「一花一果」──緣覺乘、「先果後花」──初果須陀洹、「先花後果」──菩薩乘。這種種花都不能比喻這個妙法，唯獨蓮花是有花有果，花果同時，這表示「即實即權」，「爲實施權，開權顯實」。

這種精闢獨到的見解更是前所未見。上人自性所流露出來的智慧光是這麼的朗朗明淨，不禁令人嘖嘖稱奇，嘆爲觀止。

欲續佛慧命，必須法輪常轉，而法賴僧傳，故上人非常重視僧伽的素質與培養，教育人才，使之成爲有用的人。雖然上人的色身不在，但其法身是盡虛空、遍法界，無所不在的，法師們就像是上人的化身。所謂「師父領進門，修行在個人。」在緬懷師恩之餘，要依法不依人，更要迴光返照，返本還原，諸惡莫作，眾善奉行，勤修戒定慧，息滅貪瞋癡。上人說：

有大智慧，才不會做糊塗事。
不要懵懂傳懵懂，一傳兩不懂，
師父下地獄，弟子向裡拱。

但願眾生能依止善道，了生脫死，早證菩提，龍華三會再相逢。

provisional to reveal the real." There are various kinds of flowers: sterile blooms bearing no fruit represent externalists; a single bloom bearing many fruits represents ordinary people; many blooms bearing a single fruit represents Hearers; a single bloom yielding a single fruit represents Those Enlightened to Conditions; the fruit being borne before the flower blooms represents the First Stage Arhats; the flower appearing before the fruit represents the Bodhisattvas. However, none of these kinds of flowers can be used as an analogy for the Wonderful Dharma. The lotus is the only kind of flower in which the flower and fruit appear at the same time. Thus it is used to represent the identity of provisional and actual teachings. "The provisional is set forth for the sake of the actual, and then the provisional is opened to reveal the actual.

This unique understanding of the analogy is unprecedented. One cannot help but admire the bright, pure wisdom that flowed from the Master's inherent nature.

To perpetuate the Buddha's wisdom, we must constantly turn the Dharma wheel. Because the Dharma depends on the Sangha to propagate it, the Master set a high standard for the Sangha and emphasized the education and training of its members. Though the Master has left us physically, his Dharma body is omnipresent throughout the Dharma Realm and to the end of space. The Master's left-home disciples are like his transformation bodies. There is a saying, "The teacher leads you in the door, but you yourself must cultivate." While we should remember our teacher's kindness, we must rely on the Dharma, not on people, to guide us in our cultivation. We should also reflect upon ourselves, return to the source, refrain from evil and do good, diligently cultivate precepts, samadhi, and wisdom, and extinguish greed, hatred, and stupidity. The Master said,

One with great wisdom does not do muddled things.

" It should not be that:

*The confused transmits confusion.*
*With one transmission, both are confused.*
*The teacher falls into the hells,*
*And the disciple follows right along.*

May all living beings follow a wholesome path, end birth and death, realize Bodhi, and meet again in the threefold Dragon Flower Assembly.

---

或見師子吼　殊勝無比身　示現最後生　所說無非實
──《大方廣佛華嚴經》〈光明覺品第九〉

*Perhaps someone sees him emitting the lion's roar,*
*As he, in his supreme and incomparable body*
*Manifests his final birth,*
*That which he proclaims is actual.*

Flower Adornment Sutra, Chapter Nine, Light Enlightenment

# 緣在聖城——售屋奇遇記
## AFFINITY IN THE CITY--A STORY OF HOUSE SELLING

### 賣房子畢竟是大事，我的內心深處要經過極大的掙扎。
#### Since selling a house is not a small matter,
#### I went through several grave struggles in my mind.

陳果珠　Guozhu Chen

　　我是從臺灣來的，現住聖城，我不敢說是跟大家講法，不過跟了上人後，多少也有些許的心得和感應。我把最近一次賣房子的事情告訴各位，因為我的房子在短短一個月之內，賣了三次，而且三次都成交，現在我說出來與大家分享分享。

　　前一陣子，臺灣局勢不太安定，在這之前好像就有一股力量要我來聖城，但是賣房子畢竟是大事，我的內心深處要經過極大的掙扎，後來經家庭數次會議，家人一致決定：「如果房子賣了，小孩和我可以去聖城；賣不出去，就照原來的日子過活。」當時臺灣的房地產非常不景氣，尤其受中共試射飛彈的影響，大家存觀望的態度，沒有人敢買房子。許多大房地產公司，每月的成交量幾乎等於零，尤其我住的地方——臺中，空屋的比率佔全省第一位。家人所以會答應賣房子，是認為根本賣不出去，所謂答應不過滿我一個願而已。

　　去年十一月，忙完了上人的追思法會後，回到家裏桌上放了一張名片，兒子說是來看房子的，我看了名片後告訴兒子這個人可能會買。我是開價六百六十萬元，他希望以六百萬元成交，我一口氣答應下來。在他認為我是怕房子賣不出去，才以這麼低的價錢出售，而我認為這個人可能是師父帶來的，為避免橫生枝節，就很爽快答應，所以收了他二十多萬元的訂金（這是第一位買房子的人，姓李）。

　　第三天，隔壁的鄰居帶了他的朋友來，說中意我的房子很久了，他們希望以六百三十八萬元來買這個房子。在這之前，我發覺第一個買主——李先生——看我不懂，所以在簽約時，佔我很多便宜，我發覺後，找他商量，他吃定我認為約都簽了，妳拿我沒辦法，誰叫妳當初不懂，不看好，再簽約。那時我告訴他：「……也許會因為這樣，我會賠你二十萬而不賣你房子。」（所謂賠二十萬，就是收訂

I came from Taiwan and presently live in the City of Ten Thousand Buddhas. I dare not say that I am going to speak Dharma to you. However, since I have followed the Master for some time, I do have some thoughts and stories. Let me tell you the story of how my house was sold recently. My house was sold three times within a period of one month, and the sales contract was successfully entered each time. Now let me share this story with you.

Not long ago, the situation in Taiwan was not stable. Before that, there seemed to be certain force pulling me to the City. However, since selling a house is not a small matter, I went through several grave struggles in my mind. Finally, after many meetings, our family decided that if the house were sold, the children and I would go to the City; otherwise, we would continue living as before. At the time there was a serious slump in the Taiwan housing market, and it was further adversely affected by the missile testing conducted by mainland China. Everyone assumed the attitude of waiting; no one dared to buy a house. Many large brokerage firms found their monthly sales was almost nil. It was especially so in Taichung (where I lived), which had the highest vacancy rate on the entire island. My family gave me the okay only because they saw no chance at all that I could sell the house. They just went along to satisfy my wish.

In November last year, when I came home after helping out with the Master's memorial ceremony, I found a name card on my desk. My son told me it had been left by a person who had come by to see the house. I looked at the card and told my son that this person could be our buyer. My asking price was NT$6,600,000 and he offered NT$6,000,000. I accepted without hesitation. On his part, the buyer thought I had accepted his low bid because I was afraid I could not sell the house. On my part, I was thinking that if this person was sent by the Master, I'd better accept quickly lest any complication might occur. So I took NT$200,000 in down payment. (This was the first buyer whose name is Lee.)

Three days later, my neighbor brought his friend over and said that they had long wanted to buy my house. They hoped to be able to buy it at NT$6,380,000. Before this happened, I had discovered that the first buyer--Mr. Lee--had thought I was naive and had taken advantage of me in the contract. When I went to talk to him, he thought there was nothing I could do since the contract had been signed. He basically let me know that it was

金二十萬，如果毀約就必須賠二十萬。）

　　我與第二個買主莊先生很快簽了約，簽約前我跟上人説：「上人！第二個買主與第一個買主兩人相差出價三十八萬，扣掉被罰二十萬，扣掉仲介費二萬，還多十六萬，如果成交多出的十六萬，我悉數捐出。」所以前後三天這個房子就賣了二次。但是很奇怪的一件事，正在莊先生付我訂金時，他的大兒子匆匆跑來説：「爸爸，妹妹被汽車撞了，現在送去醫院中。」所以他們一付完訂金二十萬，馬上趕去醫院。第二天一早我掛電話問他女兒傷得如何？他説只輕微的腦震盪，幾天後即可出院，我才寬心。我告訴莊先生説：「臺灣人有一種禁忌，買賣屋時，家中有人出意外，代表不吉祥，你要不要考慮看看，如果想解，錢可以還你。」莊先生説：「沒那回事，我女兒撞車是一回事，我買房子是一回事，我這人最不信邪，這屋子我買定了。」

　　五天後，記得那天是禮拜四，是十月八日佛入涅槃日，那天作的功德比平常作的功德，勝過十倍、十百倍、十千倍，所以我希望以這多出的十六萬，做他們全家人的功德，希望他們入我家後都能平安順暢。我掛個電話給莊先生，他爸爸接的，説：「他不在！」「他去哪裏？」「去市場殺雞做生意。」我想這一下完了，我竟然賣給一個殺雞的，本來我一直不懂，為什麼他買我房子的同時，他女兒會出車禍，現在我才恍然大悟。

　　那天下午，莊先生回了電話，我再確認是否買這個房子，他的回答仍然是肯定的，並又托人送來二十萬，所以我以他們全家的名字作功德，寄了十六萬元出去。星期天晚上，我們約好付尾款，但是那天我心裏就是不安，所以留在家裏誦《楞嚴經》。下午四點多，莊先生托人打電話來，説不能來付款，他大兒子又出了車禍，腿撞斷了，現在趕去醫院中。

　　第二天一早，莊先生三兄弟一起來説，他們非常遺憾不能買我的房子，接連著兩起車禍，讓他們不得不考慮放棄購買此屋的念頭，並希望我能還他們訂金二十萬，我答應了。

　　離開時，他們告訴我：「這個房子沒有福德的人，住不起！當簽約時，妳説妳們家都是阿彌陀佛時，我嚇一跳，心想『我是殺雞的，可以住嗎？』結果還是進不了你家門。」那時我真是謝謝

my own fault that I didn't read the contract carefully before signing it. I told him, "I probably will cancel the contract under penalty because of your attitude." (The penalty was the down payment.)

I lost no time in signing the contract with the second buyer, Mr. Zhuang. After the contract was signed, I said to the Master, "The price the second buyer offered was NT$ 380,000 higher than the first offer. Taking out the NT$200,000 penalty that I have to pay for voiding the first contract and the brokerage fee of NT $20,000, I still come out gaining NT $160,000. If this deal goes through, I will donate the extra NT $160,000." Thus, the house was sold twice within a three-day period.

However, strange things started to happen. Just when Mr. Zhuang was paying me the down payment, his eldest son rushed in and told him, "Dad, Sister had a car accident and is now being sent to the hospital." So they left for the hospital in a hurry after they made the NT$200,000 down payment. The next day, I called him early in the morning and asked him how his daughter was doing. He said it was nothing serious--just a minor concussion--and she would be discharged from the hospital in a few days. I felt relieved. I told Mr. Zhuang, "People in Taiwan have a taboo. That is, if an accident occurs to a family member when a house is being bought, it is an inauspicious sign. Do you want to think about it? If you would like to back out of the deal, I will give the down payment back to you." Mr. Zhuang said, "Nonsense. These are two unrelated matters. I am not a superstitious person. I am buying this house, and that's it." Five days later--I remember it was a Thursday, October 8th--it was the anniverary of the Buddha's entry into Nirvana. Meritorious deeds done that day will generate tens, hundreds, and thousands of times more merit than those done on ordinary days. I wanted to donate the NT $160,000 in the name of his entire family and hope that things would go smoothly for them after they moved into my house.

I called Mr. Zhuang and his father answered the phone. He said, "He is not home." "Where did he go? "He went to the market to kill and sell chickens." I thought to myself, "Now that did it. I sold the house to a person who kills chickens for a living." I had not understand before why his daughter had had an accident at the same time he was buying my house, but I did then.

That afternoon, Mr. Zhuang returned my call. Once again, I asked him whether he still wanted to buy the house. He confirmed it and also had someone deliver NT $200,000 to us that evening. So I mailed a check for NT $160,000 as a donation in the name of his family. According to the contract, he was to pay the balance on Sunday evening. I felt uneasy that day, so I stayed at home and recited *Shurangama Sutra*. At around four o'clock that afternoon, Mr. Zhuang asked someone to call and say that he could not come to make the payment because his eldest son had broken his leg in a car accident and he was on his way to the hospital.

Early the next morning, Mr. Zhuang and his two brothers came together. They said they regretted that they could not buy my house. Two consecutive car accidents forced them to give up the idea of buying my house. They hoped that I would return the NT $200,000. I agreed to do so.

Before leaving, they said, "A person without blessings and virtue cannot live in this house! When you told me your family was

他們，不但沒怪罪我家不好，反而怪自己是殺雞的。

但是這一下可好了，一邊是自己毀約付了二十萬給對方，一邊是不但訂金要還人家，還替他們作了功德，現在兩邊都落空，還淨賠三十六萬，房子卻擱在那裏，我知道這是一場考驗，我想如果我沒有做錯的話，應該還會有人來買房子。

兩個禮拜後，一個晚上，第一個買主打電話來，問我房子賣了沒？我告訴她出一點狀況，所以沒賣成。她笑了，她說昨晚她家的土地公告訴她，屋子沒賣成，叫她趕快來買，她認為不可能，所以來電問我看看，才知道土地公告訴她是真的。不過李太太因價錢的關係，仍然沒有成交。

李太太來電話的第二天，有個學佛的師姊帶了一個朋友來看房子，一個小時內，以六百五十二萬元成交，當場付了訂金。至此，房子的處理總算告了一個段落，我也把多出的錢全部捐出去了。一個禮拜後，第一個買主李太太又打電話來說要買，我告訴她已沒機會了。朋友說：「妳好屬害，房子這麼不景氣，妳竟可以在短短一個月內賣三次，而且一次比一次的價錢好。」我說：「不是我屬害，上人屬害，佛菩薩屬害。」

這裏有一個巧合，第一位買主，家的住址是一○八號，雖然買了但是沒有成，第三位買主的介紹人，也就是學佛的那位師姊家住址也是一○八號，而我們長串佛珠是一○八顆，所以，當第一位買主給名片時，我說可能會成交，就是這個緣故。

我有一個很小的佛具店，是爸爸那一代跟房東租的，前後四十幾年，地點非常好，但就在第三次房屋成交的第二天，房東希望結束租期，我知道這一切都是上人的安排，所以毅然決然的把店關掉，結束了經營多年的佛具店生意。

東勢有一位師兄問我：「聽說妳房子賣了，而且賣得很順，妳還說是上人幫妳的，上人怎麼幫妳呢？」旁邊一位師姊接口說：「唉呀！你不知道的，她有多發心你知道嗎？」其實不是發心不發心的問題，我只知道只要上人這邊有事情時，我一定用我的心，盡所有的力量把它做好，其他的事就交給上人，上人自會安排好好的。如果你也這麼做，有一天你會發覺你也會跟我一樣充滿法喜，其樂無窮。

Buddhist at the contract signing, I thought to myself: 'I'm a chicken slaughterer--can I live here?' It turns out I can't." I was really grateful to them--instead of blaming our family, they blamed themselves for being chicken slaughterers.

Now the situation was really bad. On one hand I had to pay the NT $200,000 penalty for breaking the first contract; only the other, not only did I have to return the NT $200,000 down payment, but I had already made a donation of NT $160,000 in his family's name. I ended up with a total loss of NT $360,000 and the house still remained unsold. I knew it was a test. I told myself that if I had not done anything wrong, someone would come and buy the house.

One evening two weeks later, the wife of the first buyer called and asked whether the house had been sold. I told her something had happened and the sale had fallen through. She laughed and explained that the Earth God at her house had told her that my house was still available and that she should quickly come and buy it. She thought it was impossible so she called to find out. Now she knew what the Earth God told her was true. However, since we could not agree on the price, Mrs. Lee did not buy the house.

The day after Mrs. Lee called, a Dharma friend of mine brought a friend over. Within one hour, the house was sold at NT $6,652,000 and the buyer made the down payment then and there. The house was finally sold for good, and I donated the extra money. One week later, Mrs. Lee called again, saying she wanted to buy the house. I told her the chance was gone. My friend said, "You are really something. Not only you could sell your house three times within a month in such a slump market, but you managed to sell it at higher price each time." I said, "It wasn't me. It was the Buddhas and Bodhisattvas."

There was a coincidence. The street address of the first buyer was 108. Though the sales contract was signed, the deal did not go through. The address of the friend who produced the third buyer was also 108. A strand of Buddhist recitation beads has 108 beads. That was why when I saw the first buyer's address I remarked that it could be our buyer.

I had a small gift shop selling Buddhist items. The shop was leased by my father some forty years ago. The location was excellent. The day after I sold the house for the third time, the landlord called and hoped to end the lease. I knew it was all arranged by the Master. So I resolutely closed down my little shop and the business I had managed for years.

A Dharma friend from Tongshi said, "I heard that you have sold your house and that the sale went very smoothly. You said the Master had helped you. How did he help you?" Another Dharma friend who was standing right next to us said, "Do you know how great a resolve she has brought forth?" Well, I do not think it is the matter of bringing forth the resolve. I only know that as soon as I discover that the Master's Way-places need something, I do my best to help with a sincere heart. I give everything else to the care of the Master. The Master always makes sure things turn out all right. If you can also have this attitude, you will be as full of the joy of Dharma as I am.

# An Interesting Recollection about Studying Chinese

# 中文課趣事一則

Gwo Jye

果傑

I wanted to submit this recollection of my experience with the Venerable Abbot while I was living at the Monastery in 1973. I feel that all those who are given a chance to read this will enjoy the mysticism and lesson learned. I entered the Monastery in the Fall of 1973. One thing that the Monks and Nuns made absolutely clear was that I should not expect the Venerable Abbot to speak to me directly for some time. He wanted to be sure that I was there for my own cultivation rather than being there for him. That was fine by me, and I went on with my duties and participated in the rigorous daily schedule.

Every evening we would have the Dharma lecture; it was given by the Venerable Abbot in Chinese and immediately translated thereafter. I sat next to Heng Kuan. He was the senior monk at the time, and like a big brother. He would often give me quick translations before the official version came across just so I could keep up.

One evening the Venerable Abbot was lecturing and he asked the Sangha the Ten Powers of the Buddha. Although he had lectured on this about a year before, it was one of those things that the members of the assembly just couldn't remember. The Venerable Abbot told everyone that he would like them to study up on it again and by the next evening be prepared to answer him. Heng Kuan nudged me and said, "See me after the lecture, I've got an idea." After the lecture, Heng Kuan and I got together and he said, "Look, I know you don't know any Chinese. Why don't I teach you the Ten Powers of the Buddha in phonetic Chinese. Then tomorrow night when the Abbot asks, you can raise your hand and answer him. That will give him a big thrill. After all, he knows you don't know this." I agreed, and by the next evening I had learned phonetically the Ten Powers of the Buddha. During the lecture I sat diligently waiting for the Venerable Abbot to ask the big question. Of course, he didn't. He didn't ask the next night. By the end of two weeks of sitting in lectures I'd completely forgotten about our scheme.

Now, every day after our meal, we had about forty-five minutes to get ready for the Great Compassion Repentance Ceremony. This was when the Monastery was still located in the old "ice box" down in the warehouse section of San Francisco. Every day during this time I would climb up the two flights of stairs to the Library level. From the window located immediately at the

我願提供一樁我與宣化上人的經歷，那時是一九七三年，我住在廟裡。我想讀者會很歡喜讀到這一樁有趣的事情。一九七三年的秋天我住進廟裡。當時那裡的比丘及比丘尼，很清楚地告訴我，不要期盼上人會有很多時間跟我談話，並且上人希望我住到廟裡是為了修行，而不是為了他。對我而言，這沒問題，該做什麼我就做什麼，而且每天參加緊湊的功課。

每天晚上都聽經，上人以中文講經，當場就有人翻譯英文。當時我坐在恆觀法師的旁邊。那時他算是老資格的比丘，就像老大哥一樣。他常常在正式翻譯前，就很快地先將上人講經的內容翻譯給我聽，好讓我跟得上進度。

有一天晚上，上人講經時，他問那些出家人，佛的十力是什麼。雖然上人已經在一年前就講過這個，但這問題仍是參加法會的人所無法記住的一個問題。上人告訴每一個人，要再好好研究這個問題，第二天聽經課時答覆。恆觀法師用手肘碰了我一下說：「聽完經找我，我有一個主意。」聽完經，恆觀法師與我碰到面，他告訴我：「我知道你一點也不懂中文，何不讓我教你用中文講這佛的十力，等明天晚上上人問起，你可以舉手回答。那會給他一個大驚喜，他知道你一點也不懂這問題。」我同意了，而且，在第二天晚上之前，我就學會了用中文發音講佛的十力。在聽經的時候，我很專心坐在那等著上人問這個大問題。當然，上人沒有問。他第二天晚上也沒有問這個問題。在後來兩個星期聽經，我已經完全忘了我們的計劃。

每天午齋後，我們有四十五分鐘時間拜《大悲懺》。這是從我們的廟尚在三藩市倉庫區一座「冰箱」樓房就開始有的功課。每天這個時候，我會爬上兩段樓梯到圖書室那一層。從這樓梯頂的窗戶，我

top of the stairs, I would quickly lean out, look up, and say "Hello" to the Sun. It was just my way of keeping in touch with the outside world. Of course, before I would ever look out the window, I would make absolutely sure nobody had followed me up the stairs. So one day, having come up the stairs, making sure I was alone, that nobody was behind me on the stairs, and no one was on the floor of the Library, I quickly ducked my head outside. Simultaneously, I heard someone behind me, I whipped around and there standing one foot from me was the Venerable Abbot.

Looking directly at me he said, "Say the Ten Powers of the Buddha." I was so completely taken aback by the fact that the Venerable Abbot was speaking to me, I didn't even think about how he could have appeared so immediately and mysteriously next to me. Of course, the first thing out of my mouth was a great mishmash of phonetic Chinese saying absolutely nothing. Having realized my mistake, I quickly regained my composure and said The Ten Powers of the Buddha. Immediately afterwards, the Venerable Abbot said. "Very good. Next time study harder." I went back downstairs and over to the kitchen area where Heng Kuan and the other Monks and Nuns had gathered for some tea. I walked in and said, "You know, the Venerable Abbot just spoke to me, and asked me The Ten Powers of the Buddha." Every one just froze in place, and with the utmost seriousness, almost in unison replied, "No he didn't."

很快的彎身出去仰視天上，對著太陽說「嗨！」那是我唯一與外面世界接觸的方法。當然，每次我上樓梯前，都看清楚沒有人跟在我的後面。有一天，我確定是自己一個人爬樓梯上去，而且也沒有人在圖書室那一層樓，我就很快的伸頭出去。就在那同時，我聽見有人在我後面，我很快的轉過，就看見上人離我一尺遠站在那。

上人看著我說：「說一說佛的十力？」在覺得非常意外，上人是正在跟我說話，我都沒想到他是如何這麼快的、神秘的出現在我身邊。從我嘴裡說出來的，當然是亂七八糟的中文發音，不知說些什麼。我一發覺講得不對，就立刻恢復了鎮靜，然後說出佛的十力。上人馬上接著說，「非常好，下次再努力學習。」我下樓去，走過廚房，恆觀及其他的比丘、比丘尼正在廚房收集茶葉。我走進去說：「你們知道嗎？上人剛剛跟我說話，而且問我佛的十力。」每個人都愣在那裡，然後一致極嚴肅的說：「不，不可能的。」

---

其性本空寂　　內外俱解脫　　離一切妄念　　無等法如是
體性常不動　　無我無來去　　而能悟世間　　無邊悉調伏
──《大方廣佛華嚴經》〈光明覺品第九〉

*His nature is basically empty and still;*
*Inside and out he is completely liberated.*
*Apart from all false thoughts,*
*The unequalled Dharma is also like this.*

*His substance and nature are constantly unmoving,*
*He is without a self and without a coming or going.*
*He is able to enlighten the world*
*So that all its boundless beings are completely subdued.*

*Flower Adornment Sutra, Chapter Nine, Light Enlightenment*

# 難報的恩澤

## KINDNESS THAT IS DIFFICULT TO REPAY

父母生我、育我之恩雖大，
師父卻是以善法滋潤我法身的恩人。

**My parents bore me and raised me,
but the Master nourished my Dharma body with wholesome Dharma.**

葉果貞　Guozhen Ye

恩師宣公上人入涅槃已接近一年了，幾番提筆欲將心中對恩師種種惠澤的感懷表明於萬一，但礙於太多的感懷，不知從何表達，因此躊躇良久，才於今日做一個簡陋陳述。

當我聽聞恩師入涅槃時，不禁嚎啕大哭，比喪父更痛心。自己深感慚愧，平時不修行，一點定力也沒有，每番想控制自己的失態，可是欲罷不能。自覺自己竟是那麼執著得可憐，那麼愚癡得可憐！雖常自責：「依法不依人啊！妳執著師父的色身做什麼呢？」儘管如此，只因師恩比父母恩更重大難報。父母生我、育我之恩雖大，師父卻是以善法滋潤我法身的恩人。他老人家教化我棄惡向善，引導我由地獄門的邊緣逐漸走向佛國的光明大道，此恩此德，難以言表。如沒有恩師過去苦口婆心的教誨，自己中了貪、瞋、癡三毒那麼深都不知道，經常在犯十惡五逆的大罪也都渾然不覺，因果不懼，犯錯不悔，可謂愚癡到了極點。

恩師的教誨不僅改變我的人生觀，更是在我最困苦煩惱時，於夢中指點我如何去修行的一盞明燈。他老人家過去在開示中，幾番提到：

煩惱即菩提，就如翻掌這麼容易。

同時在開示中，反覆翻著手掌的動作，如今記憶猶新。

於此表明再多的感懷，也不能報答恩師的惠澤於萬一。唯有時時勉勵自己，在修行的道路上要精進不退，刻刻在日常生活中反省自己的過錯，警惕自己「諸惡莫作，眾善奉行。」在餘生中多做善事，藉此報答師父的恩澤於萬一。

It has been nearly a year since the Venerable Master Hua entered Nirvana. Several times I started to set down a little bit of my feelings towards my kind teacher, but I didn't know where to start, because there were too many things to say. Thus I have delayed until now to give this inadequate report.

When I heard the news of the Master's Nirvana, I couldn't stop myself from crying piteously. It grieved me more deeply than the death of my father. I was very ashamed that due to my lack of cultivation, I had no samadhi power. I tried without success to compose myself. Pitying myself for being so foolish and attached, I often rebuked myself, "We should rely on the Dharma, not on a person. Why be so attached to the Master's physical body?" Indeed, it is only because the Master's kindness is more difficult to repay than that of my parents. My parents bore me and raised me, but the Master nourished my Dharma body with wholesome Dharma, teaching me to renounce evil and aspire to goodness, leading me from the gates of the hells onto the bright path to the Buddha's land. Such great kindness is hard to describe in words. If it were not for the Master's earnest remonstrances, I wouldn't even know that I was poisoned by greed, hatred, and stupidity, or that I was committing the ten evils and five rebellious acts. I would not know to fear cause and effect, or to repent for my errors, for I was extremely foolish. The Master's teachings changed my outlook on life; when I was in trouble, he appeared in my dreams and gave me guidance in cultivation. He often said in his talks,

*Turning afflictions into Bodhi
Is as easy as a flip of the hand.*

He would demonstrate by flipping his hand over as he said this. The memory is still fresh in my mind.

No matter how many feelings I write down, I could hardly repay the Master's kindness. Only by urging myself to advance vigorously on the Path, to constantly reflect on my faults, and to remember to "do no evil and practice all good," doing as much good as I can for the rest of my life, can I hope to repay a tiny bit of the Master's kindness.

# 心有靈犀一點通

## THE SPIRITUAL CONNECTION BETWEEN MINDS

我們誠心修行，返本還原，永遠都是與上人常在的。

**If we sincerely cultivate and return to the source,
we will always be together with the Master.**

釋恒雲　Shi Hengyun

上人說了「我從虛空來，回到虛空去」，上人已經圓寂了，上人是不是還是跟著我們呢？是不是在我們的旁邊呢？我個人覺得，上人來到人間示現，就是要把了生脫死的法，教導我們。上人所教導我們的，都是非常真實、非常真切的。譬如說，我們有一個師兄弟，她為什麼要跟上人出家？其實她以前沒見過上人，只看到上人的開示裏面說「修行要斷慾去愛」，她一看到這個地方，就覺得這是一個非常難得的大善知識，因為這不是一般人能教導出來的。

上人在這末法時代，特別要在這很複雜、多花樣的社會裏面，帶給我們真正修行的方法，帶給我們一股清流。他的化緣盡了嗎？其實還沒有盡。上人還是跟著我們，他老人家只不過用另外一種方式來教導我們，儘管上人的色身不在了，但是我們要深信，上人的精神教化是永遠存在的。

在上人沒有圓寂的時候，三藩市有一位女居士，她有一則真實的故事。有一次，在萬佛城一個大法會裏，一位老太太急著要回到沙加緬度的地方，就請這位女居士幫她找車子。可是這個女居士找來找去，都找不到有人可以順路載這位老太太，最後她就只好自己送她回沙加緬度後再回去，兜這麼一個大圈就要五個鐘頭。那時候她的小男孩也跟著，這孩子非常調皮，平常坐車時，車窗上都會留有他的腳印！就這麼調皮。可是那一天，在好幾個鐘頭裡，他的孩子在後座坐得很端正，不動來動去，也不抓來抓去。她覺得很奇怪，就跟他說：「沒關係！路途還很遠，你可以躺下來休息。」那孩子依然不動，做媽媽的很不忍心就說：「沒關係！你可以休息一下。」這個時候，這小男孩一本正經對她說：「媽媽！不可以的！師父就坐在我的旁邊。」這是

The Venerable Master said, "I came from empty space, and I will return to empty space." Now that the Master has perfected the stillness, is he still with us? Is he still around us? Personally I feel that the Master manifested in the world in order to teach us the Dharma for gaining liberation from birth and death. What the Master taught us is extremely real and genuine. For example, one of my Dharma brothers explained why she left the home-life with the Master. She had never met the Master, but when she read the sentence, "In cultivation, we must cut off desire and get rid of love" in the Master's instructional talks, she felt that he was an extremely rare Good and Wise Advisor, for this is not a teaching that an ordinary person can give.

In this Dharma-ending Age, the Master took special pains to bring to us the method of real cultivation, a pure and clean stream in this complicated society. Have his affinities for teaching come to an end? Not really. The Master is still with us. He is simply teaching us in a different way. Even though his physical body is gone, we should deeply believe that the spirit of his teachings will last forever.

I will now tell a true story that happened to a laywoman who lives in San Francisco before the Master passed into stillness. Once, during a major Dharma gathering at the City of Ten Thousand Buddhas, an elderly lady needed to return to Sacramento right away and asked this laywoman to help her find a ride. She asked around but was unable to find a ride, so she decided to drive the elderly lady herself. It was a five hour drive from the City of Ten Thousand Buddhas to Sacramento and back. Her son was with her, and the boy was so naughty that whenever he was in the car, he would leave his footprints on the car's windows. That day, however, during the long trip the boy sat very still and upright in the backseat, not crawling all over the place as usual. Finding this strange, his mother told him, "There's still a long ways to go. You can lie down to rest." When the boy didn't move, the mother again told him, "Don't worry, you can rest for a little while." The boy then told her very solemnly, "Mom, I can't, because the Master's sitting next to me."

This is a story of how the Master manifested to teach living beings, and it happened before he physically passed away.

上人在色身還沒有離開我們的時候，有這麼一個上人示現來教化眾生的故事。

在上人圓寂了以後，上人的精神教化還是存在的。譬如說，臺灣法界佛教印經會，是專門流通上人法音的地方，在上人圓寂後，請上人書的人，反而比以前更多，而且都是一箱一箱的，或者一大袋一大袋，這樣子來請的。有很多人在上人圓寂以後，受到上人的教化，反而更有信心。

有一位姓王的居士，他以前會有些許抱怨，說上人在美國那麼遠，也教化不到他，有什麼事情也不能請上人幫忙，可是上人圓寂了以後，他受到很多上人各方面的教化，所以他常常帶了很多人到廟裏來護持道場。

最近在臺灣辦追思法會，也有一個公案。一位女居士，有一天突然來跟我們講，她說有一個作素食店的女老闆，她因為生意不好，就想改作葷菜，也想到國外去，別人勸她也沒辦法。有一天夢到上人跟她說：

妳不要到國外去，我在十一號、十二號、十三號，在臺灣這兒有一個法會，妳要來幫忙！

結果她一打聽，真的有這麼一回事，所以她也不再想作葷菜了，在法會期間就到法界香積組來幫忙。

講到這些，這其實都是上人隨機來教化眾生的一些方法，我們也不執著這些，用這些來說上人是無所不在。其實諸佛菩薩的境界是永遠存在的，最重要的是我們自己要誠心懇切地來修行。

為什麼我們見不到上人？其實是我們自己障重。上人常常都是跟我們在一起的，我們誠心修行，返本還原，永遠都是與上人常在的，也就是上人的化身，才不會辜負上人來世界這一趟，來教化我們。

Although he has passed into stillness, the spirit of the Master's teaching is still present. For example, at the Dharma Realm Buddhist Books Distribution Society in Taiwan, even more people have come to request the Master's books after his passing, and they request them by the boxful and by the bag. Many people have been influenced by the Master's teaching since he passed away, and their faith is very deep.

One layman named Wang used to complain that, with the Master so far away in America, he couldn't expect the Master to teach or help him. Yet, after the Master's passing, he has received even more teachings from the Master, and so now he often brings people to the temple to attend the Dharma events.

There is a true story from the recent Memorial Ceremony in Taiwan. One day a laywoman suddenly came and told me about a woman who owned a vegetarian restaurant. Since business was poor, she decided to start carrying non-vegetarian food and to move abroad. No one could dissuade her. One night she had a dream in which the Master said to her,

You should not go abroad. I'll be having a Dharma assembly here in Taiwan on the 11th, 12th, and 13th. You ought to come and help out.

Then she found out that it was really the case, and so she dropped the plan of carrying non-vegetarian food. She also helped with the food service during the Dharma assembly.

These are just some of the ways in which the Master teaches people according to circumstances. We should not become attached and use these to prove that the Master is present everywhere. Actually, the Buddhas and Bodhisattvas are always present, but the most important thing is that we must sincerely cultivate.

Why can we not see the Master? It's because of our heavy obstacles. The Master is constantly with us. If we sincerely cultivate and return to the source, we will always be together with the Master. We will be a transformation body of the Master. Then we will not have let down the Master, who came to the world to teach us.

---

佛於甚深法　　通達無與等　　眾生不能了　　次第為開示
——《大方廣佛華嚴經》〈光明覺品第九〉

*The Buddha has penetrated the most profound Dharmas.*
*No one can equal him.*
*Living beings are not able to understand it,*
*And so in sequence he explains it for them.*

Flower Adornment Sutra, Chapter Nine, Light Enlightenment

---

# 我對師父的信心
## MY FAITH IN THE MASTER

我對師父的信心，是不需要這些表信的。

**I have faith in the Master and thus
felt no need for these superficial things.**

王鴻義　Joseph Wang

我在一九八七年佛誕日那天，第一次見到師父的。從那一天到現在，便與師父結了不解的今世緣，可以說趕也趕不走，罵也罵不走，跟定了！有些人給師父罵兩句話就跑了，或者見師父罵別人，或者見師父臥病床，就跑了。我告訴你：「這就是緣不深，我相太重，或者道心不堅，或者是對面不識觀世音。」

想要訪師學道，罵兩句就跑了，豈不是忍辱太差！今天是師父罵你，就跑，那換一個旁人，豈不是要大吵一場？我告訴你，師父曾經用很難聽的話罵過我，什麼邪知邪見啦，罪惡啦，下地獄啦。我也不跑，因為全罵中了；如果今世我沒遇到師父，那真就罵中了。

我也可以告訴你，你看到師父發脾氣時，那是演戲，不是真的。有一年佛誕日，師父好像脾氣不好，指著浴佛的行列，一下子要人家靠右邊站一點，一下子又要人家靠左邊站一點，搞得人家不知所措。那一天，我負責在大爐插香，心裡想：「老和尚今天又要玩什麼花樣？」一剎那間，看到師父朝著我這半邊的臉，咧著嘴笑，而同時又指罵著浴佛的行列。

在皈依師父的這些年來，師父托了好多次夢給我，包括在夢裡給我治病，在夢裡允許我出家（慚愧），在夢裡降魔，在夢裡跟我一起撿他的舍利（荼毗那天午睡時），在夢裡示我拳的開合相（不悟，愚癡！）還有很多，真是夢中說夢兩重虛，你信不信都是無所謂的。

有人見師父臥病床，信心就動搖了，有人擔心燒不出舍利，可是我對師父的信心，是不需要這些表信的，可以說是一點也沒放在心上。雖然師父說，

I met the Master for the first time on the Buddha's Birthday in 1987. From that day on, I have created an affinity with the Master that cannot be dissolved. You may say that nothing can drive me away from the Master. Some people ran away after being scolded by the Master. Some left upon seeing how the Master scolded others or how sick the Master had become. Let me tell you: this indicates either shallow affinity, strong egotism, a weak resolve for the Way, or failure to recognize Guanshiyin Bodhisattva when seeing him face to face. Doesn't it show a lack of endurance if you want to seek a teacher and study the Way, and yet you run away after being scolded a little? Now, you ran away when the Master scolded you. If it had been someone else, wouldn't you have gotten into a fight with him?

Let me tell you, the Master scolded me very harshly sometimes, saying that I had deviant views and evil offenses, that I would fall into the hells, and so on. But I did not run away because his scoldings always hit the mark. And they would be really true if I did not meet the Master in this life.

I can also tell you, when you saw the Master losing his temper, he was just putting on an act. It was not real. One year on the Buddha's Birthday, the Master seemed to be upset. He pointed at the lines of people waiting to bathe the Buddha, instructing them to move to the right, and later to the left. People were confused and did not know what to make of it. I was in charge of putting the incense sticks into the big censer that day. I wondered, "What is the Venerable Master up to today?" At that moment, I noticed the Master was smiling as he pointed and scolded people who were in line.

During these years of being the Master's disciple, I dreamed of the Master many times. In those dreams he treated my illnesses, granted me permission to leave the home-life (I am ashamed), subdued demons, sifted through his ashes to find sharira along with me (I dreamed this during the nap I took in the afternoon of the day of cremation), and showed me his fist opening and closing (but I am too stupid to grasp the meaning), and many others. It's said, "Speaking of dreams in a dream is doubly illusory." So it doesn't matter whether or not you believe me.

Some people wavered when they saw how ill the Master was. Others were worried that no sharira would come out of the cremation. I have faith in the Master and thus felt no need for these superficial things. Therefore, I did not care about them.

要是聽到有人誹謗他，要向這人叩頭。這對我是很難的，要不臉紅脖子粗是很難的，也許是師父知道很多弟子對他都很執著，所以才這樣勸我們。

我對師父這種近乎執著的信心，有一天終於得到了答案，在聞思修居士林慶祝成立那一天回程的車上，師父告訴我：

你跟我不止一世的因緣，所以才信得過。

哦！原來如此！我也知道，不只過去世、這一世，乃至盡未來際，我們師徒都有不盡的法緣，末了發願曰：「願生生世世護持正法，護持宣公上人。」

The Master had instructed us to bow to those who slandered him, but I find it hard not to get red-faced and stubborn under such circumstances. Maybe the Master gave us such advice because he knew that many of his disciples were very attached to him.

My strong faith in the Master, which is almost to the point of being obstinate, was finally explained one day. Returning from the opening ceremony of Bodhi Way Association, the Master told me in the car,

You have deep faith in me because you have followed me for more than one lifetime.

So that is why! I know, too, that not only in past lives, or in this life, but in future lives to the end of time, the Master and I will have an unlimited affinity in Dharma. Finally, let me vow that, "May I protect and support the Proper Dharma and the Venerable Master in life after life."

# THE PROPER DHARMA NOURISHES THE MIND AND THE FIVE PRECEPTS DISPEL THE THREE POISONS

# 正法灌心田　五戒驅三毒

Kuo Chai　史果齋

In 1975, the Master came to my hometown and gave a talk at the university. The first time I saw the Master and the Bhikshus and Bhikshunis who were with him, it made a very strong impression on my mind. Through the help of my friend, I attended some of the meditation sessions and Dharma lectures that were held in San Francisco at Gold Mountain Monastery. Gradually I became interested to the extent that I volunteered my time to live inside the monastery and help out with the work there. Later I moved to the City of Ten Thousand Buddhas and lived there for some years. In that time of my life I had a lot of problems, and I was very lucky to become involved with the Buddhadharma and to become a disciple of the Venerable Master.

Through the teaching that the Master gave to his disciples, I was able to understand my faults and to understand how to change myself and improve my life. One of the most important things I learned from the Master was how to make the five precepts part of our own thinking and activity every day, so that we can gradually overcome the three poisons of greed, hatred, and stupidity. The Master was always an excellent example of this. He showed us all what it really meant to practice and follow sincerely the rules of the Buddhadharma. Now, although I no longer live at the City, I still stay very close to the left-home people there, and I just had this opportunity to come and take part in this Dharma lecture. Thank you very much.

一九七五年時，上人到我的家鄉的一個大學來演講。我第一次見到上人和跟隨上人的比丘和比丘尼時，在我心裡就留下了很深刻的印象。透過友人的幫助，我去金山寺參加了幾次禪坐和聽過幾次法。慢慢地我的興趣越來越濃，所以我就搬進了金山寺去住，並幫忙工作。後來，我又搬到萬佛聖城去住了幾年。我那時生活中有許多的問題，所以我能接近佛法又皈依老和尚，實在是一件很幸運的事。

由老和尚給弟子的教誨中，我看到了我的過錯，也知道了應該怎樣改正自己。我從上人那兒學到的一件最重要事，就是怎樣將五戒融入我每天的思想生活中，並逐漸克服我們的貪瞋癡三毒。上人自己就是一個最好的榜樣。上人以身示範怎樣真心誠意修行佛法。現在雖然我不再住在萬佛城，我還是跟那兒的僧眾很接近的，還有這個機會和大家一齊參加這個法會。

# THE ABILITY TO REACH MILLIONS

# 廣度眾生　無遠弗屆

Roger Kellerman
果民

On reading the first two volumes in memory of the Venerable Master, I was struck by the diverse ways that he was able to influence so many people from so many different cultures and backgrounds. I would like to share with everyone something I witnessed where the Master was able to move a total stranger.

In 1991, when the Venerable Master was admitted to hospital, some of the Bhikshus went to see him. In his hospital room, we joined the monks who were staying with him night and day. We were all sitting on one side of the room and the Master was sitting on the edge of his bed. A doctor came in. She wanted to explain to the Master the two different types of treatment that could be used for his condition. At the end of her explanation she asked the Master: "And which one would you prefer?" The Master, with one sweep of his arm indicated to the doctor the assembled monks, and said:

You'd better ask them. They are the ones who are putting me through this. To me, life and death are one and the same.

The doctor carefully scrutinized the Master. She inclined her head first one way and then another. After a while she said: "You know, I believe you are qualified to say that." Now here was someone who didn't know anything about the Master. He was just another patient to her, and yet she was touched by that invisible something that emanated from the Master. That something special which goes beyond words and has moved all of us--some to look or listen, some to take refuge and some to leave home.

While these books are memorials, it is essential that we look towards the future. The Master did not want these books in memory of him. He thought of himself as an ant who came into the world without a trace and wanted to leave without one too. However, he came to America with the sole wish of bringing the Proper Dharma to the West. He emphasized three areas: cultivation, education and translation of the Tripitaka. These will be the foundation of Buddhism in the West. Thus, we who have had our light, however meagre, lit by the Venerable Master, should see that his wish is carried out.

A few days ago, I came across these words penned over one hundred years ago by the Russian writer, Fyodor Dostoevsky. Although they weren't written with the Venerable Master in mind, yet, because they describe him so beautifully, I would like to leave them by way of a conclusion:

閱畢兩冊的上人紀念專輯後，令筆者印象最深的，上人能以種種不同的法門，感化無數不同文化背景的人。以下願意和大家分享筆者親睹上人教化一位素昧平生者的故事。

一九九一年上人住院期間，數位出家弟子前去探病。師父坐在床緣，而弟子們則坐在病房的一邊。此時，醫生進來向上人解說兩種不同的療法，然後她問上人希望採用哪種療法。上人揮手指向弟子們答道：

妳應該問他們，是他們令我病到這個地步的。對我而言，生和死本是同一回事的。

那位醫師聽了非常訝異，她仔細端詳上人好一陣子後，說：「我相信您夠資格說這席話。」你瞧！這位醫生根本不認識上人，上人不過是她眾多病患之一罷了，然而她卻為上人不可言喻，無形的力量所攝化。正是那不可言諭的力量攝受了你我；有些人因而前來聽法，有些人因而皈依，更有些人因而出家！

在追思上人之外，我們更應該向前看。上人並不希望看到這些紀念他的專輯，他說過他是一隻小螞蟻，悄悄地來到這個世界，離開時他也不希望留下任何痕跡。然而他萬里迢迢遠來美國的唯一願望，是將正法傳到西方。他再三強調修行、教育及譯經，這三項事業將成為西方佛教的基石。因此，所有曾為上人點燃心燈的弟子們，無論我們的心燈是多麼微渺，均有責任去實踐上人的願望。

不久前，筆者碰巧讀到一百多年前俄國作家杜斯托也夫斯基寫的一篇文章，雖然他不是在描述上人，然因這段文字用來描述上人傳神至極，筆者遂引用作為本文之結尾：

*The people are irresistibly drawn to Him, they surround Him, they flock about Him, follow Him. He moves silently in their midst with a gentle smile of infinite compassion. The sun of kindness burns in His heart, light and power shine from His eyes, and their radiance, shed on the people, stirs their hearts with responsive love. He holds out His hand to them, blesses them, and a healing virtue comes from contact with Him.*

人們不自禁地接近他，圍繞他，追隨他。

他帶著無盡悲憫的微笑悠遊在人群中。

他的心中燃燒著仁慈的火燄，

他的雙眼所放射出的光及熱照在人們身上，

激發起人們內心深處的愛心。

他伸出手去加持他們，

所有被加持者均得到大利益。

# 懷念師恩

# IN MEMORY OF THE KINDNESS OF OUR TEACHER

Shramanera Gwo Wei, age 15

釋果維　十五歲

　　在我的印像中，師父跟信眾開示時，簡單扼要，都不會講的很多。但是他所說的話，儘管是幾個字而已，卻常令人受用不盡。他的語氣及態度就表現出他是一位親切、慈祥、和藹的老人。

　　我雖然沒有太多機會跟他老人家多講幾句話，可是這並不表示他就因此而忘記我們這些弟子。相反的，他時常注意弟子們的舉動，是否有認真修行等等。我還記得在他老人家圓寂以前，因為他病得很重，所以不能隨意走動，只能坐在黑色的沙發椅上。有一天他坐在沙發椅上，一面握著一位出家弟子的手，一面親切的鼓勵他認真修行，這時候我突然注意到他老人家的眼框濕潤了，而那一位弟子也低下頭來。如果你親眼看見這個情景，你一定會感動得流淚。從這裏我們可以看的出來他的胸懷是多麼的偉大、寬厚、慈悲。在生病時，忘了自己的痛苦，救度眾生心切；在往生前，也不忘講法。這種精神真是可敬可佩。所以我覺得我們身為一代高僧的弟子，不應該妄自菲薄而不勤加修道。更要努力的修道，而讓正法遍及於世界各地。這樣才不辜負師父苦心的教導。

I do not remember the Venerable Master speaking often to his disciples, but when he spoke he was concise. His meaning was full and very useful. In his speech and deeds he was cordial and kind.

Although I didn't have many opportunities to speak to the Master, this does not mean he forgot us. He always paid attention if we were diligent in the path. I remember that before he passed away one day he was very sick and was sitting on a black sofa. He held a disciple's hand and kindly encouraged him. If you had seen this with your own eyes, I am sure you would be moved by it and would even cry perhaps. From this we know the holiness in his heart, so deep and kind. He forgot the pain of his own sickness and encouraged that disciple. Right up to his dying breath, he was always teaching; this spirit is truly admirable and worthy of respect.

Therefore, I feel that, as disciples of such a lofty teacher, we should not look down on ourselves, but should diligently cultivate and cause the proper Dharma to be propagated throughout the entire world. Only then will we repay the Venerable Master for the hardships that he underwent to teach us.

# 緬懷恩師
## IN MEMORY OF OUR KIND TEACHER

電話裡的師父上人，卻沒有一點怒火，
還是不斷重複著那句話：忍耐、忍耐……。
**The Master's voice over the phone contained
no trace of anger as he repeated, "Be patient, be patient..."**

徐果生
Guosheng Tu

今天是師父——上宣下化上人涅槃一週年，在深深悲切的同時，不禁感慨萬分。上人把畢生的精力，全部貢獻給佛教，他不畏一切困境，在西方國家建立道場，廣行教化，接引眾生。眾生皈依佛法後，不再造罪業，要行善事，過去所做的一切罪業，都由上人來代受，這種「地獄不空，誓不成佛」的地藏菩薩精神，熏燃著每個眾生的靈魂，使他們逐漸改惡從善，依照上人教化的六大宗旨——不爭、不貪、不求、不自私、不自利、不打妄語——來淨化自己，從而使眾生能解脫生老病死的苦，成為菩薩的化身，得到大涅槃、大究竟的境界。

上人雖然離開這個娑婆世界，但他老人家的志願，這種入地獄的精神，卻深刻地烙在我的心底，永遠鼓舞著我，自強不息，沿著師父的遺訓，繼續走下去。宣公上人承接上虛下雲老和尚傳授法脈，為禪宗潙仰宗第九代接法人，摩訶迦葉初祖傳承的第四十五代傳人，這還是近年來我方才知道的。

一九七九年因緣成熟，皈依三寶後，內心深處因而有所安定，然而對佛法還是不甚瞭解，在一次偶然的機會裡，看到了上人的《開示錄》，使我心境大開，總想能有機會親自聆聽寶貴的教誨。

一九九四年，接受加拿大武術總會的邀請，舉辦武術教學講座，在這期間，得到上人恩准，有幸親近上人。當時上人身體不怎麼好，一口北方話，嗓音清亮地對我說：

你來到萬佛城，可以進一步發展你的武術事業，可以在萬佛城舉辦國際武術學院。

On the first anniversary of the Venerable Master Hua's Nirvana, I cannot help but feel deep grief and melancholy. The Master devoted his entire life's energy to Buddhism. No setback could deter him as he established Way-places and taught living beings in the West. Once people took refuge in Buddhism and vowed to stop creating evil karma and to practice good deeds, the Master was willing to suffer in their stead for all their past offenses. With the spirit of Earth Store Bodhisattva, who vowed not to become a Buddha before the hells were empty, he touched the heart of every living being and influenced them to reform their faults and purify themselves by upholding the Six Guiding Principles--no fighting, no greed, no seeking, no selfishness, no self-benefit, and no lying. In this way living beings could escape the pain of birth, old age, sickness and death; become transformation bodies of Bodhisattvas; and ultimately attain great Nirvana.

Although the Master has departed from the Saha world, his vows and his willingness to go into the hells to save beings are deeply engraved in my heart, urging me to tirelessly improve myself and continuously follow the Master's teachings. Only in recent years did I come to know that the Venerable Master had received the Dharma from Venerable Elder Master Hsu Yun, thus becoming the Ninth Patriarch of the the Weiyang lineage of the Chan School, a Patriarch of the forty-fifth generation after the First Patriarch, Venerable Mahakashyapa.

When I took refuge with the Triple Jewel in 1979, it gave me a sense of security, although I did not understand much Buddhism at that time. Later, when I happened to read the Master's *Instructional Talks*, I was greatly inspired and hoped to one day be able to hear the Master's precious teachings in person.

In 1994 I was invited by the Canadian Martial Arts Association to deliver a series of martial arts lectures. During that time I was given the Master's kind permission to visit him. The Master's health was not good. He told me in his Manchurian accent,

Why don't you come to the City of Ten Thousand Buddhas and develop your martial arts career? You can start an International Martial Arts Academy here.

雖然這一句極為普通的話，但給我的印象頗為深刻，至今還在我的耳邊不斷地迴響。

上人是一位最好的導師，他潛移默化教導眾生。想到第一次上人打電話給我時，說：「歡迎你來萬佛城出家！」當時心裡一亮，但最後還是被無明捲蓋著說：「我有太太、孩子和我的事業，還不能放下……。」上人還是用善巧的方法對我說：「你可以來萬佛城看看……。」在這期間，上人安排我在金輪聖寺和長堤聖寺，聆聽他老人家傳授「千手觀音四十二手眼」的法門，使我受益非淺。

使我更感動不已的是，上人病重快要離開我們的時候，還打電話給我，諄諄地教導：

我來美國幾十年了，這地方不好混的，
你要有忍耐心，……。

當時我非常愚癡，大聲回答說：「我來美國不是混的，我在中國怎麼怎麼地……。」電話裡的師父上人，卻沒有一點怒火，還是不斷重複著那句話：

忍耐、忍耐……。

回首當年，曾多次親近上人，他老人家總是熱忱相待，笑容可掬，教化我的情況，歷歷在目，此情此景，不能忘懷。今天是師父上人涅槃週年，面對著師父的德相，熱淚不由自主地淌流……。

這虛偽的心啊！使我造更大罪業。
這妄想的心啊！使我想入非非。
這欲心啊！使我離開了正道。

師父上人啊！當今人慾橫流，一切物化，唯利是圖的心態，極須師父的教化。今天藉著您的週年之際，我深深地向您懺悔，願您乘願再來，普渡眾生。

您的不肖弟子　徐果生
一九九六年於加拿大卡城華嚴寺

---

This ordinary-sounding statement left a remarkably profound impression upon me. Even today it continues to echo in my ears.

The Venerable Master was an excellent teacher who taught living beings in subtle and imperceptible ways. I remember once when he called me on the phone and said, "I welcome you to the City of Ten Thousand Buddhas to leave home!" My heart warmed at his words, but later I replied in my ignorance, "I have my wife, children, and career, and I can't give them up yet..." The Master expediently said, "You can still come to the City of Ten Thousand Buddhas and take a look." The Master also arranged for me to attend his lectures at Gold Wheel Monastery and Long Beach Monastery, during which he transmitted the Forty-two Hands and Eyes of Guanyin Bodhisattva. This was a very beneficial experience for me.

What touches me even more is that shortly before he left us, the Master called me on the phone and earnestly admonished me,

You've been in America for several decades. It's not easy to get by in this country, so you ought to be patient...

I very foolishly replied in a loud voice, "I'm not just 'getting by' here. In China I was this and that..." Despite my rude reply, the Master's voice over the phone contained no trace of anger as he repeated,

Be patient, be patient...

When I think back to the many visits I paid the Master in past years, I can still recall very clearly how warmly he treated me and gave me guidance with a gentle smile. I will never forget those scenes. Today, on the first anniversary of the Master's Nirvana, I cannot help but shed tears as I gaze at the Master's picture.

*This hypocritical mind leads me to commit ever greater*
*offenses!*
*This deluded mind causes me to fantasize and daydream!*
*This mind of desires leads me away from the proper path!*

Venerable Master! In the present age when human desires are out of control and profit is the only incentive, your teaching is desperately needed. Today, on the occasion of the first anniversary of your passing, I repent earnestly before you and hope you will return based on your vows to universally take across living beings.

Your unfilial disciple, Guosheng Tu,
at Avatamsaka Monastery, Calgary, Canada 1996

# 我跟師父的一段因緣
## MY EXPERIENCE WITH THE MASTER

上人已入了涅槃，但我對上人的信心依舊不變。

**Now at present, even though the Master has entered Nirvana,
my faith in him still remains the same.**

釋恆智
Shi Heng Jr

一九八三年十一月，我來到了美國，住在洛杉磯朋友家裡。因爲我在菲律賓的時候，習慣到佛教寺廟禮佛，因此我就想在住的附近找一間佛教寺廟，但是我朋友和我都沒有找到，我朋友反而帶我去天主教堂。不過我不並因此而放棄了尋找。

有一天當我搭車經過第六街的時候，我看到一間佛教寺廟，我立刻寫下名字，回到家後，在電話簿裡查到電話號碼，我打電話去問怎麼樣到那裡。第二天早上七點半，我就到了廟裡。

那是我第一次到金輪聖寺，一位比丘尼帶我到大殿禮佛。禮完佛，我就感覺到一種從未有過的、又無法形容的快樂。這位比丘尼給了我兩本《金剛菩提海》月刊；我一回到家裡，立刻就拿出來看。我注意到一篇萬佛聖城徵求義工的廣告，當時我就想「如果我能去，在那裡我會很高興地當一名義工。」這個念頭一直在我心裡打轉。同時我也定期每個星期六、星期日都會到金輪聖寺去。

過不久，師父來金輪聖寺。他遠從舊金山來，看起來似乎有一點疲倦；但是他也不休息。一位比丘尼叫我趕快給師父頂禮，但我不知道如何頂禮，那時師父就開始講經説法了。講到一半時，師父提到了當場有兩個人破戒，我很驚訝地想：「他怎麼知道的？他剛剛才到！他真的不是普通人。」

每週末我還是到金輪聖寺，但是不論什麼時回家，總是有一鼓很大的力量吸引著我再回去。因此，我開始每個星期五晚上就到金輪聖寺，直待到星期一的早上。

一九八三年十二月我皈依師父上人。有一天晚上，我作了一個夢，夢到師父看著我吃東西。醒來後，我認爲師父是來告訴我，該是我吃素的時候了。

I came to America in November 1983 and stayed with my friend who lived in Los Angeles. I was used to going to Buddhist temples to bow to the Buddhas when I was in the Philippines. I started to look for one around the area where we lived. Neither my friend nor I came across any Buddhist temple. Instead, she took me to a Catholic church. Nevertheless, I never gave up.

One day, while passing by Sixth Street, I saw a Buddhist temple. I wrote the name down quickly and looked it up in the telephone directory. I called to ask for directions, and there I was next morning at 7:30 am. That was my first visit to Gold Wheel Monastery. The Bhikshuni led me in to bow to the Buddhas. After bowing to the Buddhas, I felt an indescribable sense of happiness which I had never experienced before. Then she gave me two issues of *Vajra Bodhi Sea*. I read them as soon as I got home. I noticed the ad for volunteer workers in the City of Ten Thousand Buddhas, and I thought, "If I can go, I'll be more than happy to be a volunteer worker there." This thought remained in my mind. Meanwhile, I regularly went to Gold Wheel Monastery every Saturday and Sunday. Not long after, the Venerable Master came. He had just arrived after a long trip from San Francisco and looked tired. Nevertheless, he didn't even pause to rest. The Bhikshuni told me to bow to the Master. I had no idea what I was supposed to do. Shortly afterwards, the Master started to speak the Dharma, in the middle of which he mentioned that there were two people there who had broken the precepts. I couldn't help but wonder, "How did he know? He just barely arrived! He's certainly not an ordinary person."

I continued going to Gold Wheel Monastery every Saturday and Sunday, and whenever I left the urge to go back was very great. Hence, I started my routine of going to Gold Wheel Monastery every Friday night and staying until Monday morning. In December of 1983, I took refuge with the Master. After that, I had a dream one night. In my dream, the Master was watching me eat. Waking up from this dream, I took it as a message from the Master that it was about time I became a vegetarian. Since it was not convenient for me to be a vegetarian while staying with my friend's family, I moved out.

因為跟我朋友的家人住在一起，對我吃素是很不方便，因此我就搬出來了。

有一天我問一位比丘尼一個很天真的問題：「出家的生活是怎麼樣？」她很溫和地對我解釋出家人的生活。後來有一天，師父再來到金輪聖寺的時候，他把我叫到樓上問我：「妳為什麼想要出家？」我真的嚇一跳，他怎麼知道我心裡在想什麼？然後他問了我的家庭背景，接著問我：「妳會不會背《楞嚴經》？」我誤會〈楞嚴咒〉為《楞嚴經》，就回答：「會一點」，師父就叫我背出來。我立刻開始背〈楞嚴咒〉，當我忘記的時候，師父幫忙提示到我背完，然後很和藹地告訴我，我背的是〈楞嚴咒〉不是《楞嚴經》。我深深地體會到上人的大慈大悲。他就像一位慈父照顧我們，看每一位眾生如他子女一般。

金輪聖寺常組團租巴士到萬佛聖城參加法會，我也參加了好幾次。我記得有一次，師父從舊金山上車，跟我們一起到聖城。他坐在巴士的最後一排，我剛好坐在倒數第二排。師父看到我時，就問我：「妳好嗎？」然後他就作他自己每天的功課。當我們抵達聖城後，師父帶著我們到後山，指著一塊地，告訴我們這是將來蓋大雄寶殿的地方。然後他帶著我們到無言堂，要我們自我介紹。

一九八四年的十月，我搬到萬佛聖城，入學居士訓練班。我在那兒當了兩年的在家居士，在一九八六年十月三十日地藏菩薩聖誕日出家。當天有八個人出家，三位沙彌，五位沙彌尼。我記得師父告訴我們：「你們八位金剛，要好好護持這個道場。」直到今天這些話一直都銘記在我心裡。我不斷地提醒自己，要盡我的能力去做好，不要讓師父失望。

記得在一九八七年時，萬佛城裡人人都為舉辦水陸空法會而忙著。有一次，正在忙著搬東西時，我的腳不小心讓一台鐵車壓傷，痛得不得了，腫了好幾天，當時給聖城的一位醫生看了，又上了藥，但是腫還是不消。又有一位來訪的女醫生，建議我去看骨科醫生，照艾克斯光，但我心想：「只要誠心祈禱，一定會沒事的。」當上人來城時，與我在服務台工作的尼師跟上人講了，然後叫我不要擔心。

第二天早課後，回房休息，夢見上人在喜捨院，離我大概二、三公尺遠，上人的手指著我的腳

One day, I asked a Bhikshuni the innocent question, "What is leaving the home life all about? She very kindly explained to me the life of a left-home person. Then one day the Venerable Master came to Gold Wheel Monastery again. He called me upstairs and asked, "Why do you want to leave the home life?" I was really amazed at how he could read my mind. Then he asked about my family background. Furthermore, he asked, "Can you recite the *Shurangama Sutra* from memory?" Mistaking "Shurangama Mantra" for "*Shurangama Sutra*," I said, "Yes, a little bit." The Master asked me to recite it. I immediately started reciting the Shurangama Mantra for him. I got stuck somewhere along the line. He compassionately helped me out and kindly told me what I was reciting was the Shurangama Mantra, not the *Shurangama Sutra*. I deeply felt the profound kindness and great compassion in him. He's like a father who cares for and regards every single being as his own child.

Gold Wheel Monastery organizes group trips by bus to the City of Ten Thousand Buddhas for Dharma assemblies. I went with the group quite a few times. On one occasion, the Master joined us from San Francisco to the City of Ten Thousand Buddhas. He sat in the very last row of the bus. I was sitting in the second row from the back. When he saw me, he asked, "How are you?" Then he proceeded with his daily Dharmas. As soon as we arrived at the City of Ten Thousand Buddhas, he took us to the back property and showed us the site where the future Jewelled Palace would be built. Later he took us to his place (K Building) and asked us to introduce ourselves.

In October 1984, I moved to City of Ten Thousand Buddhas and enrolled in the Sangha and Laity Training Programs. I stayed there for two years as a layperson and then left home on Earth Store Bodhisattva's birthday (October 30, 1986). There were eight of us, three novice monks and five novice nuns. I remember the Master telling us, "You Eight Vajras should protect and uphold the Way-place." These words are inscribed deeply in my mind up to this day. I constantly remind myself to do the best I can and not let the Master down.

I remember back in 1987, while everybody in the City of Ten Thousand Buddhas was busy getting ready for the big event--Water, Land and Air Ceremony, while hauling things from one building to another, my foot was accidentally hit by a four-wheel metal cart. The impact was so strong that my foot was badly hurt. It swelled for days. Even when a Chinese doctor in the City put some medicine on it, the swelling didn't subside. A guest lady physician who happened to be in the City suggested that I see an orthopedist and have it x-rayed for broken bones. I didn't heed her advice, thinking that I'd be all right if I was sincere in my prayers. When the Venerable Master arrived at the City, the nun who worked with me at the counter told the Master about the accident.Then she came back to me and told me not to worry. The next morning after morning recitation, I went back to my room to rest. I dreamed that the Master was standing about two to three meters away from me in Joyous Giving House. His fingers were pointing at my hurt foot and his mouth was reciting something. When I woke up, my foot didn't hurt the way it used to, and I walked over to the Buddhahall to help at

，口裡念念有詞。醒來後，腳就不像早先那麼痛了，於是就到服務台開始工作。上人走過來問起我的腳，我告訴上人已經好多了。那天下午，腫也開始消了，沒看醫生，傷也癒合了。

從這件事，還有我在聖城看見上人怎樣減輕弟子們的痛苦，怎樣治療弟子們的疾病，加上聽到別人怎樣由上人那兒得到感應，都使我對上人的信心，越來越深。現在上人已入了涅槃，我對上人的信心依舊不變。我相信在我有需要時，上人一定會幫助我，因為上人這樣慈愛，一定不忍讓他的弟子受苦的。

上人的耐心也是驚人的，從上人一來美國直到入涅槃，都不休止地教化弟子們。上人為教化每一個弟子，都吃了許多苦，但是面上從不顯現出來。

有一次，上人叫我去方丈室，我跪在上人前，起先上人交代我做一件事，接著上人就像教化其他弟子一般跟我講了一些開示。在我站起來之前，他問我：「妳有煩惱嗎？」我沒講真話，答：「沒有。」因為我恐怕我講了真話，上人就會去責備某些人，而那些人會來找我麻煩。可是我心裡知道上人一定知道我的心事。上人聽了我的話，遲疑一下說：「好了。」我正要走的時候，上人又說：「妳真的沒有煩惱嗎？」我知道我不能再瞞了，所以我就告訴了上人我的煩惱。上人笑著說：「要忍耐！忍耐！」我說：「是！是！師父。」有偈曰：

忍是無價寶，
人人使不好；
若能會用它，
事事都能好。

上人的智慧和德行，不是語言所能表達的。上人是人天師表，他對眾生有著無盡的慈悲，無數的眾生因上人的教化改過遷善。上人為人忘己的精神也是人比不上的。行、住、坐、臥，上人從不休息，總是精進不懈，值得所有眾生的尊敬。

能遇到這樣的善知識，是很難得的。我很幸運能遇到上人，並在上人座下出家，獲益良多。我深信只要我遵守上人的教化，就絕不會走入歧途。我對著上人發願：「願生生世世隨上人出家！」上人說：「Try your best！」（盡妳的力！）師父！我會盡我的力。

the counter. The Venerable Master approached me and asked about my foot. I told him it was getting better. Later in the afternoon, the swelling began to subside and the wound gradually healed without my having to see a doctor.

From this incident and from seeing in the City how the Venerable Master compassionately alleviated his disciples' sufferings and cured their illnesses, and also from what I heard people say about their responses from the Venerable Master, my faith has grown deeper and deeper. Now at present, even though the Master has entered Nirvana, my faith in him still remains the same. I believe he will always be there when I need his aid. The Venerable Master is so kind that he won't let any of his disciples suffer.

The Venerable Master's patience was inconceivable. From the time he came to America until he was about to enter Nirvana, he was constantly teaching and transforming his disciples. He went through a lot of pain and hardship to teach and transform a single person, yet his face didn't show a trace of suffering.

One time the Venerable Master asked me to see him in K building. I knelt before him. First he assigned me a job, and then he talked to me and bestowed his teaching the way he usually did to all his disciples. Before I got up he asked me a question: "Do you have afflictions?" I lied and said "no" because I was afraid that he would scold some people and then those people would come back to me. However I knew very well that the Master would read my mind. He paused for a moment, then said "okay." When I was about to leave the premises, the Venerable Master asked again, "You really don't have afflictions?" That time I knew I couldn't lie again, so I said "yes," and told him a bit about my afflictions. He smilingly said, "Be patient, be patient." I said, "Yes, Shr Fu (Teacher)." A verse says:

*Patience is a priceless gem,*
*But no one knows how to use it.*
*If people were able to use it,*
*Everything would turn out fine.*

The Master's genuine wisdom and virtuous conduct are beyond words. He is a model for human and gods. His kindly compassion for living being is infinite. His teaching moved countlessly many living beings to completely change in the direction of goodness. He worked hard to the point that he forgot about himself. His vigor was incomparable. He was always vigorous in walking, standing, sitting, and reclining. He never rested. He deserves to be honored and respected by all living beings.

To be able to encounter such a good knowing advisor is very rare. I am lucky to have met him and to have become his left-home disciple. I benefitted greatly from his teaching. I strongly believe that as long as I follow the Master's teachings, I won't tread on the wrong path. I vow that I will always be his left-home disciple in life after life. I have said this to the Master before. He said, "Try your best."I will, Shr Fu; I will always try my very best.

# A RETROSPECT OF MY EXPERIENCE OF THE VENERABLE MASTER

## 夢話——回想我所認識的師父

**For over twenty years I have dreamed of the Master, regardless of time or distance; with his passing, I know that it will continue for the rest of my life.**

**二十餘年來，我無論何時何處，都會夢到師父。**
**雖然師父已入涅槃，但是我的夢在此生不會停息。**

Leland (Kuo Li) Eagleson
果璃

In the fullness of time, everyone can look back and link many seemingly unrelated events before actually meeting the Venerable Master. I believe my earliest memory of the essence of Buddhism took place when I was around three or four years old while taking naps at the family home in Columbus, Ohio. During the nap I would find myself in a beautiful country where everything was golden colored and there was no sorrow. I remember locking myself out of this state by holding my hand over my navel. I was not to understand this dream-state until many years later when I read the *Sixth Patriarch Sutra* and realized that this was a very small taste of the peace that can be found in sincere practice.

Around the same time, while banging away on our piano, I hit a chord that transported me into a waking state of completeness; it is truly a lost chord that I hope to hear again.

In November 1959, on a eerie Sunday night before Thanksgiving, there was strange weather, a very bright and silent light that tracked across the western sky, burning a knife-edged strip of clear sky through the clouds, followed by an eruption of violent weather of all kinds. At the time, as a fourteen-year-old science fiction fan, I thought, "Wow, I've seen a UFO!" In the last few years I changed my awareness of this event in light of the Venerable Master's biography (second volume) in which is described what happened in Hong Kong when the Venerable Hsu Yun's sharira were presented to the Venerable Master. As near as I can tell, the light that I saw coincided with events in Hong Kong, though what it meant is still a major mystery to me. Only one other person saw it, and my sister's recollection is not clear.

In December 1970 a waking vision of a standing golden-bodied image was the beginning of a long and haphazard search that included two dreams in January and February 1971 of the Venerable Master, where his face, form and compassionate good humor were first seen and were not confirmed until July 1975 when I finally met the Venerable Master face to face. In 1971, I

時機成熟時，每個人都可把在未遇見師父以前，所發生的許多不相干的事情，回想一下，内中脈絡可尋。

我個人對佛教真義，最早的記憶是在老家，俄亥俄州哥倫布市睡午覺時發生的。當時我大概是三或四歲，夢中我在一個美麗的地方，所有的東西都是金色的，那裡也沒有憂傷，我還記得把手按在肚臍上從夢中醒來。一直到多年後，讀了《六祖壇經》才了解夢中的情境，惟有誠心修行，才能淺嘗修行帶來的平和。

在同一段時期，我在彈鋼琴時，曾經彈出一個和音，引我至於圓滿的境界，那是我真想再聽見的和音，現在彈不出來了。

一九五九年十一月，感恩節前的星期天晚上，天氣非常怪異，西方上空裡有一道亮光如刀刃般劃過雲層，接下來的就是各種形式的險惡天氣。當時我十四歲，非常沉迷於科幻小說，心想我真是見到來自外太空的幽浮了。最近幾年，讀了師父的生平事蹟（英文版第二冊），講到虛老的舍利呈現給師父時所發生的情況，我才改變了我的看法。就我記憶所及，這道光和香港所發生的情形有關連，但是，内中含有何種意義則非我能解讀，我的妹妹也見到這道光，但是她的記憶卻不是那麼清楚。

一個鮮明的金身形象，揚開了一段長久隨緣式的尋覓，在此期間於一九七一年一月二日還夢到師父二次。夢裡第一次見到他的面相，體形和悲憫的幽

had absolutely no knowledge of the Proper Dharma or of the Venerable Master.

December 1974 found me at Buddha Root Farm helping Bill Breevort maintain his farm. The next seven months were filled with dreams four and five times a week of the Venerable Master, Gold Mountain Monastery, Bodhisattvas, and lectures. After arriving at Gold Mountain in the middle of July, 1975, the dreams continued--I found my waking contact of the Master was about the same as my dream contact, so one could say that I couldn't know if I were awake or asleep.

The opportunity to take refuge with the Triple Jewel came just a few days after my arrival at Gold Mountain Monastery, and I jumped at the chance. I was given the Dharma name Kuo Li (fruit of the crystal). I found that it was customary to present a gift upon taking refuge, and for a while, I agonized over what to give for I had a chunk of lapis lazuli and a fire opal. I decided on the lapis and went with a group of people to present it to the Master, who proceeded to tell me that my Dharma name comes from *liu li* (lapis lazuli). Quite a bit later, the Master told me that if it hadn't been for that piece of lapis, I would have been known as Kuo Meng (fruit of the dream).

For over twenty years I have dreamed of the Master, regardless of time or distance; with his passing, I know that it will continue for the rest of my life and that I will always recognize the Master because a quality of Trueness that I have come to know of the Master, that always occurs in the dreams in which he speaks his Dharma in a simple way. For example, in the fall of 1989, I had a dream in which I found myself at the City of Ten Thousand Buddhas (CTTB) where a group of people were gathered around the Master. In the dream, I bowed three times and sat down and listened and understood what he was saying. After a while, I realized that I was waking up so I told the Master, "I have to go now, Shr fu." I bowed three times and he smiled broadly and handed me a yellow rain coat, and I woke up. The following months were extremely difficult but this dream kept me aware that the Master was with me, and telling me two things: "you are safe" and "try your best." It seems that every time I was approaching difficult times internally or externally, I would dream of the Master, and some message in the dream would give me the courage to go on.

Another dream from the time I was in the middle of an agonizing decision whether to remain a monk or return to lay life (November 1977): I found myself moving through a fiery sea colored red with orange and yellow fish swimming around; suddenly the sea parted and I found myself in the presence of the Master in a stairwell at the City of Ten Thousand Buddhas. I bowed three times and as I did so I saw myself in street clothes. The Master just gently smiled as if to say "Everything's o.k." I withdrew back into the sea that was now colored green with blue and silver fish, and I woke up at my parents' house in Kalamazoo, Michigan. I had the strong sense that I had just told the Master my decision, and shortly after folded my robes and sash and put them away. In a few weeks, I did return to CTTB and formally told the Master, in public view, of my decision to return to lay life.

默，一直到一九七五年七月面見師父，才確定我的夢境。一九七一年時，我根本不認識正法，遑論師父了。

一九七四年十二月裡，我在比爾‧布瑞佛的佛根農場裡幫忙，接下來的七個月裡，一個禮拜內有四、五次夢到師父、金山寺、菩薩和講經。一九七五年七月中旬，到了金山寺後，我的夢並未停下來，我發現我清醒時，和師父的接觸與在夢中大同小異，所以你可以説，當時我不知自身是醒還是睡。我到金山寺幾天之後，便有皈依三寶的機會，我哪肯放過。我的法名是「果璃」，聽説皈依時，有送份師禮的習慣，我有一塊琉璃和一個蛋白石，不知該送那樣給師父。還煩惱了一下，最後決定送琉璃。我和眾人一起去見師父送禮，師父接著告訴我，我的法名來自琉璃。很久以後，師父才告訴我，假如不是那塊琉璃的，我法名會是果夢。

二十餘年來，我無論何時何處，都會夢到師父。雖然師父已入涅槃，但是我的夢在此生不會停息，而且我會一直記著師父。因為從夢裡我認識到師父的那份真摯，他常在夢中用最淺易的方式為我説法。比方説，一九八九年秋季，夢到我在萬佛城，一群人圍著師父，夢中我向師父三頂禮，坐下來聽並了解師父的開示，不久我覺得快醒了，就告訴師父我現在得走了，向師父頂禮三次，他對我笑著，並交給我一件黃色的雨衣。那時我醒過來了，接下來的日子並不是很順利，但是這場夢一直提醒我——
師父與我同在。此外還告訴我兩件事：第一我很安全，第二全力以赴。當時不論我內心或外在世界碰到困境，就會夢見師父，夢中的訊息又會鼓勵我往前邁進。

一九七七年十一月間，我掙扎著是否還俗時，又作一個夢。我看見自己正穿過險惡紅色的海，水中有橘色的、黃色的魚，突然間海水分開，我在萬佛城面對師父，當我向師父頂禮三拜時，發現身上穿的是俗家的衣服，師父面帶微笑好像對我説「一切都沒問題」。我又回到海上，那時海水是綠色的，充滿了藍色和銀色的魚。醒來時，我身在密西根州卡拉馬助市雙親的家裡，我強烈的感覺，已經告訴師父我還俗的決定，不久我也脫下袈裟，摺好收起來，過了幾週後，我又回萬佛城正式稟告師父和大眾，我決定還俗的決心。

This brings up an issue I know affects all of us who have left the home life only to return: please do not rack yourself with guilt now that the Master has left. I feel that being racked with guilt is the hells manifesting, and that the Master never condemned anyone for returning to lay life; and from a personal viewpoint, the Master always welcomed me back, and always told me, "Try your best." To berate yourself for not being good enough is only valuable if you can transform that energy into a genuine remorse and thus into solid reformation, for only the Master knew all the causes and conditions.

In October 1987, while at CTTB, I saw a picture of the Master in a newspaper article from September 1962. The article was about a fast for world peace the Master was carrying out. I had a profound shock followed by an epiphany of awareness of what the Master really meant to the world, by rescuing the world with its billions and billions of living beings from the horrors of total nuclear war. I wrote a poem that was kindly featured in the October 1991 issue of *Vajra Bodhi Sea*, that expresses my small understanding and deep gratitude for what the Master did by refusing to eat. Of the many many events and situations that I encountered from the Master, these stand out in my memories the most:

On the day I left the home life, during the incense offering on the crown of my head, the Master blew gently on my head eradicating the possibility of pain from burns; it was then I understood a little bit who the Master was.

*The Golden Gate Bridge incident.* While coming back from an inspection visit to what would become CTTB in the spring of 1976, I was driving the Master and one other person back. We were running really close to being late for the Sutra Lecture, and my eyes were not the best at night for driving. We were on the bridge and the right lane was clear for a long way and the middle lane was congested and the brake lights flared disorienting me, and except for the steering wheel suddenly going to the right and then left, there would have been a bad accident. As it was we missed only by inches the car in front. The Master sat up grinning and asked, "What happened?" To this day I cannot say exactly what did happen, only what didn't: there was no accident and we were only a couple of minutes late. I can only say that I don't have the driving skills to pull that off, so who was driving at that critical moment?

*The Master points out the well site at CTTB.* In the summer of 1976, the whole area was in a drought, and rain had not fallen in nearly a year and then not enough to do any good. The Master, a small group of disciples and the well driller followed as the site was shown. As we got closer, dark clouds started forming up overhead and when the Master pointed to the site, a flash of lightning, a boom of thunder and a few raindrops fell. As we walked away the clouds disappeared.

There was a time when there were gatherings in San Francisco to help end the drought, and I was at CTTB all by myself performing all the duties of a novice monk and cooking lunch. Everyone was told by the Master that if it didn't rain we wouldn't eat on the day of praying for rain. Well, I had prepared the lunch and was chanting the meal offering and looking hopefully out the

說到這裡，我要提醒我們這批出家又還俗的朋友，師父既已入涅槃，千萬不要再為我們的罪惡感而影響自己。充滿罪惡感，我覺得那正是地獄現前。師父從來也沒有責備過任何還俗的人，而且就我個人的觀點來說，師父每次見到我回來都很高興，也總是鼓勵我全力以赴。嚴責自己的過錯，沒有任何意義，除非你能真正懺悔改正，因為只有師父才明白所有的因緣。

一九八七年十月，我在萬佛城時，看見一九六二年九月報上有張師父的照片，內容是說師父為了世界和平絕食的事，深受震驚，意識裡顯現的是師父為解救這個世界中千萬億眾生，免於核子戰爭的恐懼所現於世的意義，為此我寫了一首詩登載於一九九一年十月的《金剛菩提海雜誌》裡，詩中表達我對師父絕食而為幫助世人，其中個人淺薄的了解及深深的感激之情。我和師父這麼多的接觸中，下面幾樁事情印象十分深刻：出家的那天，在頭頂燒戒疤時，師父輕輕的吹氣，讓我不會感到痛，那時我已略知師父是何許人物。

金門大橋事件：一九七六年春季我們去探訪現今的萬佛城址，回來的路上，當時由我開車，除了師父外還有另外一位人士。我的眼睛晚上開車不靈光，但是要趕回金山寺講經時間很緊迫，當時在金門大橋上右線車子不多，但是中間的車道擁擠，剎車燈令我眼盲失去判斷力，車子忽左忽右，差一吋的距離我們就會撞上前車出車禍。師父坐起身子笑問：「出了什麼事啊？」直到今天我還是說不出來怎麼回事，我只知道沒有出什麼事，車禍沒有發生，講經只遲到幾分鐘，我只能說我的駕駛能力不能達成這些結果，所以在那緊急的時分到底是誰在開車呢？

師父指點我們在萬佛城掘井的地點：一九七六年夏天裡整個地區都有旱災，將近一年沒下雨了，即使有雨量也太少起不了作用。師父帶著些徒弟、鑿井工人到井址去，走的愈近，頭頂上烏雲密集，當師父指出井址時，一道閃電夾著雷聲，幾滴雨水隨之而來，當我們走開時，烏雲也散去。

有一次大家到舊金山祈雨解除旱象，而我留守萬佛城煮飯，做沙彌的工作。師父告訴大家：「要是祈雨時，沒下雨，大家那天都不可以吃飯。」好吧，我飯已經燒好了，上供時做維那，上供到一半時，滿懷希望看著窗外是否有下雨的跡象，真的開始下起雨來了，當時上供的氣氛增加了一股新的活力

window for rain, when during the middle of the meal offering, it actually started to rain. At that point the offering took on a inspired zest, as I knew I could safely eat and obey the Master!

*The Master rescues an accident victim.* In May of 1988, while driving down to San Francisco, I passed a really bad accident where the passenger was very obviously dead. It really disturbed me for I had never seen a freshly dead person before. When I returned I told the Master about it, and he wanted to know when and where it happened. When I told him as clearly as I could, I saw his eyes take on a far away look and I had a very strong sense that he was there rescuing that person from the terrible confusion of a sudden death.

Once, a couple of years ago when I was working at the Burlingame office, I was moving furniture in the Master's quarters while he was there. At one point when my back was turned to the Master, who was quietly watching me work and giving directions where things were to go, I felt a tingling warmth in my upper torso. I have a very strong feeling that the Master was helping me in some way that went beyond but included the physical body. Knowing the Master preferred privacy in these matters, I did not make a big thing of it, but I felt grateful for his attention to details without any thought of thanks. Considering his illness at the time, it is just another example of his total selflessness towards all in need, all the time.

With the passing of his flesh body, I will miss the chance of bowing to him and seeing his glow and kind smile; but the dreams will continue, and as always, in a time of need he will manifest with an analogy that will be understood in time.

，因為我知道可以安心的吃飯，也同時遵照了師父的指示。

師父拯救車禍受難者：一九八八年五月間，有一天我開車去舊金山，路上看到一起很嚴重的車禍。看起來一位乘客已經死了，我平生也沒見過一個死人，這件事讓我很不舒服。等我回去時，面告師父這件意外，他想知道車禍是在何地，何時發生的，我就記憶所及回答師父時，我看到他的眼睛裡有一種身在異地的眼神，我相信師父就在現場幫助那個意外死亡者，免於迷惘。

兩年前有一天，我在譯經學院的辦公室裡幫忙，當時是在師父的方丈室裡搬傢具。師父坐在那裡，我背對著他。師父看著我做事，不時告訴我哪些東西放在哪裡，我的上身有些暖意，我的感覺是師父在幫我的忙，不單只是身體上的幫助，知道師父助人總是不欲人知，我也沒有張揚，但是我很感謝師父注意這些小節，也不求任何回報。想想師父當時的病體，不正是表現出上人隨時完全無私的幫助著所有需要幫助的眾生的身教！

師父的肉身己逝，我不再有機會向他頂禮，再見他的神采和慈祥的微笑，但是夢境如常，在需要幫助的時候，他會用比喻的方法告訴我，隨著時間的流逝我會明白的。

---

諸佛眞金色　非有遍諸有　隨眾生心樂　爲說寂滅法
發起大悲心　救護諸眾生　永出人天眾　如是業應作
——《大方廣佛華嚴經》〈光明覺品第九〉

*The Buddha's true golden color*
*Does not exist and yet pervades all existence.*
*According to that which living beings like, he makes them happy,*
*By speaking for them the Dharma of still extinction.*

*Produce a mind of great compassion*
*To save and protect all living beings,*
*And to forever leave the multitudes of people and gods:*
*This is the karma that should be done.*

*Flower Adornment Sutra, Chapter Nine, Light Enlightenment*

# 上人訓勉

## AN EXHORTATION FROM THE MASTER

張果遷　Guoqian Zhang

我又來到這山邊的小徑，像月兒彎形的，兩邊圍有高聳的長綠青樹，向前望去深不見底。我常來這兒經行和念佛號。今天大雨過後，我又來此，此時的空氣非常的清新，而這條小路就顯得格外的污濁了。我小心翼翼地向前走著，生怕泥水弄髒了褲角，心想：「眞是如臨深淵，如履薄冰啊！」咦！這兩句我好像在哪兒曾說起過。

十多年前與上人相見的畫面，清晰地呈現在我的眼前了。記得皈依那天，在金山寺樓上，上人命我跪在佛前，我流著眼淚，懺悔了過去的罪業。上人又進到小房間裡，拿出一本祖師修行的書，翻開其中一頁交給我：「妳唸這一段。」記得書裡都是教人做到吃人所不能吃，忍人所不能忍，受人所不能受，行人所不能行。我一面唸著，一面心中自問：「我能嗎？我不能，我能的……。」我越唸越緊張起來，手心出著汗，雖然是中文字，卻唸得結結巴巴的。唸完後，上人訓勉：「吃得苦中苦，方爲人上人。」沉默了一會兒後，又問：「妳覺得怎麼樣？」我呆呆地望著上人說：「如臨深淵，如履薄冰。」

上人接納了我，但我卻做了一個令他失望的弟子。現在回想起我當時的回答，是多麼的不恰當，不得體。

I have come again to this little trail by the hills, curved like a crescent moon, lined with towering evergreens on both sides. Peering up ahead, I cannot see where it leads in the distance. I often come to this trail to stroll and recite the Buddha's name. After the rainshower today, I have come here again. While the air is fresh and clean, the trail is especially muddy today. I tread gingerly, trying not to to let the mud splatter my pants. "It's like walking on the edge of a cliff or walking across thin ice," I think to myself. I seem to have spoken this phrase somewhere before.

A vision of my first meeting with the Master more than ten years ago appears clearly before me. I remember the day I took refuge with the Master, on the second floor of Gold Mountain Monastery. Kneeling in front of the Buddhas as the Master instructed, I tearfully repented of my past offenses. The Master went into a small room and came out holding a book on the cultivation of past patriarchs. He turned to a page and gave it to me, telling me to read a certain passage. As I remember, the book told us to eat what other people could not eat, bear what others found unbearable, take what others couldn't take, and practice what ordinary people could not practice. As I read the passage, I kept asking myself, "Can I do this? I can't... I can..." The more I read, the more nervous I became. My palms were sweating, and I stuttered the words even though they were in my native Chinese. When I finished reading, the Master exhorted me, "Only by enduring the bitterest suffering can you become a most outstanding person." After a pause, he asked, "What do you think?" I gazed at the Master stupidly and said, "It's like walking on the edge of a cliff or walking across thin ice."

The Master accepted me as a disciple, but I have only let him down. Thinking back now, I realize how totally inappropriate and irrelevant my answer was.

\*　　　\*　　　\*

阿彌陀佛身金色　　相好光明無等倫
白毫宛轉五須彌　　紺目澄清四大海
光中化佛無數億　　化菩薩眾亦無邊
四十八願度眾生　　九品咸令登彼岸
南無西方極樂世界大慈大悲阿彌陀佛
南無阿彌陀佛……

*Amitabha's body is the color of gold.*
*The splendor of his hallmarks has no peer.*
*The light of his brow shines 'round five Mount Sumerus.*
*Wide as the seas are his eyes, pure and clear.*
*Shining in his brilliance by transformation*
*Are countless Bodhisattvas and infinite Buddhas.*
*His forty-eight vows will be our liberation.*
*He enables all those in the nine lotus-stages to reach the farthest shore.*
*Homage to the Buddha of the Western Pure Land,*
*  kind and compassionate Amitabha.*
*Namo Amitabha Buddha...*

這幾天我一遍又一遍的放著這捲錄音帶，我亦跟著莊嚴的佛號聲一遍又一遍的念著阿彌陀佛……。剛開始念著，我會流下淚來，慢慢念下去，又會到一種清靜無我的境界。我也會一面念一面觀想著阿彌陀佛金色身呈現在眼前。那天去金山寺拜佛，拿出了一本廣欽老和尚的書，翻看了前面幾張照片，以及老和尚與上人之間的禪機對話，便放回到書架上去。有一天，睡覺快醒時，好像是廣欽老和尚，又好像是師父上人提醒著我要觀想著蓮花，頓時一朵好大的金色、桃紅色、白色的蓮花呈現在我的眼前。我醒來後，豁然大悟，啊！對了，也應該觀想蓮花，觀想阿彌陀佛端坐在蓮花台上才是啊！我不能忘了。

For the past few days I have played this tape and followed along in chanting Amitabha Buddha's name, over and over. When I first began reciting, tears would come to my eyes. Continuing to recite, I entered a state of stillness in which there is no self. While reciting, I contemplated Amitabha Buddha's golden body appearing in front of me. One day when I went to Gold Mountain Monastery, I took a book on the Elder Master Guangqin from the shelf and skimmed through the photographs and the dialogue between him and the Venerable Master. Another day when I was just waking up, I seemed to see either Elder Master Guangqin or the Venerable Master reminding me to contemplate a lotus flower. Immediately a golden, peach, and white lotus appeared in front of my eyes. When I fully woke up, it dawned on me: "Yes, I should contemplate the lotus upon which Amitabha Buddha is seated. I must not forget."

\*　　　\*　　　\*

我最近參加了「國際譯經學院」謄稿及複聽的工作，就是將上人講經說法的錄音抄寫下來。法師交我的是上人二十多年前講的《大方廣佛華嚴經》卷十六，十住品第十五。相信很多人還沒有聽或看過上人講的這一段，我將它抄寫如下：

I have recently been helping to transcribe tapes of the Venerable Master's lectures on the Sutras for the International Translation Institute. I have been transcribing the Master's lectures from over twenty years ago on the Ten Dwellings Chapter, Part Fifteen, of the *Flower Adornment Sutra*. Since not many people have heard or read his explanation, I have given it below:

……來建立道場，或者我們自己造，自己建立道場，這都要用誠心，我們這兒修這個空，就快完了，完了之後呢，我們要建立一個大的道場。因為，你們各位跟著我時間久的都會聽說過，我呢，這個佛教是以法界為佛教，我這個身體是以法界為身體，所以我們做的事情一定要大，要盡虛空遍法界的，所以要大，一定要有一個大的基礎；有大的基礎了，然後令這個佛教發揚光大，到每一個世界去，每一個角落去。

Establishing a Way-place, perhaps constructing it ourselves, requires sincerity of mind. We are almost finished cultivating "emptiness," and after we finish, we want to build a great Way-place. Those of you who have followed me for a while know that I take the Dharma Realm to be the scope of Buddhism; I take the Dharma Realm as my body. Therefore, the things we do have to be great; they have to exhaust empty space and pervade the Dharma Realm. We have to have a great foundation, and then we'll be able to spread and propagate Buddhism into every world and every corner.

我們這樣子呢，我們首先要拿出一個真心來，誰願意拿出真心都可以，誰不願意拿呢，那也不勉強。這個真心，就是做什麼事情要認真去做，好好地去做。我們所行、所做，所修行的都為這個道場迴向。願意念佛的人，就念佛為這個道場迴向；願意誦經的人，就誦經為這個道場迴向；願意持咒的人，就持咒為這個道場迴向；你願意拜佛的人，拜佛的時候，也迴向我們這個道場成就；你拜經的人，也以這個拜

In order to do this, we have to bring forth a true mind. Anyone is welcome to bring forth a true mind, but no one is forced to do so. A true mind means that one does everything with sincerity. No matter what we do, or what we cultivate, we should dedicate the merit to this Way-place. People who want to recite the Buddha's name can dedicate the merit of reciting the Buddha's name to the Way-place. Those who recite Sutras can dedicate the merit from doing that to the Way-place. Those who hold mantras can hold mantras and transfer merit to the Way-place. If you like to bow to the Buddha, then when you bow, pray that our Way-place will be established successfully. People who are bowing to a Sutra can also transfer their merit so that our Way-place will be finished sooner--the sooner the

經的功德來迴向，我們所要建立的道場，早一點成就，越快越好。因為這個世界的人等著我們去救呢！我們連一個道場都不能成就，那就對不住這個佛菩薩。

我們信佛一場，一定要在佛教裡有所貢獻，還有我們無論做什麼，都是為這個建立道場來迴向，表現我們的真心。所以有人願意打餓七也好，有人願意打睡七也好。怎麼叫「打餓七」呢？打餓七就是不吃飯；怎麼叫「打睡七」呢？就是在那兒坐禪，坐著不起來。有人願意打站七也好，站在那個地方，白天也是站著，晚間也是站著，那麼站著不坐。我們一定要拿出真心來，要拿出真心，一定有感應。「如果這個道場不成功，我就永遠不吃飯，我永遠不睡覺，永遠是站著。」發這種至誠懇切的心，一定會有感應的。

並且現在這一切護法天龍八部趕快出去做工去，趕快把我這個事情給我做完成了它，用種種的法門，要把這個事情一定要做成了，不做成呢，那是你們天龍八部，一切護法就放棄你們的責任了。我們是預備把這個佛教發揚光大，推行到每一個世界去，所以這個天龍八部現在都不可以閒著，一定要趕快去做你們應做的工作；你們應做的工作若不做，那就是懶惰。無論是誰，我們人也好，神也好，護法金剛也好，都要趕快去做你們應做的工作。還有，在過去皈依我的人和鬼，和一切的眾生，和現在的、未來的，都應該要各顯你們個人的能力，各顯各的神通去感應這種事情，令這種事情早一點成就。

上人這種廣大無邊的願力，所以成就了現今的萬佛聖城。真是願力有多大，法力就有多大。上人一生的事蹟，就是最好的證明。

better--because the people of the world are waiting for us to rescue them! If we can't even successfully build a Way-place, then we've really let down the Buddhas and Bodhisattvas.

If we believe in Buddhism, we definitely have to make a contribution to Buddhism. So, as a token of our sincerity, we should transfer the merit from everything we do to the successful completion of this Way-place. If people are willing to go on a starving session, that's fine. If people want to have a sleeping session, that's also fine. A "starving session" means you fast, you don't eat. A "sleeping session" means you sit in Chan without getting up. If people want to hold a standing session, standing up day and night without ever sitting down, that's fine, too. We must bring forth a sincere mind. If we are sincere, there will certainly be a response. "If the Way-place is not accomplished, I will never eat or sleep again, and I will remain standing forever." If you make an extremely sincere vow like that, you will definitely obtain a response.

Furthermore, all of you gods, dragons, and the rest of the eightfold division of Dharma-protecting spirits should quickly come forth and, by means of various methods, do your job so that we can accomplish our task. If we fail, it will be because you Dharma-protecting spirits have neglected your responsibility. We are planning to propagate Buddhism into every world, so you Dharma-protecting spirits cannot be idle. You should certainly hurry up and do the work you're supposed to be doing. If you don't, then you're being lazy. No matter who you are, whether you are a human, a spirit, or a Dharma-protecting Vajra, you should do your proper job. Also, all the humans, ghosts, and other living beings who took refuge with me in the past, are doing so in the present, or will do so in the future, should demonstrate your abilities and spiritual powers in response to this matter, helping to bring it to fruition a little sooner.

Through the boundlessly vast power of the Master's vows, we now have the City of Ten Thousand Buddhas. Truly, one's power in Dharma can be as great as the strength of one's vows. The Master's own life is the very best proof of this.

# IN REMEMBRANCE OF THE GREAT MASTER

# 緬懷上人

## The Master announced, "I am going to leave you all."

## 上人宣佈：我就要離開你們了！

Shi Heng Ji　　釋恆寂

On Chinese New Year of 1993, the Great Master came to Gold Mountain Monastery, and the scene became enormously blissful and cheery. Buddhist followers congregated there in large numbers; everyone was anxious to bow to the Master and listen to his New Year speech. Normally, the Great Master delivered his speech right after lunch time, but that day he left without saying a word. Everyone was very disappointed and sad. After a short while, he suddenly came back, and all of us rejoiced. The Great Master said,

> I wanted to go away, but knowing that many of you have false thoughts, I came back.

The Great Master gave a lively and cheerful speech. At the end, he announced,

> I am going to leave you all.

That sentence saddened all of us. The Great Master preannounced his departure from this world so that we would be prepared. Those who have not made the Bodhisattva resolve need to take a giant step up. Those who are already walking on the Bodhisattva path need to be earnestly perseverant, courageous, and determined.

The first time I went to the City of Ten Thousand Buddhas, I saw the Mountain Gate painted in red and black colors. Inside this Gate, there were several big trees, and it was very peaceful. I suddenly remembered that I had seen similar scenes in my dreams more than twenty years ago; and I became devoted to the City of Ten Thousand Buddhas with all my heart. Although I did not know the Chinese language and could speak only limited English, without being afraid and intimidated, I wished then that I could be at this monastery to cultivate the Bodhi path. The Great Master's kindness and compassion were exceptional in this world. He used all possible means to cross over living beings, the intelligent as well as the ignorant.

The Great Master's Birthday was celebrated in Long Beach in 1993. That year the bad weather made me very ill. My heart was weak, so I went to Long Beach to recover. Since I could not take care of myself, other nuns attended upon me compassionately. We slept on the lower floor; the Master stayed on the floor above us. One night I dreamed that I was drinking water from a small cup made of cinnamon shells. The clear water was so sweet and fragrant. I looked around the room; there was no one but the

一九九三年中國的新年，上人來到了金山寺，景象呈現出一片喜悅及歡愉。信眾大批地湧到那兒道賀，每個人都興奮地頂禮上人，並聆聽他的開示。通常上人都在午齋後開示，那天，他沒留下隻字片語就走了。我們都很失望、傷心……。不一會兒，上人突然又回來了！我們大家都相當的開心，上人說：

> 我本來想要走的，可是你們很多人打了妄想，所以我又回來了！

上人說的很生動，很高興。最後上人宣佈：

> 我就要離開你們了！

那句話令大家都難過了起來。上人預先告知他將離開這個世界，好讓我們做好準備。對於那些個還沒修菩薩行的人，要更加緊腳步。至於已經開悟者，則更要有毅力、勇氣及決心。

當我第一次到萬佛聖城時，我看見山門漆著紅、黑兩種顏色。門的裡面有幾棵大樹，看來是如此地祥和。我突然想起二十多年前，我曾作過一個和此景類似畫面的夢，從此我開始對聖城產生了執著。雖然我不懂中文，而且只能講有限的英文，但我沒有任何的恐懼及勉強。當時就盼望著能在這所寺院發菩提心出家。上人的慈悲在這世上是稀有的，他用盡所有可能的方法度化眾生，不論他們是聰明還是愚笨，他的態度始終一如——平等對待。

一九九三年，信眾在長堤聖寺慶祝上人的生日。那一年惡劣的氣候使我病重，因心臟虛弱，所以就到長堤休養，我不能照顧自己，其他的比丘尼好心地看護我。我們睡在樓下，上人就住在我們的樓上。一日，我夢見自己在喝一個小杯子裡頭的水，這杯子是肉桂殼做的。清水是如此的香甜，我環顧房間的四周，除了上人外，沒有其他的人，他坐在桌

Master sitting at the end of the table, while I was near the middle of this table. Since then my health improved, and I became even stronger than before. I could handle more religious tasks afterwards.

I kept remembering what the Great Master had announced to us and was worried about the day when he would enter the Nirvana; the whole world would then face even more calamities and people would be even more afflicted. We would lose a great teacher and a compassionate father. He was equally kind and compassionate to all people, regardless of their nationality, social class, religion, reputation, and wealth. When the Great Master got sick, I was very sad. One night I dreamed that I was standing in front of the City of Ten Thousand Buddhas and the Great Master was riding a bicycle coming from the monastery toward me. He looked healthy and active. After passing through the Mountain Gate, the Great Master stopped, got off his bike, and talked to a man working at the Gate. I've never seen the Great Master riding any bicycle. Seeing him riding a bicycle meant that he wanted to let us know that he was still healthy and could work normally, as if he were not sick at all. He only appeared sick to teach us and remind us to recognize the impermanence of the four transitory phases of life (birth, old age, sickness, and death). The Great Master wanted all of us to extricate ourselves from suffering and become Buddhas. He incurred sickness and endured misery for us. Because human beings are still sick, the Great Master became ill to save our souls. I told a nun about this dream. She asked the Great Master about its meaning, and he said that our interpretation of this dream was right.

About six or seven years ago, there was an American gentleman who came to the City of Ten Thousand Buddhas with his lovely three-year-old son. He asked me to help his son take refuge with the Great Master. After the ceremony, he thanked me and was very happy. He explained to me the meaning of his son's Dharma name. I said to him, "Your son is very fortunate. He is only three years old but has already taken refuge with the Great Master." He smiled. Later I saw him, his wife, and his son again at the City of Ten Thousand Buddhas. His wife was very happy to see me. Although she had just met me, she spoke to me as if we were old friends. She told me that her son recited "Namo Buddha" and then "Namo Master" a couple dozen times every night before going to bed. At the meal offering, I saw this American gentleman kneeling in front of the Great Master and reciting the verse for repentance and reform. He was reciting and crying at the same time. He later told me that because his son had been unmanageable, he had beaten his son to death. He was then so afraid that he prayed to the Great Master, who was not even there, and his son miraculously revived. At that time, I fully understood why he had so sincerely wanted his son to take refuge with the Great Master; the Great Master had saved his son's life.

At one time I was very sad seeing that one of my own children was totally preoccupied with the secular world and did not want to cultivate. I thought that I would ask the Great Master the next day to let me go to Taiwan--a very distant place--to see whether my child would wake up. At night, in my dream, I saw the Great Master come to where I was standing. I held onto his arm as we walked toward a small house. The Great Master took a key from his pocket and opened the door. I saw some garbage near the entrance; the

子的另一頭，而我則是在靠近桌子的中間。以後，我的健康是改善了，變的比生病前更加強壯，而且可以處理更多的法務。

我不斷地想著上人對我們宣佈的事情，並且擔心著上人入滅那天的到來；整個世界會面臨更多的災難，人們會更加地煩惱。我們即將失去一位大導師、大慈父。他等慈一切、不分國籍、階層、宗教、職業、貧賤。

上人生病時，我很傷心，一天夜裡我又夢見自己站在聖城前，上人騎在自行車上從廟裡頭向我這邊騎來。他看起來健康又活潑。穿過山門時，上人停住了，他從車上下來，和一個在山門工作的男子講話，我從沒見過上人騎腳踏車的樣子。看見他騎車意味著他想讓我們知道，他還很健康，還能正常地工作，好像一點病也沒有，但他示現病容來教化我們，是要提醒我們，要我們去認識生命中，生、老、病、死這四個階段的無常，上人要我們自己從病苦中解脫出來，然後成佛。他為我們承受病痛和苦難，因為人們仍然有病，上人也就示寂來拯救我們的靈魂，上人答說我們這樣解釋是對的。

大約六、七年前，有位美籍男士和他一個三歲大可愛的兒子來到聖城，他要求我幫他兒子向上人求皈依。結束後，他向我道謝，而且很興奮，他對我解釋他兒子的法名之意義，我對他說：「你兒子很幸運，他才三歲就皈依了上人。」他微笑著。之後，我又在聖城看見他與他妻子及兒子，他太太很高興看見我，她只不過初次見我面，說話的口氣卻很友善，好像我們認識了很久似的。她說她兒子每晚臨睡前，都會念幾十聲「南無佛」，接著又念「南無師父」。在一個彌陀法會的午供，我見到這位美國男子跪在上人面前唸懺悔文，他邊唸邊哭。之後他告訴我，說他兒子以前很難管教，所以他失手就把他打死了。他很害怕，就對著上人禱告，上人當時並不在場，可是他的兒子卻奇蹟似的活過來。就從那時起，我才徹底了解，他這樣誠心地要他兒子皈依的理由，原來上人救了他兒子一命。

曾經一次我非常傷心，看見我的一個孩子耽染世樂而不想修行，想隔天向上人請求讓我到臺灣，好遠離我的孩子，看看他們會不會醒悟。當晚在夢裡上人來到我站的地方，我抓著他的手臂進

interior of the house was dim. I was still holding onto the Great Master's arm. I saw a small can on the floor. Worrying that the Great Master might trip over the can, I kicked it away so hard that I woke up. The small and dim house with garbage in front represents the secular world. It is small and dirty, as compared to the vast, bright, and peaceful state of Nirvana. The Great Master once said that

> Those who left the home life and stayed at the City of Ten Thousand Buddhas had done this in past lives several kalpas before, not just in this lifetime. Those who meditate together at the monastery have also met each other in previous kalpas.

This means that whether we are the Master's left-home and lay disciples, we have all followed the Master many kalpas before. We vowed to follow the Great Master to help him propagate the Buddhadharma and save living beings; that was why the Great Master took us to this world (the small house). Opening the door with a key means that the Great Master opened the Buddha way. Holding onto the Great Master's arm means that we vowed to help him. All the various tasks of speaking Dharma, translating sutras, teaching, working in the office, cooking in the kitchen, and gardening are done for the sake of propagating the Buddhadharma and saving living beings. They are all considered the Bodhisattva conduct. When I woke up, I did not want to go to Taiwan anymore and was no longer sad. One day before the ceremony commemorating the forty-ninth day after the Great Master entered Nirvana, I dreamed that at the left side of the Long Beach Monastery, there were three flags flying in the sky with lacing around them. The two flags on either side were pinkish-violet; the one in the middle was light yellow with a picture of the Great Master in a dark yellow robe. The Great Master had a happy, kind, and compassionate smile on his face; he was wearing recitation beads and did not have a black scarf around his neck. Seeing the Great Master with a happy smile is an auspicious sign; maybe the Great Master could foresee that his disciples would unite to continue his work to propagate the Buddhadharma. Although the Great Master has entered Nirvana, we still have the Buddhadharma and the six great principles (no fighting, no greed, no seeking, no selfishness, no self benefit, and no lying) to follow so that we can achieve the Bodhi fruit.

入一間小屋子，上人從口袋裡拿出一支鑰匙，開了門，我看見入口處有一些垃圾，屋內昏暗沒有光線，我一直抓住上人的手，我看見地上有個小罐子，我怕上人絆倒，於是用力一踢，就醒過來了。屋前有著垃圾的小暗房，代表這個世俗，比起廣大、明亮而又祥和的涅槃境界，它既渺小且骯髒，上人曾說過：

> 在聖城的出家人，從過去世幾個大劫以來，
> 一直都是這個樣子，不光只是這一劫而已。
> 那些共坐道場的人，累劫以來都見過面的。

意思是說我們不論是出家、在家者，都以追隨上人好多個大劫了。我們發願跟隨上人，幫他弘揚佛法，救度眾生。那是上人帶領我們進入這個世界（小屋子）的原因。而用鑰匙開門，意味著上人打開了佛道；抓著上人的手，代表發願幫助上人，凡舉講經、譯經、教書、辦公室行政工作、廚房煮飯、乃至園藝等工作，都是為了弘揚佛法，救度眾生。任何一種工作都可視為一種菩薩行。當我醒來後，我不想去臺灣，也不再傷心了。

上人入滅後，在四十九日法會前的一天，我夢見長堤聖寺，左邊有三面旗子在空中飄揚，周圍有花邊圍繞著，兩邊的旗子是淡紅色、有著紫蘿蘭色的帷幔，中間的一面是淡黃色，有著一張上人深黃色袍的法相，上人臉上帶著愉快慈悲的笑容，他脖子上掛著念珠，並沒有圍上黑色的圍巾。看到上人愉快的微笑，好像有種祥瑞的徵兆，大概是上人預見到他的弟子將來會結合起來，繼續他未完成的佛事和弘揚佛法。此時此刻，上人雖已入滅，我們仍舊有佛法及六大宗旨，不爭、不貪、不求、不自私、不自利、不打妄語，可以依著來發菩提心。

---

常樂觀寂滅　一相無有二　其心不增減　現無量神力
——《大方廣佛華嚴經》〈光明覺品第九〉

*He is constantly happy contemplating still quiescence*
*Characterized by one mark and non-duality.*
*His mind does not increase or decrease,*
*While he manifests spiritual powers*

Flower Adornment Sutra, Chapter Nine, Light Enlightenment

---

# 恩師惠我良多

## MY TEACHER'S GREAT KINDNESS TO ME

原來終日想行菩薩道，要效法師父上人的「我」，
卻是那麼樣的捨不了「我」，總是怕「我」吃了虧。

**If I want to practice the Bodhisattva path,**
**I must learn to have the kind of "self" the Master has.**
**I'm always reluctant to let go of my ego, always afraid of taking a loss.**

余果同　　Guo-tong Yu

恩師圓寂將屆週年，這一年來弟子仍然時常得到恩師加持、教誨，真是感激不盡！

記得去年七月，我隨團到萬佛聖城參加師公上人的茶毗法會，到達舊金山前，在飛機上我預購了當日晚餐，入境之後晚餐便當送到，大家就在往聖城的巴士上吃，想不到這便當那麼大，無論如何努力也吃不完，最後只好丟棄。當時心裡非常慚愧、自責，想到師父一生節儉、苦行，弟子我卻貪吃晚餐，且又浪費，丟棄食物，這如何對得起師父，如何配作上人的弟子？當下我就極為至誠懇切的發了一個懺悔的願：法會期間，我要跟隨法師們日中一食，並祈求師父原諒、護持！

法會期間，我不但圓滿了這個願，嚐到日中一食的自在，而且每天除了少少的睡眠外，就趕往「無言堂」念佛。瞻仰、陪伴師父，或參加其他功課，竟忘記吃降血壓的藥，直待回到臺灣家中才想起吃藥的事，然而身體狀況竟比平時在家還要好。我多麼感激師父上人慈悲，如此的護持我、教化我！

良師難遇今已遇，佛法難聞今已聞，
今生不將此身度，更待何生度此身。

這些話時常警惕我，告訴我歲月不待人，再不趕緊念佛就來不及了。所以這一年來我比以往加緊用功，常告訴自己要專心念，不要生雜念，要照師父說的把佛號念得「風也吹不進，雨也打不透。」可是呀垢習太重，念佛的心時常跑掉，無法專一。有一次竟跑去找我家人的所謂「錯」（什麼樣的錯現已忘記），把這個「錯」禁錮在心不

It is nearly a year since my kind Teacher entered Nirvana. In this year I have continued to receive constant aid and teachings from my Teacher. My gratitude knows no bounds.

In July last year, I came with a group to the City of Ten Thousand Buddhas to attend the Venerable Master's Cremation Ceremony. Before we arrived in San Francisco, I ordered that evening's dinner on the plane. The dinners were delivered after we passed through customs, and everyone ate on the bus ride to the City. The dinner was so large that I could not finish it all, and had to throw away the leftovers. I felt very ashamed and castigated myself as I thought of the Master's frugal lifestyle and ascetic practices. I had not only been greedy for dinner, but had thrown away and wasted the uneaten food; how could I face the Master? How unworthy a disciple I was! At that point I very sincerely repented and vowed: During the Dharma session, I would follow the example of the Dharma Masters and take only one meal a day. I prayed the Master would forgive me and lend me his support.

During the Dharma session, I successfully fulfilled my vow and tasted the comfort and ease of taking one meal a day. And aside from a few hours of sleep each day, I rushed over to Wordless Hall to recite the Buddha's name. While beholding the Master and keeping him company, or taking part in various ceremonies, I totally forgot about taking my medicine for lowering blood pressure. I remembered only after returning to my home in Taiwan, but by then my health was much improved. How grateful I am to the Master for protecting me and teaching me so compassionately!

*It's difficult to meet a good teacher; I have met one.*
*It's difficult to hear the Buddhadharma; I have heard it.*
*If I don't liberate myself in this very life,*
*In what life will I ever liberate myself?*

These words always serve as a reminder to me that time does not wait. If I don't hurry up and recite the Buddha's name, it will be too late. In the past year I have been practicing more diligently than before. I always tell myself to recite single-mindedly and not let random thoughts arise. I try to follow the Master's instructions and recite to the point that "the wind cannot blow through and the rain

肯放下，表面上似乎仍遵著師父說的「不要生
氣，不要放原子彈，不要放氫氣彈。」內心卻
無限鬱悶氣惱，幾至淚下。忽然間一抬頭，看
見牆上師父的偈頌：

一切是考驗　看爾怎麼辦
覿面若不識　須再從頭煉

阿彌陀佛！慈悲的師父，您老人家好像就在我
身邊，親見我生起了三毒苦惱，立刻給我當頭
棒喝，適時點化。我猛然驚覺，便自然又快速
的放下了這個無明苦惱，連個「放下」的念頭
也不曾生，就輕鬆自在的一心念佛了。

又有一次，也是貪瞋癡作祟，擔心帶孫子時
間太長會累到自己，因而悶悶不樂，苦惱不已
，雖然口裡念佛，心裡卻妄想連連。又是一個
不經意，看見牆上師父的偈頌：

捨不了死　換不了生
捨不了假　成不了真

慈悲的師父啊！這一次您老人家讓弟子發現了
自己垢病的根源。原來終日想行菩薩道，要效
法師父上人的「我」，卻是那麼樣的捨不了「
我」，總是怕「我」吃了虧。現在狐狸尾巴終
於露出來了，知道這個「我」是如此自私、愚
癡！當時面對偈頌，禁不住會心一笑，頃刻間
煙消雲散，無影無蹤，出現一片晴空。恩師又
一次救度我！

師恩浩瀚，惠我良多，今謹以真心懺悔，實
心念佛供養恩師上人，並再言數語表寸心

懷師恩　勤煉功
剝皮脫殼覓真心
法語滌淨心頭垢
慧炬注照破闇冥

緊努力　莫遲疑
恩師度人不失時
但依教誨勤修習
一句彌陀直生西

cannot seep in." However, my habits are too heavy, and my mind often wanders as I recite the Buddha's name. I cannot concentrate. One time my mind became so caught up in thinking about some past event in which I was wronged (which I can't remember now) that even though I appeared to be following the Master's instructions--"don't get angry, don't set off atomic bombs and hydrogen bombs"--my heart was filled with discontentment and frustration, and I was driven to the point of tears several times. Suddenly I looked up and saw the Master's verse on the wall:

*Everything's a test*
*To see what you will do.*
*If you don't recognize what's before your face,*
*You'll have to start anew.*

Amitabha! Compassionate Teacher, you seemed to be right there beside me, giving me a swift and timely "blow on the head" as soon as you saw me afflicted with the three poisons. I awakened and let go of those afflictions of ignorance at once. I didn't even have the thought of "letting go," and I was able to single-mindedly recite the Buddha's name with ease.

Another time, greed, anger and stupidity took over as I unhappily brooded over how tired I would be because I had to babysit my grandchildren for a long period of time. Although I was reciting the Buddha's name with my mouth, my mind was full of affliction and idle thoughts. Again, I happened to see the Master's verse on the wall:

*If you can't give up death, You won't obtain life in exchange.*
*If you can't renounce the false, You won't realize the truth.*

Kind Teacher! This time you allowed your disciple to discover the root of her sickness. If I want to practice the Bodhisattva path, I must learn to have the kind of "self" the Master has. I'm always reluctant to let go of my ego, always afraid of taking a loss. Now I finally realize how selfish and foolish the ego is! When I saw the verse, I couldn't help but smile...in an instant the clouds dispersed and there was only the clear blue sky. Another rescue from my kind Teacher! How vast and great is my Teacher's kindness! He has taught me so much. I can only repent sincerely and recite the Buddha's name in earnest--making that an offering to the Venerable Master. Further, with these few words, I attempt to express my feelings a little bit:

*Mindful of my Teacher's kindness, I diligently practice;*
*Peeling off my skin and removing my shell,*
*    I search for the true mind.*
*Words of Dharma wash away the filth of the mind;*
*The brightly shining torch of wisdom chases away the darkness.*

*Work hard; don't be lazy or doubtful.*
*Our kind Teacher doesn't lose any time in teaching people.*
*Simply follow his instructions and diligently practice.*
*With a single recitation of "Amitabha," you'll be born*
*    in the West.*

# 人去法猶在

# THE MASTER IS GONE, BUT HIS DHARMA REMAINS

**有心人信上人留下的法寶，依舊大放光明……。**

**Those with a resolve
who have deep faith in the Dharma left by the Master,
continue to shine brightly...**

釋恆日
Shi Hengri

以前曾有人問起過我心目中最偉大，最值得我敬佩的人是誰，我無從回答。因爲過去的種種無明，業重情迷，累劫所造諸惡業，加上助緣不具，未能早日如願跟隨上人學佛。等到機緣成熟到了聖城，又未能好好珍惜與善知識的一份緣，不及時修行，覿面不識如來佛。也許這就是末法時期，難調難伏、剛強眾生的悲哀。上人曾説：

生在這個末法時代，一切諸佛也很少到世界上來，一切的菩薩也很少到世界上了。

除了上人，若想再遇到一位明眼善知識，猶如緣木求魚，難遭難遇。所謂「人生如夢幻泡影」，「歲月不留人」，我們要趁著身體尚健時，珍惜每一分命光，以及上人流血汗，爲弟子們創下的道場，教育等等現有機緣，決心努力克服自己的習氣毛病，面對現實，嘗試以忍辱消除業障。

我們更應抽出時間來，細心研讀上人講解的經典，常聽上人深具智慧的法雨開示，解行並重，堅固道心，腳踏實地，奉師命以戒爲師，穩重慢步於恆長的佛道，福慧雙修，才不至於途中缺乏資糧，落得來生「披毛帶角還」，或輕慢戒律，墮無間獄，百劫不得出離三惡道，這就是不孝的弟子，反之，嚴持戒律者即見如來，便得自在。所謂：

師父領進門，
修行在個人。

Someone once asked me who was the person I admired the most. I could not answer. Due to my ignorance, heavy karma, confused emotions, offenses accumulated over many eons, and the lack of conditions, I was not able to study Buddhism under the Venerable Master as early as I would have liked. When conditions finally ripened, allowing me to come to the City of Ten Thousand Buddhas, I again failed to cherish my affinity with the Good and Wise Advisor and didn't apply myself to cultivation right away. I didn't recognize the Buddha who was right in front of me! This is the sorrow of all the obstinate living beings of the Dharma-ending Age. The Master once said,

In the Dharma-ending Age, the Buddhas and Bodhisattvas rarely come to the world.

To find another clear-eyed Good and Wise Advisor such as the Venerable Master would as difficult as looking for fish in the trees. As it is said, "Life is like an illusory dream, a bubble, and a shadow." "Time does not wait for us." While we are still healthy, we must cherish every moment of our life, as well as Way-places, education, and various conditions that the Master toiled so hard to provide for his disciples. We must resolve to overcome our habits and faults, face reality, and patiently try to eradicate our karmic obstacles.

Moreover, we should take the time to carefully study the Master's commentaries on Sutras, frequently listen to the Master's wisdom-filled Dharma talks, and practice as much as we understand. With our minds firmly set on the Way, we should honestly follow the Master's instruction to take the precepts as our guide. With steady footsteps let us tread the long path to Buddhahood, cultivating wisdom and blessings hand in hand, so that we won't run out of supplies on our journey and fall into the animal realm to repay our debts. If we were to treat the precepts with contempt, we would fall into the unintermittent hells and not be able to escape the three evil paths for hundreds of eons--we would be unfilial disciples. Conversely, if we strictly uphold the precepts, we will see the Buddha and obtain comfort and ease.

The teacher leads you to the door:
you yourself must cultivate.

自己吃飯自己飽，自己生死自己了。

世界上萬事萬物都是在說法，都離不開佛法，所以

一切是考驗，看爾怎麼辦？
覿面若不識，須再從頭煉。

上人適時對弟子們的考驗，也是成就弟子們，是我們真心迴光返照，反求諸己的時候了。弟子們過去對上人依賴性強，一時之間失去上人，彷彿失去了明燈，前途充滿荊棘，危險重重。往後的日子，在戰戰兢兢中摸索著前行。然而，有心人，深信上人留下的法寶，依舊大放光明，猶如日月星辰，普照大地，只要依法修行，一切都在默默感應中。《華嚴經》云：

諸佛遍世演妙音。

十方世界裡都有諸佛在那裡演說妙音。如來的智慧音聲是盡虛空遍法界，沒有邊際的。佛的妙言，是無說無不說。佛的清淨法身是無在無不在。《金剛經》云：

凡是經典所在之處，
即為佛的法身所在。

而佛菩薩的慈悲光，由始至終皆是無私，無分別心地加持著每一個佛弟子，佛菩薩永遠不會捨棄任何一個眾生。記得上人的教誨：

真正的修道人，是要用戰戰兢兢的心情來
修道，如臨深淵，如履薄冰，時時刻刻要
謹慎，要提高警覺，這樣才可以修道。一
言以蔽之，少說話，多打坐，這是修道的
基本法。

每逢遇到境界考不過時，或造了身口意業時，唯有對著上人的法像懺悔，心理才安樂，可以說上人常住我心。當我業障現前，當我身心散亂，迷失方向時，只要我真心想回頭，願意改惡向善，隨意拿起老和尚的開示錄，或經典細讀時，永遠不會讓我失望。上人的甘露法雨，

*You yourself have to eat to get full;*
*you yourself must end your own birth and death.*

Everything in the world is speaking Dharma; nothing is apart from Buddhadharma. Thus,

*Everything's a test to see what you will do.*
*If you fail to recognize what's before you,*
*you'll have to start anew.*

When the Master tests his disciples, he is trying to help them succeed, giving them a chance to reflect upon and improve themselves. In the past, we disciples were overly dependent on the Master. Suddenly losing the Master, it is as if we have lost a bright lamp while traveling on a dangerous, dark road filled with thorny brambles. We must cautiously grope our way forward from now on. However, those with a resolve who have deep faith in the Dharma left by the Master continue to shine brightly upon the earth like the sun, moon, and stars. If we can cultivate according to the Dharma, there will always be an imperceptible response. The *Avatamsaka Sutra* says:

The Buddhas pervading worlds proclaim the wonderful sound.

Throughout the worlds of the ten directions, the Buddhas are proclaiming the wonderful sound. The Thus Come Ones' boundless wisdom sound exhaustively fills space throughout the Dharma Realm. The Buddhas' wonderful speech is unspoken, yet nothing is not spoken. His pure Dharma body is nowhere and yet there is no place it is not. The *Vajra Sutra* says:

Wherever the Sutras are found,
the Buddhas' Dharma-body is present.

The compassionate light of the Buddhas and Bodhisattvas constantly shines on every disciple of the Buddha, without selfishness or discrimination. The Buddhas and Bodhisattvas would never renounce a single being. I remember the Master's instructions:

A genuine cultivator of the Way cultivates with extreme caution,
as if he were walking along the edge of a cliff or over thin ice.
He must be alert and careful at all times. To sum up the basic
method of cultivation: speak less and meditate more.

Whenever I fail to deal appropriately with a difficult situation, or whenever I create bad karma in my actions, speech, or thoughts, I have to repent in front of the Master's picture before I can feel at peace again. The Master dwells in my heart always. When I encounter karmic obstacles, am scattered or have lost my direction, if I'm sincere about turning around and changing my faults, all I have to do is pick up the Venerable Master's Dharma talks or commentaries on the Sutras and read carefully--they never let me down. The Master's words of Dharma are like sweet dew nourishing the Bodhi sprouts of my mind--consoling me, exhorting me, guiding me onto the right

滋潤我菩提心苗，安穩我、勉勵我、引導我走向正道，續我慧命，不至墮落。上人講解的經典，是世上稀有的法寶。

上人圓寂，至今將近一年，每每念起上人，卻因自性塵垢污染，處於黑暗，不能得見，弟子當生懺悔心、慚愧心。修道的最終目標，無非是要明心見性，了生脫死。弟子們和恩師宣公上人的緣雖非深厚，亦非淺薄，若想來世與師續出家緣，先得觀察自己，是否真把生死問題掛在眉梢上；問自己是否抱定三大宗旨：

捨命爲佛事，
造命爲本事，
正命爲僧事。

反省自己是否誠心做到；

真認自己錯，莫論他人非，
他非即我非，同體名大悲。

捫心自問是否以六大宗旨作爲座右銘？切記這不貪、不爭、不求、不自私、不自利、不打妄語，是修道人的根本，清淨行之則不愧爲眞佛子，續佛慧命的傳法人。

荼毗後，上人留在世間之眞身舍利，實是上人法身所在，雖說上人回到虛空去，也就是無來亦無去。老和尚從來一直都在觀照著這些愚癡弟子，沒有離開過我們，佛法就是這麼的微妙不可思議。

宣公上人是永遠活在弟子們心中最偉大、最有智慧、最直得效法，爲人尊敬的一位人天導師。也是一位最民主、最無私無我的大慈悲父，更是救我慧命的恩師。

當我憶念上人時，我從心裡懺悔往昔所造諸惡業，但願生生世世斷一切惡，修一切善。當我憶念上人時，我由衷感恩今生成就袈裟緣，但願生生世世永不捨離，趣向菩提。

path, prolonging my wisdom-life, and preventing me from falling. The Master's explanations of the Sutras are rare treasures of Dharma.

Nearly a year has passed since the Master entered perfect stillness. Every time I think of the Master, I ought to feel repentant and remorseful for the defilement in my own nature prevents me from being able to see him. The final goal of cultivating the Way is to understand the mind and see the nature, and to end birth and death. While our affinities as disciples with the Venerable Master are not that deep, they are not shallow either. If we would like to leave home with the Master again in future lives, we ought to contemplate to see if we have truly suspended the matter of birth and death upon our brows." Have we adhered to the Three Great Principles?

*We renounce our lives to do the Buddha's work.*
*We take the responsibility to mold our own destinies.*
*We rectify our lives as the Sangha's work.*

Have we sincerely been able to

*Truly recognize our own faults,*
*Not discuss the faults of others.*
*See others' faults as our own, and see ourselves*
*as identical with others in great compassion?*

Have we made the Six Guiding Principles our personal credo? We should remember that "no fighting, no greed, no seeking, no selfishness, no pursuit of personal profit, and no lying" are the foundation for cultivators. Those who purely practice these rules are true sons of the Buddha, heirs of the Dharma who can perpetuate the Buddha's wisdom.

The sharira left by the Master represent the Master's Dharma-body. Although the Master is said to have returned to empty space, he actually neither came nor went. The Venerable Master has always been watching over his foolish disciples; he has not left us. That's how wonderful and inconceivable the Buddhadharma is.

The Venerable Master Hua will live forever in the hearts of his disciples as the greatest, wisest, and most respected teacher of humans and gods who serves as the best model for us. He is also the most democratic and most selfless compassionate father, as well as the savior of our wisdom lives.

Whenever I think of the Master, I repent in my mind for all the evil karma I created in the past, and I vow to cut off all evil and cultivate all good in life after life. When I think of the Master, I am deeply grateful for being able to wear the *kashaya* sash in this life, and I vow never to leave it in life after life as I walk the path towards Bodhi.

# 師父與我
# THE MASTER AND I

上人處處表現出家人的大丈夫氣質，
日日講經説法，使人徹底了解佛法是多麼的寶貴。

**The Master constantly manifested the heroic deportment of a monk, speaking Dharma and explaining Sutras every day without fail, thus giving people a chance to appreciate the true value of the Buddhadharma.**

謝發燕　Fayan Xie

皈依上人已有十三個年頭，總覺得「佛法無邊，師恩難報。」十二年前爲了親近上人的法，我放棄了臺灣的一切，來到一個全然陌生的環境；從餐廳的小弟、洗碗工幹起，又當上經理，然後又考上工程師執照，幫上人在長提聖寺蓋了一座大殿。現實生活的壓力以及少數民族在美國的煎熬，常常令人喘不過氣來，但是對於佛法的追求，以及達到身心合一的寧靜，卻是我一生不曾鬆懈的。以下幾段眞實的故事，是在這十三年中發生的，謹記錄如下，以饗諸位同修道友：

一、奇夢記一九八零年一個深秋夜裡，在臺灣臺北市的家裡，那一天和朋友有一個聚會，心裡不知怎麼搞的，總是毛毛的，心緒很不寧，那時候回到家裡都已近午夜，洗過澡，上過香，頂禮佛三拜之後，看看錶正好十二點。進了房間倒頭便睡，心緒仍不定，但是由於白天應酬太多，精疲有盡，只得草草入睡……。

才一刹那，只見自己在恍惚中，已經走到了松山山腳底的一片公墓中，天色已經昏暗，而我卻是漫無目地的在墓中游蕩，後來走到了一個墓前，駐足觀看墓碑上寫了一副要命的對聯：「見碑必死，無常鬼今夜索命！」才看了這右邊一聯，我已魂飛九霄，拔起腳就跑，直接衝到父母親的老家樓上佛堂，看到父母正要課誦，趕快稟明上情，請兩位大人幫忙念觀音菩薩聖號，以免無常鬼來索我的命。父母親聞訊亦焦急不堪，都急忙穿上了黑色法衣，陪著我大聲念誦大悲觀世音菩薩，而我跪在佛堂正中，對著佛像也虔念聖號；父親拿引磬站在左邊，母親拿著木魚站在右邊，

I took refuge with the Venerable Master thirteen years ago. I have always felt the boundlessness of the Buddhadharma and the difficulty of repaying the Master's kindness. Twelve years ago, in order to draw near the Master, I gave up everything I had in Taiwan and came to a totally unfamiliar environment. Starting out as an errand boy and dishwasher in a restaurant, I later became the manager. After I passed the exam and became a licensed engineer, I helped the Master construct the Buddha hall at Long Beach Monastery. Although the pressures of making a living and the torment of being a minority in the United States are sometimes unbearable, I have never slacked off in pursuing the study of Buddhism and in striving to attain peace of mind and body. I have recorded the following true events, which occurred in the past thirteen years, for the enjoyment of my fellow cultivators.

*I. A Strange Dream*: One autumn night in 1980, I was at my home in Taipei, Taiwan. That day I had been to a party with friends, and I felt nervous and ill at ease without knowing why. It was almost midnight when I returned home. After I had taken a shower, I lit incense and bowed three times to the Buddha. My watch said it was exactly twelve midnight. I went to bed immediately. Although I still felt uneasy, I was exhausted from the day's socializing and soon fell asleep...

Suddenly I saw myself walking through a public cementery at the foot of Mount Song (Songshan). It was already dark, and I was wandering blindly among the graves. I stopped before a tombstone and read a terrible couplet engraved on it: "Whoever sees this tombstone shall die; the Ghost of Impermanence will come for him tonight!" After reading the first line, I ran in terror. I ran all the way to my parents' old home. I went upstairs to the Buddha hall and saw my parents preparing to do their recitation. I quickly told them what had happened and asked them to recite the holy name of Guanyin Bodhisattva to prevent the Ghost of Impermanence from coming to get me. My parents were very distressed by the news. They hurriedly put on their black Dharma robes and recited "Greatly Compassionate Guanyin Bodhisattva" loudly. I knelt in the middle of the Buddha hall and recited sincerely; my father stood on my left

正磬鼓齊鳴，努力念佛。

一會兒，我忽然看到兩個面目可憎的無常鬼，正在我的斜上方，迎面而來，兩鬼手上各拿著一條鐵索，就靠近我，把兩條繩索都套到我的頭上來，又徐徐上升把我用力往上拉。一時間我覺得呼吸困難，心中還拼命念佛，而眼睛卻無力的看著父母親；看到雙親都瞪大了眼睛，眼睜睜地任著兩鬼拖著我去，驚得不知如何是好，尤其是母親，一會兒才放聲大哭。

兩鬼拖著我離開佛堂時，最後一眼，我還看著佛堂的觀世音菩薩，一時間，就進入一個漆黑無光，伸手不見五指的世界，眼、鼻、舌、身都毫無感覺，只有耳根仍然有感覺，只聽到了身體穿過黑暗中所引起的「呼呼聲」。也不知道過了多久，只感覺黑暗、恐怖、往下墜。

突然間眼睛一亮，看到一個小孩，大約一歲半左右，可愛極了，從小就喜歡小孩的我，心中馬上升上了歡喜心，看著他一步一步，很艱難的舉步在馬路，一搖一擺的走著。走到了路肩，他忽然走歪了，整個身子都倒下來了，頭也倒了下來，眼看著正要撞上馬路旁拱起來的堅硬水泥護提，我立刻把手伸得好長好長，放在水泥護堤上去托住小嬰兒的頭，以免小孩的頭撞得頭破血流，還記得那個小嬰孩的頭，掉到手上，有一股溫熱以及好軟好軟腦殼的感覺。這一下，天地大變，從漆黑的一片突然又變回了五彩繽紛的世界，感覺好暖和，好舒服。

眼前又看到一位師父（那時並不知是上人），身形高大背有一點駝，雙手拿著一根柺杖，站在路當中，全身一襲僧袍，非常慈祥又很有威嚴的樣子。他雙眼看著兩鬼，又看著我；兩鬼看到了上人立刻變得很謙卑的樣子，而且身上的顏色也變得五彩繽紛，樣子也可親多了。

上人用手拿起柺杖，向著地下點了一點說：「這是東山盡，西山頭，你不能再過去了。」此時的我，還沒有完全清醒，還以為是土地公來指點迷津（小時候，西遊記看多了，一次孫悟空有事時，向下一指，土地公就冒出來回話。）也不懂得向上人頂禮，還問上人：「我沒有鞋子，怎麼回去？」上人笑笑，什麼也沒說，倒是其中一鬼回話說：「我可以揹您回去的。」也不等我回話，就把我揹了起來，並且用鬼手在我的大腿上抓

holding the handbell, and my mother stood on my right playing the wooden fish. We all recited vigorously in unison with the bell and fish.

Suddenly I saw two detestable ghosts of impermanence appear above me and come toward me, each holding an iron chain. When they came near enough, they slipped the chains over my head and pulled upwards with force. All of a sudden I could hardly breathe. I desperately kept reciting the Buddha's name in my mind. I didn't have the strength to keep looking at my parents, who were staring wide-eyed as the two ghosts dragged me off. They were too startled to do anything, especially my mother, who started crying. As the two ghosts dragged me out of the Buddha hall, the last thing I saw was Guanshiyin Bodhisattva's image. After that I was in a pitch black world; I couldn't even see the fingers of my extended hand. My eyes, nose, tongue, and body ceased to feel anything. My ears could only hear the whooshing sound as my body passed through the darkness. I had no idea of time. All I could perceive was darkness, fear, and the sensation of falling.

Suddenly I saw an extremely cute child around one and a half years old. I have always loved children, and I was delighted as I watched him waddle laboriously toward the street. When he reached the curbside, he suddenly tripped and was about to hit his head on the concrete curb. I immediately stretched out my hand to cushion the child's head from the fall. I remember his head feeling warm and very soft as it fell on my hand. At that instant, the pitch darkness turned back into the ordinary colorful world. I felt a sense of warmth and great comfort.

I saw a monk (I didn't recognize him as the Venerable Master then) before me. He was very tall, slightly hunched over, and holding a walking cane with both hands. Standing in the middle of the street wearing a long monk's robe, he looked extremely compassionate and yet stern and dignified as he gazed at the two ghosts and at me. The two ghosts, upon seeing the Master, had immediately assumed a humble appearance; their bodies regained color, and they seemed much friendlier. The Master tapped his cane on the ground and said, "This is the end of the Eastern Mountain and the beginning of the Western Mountain. You may not pass beyond here." In my half-asleep state, I thought he was the local deity giving directions to us. I didn't even know enough to bow to the Master. I asked the Master, "How can I go back? I don't have any shoes." The Master smiled but didn't say anything. One of the ghosts said, "I can carry you on my back." Then, without waiting for a reply, he hoisted me onto his back. While straddling the ghost, I felt extremely buoyant and quite happy. We flew back to my old home in a moment; the whole journey was filled with light and peace.

As soon as we passed through the roof and entered my house, I saw an image of the great, compassionate, and splendid-looking Guanyin Bodhisattva hanging on the wall of the living room. I broke down crying, rejoicing at being able to return to life. While crying, I woke up from the dream. My whole body was drenched with perspiration, and my heart was beating fast. I felt as if my soul had just returned. It was two o'clock in the morning. In two short hours, I had made a trip to the realm of the ghosts. If the Master

了一下。當我跨在鬼背上時，感覺輕飄飄的，心情也愉快很多，一下子就飛回老家了，沿途一片光明，一片祥和。

從屋頂上降到老家時，剛穿過天花板，就看到一幅「又大又慈祥又莊嚴」的觀音菩薩聖像掛在大廳的正牆上，我一下子就放聲大哭，慶幸自己又生還了。就在大哭聲中，突然驚醒，大汗流滿全身，心臟也跳得好快好急，好像才回魂似的，在半夜中看著錶，已是凌晨兩點，原來是南柯一夢，在二個時辰之中居然去了一趟鬼門關，若非師父搭救，早已魂斷西山，那有回頭的道理？那時我已皈依其他法師，所以我很清楚，夢中來救我的師父並非其他的法師，所以我也一面尋找，一面念佛，祈求菩薩靈感，幫我找到這位師父。

二、拜見上人記。有本書叫《度輪禪師事蹟》薄薄的幾十頁，以文言文寫的，是記載上人在香港的一些靈異事蹟，我看了大受感動。

一九八一年三月不知誰又看到一本《夜半鐘聲》，上面很清楚的介紹度輪禪師開闢了加萬佛城的種種情況，以及有狐狸、蝙蝠來皈依的奇事。那時，我就想這位老法師大概就是我所要尋找的師父吧。從這個時候，我們不但向三寶禮拜，也向遙遠的西方禮拜，祈求老法師法體康安，能早日來臺灣弘法。

一九八一年十月初，突然有道友告訴我一個天大的好消息：「度輪法師要來臺灣參加世界僧伽會議。」大家都興奮得不得了，尤其是我。當道友指定我成立一個車隊，專門負責接送「度輪法師訪問團」的團員，我又高興，又惶恐；高興的是可以親自載上人，惶恐的是怕辦不好事，急慢了法師。

在期待中度日如年，總算等到了一九八一年十二月一日，早已有幾百人在中正機場迎接，又準備了一幅金字橫幅，上書：「恭迎度輪法師蒞臺訪問團」。半小時之後，上人率領十二位中外弟子出現在出境大廳上，大家早已跪地迎接；看到上人我心中感動到了極點，這正是在我夢中救我一命的師父，也是我多年以來追尋的明師，急忙倒頭跪地拜了三拜。

當晚住進圓山飯店，上人立刻不辭勞苦要到普門文庫講經說法；經過緊急通知，來了一百多位，把個普門文庫擠得水洩不通。

hadn't saved me, my soul would have gone over to the Western Mountain. I knew that the monk who saved me in my dream was not the Dharma Master I had taken refuge with. And so I began searching for this monk on the one hand and reciting the Buddha's name on the other, praying for the Bodhisattvas to help me find him.

*II. Meeting the Master* : There is a thin book of several dozen pages entitled *The Life of Chan Master To Lun,* which is written in classical Chinese and records some miracles that happened when the Master was in Hong Kong. I was greatly moved when I read it.

In March 1981 someone read a book called *The Tolling of the Bell at Midnight.* It relates in great detail how Chan Master To Lun established the City of Ten Thousand Buddhas in California, and how foxes and bats took refuge with him. At that time I thought this was probably the Master I was searching for. Starting then, we bowed not only to the Triple Jewel, but also toward the West, praying that the Elder Dharma Master was healthy and that he would soon come to Taiwan to spread the Dharma.

In early October of 1981, a Dharma friend told me the good news: "Dharma Master To Lun is coming to Taiwan to attend the World Sangha Conference." Everyone was very excited, especially me. When a friend suggested that I organize a car escort to pick up and transport the members of Dharma Master To Lun's delegation, I was both delighted and apprehensive--delighted because I would be able to personally drive the Master, and apprehensive that I might make a mistake and be rude to the Master.

Every day of waiting for the Master to arrive seemed like a year. On December 1, 1981, several hundred people went early to the Chiang Kai-shek Airport to welcome the Master. We prepared a yellow banner with golden words saying, "We Respectfully Welcome Dharma Master To Lun's Visiting Delegation to Taiwan" Half an hour later, the Master and twelve Chinese and Western disciples arrived at the main lobby, where everyone was kneeling in welcome. I was extremely moved by the sight of the Master--he was the monk who had saved my life in my dream, the wise teacher I had been searching for during all these years. I immediately bowed three times to him.

That evening after checking in at the Grand Hotel, the Master immediately wanted to give a Dharma talk at Universal Door Bookstore despite his tiring journey. Despite the short notice, over a hundred people arrived for the lecture, crowding the bookstore until there was no space left.

The Master arrived punctually with his twelve disciples and commenced the lecture. Everything he said had Chan meaning and was very interesting. To the surprise of the audience, the Master had all his disciples give short speeches and he spoke only at the very end. Then disciples asked questions and the Master gave simple but thought-provoking answers. After the lecture, everyone felt as if they had been bathed in a spring breeze and had grown in wisdom.

On the morning of the fourth, I received an urgent message to take the car escort to the Grand Hotel because the Master wanted to pay a visit to Elder Master Guangqin. When I arrived at Yuanshan Hotel, the Master immediately got into the front seat and three Dharma Masters sat in the back. I was overjoyed to have the chance

上人帶領十二大弟子準時到達，隨即開講，上人講說很有禪味，很風趣。更令大家驚奇的是，每個弟子都要講一段話，最後師父再總結，然後由每位弟子提問題，由師父親自回答，簡明扼要，發人深省。事後每個人都覺得如沐春風，智慧都增長了許多。

四日早晨，我又收到緊急通知，要我帶領車隊去圓山飯店，因上人要親訪廣欽老和尚。當我準時帶著車隊到達圓山飯店時，上人很快就坐上我的車，另有三位法師坐在後座。我的心高興到了極點，我居然載著上人去承天寺。路上，大家都不太說話，車很安靜，但自有一股力量；只有偶而上人問一些問題，法師們則簡要回答了。

到了承天寺，有幾位法師親自到車旁來為上人開車門以及頂禮，那時大殿正在修建，廣老在地藏殿等上人來。進入殿裡，上人禮佛之後，就和老法師緊緊地握手，開始心電交流，並且各自在一個藤椅坐下來，開始對談，這一次世紀對談留傳千古，直到現在還有很多人津津樂道，我也帶著照相機努力拍照，其中一張就是「上人和廣欽老和尚坐在藤椅的合照」，直到現在，不但有許多人珍藏膜拜，還被佛教雜誌採用。

下山時，仍是我的車載著上人，一路上也和我說了一些關於廣老的事蹟，以及問了我一些問題，當然我也迫不及待地向上人請教一些問題，上人也很耐心地一一解答。那一天，我突然有一種騰雲駕霧的感覺，又感覺自己就像一條五爪金龍，載著大慈大悲救苦救難的觀世音菩薩四處去尋聲救苦；又像一匹千里名駒，載著從西域歸來的唐三藏（玄奘）法師，準備回到東土來，大大弘揚佛法。雖然在年前之夢中見過師父，如今師父就活生生坐在我車上，相處了一天；這般的幸運，也是我畢生的榮幸。

四天後，師父又回到美國去，我們幾個是一心去萬佛城追隨上人的積極份子，每日把下班後和假日的時間都安排得滿滿的，除了參加法會，就是念佛、朝山、探訪醫院、放生，大量積蓄去萬佛城之資糧（那味道還真像積蓄往生資糧，一心要去西方極樂世界，常常念佛念到茶飯不思，心中常有菩薩在正定正坐，心中常有甘味，很不可思議。）

那年的暑假中，我們聽說師父又法體欠安，我們又難過又著急，乃在一位鄭老居士家中，發起「楞嚴咒誦持七永日」，也就是在七天七夜中二十四小

to drive the Master to Chengtian Monastery. On the way there, they spoke very little and it was quiet in the car, although there was a powerful feeling. The Master asked a few questions from time to time, and the Dharma Masters gave brief answers.

When we arrived at Chengtian Monastery, several Dharma Masters came to open the car-door for the Venerable Master and to bow to him. As the main Buddha hall was under construction, Elder Master Guangqin was waiting to receive the Master in the Earth Store Hall. After the Master entered and bowed to the Buddhas, he grasped the Elder Master's hand in a firm handshake. Then they each sat in a rattan chair and began a heart to heart exchange. Their historic conversation will be remembered for many generations. Even today many people like to talk about it. I had taken my camera and was shooting pictures left and right. One shot of the Venerable Master sitting next to Elder Master Guangqin on the rattan chair has become a treasured picture that many people bow to. It was even published in a Buddhist magazine.

As I was driving the Master back, he told me about Elder Guangqin's life and asked me some questions. I also took the opportunity to ask the Master some questions, and he patiently answered them all. That day, I felt as if I were a golden dragon flying through the clouds, carrying the greatly compassionate Guanyin Bodhisattva on my back as she went around rescuing suffering beings. I also felt like a brave steed of enduring stamina carrying Tang dynasty's Tripitaka Master Hsuan Tsang from India back to China, where he would widely propagate Buddhism. Although I had seen the Master in my dream a year ago, it was a great honor to drive the Master around for a whole day in real life.

When the Master returned to America four days later, several of us eagerly wished to follow him to the City of Ten Thousand Buddhas. We packed our after-work hours and holidays with activities such as attending Dharma sessions, reciting the Buddha's name, making pilgrimages, visiting hospitals, and liberating lives, thus accumulating the "provisions" for making a trip to the City of Ten Thousand Buddhas.

That summer when we received news that the Master was unwell, we were very sad and worried and began a seven-day 24-hours-a-day recitation of the Shurangama Mantra at the home of the elder Upasaka Zheng. We recited the mantra 10,000 times and dedicated the merit to the Master, praying that the Dharma-protecting gods and dragons and the Buddhas and Bodhisattvas would aid him. For seven days and nights we did not leave the Chan hall, and finally, exhausted to the bone, we fulfilled our goal. We recited until we were parched and dizzy, but filled with the joy of Dharma. There were various responses during the seven days. Some people saw the Master sitting beneath the Buddha image, smiling. A rare fragrance pervaded the Chan hall for the duration of the session.

In the ninth month, before Guanyin Bodhisattva's Anniversary, we held another seven-day session for reciting the Great Compassion Mantra. Our goal was to recite the mantra 100,000

時都不能間斷地念誦〈楞嚴咒〉，而且在七天中
的圓滿日要誦完一萬遍，迴向給師父，祈求龍天
護法，諸佛菩薩加被。在幾位主辦人通力合作之
下，七日七夜我們都沒有離開禪堂一步，又要努
力念咒，又要照顧大家，最後在精疲力盡之餘，
總算圓滿達到了目標；真是念到口乾舌燥，眼冒
金星，但是真是法喜充滿。七日夜間還有許多奇
妙的感應，有人看到師父就坐在佛像之下微笑著
，禪堂之中異香撲鼻，七日不散。

　　九月觀音誕前，我們再接再厲，在原址又舉辦
「大悲咒誦念七永日」，這一次目標是念誦〈大
悲咒〉十萬遍，仍然是七天七夜，二十四小時不
間斷，我們仍然七日夜都不敢離開一步，那一次
來了一百八十位居士通力合作，仍然準時在七日
之內達到十萬遍的目標，那一次我足足念誦了八
萬多遍的〈大悲咒〉，最快時約十五秒就可以念
一次而且快到口不需念而只要閉眼，〈大悲咒〉
文自然浮現在空中，只要在心中默念即可，還記
得好幾次都看到幾個大梵字浮在空中，（這些梵
字後來我在佛學辭典中查過）都有特別的意思；
那時真有些了解「念佛三昧」是什麼意思。

　　總計在二次法會中參加的居士中，後來就有了
一、二十位居士出家去修行，有一些去萬佛城，
大部份都留在臺灣的寺廟中努力修行，也是有一
段很好的因緣。師父上人是回到美國，可是精神
卻留下來，那種六十年如一日，日中一食、夜不
倒單的頭陀行，以及真修實證的真功夫，不攀緣
、不求緣、不化緣的三大宗旨。上人處處表現出
家人的大丈夫氣質，日日講經說法，使人徹底了
解佛法是多麼的寶貴。

　　三、成立「臺灣法界佛教印經會」的緣起及發
展。一九八二年十月，懷著滿腔歡喜及憧憬，我
和十多位同修一同來美參拜上人及萬佛聖城。費
盡千辛萬苦來到萬佛城，看到山門，我馬上跪在
地上，以三步一拜的方式拜到山門下才起身。也
許思念很久，所以一點也不生疏，倍感親切，見
到上人心中更是歡喜，那一夜和上人，一同趨車
回到舊金山的金山寺住了一晚。當夜心情極為清
明，夢見上人和廣欽老和尚站在我身邊，我向二
位大師頂禮，而且向上人請求傳授四十二手眼。
廣老抬頭看看上人，上人點了點頭；廣老就在金
山寺的大殿中，傳了三手四十二手眼給我。那情

times, reciting 24-hours-a-day for seven days and nights without leaving the hall. This time 180 laypeople came to join the session, and we finished 100,000 recitations within the seven days. I personally recited the Great Compassion Mantra over 80,000 times. I reached the point where I could recite the mantra in 15 seconds. When I closed my eyes, the words of the mantra appeared in my mind, and I could recite it silently instead of out loud. I also had several visions of large Sanskrit letters with special meanings. I came to understand a little of what the Buddha-recitation samadhi was all about.

Between ten and twenty of the laypeople who participated in these two seven-day sessions later left the home-life, some going to the City of Ten Thousand Buddhas, the majority staying in Taiwan to work hard at their cultivation. These were very good circumstances.

Although the Master returned to America, the spirit of his cultivation remained in Taiwan. He cultivated in the same way for over sixty years, taking only one meal at midday and not lying down to sleep. He achieved genuine spiritual skill following the three principles of not scheming, not begging, and not asking for anything. The Master constantly manifested the heroic deportment of a monk, speaking Dharma and explaining Sutras every day without fail, thus giving people a chance to appreciate the true value of the Buddhadharma.

*III. The History of Dharma Realm Buddhist Books Distribution Society in Taiwan*: In October 1982, with great joy and excitement I came with a dozen fellow cultivators to America to visit the Venerable Master and the City of Ten Thousand Buddhas. When I saw the Mountain Gate of the City after all the hardship I went through to come here, I got down on my knees and began bowing down once every three steps until I reached the Gate. Because the City had been in my mind for so long, I did not feel like a stranger at all. I felt very much at home, and I was overjoyed to see the Master. That evening I rode in the same car as the Master back to San Francisco's Gold Mountain Monastery, where I spent the night. That evening I was in euphoric high spirits. I dreamed that the Venerable Master and Elder Master Guangqin were standing beside me. I bowed to both teachers and then requested the Venerable Master to transmit the Forty-two Hands and Eyes to me. Elder Master Guangqin looked at the Master, and the Master nodded. Then, in Gold Mountain Monastery's Buddha hall, Elder Master Guangqin transmitted three of the hands and eyes to me. The dream was extremely real. When I woke up in the early morning and did morning recitation, I could still see it clearly in my mind, and I will never forget it.

In the two years that followed, I lived in San Francisco and worked and went to school. Every week I had one and a half days off, during which I would take the cable car to Gold Mountain to help edit the *Vajra Bodhi Sea* journal. That's how I developed a very close relationship with Upasaka Guoli Zhou, who lived at Gold Mountain for many years transcribing the Master's lectures on Sutras and serving as editor of *Vajra Bodhi Sea*.

I was in closer contact with the Master during those two years

形就像真的，即使在清晨醒來誦早課時，仍然歷歷在目，永遠也忘不了。

此後的兩年中，我都住在舊金山，一面工作，一面上課，每個星期固定有一天半的休假，我都搭電車到金山寺去幫忙編輯『萬佛城月刊』（金剛菩提海雜誌），因此和長年住在金山寺抄經、編月刊的周果立居士成了莫逆之交。這兩年是我一生中最接近上人的時期，每個星期上人從萬佛城來此，總會和我談一談，教導我一些事，令我受益無窮。由於當在金山寺幫忙，才知道上人的大願，乃是將中文《大藏經》，要翻譯成全世界的語言文字，令全人類都能夠念佛經；也才知道上人講經說法有數十年，幾部大經，像《楞嚴經》、《法華經》、《華嚴經》都已有詳細的白話解說，《金剛經》、《地藏經》……等等亦有白話解釋及英文翻譯。太了不起了，上人講經說法數十年如一日的精神，令人歎服！

兩年來，我常常親近上人，工作之餘又天天看上人的佛經的白話解說，我簡直入迷到了極點，有時看到天亮才睡，有時又幫周果立居士校對各種佛經上的白話解說。說真格的，我一生中從沒有看書看得如此認真又仔細。那時，上人和周居士也都鼓勵我多寫一些佛教的感應故事以及因果故事，以勸世人多學佛。所以那二年中，我就寫了十幾篇文章陸續刊登在「萬佛城月刊」上。

一九八四年暑假，第一次回臺省親，行前我突然有一個構想，即是以會員方式在臺灣成立「法界佛教印經會」，專門以最精良的印刷，流通上人的法寶，令臺灣及東亞及全世界看得懂中文的千萬人士能夠深入經藏，智慧如海。

在金山寺大殿，我跪在上人面前辭行，並向上人報告成立「法界佛教印經會」的構想。上人一口就答應，並指示小心財務處理，並要周居士負責聯絡及監督之責；周君士對我也信任有加，滿口答應。

回到臺灣，看到舊識佛友，相見甚歡，都有說不完的話題。接著我正式召集會議，邀請八位居士提出「法界佛教印經會」的構想，大家都一致同意；但是經費毫無著落，會址也是問題。為了照顧方便，乃決定第一年會址就設在我老家二樓。總算在一九八五年十月初正式成立了「法界佛教印經會」；其中艱辛，非筆墨所能形容。

than at any other time. Every week when the Master came down from the City of Ten Thousand Buddhas, he would chat with me and teach me a few things, benefitting me greatly. It was while helping out at Gold Mountain that I became aware of the Master's great vow to translate the Chinese Buddhist Canon into the languages of the world, so that the entire human race would be able to read the Buddha's scriptures. I also found out that the Master had been lecturing on Sutras for several decades and had given detailed modern-language explanations of such major Sutras as the *Shurangama*, the *Lotus*, and the *Avatamsaka*. His colloquial explanations of the *Vajra Sutra*, the *Earth Store Sutra*, and others had already been translated into English. The Master's spirit to lecture on Sutras and speak Dharma every day for several decades is truly admirable and praiseworthy!

In those two years I was often together with the Master. In my spare time I read the Master's commentaries on the Sutras. I was totally engrossed in the Dharma, sometimes not going to bed until dawn. Sometimes I helped Guoli Zhou to proofread the Master's commentaries on various Sutras. Truthfully speaking, I had never read books so diligently or carefully before. At that time, the Master and Upasaka Zhou both urged me to write some stories of responses and of cause and effect to encourage people to study Buddhism. I wrote a dozen or so articles which appeared serially in *Vajra Bodhi Sea*.

In the summer of 1984, I returned to Taiwan for the first time to visit my parents. Before the trip I conceived the idea of starting the Dharma Realm Buddhist Books Distribution Society in Taiwan on a membership basis, for the purpose of printing and distributing high quality books of the Master's Dharma so that the ten million Chinese-speaking people in Taiwan, Southeast Asia, and the world would be able to deeply enter the Sutra Treasury and have wisdom like the sea.

As I knelt before the Master in Gold Mountain's Buddha hall to bid the Master good-bye, I told him of my plan. The Master agreed immediately and advised me to be careful in handling the financial matters. He wanted Upasaka Zhou to communicate with me and supervise the project. Upasaka Zhou had full faith in me and heartily agreed.

In Taiwan I met with my old Buddhist friends. We were all very happy to see each other and had endless things to talk about. Then I formally called a meeting and asked eight laypeople to present the proposal for setting up the Dharma Realm Buddhist Books Distribution Society. Everyone gave their unanimous approval, but there were no funds and a location had yet to be decided on. For the sake of convenience, we decided to house the Society on the second floor of my old house for the first year. The Society was formally founded on October 1, 1985. The toil and suffering that made it possible can never be fully described or recorded.

In that period of time, I myself and the Vice-President of a construction magazine would often go to the printing shop and the binding shop, and we did much of the layout work ourselves. I remember that for the first edition of *Commentary on the Sixth Patriarch Sutra*, I single-handedly oversaw the proofreading, lay-

那時我身兼有一個建築雜誌的副社長，下班後還常到印刷工廠、裝訂工廠、排版工廠去監督品管。爲了省錢，就只好樣樣自己去分色，去盯工作。還記得第一本書《六祖法寶壇經淺釋》出書時，從校對、排版、封面設計、印刷、紙張及發刊辭，是我一手包辦及監督之下印出來的，我看到書，捧著它，眼淚奪眶而出，實在是太珍貴、太美好！我跪在觀世音菩薩及上人聖像前，久久都不能自己。心中在想：總算沒有對不起上人的法及上人的吩咐，更沒辜負周居士的期望。放眼當時，無論設計、編排、用紙，全是最好的，那時候的想法是要糾正許多人的錯誤觀念，當時許多佛經都是免費贈閱，紙張、印刷粗糙不堪，大家看完就亂丟，實在是辱沒了「法寶」，而我要大家捧著上人著作的佛經白話解說，就像捧著一盒金銀財寶，從裡到外都是十足有份量的。這一點是成功了，後來的佛書，都以此爲範本。

這以後，每月出書一冊，將上人的法，源源不絕，作有系統的介紹，後來當會員迅速增加，從原先幾十人到了幾千人，我們又陸續購入電腦設備，增加人手，並將會務分成出版部、印刷部、總務部、會計部、以及秘書部，在大家通力合作之下，有秩序地擴大了會務。

我們又陸續辦過朝山、探訪弧兒院、定期舉辦法會。在大眾共同地努力下，已正式成爲美國法界佛教總會在臺的分支機構之一，由萬佛城派法師常住，並在松山買下固定會所。除了已茁壯成長爲一個有組織的印經會外，亦是一個弘法、共修的清淨道場。從這裡也訓練出許多佛教人才，還有許多工作人員及會員都出家認眞修行。可謂當年我對上人的承諾及努力都美妙地開花結果了，也了卻我當年追隨上人時所發下的大願之一。

四、蓋廟記：一九八二年來到美國重新生活，也跟隨上人幾近二年，當時我曾立下幾個大願：

一、成立一個專門機構，以便流通上人幾十年來講經說法的珍貴「法寶」，令世人智慧增長，趣向佛道。關於這一點，我於一九八五年召集有志一同的同修，成立「法界佛教印經會」，專門以高水準的印刷，發行了上人各種演講集、佛經白話解說，至今已有數百本之多，後來又委託製作錄音帶及錄影帶，都曾經風靡一時。印經會至今已歷經九個年頭，雖然我早已來美，不再幫忙

out, cover design, printing, and announcement of printing. When the book came out, I held it up respectfully with tears of joy in my eyes: what a treasured and beautiful book it was! I knelt before Guanyin Bodhisattva and the Venerable Master for a long time, unable to compose myself. I thought to myself, "Well, at least I haven't let down the Master. I've followed his instructions. I haven't disappointed Upasaka Zhou's hopes either." I remember using the highest quality design, editing, and paper to print that book, because I wished to correct a popular misconception. At that time there were many Buddhist Sutras being given away free. They were printed very poorly and on cheap paper, and people would throw them away after reading them. This was truly an insult to the Dharma. I wanted people to carry the Venerable Master's modern-language commentaries on the Sutras as reverently as if they were carrying a box of gold. If I could publish a serious and high quality book the first time, it would set an example for other Buddhist books to follow.

From then on, we published one volume every month, and the spring of the Venerable Master's Dharma bubbled forth ceaselessly, giving a systematic introduction to Buddhism. The membership soon grew from several dozen to several thousand people. Gradually we purchased computers, increased our staff, and divided the Society into various departments: publications, printing, manager, accounting, and secretary. Under everyone's cooperative efforts, the Society continued to expand.

We organized pilgrimages, visits to orphanages, and regular Dharma assemblies. Due to everyone's hard work, we were formally recognized as a branch of the Dharma Realm Buddhist Association in America. The City of Ten Thousand Buddhas sent Dharma Masters to reside at the Society and bought a permanent location in Songshan. Aside from printing Sutras, the Society propagated the Dharma and served as a pure Way-place where people could gather to practice. The Society trained many people and provided them with the skills to work for Buddhism. Many of the volunteers and members also left the home-life in order to devote themselves to cultivation. The promise I made to the Master and the toil I put forth have blossomed and borne wonderful fruits. I have thus fulfilled one of the vows I made when I decided to follow the Master many years ago.

*IV. Temple Construction :* When I came to America to begin a new life in 1982, I followed the Master for nearly two years and made the following major vows:

1. To set up a center to distribute the Master's precious Dharma treasures of several decades' worth of Dharma talks and lectures on Sutras, in order to help people grow in wisdom and approach the Buddhist path. Regarding this, I got together with fellow cultivators who shared my vow and we set up the Dharma Realm Buddhist Books Distribution Society in Taiwan. The Society is devoted to printing and distributing high quality books of the Master's talks and lectures. To date it has published several hundred books. Later it also began publishing audio and videotapes, which have been very popular. The Society is now in its ninth year. Although I have come to America and am no longer involved in managing the

管理；但是接手的居士們，都能夠繼續努力，如今已正式成為萬佛城法界佛教總會在臺的分支道場之一，所以我的第一大願算是實現了。

二、為萬佛城蓋一座大殿，在臺灣時，我的職業是室內設計，曾有機會為一些寺廟做過裝修；所以我來美時，總希望能幫自己的師父蓋一座大殿。

一九八二年至一九八六年初，我大部份都在餐廳服務，但我總念念不忘希望能回到工程界來。一九八六年初，果然有機會回到了美國大中公司工程部上班。我日夜勤奮努力學習，以便早日吸收一些專門知識及蓋房子的技術，將來好為師父蓋廟。經過五年多的建築經驗及經歷，再加上一位曾老師的教導，皇天不負苦心人，終於在一九九一年二月考上「加州營建工程師」。隨後在一年，幾乎去了五趟萬佛城，帶領工人在各個精舍隔間、做水電，忙得不亦樂乎。

九二年春節我隨著「美國法界佛教總會弘法團」一行，回到臺灣去幫忙，協助法師們設置了「法界佛教印經會」之永久會所。九二年二月接獲上人弟子胡果相之邀請，在加州洛杉磯長堤寺新建一座三千二百呎的大殿。接到市政府所批准之建築執照及建築藍圖，我實在太興奮又感激，觀音菩薩真慈悲，我祈求多年的蓋廟願望，如今就要實現了。

九個月當中，師父也來住了幾次，我和師父又像從前在金山寺一樣常常見面，師父不時下來督工，也會把我和恒章師叫去詢問許多事情。

九三年四月初終於破解種種困難，準時完工了。弟子們並為長堤聖寺之大殿開光啟用，以及與上人的聖誕而合併舉行了隆重盛大慶祝典禮。

長堤聖寺大殿開光大典及上人壽筵當天，約有一千多人參加，筵間上人談笑風生，賦詩吟偈，眾人都為上人之幽默及才學折服。最後弟子們又獻上許多節目，並在放生儀式舉行圓滿結束典禮，接著又舉行梁皇寶懺大法會，直到四月中旬才結束。最高興的莫過於我，我幫上人蓋廟的大願終於達成了，心願又了一樁。

Society, the laypeople who run it continue to work very hard. Now that the Society has become a formal branch of the Dharma Realm Buddhist Association, my first vow has been fulfilled.

2. To build a great Buddha hall at the City of Ten Thousand Buddhas. My profession in Taiwan was interior design. Having done renovation work on various temples in Taiwan, I hoped to build a great Buddha hall for my own teacher after coming to America.

From 1982 to early 1986 I spent most of my time working in a restaurant, but I always hoped to return to the field of engineering. In the beginning of 1986, I found a job working for the engineering division of Dazhong Corporation. I studied like crazy day and night, hoping to acquire professional knowledge and skills in housing construction so that I would be able to build temples for the Master. After five years of working in construction and receiving guidance from a Mr. Ceng--heaven never disappoints a person with a will--in February of 1991 I finally passed the test and became a licensed building engineer in California. The following year I made five trips to the City of Ten Thousand Buddhas, bringing workers to set up partitions and install water and electricity in various dormitories. I was busy but happy.

On Chinese New Year in 1992, I accompanied the Dharma Delegation of Dharma Realm Buddhist Association to Taiwan to help the Dharma Masters fix up the permanent location of the Dharma Realm Buddhist Books Distribution Society. In February of 1992, I received an invitation from Guoxiang Woo, a disciple of the Master, to construct a 3,200 square foot Buddha hall at Long Beach Monastery in Los Angeles. Upon receiving the government permit and the building blueprints, I was overwhelmed with excitement and gratitude. Guanyin Bodhisattva was so kind! Now I could finally fulfill my vow of building a temple.

In mid-September, the Master came for several short stays, and we were often together, just as we had been at Gold Mountain Monastery in the past. The Master often came to inspect the work, and would also summon Heng Zhang Shi and myself to ask us about various matters.

In the beginning of April 1993, we overcame various difficulties and completed the Buddha hall on time. It was used for the combined celebration of the grand opening of Long Beach Monastery and the Venerable Master's birthday.

Over a thousand people attended the celebration. The Master smiled and chatted gaily, and composed and recited poems. No one could match the Master's wit and learning. Disciples performed and organized various programs, and the celebration concluded with a Liberating Life ceremony. It was followed by the Repentance of the Emperor of Liang, which lasted until mid-April. I was the happiest person of all, for I had fulfilled my vow of helping the Master build a temple.

# 夢中佛事
# DOING THE BUDDHA'S WORK IN A DREAM

只要你誠心，無論你在哪兒，
師父都會去教你，教化你的。

**As long as you are sincere,
I will go to teach you no matter where you might be.**

適興　Xing Shi

　　爲了緬懷師父上人他老人家對弟子的教化，故而將教化事蹟寫下，不爲別的，只因爲他是我的師父；我在臺灣，師父在美國，他老人家曾説過：

　　只要你誠心，無論你在哪兒，
　　師父都會去教你，教化你的。

　　師父上人色身離開我們近一年了，但是徒兒卻不認爲師父離開了我們；事實上，師父一直在虛空中看著我們如何修行。今將緬懷師父於夢中之教化和若干感應列舉如下，只將事實簡短敍述，不添加任何感想，由讀者自行參悟。

　　一九九三年皈依師父後，數度夢見師父和身披紅祖衣的一些比丘僧來臺弘法，這些身披紅祖衣的比丘僧非常高，乃至我仰望也無法見到他們的容貌，但是他們走路都很莊嚴。有一次，約在一九九三年初，夢見師父又帶領他的出家二眾弟子來臺。其中一幕，師父坐在鋪有紅地毯的會客室，此廳是長方形，沒有任何傢具和裝飾，只有三把木頭椅子倚牆而靠，此時所有的出家眾都已迴避，師父表情非常嚴肅，一人獨自坐在中間的木椅上，面對空曠的長廳，準備接見訪客。待一切就緒後，吾已立於門外，對這一些要來晉見皈依師父的眾生們説：「要皈依師父宣公上人的，現在可以一個個進去。」當時這些眾生是滿心歡喜，恭敬合掌，一個個排隊規規矩矩，安安靜靜等待進入；他們是綠色的鼻子，綠色的眼睛，綠色的臉，全身都是綠色。（當時我是維持秩序的），夢中所看到的這一切一切都很平常；但我有兩個疑念，自忖：「這些人怎麼有這麼多隻手？其中一對手是合十的，那麼多的

In remembrance of the Master's teachings to me, I have recorded these teachings in writing. I have done so for no other reason than that he is my teacher. I live in Taiwan, while the Master was in America. He once said to me,

As long as you are sincere, I will go to teach you no matter where you might be.

It has been nearly a year since the Master left us, but I have never thought that he is gone. In fact, the Master has always been watching us from empty space to see how we cultivate. I would like to share some of the teachings that I received from the Master in dreams. I will just briefly relay what happened and not add any of my own thoughts so that readers can draw their own conclusions.

After I took refuge with the Master in 1993, I had several dreams in which the Master appeared with several very tall Bhikshus wearing red robes. They were so tall that I couldn't see their faces, but they walked with dignity. In early 1993, I dreamed that the Master came to Taiwan accompanied by some monks and nuns. In one scene, the Master was sitting in a rectangular, red-carpeted reception room that was bare of furnishings except for three wooden chairs set along the wall. All the left-home disciples were gone, and the Master was sitting in the middle chair facing the empty hall waiting to receive visitors. After everything was set, I stood outside and said to those beings who were waiting to see the Master, "Those who want to take refuge with the Venerable Master may go in now, but one at a time." The beings were all very delighted. They stood in line with their palms respectfully pressed together and quietly awaited their turn. They had green noses, green eyes, and green faces; in fact, their whole bodies were green. (My duty was to maintain order.) All these things seemed perfectly normal to me in the dream, but I did have two questions. I wondered, "How come these people have so many hands (one pair of which was placed together,

手，就好像萬佛城的千手千眼觀世音菩薩一樣，可是菩薩也不是綠色的？」第二念是：我已經夠矮了，怎麼這些綠色的眾生也這麼矮？和我一般高？所以我能清清楚楚的看見他們綠色的臉部表情和容貌等。其中排首的，非常友善凝視我，並對我露出會心的微笑，感恩歡悅之情洋溢於臉上，等待門開晉見師父。喔！我還發現排首的眼睛大大的，是雙眼皮，非常可愛，高興的還對我眨一眨眼，所以我知道他是雙眼皮。

由於他們是一個個魚貫進入長廳晉見師父，我是站在門外維持秩序的，所以不知道裡面的情形。全部皈依晉見師父後，師父走出來室外，突然我發現室外旁邊的土牆上不知何時濺滿了血跡，我非常驚訝地告訴師父：「師父！師父！您快瞧，怎麼牆上都濺得血跡斑斑呀？發生什麼事啦？」師父不語，隨手將地上的泥土拾起，把有血跡的土牆「糊」上新的泥土；我也跟著師父，用我的小手由地上將現有的泥土拾起，「糊」在牆上，把所有的血跡都蓋住了。

夢醒，清晨約四至五點，左思右想，才明白夢中排成一排的眾生，是一棵棵的樹。這麼多隻手，是樹枝；和我一樣高，是「跪」在門外等候宣見。我甚至看見一個個跪著進入，它們搖搖擺擺的枝葉，非常可愛。其中排首的雙眼皮的眾生眼睛一眨，高興的對我微笑，令我印象深刻無比。我並不在意此夢，沒有多久也就忘了；一年後聽到普陀山樟樹皈依師父，才又想起來。我一年前的這個夢是有些特別，而且皈依的並不是一棵，而是一長排哩！

一九九四年農曆七月，我到臺灣法界佛教印經會打地藏七的前兩天，夢到一長相有點怪的大富長者，身著中國的長衫馬褂；有隨從恭敬於側，猶如現在大企業家的董事長。其隨從領我進入他的辦公室見他，吾遂立於側，辦公室外有花草，假山流水，非常雅緻，有點像溫室，但又很涼爽。他告訴我：「今年臺灣颱風太多（這一年的夏天，兩個月的暑假就有九個颱風，都是強烈化中，中化小，小化無的颱風），妳師父扛眾生的業，扛得生病了，不回臺灣了，妳到美國去看妳師父去！」說著並交代我一只透明的塑膠袋，內裝的是薄薄的新臺幣，也沒封口，並對我說：「妳見到妳師父宣化上人，把這個交給他，他就明白了。」我恭恭敬敬地雙手接過後，並就地叩首三拜。我心中難過，自始至終未開

joining palms)? They look sort of like the image of Guanshiyin Bodhisattva at the City of Ten Thousand Buddhas, but the Bodhisattva is not green." My second question was: I'm already very short, but how come these beings were just about my height? I could see their green faces and their expressions very clearly. The one at the front of the line gave me a friendly look and a smile. His face was filled with joy and gratitude as he waited to see the Master. I also discovered that he had big eyes with double eyelids, quite cute. He winked at me, which was how I found out he had double eyelids.

Since they went in one by one while I stood outside maintaining order, I didn't know what was going on inside. After they had all seen and taken refuge with the Master, the Master walked out. All of a sudden I noticed the mud wall outside the hall was covered with blood stains. I was astonished and told the Master, "Master, take a look! How come this wall is covered with blood stains? What happened?" The Master said nothing, but picked up some soil and rubbed it on the wall to cover the stains. I followed suit. With my small hands I also picked up some soil and rubbed it on the wall and covered all the blood stains.

When I woke up, it was four or five o'clock in the morning. It dawned on me then that the beings in my dream were trees. Their multiple hands were branches, and they were my height because they were "kneeling." I thought they were very adorable as they walked into the room on their knees, swaying their branches back and forth. I remember especially well the one in front with the double eyelids who winked and smiled at me. I soon forgot the dream, and only thought of it again a year later when I heard that a camphor tree at Mount Putuo in China had taken refuge with the Master. In my dream, not only one tree, but a whole line of them, took refuge!

In the seventh lunar month in 1994, two days before I went to Dharma Realm Buddhist Books Distribution Society in Taiwan to attend an Earth Store Recitation Session, I dreamed of an elder who looked a little peculiar. He wore a Chinese style long robe and had attendants respectfully standing to the side, very much like the modern day president of a large enterprise. His attendant led me into his office. I remained standing to one side. Outside of the office was a elegantly designed landscape with flowers, shrubs, small hills, and water falls. He told me, "There were too many typhoons in Taiwan this year. (Within a two-month period this summer, there were nine storms. However, all of them either became milder or disappeared all together.) Your teacher has been burdened too much by living beings' karma and could not come to Taiwan. You should go to America to see him." He handed me an unsealed transparent plastic bag with some Taiwan dollars in it and said, "When you see the Venerable Master Hua, give this to him. He will understand." I took the plastic bag respectfully and bowed three times to him. My heart was saddened and I remained silent throughout the meeting. I am used to keeping silent in front of the elderly to show my respect. This elder seemed to know the Master well; he called the Master by name, talked to me in a amiable manner, and accepted my bows.

口言語，因爲我已習慣長輩講話，做晚輩的雖立於側，不得言語、喧嘩，以示恭敬。同時此長者似乎和師父是很熟悉的老朋友，並直稱師父的字號，說話語氣祥和，對我和藹，並受我三拜。

醒後，百思不解，我目前不可能去美國，一無假期，二無路費，如何前去交給師父？翌日突然想到：「我剛領了薪水。扣除固定之支付，所餘的是我本月的生活費；故由生活費中取出供養金，代替塑膠袋內的新臺幣，明日打七好供養師父。」

一九九五年三月底來美國參加梁皇懺，師父病重，未克見師父，將此夢解圓，故而誠心拜懺，又發願，七天的梁皇懺，其中感應令我七天淚水潸潸。法會結束，四月九日深夜返抵家門，未久即夢見師父推門而過，手持柺杖，步履蹣跚，身著厚黃袍和黃袈裟，黑色的圍巾將頭臉和脖子都包起來，只露出一對眼眸（師父不讓我看見他的病狀），此時我正面對一些空空無也的事，忙得不可開交。師父一推門走進來，無須言語，我知道師父抱病來看我，我立刻匍匐前進迎著師父，抱著師父的雙腿失聲痛哭，並問師父：「您老人家的病是否好一點？」（這句話是回應那富貴長老告訴我的話，言下之意是請問師父，眾生的業是否減輕些？因爲所有的弟子大家都誠心拜懺。）

一九九五年五月初，第一次於夢中只聽聞師父的聲音，未見其人；說：

我出關了！

聲音響徹雲霄，劃破虛空，此時芸芸眾生，只見萬頭鑽動，每個人臉部都茫茫然，仰望虛空，而我此時仍在玩溜滑梯，我在滑梯最上面的平臺上，而在我下面的是一層層的男男女女。當我聽到師父的聲音時，馬上爬起來不玩了，說了聲：「該死！我師父來了，來找我了，我仍在這六道裡玩耍！」說著就起來，同時告訴這些芸芸眾生，他們一臉茫茫然，一副不識此人聲音是誰的表情。我焦急的說：「這是我師父宣化上人呀，你們怎麼不認識他呀？我要走了，去我師父那兒了。」遂醒！

一九九五年，水陸空法會和觀音七期間，夢中師父已將入涅槃相，我哭得好不傷心，師徒一番對話後，我問師父爲什麼提前走？不是要一百歲嗎？同時我又發了什麼什麼願啦！爲什麼師父您還要走？師父剎那

When I woke up, I could not figure out the dream. I couldn't possibly go to America at this time. I did not have days off for one, and secondly, I couldn't afford the trip. How was I going to give the money to the Master? The next day it dawned on me that I had just received my paycheck. After all the fixed expenses were paid, I took some of the remaining money, which was used to pay for my monthly living expenses, to substitute for the money in the plastic bag and made an offering to the Master at the Session.

I came to America at end of March 1995 to bow the Jeweled Repentance of the Emperor of Liang. As the Master was gravely ill, I could not see him and ask him to explain my dream. I bowed the repentance very sincerely and made several vows. The responses I received during the seven-day bowing session moved me to tears. After the session was over, I arrived home late in the evening on April 9. Soon I dreamed that the Master opened the door and walked in unsteadily, leaning on his cane. He wore a thick yellow robe and yellow sash, and a black scarf covered both his face and neck, so that only his eyes showed. (The Master did not want me to see his sick condition.) At that time I was busy doing some unimportant chores. When the Master came in, I knew he had come to see me despite his illness. I immediately dropped to my knees and crawled toward him. I held his legs and wept. I asked him, "Master, have you gotten any better?" (This was in response to what the elder had told me. What I really meant was whether the karma of living beings had been lessened since all of his disciples had bowed the repentance very sincerely.)

In early May of 1995, for the first time in my dream I only heard the Master's voice but did not see him. He said,

I have come out of seclusion.

His voice penetrated the clouds and cut through empty space. At that time, I saw the multitude of living beings looked up into the air wearing a blank expression. I was still playing at the slide. Looking down from the top platform of the slide, I saw layer upon layer of men and women. When I heard the Master's voice, I quickly got up and quit playing. I said, "Darn! My teacher's come to look for me and I'm stilling playing in these six paths." I also told the multitude of beings, but their blank faces indicated they did not recognize the voice. I said anxiously, "That was my teacher, the Venerable Master Hua! Don't you know him? I've got to go." Then, I woke up.

During the Guanyin Session and Water, Land, and Air Dharma Session in 1995, I dreamed that the Master manifested the appearance of having entered Nirvana. I cried bitterly and asked the Master why he left the world so early? Wasn't he going to live to be one hundred years old? Besides, I had already made certain vows; why did he still want to

間將眼闔上，淚水如泉，非常傷心，不言語。我再度傷心欲絕哭著，如是等等說了一些話，再問師父，為什麼要提早走？師父二度落淚，只說一句話：

眾生太福薄！

就不再多言了；自始至終，師父所有出家二眾弟子長跪於側。我又問師父您老人家什麼時候回來？……此時我已知道不能再耽誤師父的時間了，故而隨側送師父上車。在車上，師父傳見某法師，並交代有關佛學院一事，該尼師早已在外等候，我隨即下車。奇怪！師父到底要去哪裡？怎麼坐的是軍用的吉普車？無人駕駛？即使我問師父，師父也不會告訴我。

leave? Master closed his eyes and instantly tears streamed down his face. He was grieved and remained silent. I continued to cry and asked the Master again why he decided to leave the world early? The Master's tears fell for the second time and he said,

Living beings' blessings are too scanty.

And he said no more. The Master's left-home disciples had been kneeling to the side all this time. I asked the Master when he was coming back. At that time, I knew I could not detain the Master any longer so I walked the Master to his car. In the car, Master asked for a certain Dharma Master to give her instructions regarding the Buddhist Academy. That Dharma Master had been waiting outside for a long time so I got off the car. Strange! Where the Master was going? How come he was riding a jeep? And where was the driver? I knew the Master would not tell me even if I asked.

| | | | |
|---|---|---|---|
| 或見坐道場 | 覺知一切法 | 到功德彼岸 | 癡暗煩惱盡 |
| 或見勝丈夫 | 具足大悲心 | 轉於妙法輪 | 度無量眾生 |
| 或見師子吼 | 威光最殊特 | 超一切世間 | 神通力無等 |

——《大方廣佛華嚴經》〈光明覺品第九〉

*Perhaps someone sees him sitting in the Way place,*
*Enlightening to and knowing all dharmas.*
*Arriving at the other shore of merit and virtue*
*He exhausts the darkness of stupidity and afflictions.*

*Perhaps someone sees him as a victorious hero,*
*Replete with a mind of great compassion,*
*Turning the wonderful Dharma wheel,*
*Crossing over limitless living beings.*

*Perhaps someone sees him sounding the lion's roar.*
*His awesome brilliance has no peer.*
*Excelling all in the world,*
*The power of his spiritual penetrations is unequalled.*

Flower Adornment Sutra, Chapter Nine, Light Enlightenment

# 正法震撼師子吼
## THE LION'S ROAR OF
## THE PROPER DHARMA STIRS PEOPLE'S SOULS

（編按：此文節錄自華梵東研所佛學組學生陳由斌居士所作之「試論宣化老和尚的佛學貢獻」論文）

(Editor's note: This article is excerpted from the thesis, titled "Discussion of Venerable Master Hsuan Hua's Contributions to Buddhism," written by Upasaka Youbing Chen of the Huafan Institute of Literary Skills, Department of Eastern Thought, Buddhist Studies Division.)

從一九八九年皈依宣化上人，至今也已六年了，千千萬萬沒想到師父上人會這麼快就離開娑婆，難道是眾生薄福？

上人千里迢迢，將佛法帶到美國去，就是希望建立「如法」的佛教制度，所以上人的開示往往「冷酷無情」，有時甚至令人吃不消，認為老和尚只會一味地批評別人，卻不知他老人家用了多少苦心在教化頑劣的眾生？嚴厲的說詞背後隱藏多少「血淚」？上人曾說：

我到這兒來啊！是預備教化美國人。

我教化的對象是美國人，而不是中國人，中國人只是附帶的。

要我上天也不難，教化美國人最難；

要我下地也不難，教化美國人最難；

要公難下蛋也不難，教化美國人最難。

由此可知上人要教化美國人的決心。這雖然是相當困難的事，但上人終究做到了，他創造了美國始有僧相的紀錄，建造了如法的道場，及僧伽制度。

認識老和尚的人都知道，上人一生嚴持「日中一食，夜不倒單」，執行「六大宗旨」。尤其在混亂的末世，上人更是正法的代表，眾生的光明。

上人不畏魔的譭謗，到處提倡《楞嚴經》，講正法，破邪顯正。雖然末法時佛門中「魚目混珠」的現象很多，然而上人的願力卻是：

From l989 when I took refuge with the Venerable Master Hsuan Hua and all through these six subsequent years, it never in the least occurred to me that the Master would leave the Saha so soon. It would be hard to call it anything other than the scanty blessings of living beings.

The Master traveled thousands of miles to bring the Buddhadharma to America, with the hope of establishing rules governing the Sangha that were "in accord with Dharma." For that reason sometimes the Master's instructions seemed ruthless. Sometimes they were even impossible for people to accept, for they thought the Elder Master was only capable of criticizing others. Why did they never stop to realize how hard the Master was working to try to teach and transform obstinate living beings with inferior faculties? Or how behind his stern words and tough talk was hidden so much "blood and tears." The Master said:

I've come here prepared to teach and transform Americans. My teaching is aimed at Americans, not the Chinese people. The Chinese are incidentally gathered in.

Were you to ask me to go up to the heavens,
   that wouldn't be hard, but teaching Americans is hard.
Were you to ask me to bore into the earth,
   that wouldn't be hard, but teaching Americans is hard.
Were you to ask a rooster to lay an egg,
   that wouldn't be hard, but teaching Americans is hard.

From that we can realize the Master's determination to teach and transform Americans, even though it was going to be an extremely difficult task. However, the Master did it. He has a record of creating an American Sangha and of establishing Way-places that accord with Dharma and rules for governing the Sangha.

Those who knew the Venerable Master are aware that throughout his whole life he strictly upheld "taking only one meal at noon and not lying down at night," and that he put into practice the Six Guiding Principles. Especially in the turmoil of the Dharma-ending Age, the Venerable Master was even more a sure sign of the Proper Dharma and a light for living beings. The Master did not fear the slander of demons; everywhere he went he advocated the *Shurangama Sutra,* proclaiming the Proper Dharma to destroy the deviant and manifest the proper. Although during the Dharma Ending Age there are a lot of cases of "mistaking fish eyes for pearls" even within Buddhism, still, the Master's vow-power was decisive:

我一定要復興正法，我只許可佛教有正法，沒有末法！我走到那兒，那兒就有福慧、減少災難；這是我的願力。因此我就不自量力，到處說正法、行正法。

上人更感慨地說：

佛法未滅僧自滅，
道德應修人不修；
老實真誠招物議，
虛偽狡猾受褒優。
舉世五濁清甚鮮，
眾生三醉醒無秋；
殷勤寄語僧青輩，
振興吾教在比丘。

佛法沒有百分之九十九的，佛法有一分假，便不是「正法」。所以我們應該認清楚，即使在寺院中，都有「邪法與外道」，這話是一點都不過份的。甚至有些「稱師作祖」的人，也許正傳著「摻了水的佛教」。上人對此早已開示說：

你要知道這個道場啊，你不相信也不行的！有佛就有魔，那個魔他是來攪鬧道場的，他故意來混的！

佛門中有句話說：「寧可千年不往生，不可一日入魔道。」尤其處在宗教「非常發達」的臺灣，到處充滿了「大師、上師、無上師、現代佛、活佛、師尊」的「盜版」職業宗教家。這些打著「如來佛」的廣告，販賣著如來「家業」的傳教師，如果我們不具「四種清淨明誨」的慧眼，恐怕永遠也無法跳出「上師」的手掌心，而成為他們的眷屬，最後終落得——弟子與師，俱陷王難，墮無間獄。

曾經有一位信徒問道：「上人常說：『真認自己錯，莫論他人非，他非即我非，同體名大悲。』為何上人常在萬佛城月刊中，公開批評談論他人的是非？這豈不是言行不一嗎？」上人答道：

I am definitely going to revive the Proper Dharma. I will only allow Buddhism to have Proper Dharma and will not let there be any demise of the Dharma. Wherever I go, that place will have blessings and wisdom and there will be a diminishing of disasters. That is my vow. Because of that, ignoring the limits of my capabilities, I go everywhere speaking the Proper Dharma and practicing the Proper Dharma.

The Master painfully remarked:

*When the Dharma becomes extinct, it is the Sangha itself
    that becomes extinct.
Virtue in the Way should be cultivated, but people won't cultivate it.
Those who are honest and sincere are ridiculed.
Those who are false and cunning receive praise and precedence.
The whole world is full of five turbidities; it's rare to find any purity
Beings are made drunk by the three poisons and one knows not
    when they'll wake up
Earnestly remind the young Sanghans that the flourishing of
    Buddhism depends on the Bhikshus.*

In Buddhism there can't be just 99 percent. If even one part of Buddhism is false, then it is no longer "Proper Dharma." And so we must distinguish clearly, because in temples there are both "deviant dharmas and externalists"--and that's no exaggeration. (The *Shurangama Sutra* said so long ago.) There are even the ones who "call themselves teachers and make themselves patriarchs," whose transmissions are "tainted Buddhism," secretly advertising their own private brand of "talismans and incantations, secret dharmas, and mudras." The Master gave instruction about this early on:

You should recognize this Way-place--you should not fail to believe in it. Where there are Buddhas, there are also demons. That demon has come to make trouble in the Way-place. He's come deliberately to create chaos.

There's a saying in Buddhism: "I would rather not get rebirth for a thousand years than to enter the paths of demons for a single day." This is especially applicable to Taiwan where religion is "flourishing extraordinarily"--you can find religious professionals who are "Great Masters, Superior Masters, Unsurpassed Masters, Contemporary Buddhas, Living Buddhas, and Honored Masters" everywhere you go. Those Masters who transmit their teachings put out "Thus Come One Buddha" advertisements and sell off the Thus Come One's "family estate." As to the likes of them, if we lack the wise vision found in the "Four Clear Instructions on Purity," it's to be feared we will never be able to get out of the clutches of those "Superior Masters," but will become part of their retinue until finally we end up: *Then both the disciples and the teacher get in trouble with the law and fall into the unintermittent hells.* Once a disciple made this inquiry, "The Master often says: *Truly recognize your own faults. Don't discuss the faults of others. Others' faults are just my own. To be one with everyone is called Great Compassion.* And so why is the Master always openly criticizing others in the Buddhist journal, *Vajra Bodhi Sea*? Isn't that a case of saying one thing and doing another? The Master answered:

墮地獄的是我，不是你。要是真的，這也不是是非；要是假的，一定墮地獄。若說大修行人沒有因果，則墮五百世做狐狸的果報。我如果是撥無因果的話，拿黑的當白的，拿白的當黑的；拿是當非，拿非當是，說錯話，我入拔舌地獄。如果我沒有說錯話，那我沒有罪的。孟子說過「予豈好辯哉？予不得已也。……楊墨之道不息，孔子之道不著。」我爲什麼好說是非？因爲佛教裏頭是非太多了！又什麼黑教、白教、黃教、紅教……都變成顏色不一樣了，把人的眼睛都弄得眼花撩亂，連黑的也不知道是黑的，白的也不知道是白的。所以我要說人所不敢說的話，你們誰如果不高興的話，那沒有關係，我不在乎的！我是專門破人邪知邪見的！

由以上這段話，我們可以了解上人那心中「不忍眾生苦」的徹底慈心。所謂「大慈大悲，近乎殘忍」，正是菩薩教化眾生的方便。上人也曾提一詩以明其志：

我要說真話　不怕打與罵
殺我無所畏　解脫有何罣

上人對於護持正法，則多次地開示說：

在佛教裏，所有的經典都很重要，唯獨《楞嚴經》更爲重要，凡是有《楞嚴經》所在的地方，就是正法住世。《楞嚴經》沒有了，就是末法現前。《法滅盡經》上說：「末法時代，《楞嚴經》先滅，其餘諸經，逐漸而滅。」《楞嚴經》是佛的真身，佛的舍利，佛的塔廟。如果《楞嚴經》是偽經的話，我願墮無間地獄，永遠在地獄裏，不再到世間見所有的人。

哪一位能把《楞嚴經》背得出，能把《楞嚴咒》背得出，那才是真正的佛子。

法雖無正、像、末，但人心卻有正、像、末。上人認爲，什麼時候有人用功修行，什麼

The one who will fall into the hells is me, not you. If what I say is true, then it's not gossip; if it's not true, then I will definitely fall into the hells. If someone says great cultivators are not subject to cause and effect, then the retribution for that is 500 lives as a fox. If I deny cause and effect--calling black white and white black, calling right wrong and wrong right--saying things that are not so, then I will go into the Hell of Pulling Tongues. If I haven't spoken incorrectly, then I have no offense. Mencius said: "I don't like to debate, but I have no choice...if the teachings of the Yang School and the Mo School aren't put to rest, then the teachings of Confucius cannot prevail. " Why do I like to talk about what's right and what's wrong? It's because in Buddhism there are entirely too many rights and wrongs! There's the black teaching, the white teaching, the yellow teaching, the red teaching--they've become all kinds of different colors that confuse the eye. It's gotten to the point that the blacks don't know they are black and the whites don't know they. are white. And so I like to say things that others don't dare to say. If any of you are offended, it doesn't matter--I'm not concerned. I specialize in breaking through people's deviant knowledge and deviant views.

From the above passage we can recognize the depth of the Master's compassionate mind, which couldn't bear to see living beings suffer. The so-called great kindness and compassion that borders on being harsh is actually an expedient used to teach and transform living beings. The Master once wrote a verse that clarifies his determination:

*I am going to speak the truth
And I'm not afraid of being beaten or scolded.
Kill me, I have no fear.
What inhibitions are there in liberation?*

The Master repeated his instructions about protecting and supporting the Proper Dharma many times:

In Buddhism all the sutras are very important, but the *Shurangama Sutra* is even more important. Wherever the *Shurangama Sutra* is, the Proper Dharma abides in the world. When the *Shurangama Sutra* is gone, that is a sign of the Dharma Ending Age. In the *Extinction of the Dharma Sutra* it says that in the Dharma Ending Age, the *Shurangama Sutra* will become extinct first. Then gradually the other sutras will also become extinct. The *Shurangama Sutra* is the true body of the Buddha; the sharira of the Buddha; the stupa of the Buddha. If the *Shurangama Sutra* is false, then I am willing to fall into the unintermittent hell, stay there forever, and never again come back to the world to see all of you.

Whoever can memorize the *Shurangama Sutra*, whoever can memorize the Shurangama Mantra, is a true disciple of the Buddha.

There's no such thing as Proper, Image, or Ending Dharma ages; it's the minds of beings that have the concept of Proper, Image, and Ending. The Master considers that any time people work hard at cultivation is a time when the Proper Dharma abides. If no one cultivates, if no one reads,

時候就是正法。如果沒人修行，沒有人讀誦或背誦《楞嚴經》，那就是末法時代了。因爲《楞嚴經》中說的「四種清淨明誨」殺盜淫妄，及「五十種陰魔」，把天魔外道的骨頭都給看穿了，說破了。沒有人持戒就是末法，戒在佛法即在也。

上人在一九九〇年返臺於高雄勞工中心語重心長地開示，末法是由在家人「單單」護持「一個」出家人造成的。爲什麼會這樣呢？上人說：

出家人一個人住一個廟，稱王稱霸做皇帝；在家人護法沒有擇法眼，護來護去，護到地獄去。在正法時代，大眾都同住在大叢林大廟中，一起用功修道；而末法時代，人都不願住叢林，一個人住一個廟，你有你一套，我有我一套，把在家人弄得迷糊了。看這個和尚生得很漂亮，我護他的法，給他造個廟；那個又不錯，又給他造個廟。護來護去，把出家人弄得生出貪利心，讓他還俗去了。

希望佛教界對這些話都能痛定思痛，不要再掩耳盜鈴，欺騙眾生。今天臺灣的佛教亂相已經非常嚴重，但都沒有人敢站出來呼籲，眼睜睜看著佛教走向滅亡之路。三步一精舍，五步一大廟，拚命地做法會、超渡、灌頂、傳法、建寺……，而不知去弘揚教義，教導眾生如何了脫生死。佛的根本教義就是教育，使人人都有智慧有擇法眼，知因知果，斷惡修善，而非一味以蓋廟建寺做法會爲務。上人嚴厲的說詞，背後隱藏了多少心酸血淚？所謂「但能光照遠，不惜自焚身」，「雖千萬人吾往矣」，正是上人最佳的寫照。

過去中國的佛教，常常讓人誤以爲是專門超渡死人的宗教，這令一些知識份子排斥、輕視佛教。上人在圓寂前二年大聲疾呼說：

中國的佛教，打水陸、放燄口、做佛事、超渡人……這是中國佛教的一種「形狀」、「樣子」。他們就沒想一想，這樣子下去，養成了一班無業的遊民，在佛教裏混

recites, and memorizes the *Shurangama Sutra*, then that's the Dharma Ending Age. That's because the *Shurangama Sutra*'s "Four Clear Instructions on Purity" that discuss killing, stealing, lust, and lying and its "Fifty Skandha Demon-States" that expose the very bones of all the heavenly demons and externalists, both say flat out that when people don't hold the precepts, then that's the Dharma Ending Age; whenever there are precepts, there is Buddhadharma.

In l990, in a serious talk given at the Labor Hall in Kaohsiung, Taiwan, the Master said that the Dharma Ending Age results from the laity singling out individual left-home people to protect and support. What did he mean? The Master said:

Left-home people go off to live alone in their own temples and act like kings, like dictators, like emperors. The laity lack the "Dharma-selecting eye" and go about protecting here and protecting there until they protect people right into the hells. In the Proper Dharma Age, everyone lives together in large monastic complexes and cultivates together. In the Dharma Ending Age no one wants to live in large monastic complexes. It's one person per temple. You have your way of doing things and I have mine. And this throws the laity into a real quandary. They see that a certain monk is good-looking and decide to support his Dharma, so they set him up with his own temple. Then they notice another monk who's not bad and build a temple for him. Supporting this way and supporting that way, they cause the left-home people to get greedy for benefits to the point that they return to lay life.

I hope Buddhism will take these words to heart and not continue to "plug up its ears while stealing a bell"--cheating all of humankind. At present the signs of turmoil in Buddhism in Taiwan are alarmingly serious. But no one dares to stand up and shout. Everyone just stands by and watches while Buddhist followers race toward their demise. Three steps and a hermitage; five steps and a big temple--they run around having Dharma Assemblies, crossing over souls, anointing crowns, transmitting dharmas, and setting up temples. They never stop to realize that they should be propagating the teachings and explaining their meanings--instructing and guiding living beings in how to end birth and death. The fundamental intent of the Buddha's teaching is education--to cause everyone to develop wisdom and the Dharma-selecting eye, so that they recognize cause and effect, cut off evil, and do good. The intent is not to focus on building monasteries and setting up temples. One wonders how much blood, sweat, and tears are hidden behind this stern instruction by the Master. As it's said, such a one "only wants the light of the torch he's holding to shine as far as possible; he's never concerned about getting burned." "Despite the odds, I will stick to my intentions." This is the best description of the Master.

In the past, Buddhism in China always gave people the mistaken impression that it was a religion that specialized in crossing over dead souls and so the intelligentsia looked down on and tried to get rid of Buddhism. Two years prior to the Master's Nirvana, he cried out in dispair:

飯吃，這有多可惜！只知道賺錢、做超渡！其實超渡，你必須要有根基，有德行。不要說念經、念咒語，你有德行的話，就說一句話：「你往生去了。」他就會往生極樂世界去的。你既無道德，又沒有一個行持，這你憑什麼去超渡人？可以說是負這個施主的債務，並且也把佛教的根本制度都弄得不存在了。

的確，佛教有的是三藏十二部經，這麼多無量無邊的智慧寶藏，不去開發它的教義，卻盡在「表面」上用功夫，這實在是很可惜的事。

在亞洲，佛教徒流行著一種錯誤的觀念，大家都以爲皈依的師父愈多愈好，這是一種末法的跡象。左皈依一次，右皈依一次，弄得一些法師們水火不容，互相競逐法緣及徒弟。而上人常要求已受過皈依的人，不必再登記皈依證了，只要在一旁隨喜皈依就可以了。上人開示說：

有些人說：「善財童子五十三參，爲何我不可以多拜幾個師父？」但須知善財童子是由他的善知識親自遣他去參師的，而不是他貪慕旁的法師有德行，便違背原有的師父，偷偷溜去皈依。中國很多老佛教徒，一生皈依幾十百次；你問他什麼是「皈依」，他卻不知道。你說這可不可憐？他說，所有出家人都是他師父；但我說他一個師父都沒有，因爲他的心不相信。那怎能得救？

其次是「紅包」的問題。上人一向很反對紅包的習俗，因爲這裡包含著一種欺騙的性質。在亞洲佛教徒幾乎把皈依與紅包劃上等號。上人說道：

善財童子在《華嚴經》上，佔了很重的地位，卻對中國佛教起了很複雜的影響。多數的法師也曉得，同一個人皈依很多個師父是不對的，不合佛法的。但若不這樣做，「果儀」（指紅包）就少得很多了。故直到現在，沒有人公開反對這風俗。明明

Chinese Buddhism's Water Lands, Flaming Mouths, and other ceremonies and their saving of souls have become the "status quo" in Chinese Buddhism. They never stop to think that if they keep it up, they are going to be doing nothing but handing out free meals to unemployed vagrants under the guise of Buddhism. What a terrible shame! All they know how to do is make money saving souls! Actually, in order to save souls, you must have a foundation in virtuous conduct. Then, not to speak of reciting mantras or reciting sutras, the single sentence "you can go to rebirth" is sufficient for a soul to be able to gain rebirth in the Land of Ultimate Bliss. For those of you who lack any virtue in the Way, who don't have any cultivation, I ask you, what's your basis for being able to save souls? What you are actually doing is running up a debt with the donor. Besides that, you are destroying the basic system of Buddhism.

Right! It's a real shame that they don't open up the Tripitaka [Buddhist Canon] with its Twelve Divisions--a precious treasury of infinite wisdom--and learn to teach from it instead of applying all their effort to superfluous things.

Among Asian Buddhists who have taken refuge there is a popular misconception. Everyone thinks that the more teachers you take refuge with, the better. This is a sign of the Dharma Ending Age. By taking refuge with this one and then taking refuge with that one, they cause contention among the Dharma Masters, who quarrel with each other over who has the Dharma affinities and who gets the disciples. But the Master always asked those who had already taken refuge not to sign up to take refuge again--that they could just follow along and rejoice from the sidelines. The Master said:

Some people say, "The Youth Good Wealth visited fifty-three teachers; why can't I bow to a few more teachers?" But you need to realize that the Youth Good Wealth was always sent on by his previous teacher to the next teacher. It wasn't that he greedily longed for another Dharma Master endowed with virtuous conduct and so turned his back on his current teacher and stole away to take refuge with another. A lot of older Chinese Buddhist disciples have taken refuge tens or hundreds of times. But when you ask them what "taking refuge" means, they don't know. Isn't that pathetic? They say that all left-home people are their teachers. But I say they don't have any teacher at all because their minds lack faith, so how can they be saved?

Actually when it comes to the question of red envelopes, all along the Master was very opposed to the custom. That's because there's an element of cheating in it. No one knows how much money is in those red envelopes. For Buddhist disciples in Asia, taking refuge and red envelopes amount to the same thing. That being the case, people who can't come up with red envelopes and those of externalist ways don't dare believe in the Buddha and take refuge. The Master said:

In the *Avatamsaka Sutra*, the Youth Good Wealth holds a very important position and yet he has had a very complicated influence on Chinese Buddhism. Most Dharma Masters know

　　　　　　　　　　　　　　　宣化老和尚追思紀念專集

知道不對，也要去做，你說是不是很複雜呢？爲什麼呢？第一是爲了「童子」（拉信徒），第二是爲了「善財」（分紅包）；這是佛教中最壞的習氣。

上人的眞知灼見，確實與眾不同。爲了「不忍聖教衰」，上人的獅子吼背後隱藏了多少「慈悲」？

臺灣很多「明星師父」，被皈依弟子捧得高高的，卻忘了自己「荷擔如來家業，度化眾生」的責任，每天只沉醉在名利中，忽略了生死大事。其實三寶弟子碰到出家師父，應該請示佛法，而不是一味地供養紅包。所以上人也都要求弟子能儘量持銀錢戒，儘量少跟錢「結緣」，上人說：

因爲出家人若沒有錢，他還能修行；一有了錢，絕對不修行了！這是我敢保證的。你看一看！你研究研究，道士講「貧道」，僧人叫「貧僧」，沒有說「富僧」、「富道」的。所以你們弄這個錢，去供養「富僧」、「富道」的話，這是等於造罪一樣的。我說這話會得罪很多人，我雖然得罪，我也要說眞話。

大家都知道「搭衣與一食」，是萬佛城的特有家風。上人尤其特別聲明，凡是跟他出家的，都必須遵守佛制：「日中一食，衣不離身。」所以無論外界如何地批評，甚至排斥、譭謗萬佛城標異現奇，上人也絕不因此改變家風。對於這些流言的詆毀，上人只是說：「這不是我定的，這是佛制，我們要遵守佛制！」但對於比較年老的出家人，上人則方便讓他們吃三餐。這個規矩，一直到上人圓寂前的遺囑交代，始終都沒有變過。上人他自己說：

跟我出家的，如果能吃一餐，我才收他；不能吃一餐，我不收。這是跟我出家的一個鐵定的條件。任何時候、任何環境的壓迫下，也不可以改變的。

你叫我死可以，叫我不搭衣不可以；你

very well that for one person to take refuge with lots of different teachers is incorrect. It is not in accord with the Buddhadharma. But if they don't let it happen, their "tokens" (the red envelopes) will diminish significantly. And so to this day no one openly opposes this custom. Knowing full well it is wrong, they still do it. Complicated, huh? Why? First, it's for the sake of the "youths" (the laity that get pulled in) and second it's for the sake of "Good Wealth" (one's share of red envelopes). This is the worst habit going in Buddhism.

The Master's true knowledge and brilliant views are decisively different from those of the multitudes. How much compassion there is behind the Master's lion's roar that he emits because he "cannot bear to watch the sagely teachings decline"! A lot of "star teachers" in Taiwan, being put on pedestals by their disciples, forget all about their responsibility to "carry on the Thus Come One's work of saving living beings." Every day they wallow in their intoxication with fame and profit and neglect the great matter of birth and death. Actually when disciples of the Triple Jewel encounter left-home teachers, they should inquire about the Buddhadharma, not just be intent upon giving them red envelopes. That's why the Master encouraged his disciples to hold the precept against possessing money as much as possible; to avoid "tying up conditions" with money as much as possible. The Master said:

That's because left-home people can cultivate if they don't have money. As soon as they have money, then they certainly won't be able to cultivate. I can guarantee it. Look into it! Investigate it. Taoists are referred to as "poor Taoists." Sanghans are referred to as "poor Sanghans." Nobody talks about "rich Sanghas" or "rich Taoists." And so when you use your money to make offerings to "rich Sanghas" and "rich Taoists," it's the same as if you were committing offenses. I'm going to offend a lot of people by saying this. But although I am offending you, I still have to tell the truth.

Everyone knows that "wearing the precept sash and eating one meal a day" are the tradition of the City of Ten Thousand Buddhas. The Master specifically announced that anyone who left home with him had to honor the Buddha's regulations of eating one meal a day at noon and always wearing the precept sash. And so no matter how must the City of Ten Thousand Buddhas came under criticism by those outside--even when people slandered the City as doing new and strange things to show off, the Master would never, ever change his policy because of that. Regarding the barrage of slander, the Master merely said: "This is not some rule I made up. This is the Buddha's reguation. We want to honor the Buddha's regulations." But the Master was expedient with the older left-home people and allowed them to take three meals a day. This rule remained right up to the final instructions given by the Master just before his Nirvana--it never changed. The Master himself said:

If people who want to leave home with me can eat one meal a day, then I will accept them. If they cannot eat one meal a day, I will not accept them. This is a fixed requirement for anyone who leaves home with me. In spite of any pressures whatsoever regarding the times and circumstances, this cannot be changed.

叫我死可以，叫我不吃一餐不可以。有這樣堅決的定力，有這樣的信心，才是萬佛聖城的一份子。

有人認爲戒律是一種「因時因地因人」所造成的，所以「非時食」只是印度人所持的戒，中國人並不適合持此戒。其實這是不對的，因爲戒律是佛法中「戒定慧」三無漏學的一部份，都是釋迦牟尼佛親口說的法，如果「戒」學不適合中國人，那麼「定慧」之學也必定不適合中國人了，豈有此理？

下面再談老和尚對「搭衣」的看法。上人嚴格要求跟他出家的人一定要時時搭著衣，衣不離體的。上人說：

出家人不搭衣，就等於還俗一樣的，和俗人沒有分別。並不是穿這個「長衫」，穿這彎彎領，就證明你是出家人了。不要說穿這彎彎領，就是搭著衣，你還天天總在犯戒，總在不老實，何況你不搭衣！

現在中國的出家人，乃至於其他各地的出家人，多數在大乘的佛教，都不搭衣。這不搭衣，他們認爲就是天公地道，就是應該這樣子。可不知道，不搭衣已經沒有比丘相了。

上人斬釘截鐵地認爲：「出家人一定要搭著衣，否則就沒有比丘相了。」而搭衣本身就是佛弟子的標誌，佛陀本身就是三衣缽具，衣不離體的。這在《陀羅尼集經》中有說：「佛身形作眞金色，被赤袈裟。」又《要略念誦經》云：「佛身猶如紫金，三十二相，八十種好，被赤袈裟，跏趺而坐。」可見上人提倡搭衣，並不是沒有道理的。

上人一生講述的經典，大約有《華嚴經》、《法華經》、《楞嚴經》……等三十多種。國學部份有《四書》和《易經》、《藥性賦》。其中有三部著作是很特殊，很少人講述的，即《楞嚴咒疏句偈解》、《水鏡回天錄》及《佛祖道影白話解》。

《楞嚴咒疏句偈解》，這是上人在一九七

I'm prepared to die, if you want, but I refuse not to wear my precept sash. I'm prepared to die, if you want, but I refuse not to eat only once a day at noon. Those who have that kind of strong samadhi-power--that kind of faith--rightfully belong at the City of Ten Thousand Buddhas.

Some people look at it this way: "This is not the time of the Buddha and we are not in India now; what is more Chinese people are not Indians, and so, since the precepts were created for the times, the locations and the people, then they are precepts only applicable to the people of India and are not appropriate for the people of China." Actually that is incorrect because the precepts are one of the three non-outflow studies of precepts, samadhi, and wisdom in Buddhism, all of which were explained by Shakyamuni Buddha himself. If "precepts" are not appropriate to the people of China, then does that mean that "samadhi and wisdom" are also not appropriate to the people of China? Ridiculous!

The Master sternly insisted that those who left-home under him absolutely must wear the sash at all times--the precept sash must never leave their bodies. The Master said,

For left-home people not to wear their precept sashes is the same as going back to lay-life. You are no different from ordinary people. It's not that wearing the long robe that fastens on the side proves that you are a left-home person. Not to speak of just wearing the long robe--even when you wear your precept sash--all you do every day is violate the precepts and be dishonest, how much the more so when you don't wear your sash!

Chinese left-home people of today, even the left-home people of other countries as well--the majority of Great Vehicle Buddhists--do not wear their precept sashes. They think that's the status quo--the way things are supposed to be. What they don't realize is that as soon as they don't wear their precept sashes, they lose the appearance of Bhikshus.

The Master decisively thinks that left-home people absolutely must wear their precept sashes, otherwise they don't have the semblance of being Bhikshus. Besides, wearing the sash is the trademark of Buddhist disciples. The Buddha himself had three robes (sashes), a bowl, and a sitting cloth, and his robe (sash) never left his body. This was mentioned in the *Compilation of Dharanis Sutra* where it says: "The Buddha's body was the color of true gold and he was wearing a saffron *kashaya*." Also the *Essentials Regarding Recitation Sutra* says: "The Buddha's body, like azure, is endowed with thirty-two hallmarks and eighty subtle characteristics. He is wearing a saffron kashaya and is seated in full lotus posture." We can see that the Master is not unreasonable in advocating wearing the precept sash.

The Sutras which the Master lectured during his life are generally listed here: *Avatamsaka Sutra, Dharma Flower Sutra, Shurangama Sutra*--more than thirty different ones. Also among the Chinese classics he lectured: *The Four Books*, the *Book of Changes*, and the *Nature of Chinese Medicine*. Among all these are three that are quite unusual--very few people have ever explained them. They are: *Verses and Commentary on the Shurangama Mantra, Reflections in Water and Mirrors Turning*

九至一九八七年所講述的，共講了八年。這部咒在佛教歷史上罕有人解釋，唯有清朝的續法大師及武林慈雲寺的柏亭法師曾註解過。上人在一九四九年時獲得《楞嚴咒疏》單行本，自述

得未曾有，時刻研究，頗窺祕境，隨身攜帶，未曾或離。

又云：

俾能正法久住，邪說永息，人手一編，同入究竟堅固大定。

之後，上人即在美國宣講《咒疏》，對全咒五百五十四句，逐句以「七言詩」解之，並白話述之，真可謂「空前絕後」的作品，相當珍貴。上人說：

用四句偈來解釋每一句咒語，也是解釋不完的，因為咒的妙義是無窮無盡的，四句偈只是拋磚引玉地大概說一說而已。這四句偈頌看起來很簡單，但它是從我心裏流出來的，也可以說是等於我的血，我的汗，並不是尋章摘句，從其他的書本上抄來的！

我現在給你們講〈楞嚴咒〉，這〈楞嚴咒〉，百千萬劫也沒有人講一次，也不容易講一次。在我給各位講時，我知道沒有人聽得懂，就是有人自以為懂得，也不是真懂！可是十年、百年、千年後，有人見到這樣淺的註解，那時對〈楞嚴咒〉就會深深地明瞭了。

《水鏡回天錄》，是上人在一九八五至一九八九年講述的書，共四年。內容是上人詠讚諸佛菩薩、羅漢、歷代高僧大德、在家居士、古今中外的大德、異人、元首、文豪⋯⋯等，作一個客觀的評語。正如孔子作《春秋》一樣，上人本著忠貞愛國的心，欲挽回末世的混亂，可以套句孔子的話說：「知我者，其惟水鏡乎！罪我者，其惟水鏡乎！」《水鏡回天錄》正是春秋史筆的一脈薪傳，也是當今世上一本活生生的因果錄。這本書，

*Back the Tide of Destiny*, and modern-language explanations of the *Biographies of the Buddhist Patriarchs.*

The Master' lecture series on *Verses and Commentary on the Shurangama Mantra* lasted for eight years, from 1979 to 1987. Throughout all of Buddhist history this mantra has rarely been explained. Only Great Master Xu Fa of the Qing dynasty and Dharma Master Bo Ting of Compassionate Cloud Monastery in Wulin ever explained it. When the Master came in possession of a copy of the *Commentary on the Shurangama Mantra* in 1949, he records:

I obtained what I'd never had before. I got a glimpse of the state of the esoteric, carrying it always with me and never being apart from it.

He also said

For the Proper Dharma to remain long in the world, and to stop the deviant discourses once and for all, everyone should carry a copy, and we should enter the ultimately firm great samadhi together.

Later, after the Master came to America, he himself explained the Shurangama Mantra, writing verses of seven-character lines to explain each of the 554 lines and further giving a modern-language commentary. Truly this masterpiece is unprecedented. It is exceptionally valuable. The Master said:

The four-line verses used to explain every line of the mantra don't by any means exhaust the meaning, because the wonderful meanings in the mantra are infinite and endless. These four-line verses are a mere mention of the broad idea--just tendering a bit of brick, hoping someone will come up with jade. These four-line verse appear to be very simple, but they flow out from my heart. You could say they are my blood and sweat. They certainly aren't plagiarized--copied from someone else's work!.....

I'm explaining the Shurangama Mantra for you now, and throughout hundreds of thousands of eons, no one even explains it once. Also, it's not easy to explain in its entirety. When I'm explaining it, I know that none of you really understand what I'm saying. Even if there are those who think they do, they don't really. But perhaps ten years from now, or a hundred, or a thousand years from now, someone will read this simple explanation and gain a profound understanding of the mantra.

*Reflections in Water and Mirrors Turning Back the Tide of Destiny* is a series of essays composed and explained by the Master during the four-year period from 1985 to 1989. It includes praises and objective critiques of Buddhas, Bodhisattvas, Arhats, lofty Sanghans of great virtue, Buddhist lay persons, men and women of great virtue throughout history both in and outside of China, remarkable individuals, national leaders, literati, and so on. Just as Confucius compiled the *Spring and Autumn Annals*, the Master wrote *Water and Mirrors* out of his patriotic loyalty and his wish to save the world from impending chaos and turmoil. We could alter Confucius' quote to fit the Master: "If people understand me, it is because of *Water and Mirrors*; if people blame me, it is also because of *Water and Mirrors*." *Water and Mirrors* carries on the spirit and intent of

上人先對人物的一生作簡單介紹，再以八句四言詩去歌讚他，結尾再加「又說偈曰」七言律詩。此書很值得再三翫味，可以讓人知因果、鑑往知來、斷惡修善。

《佛祖道影白話解》，這是上人於一九七二至一九八五年所講，計十三年，共宣講了三百四十六次。這部書主要是自釋迦佛在拈花微笑後，傳法給迦葉尊者，迦葉尊者再傳給二祖阿難尊者，一直到第二十八代東土初祖達摩禪師，才正式將禪法傳入中國。到了三十三祖（即東土六祖）的惠能大師以後，又「一花開五葉」。後來五家又成爲七宗，也就是法眼宗、曹洞宗、雲門宗、潙仰宗、臨濟宗、黃龍派及楊岐派，加上牛頭支、兩土聖僧（東土及西土）、天台宗、華嚴宗、慈恩宗、瑜伽宗、律宗、蓮社宗，及近代十大高僧，計三百三十八尊。每尊上人都做「或說偈曰」（即七言八句的律詩）去讚頌之，並於蓮宗六祖永明延壽大師後，又各再加四言八句的詩讚之，可謂對此三百三十八尊祖師都做了詳細的講述。因爲原文書是古體文，完全沒有標點符號，加上都是一些禪門的「境界語言」，所以更是難上加難，很難去理解古來大德深祕的境界，只能說「不可說」及「如人飲水，冷暖自知」。

其實上人講述這部《佛祖道影》是有一大因緣的。因爲這部書當初是由虛雲老和尚於一九五八年寄給上人，信上寫著

茲寄奉近年增刻佛祖道影一部，好閱留念，並希自利利他，爲道珍重。

且虛老早在一九五六年四月初九，書信傳上人爲第九代潙仰宗祖師，書信內容言及

座下爲法心切，續佛祖慧命，當滿座下之願，附寄源流俾承祖脈，祖道賴以重興，是所至望，專覆不盡。

可見上人秉持師訓，將《佛祖道影》講述成白話，令眾生皆得法益，這也是「空前

Spring and Autumn Annals, and is a living record of causes and effects as they occur in the world today. After giving a brief biographical sketch of each person, the Master praises or critiques him or her with a four-line verse of eight characters per line, and then gives another verse of seven-character lines in conclusion. This book is worth repeated reading and reflection, for it teaches us about cause and effect. Studying the past, we can know the future and be warned to stop evil and cultivate goodness.

The Master gave modern-language explanations of the *Biographies of the Buddhist Patriarchs* from 1972 to 1985. During those thirteen years, the Master delivered a total of 346 lectures on the topic. The book begins with Shakyamuni Buddha holding up a flower and smiling, transmitting the Dharma to the Venerable Kashyapa. The Dharma was then transmitted to the Second Patriarch Venerable Ananda, the Third Patriarch Venerable Upali, and so on, all the way to Great Master Bodhidharma, the Twenty-eight Patriarch, who brought the Dharma of Chan to China and become the First Patriarch in China. After the time of the Thirty-third Patriarch (the Sixth Chinese Patriarch) Great Master Huineng, Buddhism divided into five sects, which later became seven sects: Fayan, Caodong, Yunmen, Weiyang, Linji, Huanglong, and Yangqi. With the addition of the Niutou branch; the Indian and Chinese Sanghans who certified to sagehood; the patriarchs of the Tiantai, Huayan, Cien, Yogacharya, Vinaya, and Lotus Society Sects; and ten contemporary eminent Sanghans [Dharma Masters Hsu Yun, Ci Zhou, Hong Yi, Tai Xu, Di Xian, Yuan Ying, Ci Hang, Tan Xu, Chang Ren, and Guang Qin], the book covers 338 people in all. The Master wrote an eight line verse (seven characters per line) in praise of each one. And for all the individuals from Great Master Yongmingshou, the Sixth Patriarch of the Lotus Sect, to the last one, Venerable Master Guang Qin, the Master wrote an additional eight line verse (four characters per line) of praise for each. With his lectures and verses, the Master provided a detailed explanation of each patriarch. The original text, in classical Chinese, devoid of punctuation, and couched in the abstruse jargon of the Chan School which is used to describe states of awakening, was extremely difficult to understand. Unable to fathom the profound states of the great cultivators of the past, one could only say they were "ineffable" or make the comment that "Only the person who drinks the water will know how hot or cold it is."

Actually there was a compelling reason for the Venerable Master to lecture on the *Biographies of the Buddhist Patriarchs*. The book was mailed to the Master in 1958 by the Venerable Elder Master Hsu Yun, who wrote in a letter,

I am sending a copy of the recently published book of prints of the Buddhist Patriarchs for you to read and keep as a remembrance. I hope that you will benefit yourself and benefit others in your work for Buddhism and that you will take care.

On the ninth of the fourth month, 1956, the Venerable Yun sent a letter to the Master making him the ninth patriarch of the Weiyang Sect. Part of the letter states:

…You, Venerable One, have concern for the preservation of the Dharma and for the continuation of the wisdom life of the Buddhas and Patriarchs. I am sending you the Source, the inheritance of the Patriarchs' pulse. It is my sincere hope that, entrusted to you, the Patriarchs' Way will prosper. This letter has been brief because there is no way to express all there is to say.

宣化老和尚追思紀念專集

絕後」的。所以，我以爲這三部著作是上人
的「三訣」，也是眾生的福報，才可以得閱
如此珍貴的法寶。

縱觀上人一生，詩詞橫溢，我大略估計最
少有二千首詩以上，每句詩都是對仗押韻的
，不得不佩服上人甚深的般若智慧。尤其把
〈楞嚴咒〉以偈解之，這是前所未有的事，
如果沒有證入「楞嚴大定」的祕境，如何能
解之？還有上人在講《佛祖道影》時，有時
又超出了歷史文獻資料，讓人聯想起上人真
有「宿命通」？上人的願力是

只要我有一口氣在，我就講經說法。

所以上人的著述很多，加上上人的願力──
要把佛經翻譯成世界各種語言，這可說是無
量無邊的功德。目前法界佛教總會已經譯出
上百部的佛經及開示錄；上人圓寂後，這譯
經的工作永遠不會間斷，永遠領導著眾生，
由黑暗走入光明，由此岸到達彼岸的究竟涅
槃。

縱觀上人一生的開示及行持，都很有老子
哲學的味道。且上人在《水鏡回天錄》中，
對摩訶迦葉尊者評道：

化身老子遊震旦，
接引有緣登彼岸。

可見上人以爲老子乃摩訶迦葉尊者的化身也
。而老子一生只五千言，卻深受歷代百姓及
修道人所喜愛。上人的言行，很多都與老子
不謀而合，如老子言：

正言若反。

信言不美，美言不信。

反者道之動，弱者道之用。

上人也常以反面的教化來激勵眾生，如：有
人問如何消滅家中的小蚊蟲？上人答：

你要消滅小蚊蟲，就得先消滅我。

這是上人何等的慈悲！上人一生以「不爭、
不貪、不求、不自私、不自利、不妄語」六

And so the Master followed the Elder Master's instructions, giving modern-language explanations of the *Biographies of the Buddhist Patriarchs* and benefiting living beings with this Dharma. This was an unprecedented contribution. Thus, I have considered these three works to be the Master's "three treasures." Only those with blessings have the opportunity to read such precious Dharma treasures.

Surveying the prolific verses that the Master wrote in his life, I estimate that there must be at least two thousand, each and every one of them matched and rhymed. How can we not admire the Master's profound Prajna wisdom? To explain the Shurangama Mantra in verses is an unprecedented achievement. How could he have done this if he had not entered the esoteric realm of the Great Shurangama Samadhi? Moreover, the Master's explanations of the *Biographies of the Buddhist Patriarchs* sometimes went beyond the documented historical records, making us suspect that he really did have the power of knowing past lives.

The Master vowed,

As long as I have a breath left, I will expound the Sutras and speak the Dharma.

That is why he composed so prolifically. His vow to translate the Buddhist canon into the languages of the world will generate infinite and boundless merit and virtue. The Dharma Realm Buddhist Association has already published over a hundred volumes of translations of Sutras and Dharma talks. After the Master's passing, the work of canonical translation will continue without interruption, eternally leading living beings from darkness into the light, from this shore of suffering to the other shore of ultimate Nirvana.

If we survey the Master's teachings and conduct, we find that they carry the flavor of Lao Zi's philosophy. In his verse on Venerable Mahakashyapa in *Water and Mirrors*, the Master says,

*Transforming himself, he appeared as Lao Zi and wandered throughout China,*
*Guiding those with affinities to ascend to the other shore.*

Clearly the Master considered Lao Zi a transformation body of Venerable Mahakashyapa. Lao Zi's one and only 5000-word composition became widely popular among the people and cultivators of China. Many of the Master's words and deeds bear a striking resemblance to those of Lao Zi. For example, Lao Zi said:

Straightforward words seem paradoxical.

Truthful words are not beautiful; beautiful words are not true.

Turning back is how the Way moves;
Yielding is the means the Way employs.

The Master often used contrary teachings to stimulate people. For example, when someone asked whether it would be permissible to kill small insects in the household, the Master replied,

If you want to kill little insects, you must kill me first!

How compassionate the Master was! The Master always taught living beings the Six Guiding Principles (equivalent to the five precepts): no

大宗旨來教化眾生（其實就是五戒）。很多人不以爲然，認爲這三歲小孩都知道的，何必再開示？可是上人不知開示了多少次：

我這一生的成就，都是由這六大宗旨走過來的，你們任何人想修行佛道，必須也要走這六大宗旨。

老子不也說過

吾言甚易知，甚易行，
天下莫能知，莫能行。

大道甚夷，而民好徑。

本來修行就是很簡單的，「道在邇，莫求諸遠」，可是人們總想走捷徑，到處去打游擊，去找「密法」修，眞是「人之迷，其日固久」。孰不知「密在汝邊」，能放下一切物欲的追求，及分別執著心，能不發脾氣、不打妄語，當下就是「密法」，就是「道」了！上人一生辛苦體悟出來的六大宗旨，以熾熱的心情，希望貢獻於世，有益於眾生。但是人們卻不屑予以一顧，甚至嗤而笑之，這眞是老子所說的：

上士聞道，勤而行之。
中士聞道，若存若亡。
下士聞道，大笑之，
不笑不足以爲道。

上人一生倡「不爭」的哲學，跟老子的「不爭」是一樣的。眞正不爭的人就是沒有脾氣的人，能「得饒人處且饒人」的人。
上人題詩曰：

爭是勝負心　與道相違背
便生四相心　由何得三昧

事事都好去　脾氣難化了
眞能不生氣　就得無價寶
再若不怨人　事事都能好
煩惱永不生　冤孽從那找
常瞅人不對　自己苦沒了

fighting, no greed, no seeking, no selfishness, no pursuit of personal benefit, and no lying. Many people were unconvinced, wondering why the Master bothered to lecture on principles that any three-year-old could understand. Yet the Master said over and over,

Everything I have accomplished in this life came from practicing the Six Guiding Principles. If any of you want to cultivate the path to Buddhahood, you also must practice the Six Guiding Principles.

Lao Zi himself also said:

My words are very easy to understand and very easy to put into practice, yet no one in the world can understand them or put them into practice.

The great Way is easy, yet people prefer by-paths.

Cultivation is basically a very simple affair. "The Way is near; don't seek it afar." Yet people like to take shortcuts, to visit various teachers in search of "secret dharmas" to cultivate. "Indeed, it is long since the people were perplexed." Little do they know that the secret is within them: if they can stop pursuing material pleasures, let go of discriminations and attachments, and refrain from anger and lying, then that's the "secret dharma" and the Way right there! Having awakened to the Six Guiding Principles after a lifetime of bitter cultivation, the Master fervently wished to offer them to the world for the benefit of living beings. Yet people paid no attention to them, and even snorted and laughed at them. It is exactly as Lao Zi said:

When the best student hears about the Way,
He practises it assiduously;
When the average student hears about the Way,
It seems to him one moment there and gone the next;
When the worst student hears about the Way
He laughs out loud.
If he did not laugh,
It would be unworthy of being the Way.

The Master's lifelong philosophy of noncontention is the same as Lao Zi's. People who truly do not contend have no anger. They forgive people whenever it is possible to forgive them. The Master wrote these verses:

Fighting involves the thought of winning and losing
And so it goes against the Way.
Giving rise to the mind of the four marks,
How can you obtain samadhi?

All things easily come and go,
But a bad temper's truly hard to change.
If you can really never get angry,
Then you've found a precious jewel.
When you stop putting the blame on others,
Then everything goes your way.
If you never let your mind get afflicted,
Then the karma born of hatred won't return to trouble you.
But whoever dwells on others' faults
Simply proves that his own suffering hasn't reached an end.

上人除了六大宗旨外，另有二首詩，很值得我們終身信受奉行，那就是：

眞認自己錯　莫論他人非
他非即我非　同體名大悲

一切是考驗　看你怎麼辦
覿面若不識　須再重頭煉

在《論語》、《孟子》書中，聖人也教我們要「行有不得，反求諸己」。上人的教導也是「反求諸己」的，且上人的身教有時令人措手不及。如一九九三年二月十日，竟發生上人戴著面紗出現在萬佛聖城；原因是弟子違背日中一食及搭衣的規矩，上人在痛心疾首之下，戴著面紗回城。上人説：

我在去臺灣之前，我就知道萬佛城從我開山以來到現在，所有的宗旨就一掃而光，人都不遵守了。因爲這個，令我大失所望，我對你們，是沒有面目回來見你們各位的。……我要帶一個假面具，免得用眞面目看你們大家。

上人如此的舉動，眞可説是打破佛教界師父蒙羞戴面紗的例子，其實該戴面紗的是犯戒的我們，而不是師父。另外，在一九九二年春天，聖城舉辦了一次空前絕後的「無遮大會」，在大會中上人開示説：

我自己痛痛打自己，痛痛打了幾大頓，打得幾乎昏去，因爲我沒有德行，教育出這樣的徒弟。

如果懺悔是眞的，有什麼過錯，我都願意承擔過來。但你不説眞話，要快點下地獄，我是沒辦法救你的。

這是我所知道，有師父因爲徒弟不孝，而痛打自己的例子，眞令人震撼及心痛難過。上人對實踐「他非即我非，同體名大悲」的精神，在此一覽無遺，就如《華嚴經》二十五品所説的：

我當普爲一切眾生備受諸苦，令其得出

Aside from the Six Guiding Principles, the Master gave us two other verses that are worth remembering and practicing for the rest of our lives:

*Truly recognize your own faults,*
*Don't discuss the faults of others.*
*Others' faults are just my own.*
*Being one with everyone is great compassion.*

*Everything's a test*
*To see what you will do.*
*If you don't recognize what's before you,*
*You'll have to start anew.*

In the *Analects* and the *Mencius*, we can read the teachings of sages: "If you fail in your endeavor, look for the reason in yourself." The Master also taught people to seek within themselves, and his teachings sometimes caught them off guard. For example, on February 10, 1993, the Master appeared wearing a veil over his face at the City of Ten Thousand Buddhas because his disciples had broken the rules of eating only one meal a day and always wearing the sash. He said,

Even before I went to Taiwan, I knew that all the principles I had laid down since the founding of the City of Ten Thousand Buddhas were completely gone, no longer being followed. That's why I am terribly disappointed and feel I have no face with which to see you…I have to wear a veil so that I will not see you with my naked face.

That was the first time in Buddhist history that a teacher had veiled his face before his disciples in order to hide his shame. Actually, we who broke the precepts are the ones who should have veiled our faces, not the Master. In the spring of 1992, the City of Ten Thousand Buddhas held an unprecedented Unrestrained Repentance Assembly (for details see issues 261-265 of *Vajra Bodhi Sea*), during which the Master said:

I gave myself several painful beatings until I nearly fainted, because due to my lack of virtue, the disciples I taught turned out to be like this.

If your repentance is sincere, then no matter what mistakes you have made, I can be responsible for them. But if you refuse to tell the truth and you want to fall to the hells faster, then I have no way to save you.

I know of no other teacher who beats himself when his disciples are disobedient. It really shakes me up and makes me feel bad. The Master's actual practice of the philosophy that "Others' faults are just my own; / To be one with everyone is great compassion" is very obvious. It is just as Chapter Twenty-five of the *Flower Adornment Sutra* says:

I should undergo every suffering for the sake of all living beings, enabling them to escape the great pit of limitless births and deaths. I should, for the sake of all living beings in all of the evil destinies in all worlds, undergo all sufferings to the end of time… I wish to

無量生死大壑。我當普爲一切眾生，於
一切世界，一切惡趣中，盡未來劫，受
一切苦……我寧獨受如是眾生苦，不令
眾生墮於地獄。當彼於地獄、畜生、閻
羅王等險難之處，以身爲質，救贖一切
惡道眾生，令得解脫。

孔子在《論語》中也說：「躬自厚，而薄責
於人，則遠怨矣。」商湯王在祭告天地時也
說：「朕躬有罪，無以萬方，萬方有罪，罪
在朕躬。」這些聖人的言行教誨，都是一樣
的。唯有以身作則，降伏自己，才能感動別
人。此外上人亦有一詩曰：

> 浩然正氣塞地天
> 大而化之學聖賢
> 行有不得求諸己
> 迴光返照莫攀緣
> 養成老拙勿使巧
> 勤掃心塵去私奸
> 若能如此時鞭策
> 不久佛法滿三千

最後談談上人的「叩頭」哲學。上人曾說他
一生修行的祕訣，就是向人叩頭、吃虧來的
。上人常對新皈依的弟子說：

> 要是有人罵我，你要向他叩頭；
> 無論誰誣謗我，不要爲我辯護。

甚至上人在美國，還常向徒弟來叩頭；徒弟
若不聽話，上人就向他叩個頭，徒弟就聽話
了。如早期在美國，有天晚上，上人在聖城
妙語堂講經時，沒有一個出家人願意上台講
；等講經結束後，從妙語堂回佛殿時，上人
是跪著看大眾出門的。他嚴厲責備自己，行
無言之教，這眞是「太空時代」的修行，居
然有師父向徒弟叩頭的事，更證明了上人已
達「無我」的精神。此外上人對請來聖城講
經的法師，都是親自領眾跪著聽的，這絕非
常人所能爲的，並不是像外人所說上人有股
「傲氣」。

而現在有些學佛者，每天只會向外面的佛
來叩頭，而不會向自己心中的佛來叩頭，更

undergo the sufferings of such living beings myself so that they do not have to fall into the hells. When they are in the hells, the animal realm, King Yama's court, or other dangerous places, I shall give up my own body to ransom them and enable them to gain liberation from the evil paths.

Confucius said in the *Analects*: "He who makes liberal demands upon himself and small demands on others, will keep resentment far from himself." (Chapter Fifteen "Weilinggong") King Tang of the Shang dynasty made a sacrifice and appealed to heaven, saying, "If I have offenses, the people are not to blame. If the people have offenses, the blame rests with me." The words, deeds, and teachings of the sages are all the same. The only way to influence others is to set an example for them and subdue oneself. The Master once wrote a verse:

> *With vast, proper energy suffusing the universe,*
> *Achieve greatness and transform it, learning from the sages.*
> *When you fail, look within yourself.*
> *Turn the light around and illumine within; don't exploit situations.*
> *Act like an old fool; don't be too clever.*
> *Diligently sweep the dust from the mind, get rid of selfish treachery.*
> *If you can constantly urge yourself on in this way,*
> *The Buddhadharma will soon fill the trichiliocosm.*

Finally, let's discuss the Master's philosophy of kowtowing. The Master once remarked that the secret of his lifelong cultivation consisted of kowtowing to others and taking losses. The Master often exhorted new disciples who had just taken refuge with him:

> If someone scolds me, you should bow to him. No matter who slanders me, never speak in my defense.

In America the Master often bowed to his disciples. Whenever he bowed to disobedient disciples, they became obedient. In the early days in America, one evening when the Master was lecturing on a Sutra at Wonderful Words Hall in the City of Ten Thousand Buddhas, none of his left-home disciples would go up on stage and speak. After the lecture, when everyone was leaving Wonderful Words Hall to return to the Buddha hall, the Master knelt by the door and watched as the entire assembly walked out. His stern self-castigation was a wordless teaching to all. It was truly an example of Space Age cultivation. The fact that he could kowtow to his disciples proves that he had realized the state of egolessness. When the Master invited other Dharma Masters to lecture at the City, he personally led the assembly in kneeling to listen to the lecture. He certainly was not arrogant as some people have described him.

Many contemporary Buddhist scholars only know to bow to the Buddha outside; they do not know to bow to the Buddha in their own mind. Nor do they know to admit their mistakes before their parents and all living beings. Thus their practice is not complete. We should learn to bow and repent daily before our parents and all living beings. We should constantly seek within ourselves, reflect upon ourselves, and listen to our own nature. Seeing worthy ones, we should strive to emulate them. Seeing unworthy ones, we should examine our own faults.

The ultimate goal of studying Buddhism is to put an end to birth and

不會向父母及一切眾生認錯，這是不圓滿的。我們應該學學天天向父母及一切眾生來叩頭問訊，要不斷地「反求諸己，迴光返照，反聞自性」，要「見賢思齊，見不賢內自省也。」學佛法最終目的就是要了脫生死，古德云：

愛不斷不生極樂，罪不重不生娑婆。

不斷除情欲的話，是不可能了生死的。《楞嚴經》上云：「淫心不除，塵不可出。」及「若諸世界，六道眾生，其心不淫，則不隨其生死相續。」「淫欲」為生死的根本。所以上人一生倡不邪淫、不淫欲，一直到他老人家圓寂前一年，仍不斷地重呼：

人生於色，死於色，如此而已。

上人說萬佛城是很古老的，仍然採男女分校的制度，就是要我們每個人都能守規矩，不邪淫、不墮胎、不吃避孕藥。因為這個「色欲」使這世界變壞的最重要因素。上人說：

男孩子要到二十五歲以後才找對象，女孩子要到二十歲以後才可以找對象。

倘若你不能斷欲去愛，你就是出家了八萬個大劫，也只是在佛教裏混光陰，吃造業飯。

現在報紙每天都是些殺盜淫妄的犯罪案件，尤其「殺」跟「淫」，更是氾濫，上人說：

在因果律上，犯淫邪者最嚴重，其懲罰尤為凌厲。根據因果律，一個人生前曾邪淫多少次，死後就會有把大鋸子，把人從頭頂鋸到腳尖多少次，生前曾結婚一百次，死後便分開一百次。

在《印光大師文鈔》中對「邪淫」的事，大師更有嚴厲的說詞：

至於邪淫一事，無廉無恥，極穢極惡，乃以人身，行畜生事，現生已成畜生，來生便做畜生……邪淫之人，必生不貞

death. There is an ancient saying:

*If love is not cut off, one cannot be born in the Land of Ultimate Bliss.*
*If one's offenses weren't grave, one would not have been born*
*in the Saha world.*

If we do not eliminate emotional desires, there is no way we can end birth and death. The *Shurangama Sutra* says: "If you don't renounce your lustful thoughts, you will not be able to get out of the dust." "If living beings in the six paths of any mundane world had no thoughts of lust, they would not have to follow a continual succession of births and deaths." Lustful desire is the fundamental root of birth and death. That's why the Master always spoke out against sexual misconduct and lustful desire. Even up to the year before he entered the stillness, he continued to repeat:

People are born because of lust and die because of lust. That's all there is to it.

The Master said the City of Ten Thousand Buddhas is very old-fashioned in that boys and girls study in separate schools. The purpose of this is to encourage everyone to follow the rules and not engage in sexual misconduct, not have abortions, and not take birth control pills; lust is the primary reason the world has gone bad. The Master said:

Boys should wait until after they are twenty-five to look for a girlfriend; girls should wait until after they are twenty to look for a boyfriend.

If you cannot cut off love and desire, then even if you are a monk or nun for eighty thousand great eons, you are merely wasting your time in Buddhism and creating karma with every meal you take.

Today's newspapers are filled with reports of murder, robbery, lust, and fraud, with the incidences of murder and lust being especially high. The Master said:

In terms of cause and effect, sexual misconduct is the gravest offense, and those who engage in it are punished very severely. According to the law of cause and effect, however many times a person commits adultery, after death he or she will be sawed from head to foot that many times by a huge saw. If they were married a hundred times in life, they will be divided into a hundred parts after death.

Great Master Yinguang spoke very sternly with regard to sexual misconduct:

Those who engage in sexual misconduct have no shame or modesty and are filthy and evil to the extreme. Although they have human bodies, they conduct themselves like animals and become animals in this very life. In their next life they will be reborn as animals... Those who engage in sexual misconduct will have children who do not preserve chastity... Those who engage in masturbation, even if they engage in no other form of sexual misconduct, will fall into the great hells. After leaving the hells,

潔之兒女……或手淫以戕身命，此人能不邪淫，亦當墮大地獄，從地獄出，或作母豬母狗，若生人中，當作娼妓。……

有人也許會懷疑祖師的開示有「言過其實」，或「矯枉過正」的嫌疑，其實不然。正因爲末法眾生已造惡到非以「過正」，不足以「矯枉」的地步。祖師的開示，必有他特別的用意，我們不必加以懷疑或揣測，這也是老子「正言若反」的哲學。

上人一生的問答錄相當多，每當上人回答信徒問題時，總是「不按牌理出牌」的，令人出乎意料之外。上人常常令信眾措手不及，而法喜充滿，連連拍手叫好。上人幽默的答案總是「充滿禪機」的「當下棒喝」！直指人心。我們可以由《六祖壇經》〈頓漸品第八〉中一段話，來看上人的「般若幽默智」，經文曰：

見性之人，立亦得，不立亦得，去來自由，無滯無礙，應用隨作，應語隨答，普見化身，不離自性，即得自在神通遊戲三昧，是名見性。

這段意思就是真正明心見性開悟的人，立這個辦法也可以，不立這個辦法也可以，無障無礙；願意來就來，願意去就去，這是指生死自由了；若有人問我問題，就隨便答而不經過思索，但要答得有道理，不是亂講的；這時，到處都是化身，化身不離自性，那麼隨時隨地都得到觀自在和五眼六通。這是指見性的人，可以有這種的功夫，可以隨問隨答，而不會答錯而誤人。下面就舉一些上人對信徒的答覆：

問：佛像沒有開光，可不可以拜？
答：你心裏沒有執著了，佛像隨時都是開光的。你若心裏有執著，開了光也等於沒開光。

問：如何避免地震？
答：人不生氣，就沒有地震。

問：如何了生死？
答：吃飯、穿衣、睡覺。

they will be reborn as female pigs or female dogs. If they are born among humans, they will be prostitutes...

Some people may wonder if the patriarchs' instructions are blowing things out of proportion or going to far to the other extreme in trying to correct the trend. Actually, living beings in the Dharma-ending Age have committed so much evil that if they didn't "go too far," they wouldn't be able to correct the trend. The patriarchs have their reasons for giving such instructions, and we need not entertain doubts or speculations. As Lao Zi said, "Straightforward words seem paradoxical."

In the numerous question-answer exchanges between the Master and those in the audience, the Master's unexpected answers often caught people off guard and filled them with the joy of Dharma, evoking cheers and rounds of applause. His humorous answers, fraught with hidden Chan meanings, always hit right on the mark and pointed straight at the mind. Let us quote a passage from Chapter Eight "Sudden and Gradual" of the *Sixth Patriarch Sutra* to shed light on the Master's Prajna humor:

Those who see their own nature can establish dharmas in their minds or not establish them as they choose. They come and go freely, without impediments or obstacles. They function correctly and speak appropriately, seeing all transformation bodies as integral with the self-nature. That is precisely the way they obtain independence, spiritual powers, and the samadhi of playfulness. This is what is called seeing the nature.

The meaning of this passage is that people of genuine enlightenment who have understood the mind and seen the nature can establish methods or not establish them. They come and go without obstruction. They have freedom over life and death. If someone asks them a question, they can answer without thinking, but their answers have principle. They don't speak recklessly. They see transformation bodies everywhere, but these transformation bodies are within the self-nature. At all times they contemplate with independence and have the five eyes and six spiritual powers. People who have seen their nature can answer spontaneously without fear of answering wrong and misleading others. Below are some of the Master's answers to questions asked by the audience:

If no one has blessed ("opened the light on") a Buddha image, can we bow to it?
**Answer:** If your mind is free of attachments, the Buddha image is always blessed. If your mind is attached, then even if it is blessed, it just the same as if it hadn't been blessed.

How can we avoid an earthquake?
**Answer:** If no one gets angry, there won't be any earthquakes.

How can I end birth and death?
**Answer:** Eat, dress, and sleep.

問：念何經咒最易成佛？
答：念不生氣的經，念不罵人的經，念不發脾氣的經。有這三種經，很快就成佛！

問：如何斷淫心？
答：不想就斷了！你跟著它想，怎麼會斷？「念起即覺，覺之即無」嘛！

問：法師圓寂後往何處去？
答：沒有地方去！

問：如何破執著和妄想？
答：誰給你執著？誰給你妄想？

問：何謂「應無所住而生其心」？
答：你心在什麼地方？先告訴我！

問：究竟是人怕鬼？還是鬼怕人？
答：你心裏有鬼，就是人怕鬼；你心裏要是沒有鬼了，就是鬼怕人。

問：往生如何處理？
答：你要往生做什麼？你帶這麼多垃圾東西，怎麼會去得了？

曾有人問上人說：「見師父上人拿著拐杖，為了眾生擔當太多的業力，心裏很難過，請師父慈悲多住世。」上人聽完後，當場把拐杖丟了出去，立刻引起一陣掌聲，上人卻說：「你不難過了吧！」這真是上人「即一切相，掃一切相」的妙般若，您不覺得很有意思嗎？又上人一生很注重「不發脾氣」及「忍辱行」，因為「佛法不離世間法」，「離世覓菩提，猶如求兔角」，上人說：「人能不發脾氣，什麼業障都能一筆勾消的。」更有趣的，上人曾發明兩句咒語，如：

忍耐！忍耐！多多忍耐，娑婆訶。

肝中若無火
何病都能躲
即此妙伽陀
亦被置高閣
娑婆訶

What Sutra or mantra should we recite that will make it easiest to become a Buddha?
**Answer:** Recite the Sutra of not getting angry, the Sutra of not scolding others, and the Sutra of not losing your temper. With these three Sutras, you'll become a Buddha real soon!

How can we cut off lust?
**Answer:** Don't think about it, and you will have cut it off! If you keep thinking about it, how can you cut it off? Be aware of each thought as soon as it arises; once you are aware of it, it goes away.

Dharma Master, where will you go after you enter perfect stillness?
**Answer:** Nowhere at all!

How can we break through attachments and random thoughts?
**Answer:** Who gave you attachments? Who gave you random thoughts?

How can we "produce the thought which is nowhere supported"?
**Answer:** Where is your mind? First tell me that.

Ultimately, is it people who fear ghosts or ghosts who fear people?
**Answer:** If you have ghosts in your mind, then people fear ghosts. If there are no ghosts in your mind, then ghosts fear people.

How can we secure rebirth?
**Answer:** Why do you want to be reborn? How can you make it when you're dragging so much junk around?

Someone once said to the Master, "It makes me feel so bad to see the Master using a walking cane and taking on so much karma for living beings. I hope the Master will be compassionate and live a long time." The Venerable Master immediately flung his cane aside, evoking a round of applause, and asked, "Do you feel better now?" This was the Master's wonderful Prajna of being able to "leave all appearances while in the midst of appearances." Don't you find this thought-provoking? Throughout his entire life, the Master emphasized "not getting angry" and "being patient with insult," because "The Buddhadharma is here in the world; / Enlightenment is not apart from the world. / To search for Bodhi apart from the world / Is like looking for a hare with horns." The Master said: "If a person can refrain from losing his temper, all his karmic obstacles will be cancelled at once." It is interesting to note two famous mantras that the Master composed:

*Patience, patience, gotta have patience.*
*Don't get angry, suo po he!*

*Purge the fire in your liver,*
*And you'll be free from all illness.*
*What a shame this wonderful elixir*
*Gets stored away and forgotten altogether!*
*Suo po he.*

如果我們仔細去閱讀上人的問答錄及開示錄，你會很容易就啓發自性的智慧，因爲「粗言及細言，皆歸第一義」。就如上人常說的：

> 不要相信我，也不用相信佛，要相信你本有的智慧，發掘你自性的般若，便會獲得擇法眼。是道則進，非道則退，不要把帽子當鞋子穿。

＊　　＊　　＊

佛教裡說的五眼六通，只是修行無漏，開悟證果的過程中，循序漸進的般若顯現境界，實在不足爲奇的。只是邪正有別，且要以戒行清淨，心無貪欲爲後盾，才不至於落入邪道。其實，神通說穿了，也只是「自性通」罷了！佛性本人人具足，五眼六通，亦人人本自具足，只是被無明煩惱給遮藏去了。當然佛在世時，曾警告大眾「不可隨便顯神通」，並非完全「不可」顯神通。如果菩薩有神通，而不示現神通去方便教化眾生，那有神通又有什麼用呢？《華嚴經》〈初發心功德品〉上說得好：「已住究竟一乘道，深入微妙最上法，善知眾生時非時，爲利益故現神通。」

很多人都誤會上人是一位搞神通的人，不過我翻遍上人所有的開示錄及錄音帶，還沒找到上人承認過他「有」神通的事。上人說：

> 我老實告訴你們，我沒有神通，連鬼通都沒有。這種超過事實的說法，不是我所希望的。

如果你認識的上人只限於「神通」而已，那真是太可惜了，可謂非上人真正的弟子。而我所認識的上人不是一位只具「五眼六通」的人，而是一位真正慈悲無我的老長者。所以我所認識的上人是一位用拐杖鞭打自己；沒收每一個人的脾氣，向每個人化緣脾氣；爲世界和平免戰爭而絕食；坐輪椅還到處說法；天天向眾生叩頭頂禮的師父，是一位「流血汗，不休息」的大菩薩行者。如果佛教徒只知道他自己的師父是否具有「特異功能」，而不知道師父教化眾生的精神及慈悲，那未免太本末倒置了，可

If we read the Master's talks and answers to questions with careful attention, they will easily activate the wisdom inherent in our natures. As it is said, "General summaries and detailed explanations all express truth in the primary sense." As the Master often said,

> You don't have to believe in me or believe in the Buddha. Believe in your own inherent wisdom. Discover the Prajna in your own nature. Then you'll attain Dharma-selecting Vision. You'll know to advance upon the Way and to retreat from what is not the Way. Don't wear your hat like a shoe.

＊　　＊　　＊

The five eyes and six spiritual powers discussed in Buddhism are merely manifestations of Prajna that occur as we cultivate towards the goal of attaining freedom from outflows and becoming enlightened. They are not to be regarded as extraordinary. In order to avoid falling into deviant paths, we should uphold the precepts purely and keep our minds free from greed and defilement. Actually, spiritual powers are merely powers inherent in our own natures. Everyone is endowed with the Buddha nature, and so everyone possesses the five eyes and six spiritual powers. It is just that they have been covered by our ignorance and afflictions. The Buddha warned people not to casually reveal their spiritual powers, but he didn't absolutely forbid it. If a Bodhisattva has spiritual powers but does not use them expediently to teach living beings, then what's the use of having them? The chapter "The Merit and Virtue of Bringing forth the Mind" in the *Flower Adornment Sutra* says, "Dwelling in the ultimate path of the One Vehicle, deeply entering the wondrous and supreme Dharma, knowing well when living beings are ready and when they are not, he manifests spiritual powers in order to benefit them."

Many people mistakenly view the Master as someone who showed off his spiritual powers. Yet, going through the Master's instructional talks and taped lectures, I have yet to find an instance in which the Master acknowledged that he had spiritual powers. The Master said:

> I'm telling you the truth: I don't have spiritual powers; I don't even have ghostly powers. I hope people will not exaggerate the facts and stretch the truth.

If you knew the Master only as someone who had spiritual powers, it's a great pity, for you were not truly his disciple. I knew the Master not as someone who possessed the five eyes and six spiritual powers, but as an elder who was truly compassionate and selfless. I knew him as a teacher who painfully hit himself with his own cane, who begged for and confiscated people's bad tempers, who fasted for world peace, who traveled everywhere speaking Dharma even when confined to a wheelchair, and who prostrated himself to living beings every day. He was someone who spared no blood or sweat and never paused to rest as he practiced the Bodhisattva Way.

If a Buddhist knows only whether his teacher has special powers but does not understand his teacher's attitude and compassion in teaching beings, he has confounded what is important with what is

謂非佛弟子也。

上人說他萬里迢迢從亞洲一個人跑到美國來，單人匹馬，匹馬單槍地深入這個外道的地方（完全沒有佛法的地方），就是為了將正法帶入西方。如今萬佛聖城已成為西方最重要的道場，此外還成立許多分道場。上人帶領著萬佛聖城各方弟子，為弘揚正法並團結宗教界而努力，這條漫漫長路，上人正以無比堅忍的腳步走著。上人的願力是所有的眾生要在他之前成佛，他要協助所有眾生，離苦得樂，找到真正的智慧，自在解脫。上人開示說：

我是一隻小螞蟻，甘願走在一切佛教徒的腳底下；我是一條道路，願所有的眾生走在我的身上，從凡夫直達佛地。

凡我弟子，如墮地獄，我願以身相代。願見到我，或聽到我的聲音，乃至間接聞到我的名字的人，都趕快成佛，我願意在娑婆世界等待著，直到你們完全成佛。

上人一生對佛學的貢獻同如虛空，豈是這篇文章所能道盡？他老人家已留給我們無數的法寶，今後我們要更精進修行，遵照六大宗旨去實行，才不至辜負上人一片苦心，並期上人早日乘願再來度眾生。

trivial; he is not a true Buddhist disciple.

The Master spoke of how he came alone from Asia to America, a land where Buddhism was virtually unknown, with the sole purpose of bringing the Orthodox Dharma to the West. The City of Ten Thousand Buddhas has now become the most important Buddhist monastic complex in the West, and there are various branch monasteries as well. Leading his disciples at the City of Ten Thousand Buddhas and other places, the Master tread the long, hard road with steady and determined footsteps, working to propagate the Proper Dharma and to unite all religions. The Master vowed that all living beings had to become Buddhas before he would do so; he wanted to help all living beings to escape suffering and attain bliss, and to discover true wisdom, comfort, and liberation. The Master said:

I am a little ant that wishes to walk beneath the feet of all Buddhists; I am a road that all living beings can traverse from the state of ordinary people to Buddhahood.

If any disciple of mine falls into the hells, I am willing to stand in for them. May anyone who sees me, hears my voice, or even hears my name quickly attain Buddhahood. I'm willing to wait in the Saha world until all of you have attained Buddhahood.

The Master's lifelong contributions to Buddhism are as vast as space itself. How could this article completely describe them? He left us countless treasures of Dharma. From today onwards, in order to repay the Master's efforts, we should increase our vigor and follow the six guiding principles in our practice. We hope the Master will soon return, based upon his vows, to cross over living beings.

法界佛教總會・萬佛聖城
**Dharma Realm Buddhist Association**
**The City of Ten Thousand Buddhas**
2001 Talmage Road, Talmage, CA 95481-0217 U.S.A.
Tel: (707) 462-0939   Fax: (707) 462-0949

法界聖城 **The City of the Dharma Realm**
1029 West Capitol Ave., West Sacramento, CA 95691 U.S.A.
Tel: (916) 374-8268

國際譯經學院 **The International Translation Institute**
1777 Murchison Drive, Burlingame, CA 94010-4504 U.S.A.
Tel: (415) 692-5912

法界宗教研究院
**Institute for World Religions (at Berkeley Buddhist Monastery)**
2304 McKinley Avenue, Berkeley, CA 94703 U.S.A.
Tel: (510) 848-3440

金山聖寺 **Gold Mountain Monastery**
800 Sacramento Street, San Francisco, CA 94108 U.S.A.
Tel: (415) 421-6117

金輪聖寺 **Gold Wheel Monastery**
235 N. Avenue 58, Los Angeles, CA 90042 U.S.A.
Tel: (213) 258-6668

長堤聖寺 **Long Beach Monastery**
3361 East Ocean Boulevard, Long Beach, CA 90803 U.S.A.
Tel: (310) 438-8902

福祿壽聖寺 **Blessings, Prosperity, & Longevity Monastery**
4140 Long Beach Boulevard, Long Beach, CA 90807 U.S.A.
Tel: (310) 595-4966

華嚴精舍　**Avatamasaka Hermitage**
11721 Beall Mountain Road, Potomac, MD 20854 U.S.A.
Tel: (301) 299-3693

金聖寺　**Gold Sage Monastery**
11455 Clayton Road, San Jose, CA 95127 U.S.A.
Tel: (408) 923-7243

金峰聖寺　**Gold Summit Monastery**
233-1st Ave. West, Seattle, WA 98119 U.S.A.
Tel: (206) 217-9320

金佛聖寺　**Gold Buddha Monastery**
301 East Hastings Street, Vancouver, BC, V6A 1P3 Canada.
Tel: (604) 684-3754

華嚴聖寺　**Avatamsaka Monastery**
1152 10th Street SE, Calgary, AB, T2G 3E4 Canada.
Tel: (403) 269-2960

法界佛教印經會
**Dharma Realm Buddhist Books Distribution Association**
臺北市忠孝東路六段85號11樓
11th Floor, 85 Chung-hsiao E. Road, Sec. 6, Taipei, R.O.C.
Tel: (02) 786-3022

紫雲洞觀音寺　**Tze Yun Tung Temple**
Batu 5-1/2, Jalan Sungai Besi, Salak Selatan,
57100 Kuala Lumpur, Malaysia.
Tel: (03) 782-6560

佛教講堂　**Buddhist Lecture Hall**
31 Wong Nei Chong Road, Top Floor, Happy Valley, HONG KONG.
香港跑馬地黃泥涌道31號12樓
Tel: 2572-7644

# 宣化老和尚示寂週年暨
# 萬佛聖城成立廿週年紀念專集

西曆1996年6月25日‧中英文版
佛曆3023年5月10日‧宣公上人示寂週年紀念日‧初版

---

發行人　　法界佛教總會
出　版　　法界佛教總會/佛經翻譯委員會/法界佛教大學
地　址　　1777 Murchison Drive
　　　　　Burlingame, CA 94010-4504 U.S.A.
電　話　　(415) 692-5912

倡　印　　法界佛教印經會
　　　　　臺北市忠孝東路六段85號11樓
　　　　　Tel: (02) 786-3022
　　　　　劃撥帳號：1321798-5
　　　　　帳戶：張淑彤

　　　　　法界文教基金會
　　　　　高雄縣六龜鄉興龍村東溪山莊20號
　　　　　Tel: (07) 689-3713